Contents

Acknowledgements   viii
List of Maps and Figures   ix
Translator's Note   x
Preface to the English Edition .   xii
List of Abbreviations   xv

*Part I   The State of Knowledge: General Characteristics
of Medieval Military History*   1

1   THE BARBARIANS FROM THE FIFTH TO THE NINTH CENTURY   3
    The decline of the Roman Empire in the West: military
        problems   3
    War and society in the Barbarian kingdoms during the
        sixth and seventh centuries   13
    The strengths and weaknesses of Carolingian armies in the
        eighth and ninth centuries   22

2   THE FEUDAL AGE FROM THE BEGINNING OF THE TENTH
    TO THE MIDDLE OF THE TWELFTH CENTURY   30
    General characteristics   30
    The Holy Roman Empire   32
    The kingdom of France   41
    England   50
    Norman Italy   54
    The Iberian world and the *Reconquista*   55
    The crusades and the Latin states in the East   59

3   MEDIEVAL SOCIETY IN ITS PRIME FROM THE MID–TWELFTH TO THE
    EARLY FOURTEENTH CENTURY   65
    Combatants and arms   67
    The Orders of Knighthood   74
    Obligations and military services   77
    Money, paid services and mercenaries   90
    Fortifications   101
    Conclusion   115

4 FREE COMPANIES, GUNPOWDER AND PERMANENT ARMIES FROM THE
BEGINNING OF THE FOURTEENTH TO THE END OF THE FIFTEENTH
CENTURY 119
The presence of war 119
The Age of the Horse 126
The transformation of the infantry 132
Gunpowder 137
Contracts, salaries and volunteers 150
The first permanent armies 165

Part II Themes and Perspectives 173

5 ARMS AND ARMOUR 175
Barbarian armament 175
The problem of the stirrup 179
Mail shirt, hauberk and haubergeon 184
Collective equipment and uniforms 188

6 ARTILLERY 193
The end of trébuchet artillery 194
Powder and cannon balls 196
The role of gunpowder artillery in pitched battles 198
Siege warfare: attack and defence 200

7 THE ART OF WAR 208
Teaching on the art of war 210
Strategy: the mastery of space and time 219
Tactics: the pitched battle 228

8 WAR, GOVERNMENT AND SOCIETY 238
In connection with social structures 239
In connection with political structures 242

9 TOWARDS A HISTORY OF COURAGE 250
Courage among the virtues and vices 250
Motivation, behaviour and hopes 253
The extent of risk 255

10 JURIDICAL, ETHICAL AND RELIGIOUS ASPECTS OF WAR 260
The early Middle Ages: Germanic practices, the church
fathers and Carolingian Christendom 260
The Peace and Truce of God, the chivalric ethic and the
crusade 270
War and scholastic thought 280
The law of arms and justice: relations between ethics and
practice in the wars of the late Middle Ages 284
Medieval pacifism and its limits 292
Integrated war 296

CONCLUSION   303

Part III   Bibliography   309

1   GENERAL   311

2   THE ART OF WAR: CONFLICTS, CAMPAIGNS, SIEGES AND BATTLES   311
    Sources   311
    Secondary works   312

3   INSTITUTIONS, SOCIETIES AND MILITARY ATTITUDES   315
    General   315
    Sixth–ninth centuries   317
    Tenth and eleventh centuries   319
    Twelfth and thirteenth centuries   321
    Fourteenth and fifteenth centuries   325

4   ARMS, ARMOUR AND WAR ENGINES   337
    Sources   337
    Catalogues, inventories and lists   337
    General studies   338
    Particular studies   340

5   CANNONS AND GUNPOWDER ARTILLERY   343

6   CASTLES AND FORTIFICATIONS   345
    General accounts   345
    The Empire and the Germanic world   346
    France and its sphere of influence   347
    The British Isles   351
    Italy   352
    The Latin East   353
    The Iberian peninsula   353

7   WAR, ECONOMY AND TAXATION   353

8   WAR AND PEACE: LAWS, ETHICS AND CHRISTIANITY   355
    Selected sources   355
    War and Christianity: the notion of the Just War   355
    The early Middle Ages   357
    The Peace and Truce of God   357
    The crusade and Holy War   359
    Landfriede: the public peace   359
    Chivalry and religion   360
    The laws of war   360

Index   361

Acknowledgements

The publishers are grateful to the following persons and institutions for permission to reproduce photographs and other illustrations.

Plate

1   La Ville de Bayeux
2   Le Musée Historique Lorrain, Nancy (photo Gilbert Mangin)
3   Aerofilms
4   Giraudon
5   Aerofilms
6   Castello Sforzesco, Milan
7   New College, Oxford
8   Giraudon
9   Bibliothèque Sainte-Geneviève, Paris
10 Riksantikvarieämbetet, Stockholm
11 Riksantikvarieämbetet, Stockholm
12 British Library (Add. MS 42130, fo. 202v)
13 Bibliothèque Nationale, Paris (MS Fr. 22495, fo. 265v)
14 Scala, Florence
15 Mansell Collection
16 The Trustees of the Wallace Collection
17 Bernisches Historisches Museum
18 The Trustees of the Wallace Collection
19 The Trustees of the Wallace Collection
20 Institut Royal du Patrimoine Artistique
21 Österreichische Nationalbibliothek (Cod. 3033, fo. 34r)
22 Bibliothèque Nationale, Paris (MS Fr. 38, fo. 157v)
23 Burgerbibliothek, Bern (MS hist. helv. I.3, fo. 757)
24 Bodleian Library (247139 c 1, fo. 53r, v)

Plates appear between page 80 and page 81.

Maps and Figures

MAPS

1 The theoretical order of battle of the Roman army at the beginning
of the fifth century, according to the *Notitia Dignitatum*   8
2 The first crusade (1096–99)   63
3 Defence in depth: the principal French garrisons north and south
of the Garonne (September 1340)   221
4 The frontier between Perche and Normandy in the twelfth century   222
5 The first campaign of the Hundred Years War: the charitable
mission of Bernard Carit in the Cambrésis (1340)   224
6 The first raid of Edward, prince of Wales (October–November
1355)   225
7 Morat 1476: Charles the Bold's battle plan   235

FIGURES

1 Rhuddlan castle, Wales: plan   112
2 Rhuddlan castle, Wales: cross-section   113
3 Order of battle of the Swiss at Morat, 1476   232
4 Ideal battle plan of Charles the Bold, Lausanne, May 1476   234

Translator's Note

A characteristic and essential feature of works first published in the *Nouvelle Clio* series is their extensive bibliographical apparatus. This has been revised for this English edition by the author. To reduce the length of the footnotes, references to works in the bibliography are signified by a number in brackets after the author's name and/or shortened title of his work. For books and articles cited only once or infrequently fuller details are given in the relevant footnote. Quotations from primary sources in English or from the works of historians writing in English have normally been taken directly from the editions or authors cited. Unless otherwise acknowledged, I have normally translated quotations from similar sources in languages other than English for this edition.

The various coins and currencies mentioned in the text are those cited in the documentary sources. Where the major unit for accounting purposes was the pound (£), this subdivided normally into 20 shillings and each shilling into 12 pennies, a system which goes back to Charlemagne and beyond. A distinction is normally made in the text when citing French sources from the turn of the thirteenth century between the *livre tournois*, *l.t.* (and its subdivisions – *sous tournois*, *s.t.* and *denier tournois*, *d.t.*) and the *livre parisis*, *l.p.* The former currency had dominated in the Angevin lands of the French kings annexed by Philip Augustus, while the *livre parisis* had been the main money of account for the traditional Capetian lands. The usual ratio between them was 5 : 4. The £ sterling in the later Middle Ages normally exchanged with the *livre tournois* at the rate of 1 : 6.

Apart from the full co-operation of M. Contamine, which has been particularly valuable in the selection of the illustrations for this English edition, I have also incurred other debts to friends and colleagues. Without in any way burdening them with any responsibility for errors committed, I should nevertheless like particularly to thank Christopher Allmand, Anthony Goodman, Robert Markus, Malcolm Offord and Malcolm Vale for helpful historical and stylistic assistance. Keith Bowler, Department of Geography, University of Nottingham, has kindly redrawn maps and diagrams for this edition for which the translator and publisher are very grateful. The editorial assistance of Harriet Barry at Basil Blackwell has been much appreciated. Finally, my wife has cheerfully helped at all stages which began with drafting chapter 1 on the Plymouth-Roscoff ferry and finished with the index.

M. J.

Preface to the English Edition

When I began the work of which this book is the end product, I had a feeling that the progress of medieval studies had led to an underestimation of the phenomenon of war. Medieval warfare is a massive and hence impossible subject. Save for a few exceptions, scholars have understandably, but in a sense strangely, retreated before the imperatives of authentic scholarship. Discussion of medieval warfare has often had a tendency to fragment, even to content itself with a series of isolated, parallel or divergent, analyses. At a stroke the impact of war as a fundamental element in the evolution of medieval societies is thus diminished, whilst at the same time the reciprocal links between war and the human environment in which it arises and upon which it acts are masked.

The purpose of this book is to restore to war its decisive place both as an explanatory factor and as the product of a whole cultural, technical and economic environment. The predicament of a class, a society or a country faced with war seems to me to be a good indicator of its hopes and fears, ambitions and claims, and ultimately of the role which it has recognized for itself or which has been accorded to it at the heart of a social, national or international game. And in the Middle Ages war, intervening as an autonomous factor, never ceased to weigh, sometimes discreetly, sometimes heavily, on historical developments.

Certainly the wish to encompass in a single volume such a vast theme over such a long period is not without presumption, and I willingly associate myself with the remarks of a modern authority who has said that 'no one scholar can hope to master the sources for the history of so great a subject through a millennium.'[1] For medieval warfare is indeed a world in itself, involving knowledge of canon law as well as of propitiatory inscriptions on swords, of the use of horseshoes and the art of healing wounds;[2] of recourse

[1] R. C. Smail, *Crusading Warfare (1097–1193)*, Cambridge 1956, p.v.
[2] Guy de Chauliac, *La grande chirugie*, ed. E. Nicaise, Paris 1890, pp.15–16.

to poisoned arrows[3] as well as of the diet recommended to combatants.[4] Nor should we forget that the medieval imagination lived with obsessions about war, as is suggested by the recurrence in century after century of identical and perennially symbolic visions – in the Frankish empire in 827 it was reported that two armies had fought each other in the sky, presaging future and all too real massacres on earth;[5] in 1138 it was the turn of England to be frightened by burning coals and other sparks flashing through the air;[6] and in the mid-fifteenth century, during one of the last campaigns of the Hundred Years War, there were seen in the sky above the city of Le Mans 'two marvellous cohorts of armed men fighting each other to the death'.[7] The subject needs to be approached from many different angles if we are to comprehend it in its entirety: military skill, armament, recruitment, composition and life in the armies, moral and religious problems posed by war, the relationship between war and its political and cultural context, might constitute some of these. All this must be done with an indispensable respect for chronology (understood, moreover, both as the distinction between 'before' and 'after' and as a continuous series of events), which is to history what perspective is to classical painting.

The Middle Ages as envisaged here cover their traditional span, but I have left aside the Byzantine and Islamic worlds to concentrate on the heart of Latin Christendom: England, France, Germany, Italy and Spain. Similarly war at sea has not been systematically dealt with because treating it as it deserved would have necessitated much more considerable coverage of technical developments; thus it has been excluded simply as a matter of maintaining internal balance rather than on grounds of principle. Lastly, throughout the whole period, a certain idea of war as a collective and public phenomenon has been followed, though not without some flexibility. The book does not deal with particular, private and individual forms of violence; that again is a field for original research which deserves a specific study in itself.

Circumscribed in this way, the subject nevertheless remains vast – too vast. It has frequently been necessary to make a choice, often only indicating a series of high points and lines of development, limited here and there to a simple survey, to a suggestion of major problems rather than to the provision

---

[3] Enguerran de Monstrelet, *Chroniques*, ed. L. Douët d'Arcq, i(Paris 1857), 105; V. Gay and H. Stein, *Glossaire archéologique* (554), i.721; Abbon de Saint-Germain-des-Prés, *Le siège de Paris par les Normands. Poème du IXe siècle*, ed. and tr. H. Waquet, Paris 1942, pp.18–19; *Le livre des trahisons de France*, ed. Kervyn de Lettenhove, Brussels 1873, p.198.

[4] *Les douze livres de Robert Valturin touchant la discipline militaire*, Paris 1555, f.91r.

[5] *Annales regni Francorum inde ab a. 741 usque ad a. 829 qui dicuntur Annales laurissenses maiores et Einhardi*, ed. G. H. Pertz and F. Kurze, Hanover 1895, p.173.

[6] *Gesta Stephani*, ed. K. R. Potter and R. H. C. Davis, Oxford 1976, pp.50–2.

[7] Georges Chastellain, *Oeuvres*, ed. Kervyn de Lettenhove, iii.359–62, cited by J-C. Delclos, *Le témoignage de Georges Chastellain, historiographe de Philippe le Bon et de Charles le Téméraire*, Geneva 1980, p.328.

of complete answers to a whole range of questions. I have taken sides but in so doing I hope that the inevitable abbreviation and selectivity to which I have sometimes had to resort will not prevent the reader from grasping in all its complexity such a multiform theme which is, truly, inexhaustible.[8]

P. C.
Paris

---

[8] I am very happy to thank my colleague and friend Michael Jones not only for undertaking the translation of this book but also for improving it at several points.

Abbreviations

AEM   *Anuario de Estudios medievales*
AESC   *Annales, Economies, Sociétés, Civilisations*
AHR   *American Historical Review*
AIBL   *Académie des Inscriptions et Belles-Lettres. Comptes rendus des séances*
Arch. dép.   Archives départementales
Arch.mun.   Archives municipales
Arch.Nat.   Archives nationales, Paris
ASI   *Archivio Storico Italiano*
Bataille de Nancy   *Cinq-centième anniversaire de la bataille de Nancy (1477).*
   Actes du Colloque organisé par l'Institut de recherche régionale en sciences
   sociales, humaines et économiques de l'Université de Nancy II(Nancy, 22–24
   septembre 1977), Nancy 1979
BEC   *Bibliothèque de l'Ecole des Chartes*
Bib.Nat.   Bibliothèque Nationale, Paris
BIHR   *Bulletin of the Institute of Historical Research*
BL   British Library
BM   *Bulletin monumental*
CHE   *Cuadernos de Historia de España*
ChG   *Château-Gaillard. Etudes de castellologie européenne*
DA   *Deutsches Archiv für Erforschung des Mittelalters*
EHR   *English Historical Review*
Froissart, ed. Luce   *Chroniques de Jean Froissart*, ed. S. Luce, G. Raynaud,
   L. and A. Mirot, Paris, 15 vols. 1869–1975 (continuing)
Froissart, *Oeuvres*, ed. Kervyn de Lettenhove   *Oeuvres de Jean Froissart*, ed.
   Baron Kervyn de Lettenhove, Brussels, 26 vols. 1867–77.
Gl.   *Gladius*
Guerre et Paix   *Actes du CIe Congrès national des Sociétés savantes, Lille*
   1976, Section de philologie et d'histoire jusqu'à 1610, La guerre et la paix,
   Paris, 1978
Hist.   *History*
HZ   *Historische Zeitschrift*

JBS   Journal of British Studies

MA   Le Moyen Age

MIÖGF   Mitteilungen des Instituts für österreichische Geschichtsforschung

MS   Mediaeval Studies

OM   Ordinamenti militari in Occidente nell'alto Medioevo, Spoleto, 2 vols. 1968 (Settimane di Studio del Centro Italiano di studi sull'alto Medioevo)

Orderic Vitalis, ed. Chibnall   The Ecclesiastical History of Ordericus Vitalis, ed. M. Chibnall, Oxford, 6 vols. 1969–80.

Ords. des rois de France   Ordonnances des rois de France de la troisième race, ed. E. S. de Laurière et al., Paris, 23 vols. 1723–1849

Patr.Lat.   Patrologiae latinae cursus completus . . . , ed. J. P. Migne, Paris, 221 vols. 1878–90.

PCEEBM   Publications du Centre européen d'Etudes burgundo-médianes

PP   Past and Present

RCH   Recueil des Historiens des Gaules et de la France, ed. Dom Bouquet et al., Paris, 24 vols., 1738–1876

RH   Revue historique

RHDFE   Revue historique de Droit français et étranger

RIHM   Revue internationale d'Histoire militaire

RSI   Rivista storica italiana

SM   Studi medievali

Spec.   Speculum

TRHS   Transactions of the Royal Historical Society

War, Literature and Politics   War, Literature and Politics in the Late Middle Ages. Essays in Honour of G. W. Coopland, ed. C. T. Allmand, Liverpool, 1976

ZOF   Zeitschrift für Ostforschung

ZSSRG   Zeitschrift der Savigny-Stiftung für Rechtsgeschichte

Part I

The State of Knowledge:

General Characteristics of
Medieval Military History

1

The Barbarians from the Fifth to the Ninth Century

With the invasion of Germanic peoples between the fourth and sixth centuries, followed by the foundation of Barbarian kingdoms, new forms of political power and institutions were created, society was organized in a new way and new values were recognized and experienced. These changes were necessarily accompanied by a transformation in ideas concerning war itself, as well as by changes in how warfare was practised. Indeed, the effects of these changes were to be felt for centuries and, in some respects, even to the end of the Middle Ages. How, why and to what extent did what one can call the Barbarian style of warfare replace the Roman art of war?

THE DECLINE OF THE ROMAN EMPIRE IN THE WEST:
MILITARY PROBLEMS

'Above all it must be recognized that wild nations are pressing upon the Roman Empire and howling round about it everywhere, and treacherous barbarians, covered by natural positions, are assailing every frontier.'[1] In these terms the anonymous author of the treatise *De rebus bellicis* described the condition of Romania around the years 366–75. A generation later, according to St Jerome, the situation had deteriorated further: 'I cannot enumerate without horror all the calamities of our age. For the last twenty years and more Roman blood has been shed daily between Constantinople and the Julian Alps. Scythia, Thrace, Macedonia, Dardania, Dacia, Thessaly, Achaea, Epirus, Dalmatia and both Pannonias have lain prey to Goths, Sarmatians, Quadi, Alans, Huns, Vandals and Marcomans who have ravaged, destroyed and pillaged them.'[2]

Victories over the Barbarians in both east and west during the second half of the third century, abandonment of Dacia and of the Decumatian fields,

---

[1] Thompson, *Roman Reformer* (674), p.97.
[2] Quoted by P. Courcelle, *Histoire littéraire des grandes invasions germaniques*, Paris 1948, p.14.

contraction of the frontier (*limes*) in North Africa and the reforms of Diocletian, gave Rome a respite for 50 years. But from the middle of the fourth century, the pressure of Franks, Alamans and Saxons had broken the Rhine frontier. Without doubt Julian (battle of Argentoratum [Strasbourg], 357), and then Jovian (battle of Scarpone, 366), succeeded in re-establishing some order, but they were unable to prevent the Franks from permanently settling south of the Rhine in Toxandria. After 407 imperial troops evacuated Britain, leaving the Britons to live 'according to their own customs, without observing Roman laws'[3] and to defend themselves alone against the attacks of Saxons, Picts and Scots. From 413 Visigoths, who had crossed the Danube in 376 and spread through the Balkans before entering Italy, settled more firmly in south-west Gaul around Narbonne, Toulouse and Bordeaux, concluding a treaty with the patrician Constantine in 418 which accorded them the right to settle certain lands. After 409 large areas of Spain were briefly held by Alans and Hasding and Siling Vandals before passing into the hands of the Sueves. At the same time Alamans settled in Alsace and the present area of the Palatinate. Between 429 and 442 the Vandals conquered the eastern, most wealthy, parts of North Africa. In a generation from the mid-fifth century to 484, the Visigoths made themselves masters of the whole of Spain, apart from the kingdom of the Sueves in the north-west, and extended their power into southern Gaul. At the same time the growth of Burgundian, Alamanic and Frankish power destroyed the remnants of Roman authority in the rest of Gaul. Finally, after experiencing the stern rule of Odoacer (476–93), Italy submitted to Theodoric, king of the Ostrogoths.

The disappearance of the Roman empire was not complete. Justinian succeeded in reconquering part of North Africa (533); this region was not finally lost until it was overrun by the Arabs in the early eighth century. In Spain an attempted reconquest was limited to the region around Cadiz, Córdoba, Malaga and Cartagena. However, from 629 the last vestiges of Byzantine domination in Spain disappeared. Italy was retaken between 536 and 554, but from 568 incursions of the Lombards forced a contraction of the area under Roman domination. By the end of the sixth century, the Western Empire still held a corridor of territory running from Ravenna to Rome, which cut the peninsula in two, and Sicily, Sardinia and Corsica, as well as large parts of southern Italy. In the end the Lombards never succeeded in dominating all of Italy and it was not until the eleventh century that the Normans finally drove the Byzantines from Calabria and Apulia.

The process which led to the disappearance of Roman power in the west was not rapid, but neither was it irreversible. Many things masked, slowed down or interrupted its course; fortunes frequently ebbed back and forth.

---

[3] L. Musset, *Les invasions: les vagues germaniques*, Paris 1965, p.155 (tr. E. and C. James as *The Germanic Invasions. The Making of Europe AD 400–600*, London 1975, p.101). In fact it was only in the last years of the fifth century that the Jutes, Angles and Saxons disembarked in large numbers on the eastern and southern coastline of Britain.

Nevertheless the relative rarity of great battles and of prolonged sieges underlined the inexorable progress of the Barbarians. All this happened apparently because Roman forces often refused to confront the enemy directly, and seemed to have mysteriously disintegrated from within.

A passage from Procopius throws light on this disintegration. After recounting how the Visigoths had captured Spain and the area of Gaul lying to the west of the Rhone, he adds:

> Now the Roman soldiers, also, had been stationed at the frontiers of Gaul to serve as guards. And the soldiers, having no means of returning to Rome, and at the same time being unwilling to yield to their enemy who were Arians, gave themselves, together with their military standards and the land which they had long been guarding for the Romans, to the *Arborychi* and Germans; and they handed down to their offspring all the customs of their fathers, which were thus preserved, and this people has held them in sufficient reverence to guard them even up to my time. For even at the present day they are clearly recognized as belonging to the legions to which they were assigned when they served in ancient times, and they always carry their own standards when they enter battle, and always follow the customs of their fathers.[4]

It is true that imperial armies kept up appearances for a long time. Constantine, between 324 and 337, had endowed them with a durable organization based on overall strategic considerations. At the end of the third century, Diocletian had chiefly been concerned to protect the frontiers by concentrating the majority of troops there; Constantine now considerably increased the power and numerical strength of a mobile army, thanks to permanent levies raised at the expense of frontier troops and the addition of new regiments of cavalry and infantry. In this way the complimentarity – and also the division – became very marked between the field army (*comitatenses*) on the one hand and the frontier troops (*limitanei, ripenses* or *castellani*) on the other. Then with the division of the Empire and increasing threats of attack, the *comitatenses* were divided into several armies, each of which, in theory, was attached to a particular important region, while the Emperor or Emperors kept at their own command an elite force of *palatini*, distinct from the proper regiments of imperial guards or *scholae*.

The men who formed these military forces were subject to an apparently strict discipline and a faultless collective training. Soldiers and officers enjoyed long careers. They were true professionals, regularly supplied either by generous rations in kind (*annonae*) consisting of bread, meat, wine and oil, or by money wages, graded according to rank. The state provided them with standardized equipment, both offensive and defensive, manufactured and stored in its arms factories (*fabriciae*), of which there were about 40 scattered throughout the Empire.[5] In certain circumstances the state also provided

---

[4] Procopius, *The Gothic Wars*, ed. H. B. Dewing (Loeb Classical Library), iii.120–1.

[5] The armourers (*fabricenses, barbaricarii*) who worked in these establishments had military status.

mounts for the cavalry through the office of the *comes stabuli*, either from the imperial studs or from levies on the provinces by a special tax. All this allowed many troops to lead a normal family life; many soldiers owned slaves. The *limitanei* lived in *castella*, towers or fortified camps. Those serving in the interior sometimes used barracks but most frequently were billeted in cities with inhabitants who, in practice if not in law, were compelled to supply them with furniture, wood, heat and light. Soldiers benefited from various fiscal privileges such as exemption from taxes like the *capitatio*. After 20 years' service they received the *honesta missio*, and after 24 years, the *emerita missio*, that is discharge for fully-performed and well-merited service. Afterwards, not only could they conserve their fiscal privileges but they also received a sum of money allowing them to set up a small business, or a plot of land, often uncultivated, together with a modest *ex gratia* payment, a quantity of seed and a pair of oxen.

Anxiety to protect the frontiers led to the construction and upkeep of strategic roads, earthworks, fortlets and *castella*. A document from the beginning of the fifth century enumerates 89 *castella* along the Danube, 57 along the eastern *limes* from the Black to the Red Sea, 46 in Africa from Tripolitania to Tingitania, 23 in Britain and 24 in Gaul.[6] Experts still considered this effort insufficient: 'The frontiers' safety will be better provided for by a continuous line of forts constructed at intervals of one mile with firm walls and very powerful towers.'[7] Emperors, at least, exhorted their subordinates to continue this long-term task, as a letter in June 365 from Valentinian I to the military commander (*dux*) of *Dacia Ripensis* shows:

> On the *limes* entrusted to your eminence's rule, you should not only restore the fortifications which are crumbling but also build each year further towers in suitable locations. If you ignore my order, on completion of your term of office, you will be sent back to the *limes* and the works which you have neglected to build with military labourers and resources, you will be compelled to execute at your own expense.[8]

Nevertheless the Roman army suffered from serious weaknesses which markedly diminished its worth. At the time the overall strategy which determined its organization was criticized. Thus Zosimus contrasted Diocletian, who had strengthened the already powerful towns and garrisons on the frontiers of the Empire and had lodged the whole army there, with Constantine who 'withdrew from the frontier the great majority of soldiers to install them in towns which had no need of protection'. This resulted simultaneously in ruining the cities, overwhelmed by this military presence, and in undermining the troops' morale.[9] It is true that there is a detectable bias in this

---

[6] *Notitia dignitatum utriusque imperii*, ed. O. Seeck, Berlin 1876.
[7] Thompson (674), p.105.
[8] Quoted by A. Piganiol, *L'Empire chrétien (325–395)*, Paris 1947, p.173.
[9] Quoted by A. Chastagnol, *Le Bas-Empire*, Paris 1969, p.284.

judgement by a pagan on the first Christian Emperor. Constantine's policy, which merely repeated one first formulated by Gallienus in the third century, was certainly the better; his successors were to propose no other. But there remained the risk that, separated from immediate danger, the *comitatenses* would lose their willingness to fight. Moreover, they could easily be transformed into garrisons of the interior, lose their mobility and become absorbed in policing and the maintenance of order.

There was also the important question of recruitment and numbers. The regular army, excluding the *foederati* to be mentioned shortly, consisted of three elements. Sons of soldiers, if they were physically suitable, could follow their fathers, in conformity with the principle of hereditary professions widespread in the late Empire. There was also a regular annual conscription of troops. Landowners either alone or in groups, according to the value of their estates, were obliged to supply a man from their lands or from merchants actually providing soldiers. This system was known as the *praebitio tironum*, from which exemption could be purchased by paying a certain sum, the *aurum tironicum*, to the treasury. Finally, volunteers were accepted and enrolled on certain conditions. The weak and infirm were rejected; so were slaves, certain farm labourers (*coloni*) (except in times of crisis) and members of various trades considered degrading. On the other hand, individual Barbarians could enlist. They then served either in mixed units or in units where one race or ethnic group predominated and where the organization was at least in part still Roman.

These sources of recruitment should have sufficed. But in fact, in many parts of the Empire, Roman citizens felt no attraction to the profession of arms with its risks, hardships and often long-term or even permanent uprooting. Only those most badly off would, for want of something better, accept its rigorous discipline. The large-scale employment of Barbarians this necessitated further accentuated the separation between the inhabitants of Romania and her army.

It is thus not easy to estimate the numbers of troops raised. According to John the Lydian, a contemporary of Justinian, who may have discovered this figure in the archives of the Praetorian prefecture where he worked, Diocletian's forces numbered 435,266 men, of whom 389,704 served in the land armies and 45,562 in the navy. Agathias, also writing in the sixth century, declared that in an earlier period the army totalled 645,000 men. But the fullest, if not the most reliable estimates, are provided by the famous *Notitia dignitatum et administrationum omnium tam civilium quam militarium in partibus Orientis et Occidentis*. As it has come down to us in several fifteenth- and sixteenth-century manuscripts, all deriving from the ninth-century *Codex spirensis* (itself now lost apart from one folio), this document was almost certainly compiled by a chief notary (*primicerius notariorum*) in the West at the beginning of the fifth century. The final version of the section dealing with the Eastern Empire probably dates back to 408, whilst that concerning

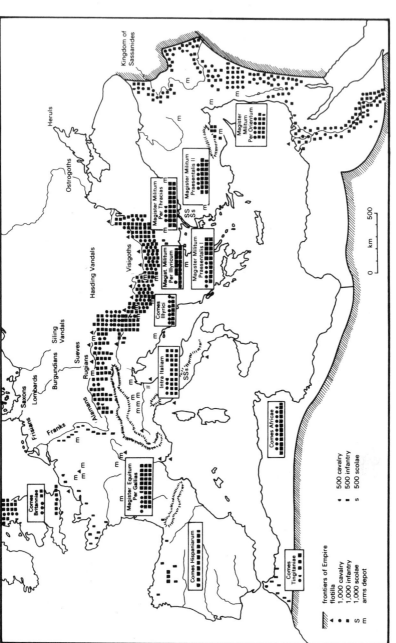

Map 1 *Theoretical order of battle of the Roman army at the beginning of the fifth century according to the Notitia Dignitatum (after A. H. M. Jones, The Later Roman Empire, 284–602. A social, economic and administrative survey, 1964)*

The figures within the boxes correspond to the number of troops in the field armies (Palatini, Comitatenses), the others to frontier troops (Limitanei). The legions have been estimated at 1,000 men for field armies and 3,000 men for frontier troops. All the other corps (Vexillationes, Auxilia, Pseudo-Comitatenses, Alae, Cohortes, Cunei, Milites, Numeri) have been estimated as 500 men.

the Western Empire was incompletely and inaccurately revised down to about
423.[10] Even if these dates are admitted, however, two difficulties arise. First,
it seems that the imperial administration added new units as they were
created; secondly, the numerical significance which can be attributed to
various formations is debatable. Ferdinand Lot, for instance, had no faith in
this order of battle which he termed a pure 'phantasmagoria'.[11] But other
historians accept a figure in the region of 600,000 men which helps to
confirm Agathias' estimate. The author of the anonymous *De rebus bellicis*
provides another contradiction: after affirming that there were too many
costly soldiers remaining for ever in the regiments, he goes on to say that
wars and desertion provoked by disgust for the military life had seriously
reduced effective numbers.[12] Perhaps the information provided by the
Notitia has a chiefly fiscal significance and corresponds to the total expenses
required for the army. Table 1, which gives numbers of troops, as well as
map 1, giving their geographical location, should thus be considered theoretical rather than actual.

To these regular forces can be added, especially from the end of the fourth
century, those troops furnished by the federates (*foederati*); that is, by those
Barbarian tribes, principally Germanic, who fought under their traditional
chieftains and received from the Roman state, when taken into its service, a
lump sum for wages and maintenance. Indeed it often appears that these
federates formed the essential core of the armies which tried to stem the
inroads of the invaders. Even in Justinian's day, especially after the great
plague of 541–43, the role of the federates remained preponderant in the field
armies at least, so that 'at times the Roman army would probably have been
as Roman as Franco's army was Spanish during the Civil War of 1936–38.'[13]

The contrast between the formidable weight of the Roman military
machine and its inefficiency is thus striking. The Roman army was an
impressive organization, impeccably structured in theory, but which in practice kept seizing up. The Emperors – and there were some energetic ones –
were unable to use the opportunities represented by facility of communica-
tion, an abundance of information and rapidity in the dispatch of orders.
Furthermore, the bureaucracy which sustained their efforts was small, easily
overloaded or discouraged; it expected only delays and adopted an obstruc-
tive role. It seems everyone was easily deluded, if we can believe Ammianus
Marcellinus, who witnessed the reaction of the imperial entourage when the
Visigoths in 376 sought permission from Valens to cross the Danube: 'Their
request produced a favourable impression rather than one of alarm. Courtiers

[10] A. H. M. Jones, *The Later Roman Empire 284–602. A Social, Economic and Administrative Survey*, Oxford 1964, iii.347–58; D. Hoffmann, *Das Spätrömische Bewegungsheer* (164).
[11] F. Lot, C. Pfister and F. L. Ganshof, *Les destinées de l'Empire en Occident de 395 à 768*, Paris 1940, p.19.
[12] Thompson (674), pp.112–13.
[13] Teall, *Barbarians* (176), p.312.

TABLE 1 Roman forces after the *Notitia Dignitatum*

	Limitanei			Comitatenses				
	Cavalry	Infantry	Cavalry plus infantry	Cavalry	Infantry	Cavalry plus infantry	Scholae	Cavalry, infantry and scholae
Eastern Empire	112,000	138,000	250,000	21,500	78,500	100,000	3,500	353,500
Western Empire	29,500	105,500	135,000	23,500	89,500	113,000	2,500	250,500
Total	141,500	243,500	385,000	45,000	168,000	213,000	6,000	604,000

Total cavalry (*limitanei* and *comitatenses*): 186,500 (30%).
Total infantry (*limitanei* and *comitatenses*): 411,500 (68%).

used every form of adulation to exalt the good fortune of the Emperor to whom, unexpectedly, recruits from the ends of the earth had offered themselves. The incorporation of these foreigners into the national army would make it invincible.'[14] Behind this disconcerting policy, there was undoubtedly the vain hope that in establishing these Barbarians in the Empire, they would in the end be peacefully settled and romanized and that in the meantime they would furnish soldiers who, if not entirely peaceful, would at least be relatively faithful and efficient. Furthermore, the Emperors were scarcely supported in their efforts by a population, long unaccustomed to military habits, deprived of initiative, indifferent to the fate of Rome, who considered the state as an oppressor rather than a protector and who refused in any event to take their own destinies and defence into their own hands.

The Barbarian warriors who brought down the Empire in the West never constituted a very numerous force. The Alamans, for example, disposed of a maximum of 25,000 combatants at the battle of Argentoratum in 357; at Adrianople in 378, the coalition of Huns, Alans, Ostro- and Visigoths which crushed the army of Valens totalled about 18,000 men, of whom perhaps 10,000 were Visigoths; in 429 Genseric crossed into Africa with some 16,000 fighting men, a third of these coming from the remaining Siling Vandals, Alans and Goths, the rest from the Hasding Vandals. In the first years of the reconquest of Italy by Justinian, Witiges may have had some 25–30,000 men to oppose the army of Belisarius, which was smaller. In the second phase of that war 20 years later, Totila at best commanded only 25,000 men. In short, each of the principal Barbarian peoples could muster forces of between 10,000 and 30,000 men.[15] In addition, because of the demographic weakness of the invaders, who lacked sufficient men, losses could not easily be made good and recourse was had, in order to avoid fighting with skeleton forces, either to other Barbarians or to subject populations whose enthusiasm was evidently lukewarm.

Ignorant of proper discipline, easily discouraged, the Barbarians used very rudimentary tactics. Their favourite ploy was to form a wedge and to launch sudden attacks on the enemy in order to break up opposing formations in a single movement. But if the initial impetus miscarried before determined resistance, they then retreated in disorder and succeeded in regaining control only with great difficulty. Nor was hand-to-hand combat favourable to them because of their lack of offensive and, above all, defensive arms. Their capacity for siege warfare – fundamental to the defeat of an urban civilization whose many powerful cities had taken care since the invasions of the third century to enclose themselves within ramparts – was considered deplorable by the Romans. For most of the time they were unable to build, let alone use, siege weapons. When Rome was besieged in 536, Witiges had wooden towers

---

[14] Quoted by Courcelle, *Histoire littéraire*, p.10.
[15] Perhaps only 5,000 men in the case of the Burgundians.

built, which were mounted on wheels and drawn by oxen, but these contraptions were soon immobilized by Roman archers shooting the oxen. The Visigothic, Ostrogothic or Frankish warrior chieftains clearly saw what was necessary but were generally incapable of undertaking enterprises of this kind with success. Supplies posed the same acute problems. There was nothing comparable to the complex and sophisticated Roman administration. Spurred on by hunger, the Barbarians were often constrained to split up into small bands to scour the countryside, which was very vulnerable unless organized defences remained. The position of the Barbarians was also more precarious because they did not simply form armies but were whole peoples on the move. Carts, baggage, livestock, women, children and the old, whom they took with them, reduced their mobility and continuously forced on them the tasks of surveillance and protection.[16]

Small armies, rudimentary tactics, an almost non-existent logistic – one should not conclude from all this that the Barbarian victory is inexplicable. Let us look first at the contrast between the military efficiency of Germanic society at the time of the great incursions and that of late imperial Rome. On the one hand was a society requiring the employment of all adult males from 15 or 16 until their physical strength deserted them, perhaps a fighting force of a quarter or fifth of the total population; on the other, a rich Empire of several tens of millions of inhabitants, just capable, at a ruinous cost, of raising some 500,000 to 600,000 men, of whom two-thirds, perhaps even three-quarters, were incapable of fighting a campaign – a ratio of combatants to civilian population of the theoretical order of 100 : 1 and in practice of 400 : 1. The superiority of imperial forces in effective terms was made even more precarious by the need of the Roman state on various occasions to confront several Barbarian peoples simultaneously. Thus between 407 and 410 Visigoths, Vandals, Alans and Sueves, perhaps some 60,000 warriors in all, numbered scarcely less than the united forces of *comitatenses* in Italy, Gaul and Spain.

If the military equipment of the Barbarians was rather deficient overall, it is nonetheless true that some of the Germanic peoples in contact with the nomads of the Steppes had become outstanding horsemen. Similarly some of their arms – the long sword, the Frankish battle-axe – were technically excellent and had no Roman equivalent. Barbarian inferiority in the art of fortification was only a decisive handicap where towns resisted energetically. In fact, many towns were lost by surprise attacks, treason or by a blockade, more or less prolonged. Others deliberately opened their gates in the hope of being spared (*sub spe pacis*: Rome 537–8). Very few succeeded in holding an adversary at bay long enough for a relieving Roman army to be raised and to

---

[16] Lactantius, *De mortibus persecutorum*, ed. J. Moreau, Paris 1954, i.88; 'The Barbarians are accustomed to set off for war with all they possess, hampered by their very numbers and incommoded by their baggage.'

intervene.[17] In other words, the efforts of the Roman state could only succeed if ably supported by willing co-operation in self-defence by the rest of the population. For various reasons, which in any case go beyond strictly military factors, this co-operation was displayed only episodically.

The reputation of the Barbarians provoked panic and paralysed response. Contemporary texts vied with one another in describing their bravery, cruelty and ferocity. Ammianus Marcellinus writes of the Huns: 'Of all warriors they are the most redoubtable.' Velleius Paterculus calls the Lombards 'a race surpassing even the Germans in savagery'. Isidore of Seville says the Franks were so called 'because of the ferocity of their customs'; Sidonius Apollinaris described the Saxon pirates as 'an enemy fiercer than any other' and the Salian Franks as having 'in their childhood a passion for war more normally associated with maturity. If by chance the number of their enemies or the weakness of their position causes their downfall, then only death will defeat them, never fear. They remain in their places, undefeated, and their courage survives, one may say, until they draw their last breath.'[18] What could one do in the face of these men who experienced 'martial ecstasy'?[19] How could one oppose the *furor teutonicus*? Was it not best to come to terms with the inevitable? In this sense the explanation of a St Jerome for whom 'it is our sins which strengthen the Barbarians, it is our vices which undermine the Roman army',[20] can be accepted if it is considered as a religious formulation of a moral diagnosis: the general loss of public spirit, the absence of civic pride, even more serious when it affected the powerful than the weak. In the words of Salvian of Marseilles: 'One foresaw slavery and feared it not. Fear had been taken away from these sinners so that they might not take heed. The Barbarians had little need to look for almost everything could be seen, all citizens living without fear and all towns without defence.'[21]

WAR AND SOCIETY IN THE BARBARIAN KINGDOMS DURING THE SIXTH AND SEVENTH CENTURIES

The political, social and religious conditions which determined the shape of the different Germanic kingdoms from the early fifth century varied widely. In the first instance contrasts may be drawn between peoples settling in

---

[17] There are a few exceptions: the more or less legendary resistance of the towns of Northern Gaul at the time of Attila's invasion (Troyes defended by St Loup, Orléans by St Aignan and Paris by Ste Geneviève).

[18] Ammianus Marcellinus, *Res Gestae*, 31,2: Velleius Paterculus, *Historiae Romanae*, 2,106; Isidore of Seville, *Etymologies*, IX,ii; Sidonius Apollinaris, *Poema*, 5,5 and *Letter to Namatino*, 8,6.

[19] F. Altheim, *Die Krise der alten Welt*, Berlin 1943, p.110.

[20] Quoted by Courcelle, *Histoire littéraire*, p.14.

[21] Salvian of Marseilles, *De gubernatione Dei*, in *Oeuvres*, ed. G. Lagarrigue, Paris 1975, ii.413–15.

regions largely devoid of inhabitants and those settling in densely populated areas. Thus the invaders of Britain, the Angles, Jutes and Saxons or even the Alamans, Bavarians and Thuringians can be contrasted with peoples who dominated regions where the earlier inhabitants had not been driven out and where, in consequence, the victors formed only a more or less substantial minority. This was the case with the Burgundians, Visigoths, Ostrogoths, Sueves, Vandals, Lombards and Franks, even if the latter were probably in the majority in some parts of Northern Gaul. A distinction can also be drawn between ephemeral, short-lived kingdoms (the Burgundians of south-west Gaul, the Vandals in Africa, Ostrogoths and Lombards in Italy, Sueves and Visigoths in Spain) and those destined for a long history like those of the Franks and Anglo-Saxons. Similarly some peoples, once settled, ceased expanding and rapidly went onto the defensive (Ostrogoths and Vandals), whilst others experienced a long period of victorious and dynamic expansion (Franks and Lombards). That is to say, during the sixth and seventh centuries the Germanic kingdoms of the West had varied military histories and had to face different kinds of threat of varying severity. Sometimes they ran up against other Germanic peoples and kingdoms, sometimes against foreign powers like the Byzantines or Arabs. However, their conception and practice of warfare present sufficiently common characteristics for an attempt to be made to study them collectively.

In every case, in fact, we are dealing with communities fundamentally organized for war, where the majority of recognized virtues are martial values, where the links between social organization and the organization of armies are close and integral, where a free man is normally a soldier, where the function of royalty is above all to provide war-leadership (*Heerkönigtum*), where the king is an 'entrepreneur of conquests', where war 'is still a way of life as much as a means of survival or expansion',[22] where the non-military episodes of public and private life nevertheless freely take on a military aspect. Hence when Chilperic gave his daughter, Rigonthis, in marriage to Reccared, king of the Visigoths, he provided her with a following of 4,000 combatants; and when Bertoald, mayor of the Burgundian royal palace, received an order to inspect the royal estates (*fisci*) along the Seine, he took 400 soldiers with him. 'The civilisation born out of the great migrations was a civilisation of war and aggression.'[23] The omnipresence of war is equally revealed in the Germanic names which became popular in Gaul amongst descendants of the Gallo-Romans in the seventh century: Baudry (Bald-Rik: bold-powerful); Richard (Rik-hard: powerful/strong-bold); Armand (Heriman: man of war); Roger (Hrot-gar: glorious spear); William (Wile-helm: will-helmet); Gerard (Ger-hard: strong lance); Augier (Adal-gari: noble

---

[22] J. M. Wallace-Hadrill, *Early Germanic Kingship in England and on the Continent*, Oxford 1971, p.151.
[23] G. Duby, *Guerriers et paysans* (158), p.60.

lance); Gertrude (Gaire-trudis: spear-might); Matilda (Macht-hildis: strong for war); Sibour (Sigeburgis: defence through victory); Louis (Chlodo-wed, Hlodovicus: famous warrior); Lothair (Chot-ari: celebrated warrior); Herbert (Chari-bercht: army bright); Guntram (Gund-chramm: war raven); Clothilda (Chloto-hildis: glorious battle); Brunhilda (Brune-hildis: breastplate-battle). Similarly among acquisitions by Roman society from Germanic peoples may be numbered several martial terms: war, guard, watch, marshal, steward, harm, spy, banish, wound, dub, sword point, helm, shield, gambeson, stirrup, spur, standard, banner, gonfanon.

One of the characteristics of the new forms of war specific to the Barbarian world, which at first sight appears radical, is its obvious break with the Roman military system. The latter had depended on the existence of a permanent army of professional soldiers, maintained by regular taxation in kind and money at the expense of the rest of the population. This implied the existence of a military and civil bureaucracy with archives, making much use of written orders. In principle, by using a continuous line of defence around Roman territory, it had been expected that peace would reign within the Empire and that there would be no reason for bearing arms, that violence would be illegal and recourse to justice would be the normal means of resolving litigious questions whatever they concerned.

But, taken together, the Barbarian monarchies did not have a regular army at their disposal; the former Roman bureaucracy which served them rapidly became rudimentary and saw its means and field of action restricted in large measure. Direct taxation shrank, indeed disappeared completely in many regions; indirect taxation, though resisting decline more effectively, was affected by the decline in economic activities. Coins circulated more slowly; hoarding became common. The resources of monarchies were largely absorbed by the immediate private expenses of kings and their entourages. The idea of a frontier (*limes*) was almost completely lost. At a stroke insecurity became general; no region was able to claim immunity from war. Each individual, every social or family group, had to look to their own security, to defend their rights and interest by arms. The bearing of arms, at first reserved to the conquerors, became a habit among the whole population, while at the same time an ethnic, juridical and cultural fusion between the victors and vanquished occurred. The differences were obliterated between public warfare and private violence, between the feud or vendetta and a conflict waged by the king in the name of his people. Even the wergild (man-price), designed to prevent a continuing train of violence, appeared in some respects like a ransom, a war indemnity paid to the injured party.

However, certain facts may be cited to modify this contrast. First, from the time of the late Empire, by force of circumstance, the military aspects of the imperial position had been vastly accentuated, even to the extent of borrowing Barbarian customs – as is shown, for instance, by the way Julian was raised on a shield by his soldiers to the accompaniment of clashing bucklers

(360). The Emperor was surrounded by military men, often of Germanic origin. From the reign of Constantine, the independence of military chiefs in relation to praetorian prefects, vicars, proconsuls and provincial governors increased to such a degree that commanders-in-chief of cavalry and infantry (*magistri equitum, magistri peditum*), dukes (*duces*) and counts were now answerable directly to imperial authority. The old practice of *cedant arma togae*, symbolizing the end of professional service, no longer held, and civilian power lost its precedence. Even service in certain civilian offices was now considered a form of military service – distinct, it is true, from *militia armata*, but necessitating the wearing of uniform and a military belt (*cingulum*). As for the *pax romana*, there were many regions of the Empire where this was but a memory. Endemic disturbances, popular uprisings like that of the *Bagaudae* in Gaul or the Circumcellions in Africa, the penetration and settlement of small groups of Barbarians even before the tidal wave of the great invasions, had destroyed peace. For their part, the powerful on their estates already lived like lords; their villas, often protected by a tower, took on defensive characteristics. Libanius, in his *Discourse on Rural Patronage*, was above all conscious of the military aspect of that institution.[24]

Conversely, the Barbarian monarchies tried to use to their full advantage the remains of the military organization of the late Empire, as did Theodoric in the Ostrogothic kingdom. Civil servants in Constantinople considered him a Roman commander-in-chief (*magister utriusque militiae*) to whom the government of Italy had been conceded. By a legal fiction he thus found himself at the head of a Roman army entirely composed of Germans and from which Romans had been expelled. The officers bore Roman titles: dukes, counts, tribunes, prefects. Some troops, installed in *castella* in frontier provinces (Raetia, Pannonia, Dalmatia and Savia) could be considered as successors to the *limitanei* of the late Empire, whilst the military commandants (*comites civitatum*) of Gothic garrisons of the interior and the provincial dukes (*duces provinciarum*) instructed to repress brigandage, were in some respects successors to the *comitatenses* of an earlier period. Similarly, just as Emperors were for their safety surrounded by guards (*scholares*), so Theodoric had his bodyguards. Certain late-imperial arms factories continued to function, as did the practice of paying bounty (*donativum*) to soldiers and sailors. At least in time of war, wages in money and kind (in the traditional form of *annonae*) were distributed to the troops; thus they did not live simply on the thirds of lands held by virtue of the regime of billeting (*hospitalitas*) which the Goths enjoyed after their victory over Odoacer. It is likely that certain laws from the Roman military code were still applied. Even the prohibition on Romans carrying arms may perhaps be understood not as a security measure designed

[24] J. H. W. G. Liebeschuetz, *Antioch. City and Imperial Administration in the Later Roman Empire*, Oxford 1972, pp.201–5.

to protect the Germanic minority against any attempted uprising but as a survival of earlier Roman legislation.[25]

In regions where they dominated, probably because the collapse of imperial military institutions was more advanced than in Italy, the other Germanic realms gained only a very feeble military inheritance from the late Roman world. But it can be noted that the Burgundians and Visigoths as well as the Franks made use of the count of the city 'who was simultaneously military chief, keeper of the public peace, judge, collector of taxes and administrator',[26] and this led to a fusion of Roman and German traditions.

According to Receswinth's code, there existed in the cities and *castella* of the Visigothic kingdom officials styled variously *erogatores annonae, dispensatores annonae* or *annonarii*, in charge of supplying the army. The *Life* of the hermit of Périgord, Saint Avitus (a late document), speaks without anachronism of a bounty (*donativum*) which King Alaric II is supposed to have distributed to his troops before the battle of Vouillé (507). As late as the seventh and eighth centuries Lombard kings, anxious to protect their power by a network of frontier posts (*clusae*), the *clusurae Italiae*, remained faithful to the strategy of the *limes*. They dipped into their treasury to distribute the *donativum* to their men. The term *sculca*, used to describe groups of warriors who in field armies were assigned special tasks, was common to both the Byzantines and Lombards.

Recruitment of armies in the Barbarian kingdoms started everywhere from the same principle: the obligation incumbent on every free man as soon as he was old and strong enough to obey the military summons of the king and to serve throughout the campaign (*expeditio*), providing his own supplies and equipment.[27] Any failure incurred a punishment which often took the form of a heavy fine. Thus Article 21 of Rothari's edict (643) reads: 'He who refuses to join the army or the *sculca* shall pay 20 shillings to the king or to his duke.' Similarly Gregory of Tours says that after the siege of Comminges by the troops of King Guntram in 585 'an edict was issued by the judges condemning those who had delayed to join the expedition.'[28] Or as in chapter 51 of the laws of Ine, king of the West Saxons (688–94): 'If a gesithborn man who owns land, neglects military service, he is to give 120 shillings and to forfeit his land; one who owns no land, 60 shillings, a ceorl 30 shillings, as a fine for [neglect of] military service'.[29] However, the

[25] cf. Anonymus Valesianus in Ammianus Marcellinus, *Res Gestae*, ed. J. C. Rolfe (Loeb Classical Library), iii.560: '*Item, ut nullus Romanus arma usque ad cultellum uteretur, vetuit.*'

[26] G. Tessier, *25 décembre . . .* , *Le baptême de Clovis*, Paris 1964, p.257.

[27] *Dum sanus est* according to the *Lex Wisigothorum*.

[28] Gregory of Tours, *Histoire des Francs*, tr. R. Latouche, Paris 1965, ii.121.

[29] *English Historical Documents, c.500–1042*, ed. D. Whitelock, Oxford, 2nd edn, 1979, p.371.

application of this general principle raised difficulties. It may be asked whether, in particular, this obligation had a personal character or property qualification. How, for instance, was it possible to levy a fine, often very heavy, on a defaulter or deserter who lacked wealth? Or how could efficient service be obtained from a man too poor to arm himself? It is more important still to answer the question of how far the Roman population was excluded from direct participation in warfare.

Answers vary according to time and region. In the Ostrogothic kingdom military service was formally reserved to Goths. By virtue of a division of tasks and activities, the Romans had been assigned civilian functions and trades, whilst the Germans, the *Barbari*, or *capillati*, as they were still called, were supposed to protect the community. 'They protected the commonwealth entirely through war. Whilst the Gothic army fought, the Romans lived at peace' (Cassiodorus). Meanwhile some 'honorary Goths' were allowed to fight. Indirectly Romans did take part in war by maintaining fortifications. Valets and serving men could well be Roman by birth; at critical moments – as in the reign of Totila – well-born Italians were employed. But amongst the Vandals there is apparently no parallel. After a century in North Africa, this people was still not assimilated into the indigenous population, and they treated the natives as vanquished, expecting no help from them when the Byzantine counter-offensive was launched. The position is less clear amongst the Burgundians where the kings, faithful to their policy of conciliation displayed in the laws of Gundobad, sought to use the military assistance of Gallo-Romans, who can be seen participating, at least, in an expedition to the Auvergne.

In the Visigothic kingdom, authorization for mixed marriages between Romans and Goths which was accorded in the reign of Leovigild (567–86), the conversion of Reccared (587), the disappearance of separate tribal laws and the promulgation of the *Liber judiciorum* (654) comprehending the whole population, suppressed the juridical obstacles which might have prevented the Hispano-Romans from joining the army. In fact, if, since the redaction of the most ancient Visigothic laws in the middle of the fifth century, the terms *Gotus* and *miles* had been synonymous, then from the reign of Alaric II at the beginning of the sixth century some Romans at least had fought in the ranks of the army. Their presence could only increase in following generations, and under Wamba (672–80) the monarchy attempted to impose military obligations on all the population, who were without doubt opposed to this. A movement of a similar kind occurred in Gaul. If the presence of Gallo-Romans in the Frankish armies was exceptional in the time of Clovis, by that of his sons and grandsons the situation had been reversed. Not only were Gallo-Romans allowed to fight, they were now theoretically obliged to do so. Finally, the Lombards, whose position remained precarious, resisted longest this general movement which led to the equalization of rights and duties amongst the descendants of both victors and vanquished. It was only in the eighth century under Aistulf that Romans could be sure of entering the army freely.[30]

Alongside these differences of an ethnic kind, others appeared based on differences of a juridical nature or on rank in society. In principle neither secular clergy nor those in monastic orders could be forced to do military service. Though it remains true that clerics involved in warfare appear sometimes in the sources, it is most frequently a question of spontaneous martial action not resulting from any military obligation. Amongst the Visigoths, the Fourth Council of Toledo especially concerned itself with clerics who might willingly take up arms in a rebellion or who had already done so, and condemned them for this. But sometimes kings were obliged to force clerics to fight. On 1 November 673, returning from a campaign in Septimania, Wamba, king of the Visigoths, proclaimed a law which, amongst other matters, severely punished those who had not contributed to the defence of the country against the Basques and Franks in threatened areas. Even clergy were included in this law, which was also to remain in force in cases of internal rebellion. In Lombard Italy there was the case of Vualprand, bishop of Lucca, who, according to his own statement, had to join the army 'by order of our lord, King Aistulf'.[31]

Nor does it seem that military obligations were reserved to the rich. Gregory of Tours shows Chilperic exacting from peasants and young servants of the cathedral and basilica the fine imposed for failure to join the army. He adds: 'Yet it was not the custom that such people should be subject to public charges.'[32] Was this exemption due to their dependence on a church, their age or economic position? Another passage from the same author shows that the first explanation is valid.[33] An effort can be detected to force military obligations on another group who stood somewhat apart from the rest of society: merchants. A passage in the law of Aistulf (750) speaks of men who are engaged in commerce and should have arms appropriate to their wealth (for the richest and most powerful, a full set of armour, shield, spear and horses; for those not so rich, a quiver, bow and arrows).[34] It is likely that the semi-free, or *lidi*, of Frankish society had restricted military obligations, and even slaves (*servi*, *mancipia*), the property of both Germans and Romans, did not entirely escape military service.[35]

The law of Gundobad mentions the *servi ministeriales sivi expeditionales*. Still more specific is this passage from a Code of Ervig (680-7): 'By a special decree we have decided that all men, Goth or Roman, on joining the army, shall be accompanied during the campaign by one out of ten of their slaves,

[30] P. Rasi, *Exercitus italicus* (173).
[31] *Ibid.*, 75: '*ex jussione domini nostri Aistulfi regis*'.
[32] Gregory, *Histoire des Francs*, i.288.
[33] *Ibid.*, ii.121.
[34] F. Beyerle, *Leges Langobardorum 643–866*, Göttingen 1962, p.360.
[35] E. Zöllner, *Geschichte der Franken*, Munich 1970, p.115.

in such a fashion that this tenth shall not be without arms but provided with various sorts of weapons so that for each one brought to the army, some shall wear armour and most shall have bucklers, swords, axes (*scramasax*), spears and arrows.'[36] Ervig complained that slave-owners were not even bringing 1 in 20. Egica (678–702) exacted military service from royal, legally enfranchised, slaves and their descendants. It has been said that the greater part of the Visigothic army in the seventh century was made up of slaves sent by their masters.[37] Another procedure, attested among the Lombards, was to augment the army by freeing slaves.[38]

From a geographical point of view, the basis for recruitment should have been very broad. Against the Bretons, Chilperic summoned men from Touraine, Poitou, Bayeux, Le Mans and Angers. Against the Poitevins, Guntram used men from Touraine and Berry.[39] In the fifth century when the Visigothic king decided on an expedition, he sent his slaves (*servi dominici, compulsores*) through the realm. Each Goth had to be individually summoned and the *compulsor* was forbidden to accept any goods or money whatsoever to purchase exemption. The warriors were formed into units commanded by a hierarchy of *prepositi exercitus*, responsible respectively for 10, 100, 500 or 1,000 men, under the control of the count of the city. In the seventh century the *thiufadus* was not, as has long been thought, the equivalent of a *millenarius*, but a 'captain of servants' (from *thius*: a valet or servant), that is of the non-free.[40]

Ethnic divisions had to be respected. In the army Alboin led in Italy, alongside Lombards are mentioned a certain number of peoples who had conserved their cohesion and homogeneity: Gepids, Pannonians, Sueves, Thuringians. This habit is still apparent in a passage from Fredegar's *Chronicle*:

> In the fourteenth year of his reign, since the Gascons were in revolt and were making severe raids into the Frankish kingdom that had been Charibert's, Dagobert raised his forces throughout Burgundy and put in command of them the referendary Chadoind. . . . He made for Gascony with his army in company with ten dukes and their forces – namely the Franks Arnebert, Amalgar, Leudebert, Wandalmer, Walderic, Hermenric, Barontus and Chaira, the Roman Chramnelen, the Burgundian patrician Willebad, the Saxon Aighyna and in addition many counts who had no duke over them.[41]

---

[36] IX, 2, 9. Certain manuscripts speak of half of a man's slaves up to a maximum of 50.

[37] E. A. Thompson, *The Goths in Spain*, Oxford 1969, p.318, and cf. P. D. King, *Law and Society in the Visigothic Kingdom*, Cambridge 1972, pp.71–7.

[38] Paul the Deacon, *Historia Langobardorum*, i.13.

[39] Gregory, *Histoire des Francs* i.288; ii.88.

[40] D. Claude, Millenarius und Thiuphadus, ZSSRG, *Germ. Abt.*, *88* (1971), 181–90.

[41] *The Fourth Book of the Chronicle of Fredegar*, ed. and tr. J. M. Wallace-Hadrill, London 1960, p.65.

Nevertheless the principle of general recruitment should not obscure reality. In fact it was in most interests to summon for preference the rich, the *robustiores*, rather than the *populus minus*, *inferiores* or *pauperes*. Visigothic Spain shows the continuing predominance of the Germanic aristocracy. Alongside a massive implantation, a proper colonization by the invaders of the Castilian Meseta, there was a general dissemination throughout the peninsula of an elite who progressively assumed politico-military power. Such were the *seniores Gothorum*, magnates living in more or less closed societies or the 'very prosperous Gothic people' mentioned by Isidore of Seville at the beginning of the seventh century; in all, perhaps, some 500 families of *primates*, who with their protégés, their free and unfree domestic servants, their faithful followers, formed the only truly solid part of the Visigothic army, to which the provincial levies hardly added anything of value.[42] From this springs the importance that must be attached to the military entourage of the great: around the king, the *gardingi*, around the lords, the *buccellarii* ('biscuit-eaters') who, according to Euric's code, received arms from their patrons, which they had to return if they transferred to the service of another master. As for the former royal messengers (*saiones*), they could still be discovered amongst both the Visigoths and Ostrogoths. In the latter case, the job of these maids of all work was certainly to bring the army together, organize transport and supplies, requisition men and timber for the war fleet, as well as to supervise the collection of taxes and the efficient functioning of the postal system. In the Lombard state the *faramanni*, members of a *fara* or lineage group, installed in a *castrum* or *castellum*, a strategic position of any sort, and gravitating around the dukes, were distinct from the *arimanni*, who in the eighth century became the most trusted dependents of the king, his *fideles*, more than just soldiers.[43] The Anglo-Saxon kingdoms had their *gesiths* and *gesithcundmen* whose position fluctuated. Some at the bottom of the scale seem like *hlafaeten* or 'bread-eaters' who received food and clothing from their lord (*hlaford*: giver of bread), whilst others, more independent, had their own possessions or had even received concessions of land held by precarious or more definite tenures from their masters.

Finally, there is the Frankish realm where, at first, around the king we find *antrustions* (from Salian Frankish *trust*, a term translated in glosses by *adjutorium*, helper), and around the great men, a whole variety of figures described by almost synonymous terms for the same relationship: *satellites*, *sicarii*, *pueri*, *viri fortes*, *amici*, *lictores*. A clear distinction is drawn between members of the *scara* or *scariti*, small groups of men ready at a moment's notice, especially to wage war, and the army (*exercitus*) of the *pagenses* whom it is the count's duty to summon and command. Later, the *antrustions* are called

---

[42] R. d'Abadal i de Vinyals, A propos du legs visigothique en Espagne, *Carrateri del secolo VII in Occidente*, Spoleto, 2 vols. 1958, ii.541–85.

[43] P. Toubert, La liberté personnelle au haut moyen âge et le problème des *arimanni*, *MA*, *73* (1967), 127–44.

leudes, whose role is defined in two passages from Fredegar's *Chronicle*: one relates to the reign of Sigebert 'who ordered all the leading men (*leudes*) of Austrasia to assemble in arms', then 'crossed the Rhine with this army, and was joined by all the peoples of his kingdom who lived in the districts across the river'; the other, in Dagobert's day, refers to the way in which he assured his peaceful succession by 'ordering all his Austrasian followers (*leudes*) to assemble in arms'.[44]

THE STRENGTHS AND WEAKNESSES OF CAROLINGIAN ARMIES
IN THE EIGHTH AND NINTH CENTURIES

In the seventh century the Merovingian monarchy experienced a very severe crisis; it was overtaken by a sort of general paralysis, brought on both by the growth of aristocratic power as well as by dissensions and civil wars. The decline was only halted at the moment when Pepin II of Herstal, victorious over the Neustrian army at Tertry, was recognized as mayor of the palace for the whole of the kingdom (687). Then campaigns could be undertaken against neighbouring peoples like the Alamans, the Frisians and the Saxons who had previously threatened the borders of Frankish territory and had refused to submit even in symbolic form. Whilst this was a beginning, the political and military crisis which followed the death of Pepin II (714) threatened to undermine the effort to redress the balance. A bastard of Pepin, Charles (the future Charles Martel) succeeded, however, in establishing himself by defeating the Neustrian army, first of all at Amblève near Malmédy (716), then at Vinchy, near Cambrai, on Sunday, 21 March 717. Thereafter Charles Martel led a military campaign in one direction or another almost every year.

In his turn, Pepin III the Short displayed the same energy as his father. In a reign of 28 years he led an expedition against the Muslims, two against the Alamans, two against the Bavarians, two against the Lombards, three against the Saxons and eight against the Aquitainians. Sometimes two campaigns occurred the same year; thus in 745 when Pepin commanded part of the Frankish forces against Teobald, duke of the Alamans, his brother Carloman fought against the Saxons at the same time. In 767 a first campaign in Aquitaine begun in March and marked by the capture of Toulouse, Albi and Rodez, was followed by a second which began in August with the assembling of an army at Bourges and continued with a raid as far as the Garonne.

It is true that the annual rhythm of war was interrupted at times. After the campaign in 749 against the Bavarians, one of the continuations of the chronicle of the Pseudo-Fredegar states that 'for two years the land had peace', a respite from warfare which was repeated, according to the same source, in 757–8.[45]

---

[44] Fredegar, pp.47 and 73.
[45] *Ibid.*, pp.102 and 108.

An effort of similar intensity occurred throughout the major part of Charlemagne's reign. Years without military expeditions were always sufficiently exceptional for them to be mentioned in the Annals, as was the case in 790 and 792 when the principal narrative source, the *Annales regni Francorum*, states: 'No military campaign (*iter exercitale*) was undertaken this year.'[46] But the conquest of Frisia, the submission of Bavaria and Saxony, the struggle against the Avars and Bretons, the settlement beyond the Pyrenees and the destruction followed by the annexation of the Lombard kingdom, necessitated the regular summons and systematic use of Frankish armies, frequently commanded by the king in person.[47]

After a century of wars, the success of the Carolingian dynasty was undeniable: at the start controlling Austrasia alone, it succeeded not only in retaking Neustria and bringing back under its domination the huge region of Aquitaine, but it also reached the south of the Danish peninsula, controlled all the region to the west of the Saale and Elbe, advanced into Carinthia, seized the Italian peninsula down to the duchy of Spoleto and occupied Barcelona and Pamplona. Even beyond these official limits its protectorate extended over the lands of the Sorbs, Moravians, Avars and Croats as well as over the duchy of Benevento and the region lying between the March of Spain and the Ebro. Certainly many of these conquests had been achieved patiently, step by step, without those striking successes which a few generations earlier had marked Arab expansion, but they also revealed both the tenacious will of the leaders and the high quality of the military machine at their disposal.

The Carolingians had to overcome many obstacles in their vast enterprise of territorial expansion. In particular it was often necessary for them to fight far from the material and spiritual bases of their power, away from the centre of their domination between the Rhine and the Meuse. They had to confront peoples whose martial habits were very different from one another and thus they had to adapt to their adversaries. On the other hand, vis-à-vis these enemies, the Franks enjoyed a large superiority in both men and arms. In addition, the political systems of the societies which they faced were often insubstantial and riddled by division. The sudden disappearance of the Lombard monarchy cannot be easily explained unless one considers the struggles which had for a long time brought it into opposition with its dukes. It was the intrigues of Muslim chiefs in Spain, rebels from the authority of the emirate of Córdoba, which allowed Charlemagne to extend Frankish influence south of the Pyrenees. It has been suggested that reasons for the conquest of Saxony may be found in the division of Saxons into two parties, on the one hand a seigneurial class who were prepared to accept Charlemagne

---

[46] *Annales regni Francorum*, ed. G. H. Pertz and F. Kurze, Hanover 1895, pp.87 and 92.
[47] For the principal military capitularies see *Capitularia regnum Francorum*, ed. A. Boretius and V. Krause, Hanover 2 vols. 1893–7: 807 (i.134–5); 808 (i.136–8); 811 (i.166–7); 825 (i.324–5); 846 (ii.65–8); 866 (ii.94–6).

with few regrets and, on the other, the lower orders – free and semi-free – fiercely hostile to the foreign conqueror. Finally, in this progress of expansion, diplomacy played a role which was sometimes as great as that of the strictly military.

The personal qualities of these three sovereigns were just as important in explaining Frankish success as the weaknesses of their adversaries and the complexity of the diplomatic scene. If there is nothing to prove that Charles Martel, Pepin or Charlemagne were inspired strategists, at least one cannot deny their extraordinary physical and moral endurance or their genuine enthusiasm for war. They also had a consummate aptitude for leading men, for getting the best out of their own vassals as well as from the different aristocracies who, with varying degrees of sincerity and opportunism, found themselves progressively integrated into the Frankish political system.

At the end of the eighth century and the beginning of the ninth, thanks to the capitularies, our knowledge of the Carolingian military system becomes less imprecise. Concerning recruitment, one of the most important aspects of the power to order, prohibit and punish which the Carolingian sovereign enjoyed under the term *bannum* resided in the fact that all his subjects, including those who had most recently submitted to him or been conquered, owed him military service. However, in practice this service was only fully exacted in the event of an enemy invasion and then only in the threatened province. This constituted the general summons to arms or *lantweri*, absence from which entailed death, at least if the invasion that had necessitated the summons actually occurred.

For a long time the formulae for convocation of the army remained very vague, doubtless because the men who responded were sufficient in numbers for most needs. Then from 806 the formulae became more precise. A distinction appeared between simple freemen whose obligations were limited and vassals, maintained either directly or indirectly by the king, bishops, abbots and abbesses, counts or lords, who had very strict duties. A memorandum of 807 prescribed, for example, that 'beyond the Seine all should do service in the host. First of all, those who had benefices should come to the army. Then every freeman who had five *manses* should come to the army, then those who had four should appear and then those with three. When there were two men, each with two *manses*, each one should help the other and the most competent of the two should come to the army. As for those who had only half a *mansus*, five of them should equip a sixth, and he who was poor, having neither slave nor lands of his own worth [blank] shillings, then five of these men should also equip a sixth and to each of these latter, five shillings should be handed over jointly by the aforementioned five poor men who appeared to have no land'.[48] Complex as this system was for those who actually participated and those who merely contributed (between whom some exchange was perhaps

[48] *Ibid.*, i.134.

envisaged), it remained in force under Louis the Pious and was even introduced into Italy in the reign of Lothair II by a capitulary of 825.

In the absence of registers of troops who could be mobilized which, according to an act of Louis the Pious in 829, should have been compiled county by county, it is impossible to be exact about the number of effectives which could be assembled. H. Delbrück, F. Lot and F. L. Ganshof agree in thinking that the Carolingians even at their most powerful were unable to raise more than a few thousand combatants, 5,000 being an acceptable total.[49] J. F. Verbruggen is a little more generous – a large army might number between 2,500 and 3,000 horsemen and 6,000–10,000 foot soldiers. His figures allow him to split up the men into several divisions coming from different regions and peoples which could then merge and together attack a strategic objective.[50] K. F. Werner, examining the whole question, has shown weaknesses in Lot's reasoning and has insisted on the wide extent of territory from which Charlemagne could raise his armies.[51] He has proposed two methods of estimation which, though depending on different bases, nevertheless give convergent results. A statistical survey of the *regna* of which the Carolingian Empire was composed reveals the existence of at least 200 *palatia*, 600 *fisci*, 500 *abbates* (of whom 200 directly depended on the king) and 189 *civitates* or bishoprics (of which 140 at least were *castra* of real importance), perhaps some 1,500 human settlements where royal authority was exercised directly. The other line of reasoning is that the Empire at its greatest extent included at least 700 districts (*pagi*) of which 500 had a count at their head. It can be seen that in these circumstances the figure of 5,000 horsemen is too low; at only 50 horsemen per county that would give 35,000 for the whole of the Empire. One could also start from the number of direct vassals whom Charlemagne had: 100 bishops, about 200 abbots, 500 counts and, as an estimate, perhaps 1,000 *vassi dominici*, a total of 1,800 men. If each one of them brought to the army 20 horsemen raised from his own vassals that would again give a force of 36,000 horsemen. *A priori*, this figure of 20 does not appear too high. Under Louis the Pious, the abbot of Corvey, for example, had 30 vassals for his own needs, who were exempt from royal military service, and in numerous acts issued by counts it is common to find the attestation of 30 vassals. That is to say, Werner estimates that between 800 and 840 the Empire could provide some 35,000 well-equipped horsemen, to whom should be added a vast mass of foot soldiers and auxiliaries, perhaps some 100,000 men. From these potential resources only a fraction was actually raised for particularly important expeditions like that directed in 796 against the Avars when, with all the columns united, Charlemagne's forces may have numbered between 15,000 and 20,000 horsemen.

[49] H. Delbrück, *Geschichte des Kriegskunst* (3); F. Lot, *Art militaire* (6); F. L. Ganshof, L'armée sous les Carolingiens (159).
[50] J. F. Verbruggen, L'armée et la stratégie de Charlemagne (177).
[51] K. F. Werner, Heeresorganisation und Kriegsführung (214).

Even if the preceding estimates appear too optimistic, it remains true that Werner has pertinently emphasized the extent of territory of which Charlemagne and Louis the Pious were masters. To the degree that they were capable, thanks to their methods of government, of enforcing their will or, more modestly, of issuing orders throughout this immense realm, it would have been possible for them to raise relatively large numbers even when each region furnished only a modest contingent in relation to the total population legally obliged to serve.[52] What is more, Werner's reasoning implies that from at least the beginning of the ninth century the core of the Carolingian army comprised men who were attached to their sovereign by a specially strong link, which had a public character in the case of counts, or a private one in the case of vassals.

The existence of fairly precise rules of recruitment leads one to think that the authorities feared that in many circumstances there would be a lack of soldiers. Recourse solely to volunteers attracted by a sense of adventure and search for booty was insufficient. But one should not forget that the maintenance of military obligations also had an economic and fiscal purpose. Absence from the army was, in fact, punished by a heavy fine (*heribannum*). In 805, for instance, defaulters who possessed moveable goods worth six pounds (gold, silver, leather jerkins, livestock, clothes etc.) owed a heriban of 60 shillings, those with goods worth three pounds paid 30 shillings and those with two pounds paid ten shillings.[53] Raising the heriban and summoning the army were tasks frequently entrusted to the same officials who undertook the two missions simultaneously. Falling on those who held *manses*, the *carnaticus* was an obligatory purveyance of livestock, especially sheep, destined to supply the army, whilst the *hostilense* or *hostilitium* was a levy in oxen and carts.

The importance attached by Carolingian legislation to the problem of supplies in itself implies that the numbers participating in expeditions were not necessarily derisory. A capitulary dating from the last years of Charlemagne's reign states that each count should reserve in his county two-thirds of the grazing for the needs of the army. In a letter to Abbot Fulrad, in all likelihood dating from 806, Charlemagne, after having indicated to him the place and date of the rendezvous, invited the abbot to provide himself with carts loaded with all kinds of tools, foodstocks for three months and arms and clothing for half a year. As for the royal demesnes, they were to provide carts of standard size, covered with leather and waterproofed for crossing rivers.

For a long period the Carolingian armies fought essentially defensive campaigns, the date of departure for which, if not the duration, could be fixed long in advance. However, the authorities sought to speed up the process of

---

[52] cf. the *terribile imperium* of which Hetti, archbishop of Trier, speaks in a letter to Frothard, bishop of Toul (*RCH*, vi.395).

[53] *Capitularia*, i.125.

mobilization. From at least 790, this took place in two stages: first of all local authorities (counts, bishops, abbots and abbesses, important royal vassals) received an order to arm from the *missi*. They would then compile a list of those who would fight and those who would send aid, inventory and inspect available arms and gather supplies. Then when the order to join the army arrived, all was ready for a rapid departure which, according to an act of Louis the Pious, should occur within less than 12 hours.

Together with the household warriors, directly dependent on the Carolingians, the army consisted of contingents from the different great provinces or *regna* into which the Empire was divided. Thus, according to the Royal Annals, the campaign which Charlemagne led in 778 against Saragossa included men who had come from Burgundy, Neustria, Bavaria, Provence, and Septimania, and even a contingent of Lombards. These great units, which were both ethnic and administrative, each included a series of more or less specific and autonomous formations.

Other forms of military activity required a different personnel. First, in frontier zones (*marcae*), labour services were exacted for the upkeep and construction of fortresses and their defence was entrusted as much to the local population (*wacta, warda*) as to professional and permanent warriors. The latter sometimes constituted proper military colonies and formed the backbone of those small task forces which had determined and limited objectives, groups which are called in the sources *scarae* (from the German *Schar*: troop), *excariti* or *scariti homines*.

Despite their limitations, the military successes of the Franks throughout the eighth century in no way foreshadow the reverses of the following age. In fact during the reign of Louis the Pious (814–40) the defence of the Empire along its different frontiers was more or less assured. Various attempts were made to seize Brittany. The *limes danicus* held. The Bulgar invasions of 827 and 829 had only limited consequences, as did the penetration of the Saracens into the March of Spain (826–7) and the progressive isolation of Corsica, Sardinia and the Balearic islands. It is difficult to decide whether this lull was due to the maintenance of Frankish prestige, to the continuing efficiency of the system of imperial defence or to the weakness of the attacks or threats coming from outside the Empire. In any event, from the 840s Saracen pirates increased their attacks in the Mediterranean. The Italian peninsula was assailed from all sides and coastal towns fell into Muslim hands, sometimes for a long time.

But it was the Viking threat, menacing the heart of the Empire, which was the most serious. It was during the first 20 years of Charles the Bald's reign that the Northmen achieved their greatest success and amassed their richest booty. Later, resistance was organized and the Vikings changed both their tactics and, even more, their objectives. Instead of pillaging indiscriminately, they began to exploit their victims more carefully and then to form lasting settlements in lands which became recognized as their own. This was the case from 878 in north-east England (the future Danelaw) and from 911 in the Caux region and the counties of Rouen, Evreux and Lisieux, abandoned to Rollo by Charles the Simple. The first wave of Scandinavian expansion then came to an end, and a period of calm ensued, lasting for about 50 years.

It is not necessary to seek superior numbers as an explanation of Viking victories. Nor were the Viking bands, usually totalling a few hundred men, better armed than the Frankish troops. Their swords, for example, often came from the Carolingian empire; though the great, two-handed Danish axe was unique to them and could prove horribly effective in massed hand-to-hand combat. For siege warfare, of which we have a good account thanks to Abbo, the Vikings – helped by deserters – had only to borrow or copy the siege engines of their enemies.[54] A major advantage, however, was their mobility. Primarily this was because of their ships, 'the instrument par excellence of Viking imperialism',[55] and then because of the horses which they learned how to obtain at the expense of their enemies, so they could undertake amphibious operations and succeed in surprising their adversaries without ever being surprised themselves. Later they began to lose a little of this capacity for movement. Transforming themselves into 'half-sedentary buccaneers',[56] they built camps, protected in all likelihood by earth and wooden ramparts similar to those they used in Scandinavia, where they could safely store food, weapons and the produce of their raids. Contemporaries considered these wild, sacrilegious pagans, the product of a profoundly military society where everyone lived in constant familiarity with arms from adolescence to death, capable of every form of cruelty, deceit and audacity.

During the first phase between 840 and about 865, the Franks, clearly helpless, only reacted feebly. Many bishops and counts fled, abandoning the rest of the population to their fate. Everyone jibbed at involving themselves in this bitter and profitless warfare. Deceptive respite was gained by paying heavy indemnities. Even cities possessing walls did not know how to defend themselves. In brief, there was a total denial of responsibility which, however good his intentions, Charles the Bald could do little to repair. Then resistance was organized. It took the form of a territorial defence system, no doubt too static, but relatively effective. From the Loire valley to the Rhine, with royal initiative or without fortified bridges (like that at Pitres on the Seine), *castella* and *castra* were built, town walls were restored and monasteries provided with defences. The chronicles even report some cases where the common people shared in the struggle.

It is not certain, however, whether the results achieved owed their success to the Frankish counter-attack or to a decline in Viking aggression. When this

---

[54] Abbon de Saint-Germain-des-Prés, *Le siège de Paris par les Normands. Poème du IXe siècle,* ed. and tr. H. Waquet, Paris 1942.

[55] A. d'Haenens, *Les invasions normandes* (156).

[56] M. Bloch, *La société féodale* (99), i.47 (tr. L. A. Manyon as *Feudal Society*, London 1961, p.21).

revived, as in the period 879–87, the Franks scarcely contained their enemies better than before and they often finished by purchasing the departure of the Vikings with a heavy tribute. But whereas in Gaul the Northmen obtained a permanent base, in Italy the Saracens, threatened first by the energetic offensives of Lothair (846), then by Louis II (expedition to Benevento in 866, recapture of Bari in 871), and by vigorous local reaction and from 885 by methodical Byzantine counter-attack, could only obtain temporary bridgeheads.

In the end, Scandinavian successes may be explained principally by the destruction of 'fraternity and concord' amongst the descendants of Louis the Pious and by the rapid disintegration of central authority, because of which the rulers of *Francia occidentalis* and *Francia media* were placed in tutelage by the *proceres*, losing at a stroke both their support and means of action. Charles the Bald might well in his capitularies repeat the legislative arrangements of his glorious predecessors. But in the military sphere it was simply a façade behind which existed only a simulacrum of power.

2

The Feudal Age from the Beginning of the Tenth to the Middle of the Twelfth Century

The death of Louis the Pious (840) marked a decisive turning point in the history of the Carolingian Empire. Its unity was never firmly re-established. Though an Emperor whose prestige was envied survived, the kings who headed the different parts of the Empire were always Carolingians and, for a brief period during the reign of Charles the Fat, it seemed that the whole inheritance was going to return to a single ruler for a long time. But it was an illusion, dissipated by the events of 887–88. These definitively marked the fading of the great Carolingian dream; with new political circumstances, the military activities of the West took on a new shape.

GENERAL CHARACTERISTICS

Once the battle of the Lechfeld (955) had halted the Magyar threat, once the last Viking raids had ceased and the final fears of Saracen attack had been removed at the beginning of the eleventh century, the West found itself no longer on the defensive and succeeded in a few generations in notably extending its area of dominance. Not only did the conversion of Poland, Hungary and the Scandinavian kingdoms enlarge the zone of influence of Latin Christendom to the north and east, but Islam fell back in Spain, through the progress of the *Reconquista*, and in the Mediterranean, with the annexation of Sicily and the establishment of Latin states in the Middle East. At the same time, in the wake of a movement that was not only military but also economic and demographic, a new Germany was created beyond the Elbe. Facing their enemies, neighbours or rivals, the warriors of the West marked up a string of successes.

This expansion is all the more remarkable because it occurred at a time of increasing fragmentation of power. It is true that between the tenth and twelfth centuries some relatively powerful, unified states survived or were created, like the kingdom of England, the Norman kingdom of Southern Italy or the kingdom of Castile. In France, however, as well as in the Empire, despite the survival of certain earlier political institutions, duchies, marquisates, counties, baronies or simple lordships multiplied. All formed political units enjoying increased autonomy, even quasi-sovereignty. Even more than the relationships between one man and another, the rites of homage and vassalship, this is the outstanding feature of that complex phenomenon which historians call feudalism. In tens and hundreds, principalities of every size became centres of independent military systems, including, in addition to specific means of attack and defence, the right and power to declare, pursue and terminate war. From this sprang that multitude of skirmishes, sieges, raids, burnings, encounters and battles, often on a very small scale, whose recital constitutes the daily fare of contemporary annalists and chroniclers. It was warfare of short duration that predominated, if we leave aside major military expeditions which necessitated assembling armies from each nation and kingdom or from the whole of Latin Christendom.

The feudal period was also one in which slowly, everywhere, heavy cavalry, armed with lance and sword and protected by a conical helmet and a chain-mail hauberk, came to predominate. In Richer's *History of France*, written at the very end of the tenth century, one finds the expression *milites peditesque*, which implies that the *miles*, the soldier *par excellence*, is a mounted warrior. The same author speaks indiscriminately of the *ordo equestris* and the *ordo militaris*.[1] Monopolizing for their own profit military techniques and prestige, the *milites* were not only specialists in fighting but also became the predominant element in the social structure. Nevertheless, though they constituted, after the *nobiles* properly so-called, a true aristocratic group, they remained a relatively open order to which all those who were able to demonstrate their military abilities, whatever their birth or wealth, could accede.

Similarly, the lower social orders were more or less systematically and completely excluded from a military role, or played in this sphere only an auxiliary role, doubtless useful, even indispensable, but scorned. The mass of the peasantry were thus described as *imbelle* or *inerme vulgus* (unarmed), in contrast to the elite of *pugnatores* (fighters). At a time when throughout most of the West towns were few and tiny, often strangers to the rural world which surrounded them, the militias which their inhabitants could raise intervened ineffectually and were scarcely capable of ensuring their own defence from behind the safety of the town's walls. Moreover, towns were far from being the only fortified structures, for it was at this period that castles multiplied. These were rudimentary, made in many regions of wood rather than stone, built on an artificial mound (*motte*) or natural spur, and surrounded by a palisade and ditch. Each of these fortresses, serving both as a civil residence and for defence, was the nerve centre of which a network allowed control and exploitation of the countryside for political, military and economic purposes. The castle housed an almost permanent group of warriors.

[1] Richer, *Histoire de France*, ed. R. Latouche, Paris 1937, ii.180.

Money remained scarce almost everywhere. Rulers and powerful men had limited and intermittent supplies of cash. The maintenance of soldiers in their service was preferably assured by lands which were conceded to them, in practice in heredity, in return for performance of a certain number of duties of a military character. Certainly the payment of soldiers was not an entirely unknown phenomenon, but it was a secondary, marginal one, less important in any case than the upkeep of castle garrisons at the expense of the rich, powerful lords.

Finally, military activities and attitudes were more or less deeply affected by the influence of the Church which proposed or prescribed a new ideal of a Christian soldier, sometimes seeking to exalt military virtues when it was a question of fighting the Infidel, sometimes seeking to limit and purge them when it was a matter of internal disputes. However, within the broad framework of conditions common throughout the West, important differences existed which can best be surveyed by looking separately at the great regions of which the West was composed.

THE HOLY ROMAN EMPIRE

'Your land is fecund in valorous men. It is renowned for being populated with a vigorous youth. Thus the whole world praises you and the fame of your courage has filled all the earth.'[2] An expression of the most powerful state of the West, the military forces of which the Roman Emperors and German kings of the Saxon and Salian dynasties could take advantage were simultaneously the most numerous and the most redoubtable. It is true that their task was particularly difficult. They had at the same time to fight in Germany in the internal wars (*bella civilia*) in which they confronted the armies of territorial princes when they attempted to free themselves from central authority, to repulse the Danes, subject the Slav tribes beyond the Elbe (Wends and Sorabs), bring the kingdoms of Poland and Hungary and the duchy of Bohemia to heel, protect or push further to the west the limits of the Empire and, lastly, impose the Germanic yoke on the kingdom of Italy. In this sense the Ottonians and Salians were true successors to the Carolingians, with a huge territory to protect, pacify and extend, and the obligation to lead almost annual expeditions in one direction or another. Moreover, several German sovereigns like Otto the Great, Henry II, Conrad II and Henry IV were war leaders of note.

Among their major military successes may be numbered victory over the Hungarians or Magyars. This people, related to the Huns, Avars and

---

[2] St Bernard, *Epistola* 363. According to Walter Map, Louis VII used the same words: 'The Roman Emperor, whom one calls German, has men who know how to wage war and warhorses' (*De nugis curialium*, ed. M. R. James, Oxford 1914, p.225).

Bulgars, settled at the end of the eighth century on the lower Danube in the region which later became the provinces of Bessarabia, Moldavia and Walachia. Undoubtedly the Magyars were themselves under pressure from other migrating peoples, especially the Petchenegs. The Byzantine Emperor Leo VI (886–912) used the Magyars against the Bulgars. But the latter allied with the Petchenegs and the Magyars were forced to start their march westwards again and to cross the Carpathians (895). They debouched onto the Pannonian plain, driving off or subjugating the few small tribes which occupied it. Then from this remarkable base they began a series of incursions into the West. From 899 to 955 there were at least 32 raids. France and Italy were attacked, but it was Germany which suffered most.

The Magyars formed a kind of 'military republic',[3] linking several tribes. Only men fit for war exercised political rights. Each tribe elected its chieftain (Hungarian: *hadnagy;* Latin: *dux*) from the same family. In their turn the chieftains chose a *princeps*, who at the time of the invasions belonged to the Arpad family. An assembly of Magyar peoples met to decide on important issues such as, for example, military expeditions. These horsemen, armed with sword, spear and bow, were only lightly protected by a sort of felt head-piece. Their war cry (the *Hui, hui* of which Liutprand speaks)[4] frequently provoked panic. They were often regarded as hideously terrifying. Even in the twelfth century the bishop of Bamberg, Otto of Freising, passing through Hungary on his way to the Holy Land, wrote that 'it is necessary to marvel at Divine Providence for having delivered such an agreeable land not to men, I say, but to such monsters of men.'[5] They were suspected of drinking their enemies' blood. Their tactics were the same as those of peoples of the Steppes – a sudden attack, accompanied by a rain of arrows, followed by simulated flight in order to encourage pursuit; then, when their adversaries' cohesion had been broken, the Magyars wheeled about and overwhelmed them. Their encampments were protected by waggons. When they found themselves in a difficult position, they refused to fight. For a long period they lacked siege engines. Only rarely did they succeed in capturing castles and fortified towns. They contented themselves with burning suburbs and operating more or less strict blockades. Westerners admired their solidarity in combat; they tried to recover captured companions and were anxious to burn their war dead in order to carry home their ashes. The *Chronica Hungarorum* describes their total forces in this way: 'They divide themselves into seven armies, each of which is commanded by a particular

---

[3] G. Fasoli, *Le incursioni ungare in Europa nel secolo X*, Florence 1945; *idem*, Points de vue sur les invasions hongroises en Europe au Xe siècle, *Cahiers de civilisation médiévale*, 2 (1959), 17–35. See also A. d'Haenens, Les incursions hongroises dans l'espace belge, *ibid.*, 4 (1961), 423–40.

[4] Liutprand of Cremona, *Antapodosis*, ed. E. Dümmler, Hanover 1877.

[5] Otto of Freising, *Chronica*, ed. A. Schmidt and F. J. Schmale, Berlin 1965, p.192.

leader, and they establish captains of hundreds and of tens in the usual fashion; each army totals 30,857 combatants . . . some 216,000 men coming from 108 tribes, each tribe having furnished 2,000 fighters.'[6] These are all imaginary figures, yet seem in some sense to correspond to mobilizable forces in a defensive war. It has also been suggested that the Magyar raids were the action of an aristocratic minority whose style of life they reflected. This minority was clearly distinct from the mass of the population which was composed of a peasantry quickly settled and pacified.[7]

It is hard to find in their attacks a proper political design. In contrast to the Vikings and Saracens, they did not seek to settle permanently in any region, town or fortified site. However, though as a general rule they left their homeland in the first days of spring to return there towards the end of autumn, loaded down with booty, it sometimes happened that they spent the winter in a Christian land as they did in 937–8. The Magyars knew how to profit from circumstances. Sometimes they seem very well informed of conditions in the countries they wished to attack. A statement of Leo VI supports this view: 'They sought an opportune moment with the greatest care', and Liutprand shows that the great invasion of 899–900 was preceded by an exploratory phase. A minority, a regency or a civil war all evidently favoured their schemes and they were able to take advantage of inside help. Surprise remained, however, one of their greatest assets. No political or diplomatic tension needed to precede their incursions. Rising unexpectedly in small elusive groups, these 'lubricious vipers', as they were called by the compiler of the *Chronicon Ebes pengense*, seized control as quickly as possible of roads and passes, leaving authorities no time to prepare or to form any defensive plan.

As in the Viking period, the reaction of the West was slow. The inhabitants of threatened regions preferred to seek refuge in towns and castles or even to hide themselves in forests and marshes. An attempt was made to buy them off. Truces, sometimes long-lasting, were arranged. Eventually it was recognized that the invaders were not invulnerable. Religious leaders came to the fore: the abbot of Fulda in 915 or the abbot of St-Gall in 926. German counts and dukes in the reign of Conrad I (911–18) began to show determination. Conrad's successor, Henry the Fowler (919–36), first agreed to pay tribute. Then he thoroughly reorganized his military system by founding new towns and ensuring their protection.[8] 'Choosing one in nine soldier-peasants, he compelled him to live in a town so that he could build eight dwellings for his companions, receive and store a third of all the harvest, whilst the eight others would sow, reap and harvest for the ninth, putting his share on one

---

[6] J. de Thworcz, *Chronica Hungarorum*, Frankfurt 1600, ii.7.

[7] G. Török, Die Bewohner von Halimba im 10. und 11. Jahrhundert, *Archaeologia Hungarica*, *39* (1962).

[8] E. Sander, Die Heeresorganisation Heinrichs I (208).

side.'[9] The king also appealed to the Saxon peasantry, who it seems had some military experience, gained by contact with the Slavs, and even to bandits and criminals whom he employed as mercenaries, installed in a suburb of Merseburg (the *legio Mesaburiorum*). After gaining several victories over the Slavs, Henry I considered that he now had an army sufficiently skilled in mounted warfare, of which the core was formed by the *milites armati* mentioned by Widukind of Corvey. In agreement with the great nobles, he refused to purchase peace from the Magyars any longer. A later legend even relates that instead of the tribute demanded, the king sent them a dog whose ears and tail he had cropped. A response was not long delayed: the Magyars invaded Saxony. Henry the Fowler dared to oppose them and emerged victorious from the battle of Allstedt (15 March 933).

In 955 Henry's son Otto the Great consummated this success. Having advanced into Swabia, the Magyars undertook the siege of Augsburg on 8 August. The town had a circuit of stone walls, though this was not very high and lacked towers. Nevertheless while the bishop's knights took up positions outside the walls to meet the first assault, the population worked feverishly on the ramparts to reinforce weak spots. Next day the Magyars approached with siege engines. Learning of the arrival of Otto with his Swabian, Bohemian, Saxon, Franconian and Bavarian contingents, they interrupted this manoeuvre to await the enemy. All day on 9 August the German soldiers fasted according to their custom. The following morning at the Lechfeld they swore peace and mutual aid. Otto's army consisted of eight cavalry units (*legiones*). After a first unfortunate skirmish, Otto disposed his troops in line of battle (*acies*). A frontal attack by the heavy German cavalry forced the Magyars to flee, since the majority lacked shields, helmets and hauberks. The pursuit was most effective. To weaken his enemies permanently Otto ordered the massacre of captured chieftains. His gamble paid off: according to the annals of the German kingdom it was 1030 before another sovereign had to lead another great army against the Magyars.[10]

The *expeditio italica* (or, similarly, the *expeditio ultra Alpes*, or *trans Alpes*, or, from 1135, the *expeditio romana*) was another major kind of military activity. This was far from being just a martial enterprise. Crossing the Alps after his succession, the German king's first ambition was to wear the iron crown of Lombardy and to obtain the imperial crown from the papacy. Confirming his status as ruler of Italy, it was then necessary for him to govern, administer and negotiate. But very often his simple presence did not at a stroke cause rebels and recalcitrants to submit; so he had to resort to force, which was also equally directed against his Byzantine and Norman

<hr>

[9] Quoted by D. Schäfer, Die *agrarii milites* des Widukind, *Sitzungsberichte der königlich-preussischen Akademie der Wissenschaften*, *27* (1905), 569–77.
[10] K. Leyser, The battle at the Lech (67); *idem*, Henry I and the beginnings of the Saxon Empire (201).

adversaries. During his stay (often lasting several years) his court took on the form of a military camp, staffed by princes and German knights always ready to start fighting again. From the accession of Otto the Great (936) to the death of Lothair of Supplinburg (1137), 20 Italian campaigns may be listed, without counting the almost solitary journey of Henry IV in 1076–77, notable for the interview at Canossa. In general, the armies passed through the Brenner pass, after assembling at Augsburg or Ratisbon; more rarely they used the St Gothard or Mont Cenis passes. In most cases the Alps were traversed at the beginning of August or September, though sometimes also in early spring or even in November, December or February. Once the Brenner pass had been negotiated the army reassembled in the plain of Roncaglia where there was a muster of troops.

> The custom of the Frankish and German kings was such that every time they had compelled cavalry to cross the Alps to obtain the crown of the Roman Empire, they halted in the plain. There a shield was hung high on a wooden post and a court herald summoned the army of vassals to mount watch near the king the following night. The princes, each accompanied by his own retinue, then summoned, through the heralds, their own vassals. Next day whoever was found missing from this muster was summoned again in the presence of the king, princes and great men, and all vassals staying at home without the permission of their lords were condemned to lose their fiefs.[11]

Return was frequently effected during the good weather from May to September, but it could equally happen in the depths of winter.

For the defence of the country, Italian expeditions, and fighting against peoples on the eastern frontier, the German king used his right of *bannum* to collect the troops which he required. This was the fundamental legal power of 'the king's order' or 'royal edict' which in case of extreme danger could be issued to everyone. The *clamor patriae* was then invoked. Those unwilling to serve, described as *desertores militiae*, were threatened with condign punishment, while from at least the end of the eleventh century a general peace was proclaimed throughout Germany during the emergency. On various occasions peasants shared in warfare, sometimes mounted but usually on foot. A margrave of Austria summoned even cow- and swineherds against Bohemia. In Saxony Henry IV was opposed by popular forces, 'more accustomed to agriculture than to knighthood', wrote Lambert of Hersfeld with characteristic disdain.[12] In certain areas like Frisia, especially north of the Elbe, the division between a free peasantry, holding allods, hereditary lands held of no lord, and the knightly order (*Ritterstand*), remained vague. Merchants and townsmen occasionally served in the armies of the period. These auxiliaries were sometimes useful, sometimes an encumbrance. In fact the strength of the royal army lay mostly in its heavy cavalry of *milites electi*, *milites armati* or

[11] Otto of Freising, *Chronica*, p.304.
[12] Lampert von Hersfeld, *Annales*, ed. A. Schmidt and W. D. Fritz, Berlin, s.d.

milites loricati, to whom were added less completely armed elements described variously as *clipeati milites*, *scutiferi*, *scutarii* and *armigeri*. In any given region this constituted the *Heerschild* of a prince or abbey. The king had his own *Heerschild*, that is household troops, depending directly on him (*palatini milites*, *privati milites*). He was joined by the lay princes (*principes*, *duces*, *proceres*, *comites*) and ecclesiastical lords, abbots and bishops. No campaign could succeed without the aid or fealty of these magnates. If they defaulted – their presence was usually confirmed by an oath – the assembled forces were insufficient. Thus at the time of the invasion of France by Henry V in 1124, 'he led there few men because the Germans do not readily fight against forcigners.'[13] Each great lord led a contingent, the numbers of which were more or less fixed by custom. Poland and Bohemia, for example, were supposed to provide at least 300 horsemen for the journey to Rome. Generally service beyond the Alps was less burdensome: a feudal accord concluded between the Archbishop of Trier and the count of Arlon stipulated that the latter would furnish 40 *scutati* on the German side of the Alps and 20 beyond.

Extremely valuable information is provided by a document unique for the period, the *Indiculus loricatorum*, or list of heavy horsemen, summoned in 981 by Otto II for a campaign in Italy. The previous year the Emperor had assembled a first army which since then had been fighting the Saracens in southern Italy. It was now a question of raising a new force, leaving aside Saxon troops in particular, possibly because they were already in Italy, possibly because it was thought preferable to leave them at home to defend Germany against the Slavs. The document names 47 laymen, bishops or abbots who were each to send (*mittere*) or lead (*conducere*) a specific number of heavily armed men in chain mail (*loricati*). Erkenbald, bishop of Strasbourg, for example, was responsible for sending 100, the abbot of Murbach was to lead 20, Count Ansfred to send 10. In all about 2,080 heavy horsemen were required. If we extrapolate from this document, it appears that the bishops depending on the German king north of the Alps owed 1,822 heavy horsemen and the royal abbeys 1,200. As for the contribution of laymen, a force twice as large is credible, including, in addition to Otto II's household knights (*milites aulici*), of whom the core was represented by his Slav bodyguard, the contribution of dukes, margraves (especially numerous and important in Saxony and Bavaria), territorial divisions (*pagi*, *regna*) and, lastly, the direct vassals of the king who were neither dukes, margraves nor counts. This might give a total of 6,000 *loricati*, of whom 1,400 came from Bavaria, 900 from Alemannia, 1,100 from Lorraine, 800 from Franconia and at least 1,500 from Saxony. Otto II could also equally dispose of the resources of the

[13] Ekkehardt of Aura, *Chronica*, ed. F. J. Schmale and I. Schmale-Ott, Darmstadt 1972, p.368.

Regnum Italiae, used jointly in Italy and, though more rarely, beyond the Alps against France, Bohemia and Hungary. In the event, it was not just up to the princes from Benevento to provide troops, though they did indeed fail to do so. All this leads one to think that the defeat suffered by Otto's troops on 13 July 982 at Cap Colonna was not due to inferiority of numbers. The various sources agree in underlining the seriousness of imperial losses. So it is all the more remarkable that Otto II did not acknowledge defeat but quickly prepared his revenge; the military resources under his control allowed him to plug the gaps.[14]

Among the *loricati* some had responded to a public military obligation of a Frankish type; others came because they had received *beneficia* as the reward for *labor militis;* many belonged to that category of unfree, called knight-serfs or *Dienstleute* (Latin: *ministeriales*), who first clearly emerge in the reign of Conrad II. Because of their juridical status, the latter depended strictly on the great lords in whose service they were and for whom they primarily fulfilled military functions. A piece of land conceded by their lord provided a livelihood, but frequently they were maintained directly like privileged household servants.

A mid-twelfth century document concerning the *ministeriales* of the archbishop of Cologne gives exact details of the way in which their services were to be performed. If the archbishop's lands were threatened in any way, all his *ministeriales*, whether they had received a fief or not, had to follow their master to the limits of his territory to defend it by arms. Beyond this they were not obliged to go unless they agreed to do so or were paid an indemnity by the archbishop. They were also obliged to accompany him to the coronation of the king across the Alps. This service fell particularly on all *ministeriales* who had received a fief from the archbishop bringing them an annual income of at least 5 marks, though their lord had to provide them each with 10 marks and 40 ells of cloth for their equipment as well as a saddled pack animal, two travelling bags, four horseshoes and 24 nails for every two *ministeriales* who went. Better still, once the Alps had been reached, the archbishop had to distribute to everyone one mark a month for as long as the journey lasted. A complex procedure was established in the event of this sum not being paid regularly; an interruption in payment freed the injured *ministerialis*. Those who enjoyed an income below 5 marks could, if they wished, stay at home provided they paid an indemnity (Latin: *Herstura*, German: *Heersteuer*) equal to half their fief's revenue. In all cases the archbishop had to announce the departure of the expedition at least a year and a day in advance.[15]

It was the fief which increasingly formed the basis for military service, but neither the king nor the great lords could normally exact from their vassals,

---

[14] K. F. Werner, *Heeresorganisation und Kriegsführung* (214).
[15] Quoted by E. von Frauenholz, *Entwicklungsgeschichte* (110), i.248–53.

whether free or not, unlimited gratuitous service.[16] It became necessary to pay them by one means or another, and one even finds examples of genuine wage-earners (*solidarii, stipendiarii milites, conducti milites*),[17] this practice being particularly widespread in the western parts of the Empire and in Italy. At the end of the eleventh century an Italian, Benzo of Alba, suggested to Henry IV that he should replace feudal service by a tax which would allow him to hire mercenaries. A similar piece of advice was given by King Henry I of England to his son-in-law, Emperor Henry V, after the failure of his campaign against France in 1124.

It was a general rule that the king should command in person every important campaign. Age did not matter; Otto III was 11 when he led his army against the Saxons (991) and Henry IV 13 when he went to war against the Hungarians in 1063. However, command could sometimes be delegated. Following a Carolingian precedent, the king conferred his authority on two people, a layman (a duke) and a cleric (a bishop). Even if the structure of the army was largely feudal, some large units of which it was composed still had a territorial or even ethnic base. Each *regnum* formed a contingent under its own duke. Finally, castles now represented an important feature in military planning. Entrusted to the keeping of *Burgmannen* or *castellorum custodes*, fortresses guarded the frontiers against the Danes, Slavs and Magyars. The German term for these – *Burgward* – referred not only to the castle itself but to the whole district which it dominated and controlled.

In the kingdom of Italy (*regnum Langobardorum, regnum italicum*), the Lombard invasions and then the Carolingian annexation had almost totally destroyed Roman political traditions. In the ninth century monarchical power was represented by counts of Frankish origin. There was one count for every diocese and city. In the most threatened regions the counties were grouped into larger military commands, the Marches, each entrusted to a marquis. At the time when the Carolingian dynasty came to an end, the counts, still public officials, became vassals of the king of Italy.

Thanks to the troubles which wracked the kingdom, principally between 888 and 915, the counts and marquises succeeded in making their offices not only lifelong but also hereditary. Increasingly, by virtue of successoral practices applying to fiefs in Lombard law, on the death of its possessor the fief was divided into as many parts as there were heirs. In the first half of the tenth century, for example, there were two marquises of Ivrea and in 1014 three or four men bore the title Marquis of Liguria. This led to an increasing fragmentation of both real property and political power. Generating quarrels and incessant violence, this fragmentation, linked to the Magyar threat and

---

[16] This does not mean that knights did not have to spend anything. In 968, Milo, son of the advocate Rambert, gave to the monks of St-Vanne de Verdun, the church of St-Rémi du Mont-Saint-Vanne. In return he received silver 'of which he had great need before leaving for Italy with the Lotharingian army'.

[17] Sometimes also called *Gelduini*, that is natives of Guelders.

the eclipse of royalty, contributed to a very complex process to which Italian historians have given the name *Incastellamento*. Some of these fortresses (*castra*) were built by the king, others by the counts and marquises in their fiefs, others by holders of great allods. To ensure defence of towns, which were more numerous than elsewhere in the West, the king conceded to bishops the duty of protecting the population (*tuitio*), transferring to them some of the counts' authority. In the course of the tenth century, the bishops progressively took their place in the feudal system. Some bishoprics became proper lordships, as did the three bishoprics of Istria (Trieste, Pola and Parenzo) and the patriarchate of Aquileia, which were particularly exposed to foreign threats. This 'feudalization' of the higher clergy became even more apparent during the time of the Saxon Emperors, who chose bishops from their faithful followers and supported them against the lay aristocracy, who were much more independent and deeply rooted. Otto I conferred comital powers on the city and an area three or four miles around it for the bishops of Parma, Asti and Reggio Emilia. Otto II did the same for those of Lodi, Acqui and Tortona, and the policy was continued by Otto III in favour of the bishops of Piacenza, Ceneda, Ravenna and Brescia.

The position around the year 1000 may thus be presented schematically: marquises and counts held only a minority of cities like Milan, Pavia, Turin, Mantua, Verona and Treviso. Everywhere else they had been driven out of urban centres and their immediate environs for the profit of the bishops. For most of the time they lived on some *rocca* or in some *castello* in the countryside, surrounded by a retinue (*masnata*) of knights (*milites*) to whom they accorded fiefs. They might still draw on the assistance of local forces of *pedites*, *homines* or *habitatores*, obliged to defend the country within a limited area (*defensio patriae*). As for the bishops whom the king–emperors had invested with cross and ring, they were masters in the cities. They also had a military and administrative entourage: first of all, their direct vassals or *primi milites* or *milites majores*, among whom could be found advocates, vidames and captains of the people or gates. Then there were *milites minores* or *secundi milites*, who were the rear-vassals (*vavassores*) of the bishop or rear-rear-vassals (*vavassini*) of the king of Italy. Like the count, the bishop could use the resources of local militias or even, in emergencies, ask all citizens to help in the city's defence. Aribert, archbishop of Milan, in the early eleventh century summoned 'all the inhabitants of the parish of Ambrose . . . from the rustic to the knight (*miles*), from the poor to the rich'.[18]

In theory the king of Italy should have been able to use all these elements, of which an assembly was reputed to form the *militia regni*. In fact, the aid he received from lay or ecclesiastical feudal lords was very limited and depended on highly variable political circumstances.

[18] Quoted by G. Tabacco, *Il regno italico* (212).

THE KINGDOM OF FRANCE

In contrast with the Germanic world, during the feudal period France found itself safe from foreign attack because of its geographical position. Taken as a whole France was not a frontier province, having nothing comparable to those military territories or marches which formed the bulwark of the Empire running from north to south: the March of the Billungs, Nordmark, Lusatia, Misnia, Ostmark (centre of the future Austria), the Marches of Styria, Carinthia and Carniola. Nor did the kings of France undertake anything comparable to the great Italian enterprise of the German rulers. In other words, to the west of the Meuse, Saône and Rhône, military forces developed very largely in isolation, apart from the predominant 'French' share in great movements like the conquest of England, the Crusades and the reconquest of Spain (*Reconquista*).

Although until the reign of Philip Augustus (1180–1223) the Capetian kings were condemned to pursue an unambitious policy, they had to spend a good proportion of their time fighting, as the military annals of the reign of Louis VI the Fat (1106–37) reveal. Even before the death of his father, Philip I (1060–1106), Louis's role lay fundamentally in this sphere since he was both leader of the army (*dux exercitus*) and defender of the realm (*defensor regni*). Louis had his first experience of fighting at the age of about 16 in 1097 when he was engaged in a conflict with William Rufus, king of England and duke of Normandy. In 1098 he led several incursions into Berry, Auvergne, Burgundy and Ponthieu. In 1101 and 1102 there was the siege of Montmorency and the campaign against Dreu de Mouchy, whose castle was burnt. Still in 1102, having concentrated his forces at Reims, he fought for two months on end against Eble II, count of Roucy. In 1103 there were other operations, with the capture of the keep at Meung-sur-Loire and the burning of a neighbouring church, followed by the victorious defence of Montaigu castle in the Aisne. After a respite, in 1105 he led an expedition against Montlhéry, captured Gournay in 1107 (but failed before Chevreuse), recaptured Montlhéry and took Bréthencourt. In 1108 he campaigned in Berry to restrict the depredations of Humbert, lord of Ste-Sévère. After his arrival on 3 August he forced the town of La Ferté-Alais to capitulate.

Warfare took on a new dimension. It was no longer just a case of attacking petty lords but the king of England, Henry I. In 1109 the Capetian king summoned the royal army, which included the forces of Robert, count of Flanders, Thibaud IV, count of Blois, Guillaume II, count of Nevers and Hugues II, duke of Burgundy, as well as those of numerous archbishops and bishops. Having laid waste the lands of Robert III, count of Meulan, the forces of Louis VI met those of his principal enemy at Planches near Neaufles-Saint-Martin. There the king of France defied Henry I, challenging him to single combat, which was refused. But the following day at the gates of Gisors the Anglo-Normans were defeated in a skirmish. At the end of 1109 Mantes was taken. Next year it was the turn of Meulan and the struggle was only terminated by a peace concluded in March 1113. At the same time petty warfare against local 'tyrants' continued. In 1109 there was the siege of Germigny-l'Exempt; in 1111 the first siege of Le Puiset, when the keep (*donjon*) was taken and the castle burnt; 1112 saw the king defeated near Toury by a coalition which included among others the troops of the count of Blois and Raoul de Beaugency. In fleeing, the royal army was forced to seek refuge in Orléans, Etampes and Pithiviers. To compensate for this defeat, in 1112 there was a second, successful, siege of Le Puiset.

Had this period of concentrated action exhausted the protagonists? It was not until March 1115 that operations recommenced, with the capture of the castles of Crécy-sur-Serre and Nouvion-l'Abbesse. During an assault on the keep at Amiens Louis VI was wounded; withdrawing, he ordered a blockade which lasted two years before the town surrendered. War with Henry I also broke out again in 1116.

This time the king of France could count on the support of Foulques V, count of Anjou, and Baudouin VII, count of Flanders. Fighting took place in the Vexin, but also in Picardy, Brie and around Chartres. There were many sieges and surprise attacks (Gasny, Malassis, l'Aigle, Les Andelys, Dangu, Châteauneuf-sur-Epte) and a full-scale battle fought at Brémule on 20 August 1119 where Louis VI sustained a severe defeat, which provoked, however, a vigorous reaction. This time the objective was to take Breteuil. To achieve this Louis urged his bishops to join him with their diocesan militias. Orderic Vitalis, the contemporary chronicler, even mentions the raising on this occasion of levies *en masse* bringing together troops from the following regions: Burgundy, Berry, Auvergne, Sens, Paris, Orléans, Vermandois, Beauvaisis and Laon. Péronne, Nesle, Noyon, Lille, Tournai, Arras, Gournay and Clermont were also supposed to send soldiers. But the effort was unavailing; Breteuil held. In December 1120 peace was concluded between the two kings, allowing (among other matters) for restitution of castles and freeing of prisoners. It was like the final moves of a chess match, enthusiasm for which was incidentally just beginning to spread in the West at this very moment.

The scale of military campaigns now began to increase. In 1122 Louis VI assembled an impressive army, which included the counts of Anjou, Brittany and Nevers, at Bourges. In 1124 there was the major German invasion, with the raising of the Oriflamme at St Denis. In 1126 there was a second expedition into Auvergne; in 1127–28 two expeditions into Flanders and, in 1137, a campaign in Aquitaine, led by the future Louis VII. Simultaneously, the small local operations began to become less frequent (1128, capture and destruction of the castle of Livry; 1130, attempt to take Cosne; 1132, failure before La Fère; 1133, burning of Bonneval; 1135, capture and burning of the castle of St-Brisson-sur-Loire, the last active campaign of Louis VI).

Thus, even if most of the fighting took place within a relatively restricted area (about 40,000 km^2), and if large-scale battles were rarer than sieges, the number of troops engaged often modest, the campaigns brief, the risks and losses very limited, and devastation restricted, it nevertheless remains true that for Louis VI and his *familia*, his faithful followers, war was a continuing preoccupation, a threat which was always close.

The forms assumed by wars in this period may be primarily explained by the political fragmentation which, in differing degrees, had afflicted the whole of *Gallia* from the end of the ninth century. Several stages may be distinguished in this development. Between 888 and 920 the principalities on the periphery of the kingdom were formed; their distant origins go back to the great commands which Emperor Charles the Bald entrusted to certain powerful figures. This was the case in Flanders, Burgundy and Aquitaine, to which may be added the Normandy of Rollo and Brittany ruled by Alan Barbetorte. Each of these principalities, governed hereditarily, formed 'a veritable state in which the prince exercised the authority which had previously devolved upon the king'.[19] Each of them also brought together several districts (*pagi*) some of which were held directly by the territorial prince, others of which were subjected to a less rigorous control by him.

In a second phase, roughly corresponding to the years 940–70, counts, holders of a single *pagus*, profiting from the battles between the Carolingians and the Robertians (ancestors of the Capetians) were able to make themselves politically autonomous, as happened in Anjou, the Mâconnais, Auxerrois and Nivernais. The same thing happened in the Midi; around the year 900 the whole of France south of the Loire was dominated by about a dozen families, but by 975 it was divided amongst some 150 lineages of independent counts and viscounts.[20] Then, from the end of the tenth century, even the *pagi*, small though they were, could not maintain their integrity. New political formations appeared in their midst: the castellanies, whose holders possessed the *ban*, that is, military command. In the county of Mâcon, for example, the castles which the count had entrusted to *fideles* or to vassals became centres of these small practically independent units. At the same time, the monasteries of Tournus and Cluny or the cathedral church of Mâcon assumed responsibility for a distinct lordship within which they also exercised the *ban*. But this new form of dispersed authority did not triumph everywhere. It ran up against the resistance, sometimes precocious, sometimes more tardy, of certain territorial princes like those in Normandy and Flanders. After a time of dissolution came one of consolidation, a movement which also affected regions like Champagne, Burgundy and the Île-de-France.

[19] J. Dhondt, *Etudes sur la naissance des principautés territoriales en France*, Bruges 1948, p.254. See also J. F. Lemarignier, *La France médiévale: institutions et société*, Paris 1970, pp.107–25, for this development.
[20] A. R. Lewis, *Development of Southern Society* (200).

This double movement could not occur without wars and rivalry. Free rein was given to the opposing ambitions of many oppressive and greedy dynasts. Even if it is unsafe to believe the lamentations of monastic chroniclers, it still seems that the classic expression 'feudal anarchy', rejected by many contemporary medievalists, does in fact describe at least part of that reality.

In the innumerable military vicissitudes which accompanied political action, the castles played an essential role. During the feudal period France was a country of castles, where a 'great stone civilisation' spread.[21] Doubtless as early as the Merovingian period in certain areas, especially mountainous ones like the Auvergne, fortifications called *castella*, *munitiones*, or *castra* existed. Gregory of Tours uses these expressions to describe the naturally defensive site of Chastel-Marlhac, an isolated plateau covering some 40 hectares, without ramparts but encircled by cliffs some 30 metres high.[22] Under Pepin and Charlemagne, Frankish troops undertook not only the siege of ancient cities, fortified by a circuit of walls built during the late Roman Empire, but also of proper rural camps and fortresses, defended by earthworks, many of them only used temporarily during emergencies by the population at large. But the *curtes*, those administrative and social centres of aristocratic or royal estates, generally had some defensive element. Buildings were arranged within an area of about a hectare or hectare and a half which was ringed about with an earth bank, sometimes preceded by a ditch, and often reinforced by a palisade of logs, stakes and interwoven branches (Latin: *haia;* French: *plessis;* hedge, enclosure). The *curtis* properly so-called was itself enclosed within a second similar fortification or enceinte which was much larger, whose irregular outline was determined by the inclusion of gardens and small cultivated plots. The whole settlement formed a very loose extended ensemble, lacking flanking elements or even points for resistance, and was usually incapable of resisting a siege since the number of defenders was too small. However, a number of more imposing and complex fortifications with walls, towers and war-engines existed, such as the palace which St Nicetius, bishop of Trier, built near Coblenz in the sixth century.[23]

In the course of the tenth and eleventh centuries a new type of fortification appeared or became widespread. It was characterized by the presence of a motte (*motta*, *agger*, *dunio*) or conical shaped mound. The average size of such a motte was 30 m diameter at the base, 10 m diameter on top, with a height of 5 or 6 m. But much more impressive mottes can be found, with a base diameter of 60 m, 20 m at the summit and 10 m high. The surface area of a motte at its base was usually between 7 and 30 ares (1 are = 100 m²), and at the level of the platform, between $\frac{3}{4}$ and 3 ares. Around the base of the motte there ran a ditch, and on its summit would be a wooden palisade. A

---

[21] R. Boutruche, *Seigneurie et féodalité* (102), ii.39.
[22] G. Fournier, *Le château dans la France médiévale* (788), pp.28–32.
[23] Venantius Fortunatus, *Opera Poetica*, Lib. III, xii.

classic account of such a fortified motte in Flanders at the beginning of the twelfth century describes it thus:

> It is the custom of all the richest and most noble men of this region . . . to construct, piling up the earth, a motte as high as they are able, digging all around it a ditch as wide and deep as possible, and fortifying it on the outer side of its enclosure with a palisade of planks solidly joined together in the form of a wall. They furnish the circuit with as many towers as possible and on the inside they build in the centre a house or rather a fortress which dominates everything else, set up in such a fashion that the entry into the dwelling is only accessible by means of a bridge which, starting on the outer edge of the ditch and resting on a series of pillars, grouped in twos or, even, threes and placed at the appropriate spot, slowly rises over the ditch, sloping in such a way that when one reaches the level of the platform of the motte, the bridge has attained the same level directly before the gateway.[24]

Many castles were built on naturally favourable sites (on a rocky spur, and plateau, or isolated hillock), but even there, earth was brought in and undoubtedly used, in conjunction with wood, for the construction of the tower which crowned the motte.

Against this general background a number of variations may be mentioned:

1   These castles might be built on a virgin site, but they could also be located in former *curtes*. In this case, modifications could take various forms. Sometimes everything was sacrificed to military needs and the former layout was totally destroyed in order to obtain a more coherent and compact plan; sometimes an artificial motte placed at the most favourable spot was simply added to the former settlement. The example of the two sieges of Le Puiset in 1111 and 1112 shows how a lord of the early twelfth century under the pressure of events gave up this second type for the first.[25]

2   From a political point of view these castles may be divided into three categories. First, those which the holder of public authority (duke, count or simple lord having the right of command; *bannum*) kept in his own hands; second, those which he had entrusted, usually in the form of a fief, to his officers, relatives, faithful lieges or vassals. Lastly there were private, adulterine, fortresses, illegally erected without the knowledge of the territorial prince, perhaps by adventurers, but mostly by powerful nobles.

3   Even when their location had a strategic character (control of a river, road or fine position), many castles were not integrated into a network of forts forming the defended frontier of a political unit. For the purpose of castles was simultaneously to form a protected refuge for those who lived there and to control the neighbouring population. A castle was the centre of an area of

[24] C. M. de la Roncière, P. Contamine, R. Delort and M. Rouche, *L'Europe au Moyen Age. Documents expliqués, II: Fin IXe siècle–fin XIIIe siècle*, Paris 1969, p.152.
[25] G. Fournier, Château du Puiset (789).

command, protection, power, judicial authority and territory (*mandamentum, salvamentum, potestas, districtus, territorium*).

4 Although it is impossible to establish reliable statistics, given the insufficiency of written sources and the still very incomplete archaeological evidence, it does appear that the number of castles, without ever being very large, did increase. In Poitou, three castles are mentioned before the Viking incursions, and 39 in the eleventh century. In Touraine there were 9 at the end of the ninth century and 26 by the mid-eleventh. In Maine, none has been found before the tenth century, 11 in 1050 and 62 in 1100; in Auvergne, there were 8 just before 1000 and between 21 and 34 around 1050. In Normandy there were a dozen ducal castles around 1035 and 20 around 1100. In the area round Chartres in the twelfth century, there were 20 castles in 6,000 km². However, certain regions obtained their quota of proper castles very early;[26] this was the case in the Mâconnais where, thanks perhaps to a more abundant documentation than elsewhere, 16 castles can be listed about the year 1000 to which only a single one could be added between then and 1150. This list is somewhat deceptive in that it includes only proper castles and not those more or less fortified residences which could be found in the countryside. An exhaustive study of the Cinglais, a small area in Lower Normandy, on the plateau bounded on the west by the Orne, on the east by the Laize and to the north by the confluence of these two rivers, measuring some 12 km by 20 km (say 240 km²) and today including 48 communes, has enabled Fixot to list 3 or 4 stone castles and 28 earthwork fortifications, of which 20 still remain visible on the ground (13 mottes but also 7 ringworks, a term used by archaeologists to describe a simple enclosure, with ditch, bank and palisade, delimiting an enclosed space where there were dwellings).[27]

The differences between various types of fortification appear, among other matters, in Article 4 of the *Consuetudines et Justicie*, a Norman document of 1091 referring to William the Conqueror's reign:

> No-one in Normandy may dig a ditch in open country unless from the bottom of this ditch the earth can be thrown out of it without the aid of a ladder, nor may he set up more than a palisade which must have neither redan nor rampart-walk (*propugnaculis et alatoriis*). Nor may anyone build a fortification on a rock or on an island, nor raise a castle in Normandy, nor may anyone in Normandy refuse to deliver his castle to the lord of Normandy should he wish to take it into his own hands.[28]

5 Stone castles appeared, the central feature of which was the keep, for a long time square, then, from the end of the eleventh century, cylindrical or

---

[26] The author is thinking of the distinction in French betweeen a *château-fort* and a simple *château*, between a fortress utilizing all possible contemporary means of defence and a building provided with only a limited number of these elements. See the next sentence.

[27] M. Fixot, Fortifications de terre (784).

[28] C. H. Haskins, *Norman Institutions*, Cambridge, Mass., 1918, p.282.

prismatic. These particularly assisted those authorities who were best established, the richest and most powerful lay princes and ecclesiastics. The spread of the use of stone occurred slowly according to circumstance and region (more quickly in central France, later in Flanders). The earliest stone keeps (*donjons*) were probably Langeais (if the date of 994, disputed by some, is accepted), then, about 1000, that of Sault near St-Benoît-de-Sault in Berry. At the same time, because of the weight of stone, the earthen motte often disappeared.

Possessing the plenitude, or quasi-plenitude, of regalian rights, the political leaders did not simply have one or a few castles at their disposition. They exercised over their dependants and subjects rights enabling them to control the construction and maintenance of their castles, to direct soldiers to defend them on occasion or permanently and to wage full-scale war. This last was the most important. For in this sphere, in a more categorical fashion than in other parts of the West, the warrior par excellence was the heavy horseman. It was necessary to have such men ready at a moment's notice, practised in the art of mounted combat and swordsmanship. Where could such specialists, necessarily detached from normal daily concerns, be found? First of all in the entourage of the powerful men. There were also domestic servants who, carrying out functions judged prestigious, were called to serve as companions in arms. Fealty, or better still homage, tied them to their lords, whose lifestyle they shared and from whom they received military equipment (*arma militaria*). Lastly there were vassals who had received a benefice or fief and who sometimes were entrusted with a castle. Until the early eleventh century, the level of population, economic stagnation, fragmentation of power, the mediocrity of monetary resources available to the aristocracy, all conspired to limit the numbers of *milites* who could engage in warfare. But around 1050 things began to change with a slow rise in population, reconstruction of political authority and the increasing practice of enfeoffment and sub-enfeoffment.

At the same time, because it was in the interests of lords and especially of vassals, the military services (*militare obsequium*) falling on these latter in return for their fiefs were progressively defined and restricted. If the authenticity of the customs which Bouchard, count of Vendôme, established about 1025–30 for the guard of the castle in that town may be accepted, it would appear that the count himself undertook to secure this during the months April to August from his own pocket; during the first two months he did this from the comital treasury (where it was a question of paying wages to *stipendiarii, conducticii, solidarii, milites externi*), and for the next three months with the aid of a tax called the *gaitagium* raised on inhabitants of the *burgus* of Vendôme. Then seven vassals (of whom two at least had residences in Vendôme) each had to serve for a month by virtue of the lands they held. The service was fairly heavy since five watches had to be set each night –

three fixed ones, including two for the gates, and two itinerant ones, patrolling the tower of the castle throughout the night. Similar regulations determined service in the host and on campaign.[29] At the beginning of the twelfth century impressive numbers of troops could sometimes be raised. The example of Louis VI in 1124 may be cited again: in order to repulse Emperor Henry V, the Capetian king benefited from the aid 'of such a quantity of knights and foot-soldiers that one might say that they were like locusts hiding from sight the earth with its rivers, mountains and plains'. His army appeared to be already organized: a vanguard combined the contingents of the duke of Burgundy and the count of Nevers; on the right wing was Raoul, count of Vermandois, the king's cousin, and on the left, the men of Ponthieu, Amiens and Beauvais. Then there came four battle formations (*acies*): the men of Reims and Châlons, those of Laon and Soissons, those of Orléans, Etampes and Paris (with the troops from St-Denis mentioned by our source, Abbot Suger, and finally the cavalry forces of Thibaud, count of Chartres, Blois and Brie, and of Hugues, count of Troyes and Champagne. The royal army also further included a rearguard led by Charles the Good, count of Flanders, in which there could also be found the more modest retinues of the duke of Aquitaine and the counts of Brittany and Anjou.[30]

Doubtless 'the appeal to France', to repeat Suger's expression, in these critical circumstances elicited an exceptional wave of enthusiasm amongst the vassals and lieges of the Capetians, for their strict obligations fell far short of this. Thus, at the beginning of the twelfth century, Philip I had concluded an agreement with Robert, count of Flanders, by which the latter could fulfil the military service (*auxilium*) owed to his lord and sovereign by taking part in royal expeditions accompanied by only 20 knights. In 1133 an enquiry into the fiefs possessed by the bishop of Bayeux brought the following reply from Robert, earl of Gloucester, illegitimate son of King Henry I Beauclerc, baron of the church of Notre-Dame de Bayeux and its hereditary standard-bearer: the earl recognized that he held in fief from the bishop the honour of Evrecy, comprising ten knights' fees, but that he owed only a single knight for 40 days service with the king of France and two, for the same period, for service with the duke of Normandy and king of England, provided that service was within the frontiers of the province. His full contingent could only be summoned when the host was being prepared for a *proelium*, that is a full-scale war which threatened to end with a great public battle. The same document adds that all *vavasseurs* of the bishop, freely holding 50 or 60 acres or more, owed service to the duke of Normandy when he summoned his army for battle.[31]

In other words, the returns to summonses varied according to circum-

[29] *Cartulaire de la Trinité de Vendôme*, ed. C. Métais, Paris, 2 vols. 1893, i.6–8.
[30] Suger, *Vie de Louis VI le Gros*, ed. H. Wacquet, Paris 1929, pp.218–30.
[31] H. Navel, *L'enquête de 1133* (270).

stances; the conquest of England and the first Crusade, for different reasons, attracted large numbers and created the logistical problems this entailed. But when the proposed operation was unattractive, every pretext, juridical or otherwise, was used in order to disobey 'supplications' and 'orders' for service.

The army raised in 1124 also demonstrates that footsoldiers, *pedites*, in spite of their subordinate role, were present in large numbers. It is even possible that they were often in the majority. Yet this infantry may well have been conscripted, for mass military service had not completely disappeared. Not only did country-dwellers have to work in fortresses, provide foodstuffs and carts; they also had to fight, especially locally, with their primitive arms. In the county of Anjou, free men were summoned in the event of general war (*proelium generale*) for the defence of the kingdom and the prince (*pro defensione regni et principis*). In Poitou, when lords founded monasteries, they expressly reserved their military prerogatives over their former dependants. In Flanders, the count had the right to order all the male population of each castellany to work there on the upkeep or construction of *castra* (the right of *balfart*). Alongside the *Landesbanwer*, the national feudal army, there also existed the *Landwere*, local militia, with its double form, offensive and defensive.

In bringing this survey to a conclusion, attention may be drawn to a famous document which shows the degree of precision reached in the best of examples at the beginning of the twelfth century. It is the treaty concluded at Dover on 10 March 1101 between Henry I of England and Robert II, count of Flanders.[32] Robert agreed to support Henry in the defence of the kingdom against 'all men who live and die' (*contra omnes homines qui vivere et mori possint*), saving his fealty to Philip, king of France. In particular, if Philip wanted to invade England, Robert would try to dissuade him but only by his supplications and not by gifts of money or evil council. If Philip persisted in his plan, naturally Robert as a vassal would accompany him, but with the smallest possible force consistent with avoiding any accusation that might lead to the forfeiture of his lands to his lord. When the king of England required his aid he would send letters summoning the count and he, within 40 days (a delay frequently encountered in the Middle Ages), would gather 1,000 horsemen (*equites*) or knights (*milites*), ready to embark at Gravelines or Wissant in ships sent by Henry I, in such a way that each horseman would be allowed to transport three horses. The expeditionary force would thus total 3,000 horses and probably as many men, each horseman having two aides, including one squire (*armiger, scutifer*). Robert would accompany this force, provided that (a) he was not too ill to do so, (b) he had not been summoned to the French royal host, or (c) to that of the Emperor whose vassal he also was for certain lands. For as long as they remained in England Henry I

---

[32] *Diplomatic Documents*, I, *1101–1272*, ed. P. Chaplais, London 1964, no.1.

would keep them, even reimbursing them for losses just as he was accustomed to do for his own *familia*.

The same document also made provision for service in another area of operation: Normandy. In this case, the count would send help on a similar scale but would serve at his own expense for the first eight days of the campaign. If Philip of France invaded Normandy, Robert would accompany him but with just 20 knights while the other 980 would remain 'in the service and fealty' (*in servitio et fidelitate sua*) of Henry I. A third possibility was also envisaged: service in Maine. This time the count of Flanders was only obliged to send 500 knights not more than once a year, who would for a month be incorporated into the *familia* of the king-duke. In return for these undertakings, Henry I promised to protect Robert's life, to obtain his release if he were captured and to pay him annually £500 sterling.

ENGLAND

Unlike the other Germanic peoples settled on the continent, the Anglo-Saxons, at the same time as they completed the conquest of Britain, split up into numerous kingdoms, each of which formed autonomous military entities, although coalitions might be arranged against the Celts of the West and North on occasion. The process of unification occurred slowly; at the end of the eighth century Mercia under King Offa (757–96), who could style himself *rex totius Anglorum patriae*, exercised control directly or indirectly over most of England. Then supremacy passed to Wessex under Egbert (802–39), who at the end of his reign not only dominated southern England but also Mercia, East Anglia and Northumberland. This supremacy was maintained during the reign of his grandson, Alfred the Great (871–99), despite Viking attacks which forced him by a treaty in 886 to cede all of England north-east of a line running from the Thames estuary to that of the Dee. At his death he could rightly be entitled 'king of all the English except those under the Danes'. His successors Edward the Elder (899–924) and Athelstan (924–39) succeeded not only in maintaining the political unity of the English but in defeating the Danes. Later disasters, the rule of Canute the Great and the return of the Anglo-Saxon kings with Edward the Confessor, did not break the realm's unity, expressed in and through the unity of the army which remained the king's. There developed in England nothing comparable to the territorial principalities of Eastern or Western Francia.

The sources are miserly but nevertheless permit us to obtain some idea of Anglo-Saxon military institutions in the eighth and ninth centuries. From the time of Offa there were already three great obligations weighing on the people (*folc*): the *trinoda necessitas, scilicet expeditionem, burhbotam et brugbotam* (that is, three public burdens, service in the army and work on fortresses and bridges).[33] Another phrase used to describe the same duties was *expeditio et pontis arcisque constructio*. In other words, possession of land – measured in hides or carucates (*carruca*)[34] – entailed military service and the construction and upkeep of urban settlements (*burhs*) and bridges. Linear fortifications, such as Offa's Dyke and Wat's Dyke, were as much political frontiers (*limes*) as military ones between the Anglo-Saxon and Celtic worlds. The distinguishing characteristic of the free man was his ability to fight, a rigorous principle plainly visible in the rite of manumission of a slave in which his former master put into his hands a free man's weapons to symbolize his new status – though even at this stage, mass levies of peasantry did not form the spearhead of the Anglo-Saxon armies; the preponderant role was shouldered by the king's companions (*comites, gesiths, gesithcundmen*).

On the eve of the Norman conquest, under the term *fyrd*, 'the nation in arms', a general mobilization of all free-men for the defence of, for example, the shire or borough or coasts occurred. Alongside this there was the select *fyrd*, recruited at the rate of one man for every five hides or, in the Danelaw, from six carucates. This institution, analogous to that which the Carolingian world had known with its participants and helpers, is evoked in this passage from the Domesday Book concerning Berkshire at the time of Edward the Confessor (1042–66): 'If the king sent an army anywhere, only one soldier went from five hides, and four shillings were given him from each hide as subsistence and wages for two months. This money, indeed, was not sent to the king but was given to the soldiers.'[35] The soldiers thus selected could be ordinary peasants (*ceorls, geburs*), but also, and principally, *thegns* or *thanes*, aristocrats in royal service and great lay and ecclesiastical nobles who occupied the same position as the *gesiths* of the previous age. In the kingdom at large the select *fyrd* might produce 20,000 combatants of this sort, to which may be added the mounted messengers (*radcnihts, radmanni*), together with the local militias produced by the general levy.

A similar system existed for raising warships. In addition to those special obligations which rested on certain coastal towns (of which some would become the Cinque Ports of Anglo-Norman times: Hastings, Romney, Dover, Hythe and Sandwich), it was envisaged that each group of 300 hides would equip a ship carrying 60 soldier-oarsmen with coats of mail, helmets, swords, Danish battle-axes and shields.

---

[33] John Selden was responsible for the reading *trinoda* for *trimoda* in this supposed technical phrase from a forged tenth-century charter purporting to come from Caedwalla of Wessex, but 'no usage of the kind is ever found in genuine Old English documents', though 'it is clear that in Offa's reign work on bridges and fortresses and service in the fyrd were regarded as standing apart from all other forms of common service' (Sir Frank Stenton, *Anglo-Saxon England*, 3rd edn, Oxford 1971, pp.289–90).

[34] According to Bede the hide was the land of one family (*terra unius familiae*) and was the Anglo-Saxon equivalent of the Carolingian *mansus* or Germanic *Hufe*. A carucate was the amount of land that could be ploughed by one plough team annually.

[35] C. W. Hollister, *Anglo-Saxon Military Institutions* (192), p.38.

The two months' free service owed normally sufficed for the effective prosecution of a campaign. After this time the king was allowed to maintain his army, thanks to the product of a land tax which makes its first appearance in 991 and was initially destined to pay tribute to the invading Scandinavians; the *danegeld, heregeld* or, simply, *geld*. To this could also be added commutations or purchase of exemption from service, confiscations and fines, of which that raised for absence from the *fyrd* was called *fyrdwite*. The eleventh-century Anglo-Saxons seem to have been rolling in money. Coins were used for commercial transactions as well as for paying stipendiaries, hired-men, *lithsmen, butsecarls,* and, above all, the royal bodyguard, established in 1018 by Canute the Great: housecarls, who may have numbered up to 1,000.

There is no reason to believe that the Anglo-Saxon military system displayed serious weaknesses. It was capable, for example, of achieving victories over the Scandinavians (like that at Stamfordbridge, 25 September 1066, revenge for the Norwegian victory at Fulford on 20 September). However, it was an army of foot soldiers, consequently deprived of mobility on the field of battle, while the art of fortification remained archaic. There were no motte and bailey castles before the Norman conquest except for those built after about 1050 by Normans in Edward the Confessor's entourage (Clavering in Essex, Richard's Castle in Herefordshire).[36]

On the eve of the long expedition of 1066 (a campaign of seven months), which has been described as the greatest amphibious operation since classical times,[37] the duchy of Normandy had already experienced a good half-century of demographic and economic growth. Moreover, since his victory at Val-ès-Dunes (1047) over his rival Gui de Brionne, William the Bastard had overhauled, or, better still, organized his duchy. At an assembly of lay vassals and bishops at Caen, he had proclaimed, for his own profit, 'the peace, which was called in contemporary language, the truce of God'.[38] Those lords who did not respect this were forced into exile or made to pay reparation for the damage they had caused. Alienating his demesne and robbing his churches, William multiplied enfeoffments. Nevertheless the expedition in 1066 was not strictly feudal. To the Norman chivalry were added volunteers from Brittany and Flanders and from even further afield (Champagne, Southern Italy). It was thus a geographically and militarily composite army (perhaps 7,000 men, half on horseback, half archers and infantry) which won at Hastings on 14 October 1066. Then, after an attempt to co-operate with the indigenous population, the Conqueror, at the price of enormous devastation and ruthless massacres, mastered Anglo-Saxon rebellions (1067–70). As the former aristocracy was exterminated or fled, vast lands were free for distribution while thousands of conquerors awaited their reward.

---

[36] *Ibid., passim.*
[37] J. H. Beeler, *Warfare in England* (25), p.5.
[38] M. de Boüard, Origines de la trêve de Dieu en Normandie (971).

In order to hold the country, William and his barons resorted to the construction of motte and bailey castles for which all that was needed was a group of navvies and a few specialist carpenters. These castles were established following an overall strategic plan, which entailed protection of Channel ports, crossing-points of rivers and a remarkable concentration around London and Coventry, that is around the two great nodal centres of communications in medieval England. To guard these castles and to form an army, troops were maintained. The Anglo-Norman king distributed lands (*tenures*) to some 180 lay barons and made use of the lands of bishops and abbots, now encumbered with military obligations. In total he could count on a *servitium debitum* of 5,000–6,000 knights, owing two months' voluntary service in time of war and 40 days in peacetime, not including castle-guard.

To furnish their quotas, the tenants-in-chief of the king sometimes used their own household knights, sometimes men hired for this purpose and sometimes knights to whom they had previously granted a fief. This means that the word *miles* corresponded at that time to a certain sort of soldier and not to a homogeneous social order. The process of subinfeudation was carried out more quickly by bishops and abbots than by lay barons. In any event it was well advanced by 1100. The chronicle of Abingdon abbey on the Thames near Oxford has a good account of this movement: Athelhelm, a monk from the monastery of Jumièges in Normandy who had been appointed abbot of Abingdon by order of William the Conqueror:

> considered it necessary at the beginning of his abbacy never to journey without a troop of armed knights, because with the almost daily conspiracies against the king and kingdom, he felt impelled to take measures for his own safety. Then castles were built at Wallingford, Oxford, Windsor and elsewhere for the security of the kingdom and the king ordered this abbey to furnish a guard of knights for Windsor. Knights who had come from the continent to England were considered most suited to this task. In the midst of these disturbances, the lord abbot Athelhelm defended the position which had been entrusted to him with a force of armed knights. To begin with wages were paid. Then when the troubles ceased it was noted in the records by the king's command how many knights were needed from bishoprics and abbeys for the defence of the realm in emergencies. And the abbot, after having resumed the lands which had formerly been granted, designated the manors of those who were to hold of the church and specified the obligations which they were to assume. These lands had formerly belonged to men called *thegns*, killed at the battle of Hastings.[39]

The *servitium debitum* provided an imposing, readily available, force. Though the figures are exaggerated, the description by Orderic Vitalis remains valuable. William 'allocated land to knights and arranged their contingents in such a way that the kingdom of England should always have

[39] *Chronicon monasterii de Abingdon*, ed. J. Stevenson, London 1858, ii.3. In fact by 1084 the monastery had enfeoffed 31 and 3/20ths knights' fees when its *servitium debitum* was only 30 knights: C. W. Hollister, *The Military Organization of Norman England* (195), p.54.

60,000 knights, ready to be mustered at a moment's notice in the king's service whenever necessary'.[40] At the same time, however, this same king and his sons, William Rufus and Henry I, also employed paid soldiers for whom they eagerly searched the continent. William Rufus, in particular, had the reputation of being *militum mercator et solidator*. Additionally, there is proof that the select *fyrd* continued to function for several decades and was even used abroad. On the other hand, the troop of housecarls did not survive the death of Harold. The Anglo-Norman kings kept only a modest bodyguard made up of archers commanded by constables.[41] The Conqueror's military reputation was high. In 1074 it was rumoured that he was about to take Aachen in order to gain the Empire. In 1082 people believed that his half-brother, Odo, bishop of Bayeux, was about to seize the papacy, while another Norman, Robert Guiscard, would master Constantinople.[42]

NORMAN ITALY

In England, we find a duke who became a king within a few months of the beginning of his expedition, a large army in contemporary terms, enormous booty and a massive and speedy redistribution of lands principally for military purposes; in southern Italy, there were Norman adventurers who had left their homeland to escape the reorganization of society by the prince, a small group who effectively insinuated themselves into a complex political situation and then like a snowball gradually grew, enabling its leaders to obtain official titles and authority, including royalty, though only after a century.

The account of Aimo of Salerno, monk of Monte Cassino, written at the end of the eleventh century, relates that in 1016 a group of Norman pilgrims, who were returning from worshipping Christ at the Holy Sepulchre in Jerusalem, arrived in Salerno, then under siege by Muslims. These peaceable travellers obtained arms and horses from the governor of the town, defeated the enemy, were loaded with rewards and invited to stay to defend the Christians. They declined the offer but, on returning to Normandy, they related their adventures and other Normans were inspired to copy them.

At the beginning of the eleventh century the position in the south was as follows. Sicily had been conquered from the Byzantines by Muslims from Ifriqiya, a conquest begun in 827 and completed in 969. Sicily was then divided into several emirates, whose emirs recruited mercenaries, often acting through military chiefs who, for wages, received concessions of land called *iqta*. Byzantium still controlled the extremities of the mainland peninsula.

[40] *The Ecclesiastical History of Orderic Vitalis*, ed. and tr. M. Chibnall, Oxford, 6 vols. 1969–80, ii.266.
[41] See now J. Prestwich, The military household of the Norman kings (279a).
[42] Hollister (195).

Apulia and Calabria formed the theme of *Langobardia*, governed from Bari by a catapan. The small autonomous duchies of Amalfi, Sorrento, Naples and Gaeta were, in principle, under Byzantine rule. There were three Lombard principalities: Benevento, Salerno and Capua.

During the second quarter of the eleventh century, Normans succeeded in getting themselves recognized as counts of Aversa and then of Apulia. In 1059 Pope Nicholas II addressed one of them, Robert Guiscard, as 'duke of Apulia and Calabria, by the grace of God and the Holy See'. This same Guiscard made himself master of the duchy of Amalfi in 1073 and of the principate of Salerno in 1076. Simultaneously, after 1060, the conquest of Muslim Sicily had begun through the initiative of his brother, Roger. It was completed some 30 years later. Though attempts against the Byzantine Empire constituted a long-term objective, the Norman domination of the Italian peninsula was consolidated quite rapidly. In 1129 Roger II (1127–54) added to it the principality of Capua. The following year he got from anti-pope Anacletus II the title 'king of Sicily and of the duchies of Apulia and Calabria', which was finally recognized as his by Pope Innocent II. In the mid-twelfth century he succeeded in fixing the northern frontier of his kingdom, which was not changed until 1860.

As in Anglo-Norman England, a process of enfeoffment and sub-infeudation occurred, largely for the benefit of Normans but also for some members of the former Lombard aristocracy. Three levels may be distinguished: the counts whose power centred on a town, the barons whose authority rested on a castle, and the *milites*, where one can distinguish between 'those who held nothing' and the *feudati*. The *Catalogue of the Barons*, contemporary in its first version with the last years of Roger II's reign, contains a general register of military services, excluding Sicily and Calabria. The fiefs are enumerated there according to constabularies or counties. 3,453 fiefs owing the service of 8,620 *milites* and 11,090 sergeants are listed. If the resources of Sicily and Calabria are added, figures may be obtained as great as those at this date for *milites* living under Lombard law who were not included in the survey.[43] In addition the sovereign could also seek aid from the entire population and ask the coastal towns, notably in Sicily, to provide ships for naval warfare, particularly practised under Robert Guiscard and Roger II. Muslim mercenaries, foot soldiers, mounted archers and experts in siege warfare were also employed.

THE IBERIAN WORLD AND THE *RECONQUISTA*

It has been said of Spanish society from the eighth to the thirteenth century that it was 'a society organised for war'.[44] The struggle against the Muslims,

---

[43] *Catalogus Baronum*, ed. E. M. Jamison (216); C. Cahen, *Régime féodal* (234).
[44] E. Lourie, A society organized for war (121).

the war of reconquest and religion all simultaneously shaped social structures. The events after 711 had carried the Muslim flood within a few years not simply to the Pyrenees but beyond into Septimania. However, the scattered remnants of Hispano-Visigothic power succeeded in recovering their independence in the Asturias and Cantabrian mountains. About 718 the Asturian aristocracy elected a king, Pelagius. Under Alfonso I (739–57) Islam was forced to abandon Porto, Braga, Leon, Simancas, Osma, Salamanca, Avila and Segovia. The whole of Galicia was reconquered. But, lacking manpower, it was impossible to occupy permanently territory to the south of the Cantabrian mountains, which remained a no-man's-land where Christians and Muslims fought each other incessantly. Further to the east, despite a defeat before Saragossa and the rout of Roncevaux (778), Charlemagne was able to organize to the south of the Pyrenees a March whose capital became Barcelona, conquered in 801. This March was bounded, after the capture of Tarragona in 808, by the course of the Ebro.

After a period of internal division which lasted until the mid-ninth century, the *Reconquista* began again under Alfonso II (866–911). Town-fortresses like Burgos were created. At the beginning of the tenth century the kingdom of the Asturias chose a more central capital, Leon. New political entities began to appear. Around Burgos, Castile became an independent county *c*.950; around Pamplona, Navarre became a kingdom in 925. At the beginning of the eleventh century Muslim Spain broke up into several emirates, the 'reyes de taifas', which were culturally brilliant but incapable of presenting a united front to the Christian advance. At the same time the Iberian peninsula emerged from its isolation from the rest of Christendom. Pilgrims flocked to visit the tomb of the apostle James at Compostella. The first Frankish knights appeared, eager to fight the Infidel in an atmosphere that prefigured the Crusades and which is captured in the first *chansons de geste*.

Initiative passed to the county of Castile, which became a kingdom in 1035 and then united with Leon. The reconquest changed its character and the Christians became much more daring and systematic in their attacks. The Tagus was reached and Toledo taken in 1085. Portugal took shape; a county in 1071, a kingdom in 1143. Aragon, which had become a kingdom in 1035, united a century later with Catalonia. By the mid-twelfth century a good half of the peninsula north of a line from Lisbon through Toledo to Tortosa was under Christian rule. This liberated Spain was shared between four kingdoms: Portugal, Castile and Leon, Navarre and Aragon.

The struggle against the Moors did not absorb all martial energies. Internal conflicts, divisions and dissensions broke out on many occasions. There was never a general or durable armistice between the Moors and Christians along the length of the frontier, only partial and fragile peace treaties and accords. In the process of reconquest there was never an irreversible continuous thrust, but a movement back and forth, advances and retreats, marked on both sides by daring raids and spectacular defeats. Although in the long term the Muslims retreated, this does not mean that the military system of the Caliphate of Córdoba lacked value and coherence. Close to Christian territory there were different, internal, provincial, military districts termed *thughur*. In the tenth century a March around Saragossa faced the Pyrenees, surveying and blocking the way between Aragon and Navarre. Another further to the west around Medinaceli hemmed in Leon and Castile.

The Muslim army was composed of a few permanent units (the chief one was the palatine guard of the emir or caliph, quartered in Córdoba and recruited from foreign slaves), from warriors owing service because of their *iqta*, from mercenaries temporarily recruited outside Spain, from Andalusian militias of little military worth, and from volunteers for the Holy War, anxious to fulfil at least once in their lives the Koranic obligation of *djihad*. In spite of booty, upkeep of the army required large sums, particularly because troops whose names were regularly inscribed in the rolls of the treasury (*diwan*) were paid wages.

Except during periods of truce, in principle an expedition was undertaken every year. Preparation began in June. A month later the army, where the cavalry outnumbered the infantry, was mustered in the presence of the caliph in a huge encampment to the north of Córdoba. The banners of command were distributed in the great mosque to which they were remitted on return. The object was to take fortresses, to raid and rob. Prisoners were carried back: peasants, women destined for the harem, young men lusted after by homosexual Moorish chieftains. As for the division of booty, once the state had received its share, the rest was divided according to the military and social condition of the warriors.[45]

What could the rude and archaic Christian kingdoms of the North raise to oppose these composite forces, maintained by a well-organized state which lacked neither men nor financial resources? In the kingdom of the Asturias in the eighth century the institutional break with the Visigothic period appears stark. The sources no longer mention *duces, comites, prepositi exercitus, thiufadi* or *gardingi*. The system of *annonae* had disappeared, too, whilst there is no mention of *publice expeditiones* but of *fonsado*, or *fossato*, a phrase of popular origin for which three meanings have been proposed: first, that the word comes from *fossa*, a trench, dug for tactical purposes, as can be seen by its use in wars against the Muslims in 816 and 825; second, that it derives from the verb *fossare*, to transfix the enemy; and third, that it comes from the word *foso*, a boundary or frontier. In any event it is clear that *fossato* corresponds to a major expedition, an offensive campaign led by the king or a powerful magnate. *Fossatoria* and *fonsadera* signify the indemnity paid when a man did not take part in a *fossato* when he was juridically obliged to do so.

---

[45] E. Lévi-Provençal, *Histoire de l'Espagne musulmane*, III: *Le siècle du califat de Cordoue*, Paris 1953.

It was the king's prerogative to summon the army and naturally his role as war-leader was essential. Since danger was ever-present all free men were obliged to serve. Before the campaign the king, who might have his own retinue of *milites*, gathered in his palace all the great men. Each *comes*, aided by *majordomi* or *majorini*, led and commanded his contingent. For a long period, infantry was important because a crowd of peasants, small free proprietors or those possessing emphyteutic tenures, grouped into communities, had to share in a struggle that was above all defensive (protection of *civitates*, *castra* and *villae*). Then when danger receded, destructive raids and rapid attacks formed the principal type of warfare, promoting the fortunes of cavalry troops. But the cost of arming a horseman was high. In the tenth century a horse was worth between 4 and 10 oxen, 40 to 100 sheep or 40 to 100 measures of corn. A coat of mail cost 60 sheep.[46] The king could demand such equipment or similar services only from those to whom a fief (*prestamo*, *prestimonium*) had been granted or from those who benefited from a regular wage. By the eleventh century the military obligations of the rest of the population began to decline. Infantry lost ground at the expense of cavalry provided by the towns and by the great lords, the *ricos hombres* (*nobiliores*, *proceres*, *locupletes*, *richi homines*), who had received from the king honours (*honores*) in full propriety and who were surrounded by their *fideles*, *satellites*, *vassalli* and *homines*. Many of these were light, mobile horsemen, mounted on thoroughbreds, (*jinetes*), using a short stirrup, low saddles and specially shaped bits, different from those of knights in the rest of Europe who sat on high saddles and had the advantage of a very solid seat. These horsemen used the tactic of simulated flight (*torna-fuye*) similar to that practised by the Muslims under the term *karr-wa-farr*.

Around 1050 the following military units can be discovered in Leon and Castile: (a) the *infanzones* or *caballeros hidalgos* who took part in the *fonsado* because of their fiefs or for a wage; (b) the *caballeros villanos*, particularly numerous in the Duero valley, a sort of popular cavalry whose role increased after 1080; in origin as much urban as rural, they can be compared with the non-noble citizens of the Italian communes, obliged to serve on horseback because of their economic position; (c) contingents of *pedones* provided by the towns according to the terms of their charters (*fueros*).

In general, obligations varied according to the type of war. It seems that *guerra* signified a civil war between the great men in contrast to *bellum*, war directed against the Muslims. The *hueste* (army or host) signified a great offensive led by the king or his lieutenant, whilst a *fonsado* was a restricted campaign chiefly mounted by towns, and the *apellido* was a levy en masse in the event of invasion. Lastly there was raiding into enemy territory which was described by words like *cavalgada*, *algara*, *corredura* and *azaria*. A

---

[46] In Central France in the eleventh century a saddled horse was worth between 2.5 and 8 oxen, and a hauberk between 10 and 16 oxen.

twelfth-century chronicler describes this kind of warfare in these terms: 'Every day large bodies of knights leave castles on what we call *algarades* and roam far and wide, pillaging all the territory of Seville, Córdoba and Carmona, and setting it all alight.'[47]

THE CRUSADES AND THE LATIN STATES IN THE EAST

Beginning with the appeal of Urban II at the council of Clermont (27 November 1095), culminating in the capture of Jerusalem (15 July 1099) and terminating in the battle of Ascalon (12 August 1099), the first crusade was by far the most outstanding military achievement of the feudal period. The participants themselves were aware of the enormity of their success. Listen to Anselm of Ribemont writing to Manasses, archbishop of Reims, at the end of November 1097 at the moment the siege of Antioch began: 'Be it known to you that we have certainly conquered for Our Lord two hundred cities and castles. May our Mother Church in the West rejoice that she has borne men who have won for her such a glorious name and have succoured the Church in the East in such a marvellous fashion.'[48]

On the eve of the first crusade, Byzantium had been in marked decline for about 50 years. Not only had it lost its Italian possessions and vantage points, it had also failed to stem the advance of the Seljuk Turks. The Turks had defeated and captured the Emperor Romanus Diogenes in 1071 at Manzikert, seizing control by the same stroke of most of Asia Minor. The loss of this province, so vital to the Empire because it was a great reservoir of soldiers, was completed in 1085 when Antioch fell. Since 1081 Alexis I Comnenus, a capable and farsighted man, sought to protect Constantinople from a Turkish landing in the Balkans and to recover Asia Minor and Northern Syria. The Byzantine Empire did not lack financial means, but the remnant of its national army was in no condition to undertake a counter-offensive with any reasonable chance of success. Mercenaries were needed. In this respect the Latins could do the job, provided that they did not turn up in overwhelming numbers and that they quietly accepted the political direction of their employer.

As for the Seljuk Turks, they had had considerable success under their sultans Alp Arslan (1065–72) and Malik Shah (1072–92). Their first military quality was mobility; more lightly armed than the knights of the West, the Turkish horsemen were able to harass their enemies, encircling, outrunning

---

[47] Quoted by A. P. Torres, Ejercito en los estados de la Reconquista (288).
[48] *Epistulae et chartae ad historiam primi belli sacri spectantes*, ed. H. Hagenmeyer, Innsbruck 1901, pp.145–6.

or surprising them, causing them to lose their order by feigning retreat. After firing a hail of arrows which they shot from horseback in successive waves, thanks to 'Turkish bows', they took advantage of the casualties or disarray they had inflicted to begin hand-to-hand combat. Although dating from a later period, the two extracts which follow allow us to glimpse the tactics they used at the time of the first crusade:

> [The Turk] surrounded our men and shot such a great number of arrows and quarrels that rain or hail never darkened the sky so much and many of our men and horses were injured. When the first bands of Turks had emptied their quivers and shot all their arrows, they withdrew but a second band immediately came from behind where there were yet more Turks. These fired even more thickly than the others had done. . . . [after this preparatory phase, decisive action followed:] The Turk, seeing that our men and horses were severely wounded and in great difficulties, hung their bows instantly on their left arms under their armpits and immediately fell upon them in a very cruel fashion with maces and swords.[49]

Yet if this tactic was evidently well known to the Byzantines, who could have warned the Latins even before they had crossed the Golden Horn, the latter had only theoretical knowledge of it (though some crusaders who had already been on pilgrimage to Jerusalem may have known something of the countryside and of the military habits of its inhabitants, and others may have fought in Spain where the Moors employed a very similar tactic). The Turks were also fighting in a land which they had known for a generation and in a climate with which they were familiar. On the other hand their human resources were not limitless. The different tribes had frequently been at war with one another. Nor did they know how to unite in time to face an invader whose ambitions they could not understand. Elsewhere, in Syria, the local emirs acted independently, whilst southern Palestine was falling, at least in part, under the domination of Fatimid Egypt.

The true political objectives of Urban II are unknown. Did he simply wish to ensure the safety of the route to the Holy Places, *via hierosolymitana*, or to recapture for the papacy's profit the land of Israel which he knew had once been part of the Roman Empire? The methods which he intended to employ on the expedition are better known. He wanted to unite under the spiritual and political authority of his legate Aimar de Monteil, bishop of Le Puy, with the aid of Raymond V of St-Gilles, count of Toulouse, a pious and experienced 50-year old, an army of several thousand hardened *milites*, all volunteers, recruited chiefly in southern France. Perhaps he hoped that this expeditionary force, similar in composition to that which William, duke of Normandy, had collected 30 years earlier for the conquest of England, would receive logistic support and reinforcement from Byzantine troops. In fact, the

---

[49] Thirteenth-century French versions of William of Tyre's *History* quoted by R. C. Smail, *Crusading Warfare* (286), pp.76 n.9 and 82 n.4.

army of God matched this plan very imperfectly. On the one hand, there were leaders who had avowedly temporal ambitions; politicians rather than mystics took part in the crusade. On the other, the *milites* of many regions in the West responded to its preaching with such eagerness that several armies were formed. There was an army of the Normans of Southern Italy and Sicily; that of Northern France, including Robert Curthose, duke of Normandy; that of Godefroy de Bouillon or the army of Lorraine, including Walloons, Frenchmen, Flemings and Germans, to which one may add the small troop of Hugues the Great, count of Vermandois, brother of Philip I of France. There were also popular elements which joined the movement, whether they left for Constantinople before the official date for departure (fixed for August 1096) and formed the so-called People's Crusade with Peter the Hermit and Walter Sans-Avoir, or whether they joined the official armies. These popular elements simultaneously presented advantages and disadvantages. By their presence they weighed the armies down, slowing their progress, making discipline even more difficult to maintain and complicating yet further the acute supply problems. But they also provided auxiliary combatants, infantry who were indispensable on many occasions. The People's Crusade (and its remnants once it had been largely exterminated by the Turks in the autumn of 1096) was not made up entirely of *inermes*, women and children. From this mass of poor people were recruited the troop of *Tafurs* who met the Turks in a state of ecstasy, standing firm in the front line without spear or buckler, armed simply with sticks. They terrorized their adversaries because they were reputed to eat their bodies. But the poor did not only have a military role. Helped by the lower clergy, they succeeded in maintaining enthusiasm for the crusade, fanning the flames when they threatened to go out, after the capture of Antioch and the conquest of Syria for example. Without their action the leaders might well have given up and renounced the supreme objective.

The crusading armies (*exercitus Dei*) were chiefly divided into three groups: the Franks, the Provençals and the Normans of the South, although by the nature of things, they had to co-ordinate their efforts on the battlefield. As a symbol of their unity they wore crosses sewn onto their clothes which protected them and recalled their double mission of pilgrimage and holy war.[50]

Did they at least enjoy numerical superiority? The sources do not provide a definitive answer. After mentioning the innumerable hosts of which the crusading army was composed, they refer to the even greater number of pagans who threatened to overwhelm them. Nevertheless it is likely that although the poor and auxiliaries were fairly numerous and there were thou-

---

[50] Raymond de Saint-Gilles was described as 'armed on all sides by the sign of the cross' as were the count of Flanders and Robert, constable of Prince Bohemond (*Histoire anonyme de la première croisade*, ed. L. Bréhier, Paris 1924, pp.36, 72, 84).

sands of knights (*milites*), on occasion only a few hundred were available with their mounts to lead a charge.[51] Moreover, despite generous promises, the aid furnished by the Byzantine Emperor was very modest; a contingent of troops under Taticius (*Tatikos*), some arms and a few supplies. As a result there were serious problems for the commissariat and in raising forces. In order to replenish the stock of horses, it was necessary to depend on booty.

It is remarkable, however, that during the two years and four months of the campaign, the crusaders received practically no reinforcements from the West. Thus their power continually declined through desertions and those returning home, through death, disease and injuries. They left important contingents of varying sizes to garrison towns and fortresses which they had conquered. The victorious army of Ascalon (12 August 1099) was significantly weaker than that which had won at Dorylaeum (1 July 1097).[52] Nevertheless various Christian peoples in the West were of some assistance. English and Genoese squadrons and the activities of the pirate Guynemer of Boulogne show at least a certain mastery of the sea. The crusaders' success appears all the more striking since they did not enjoy the aid of the German Emperor nor the kings of England and France. Doubtless there were those who thought the enterprise would be easier and certainly shorter (after the taking of Nicea the count of Blois wrote to his wife that unless they were delayed at Antioch, Jerusalem would be reached in less than five weeks).[53] The Latins knew not only how to utilize their attacking power to win set-piece battles (*bella campestra, proelia*), but how to prosecute clever siege warfare with the use of sophisticated engines. We may also note the frequency of military actions and a continuity of effort which was rare for the Middle Ages, when soldiers were easily discouraged. The crusaders were able to benefit from a divided enemy, allowing them time to realize the dangers of their expedition, but their success was by no means foreordained. The proof of this lies in the complete failure of the crusade of 1101 when, it seems, forces of similar size were raised and a comparable strategy adopted.

It was necessary to maintain the states of Outre Mer. This was a difficult task, first of all because of the small numbers of Latin troops. After the battle of Ascalon (1099), Godefroy de Bouillon had at his disposal only 300 knights and 2,000 infantry, to which could be added the minimal garrison at Edessa and the somewhat more important one which was installed at Antioch with Bohemond. It is possible to envisage a regrouping of all the Christian forces in the region of Jerusalem and the establishment of a bridgehead linked to the sea through Jaffa, which could then be supplied by Italian, especially Pisan, fleets. But the Franks considered it more profitable in every respect to keep

---

[51] J. Prawer, *Histoire du royaume latin de Jerusalem*, tr. G. Nahon, Paris 1969, i.204, speaks of 4,500 knights at the beginning and 30,000 infantry, plus at least an equal number of non-combatants.

[52] Perhaps 1,200 knights and 12,000 infantry at the siege of Jerusalem (*ibid.*, i.225).

[53] *Epistulae et chartae*, pp.139–40.

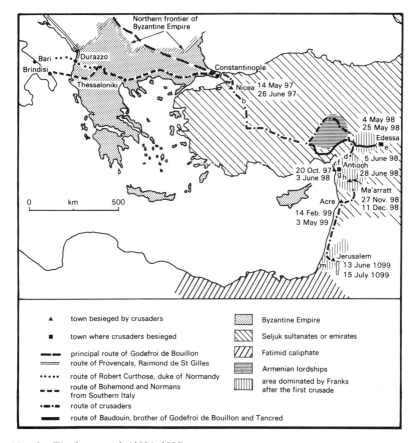

Map 2   The first crusade (1096–1099)
   Battles fought by the crusaders: a. Nicea, 21 May 1097; b. Dorylaeum, 1 July 1097; c. Heraclea, 9 September 1097; d. Iron Bridge, Antioch, 20 October 1097; e. Harran, Mid-November 1097; f. Antioch, 29 December 1097; g. Against the Muslims of Aleppo and Damascus, 31 December 1097; h. Antioch, 9 February 1098; i. Antioch, 6 March 1098; j. Antioch, 28 March 1098; k. Against Kerboga, 28 June 1098; l. Ascalon, 12 August 1099.

and consolidate their four centres of power – the counties of Edessa and Tripoli, the principality of Antioch and the kingdom of Jerusalem. The existence of these four states reflected the course of the march to Jerusalem and the divisions of the crusading army. After 1101 the route through Asia Minor was impassable. Antioch and Edessa became outposts guarding the northern flank of this territory, not staging posts on the road between Constantinople and Jerusalem. In these circumstances it would have been best to conquer all the hinterland from Antioch to Ascalon inland as far as the desert in order to create a no man's land between the Franks and the Muslims. But the task was beyond them. Near Ascalon the Fatimids held a salient to the south, while the Muslims still held Aleppo, Homs and Damascus – though this did not prevent, despite alternating defeats and successes, a certain expansion of the Latin states. Around 1118, at the close of the reign of Baldwin I, this expansion had practically reached its apogee. By 1135 under Baldwin II the establishment of the Latin states seemed secure.

What forces had been used to achieve this consolidation? In the first instance, the feudal lords and knights of the Holy Land, having received, acquired or conquered fiefs, owed to their direct lord or to their suzerain military services which were much less restricted than those known in the less threatened West. Whilst Godefroy de Bouillon maintained his knights directly in his household or conceded 'in fief, rents assigned on the revenues of markets, towns or ports', his successors Baldwin I and Baldwin II implanted 'the organic structures of feudalism: counties, baronies, castellanies, knights' fees which became the basis of service'.[54] A plausible estimation of numbers provides the following figures: in its short existence the county of Edessa never contained more than 100 knights, that of Tripoli probably had double this number, the principality of Antioch, 700, and the kingdom of Jerusalem, 1,000. In all some 2,000 knights at a time, when Henry I of England had three times that figure. Furthermore all these men could never be put into the field simultaneously. To the *milites* may be added the foot sergeants, *pedites*, provided by ecclesiastical and urban communities, who were not that numerous, for (according to a late document, it is true) 'when there was an emergency in the land and kingdom of Jerusalem' the patriarch of Jerusalem, the canons of the Holy Sepulchre, and the burgesses of Jerusalem and Acre each had to send 500 sergeants. One can estimate that the kingdom of Jerusalem could provide 5,025 sergeants, a figure which should be doubled if one includes the other three states. The crusaders could also still count on native troops (the Turcopoles, particularly notable after 1150), on armed pilgrims from the West, and, finally, on the military orders who were already powerful before the second half of the twelfth century.[55]

---

[54] Boutruche (102), ii.346.
[55] For the Military Orders see below, pp.74–77.

3

Medieval Society in its Prime from the Mid-Twelfth to the Early Fourteenth Century

Even more strikingly than in the previous age, within the period 1150 to 1300 medieval society experienced times of almost complete peace on many occasions and over comparatively large geographical areas which allowed an acceleration of demographic and economic growth. This was certainly the case for most regions of France which, though disturbed by episodic and superficial military expeditions and private wars, which were certainly very numerous, saw their effects more and more circumscribed by royal or princely authorities. In this respect Brittany, which in the half century from 1250 to 1300 knew only one war of any length, that between Duke John Rufus and Olivier de Clisson (1254–61), was by no means exceptional. During Henry III of England's reign of 56 years (1216–72), only 20 were affected by warfare – six on the continent (1225, 1230, 1242–43, 1253–54), five in Wales (1223, 1228, 1231, 1245, 1253), and two on the Scottish border (1244 and 1255), whilst in England itself there were only six years when fighting broke out (1216–17, 1224, 1233, 1264–65). Even the rivalry of Italian lordships and communes, despite their relative frequence, had only a limited impact on life and daily activities. For many sovereigns the time had now finally passed of annual military expeditions so characteristic of the earlier Middle Ages. Philip Augustus after Bouvines (1214) and St Louis, throughout the major part of his reign, only had to raise armies periodically and no longer knew the constant fatigue and dangers of military campaigns. Their links with war became very tenuous.

It was not that the chivalry of the West had lost its dynamism or its effervescent expansionist force. In the Iberian peninsula the Muslim retreat speeded up following the defeat of Las Navas de Tolosa (1212) and the loss of Córdoba (1236) and Seville (1248). Around the year 1230 the Portuguese frontiers reached their present extension. At the same time Islamic domination was reduced to a bridgehead around Malaga, Granada and Almeria. Although they achieved only ephemeral success, the crusades and other similar overseas expeditions linked to them continued. The three greatest Western rulers of the time – Philip Augustus, Richard Coeur de Lion and

Frederick Barbarossa – took part in the third crusade (1190–91). The fourth crusade (1202–3) led to the establishment of a Latin Empire in the East, the more and more precarious existence of which lasted for two generations (1204–61). The following crusades, combining military action and diplomatic initiatives, even if they did not prevent the defeat and final disappearance of the Latin states of the East with the fall of Acre, the last Frankish possession on the Asiatic continent, in 1291, nevertheless showed that a section of the warrior aristocracy, urged on and organized by states, had not entirely renounced fighting for the holy places. In the Baltic lands and in Prussia, German expansion, spearheaded by the Teutonic knights, took the form of a holy war.

It was, however, within Christendom that the major military enterprises occurred. Northern and central Italy was the scene of many attempts by the German Emperors to impose or to re-establish their domination. In their turn, the installation of the Angevin dynasty in the kingdom of Sicily and their difficulties after the Sicilian Vespers (1282) provoked bitter conflicts. Elsewhere, throughout the whole period, Guelfs and Ghibellines, respectively representing the papal and imperial cause, on a regional or local scale, incessantly opposed each other. In short, the ambitions of foreigners (German, French and Aragonese), political fragmentation, commercial rivalries (especially acute in this epicentre of the economic renaissance), turned Italy in the twelfth and thirteenth centuries into a region which experienced a high incidence of warfare. Many of the greatest battles of the period occurred there: Legnano (1176), Cortenuova (1237), Parma (1247), Montaperti (1260), Benevento (1266), Tagliacozzo (1268), Roccavioni (1275).

In the most diverse forms and for a variety of reasons, the pieces on the chess-board of German politics (towns and urban states, simple lords and territorial principalities and, lastly, the crown) expressed their rivalries and the contradictions of their interests in a multitude of conflicts which were only imperfectly stopped or limited by public peace (*Landfriede*). On several occasions the German Emperors had to face general revolts. From 1250 the great Interregnum allowed military anarchy to flourish.

If conditions look more peaceful in France and England, it must not be forgotten that the serious duel between the Capetians and the Plantagenets culminated in 1214 in the victories of Philip Augustus at La Roche-aux-Moines and Bouvines. The Albigensian Crusade and its aftermath profoundly affected parts of Occitania for a generation. At the end of this period, the renewed Franco-English struggle, the conquest of Wales by Edward I, his campaign against Scotland and those of Philip the Fair against the Flemings, stirred up conflicts which prefigure the great dynastic and national wars of the late Middle Ages.

COMBATANTS AND ARMS

'Probably few arts tend to be so dominated by tradition as warfare.'[1] A social as well as a professional group, the knights continued to form the core of armies. The majority of rulers would have agreed with Frederick II that 'The adornment of the Empire and of our power especially lies in a multitude of knights.' Even at the end of the thirteenth century there was still a widely held belief that 100 knights were worth 1,000 foot soldiers.

The Rule of the Templars precisely defines the normal equipment of a knight: a shirt (*haubert*) and mail leggings (*chausses*), a helmet or iron head-piece, *espaliers* for protecting the shoulders, sollerets covering the feet, a surcoat or jupon of arms which was worn over the haubert, and a shield, whilst a lance or spear, sword, Turkish club (*masse*) and a dagger were the offensive weapons.[2] The Assize of Arms promulgated by Henry II of England in 1181 declared: 'Let every holder of a knight's fee have a hauberk (*lorica*), a helmet, a shield and a lance.'[3] In 1260 Florence expected its knights to possess a *panziere* or haubert, mail leggings (*stivaletti*), a steel helmet, *lamières* or a breastplate and, to complete protection of the torso, encased in the haubert, a lance, and a buckler called a shield, targe or *tavolaccio* (*tabolaccium*: great board).[4]

Until the thirteenth century three remained the minimum number of mounts at the disposition of each knight, and in all probability there was a tendency to increase this number. The Rule of the Templars stipulated three horses, though a fourth was allowed by permission of the Master. In a pact concluded with Pope Gregory IX in 1239, Venice agreed to send 'three hundred knights, each of them having a warhorse (*destrier*), two rounceys and three esquires with their arms' for a campaign.[5] In the same year Raimond VII, count of Provence, promised to serve the pope and the church in the Italian peninsula with 40 knights and 10 mounted crossbowmen (*arbalétriers*) at his own expense, and each of his knights was to have at least five horses. The bull of Urban IV laying down the conditions on which Charles of Anjou was to obtain the kingdom of Sicily indicated that each knight brought by Saint Louis's brother should have at least four horses for his use.[6]

However, even among horsemen uniformity was not the rule. Certain ones were better equipped and mounted. Those belonging to the richest families had finer, probably more resistant arms, a larger following, better and more

[1] M. R. Powicke, *Military Obligation* (127), p.26.
[2] H. de Curzon, *Règle du Temple* (217).
[3] *English Historical Documents*, II. *1042–1189*, ed. and tr. D. C. Douglas and G. W. Greenaway, London 1953, p.416.
[4] C. Paoli, *Libro di Montaperti* (223), pp.373–4.
[5] P. Pieri, *Federico II di Svevia* (274), p.120.
[6] E. Berger, *Histoire de Blanche de Castille*, Paris 1895, pp.306–8.

horses. These differences, already apparent in the twelfth century with the distinction between *milites gregarii* (or *milites plebei* or *rustici*) and the *primi milites*, who were also called *strenui milites*, became institutionalized in some form in the thirteenth century with the appearance in France under Philip Augustus and in England, during the early years of Henry III's personal rule, of knights banneret, who were ranked above simple knights, knights bachelor or shield-knights. This latter category may be assimilated with the *einschildig Ritter* found at the base of the pyramid of the German *Heerschildordnung*. In 1269, seeking to limit as much as possible the costs of transport for his future crusade, Louis IX authorized every knight banneret to bring with him two horses and a following of five companions, whilst every ordinary knight, called in these circumstances 'a poor man', only had the right to bring a single horse and two helpers.

To describe these auxiliaries, whose role and qualifications are not necessarily identical, a varied vocabulary was used. Three names are found most frequently: valet (Latin: *vallettus;* German: *Knecht*), boy (Latin: *garcio, puer;* German: *Knabe, Knappe*) and esquire (Latin: *armiger, scutifer*). Thus each knight Templar had an esquire. In 1253 Matthew Paris thought it went without saying that each knight was accompanied by an *armiger* or *garcio*.[7] Charles of Anjou in 1283 ordered his financial officers to pay wages to a certain number of soldiers under the command of a knight, Mauger de Bussières. He was to be suitably armed and to have four horses and three aides – a noble esquire and two 'boys' who wore espaliers and a metal tippet to protect the neck, and carried a sword and dagger.[8] These servants were thus not only to concern themselves with supplies and the maintenance of their master and his mounts, but also had their combat role. In 1237 the *armigeri militum* of Frederick II took prisoner and chained enemies who had fallen to the ground. The Rule of the Temple made provision, when the knights had gone to fight, for some of their valets, boys or esquires to remain at the rear with the pack animals. Others bearing spears accompanied the knights, but when the charge began they were to rejoin the rearguard in order to clear the battlefield.

It is by no means certain that all those called knights or *milites* in the sources were true knights in the social sense of the term. Frederick II, having promised the papacy that he would maintain for two years in Palestine 1,000 *milites*, sent Hermann of Salza, Master of the Teutonic Order, to Germany to recruit them. His injunctions, contained in a letter of 6 December 1227, are significant: 'We have sent the Master of the House of the Teutons to pay for knights, allowing him the right, if he wishes, to make a discerning choice among courageous men, to whom he may promise wages for their personal

---

[7] *Chronica majora*, ed. H. R. Luard, London, 7 vols. 1872–84, v.398.
[8] A. de Boüard, *Documents français des archives de Naples* (*règne de Charles Ier*), II. *Les Comptes des trésoriers*, Paris 1935, p.286.

merits.'[9] In other words, some of these *milites* could have been recruited from others than the class of *Ritter*, provided they had the necessary military ability and equipment.

Conversely, possessors of knights' fees or fees of haubert (*feoda loricae*), for various reasons, chiefly economic, refused more and more frequently in the course of the thirteenth century to get themselves dubbed, thus avoiding participation in the honour and expenses of knighthood. This tendency was particularly felt in England where, by the end of the thirteenth century, there were some 1,250 knights (earls and barons included), of whom perhaps 500 were capable of effective mobilization by the monarchy, as opposed to 1,750 non-knights who had sufficient revenues and fees to become knights if they had so desired.[10] In vain did the monarchy try to force through repeated distraints of knighthood – 26 such attempts can be counted between 1224 and 1272 – on all those possessing either a knight's fee or income of at least £20.[11] In the majority of these cases it remained true that horsemen who had not obtained the *cingulum militiae* formed a category of combatants of the second rank, although they performed the same role in warfare. The texts mention them under various names: *servientes equites, servientes loricati, famuli, scutiferi, satellites equestres, clientes, servientes armati ut milites*.

In the Order of the Temple sergeants or serving brothers had the right to one mount only unless given permission for more; they did not have esquires. Their external appearance differentiated them at a glance from the knights since the latter wore a jupon and white mantles bearing red crosses, whilst the former only had the right to wear a black surcoat and a black or brown mantle. However, there was scarcely any difference between their actual equipment; the sergeants, in place of the haubert, simply had a *haubergeon* (smaller haubert) lacking *manicles*,[12] in place of the helmet an iron cap, and mail leggings without foot protectors.

The appearance during the last decades of the twelfth century of mounted sergeants clothed in the same style has a double significance. Military, first of all, to the extent that the progressively increasing weight and cost of a complete set of knight's equipment was tending to restrict its diffusion amongst an elite distinguished by wealth and birth. Secondly, it had social significance, since at the same time and in parallel with the way knighthood was exalted as a model, whose apogee may be found in the thirteenth century, men refused to call those who had not undergone the ritual of dubbing knights or *milites*. In these circumstances it was necessary to use a new expression to designate horsemen whose obscure birth and precarious fortunes prevented them from becoming knights.

[9] H. Delbrück, *Geschichte* (3), III. *Mittelalter*.
[10] N. Denholm-Young, Feudal society (238).
[11] M. R. Powicke, Distraint of knighthood (278).
[12] A kind of mail glove protecting the hand.

From this sprang the social diversity of this group of combatants. Certainly popular elements may be found among them, men of robust physique whom princes had encouraged to ride in the hope of being well served. But there were also holders of sergeants' fees, vavassours, those who in England had an annual income of £10 or £15. It is significant that almost everywhere after about 1250 the description 'horse sergeant' was being replaced by those of page or squire (*damoiseau*), esquire, man on horseback, or man at arms. At the battle of Falkirk (1298), for example, the victorious cavalry of Edward I included 111 knights banneret, about 600 knights bachelor and 1,700 *homines ad arma* or *armati*, also termed *scutiferi, valletti* and *servientes*.[13]

In certain cases all reference to social origins might even disappear. Thus in 1290 the contract drawn up between Florence and Amaury de Narbonne envisaged the latter serving with 30 horsemen *de conredo*, having a great experience of warfare, 420 ordinary horsemen (both groups having three mounts each: a warhorse, a palfrey and a rouncey) and finally 170 esquires or pages having only two horses (a warhorse and a rouncey). In 1277 the contract agreed between the same commune of Florence and a Provençal adventurer, Inghilese de Saint-Rémy, speaks only of a troop of 100 cavalry-men, provided with 100 warhorses and 30 rounceys for the baggage, with their captain alone having the right to three mounts.[14]

Neither by its equipment nor through its tactics did this second-rank cavalry constitute a genuine light cavalry. This nevertheless did exist in the twelfth and thirteenth centuries in various forms. There were the Turcopoles in the Holy Land who drew their Turkish bows without dismounting. There were also those mobile forces of which Gerald of Wales, in a justly famous passage from the celebrated *Expugnatio hibernica*, advocated use against the Irish:

> In the same way as when armies clash in the open, heavy and complicated armour made of linen as well as iron protects and perfectly decorates knights, so when one is fighting only in the hills, woods or marshes . . . a light armour is the best. For against men lacking protection, for whom the victory is won or lost at the first encounter or nearly always so, less cumbrous weapons fully suffice . . . with a complicated armour and high curved saddles, it is difficult to dismount from a horse, even more difficult to mount and yet more difficult to get around on foot when necessary.[15]

One might also add to this same category the mounted Saracen archers whom Frederick II installed at Lucera in Apulia and whom he used in several of his Italian campaigns,[16] the *alforrats* (*homens a cavall alforrats* as opposed to the

---

[13] N. Denholm-Young, *History and Heraldry 1245 to 1310. A study of the historical value of the Rolls of Arms*, Oxford 1965.

[14] D. P. Waley, Army of the Florentine Republic (295), pp.86–8.

[15] Giraldus Cambrensis, *Opera*, ed. J. S. Brewer *et al.*, vi.395–7.

[16] P. Pieri, I Saraceni di Lucera (275).

homens a cavall armats) of the Catalan armies, mounted on *jinetes*, and the English *hobelars* (light horseman) used in campaigns against Wales. There was a final type of horseman: the mounted crossbowman. John Lackland recruited a certain number of them who often possessed several mounts. In 1200 a company of 84 crossbowmen included 25 who had three horses, 52 who had two and seven with only one. Philip Augustus for his part did the same and *balistarii equites* are found in the French king's armies until the 1280s. In 1238 Frederick II fetched a troop of mounted crossbowmen from Hungary. The following year the pope engaged crossbowmen, each of whom had four horses, provided by the count of Provence. In the mid-thirteenth century the Lombard league undertook to pay, in addition to urban contingents, a permanent force of 600 horsemen. Of this number 400 were each to have three mounts including an *equus armigerus et coopertus*, 100 were to have two, and as for the other 100, these were crossbowmen and they, too, were to have two horses.[17]

Employed since Antiquity under various forms, the crossbow, after a period of relative eclipse, once again came to prominence in the last decades of the eleventh century.[18] Anna Comnena in the *Alexiad* described it as something novel:

> The cross-bow is a weapon of the barbarians, absolutely unknown to the Greeks. In order to stretch it one does not pull the string with the right hand while pushing the bow with the left away from the body; this instrument of war, which fires weapons to an enormous distance, has to be stretched by lying almost on one's back; each foot is pressed forcibly against the half-circles of the bow and the two hands tug at the bow, pulling it with all one's strength towards the body. At the mid-point of the string is a groove, shaped like a cylinder cut in half and fitted to the string itself; it is about the length of a fairsized arrow, extending from the string to the centre of the bow. Along this groove arrows of all kinds are fired. They are very short but extremely thick with a heavy iron tip. In the firing the string exerts tremendous violence and force, so that the missiles wherever they strike do not rebound; in fact they transfix a shield, cut through a heavy iron breastplate and resume their flight on the far side. . . . Such is the crossbow, a truly diabolical machine.[19]

The Byzantines were not the only ones to recognize the diabolical qualities of the crossbow. The papacy shared the same opinion and for this reason the second Ecumenical Lateran council (1139) anathematized all those who used the crossbow (and also the bow) in wars between Christians. Already in 1096–97 Urban II had condemned the action of crossbowmen and archers against Christians.[20] Naturally this prohibition was very unevenly observed

[17] *Idem* (274), p.121.
[18] A summary history is provided in *The Carmen de Hastingae Proelio of Guy, bishop of Amiens*, ed. C. Morton and H. Muntz, Oxford 1972, pp.112–15.
[19] *The Alexiad of Anna Comnena*, tr. E. R. A. Sewter, Harmondsworth 1969, pp.316–17.
[20] G. Vismara, Problemi storici (961), p.436.

according to circumstances, times and places. In 1138, for example, Louis VII had in his pay a small troop of archers and crossbowmen.[21] It is not known whether he dismissed them following the council's decision. In any case the crossbow for a long time was little known, at least in France, and Guillaume le Breton attests that it was practically unheard-of until Richard Coeur de Lion in 1185 instructed the French in its use.[22]

But from the end of the twelfth century the crossbow was widely used on land and sea, amongst horsemen as well as infantry, more deliberately in sieges than in pitched battles and more often in southern Europe than in the North. As indications of this diffusion it may be noted that in 1199 Richard Coeur de Lion was mortally wounded by a crossbow shaft when he was besieging the castle of Châlus in the Limousin. At the beginning of the thirteenth century an inventory of munitions stored in 32 places in the Capetian demesnes enumerates, in addition to 265,960 quarrels, 278 crossbows of several types, distinguished by the materials used to make them (horn or wood) or the kind of tension employed (a stirrup, one or two feet, or a stand). About 1250 it was expected that the garrison of Saphet in the Holy Land would include, amongst other troops, 300 crossbowmen. In the pact renewing the Lombard league in 1231 it was agreed that in addition to assembling 3,000 horsemen and 10,000 infantry armed with pikes, 1,500 crossbowmen on foot should be raised. In the letters of franchise granted in the same year by Thibaud of Champagne to the town of St-Florentin it was stipulated that 'everyone in my community of St-Florentin who is worth 20 pounds shall have a crossbow in his house and up to 50 quarrels (that is, arrows).'[23] In the convention drawn up in 1294 between Guillaume Piere de La Mar and Philip the Fair for the arming of Provençal galleys, each ship was to carry 60 crossbows and 6,000 quarrels. In 1314 the Venice Arsenal possessed 1,131 crossbows.[24] Even army leaders did not disdain their use. At the siege of Gaillon the routier captain Cadoc wounded Richard Coeur de Lion with a crossbow bolt and in 1218, at the siege of Toulouse, the count of Comminges grievously injured Guy de Montfort with a crossbow.[25]

Whatever may have been their importance, the crossbowmen on foot were not the only form of infantry. There were also archers, known in Italy as well as in England, where their role appears to have increased from the middle of the thirteenth century as the diffusion of the long bow, utilized in the Welsh wars, rejuvenated this traditional weapon. At the end of Edward I's reign archers enjoyed a preponderance which was almost absolute among the English infantry. The slowness with which the crossbow was reloaded

---

[21] E. Audouin, *Armée royale* (226), p.36 n.1.

[22] *Ibid.*, p.67.

[23] A. Longnon, *Documents relatifs au comté de Champagne et de Brie (1172–1361)*, II. *Le domaine comtal*, Paris 1904, p.33.

[24] L. de Mas-Latrie, *Armes existant à l'arsenal de Venise* (646).

[25] *La chanson de la croisade albigeoise*, ed. E. Martin-Chabot, Paris, 1973, iii.18.

between firing two shots led to the creation of a new corps of *pavesari* whose great bucklers or shields (*pavois*) protected the crossbowmen during this time. During the campaign of Montaperti in 1260, Florence employed 300 *pavesari* to protect the 1,000 crossbowmen she had. The need to clear a route for armies now numbering up to 15,000 or 20,000 men, to build or destroy fortifications and the desire to ruin the economic resources of the enemy often led to the formation of numerous troops of pioneers, miners, sappers and 'wasters' (*guastatores*). Many infantry, moreover, were now either armed with long pikes in order to stop cavalry charges or with weapons for hand-to-hand combat: gisarmes (battle-axes or halberds), flails, slashing-hooks, clubs (*goedendags*), swords and so on.

A large number of the infantry were now at least lightly protected with iron caps, bascinets, *cervellières* and gorgets. The shield was fairly widely used as well as the haubergeon, which was sometimes replaced by the more rustic and cheaper gambeson. Other infantry fought without any armour when they lacked the means. Urban contingents often appeared to be 'poorly armed and naked'.[26] Some infantry of high quality did, however, disdain the use of all protection out of choice in order to retain their agility, as did the English and Welsh archers and pikemen and the Almogavars of the kingdom of Aragon, whose name derives from the Arabic *mugâwir* meaning a runner, the *incensor* of Latin texts. These troops, who came from the mountains of Aragon and Catalonia, had very limited equipment in which the use of leather recalled their pastoral origins: a tunic called a *gonella*, *cassot* or *camisa*, leather gaiters, sandals with leather soles, a leather bonnet, sometimes reinforced with a kind of steel framework, and a leather knapsack containing food supplies. The Catalan chronicler Bernat Desclot described them thus:

> 'The men whom we call Almogavars live exclusively by their arms and dwell neither in towns nor villages but only in forests and mountains. They fight daily against the Saracens, penetrating a day or two's march into Saracen territory, pillaging and collecting booty and bringing back with them numerous prisoners and many goods. They live off this booty. . . . They are a very strong, quick and agile people eager in pursuit and difficult to follow.[27]

It would, then, be incorrect simply to represent the combatants of this period under the two classical headings of cavalry and communal infantry and of the Orders. In some regions at least, in the Iberian peninsula, Ireland, Scotland and Switzerland, there were also popular forces of peasants or pastoralists who in certain historical circumstances might be transformed, despite the rustic character of their arms, into formidable fighters, successfully using their knowledge of the terrain, their local clan or tribal unity and the solidarity of their way of life or language, against 'regular' armies technically better equipped.

---

[26] C. Gaier, *Art et organisation militaires* (112), p.162.
[27] R. Sablonier, *Krieg und Kriegertum in der Crónica des Ramon Muntaner* (537), p.57.

THE ORDERS OF KNIGHTHOOD

The military religious orders, made up in principle of volunteers engaged for life and which, for the most part, were created between the beginning of the twelfth century and the early thirteenth, offered through their recruitment, organization and use a very particular form of armed force. Of this phenomenon, born out of the crusades, and the spirit of the crusade, the Templars furnished the first model, soon to be imitated, though not without modification, by other foundations.

The Templars (*fratres militiae Templi*) appeared in the Holy Land about 1118. At that time they were a pious and devout handful of knights grouped around a Burgundian, Hugues de Payens, and a Fleming, Geoffroi de Saint-Omer. Their original aim was to ensure throughout the new Latin states the safety of roads which brought pilgrims to the Holy City. This tiny fraternity soon reinforced its structure and its mission by taking the triple vow of chastity, poverty and obedience. It undertook, as far as it was possible, to help with the recitation of canonical offices in the church of the Temple at Jerusalem, close to which they had been installed by King Baldwin II. By the same token they became religious, aspirants to perfection.[28] Wishing to increase recruitment, which was still very modest, Hugues de Payens journeyed to the West to encourage this vocation there. It was at the council of Troyes in 1128 that the Order received its Rule, permeated by the spirit of St Bernard, who pronounced on this occasion an encomium on the new chivalry (*De laude novae militiae*). At Troyes were established 'the theological principles of this rather novel form of life which attempted to weld together the obligations of monastic and military ways of life' (J-M. Canivez).

Bernard of Clairvaux began with a very harsh and largely radical criticism of profane chivalry of 'secular militia', whose members found themselves, in a sense, in an impossible position: either they killed and thus sinned mortally or they were themselves killed and, since they had not had time to prepare for death, were lost for eternity, with the result that the fruits of war 'could only be death or sin'. Even when a knight died without having killed anyone, he nevertheless died guilty of homicide for his intention in fighting was to deal out death. For if ordinary war was mortal for the soul, it was so above all because of what motivated it: sometimes simply a bellicose temperament and a gratuitous desire for adventure, sometimes anger, sometimes a desire for personal glory, sometimes the will to conquer.

After this very brief and rhetorical analysis, St Bernard underlined the novelty of the Templars' enterprise. It was 'such that the world had not

---

[28] It should be noted, however, that members of the military orders were not monks who had been given permission to fight and shed blood, but rather lay knights integrated into a religious rule.

known until now'. It is true that for a long time monks had bent the force of their souls in the spiritual fight against vice, evil and the temptations of the Devil in a fashion not dissimilar to men using all their bodily strength to fight against a corporal enemy. But here were these new men whom he 'admired above all words' intending to undertake this double combat of flesh and spirit, and this was a just fight, for they undertook it in the name of Christ and for Him. For them it was a question of defeating 'the enemies of the cross of Christ'. In killing malefactors they were suppressing evil and were thus not murderers. Of course murder was always an evil, but 'in our present condition' there was no other method to prevent pagans from oppressing the faithful and the just who, if they were beaten, risked falling into iniquity. What name should be given to the members of this new militia, monks or knights? 'In truth they are worthy of both.'

Not only did the purity of their motivation render their struggle legitimate, but the way in which they carried it out, their way of life, turned them into exemplary warriors. They were obedient and showed discipline in battle, whilst displaying frugality and asceticism in a communal life from which women and children were excluded. They all lived under the same roof, received from their leaders clothing and nourishment and had no private possessions. They were never inactive. When they were not fighting, they were doing menial tasks, repairing their weapons and clothes. Their hierarchy was founded not on nobility but on merit. They had repudiated the pleasures and prestige proper to secular chivalry – love of fine arms, exaggerated care of the body and coiffure, passion for games and hunting, taste for the jesting of jugglers and minstrels. *Pauperes commilitiones Christi*: this title underlines the character of the new order founded on poverty, a communal life and devotion to Christ.

The Templars' ideal – this double submission to the *disciplina militaris* and the *disciplina regularis*[29] – soon achieved great success. Not only did donations flow in from the nobility who were eager to share in the spiritual benefits of the Order, but recruits were not lacking. This led to the abandonment of the initial mission of protection for a more specifically military role against the Infidel. From this point the history of the Temple was indissolubly linked with that of the Latin states. Leaving on one side the defeats, intrigues and rash actions of the Templars, it must be stressed what a heavy tribute they paid in the crusading cause. On several occasions the majority of their knights perished in battle. Others endured captivity. In a century, five Masters of the Temple died sword in hand.

The origins of the Order of the Hospitallers of St John of Jerusalem can be found in the existence, around 1070, of a hospice in that city which provided shelter for pilgrims. The events of the first crusade could only increase its

[29] Anselm of Havelberg, *Dialogues, i. Renouveau de l'Eglise*, ed. G. Salet, Paris 1966, pp.98–100.

role and reputation. It was, it seems, in the Iberian peninsula that some of its members began its military function. This was attested in the Holy Land from 1137. The Hospitallers, whose Rule was related to that of the Augustinian canons, became emulators and often rivals of the Templars.

In its turn, the struggle against the Muslims in the Iberian peninsula provoked the appearance of several military orders, all linked to Cîteaux: Calatrava (1158); San Julián de Pereiro (between 1156 and 1176), later to become the Order of Alcantara from 1220; the *militia sancti Benedicti cisterciensis ordinis*, founded in 1162 under the patronage of Alfonso the Conqueror, king of Portugal, which became the Order of Avis in 1187 and which from 1213 formed a dependency of Calatrava; St James of the Sword, whose first mission was the protection of pilgrims and whose military function became clearer from 1175; the Orders of Turgel, Monte-Frago and St Mary; and finally the Orders of Montesa and Christ, survivors of the Temple beyond the Pyrenees.

As for the Teutonic Order (*Domus hospitalis sanctae Mariae Teutonicorum*), this appeared about 1128 in the Latin Kingdom of Jerusalem as a hospital confraternity. It was transformed into a military order in the last years of the twelfth century. The important contribution of the Germans to the Fifth Crusade (1217) and then the crusade led by Frederick II in 1228 strengthened the position of the Teutons in the Holy Land. They now kept up castles there whilst the official residence of the Master of the Order was established at Acre. But it was in the Baltic regions that the Teutonic Order found its major field of activity. Hermann von Salza, the fourth Master of the Teutonic knights (1210–39), became convinced that the Frankish domination of the Holy Land was bound to come to an end sooner or later. This led him to look elsewhere for a more favourable battlefield. After thinking first of Transylvania, he obtained in 1230 the territory of Kulm which was ceded to him by Christian, first bishop of Prussia, and Conrad, duke of Masovia. These latter had previously tried to force the Prussians into submission with the aid of a new order, the 'Knights in the service of God in Prussia', established at Dobrzyn, hence their name 'Brothers of Dobrzyn'. The Teutonic knights succeeded where the 'Dobriners' had failed. Moreover, the Order received after 1237 assistance from the Sword-brothers (*ensiferi*), an Order founded about 1200 by Bishop Albert of Riga, and confirmed by Innocent III in 1204. It was through their agency that Livonia and Courland were added to the Prussian domains.

This survey of the European scene shows how from the beginning of the twelfth century both lay and ecclesiastical powers believed that the foundation of military orders was one of the most efficacious ways of bringing pagans and infidels to submission. Some of these orders vegetated, but others went from strength to strength over the centuries. Like other medieval religious brotherhoods, the military orders benefited from the generosity of the faithful. In addition they knew well how to exploit their own wealth. Several, including the Templars, Hospitallers and Teutonic knights, engaged in banking and commerce. Having at their disposal, through their network of local houses or commanderies, an important logistical support and regular revenues, they were able to maintain their military forces permanently. These, organized into proper armies, included not only knights, but also mounted sergeants and even infantry. The sources do not allow a precise estimation of their numbers, but as an indication it may be said that in the mid-thirteenth century in the Holy Land, along the Baltic coast, in Castile and Portugal, the combined military orders could probably put between 5,000 and 10,000 troops in the field, of whom 1,500 would be knights.

OBLIGATIONS AND MILITARY SERVICES

During this period groups of human beings and the authorities who directed them attempted, in order to wage their wars, to gather in the most effective and economical fashion the military units which they judged necessary in both quantity and quality. The rulers' first idea was to rely on their own resources and to exploit as fully as possible the complex series of military obligations owed them.

The first type, as in the preceding period, arose from the feudo-vassalic system. Throughout the West, in tens of thousands, individuals, men and women, great and small, young and old, owed military service of various sorts to their lords for their fiefs. This was also the case in the Latin kingdom of Jerusalem. According to the evidence of the Assizes of Jerusalem, 'a compilation of juridical texts dating from the end of the twelfth century to the second third of the thirteenth', vassals owed 'servise d'aler a cheval et as armes' on the summons of their lord 'to any place in the kingdom' (*en toz les leus du roiaume*).[30] Some served as knights, some as sergeants, but for all of them the time of service was exceptionally long, a year in fact, so that in the most extreme conditions a vassal might spend all his life under arms. According to John of Ibelin the *servitia debita* of the kingdom of Jerusalem totalled 675 knights. The Assizes of Romania specify that every feudatory owed service in person until the age of 60, from which point his son might replace him, or in his absence, any other knight or two esquires. There the period of service was four months in a castle, four months on the frontier and the rest of the year could be spent at home.

In the German Empire after the consent of the princes assembled in the *Reichstag*, knights could be convoked by the king of Germany for the *Reichsheerfahrt* on either side of the Alps. If the army remained on the German side, according to the *Mirror of the Saxons* and the *Mirror of the Swabians* (*Sachsenspiegel* and *Schwabenspiegel*), an interval of 40 days elapsed as a rule

---

[30] R. Boutruche, *Seigneurie et féodalité* (102), ii.348 and 454.

between summons and departure. For service beyond the Alps the interval was extended to a year, six weeks and three days (410 days), a delay of remarkable length. This is mentioned for the first time in the middle of the twelfth century in the *Constitutio de expeditione romana* but was observed on a number of occasions, as for the *Romfahrt* of Henry VI and that of Henry VII which were announced, respectively, on 10 August 1189 and 15 August 1309, to begin on 21 September 1190 and 1 October 1310.

Nevertheless the increasing weakness of imperial power became apparent with various limitations on military obligations. By the *Privilegium minus* of 1156 the dukes of Austria obtained the right to participate only in imperial expeditions in neighbouring provinces and kingdoms. In the thirteenth century the margraves of Brandenburg only owed unconditional service to the kings of Germany in Saxony and Thuringia. From 1212 Bohemia was dispensed from the *Romfahrt* on payment of a sum of silver. The *Sachsenspiegel* states that a vassal's duty 'obliges him to serve in German-speaking lands subject to the Roman Empire. But all those whose fiefs are situated east of the Saale shall serve in Wendland, Poland and Bohemia. For six weeks the vassal shall serve his lord at his own expense.'[31] The same customary law adds that 'all vassals holding royal goods in fief' shall take part in the *Romfahrt*, though they might freely commute this obligation by paying a tenth of its annual value, a clear reduction in comparison with the mid-twelfth century when a defaulter was liable to a fine representing half his fief's income. Even the obligations of *Dienstleute* constantly decreased.

It is true that to royal service there must be added obligations to territorial princes which were more frequent and burdensome, despite a similar tendency to limit them in length and distance, with the possibility of monetary commutation. Yet the old Carolingian rule of three months' free service was not totally forgotten. In 1234 Pope Gregory IX informed the German princes who were on the point of coming to Italy that they would have to stay there for three months at their own expense in addition to their other service.[32]

In Italy the system of feudal obligations was far from falling into disuse, neither in the kingdom of Sicily nor in the northern principalities like the county of Savoy, marquisate of Montferrat and so on. In the papal states in the thirteenth century, the baronial vassals of the Holy See had to 'make peace and war against all men'. In 1212 Innocent III invested Azzo of Este with the March of Ancona in return for the service of 100 knights for a month each year.[33]

This crisis in the feudal system even manifested itself in the strongest and best organized states. In England, following the anarchy of the civil war between partisans of Empress Matilda and those of Stephen of Blois, Henry II, a few years after his accession, carried out a great inquest amongst his

[31] *Ibid.*, ii.432.
[32] J. L. A. Huillard-Breholles, *Historia Diplomatica Frederici II*, iv.513, vi.576 and 939.
[33] D. P. Waley, Papal armies (294).

tenants-in-chief (1166). They were asked four questions: how many enfeoffed knights had they at the death of Henry I (1135)? How many household knights had been enfeoffed since then? How many knights did their demesne properly owe? And, what were the names of the enfeoffed knights (this last information would allow the king to check those who had not taken the oath of allegiance)? Replies were contained in the famous *Cartae Baronum*: 283 tenants-in-chief declared there a total of $6,278\frac{7}{8}$ knights' fees, though the *servitium debitum* only amounted to some 5,000 knights – 1,000 supplementary knights furnishing, one might think, a sort of safety net taking into account minors, old men, the infirm and sick. The abbey of Bury St Edmunds, for example, had 50 knights dependent on it although its *servitium debitum* was only 40, and the abbey of Abingdon, which owed the king 30 knights, possessed 33 *feoda militum*.

Of the three obligations constituting the *servitium debitum*, one, *cavalcata*, *chevauchée* or riding services, which had only ever had a subordinate position, now almost completely disappeared. The second, watch service, is frequently mentioned until at least the beginning of the thirteenth century, but most frequently as a monetary tax. Jocelin of Brakelond relates, for example, that at the end of the twelfth century each of the 50 knights of Bury St Edmunds paid the abbot 29*d*. every 20 weeks when their turn to mount watch recurred. He shows how, later, thanks to the perseverance of Abbot Samson, payment was increased to 3*s*. per knight and the period of service now came round more often, every four months.[34]

There remained service in the host, where two important reductions in requirements may be traced from the reign of the first Plantagenet. The period of service fell by a third, from 60 to 40 days, and it was practically no longer exacted for service across the Channel, even if there was a question of defending the continental possessions of the English kings. In addition, under the term scutage (*scutagium*), commutation of host service, an ancient practice already attested by 1100, became general in the second half of the twelfth century at the rate of 6*d*. a day, that is 240*d*. or £1 for 40 days. Not only did the monarchy willingly have recourse to this procedure, but by a writ *de scutagio habendo* it authorized tenants-in-chief to act in the same fashion towards their own vassals on the sole condition that the quota fixed by the *servitium debitum* should be respected. Recourse to scutage on a more systematic and wider scale than in France or Germany at the same date may be explained by the demilitarization of some fief-holders, by a more abundant circulation of money and by the presence of knights, both native and foreign, of undeniable fighting worth, who were ready to serve for an unspecified period of time in return for money. Another practice was also used which recalls that of the helpers and participators once familiar in the Carolingian period. The king summoned only a part of his forces, demanding that those

[34] Jocelin of Brakelond, *Cronica*, ed. H. E. Butler, London 1949, pp.65–8.

who remained at home should support, either directly or through taxes, their companions who had been mobilized. In 1157 Henry II gathered only a third of the *servitium debitum*. Richard I did the same in 1191 and 1194. In 1197 he proposed that all his English tenants should equip a force of 300 knights for service for a year in Normandy for which they would be paid. In 1205 John Lackland persuaded his tenants-in-chief to agree that nine knights should equip a tenth and pay 2s. a day for his upkeep.

The difficulties which marked the last years of John's reign, the minority of Henry III, the long phases of peace which his reign enjoyed and the political crisis of 1258–65, all contributed to a further deterioration in the system. An obscure series of negotiations between the monarchy and its tenants-in-chief (who acted more as individuals than collectively, each following his own interests) resulted in a drastic reduction of quotas. At the beginning of Edward I's reign that of the bishops and abbots was limited to $132\frac{1}{2}$ fees and the lay nobles owed between 300 and 500 fees. Some 90 per cent of the *servitium debitum* had, in a word, evaporated, as these examples show: in 1231 Richard of Cornwall, Henry III's own brother, had received the Honour of Wallingford (Berkshire) which owed scutage for 100 knights' fees in return for the service of three knights, Hugh de Courtenay's commitment fell from 92 to 3 knights and the earl of Winchester's from 66 to $3\frac{1}{2}$. As was so often the case, the smaller tenants fared less well and failed to obtain such massive reductions. The first summons of the reign (1277) produced only 228 knights and 294 sergeants which, if two sergeants were equivalent to a knight, means a total of 375 knights. A new low was reached in 1300 when feudal service provided Edward I with only 40 knights and 366 sergeants. In that year William de Cantilupe, knight banneret, may be found fighting for pay with three knights and eight sergeants for two months; his *servitium debitum* amounted to one tenth of a knight's fee and in order to fulfil it he simply sent one of his sergeants for eight days. At the rate of 2s. a day for every knight and 1s. for every sergeant in 1277 the feudal summons was worth just £1,500, when every year between 1294 and 1298 Edward I was spending a hundred times that sum on his military operations.

Developments in France were not fundamentally different. According to the evidence of the *Scripta de feodis* and other similar documents, Philip Augustus after his brilliant conquests could certainly count on host service from several thousand knights. A list dating from the years 1210–20 indicates that the French Vexin should have furnished 30 knights, Ponthieu 60, the castellanies of St-Quentin, Montdidier and Roye, 40, 50 and 50 respectively. In comparing these relatively small administrative districts with the extent of the Capetian demesne an impression of considerable human resources is gained. Moreover, the great territorial princes responded to royal summonses with fairly generous contingents. In 1236, for example, 19 dukes and counts were summoned 'three weeks after Pentecost to St-Germain-en-Laye to do service'. The list containing their names also alludes to the service of bishops.

(above) The English
shield-wall withstand-
ing Norman attacks at
Hastings (Bayeux
Tapestry, *c.*1080)

2   Sixth- and seventh-century Frankish arms and
shield *umbo*

3 Dover Castle, chiefly twelfth and thirteenth century

4 *(left)* Carcassonne: part of the thirteenth-century urban defences

5 *(right)* Le Krak des Chevaliers, Syria, twelfth and thirteenth century

6 Milanese communal troops returning after their victory at Legnano (1176) over Frederick Barbarossa

7 Flemish communal militia (The Courtrai Chest, early fourteenth century)

8 A knight receiving communion (detail from a door in Reims Cathedral, thirteenth century)

9 A bishop blessing arms (Pontifical de Guillaume Durand, early fourteenth century)

10 *(left)* A victim of the battle of Visby (1361), buried with his mail coif

11 *(below)* Visby (1361): one of the mass graves excavated in the 1920s

12 Sir Geoffrey Luttrell leaves his family for the wars (from the Luttrell Psalter, c.1335–40)

13 The continuing crusading ideal: a miniature from the *Roman de Godefroi de Bouillon* (1337)

4 *(left)* Paolo Uccello's funeral monument (1436) to Sir John Hawkwood (*d*.1394) in Florence Cathedral

5 *(above)* Training for war: knights jousting with tournament lances (fourteenth-century ivory)

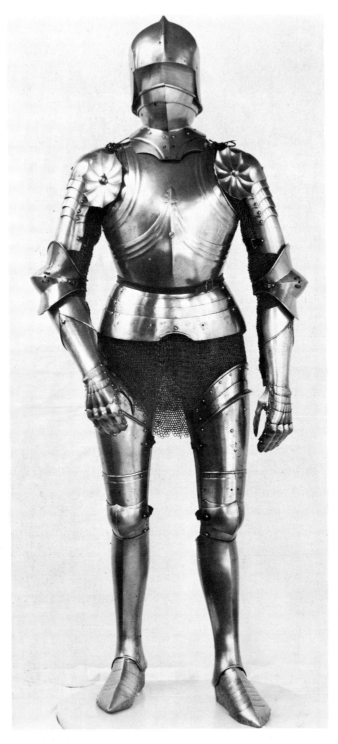

16   A composite suit of late medieval German and
Italian armour

17   Bernese and Burgundian shields, c.1470

18   Mail shirt (German, fifteenth century) and gauntlet (north Italian, late
fourteenth century)

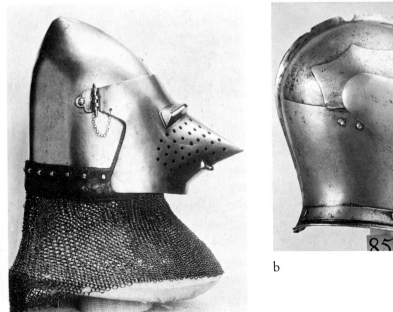

b

a

c

d

19   Four helments: (a) Visored bascinet (?Milan, 1390–1410); (b) Armet (Milan,
1440–60); (c) Barbute or sallet made by Antonio Missaglia (Milan, 1450–70);
(d) Sallet (Germany, 1450–60)

20 *(above)* Dulle Griet – Mad Margot – a giant bombard: length 5.025 m, calibre 0.64 m, weight 16,400 kg (Ghent, Old Market Place, mid-fifteenth century)

21 Emperor Maximilian visiting his cannon founders (from Hans Burgkmair's *Weisskunig, c.1515*)

Ly commence le ſixieme li
ure particulier de ce traitie

22   Artillery on shipboard, from a manuscript executed in 1482 for Louis de Bruges, lord of Gruythuse, whose bombard emblem may be seen in the margins

23   *(right)* The battle of Morat (1476) from Diebold Schilling's late fifteenth-century *Chronicle*

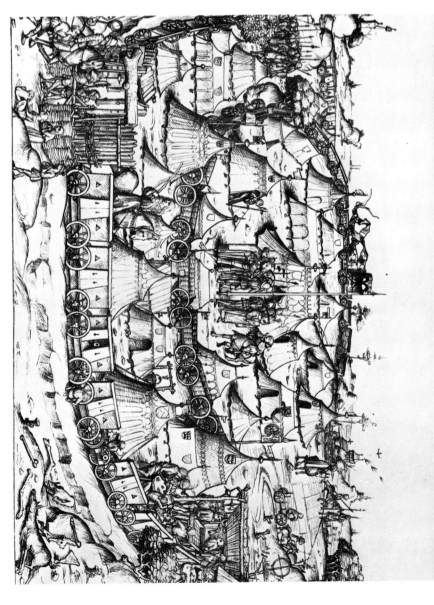

24 A late medieval military camp or *laager* (from *Mittelalterliches Hausbuch*, late fifteenth century)

It also still mentions the 'Queen of Orléans' – Ingeborg of Denmark, widow of Philip Augustus who held Orléans in dower – and 'all those who are under her and owe service at their own expense, having lands worth 60 *livres* or more'. One also finds that service was exacted through the intervention of *baillis* in the *bailliages* of Vermandois, Orléans, Sens, Gisors and the rest of Normandy. There also survives an almost contemporaneous census of all knights (a total of 75) possessing lands worth 60 *livres* per year who held of the king or others in the castellany of Melun, whilst an inquiry of a similar kind in the castellany of Corbeillists 40 there. If the other regions covered by the royal summons brought proportionately as many, the importance of the forces which Louis IX had at his disposal at this date for voluntary service within the limit of 40 days can easily be imagined.[35]

The custumal traditionally entitled the *Etablissements de Saint Louis*, which was compiled in Touraine or Anjou around 1270, specifies in fact that barons and the king's men should serve in his host for 40 days and 40 nights. After this period, which does not seem to be limited by distance, vassals may remain behind only if they wish to. Nevertheless if the king paid them and it was a matter of defending the realm, they ought to continue to serve. But they were freed from their obligations if they were asked to fight outside the kingdom, even if they were paid to do so.

The imperfections of this system appear clearly on the occasion of the summons issued by Philip III at Tours for the host to Foix (1272), an insignificant little expedition against a rebel vassal. The mechanism for recruitment of troops is known from the survival of three lists. The first provides the names of those who were convoked and from whom the king expected service. The second enumerates those who actually appeared at Tours and specified the service they thought they owed on this occasion. The third, some weeks later, lists the troops who took part and the number of days service they had already performed. It is particularly instructive to measure the difference between the support on which the king counted, following the feudal and administrative documents available in his chancery, and that which he really obtained. For example, from the bailliage of the Cotentin 80 knights or their equivalent were expected which, at 40 days voluntary service, gives a total of 3,200 days service, but only 55 turned up, offering a total of 2,165 days. This was a serious loss but it was not overwhelming. Calculated from the daily rates of pay then given to knights, the voluntary service of the Cotentin alone amounted to 811 *livres tournois* (*l.t.*). If we suppose that the Cotentin represented a fiftieth of the military resources of the king of France, that would mean the monarchy may have disposed, at a maximum of 40 days, of some 2,750 knights, equivalent to 40,550 *l.t.* But examination of other Norman bailliages (Caux, Caen, Rouen and so on) shows that the return there was distinctly lower. In addition it is

[35] *RCH*, xxiii.725–6 and 686–9.

probable that Normandy, with its strong administrative traditions going back to the Plantagenets, responded better to the royal summons than other provinces. In fact the third list reveals a total contribution of only 672 knights. Even if one adds by hypothesis contingents from the Midi who are not mentioned, the final impression is far from favourable, more especially since a number of vassals claimed that they were there at the king's expense or only had to fight within the limits of their province; whilst yet others were serving gratuitously by reason of their own good will without any legal obligation. It may be added that the proportion of those who arranged for substitutes was considerable, rising it seems to about 40 per cent.

Philip III was greatly deceived. The royal administration tried to redress the situation by imposing heavy fines on defaulters, representing 50 per cent of the wages allowed to barons, bannerets, knights and esquires, to which was also added, naturally, payment for the 40 days due thus a baron owing 40 days service in 1274 was fined 300 *l.t.* (100*s.* a day plus 50 *sous t.* fine × 40). But this procedure also proved to be ineffective. Not only was the crusade to Aragon in 1285 undertaken principally by paid units, which was normal since it was an expedition beyond the frontiers of the kingdom, but even the campaigns led by Philip the Fair against the Flemings were not used any longer to recruit troops by traditional feudal means. The list of summonses which have been conserved for the last years of the thirteenth century and the beginning of the fourteenth are very different from those of 1272 and this difference chiefly lies in the preponderance of another type of recruitment. By 1300 in the kingdom of France the traditional *servitium debitum* was in full retreat.[36]

Among the multiple factors which brought about this dislocation, without doubt the most important concerns the geographical limits which nearly everywhere fief-holders wished to impose. In 1272 inhabitants of the county of Toulouse claimed that they owed service at their own expense only within the county. In 1315 the men of Champagne similarly alleged that they were obliged to obey a royal summons only 'within the limits of Champagne' and then only on receipt of the king's wages. Outside the county they were to follow the king only if he met 'all their expenses and costs'.[37] The same phenomenon affected the territorial principalities. If in emergencies the duke of Guyenne sometimes asked his Gascon subjects to perform host service for him in regions beyond the territorial limits mentioned in their privileges, this request was accompanied, as in the Poitevin campaign of 1242–43 by a letter

---

[36] Thus in August 1294 when John II of Brittany summoned his host to Ploërmel only 166 knights and 17 esquires acknowledged owing service (Dom P-H. Morice, *Mémoires pour servir de preuves à l'histoire ecclésiastique et civile de Bretagne*, Paris 1742–46, i.1110–15).

[37] Hence efforts by the monarch to abolish geographical limitations when the king campaigned in person – cf. the list of 'dux, contes, barons, chevaliers, escuiers et autres qui doivent servise au Roy toutesfoiz que le Roy en sa personne va en guerre, en quelque lieu que ce soit' (Bib. Nat., MS lat. 9016 no.41).

of non-prejudice. Normally, in fact, the Poitevins owed military service south of the Loire, the Gascons between the Pyrenean passes and the Garonne (*inter portus et Garonam*), the inhabitants of the Bordelais within the limits of the diocese of Bordeaux and those of the Agenais within the diocese of Agen.[38]

With the commercial revolution, the rise of craft industry, changes in government and administration, even in the intellectual training of men, the twelfth and thirteenth centuries witnessed an accelerating growth of cities and large towns. A recent survey which is necessarily approximate and doubtless also pessimistic leads one to think that even before 1300 the Christian West contained at least 5 towns with more than 50,000 inhabitants, 30 or more between 20,000 and 30,000 and 56 with between 10,000 and 20,000.[39] As for towns with fewer than 10,000 inhabitants, they could be counted in hundreds, possibly even thousands.[40]

Whatever their dimension, urban centres provided important military vantage points because of their fortified walls (although there was always a number of them which were never provided with these), for the castles with which they were frequently associated and because of their resources of men, money and arms. Nor did kings and princes fail to use their often decisive aid, by inviting them to ensure their own defence and to provide men, war supplies and foodstuffs. What is more, certain towns in Northern and Central Italy, in Flanders and Rhineland Germany, were heads of urban states which necessarily meant they were forced to exploit various military obligations.

Many towns had at their own command their own military organization, controlled by municipal authorities. The inhabitants were grouped militarily, either by quarter or by craft. They had permanent control of military equipment appropriate to their social position and fortune, to ensure public order within a certain district and to share in the construction, upkeep and guard of the ramparts. In London, for example, there were 24 wards. If in peacetime they were content with a perfunctory watch, in time of war each of them, under the direction of its alderman, had to defend a sector of the walls. On campaign, command of the urban contingent was traditionally assumed by the captain of Baynard's Castle, a fortress situated within the city, near to the Thames.

The French monarchy used the resources of the towns and communes on a massive scale from the reign of Philip Augustus onwards. This is demonstrated by the celebrated *Prisia servientum* or *Prise des sergens* originating in 1194 and brought up to date down to 1204. This list shows the number of

[38] P. Chaplais, Le duché-pairie de Guyenne: l'hommage et les services féodaux de 1259 à 1303, *Annales du Midi*, 69 (1957), 14 (repr. in *Essays in Medieval Diplomacy and Administration*, London 1981).

[39] L. Genicot, Les grandes villes d'Occident en 1300, in *Economies et sociétés au Moyen Age. Mélanges offerts à Edouard Perroy*, Paris 1973, pp.199–219.

[40] Three thousand towns have traditionally been counted in late medieval Germany.

sergeants (and, additionally, of carts) which were owned by various abbeys and townships (*ville* and *communie*), some of which did not have to send men but money. It adds up to a total of 7,695 sergeants, 138 carts and 11,693 *livres parisis* (*l.p.*). It also seems that the period of service expected from these communities was three months, though, since the pay of a sergeant at that time was 8*d.* a day (a pound a month), it follows that, ignoring the carts, if the king accepted full monetary compensation, he would have received every year service was due 35,048 *l.p.* Conversely if he preferred men, he could have obtained a force of 11,683 sergeants; this would be the equivalent of host service by 2,920 knights for 40 days. Again, in certain cases, urban contributions might be even more important. A royal act of 1188 reveals that the citizens of Tournai had to provide 300 well-armed infantry when summoned. This was the figure actually mentioned in the *Prisia servientum*, but it is also specified there that if the royal army marched towards Arrouaise, then the whole commune of Tournai should join it at that spot or within an equivalent distance.[41]

Throughout the thirteenth century towns were summoned as a rule. In 1253, for example, Louis IX assembled at Issoudun the contingents of several communes – totalling 3,100 sergeants – as well as forces drawn from the following towns: Cahors, Figéac, Rocamadour, Sarlat, Martel, Périgueux, Limoges, Brive and Saint-Junien. Even at the beginning of the fourteenth century a large number of towns still sent important groups of combatants, some on horseback, some on foot, without the king having to pay their wages, at least during the first 40 days of a campaign.

The share of towns was still more massive when it was a question of war for their own ends. There could then occur general mobilization not simply in the case of siege – as at Toulouse during the Albigensian crusade – but also for a military expedition. As many burgeses and citizens as possible had to participate; at Florence this meant all men between the ages of 15 and 70, at Perugia between 14 and 60. It has been calculated that Florence in the middle of the thirteenth century might raise from its own population a force of between 3,000 and 5,000 combatants or 6,000 at the outside. In 1340 Bruges was able to raise 7,000 men from a population of 35,000 inhabitants.[42] In 1338 at Venice, according to the *Chronicon Justiniani*, 30,000 men between 20 and 60 years old were able to bear arms and, according to Giovanni Villani, at Florence 25,000 between 15 and 70 could do likewise.[43]

Yet urban communities, especially when it was a matter of helping a superior authority, a king or territorial prince, tried like all fief-holders to

[41] *Recueil des actes de Philippe Auguste, roi de France*, ed. H-J. Delaborde *et al.*, I. *1179–94*, Paris 1916, no.224.

[42] J. de Smet, L'effectif des milices brugeoises et la population de la ville en 1340, *Revue belge de philologie et d'histoire, 12* (1933), 631–6.

[43] D. Herlihy, The population of Verona in the first century of Venetian rule, in *Renaissance Venice*, ed. J. R. Hale, London 1973, pp.92–3.

contest and diminish their obligations. A fourfold attack ensued – to limit the size of the contingent, to cut short the duration of voluntary service, to limit the area within which service was due and to substitute a monetary payment for actual service. What had happened in the papal states by the thirteenth century is a typical example. Camerino, a town in the March of Ancona, only provided the pope with a full *posse* within its *contado*, five knights within the March of Ancona and two outside it. Città Papale owed six days service at its own expense if warfare broke out close by, three days only in more distant zones. Fano owed nothing outside the March.[44] The same process can be traced in Transalpine countries. In 1203 Thibaud I, count of Bar, enfranchised his town of St-Thiébault-sous-Bourmont for ten years from all his 'expeditions and armies'. At the end of that period his subjects were to appear in arms wherever he wished but service at their own costs was limited to two days.[45] In 1272 on the occasion of the summons for Foix, the mayor and burgesses of Rouen declared 'that they only owed service in the host as long as they could return home each evening'.

Military obligations were not limited simply to fief-holders and to urban communities. Almost everywhere, in various ways, authorities also tried to obtain services from the inhabitants of the countryside. These obligations were often comparable to those weighing on genuine towns; in the *Prisia servientum* certain places which were assessed at 10, 15 or 20 sergeants were in fact only villages. Similarly abbeys, in order to furnish their contingents, certainly had to call on the aid of rustics. Hence at Saint-Germain-des-Prés, a cartulary of the abbey declares:

> We are obliged to our lord the king of France when he leads his host to provide 150 sergeants with four carts, drawn by four horses, and a packhorse worth 17*l*. 10*s.p*. And if he will not accept the sergeants, carts or packhorse, we owe him 60*s.p*. for each sergeant, the carts, horses and packhorse included. If he accepts the sergeants, carts, horses and packhorse, we are not obliged to keep them at our expense beyond forty days.[46]

From charters and administrative enquiries from many French localities we learn that they owed host and riding services to their lord.

The *Etablissements de Saint Louis* express a more general principle when they relate that customary tenants of castellanies are obliged to serve barons in their *chevauchées* on pain of a fine of 60*s*., the same rate applicable to those of them who did not join the host.[47] Philippe de Beaumanoir in the *Coutumes de Beauvaisis* alludes to the military obligations of that category of peasants which was so widespread in France in the twelfth and thirteenth centuries – the customary tenants (*hospites, hôtes*). To follow him, every lord could call

---

[44] Waley (294).
[45] Arch. dép. Meurthe-et-Moselle, E 491 no.1.
[46] B. Guérard, *Polyptyque de l'abbé Irminon, i, 2e partie*, Paris 1844, p.665 n.21.
[47] P. Viollet, *Les Etablissements de Saint Louis*, Paris 1881, i.94–5 and 97.

on his peasants in case of need to defend his body or house, but exclusively within the fief on which the customary tenants depended (*dedans le fief dont les ostises sont mouvans*). Outside this fief the customary tenants might well follow their lord but only by agreement ('by their wishes') and in return for a daily payment of 8*d.* for a foot soldier and 2*s.* for a mounted man. To this service of a private nature, there had to be added that of a public kind to the count. Beaumanoir specifies, in fact, that when the count summoned his men (in the sense of vassals) and encouraged them to bring their customary tenants to a certain location, neither the count's men nor subjects of the count's men could excuse themselves.[48]

That effective mobilization sometimes occurred is proved by several passages from the administrative inquiries of Saint Louis mentioning fines paid by customary tenants who had defaulted.[49] Similarly in September 1284 Pierre de Chevry, abbot of Saint-Maur-des-Fossés, summoned the men of this community and, doubtless, of other localities under his authority, to display their weapons in the neighbouring plain of La Varenne-Saint-Hilaire. Everyone presented equipment according to his wealth. Twelve tenants of the abbey, possessing at least 60*l.*, had a haubert or a haubergeon, an iron cap, a sword and a dagger. Fifty-three others, owning less than 30*l.* had a padded coat or gambeson, an iron cap, sword and dagger; those with 10*l.* or more had to possess an iron cap, a sword and dagger, whilst the rest could present themselves bearing bows, arrows and a dagger.[50]

In Germany maintenance of public peace meant that everyone had to arm. This was the *Folgepflicht* (duty to follow) mentioned by the *Sachsenspiegel*, from which only women, shepherds, clerics and servants of churches were exempt. According to the Austrian *Landrecht* of 1237, 'all inhabitants of a country shall help to guard it'. Nor did Italian urban states deprive themselves of the advantage of the human resources of their *contado*. Those of Perugia were to supply horses, weapons, corn and men.[51] In 1292 the *contado* of Siena supplied 3,000 infantry, and in 1318 the number was 7,000. To facilitate their levying, this territory was divided into several military districts called vicariates. In 1310 there were nine of these, comprising 289 communities, each of which had to find from its own resources the troops it had to provide without having recourse to mercenaries.[52] At the time of the war of Montaperti (1260), 3,000 sappers and 5,000 infantry, possibly half the army, were drawn from the Florentine *contado*. In Scotland during the wars of independence the resources of the *communis exercitus* or *servitium scoticanum* were added to those of feudal service.

[48] Ph. de Beaumanoir, *Coutumes de Beauvaisis*, ed. A. Salmon, Paris 1899, i.492–3.
[49] *RCH*, xxi.154 no.649 and 249 no.1893.
[50] *BEC*, x (1848–49), 68.
[51] A. I. Galletti, Società comunale (250).
[52] W. M. Bowsky, City and contado (492), and *idem*, *A Medieval Italian Commune. Siena under the Nine, 1287–1355*, Berkeley, Los Angeles and London 1981, pp.117–58.

l The innovations of Philip the Fair's reign in France equally affected the sphere of military obligations. On the one hand, the monarchy tried to obtain the service of all fief-holders, whether they were direct vassals of the crown or not. That was the purpose of the king's *ban*. On the other hand, at least from 1302 and the defeat at Courtrai, the crown claimed to summon through the *arrière-ban* all those who were fit to bear arms, regardless of their position, whether they were subjects of the king, lay lords or the church.

The idea of the *arrière-ban*, which developed vigorously and on a wide scale, was not, however, a novelty. The term, probably a semantic deformation of the Carolingian 'heriban' (a kind of military tax on those whose service did not come up to scratch), appears from time to time in the twelfth and thirteenth centuries. A charter of Louis VII in 1141 speaks of an estate whose men were to send four sergeants to the king's host for the *arrière-ban* (*in exercitu regis ad retrobannum*). In John Lackland's day there are allusions to the *arrière-ban* of Normandy (*retrobannum Normandie*), meaning either the summons of all free men, or that of fief-holders who had escaped from proper host service. Thus the bishop of Lisieux owed the duke 20 knights for the host plus 10 others from the district of Lisieux who remained on guard in the city until the *arrière-ban* was convoked.[53] At the same period, an inquiry into the rights of the countess of Champagne mentions that 'all men living in the castellany of Château Thierry whoever they are owe my lady host and riding services from one day to another except the householder who owes the *arrière-ban*.' The same document signals, a little further on, that 'those of Rouvroy and Annoy owe my lady *arrière-ban* and service in court once a year.'[54] In an ordinance for the county of Albi issued on 1 December 1212 Simon de Montfort stated that 'for ordinary or particular wars or to help the count if he is besieged or for the *arrière-ban*, all barons and knights, great and small, who are cited, are obliged to reply.'[55] Literary sources like Philippe Mousket, Joinville, *Le Roman de Renart* and *La Chanson de Girart de Roussillon*, all mention the word.[56] It was thus in using an idea which, imprecise as it was, nevertheless was far from unknown, that Philip the Fair in the dramatic circumstances which followed the defeat at Courtrai attempted to generalize the principle of military service from all his subjects. This has undoubtedly too often been viewed as a means of raising a tax. Certainly it happened most frequently that proclamation of the *arrière-ban* was usually followed by the imposition of a new tax, but in some instances there is proof

---

[53] F. M. Powicke, *The Loss of Normandy*, Manchester 2nd edn 1961.

[54] Longnon, *Documents relatifs au comté de Champagne*, ii.1 and 4, 'tuit li home de Chastel Tierri qui i sont couchant et levant, cui home qu'il soient, doyvent ma dame l'ost et le chavauchie dou jour a l'endemain, fors que li aubaine qui doivent l'arriere ban . . . cil de Rouvroy et d'Annoy doivent a ma dame l'arriere ban et plaidoiement une foiz l'an.'

[55] C. Devic and J. Vaissete, *Histoire générale de Languedoc*, new edn by A. Molinier *et al.*, Toulouse 16 vols. 1872–1904, viii.625–35 no.165.

[56] Philippe Mousket, *Chronique rimée*, ed. F. de Reiffenberg, Brussels 1836, i.223 and 271, ll.5540 and 6845; P. Contamine, *Guerre, état et société* (457), p.26.

that there was, if not a massive mobilization which was technically and militarily unthinkable, at least the dispatch by a host of rural and urban communities of contingents of naturally varying sizes.

It was in England that the principle of general military obligation gave rise to the most precocious, developed and effective results. The English lead in this sphere may be explained both by the survival of the old Anglo-Saxon traditions, by the presence from the twelfth century of an organized state and a remarkable administration and by the existence of a sense of community in the realm at large which was more widespread and better rooted than in other regions of the West.

The initiative for this lay with Henry II. Whilst he was holding his court at Le Mans at Christmas 1181 in the presence of the Archbishop of Bordeaux and various prelates and barons of the province, he promulgated an edict for all his continental possessions. This did not envisage the raising of an army nor did it fix the strictly military obligations of his subjects, but indicated the weapons they were to own according to their wealth. Three categories were selected: those possessing movable goods worth £100 Angevin (equivalent to 100 *l.t.* or £25) were to have a knight's equipment including a horse; those who had movable goods worth between £20 and £40 Angevin were to have a haubergeon, spear and sword; the poorest were to be let off with a gambeson, iron cap, spear and sword, or bow and arrows.[57] The practical outcome of this assize is unknown but the emphasis on movable goods suggests that Henry was above all trying to arm the inhabitants of towns.

A few days later the same sovereign proclaimed the famous Assize of Arms for England. This document, which is much more detailed than the preceding one, envisaged as many horsemen as there were knights' fees. It prescribed for all lay men having an annual income or movable goods worth 16 marks (the equivalent of £40 Angevin) a complete set of knight's armour; for all free lay men having 10 marks (about £28 Angevin), a haubergeon, iron headpiece and lance; for other burgesses and the rest of the community of free men, a gambeson, iron headpiece and spear. All were to keep these arms ready to serve the king. The essential aim of the assize was thus to increase the stock of weapons and to prevent its further diminution, hence also the establishment of regulations against sale, pawn and export of arms.

It appeared that the monarchy was hardly interested in arming the poor, intentionally excluding the non-free from this series of measures. Two groups were interesting because they had certain resources, but also because they were unlikely to cause much trouble to public order – the knights on the one hand, and the 'free and honourable' men on the other. They alone were to be enrolled in the towns and hundreds and were to take an oath of allegiance to the king.[58]

[57] *Gesta Regis Henrici Secundi Benedicti abbatis*, ed. W. Stubbs, 2 vols. London 1867, i.269–70.
[58] *English Hist. Documents*, ii.416–18.

The system was perfected and transformed later. In 1205 John Lackland carried out a general mobilization with the assembly of burgesses in constabularies in the towns and cities and of the country-dwellers (*rustici*) in hundreds and villages. In 1212 the sheriffs were ordered to summon the earls, barons and knights, together with free-men and sergeants (*servientes*) capable of bearing arms and who had performed homage or sworn allegiance to the king, to march to Dover for defence of the king, their persons and the kingdom of England. Defaulters were to be demoted to the condition of serfs. The summons was a success. After some days so many appeared that it was necessary through want of food supplies to dismiss the least well armed, keeping only the knights, sergeants, free-men, archers and crossbowmen.

From 1230 the non-free (at this time the majority of the population) found themselves expressly integrated into the system of military obligations. That same year there appeared a division of the lowest categories into two groups: those who possessed 40s. in movables had to have an iron headpiece and a padded doublet; those having 20s. in movables were to provide themselves with an axe and a spear. A further stage was reached in 1242 when a royal writ defined those sworn to arms (*jurati ad arma*), obliged to perform defensive services, amongst whom appeared for the first time archers, corresponding to those possessing 40s. worth of land. In 1264 a process of selection was openly practised. Each village (*vill, villata*) had to pick four, six or eight foot soldiers, particularly reputed for their bravery to be armed with spears, bows, arrows, crossbows and swords. These men, grouped in tens and hundreds, were to be led by *standardarii* and mounted constables.

Edward I perfected the organization of recruitment by instituting commissions of array, which controlled and sometimes themselves selected the best fighters. Confronted, moreover, by an acute crisis with the *servitium debitum*, the king attempted to force all his subjects with an income of between £20 and £40 to serve on horseback. In addition he appealed to the devotion and loyalty of the nobles so that they would answer his summonses with the maximum number of men at arms. This attempt to broaden the base of recruitment can obviously be compared to the analogous measures taken by his contemporary, Philip the Fair.

If during the thirteenth century over most of the West military obligations springing from feudo-vassalic institutions continued to wither away to the point where they represented only a minor support, one cannot say that the authorities had given up the effort to obtain aid from the feudal knightly class. But this aid was acquired more and more in return for monetary payment whose importance we shall soon see. As for the rest of the population, the descendants of the *inermes* of the eleventh century, whilst totally ignorant of the system of conscription which modern states from the end of the eighteenth century have been able to institute by using their formidable powers of persuasion and organization, the nationalism of their public opinion and the enormous increase in production, they nevertheless found themselves subject to obligations for defence which were often heavy. These forced them to share fully in the wars of the period; and this participation, especially important at the level of the towns, was despite everything far from unknown among the rural masses.

MONEY, PAID SERVICE AND MERCENARIES

Money was the almost obligatory link between authority and soldiers. According to contemporaries themselves, this phenomenon accelerated from the mid-twelfth century. At every turn the sources mention hired men (*solidarii*), stipendiaries (*stipendiarii*), those summoned to serve for pay (*summonitiones ad denarios*), wages (*vadia*) and money gifts (*donativa*). About 1150 Peter the Venerable, abbot of Cluny, accused his predecessor, Pons de Melgueil, of having emptied the abbey's treasury by paying soldiers: 'I found all my neighbours, knights, castellans, counts and even the duke of Burgundy himself, urging me to take up arms, attracted by the smell of lucre.'[59] In the *De necessariis observantis Scaccarii dialogus*, compiled between 1176 and 1179, Richard Fitz Nigel wrote: 'Money is no less indispensable in peace than in war. In war it is lavished on fortifying castles, paying soldiers' wages and innumerable other expenses, determined by the character of the persons paid, for the defence of the realm.'[60] At the beginning of the thirteenth century in his *Liber Abaci*, Leonardo Fibonacci, the celebrated Pisan mathematician, gave some examples of calculations for the payment of hired men. From about 1140 there began to become known in the West a work from the Muslim world destined to enjoy great popularity amongst ruling groups, the *Secretum secretorum*, attributed to Aristotle; in it may be found a circular diagram clearly displaying the connections between the king, the army and money. According to the *Grandes Chroniques de France* Philip Augustus amassed treasure in a number of places and lived a very frugal life, since he thought that kings of France had lost many of their lands on numerous occasions because they had nothing with which to pay their knights and sergeants when there was an emergency.

This monetary invasion is obviously to be associated with what has been called 'the commercial revolution'.[61] It expresses in the realm of warfare the progress of a monetary economy (*Geldwirtschaft*) as opposed to a natural one (*Naturwirtschaft*). The stock of precious metal possessed by the West was from this time on more abundant, coins circulated more quickly and mone-

---

[59] G. Duby, *Le Dimanche de Bouvines* (244), p.100.
[60] *Dialogus de Scaccario*, ed. C. Johnson, London 1950, p.2.
[61] R. S. Lopez, *La révolution commerciale dans l'Europe médiévale*, Paris 1974 (tr. of *The Commercial Revolution of the Middle Ages 950–1350*, Englewood Cliffs 1971). A. Murray, *Reason and Society in the Middle Ages*, Oxford 1978, pl.II, shows an example of the 'Circle of the Sphere' from the Pseudo-Aristotelian *Secretum Secretorum*.

tary exchanges affected a greater number of social levels. Let us, however, avoid exaggeration. Even in previous centuries knights had need of money (and not barter) to buy a warhorse or armour. Not everyone paid the blacksmith who made swords by giving him his keep, a piece of land or a few sacks of corn. During great expeditions the combatants did not simply ensure their maintenance by pillage, requisition or the consumption of food coming from their own agricultural stocks. Added to the greater availability of money was the fact that kings and princes learnt at the same time to increase their own monetary resources, perhaps even at a superior rate. They did this in three main ways – thanks to demesnes which were rapidly expanding, to public taxation which continually grew and diversified and, finally, to the commutation of military services for money.

Examples of this commutation abound, like the scutage which has been mentioned, as well as the fact that in 1202–3 all the towns owing host service to Philip Augustus sent money, not sergeants. In 1227 Frederick II, preparing his crusade, ordered that in the kingdom of Sicily 'every fief-holder should pay for each fief eight ounces of gold and every eight fiefs should provide a knight'; in other words, from each group of eight fees the King-Emperor would get one knight and 64 ounces of gold which represented about a year's pay at current rates.[62] From 1255 certain communes in the papal states preferred to pay rather than serve.

Thus collected and available, what one might call (though the term is slightly anachronistic) public funds served first of all to pay for the different kinds of military obligation. At the same time they allowed consolidation of the obligations and a breakdown of the restraints on time and distance which had singularly limited their worth. At Perugia, as at Florence, in the thirteenth century, the communal militia were paid from the first day of the campaign – 5s. for a foot soldier, 10s. for a man with one horse, 15s. for a man with two horses, in the first instance; 3s. for crossbowmen, 2s. 8d. for archers, 2s. 6d. for pavesiers, 2s. for ordinary foot soldiers in the second. From 1193 in England 500 *servientes* on foot at Windsor received wages for their 40 days' service. From the reign of Henry III the rule was established that local militia services would not be exacted beyond the limits of the county of origin without payment. In France, even if many towns continued to owe voluntary service to the king, the contingents which they sent were paid at their expense.

Analogous phenomena occurred with the service of fief-holders. Not only did a number of them receive wages once they had performed their gratuitous service, but there came a time when they were paid from the start. In 1240, for example, Frederick II ordered various judges in the kingdom of Sicily to choose from their districts *milites strenui* who were to assemble at a given place. One judge was to provide 15 men, another 60, yet another 40. But for

[62] Riccardo di San Germano, *Cronica*, ed. C. A. Garufi, Bologna 1937, p.149.

the selected knights (*milites*) a wage of 10 ounces of gold for two months was fixed. A roll dating from the reign of St Louis (probably 1242), after enumerating a certain number of bishops, great lords and knights summoned in all likelihood to perform their voluntary host service, mentions 'two paid summonses for the county of Albi both of knights with a number of other men on horseback and of communes who were to send a certain number of infantry'.[63] The expansion of the cavalry under Edward I and Philip the Fair was only possible because of the payment of wages. Incontestably these sovereigns had suffered a juridical defeat which was underlined by Pierre Dubois when he wrote his *De recuperatione Terre Sancte* (1305–7):

> The lord king ought to compel each and every one of his vassals, dukes, counts, barons, castellans, and knights, and in general everyone owing him fixed services, to render and perform such services without fraud or reduction. He ought not to remit or give up any part of them or neglect to exact them – to the detriment of those who ought to be summoned only through the *levée en masse* [i.e. *retrobannum* or *arrière-ban*]. But it is reported that the lord king, unmindful of this, and placing himself and his judgment in the hands of his counsellors, has been accustomed to summon to his aid in war, sometimes at his own expense, those counts, barons, knights, and squires who, being obligated to render armed service, should have campaigned at their own expense and made recompense for their fiefs with armed service.'[64]

It is probable that in fact the financial and political advisers of Philip the Fair knew clearly what they were doing in renouncing the king's theoretical rights. They considered it impossible both psychologically and probably materially to maintain side by side a small troop of vassals performing their 40 days' service with bad grace and a mass of knights and esquires with the same social and geographical origins, receiving daily pay at the hands of the king's treasurers and their clerks.

One type of fief was nevertheless for a long time better suited than others to provide free service. This was the fief-rent, also termed money fief or *fief de chambre*. In this case, in effect, payment in cash of a type of annual pension (for the fief-rent was the true precursor of those royal and princely pensions which assume such importance, above all from the end of the fourteenth century) to a particular person appears as an advance for eventual future services, the more so, despite the clauses contained in many charters creating fief-rents, since this latter was in practice neither transmissible to heirs nor even held for life. Very often the beneficiary received it for some years then for one reason or another the contract lapsed.

The case of Fernand de Jean provides an example of a fief-rent specifying free service. According to a document of 1277 this Castilian knight had abandoned the service of the king of Castile to enter that of the king of

---

[63] *RCH*, xxiii.728.
[64] Pierre Dubois, *The Recovery of the Holy Land*, tr. W. I. Brandt, New York 1956, p.187.

France. Yet he had been in receipt of an annual income of 300*l.* from his first master. Philip III thus agreed to pay him the same sum during pleasure or for life. In exchange Fernand performed homage to him against all others except the nephews of Philip III, sons of his sister, Blanche, and Fernando of Castile. What is more, the new vassal was to serve the king of France with 10 knights freely for 40 days a year and to present himself with his company to perform this service within six weeks of summons. Nevertheless he did not have to fight everywhere, but only in the lands of the king of Aragon, Castile and Portugal, in the kingdom of Navarre, in Gascony and in the county of Toulouse. After the 40 days the king of France could employ him and his men on payment of a daily wage of 7*s.* 6*d.t.*, though there were no provisions for the restoration of lost horses.[65]

Other fief-rents, however, were not so advantageous to the authorities, like that conceded in 1294 by Philip the Fair to a knight from the county of Burgundy, Hugues de Bourgogne. He was to receive 300*l.t.* each year at the Temple in Paris on the Feast of the Purification (2 February). In return for this amount, which was in theory perpetual with the right to transmit it to his heirs, he performed fealty and liege homage to the king of France. He had to serve him, in the event of war with the king of England or other enemies, with his men, castles and fortresses and at least 60 armed horsemen. As long as he remained in his own lands he would receive nothing, but if Philip the Fair summoned him elsewhere he would benefit from wages and eventual recompense for lost mounts.[66] The details of the contract are undoubtedly to be explained by general political circumstances; in order to parry the formidable encircling movement undertaken by Edward I, Philip the Fair was looking everywhere for allies, whatever the cost. Another example concerns recruitment of combatants for the crusades. By an agreement of 1249 Alphonse of Poitiers announced that he had engaged Hugues le Brun, count of Angoulême, to serve a year at his wages during the crusade with 11 knights. But the prospect of this pay was doubtless insufficient to persuade Hugues le Brun, so in fact he received in addition an annual hereditary fief rent of £600 Poitevin and also, as a four-year loan, 4,000 *l.t.* to enable him to equip his contingent.

It is astonishing, in these conditions, what constant care the authorities displayed in order to maintain, if not reinforce, a system of obligations, when this system had resulted more and more frequently in the payment of wages and various indemnities comparable in every sense to wages, as well as other recompense to volunteers. In other words, why did they not go directly, to use the terminology of P. Schmitthenner, from feudal warfare (*Lehenskriegertum*) to free mercenary warfare (*freie Söldnertum*), rather than

[65] Guillaume Anelier, *Histoire de la guerre de Navarre en 1276 et 1277*, ed. Francisque-Michel, Paris 1856, p.642 n.1.
[66] Arch. Nat., J 622 no.33.

creating an economy of paid feudal warfare (*versöldnerte Lehenskriegertum*)?[67]
There are several reasons for this. First, the very nature of payment. As far as
amounts can be established in England from the mid-twelfth century or from
the beginning of the thirteenth century in France, it often appears less like a
proper professional salary than as a sort of campaign indemnity allowing
temporary warriors to meet supplementary expenses occasioned by their participation in military expeditions. Hence generally their daily character corresponding to short campaigns, whose duration in any case could not be
foreseen. Thus table 2 shows payments to the two major categories of knights
and ordinary foot soldiers in England and France, where developments were
similar.

TABLE 2   Daily rates of pay for soldiers in
England and France *c*.1150–*c*.1300

	Knight	Foot soldier
England (in sterling)		
1150–70	6*d*.	
c.1165	8*d*.	1*d*.
c.1195	1*s*.	
c.1215	2*s*.	2*d*.
c.1250	2*s*.	
c.1300	2, 3 or 4*s*.*	2*d*.†
France (in livres tournois)		
1202	7*s*. 6*d*.	10*d*.
1295	10*s*., 12*s*. 6*d*. or 15*s*.**	12*d*.††

* in silver: 31.12 g, 46.49 g or 62.24 g
† in silver: 2.6 g
** in silver: 33.48 g, 41.85 g or 50.22 g
†† in silver: 3.34 g

The present state of records scarcely allows us to know if the sum total of
payments normally covered expenses. One may nevertheless believe that this
was so, even if soldiers paid for what they ate, which was naturally far from
always the case. Otherwise it would be hard to understand why genuine
mercenaries agreed to serve for an identical rate of pay. The wages offered to
English foot soldiers around 1300 were of about the same level as the daily
rates of a labourer and the same is true, it seems, in France and at Florence.
There is a hint that leads one to think that the wages of knights were no less
disadvantageous. This comes in a passage from Matthew Paris's chronicle
where he describes the famine in Gascony in 1253: 'In those days famine
spread amongst the king's army in Gascony so that a chicken was sold for 6*d*.,
a bushel of wheat for 20*s*., a gallon of wine for 2*s*. or more and bread at 2*d*. or

[67] P. Schmitthenner, *Das freie Söldnertum* (131).

3*d*. a pound so that a knight could scarcely as he ought feed himself, his esquire, his page and his horses on 2*s*. a day.' If it is remembered that at that time 2*s*. was the normal daily pay of a knight (which could buy between 8 and 12 lbs of bread), it seems that even in these critical circumstances it was sufficient to prevent its recipients from starving to death, though it is true that if we accept these figures, the foot soldier with his 2*d*. a day could only buy a third of a loaf.[68]

In a word, it was not because of pay and daily wages that reasons can be discovered to explain why the system of military obligations survived the disappearance of free service. There was also the problem of investment or capital represented by the warriors. In effect, through the agency of military summonses, authorities found themselves with combatants who were not only fully equipped and mounted but who had undergone since their youth training and apprenticeship necessary to follow a career in arms. For as Roger of Hoveden, amongst many others, emphasizes, 'unless one has trained beforehand through mock battles, the art of war will not be possessed when it is necessary to put it into practice.'[69] And it was the fief which allowed its holder and his sons the leisure and necessary income to live on a level with the world of warfare, through hunting, tilting practice, jousting and especially through tournaments which from 1150 to 1350 formed mock battles in which two groups of fighters confronted each other, not without risk.[70]

But above all authorities expected holders of fiefs or those with a certain fortune, whatever its nature, movable or landed, to keep mounts and knightly equipment in permanent readiness. Yet, although precise figures are rare before the end of the thirteenth century, it is certain that such equipment alone was very dear. At Genoa between 1200 and 1250 a headpiece (*barberia*) cost between 16*s*. and 32*s*., a haubert between 120*s*. and 152*s*. and, if one adds protection for the legs and other various accessories, the total amounts to about 200*s*. or £10 Genoese, the equivalent of 800 grammes of silver.[71] In addition there was also the cost of offensive weapons, as well as that of more simple military equipment for an esquire, if not for a valet. It is thus probably no exaggeration to estimate that some 1,400 grammes of silver would be the price of the equipment of a knight and his following around 1250, that is between a month and a month and half's wages.[72]

---

[68] Matthew Paris, *Chronica majora*, ed. Luard, v.398.

[69] Roger of Hoveden, *Chronica*, ed. W. Stubbs, London, 4 vols. 1868–71, ii.166.

[70] N. Denholm-Young, Tournament in the 13th century (239).

[71] W. N. Bonds, Some industrial price movements in medieval Genoa (1155–1255), in *Economy, Society and Government in Medieval Italy. Essays in memory of Robert L. Reynolds*, ed. D. Herlihy *et al.*, Kent, Ohio 1969, pp.132–3. The Genoese shilling contained 3.947 grammes of silver at the beginning of the thirteenth century.

[72] At the beginning of the fourteenth century in England, however, according to Exchequer accounts, a complete set of armour including a *hoqueton* (haqueton or jack), haubert, bascinet and mail gloves cost on average £1, perhaps 10 days' wages at a maximum for a knight: M. R.

The mounts were even more expensive. An estimate of the value of some horses belonging to certain knights, paid by Alphonse de Poitiers in 1242, shows prices ranging from 5 to 60 *l.t.*, 30 *l.t.* being the average.[73] In 1269 various warhorses bought for the Crusade of Saint Louis at the fairs of Champagne and Brie (Bar-sur-Aube, Lagny, Provins) cost on average 85 *l.t.*, though they were probably animals of great value, sometimes brought from Spain or Apulia.[74] In preparation for the Flanders campaign of 1302, during which he was kept by the king from 26 May to 15 July, Robert II, count of Artois, bought for himself and his retinue the following horses of which the price is known: five 'grands chevaux' (one from Spain) at an average price of 280 *l.p.*, eight horses without qualification, at an average of 115 *l.p..*, two palfreys at 50 *l.p.* each, a courser for 60 *l.p.*, 14 rounceys at 34 *l.p.* and three '*roncinets*' at 12 *l.p.* each. For a knight having a great warhorse, a palfrey, a rouncey and a little rouncey that would represent a capital investment of 470 *l.p.* It is true that the announcement of the expedition against the Flemings had caused prices to rise and that at that moment money of account was being steeply devalued since the mark of silver which was worth 50*s. t.* in 1266 and 61*s. t.* in 1295 had risen to 104*s. t.* on 23 April 1302. Elsewhere, the warhorses of the Templars imported from the West were often valued at 100 besants in the Holy Land. In 1277 Florence took into its service a number of Provençal horsemen and in the clauses of their contract it was stated that each of them should have a horse worth at least £30, that is 133 days' wages.

It was for this reason that kings, princes and urban authorities sometimes enjoined all those who had the means to keep a warhorse. This was the case at Florence, Siena and a number of other Italian towns where commissioners were appointed *ad equos imponendos*. At Florence, for example, the number of horses raised in 1260 was 1,400, in 1310, 1,000 and in 1312, 1,300. In 1222, seeking to obtain an *augmentatio militiarum Crete*, Venice imposed on every Cretan knight having a *militia integra*, the maintenance of a warhorse worth at least £75 Venetian to which were added two other mounts and two esquires, who can only have been of Greek origin. As for fief-holders having only a *media militia*, they had to keep a horse worth at least £50 Venetian for themselves plus a mount for an esquire.[75] In a document of 1279 Philip III the Bold ordered all knights and all 'gentils' in his kingdom having an income of 200 *l.t.* or more from their estates and all burgesses possessing property in

---

Powicke, Edward II and military obligation (425a), 101 n.49. In France in 1295 the offensive and defensive armour of a crossbowman, including a crossbow, gorget, sheath, baldric, bascinet, padded jacket and sword, cost at least 3 *l.t.* (P. Wolff, Achats d'armes pour Philippe le Bel dans la région toulousaine, in *Regards sur le Midi médiéval*, Toulouse 1978, pp.395–402).

[73] *Layettes du Trésor des Chartes*, ed. A. Teulet *et al.*, Paris 1886, ii.658–60 no.3011.
[74] Bib. Nat., MS lat. 9016 no.15.
[75] G. L. F. Tafel and G. M. Thomas, *Urkunden zur älteren handels- und Staatsgeschichte der Republik Venedig, II. 1202–1255*, Vienna 1856, 34 no.263.

land or movables worth 1,500 *l.t.* or more, to raise a brood-mare. As for dukes, counts, barons, abbots and 'great men' possessing sufficient pasture, they were to raise four or six.[76] An order of Edward I in 1282 noting the lack of great horses 'fit for fighting' in England, instructed all his subjects having at least £30 in landed income henceforth to keep, to serve the king in time of need, 'a powerful horse suitable for war, together with proper armour'.[77]

From this bundle of fragmentary and sometimes discordant facts, it is permissible to conclude that in the thirteenth century the capital represented by the defensive and offensive equipment and the mounts of a knight and his following represents on average between six and eight months' daily wages. It has been calculated that around 1250 in England, the equipment of a knight, his horses included, was equivalent to his year's revenue, that is £20.[78] So that the authorities had available, at no cost to themselves, a considerable investment which they could use as they pleased for several days or weeks. If, on average, service was for only a few days a year, it is obvious that the wages paid, even if they were generous, in no way corresponded to the capital involved nor to its upkeep. It was indeed necessary to support this capital outlay from the revenues of the fief.

It is true that frequently there was compensation, reimbursement, sometimes called in Italy *mendum*, in French *restor* or *restaur*, in Latin *restaurum* or *restauratio*, for warhorses killed or injured during a campaign. At Perugia the sums paid ranged from £15 to £100, from which 30s. was regularly docked for the price of the skin. At Florence in the last decades of the thirteenth century warhorses were often apprised by a commission headed by the town's marshal and reimbursement was automatic if the loss was reported within three days. The expenses account for the first crusade of Saint Louis mentions *restor* of 264 horses for 6,789 *l.t.* (an average of just over 30 *l.t.* each), whilst for the '*voye d'Aragon*' in 1285, 34,681 *l.t.* was paid in compensation by Philip III (that is, for more than 1,100 horses).

If one could convoke those obliged to serve for a minimum period, in contrast an appeal to volunteers had a better chance of success if they could be guaranteed a longer term of employment. As a result, alongside daily wages, monthly rates are frequently mentioned in thirteenth-century sources. Thus when Florence was preparing for the 1260 campaign, the Signory had recourse to a Milanese lord, Pietro of Bazacape, amongst others, inviting him to come with 50 men, promising him two months' pay at the rate of £8 of small florins a month for each horseman. The same town decided to recruit at Modena in Lombardy 100 *berrierii*, including two gonfaloniers and four cap-

---

[76] *BEC, 15* (1854), 180–1.
[77] B. C. Keeney, Military service (256), 539 n.27, 'unum equum fortem et competentem ad arma una cum armatis competentibus ad eundem'.
[78] R. F. Treharne, The knight in the period of reform and rebellion 1258–67: a critical phase of a new class, *BIHR, 21* (1946–48), 1–12.

tains, all six having three horses as opposed to the single one for the ordinary *berrierius*, for a period of three months. Similarly Charles of Anjou recruited soldiers with the following monthly wages: four ounces of gold for knights, two for esquires and mounted crossbowmen, 18 tarins (at 30 tarins to an ounce) for foot crossbowmen.

The guarding of castles gave rise to contracts for even longer periods. In 1280, to defend the peninsular part of the kingdom of Sicily, Charles of Anjou, again, installed garrisons in 78 castles divided amongst five great territorial districts – Abruzzi, Principate and Terra del Lavoro; Calabria; Val de Crati and Terre Jourdaine; Bari and Otranto; Capitanata and Basilicata. The command of each was entrusted to 18 knights and 60 esquires from France, of whom only 16 held land in the kingdom of Sicily. These castellans commanded 1,037 sergeants and 15 chaplains of whom the majority in all likelihood were natives. They were to be paid every four months and received in 1280 8,852 ounces of gold (at five florins an ounce this equals 42,260 florins) which the Angevin treasurers principally paid in silver coins called *mailles charloises* or *charlois d'argent.*[79]

In fact garrison service could be prolonged indefinitely. In 1247 a Norman knight claimed that he had spent four years on the king's orders on guard at the castle of Léhon in the diocese of Dol at the daily rate of 6s.p. He complained to Saint Louis's *enquêteurs* that he had never had a penny in all this time.[80]

Paid service not only had the advantage of allowing mobilization in a few days; it also facilitated the spread of orders for an assembly, either by means of individual letters addressed to the most important men or through public announcements asking for specialized personnel who could be set to work and controlled by *baillis*, sheriffs, provosts, justiciars and other local administrators. Thus in May and June 1282 Edward I requisitioned in the English counties 3,000 workers (carpenters, pioneers, masons, woodcutters) for the sites of ten new castles which he was building in Wales. No doubt he could have limited himself to making an appeal for volunteers, but he judged it safer, using the normal administrative channels, to tax each county with a certain number in order to obtain the workforce he required rapidly and economically.

Beyond this, from the moment when it was a matter of obligatory service, the level of pay appears to result in the first instance from initiative by the authorities and not as a result of bargaining between employer and employee following market forces. At the same time those who were 'contracted' to serve found themselves in competition with those 'summoned' but paid, and were constrained in some sense to moderate their demands. The wages which

[79] A. de Boüard, *Documents français des archives de Naples* (*règne de Charles Ier*), ii.87–104 and 126–30.
[80] *RCH*, xxiv.44 no.335.

both those summoned and those who had sought employment were paid were not sufficient to turn them into true mercenaries. They came to the assembly point in family, feudal or regional groups and continued to fight in the service of their rightful sovereign (*droiturier souverain*) but under the orders of their immediate natural lords. In other words, they left home together in their customary social formations.

It is for this reason that one must not conclude from the disintegration of the traditional feudal *auxilium*, which was more and more marginal to even the smallest military operations, that the chivalric class in broader terms suffered from military weakness. In England and France around 1300 it was still these same groups, impregnated with the same reflexes and attitudes, who furnished the core of the heavy cavalry, even if their forms of service and the juridical and moral basis of the obligations which they had were largely modified. Nor can one call every soldier a mercenary from the moment he received payment in one form or another. It is better to adapt to medieval circumstances a definition recently proposed by the classicist Y. Garland, who writes: 'The mercenary is a professional soldier whose conduct is dictated not by his membership of a political community but above all by his desire for gain.'[81] In short, the mercenary is defined by three qualities: being a specialist, stateless and paid.

If we use this definition we will no longer speak of mercenaries in talking about the knights who accompanied St Louis on his two crusades, some paid wages by the king, others rewarded by virtue of *convenances* or accords made with the royal administration, some enjoying *bouche à court*, fed in the king's household, yet others concerning themselves with their own subsistence. All had in fact taken the crusading vow, hoping to benefit from the plenary indulgence, and all, or nearly all, if we read Joinville or scrutinize, for example, the lists of knights going on the expedition to Tunis (*pour la voye de Thunes*), belonged to the socially restricted class of great liegemen or leading vassals of the crown.

Even when they came from more varied geographical regions and had uprooted themselves chiefly in order to pursue a career, the knights who permanently staffed royal and princely households were in no sense proper mercenaries. On the other hand, those esquires, knights and sergeants who attached themselves to Charles of Anjou in his great Transalpine adventure were mercenaries, as were those Saracens employed by Frederick II. The cavalry engaged by Florence in the years 1270–80 were mercenaries: small constabularies of horsemen with the description *tallia militum societatis tallie Tuscie* who from 1270 prefigure the fourteenth-century *condotte* in Italy.

---

[81] Y. Garland, *La guerre dans l'Antiquité*, Paris 1972, p.67. The word *mercenarius* is rarely used to mean a paid soldier: *stipendiarii et mercenarii milites* is the phrase used by William of Malmesbury to describe Harold's housecarls at Hastings (*De gestis regum Anglorum libri V*, ed. W. Stubbs, London 1857, i.182).

Hence in 1277 the agreement concluded on the one hand between Florence and, on the other, the Provençal Inghilese de Saint-Rémy, who earlier can be found in the service of Siena, concerned a troop of 100 horsemen, each receiving 11 florins a month and commanded by two standard-bearers in addition to the captain. Every eventuality was foreseen in the contract – the number and allowances for rounceys carrying the baggage, inspection of horses and weapons of the soldiers, the settlement of disputes, the fate of prisoners, reciprocal guarantees, indemnities in case the contract was broken and its stipulations. One finds the complete mercenary like William the Catalan who had first seen service with Siena from 1277 to 1285, then with Bologna from 1288–89, then with Florence from 1290 to 1292. The geographical origins of his men are revealing in themselves. Of the 53 horsemen whose place of birth may be traced according to their names, 28 came from Occitania in the broadest sense, 8 from Northern France (including 6 from Picardy), 2 from Flanders, 7 from Italy, 7 from the Iberian peninsula (including only 3 Catalans, which is surprising considering the origin of their captain) and, finally, there was one Englishman.[82]

Recourse to different types of mercenaries on the part of states may be explained by several reasons. The first is purely military – the worth and reputation of a group of fighters whose equivalent it was impossible to find locally amongst vassals, subjects or fellow-citizens. The Saracen archers of Lucera, the crossbowmen of Pisa, Tortosa, Liguria or Corsica and Gascon infantry may all be thought of in this regard. The temporary or long-term disaffection, because of political circumstances or a changing way of life, of certain categories of dependants whom princes would have preferred to use, must also be taken into account. John Lackland, unable to obtain sufficient aid from his barons, was forced on more than one occasion to seek troops elsewhere. If Florence from the 1270s more willingly recruited horsemen from other parts of Italy, Provence, France and Germany, it was in part because the urban patriciate refused to fulfil its military duties and preferred to employ paid troops at great cost. Mercenaries, at the level of bodyguards for example, were thought to guarantee greater safety for sovereigns. But it is equally necessary to see the other side of the coin. Authorities could only use mercenaries because there existed a potential market or supply. The presence of this market may be explained in turn by demographic factors, fluctuations in economic conditions or even by successoral practices. Between employers and employees, recruiters and recruited, interaction was constant. The supply stimulated demand at the same time as demand encouraged supply. The examples of the *Cotereaux*, Brabançons and routiers of the age of Richard I, John Lackland and Philip Augustus, and then later of the Catalan company, suggest that the appearance of mercenaries as a major historical phenomenon

---

[82] Waley (295), pp.86–91, and *Condotte* and *Condottieri* in the thirteenth century, *Proceedings of the British Academy, 61* (1976), 337–71.

is less well explained by political conditions than by the economic and social background.[83]

In its most usual form medieval warfare was made up of a succession of sieges accompanied by skirmishes and devastation, to which were added a few major battles or serious clashes whose relative rarity was made up for by their often sanguinary character.

In this siege warfare towns ultimately presented tougher obstacles than isolated castles. In the twelfth and thirteenth centuries there were certainly a number of notable and long sieges of castles. During the Albigensian Crusade the citadel of Termes resisted from August to November 1210. In the Holy Land Krak des Chevaliers only succumbed to the Muslims in 1271 after a very prolonged siege. Resistance at Montségur lasted a year (1244) and Philip Augustus took five months to capture Château-Gaillard in 1204.

However, the sieges of towns, whatever their results, were much more impressive military episodes: for example the siege of Acre by the Franks, one of the longest ever recorded – apparently lasting from June 1189 to July 1191; the second siege of Constantinople at the time of the fourth crusade (November 1203 to April 1204); the siege of Toulouse by Simon de Montfort (October 1217 to June 1218), or that of Marmande by Amaury de Montfort and Prince Louis of France (October 1218 to June 1219). It was not that towns were technically better protected than castles. On the contrary, their fortifications were often very rudimentary and it was rare indeed when an enceinte did not have some weak points. But, on the one hand, they offered space, material and moral resources favourable for prolonged resistance and, on the other, while a conqueror might easily ignore an inaccessible castle, it was absolutely vital to control such centres of economic, administrative and human resources as were represented by towns. Their importance in contemporary strategy during the twelfth and thirteenth centuries is explained less by military factors than by the fact that urban centres, not castles, were the true masters of space.

By a dialectical process which may be found in all periods, progress in the art of siege was answered by progress in the art of fortification, and vice versa; thus, simply for purposes of exposition, methods of attack and defence will be treated separately here.

1 Methods of attack

In order to capture a place recourse was often necessary to psychological or political means – a mixture of threats and clemency.

---

[83] See below, chapter 8.

A promise to respect lives and property, to allow the garrison to come out freely, or the prospect of a general massacre, arson and systematic pillaging, frequently resulted in a negotiated capitulation by the besieged. The same result might be gained by blockade, scarcity of food, poisoning water supplies and the eventual spread of epidemics.

After indirect means came direct attacks. The aim of the besieger, normally superior in numbers to the besieged, being to enter the place, it was first of all necessary for him to surmount excavated defences, dry ditches or moats filled with water. Hence the need to fill them with whatever materials were available, wood, stone, earth and so on. Faggots were most usually employed, as at the siege of Pujol, occupied by the Albigensian crusaders and besieged by men from the counties of Toulouse, Comminges and Foix: 'Their forces hurriedly searched for faggots; there was not a knight nor burgess nor sergeant who did not immediately carry a load on his back which they threw into the ditches so that they were completely filled and they could approach the foot of the walls.'[84]

If the besieged were able to defend themselves, it was necessary to protect the besiegers, either while they blockaded the place, carried out approach works or mounted an attack. Hence the digging of trenches, construction of banks and palisades and, above all, the use of approach engines, various types of counter-fortifications which allowed them to continue to injure the enemy while coming up to the walls. These tower-machines, belfries or wooden castles, often depicted in manuscript illuminations, bore many names, some of which had been handed down from Antiquity or had been rediscovered in specialist Latin works: sows (*truies*), pent-houses (*vinae*), cats (*chattes*), weasels (*belettes*), sentry-boxes (*guerites*), covered ways, cats' castles.[85] Sheltering archers, knights and crossbowmen, the majority of these engines could be placed on wheels or rollers to be pushed close to the opposing walls by the efforts of dozens and dozens of labourers. Smaller ones were erected on carts. At the siege of Beaucaire by Simon de Montfort in 1216, the crusaders' leader had carpenters construct a 'castle and a cat' (*castel e gata*) out of wood and iron but also from leather, this latter material being employed without doubt to protect the engine against risk of burning. The contraption was stationed between the ramparts and the ditches, right up against the wall, and it was guarded day and night.[86] Two years later at the siege of Toulouse the same Simon de Montfort employed another cat which the *Song of the Albigensian Crusade* describes as a redoubtable monster, sheltering 400 knights and 150 archers and fearing neither trébuchets, stone-throwers (*petrariae*) nor rocks because of the iron and steel used to bind its different parts together –

[84] *Chanson de la croisade albigeoise*, ed. Martin-Chabot, ii.9.
[85] *Vineas et catos versatiles que sunt machine bellice*, says John of Garlande in his *Dictionary* (cited by H. Géraud, *Paris sous Philippe le Bel*, Paris 1837, p.599).
[86] *Chanson de la croisade albigeoise*, ed. Martin-Chabot, ii.148.

the platform, sides, beams, cross-pieces, doors and roof.[87] When he was besieging Damietta during the Seventh Crusade, Louis IX 'had two belfreys made which were called cats' castles for there were two castles in front of the cats and two houses behind the castles to protect those who mounted watch against the attacks of Saracen engines.'[88]

There were other weapons to break down, pierce, shake or rip open the walls. Sometimes simple picks and iron bars were used; sometimes battering rams (Latin: *arietes*, Occitanian: *bossons*). The same effect could be achieved using stones thrown by machines called trébuchets, *petrariae*, mangonnels and *'chaables'* (Occitanian: *calabres*). According to John of Garlande, 'Parraria (*peralia*) est tormentum minus . . . Trabuceta sunt etiam tormenta murorum (gallice, trebuchet).'[89] 'A *parraria (peralia)* is a smaller windlass for throwing missiles . . . *trabuceta* are also used to attack walls. (In French they are called trébuchets.)' The period 1180–1220 witnessed great advances in this domain thanks to the use of machines worked by balances and not only by human traction – the most rudimentary form – but by fixed or mobile counterweights. Modern experiments have shown that a trébuchet operated by 50 men and having a ten-ton counterweight is capable of throwing a stone of 100–150 kg about 150 metres, whilst in the most favourable conditions, a catapult of Roman type could only throw a stone of 20–30 kg some 225 metres. The *Album* of Villard de Honnecourt contains a drawing of a trébuchet.[90] It used to have a second, of which, unfortunately, only the caption remains:

Se vos volés faire le fort
engieng c'on apiele trebucet,
prendés ci garde. Vés ent ci
les soles, si com il siet
sor tierre. Vés la devant
les .II. windas et le
corde ploié a coi on ravale
le verge, veir le poés en cele
autre pagene. Il i a grant
fais al ravaler, car li
contrepois est mult pezans,
car il i a une huge plainne
de tierre ki .II.grans
toizes a de lonc et .VIIII.
piés de lé, et .XII.piés de

If you want to make the stong
engine which is called a trébuchet,
pay close attention here. Here is
the base as it rests
on the ground. Here in front
are the two windlasses and the
double rope with which one draws
back the shaft as you can see
on the other page. There is a great
weight to pull back, for the
counter-poise is very heavy,
being a hopper full
of earth which is two large
toises long and nine
feet across and twelve feet

---

[87] *Ibid.*, iii.157.

[88] *Oeuvres de Jean sire de Joinville*, ed. N. de Wailly, Paris 1867, p.128.

[89] Latin: *trabucium;* Italian: *trabocco.*

[90] H. R. Hahnloser, *Villard de Honnecourt. Kritische Gesantausgabe des Bauhüttenbuches. ms.fr 19093 der Pariser Nationalbibliothek*, Graz 2nd edn 1972, pl.59.

parfont. Et al descocier de
le fleke pensés et si vos en
donés garde, car il le doit
estre atenué a cel estançon
la devant.[91]

deep. Remember the arc of the
the arrow when discharged and take
great care, because it must be
placed against the stanchion
in front.[92]

The *Chronicon Sampetrinum* notes under the year 1212; 'Otto, having come into Thuringia, besieged and reduced the castle of the Landgrave at Salza with a three-armed machine called a Triboke.' And the *Annales Marbacenses* in the same year notes; 'From Salza he advanced to besiege Weissensee which he similarly reduced . . . There was used for the first time that war engine which is commonly called the Tribok.'[93]

Trébuchet artillery did not simply aim to demolish or shake fortifications. It was also used to throw incendiary projectiles and to introduce epidemics into a besieged place by throwing the carcasses of putrifying animals. In 1332 when besieging the castle of Schwanau, the men of Strasbourg captured 60 prisoners, of whom they massacred 48, including three carpenters, whose bodies they placed in barrels, together with all kinds of rubbish, which they then catapulted into the castle.[94] There was also the question of directly striking combatants, especially the leaders. Simon de Montfort perished from a stone thrown by a *petraria* which had been fired, according to various witnesses, by the women of Toulouse. They could also destroy enemy engines of the trébuchet or cat variety. An episode from the siege of Castelnaudry by the Occitanians in September 1211 shows a trébuchet in action:

> The besiegers set up their trébuchet on a road but all around they could only find stones which would have fragmented under the impact of firing. In the end they found three which they brought from a good league away. With their first shot they knocked down a tower. With the next, in everyone's sight, they destroyed a chamber. With the third shot they fired the stone disintegrated but not before causing great injury to those who were inside the town.[95]

Even for the greatest sieges throughout the thirteenth and early fourteenth centuries the number of these trébuchets was relatively small, 20 being the maximum. In 1244 round trébuchet stones were being produced in large quantities through the efforts of the English government. Some idea of their rate of fire may be obtained. In 1304 Edward I possessed 13 trébuchets for the siege of Stirling, the majority of which had names (a sign of rarity like the

[91] W. Worringer, *L'art gothique. L'Album de Villard de Honnecourt*, Paris 1967, p.128.
[92] I have adapted the translation of Theodore Bowie, *The Sketchbook of Villard de Honnecourt*, Bloomington and London 1959, pl.61 (tr).
[93] R. Schneider, *Artillerie des Mittelalters* (704), p.28.
[94] P. Martin, Aspects de l'art de la guerre en Alsace (373).
[95] *Chanson de la croisade albigeoise*, ed. Martin-Chabot, i.216.

names of the first large cannons later) – Vicar, Parson, War-Wolf, Gloucester, Belfry, Tout-le-Monde, which threw 600 stones. On 6 June 1296 when Edward I arrived with his army before the abbey of Holyrood near Edinburgh he set up three engines which fired 158 huge stones in three days.[96]

Sapping and mining were frequently practised. An instance of this may be found, for example, at the time of the siege of Château-Gaillard. If a large enough breach had not been made, an attack could be mounted with scaling ladders. At the first siege of Constantinople, Villehardouin relates the attack of some Frankish knights on one part of the walls:

> They planted two scaling ladders against a barbican close to the sea. The wall here was strongly manned by English and Danes, and the struggle that ensued was stiff and hard and fierce. By dint of strenuous efforts two knights and two sergeants managed to scale the ladders and make themselves masters of the wall. A good fifteen of our men got up on top, and were quickly engaged in a hand-to-hand contest of battle-axes against swords. Those inside the barbican plucked up courage and fought back so savagely that they drove our men out, while retaining two as prisoners.[97]

Of course none of these various methods was unknown before 1150. Even the mangonel is mentioned by Abbo at the time of the siege of Paris by the Vikings in 885: 'With beams of equal length bound together, they constructed what are called in the vernacular mangonels, engines which can throw huge stones, with which they shattered the tiny galleries of the Barbarians.'[98] It seems nevertheless that engines and war-machines were used much more frequently in the twelfth and thirteenth centuries and that various technical improvements permitted more rapid and accurate firing of heavier missiles. At the same time sapping works became more sophisticated and effective.

All this is accounted for by the more frequently attested presence in the sources of technical personnel, miners, pioneers and specialist craftsmen. Amongst these people a little group, particularly from the end of the twelfth century, began to stand out: masters of the engines or engineers, who benefited from financial advantages which underline the price people were prepared to pay for their services. The fine future reserved for this type of professional is well known, but their military origins have been insufficiently appreciated. Of course it is true that the engineer of 1200 was not a radically new figure even in the medieval West. Raimond d'Aguilers, in his account of the taking of Jerusalem (1099), names the technicians who, on the order of

---

[96] A. Z. Freeman, Wall-breakers and river-bridgers (249).
[97] Geoffroi de Villehardouin, *La conquête de Constantinople*, ed. E. Faral, Paris 1938, i.172–4; the English version is adapted from Jean de Joinville and Geoffroy de Villehardouin, *Chronicles of the Crusades*, tr. M. R. B. Shaw, Harmondsworth 1963, p.70.
[98] Abbon de Saint-Germain-des-Prés, *La siège de Paris par les Normands. Poème du XIe siècle*, ed. and tr. H. Waquet, Paris 1942, pp.420–3.

Godefroy de Bouillon and Raymond de Saint-Gilles, built numerous *lignea castra, machinae et machinamenta* during the siege.[99] But from the reigns of John Lackland and Philip Augustus mention of engineers becomes more frequent. A certain Master Urric accompanied King John to Normandy in 1201 'to make engines' (*ad facienda ingenia*). At the siege of Toulouse in 1218 two trébuchet specialists, Bernard Parayre and Master Garnier, worked for the besieged. In 1229, wishing to capture the castle of Bellême, Louis IX appealed to 'all those who know how to mine'. He had two engines worked by several masters.[100] During the crusade in Egypt, Jocelin de Cornaut fulfilled the duties of *'mestre engingneur'* and presided with his companions over the construction of 18 engines.[101] Some of these engineers had long and fairly distinguished careers, like the Gascon Jean de Mézos, called *magister ingeniorum* or *ingeniator*, who was knighted in 1254, worked in several castles in Gascony and later passed into the service of the count of Savoy until 1271–72.[102]

2   Methods of defence

When besieged, a castle, garrison or town had a number of possible means of counter-attack. It could wait for or seek the intervention of a relieving force which would place the besiegers in an uncomfortable position, forcing them to decamp. Sorties could be made to break up the blockade or spread panic. They could hope for climatic or monetary difficulties, lack of foodstuffs and discomfort, desertion and disease, to break up the siege. To the trenches of the besiegers they could respond with their own counter-mines. Towns and castles could use trébuchets and stone-throwers just as easily as their besiegers. An inventory of the weapons in fortresses belonging to Philip Augustus reveals the existence at Chinon of 'IIIIc corde ad petrarias, VIII magna chaabla canabi, I magnum chaablum et I parvum et I petraria turquesia' and at Falaise of 'due petrarie et II manguanelli et L paria cordarum'.[103] The presence in opposing camps of trébuchets led to proper artillery duels, the primary objective of the protagonists being to destroy the enemy engines.

Because of their multiple functions, to which their military purpose was in general subordinated or added later, towns possessing a system of fortifications often presented many weak points. Alongside a few cities which fully utilized the military potential of their site (on a spur or plateau, in a marsh or surrounded by water courses), there were many others which had spread out, thinking only about convenience for roads and building. Urban growth in the

[99] Raimond d'Aguilers, *Historia Francorum qui ceperunt Jerusalem*, in *Recueil des historiens des croisades, Historiens occidentaux*, Paris 1866, iii.297.
[100] J-F. Finó, *Forteresses de la France médiévale* (783), pp. 216–17.
[101] *Oeuvres de Jean sire de Joinville*, ed. N. de Wailly, pp.129 and 203.
[102] J. Gardelles, *Les châteaux du Moyen Age dans le France du Sud-Ouest* (797), p.70 n.21.
[103] E. Audouin, *Armée royale* (226), pp.190–1.

twelfth and thirteenth centuries and the relative peace from which this period benefited could only increase this tendency. Even when they existed (and many towns still lacked walls), urban fortifications were often very primitive, additionally weakened by openings and posterns which gradually multiplied. On the exterior of the ramparts, houses, barns, mills and orchards rendered defence more difficult by permitting potential attackers to approach under cover. The first concern of a threatened town was thus to block up the greatest possible number of openings and to clear the terrain around the enceinte in order to allow rapid circulation by the defenders either at the foot of the walls or on wall-walks (*chemins de ronde*). At the same time platforms, palisades, *coursières* and vaulted passages were repaired or built. Gates were the object of special attention. The majority were not only blocked up and flanking towers filled with men and material but they were provided with foreworks, barriers and barbicans (*antemuralia, barbacanae*). During the siege of 1218 at Toulouse, for example, the defences included 16 barbicans each of which was entrusted to a captain whose name was listed in the *Song of the Albigensian Crusade*.[104]

Examples furnished by the first register of Philip Augustus concerning the walls of Laon, Compiègne, Saint-Mard-en-Soissonnais, Melun and so on show that it was considered normal at the beginning of the thirteenth century for ditches to be between 8 and 11 m deep and 12 and 19 m wide, curtains to be between 6 and 10 m high to the base of the parapet, and at the level of the *chemin de ronde* between 1.20 and 2.10 m wide. The same specifications envisaged gates flanked by small towers with thicker walls. Some of these gates are described as simple, others as double. They were preceded by drawbridges (*pontes tornatiles*) whilst other small towers at variable intervals were dotted along the walls. Here are the details for Compiègne, one among many, whose construction was committed to Gautier de Mullent:

> At Compiègne he must make 300 *toises* of new limestone wall in such a manner that it is four *toises* high to the parapet, and also raise the other wall until it is similarly four *toises* high to the parapet and has a four-foot wall-walk. He must plaster and repoint the wall with limestone inside and outside and make four simple gates with double turrets and ditches fifty feet wide and thirty feet deep. And he should do this for 2000*l.* of which the inhabitants shall pay 950*l.* and the king 1050*l.*'.[105]

Some towns offered a much more complex series of defences, like Carcass-onne whose fortifications benefited from considerable attention during the reigns of Saint Louis and Philip III. At the end of these building campaigns the town first presented an exterior enceinte 1,500 m long, provided with 20 towers. This enceinte was preceded either by a ditch or, when the site

---

[104] *Chanson de la croisade albigeoise*, ed. Martin-Chabot, iii.301–19.
[105] V. Mortet and P. Deschamps, *Recueil de textes relatifs à l'histoire de l'architecture* (810), ii.215.

allowed, by a steep escarpment. Then there were the open spaces between the walls and other defences, the lists (*lices*), some 7 or 8 m wide, which allowed rapid circulation of men and materials. Then came the second circuit of walls, reinforced by 25 towers which dominated the first circuit by several metres. There were two principal gates giving access to the town preceded by imposing barbicans. The distance between towers on the eastern side was considerable but this was reinforced by the presence of the castle, a massive construction in the shape of a quadrilateral.

In these circumstances one might think that to fortify a town was a long-term project allowing room for little improvization. But in reality things were somewhat different; in emergencies, towns were capable, thanks to their human resources, of erecting in a few months summary but effective protection. This was the case at Pisa which, threatened by Frederick Barbarossa, surrounded itself in two months (July–August 1155) with a ditch 6 km long and built a wall covering the most exposed sector. The following year wooden towers, castles and brattices, results of work lasting the same length of time, completed the defences.[106] After the first siege of Toulouse Simon de Montfort ordered the razing of the fortifications 'so that anybody or anything, man or animal, might be able to enter running.'[107] This dismantling was completed in October 1216, yet it did not prevent the town from rapidly refortifying itself, thanks to the efforts of its inhabitants, and successfully resisting the siege of 1218.

The greatest, most inventive and the most calculated advances in the art of fortification occurred in castles, that is to say in buildings which, despite their residential functions, were primarily of military importance. Naturally, during this period traditional sites were frequently used, some of which had played a defensive role since time immemorial. The first Romanesque keeps were not necessarily put to other uses or demolished, but completed, modified or incorporated into a much greater and newer complex. Thus the Tower of London, whose cubic keep was begun in 1078 and enceinte in 1097, was completed by works undertaken in 1129–30, 1171–78 and 1190. In the latter year the changes were considerable, judging by the expenses incurred, which totalled £2,881. In general terms, three distinct attitudes can be discerned with regard to earlier fortresses. Sometimes for political rather than military reasons they were destroyed and the site abandoned. After the revolt of 1173–74, for example, Henry II razed several baronial castles. In John Lackland's reign at least a dozen castles were demolished in England. Sometimes the site was conserved and the ditches and foundations were used again, but the fortified works were raised from scratch and owed nothing to previous buildings. This was the case at Coucy where the new castle of Enguerran III apparently retained nothing from the preceding castle. Some-

---

[106] G. Schmiedt, *Città e fortificazioni* (860).

[107] *Chanson de la croisade albigeoise*, ed. Martin-Chabot, ii.248.

times earlier feudal works, especially stone keeps, were judged sufficiently important to be conserved.

In sum, new foundations just outnumbered destructions almost everywhere. Hence there was an increasing density of castles revealed both by archeology and by written sources, even taking into account the relative rarity of documentation from the preceding period which hides many already existing fortifications from us. Some princes undertook systematic building campaigns like Frederick II in the kingdom of Sicily, Philip Augustus throughout the Capetian demesne, and Edward I in Guyenne and Wales. The consolidation of political power led to an increased number of castles being owned by the same person or dynasty. A list of castles and fortresses held by Philip Augustus following the great conquests of his reign enumerates more than 100 places, 45 of which were in Normandy alone. At the accession of Henry II Plantagenet in 1154, England contained 49 castles belonging to the king and 225 belonging to the barons. Sixty years later in 1214 the figures were respectively 93 and 179. In 1220 the king of England had 10 castles in his duchy of Guyenne, in 1250, 14 and in 1294, 32 and another 11 held in *paréage* (that is, jointly with another lord). Around 1300 the count of Provence held about 40 castles. To the castles owned by kings and territorial princes must be added in increasing numbers the castles of vassals which were either *jurable* (sworn) when they had been remitted in return for an oath or *rendable* when it was necessary to cede them to their lord for a period judged necessary for their defence.[108] As early as 1186, in the duchy of Burgundy, 70 castles have been discovered for 7,000 km^2, the majority of those which did not belong to the duke, being jurable and rendable to him. A similar effort was made to include those forts held in rear-fief in the same system of obligations.

This period also saw the proliferation of fortified residences (as opposed to simple residences) and roughly fortified seigneurial manors whose construction was authorized by princes, the more willingly since their presence helped to display tangible reinforcement of political control over the population and offered a serious obstacle to primitive forms of banditry and violence, without in any way representing a threat to their own power. A definition of the fortified residence in the county of Forez may be applied to many regions. It was 'a private enterprise, of more or less recognised public worth, depending on its strength and the power of its lord, and endowed by the count with low justice to enable its lord to enjoy a pretence of service.'[109] Often a territorial prince established a certain number of conditions with which the fortified residence had to comply. Thus, Thibaud, count of Champagne in 1223, in respect of a residence built at Givry by a certain Henri de Mirvaux, stated: 'I

---

[108] Boutruche (102), ii.38, cf. C. L. H. Coulson, Rendability and castellation in medieval France, *ChG*, 6 (1973), 59–67.
[109] G. de Neufbourg, Châteaux et maisons fortes, *Bulletin de la Diana*, 31 (1948), 228–31.

have conceded to the said Henri that he and his successor may construct around the said house a wall 15½ feet high and two and half feet thick, without a moat, tower, wall-walk with archers' loops or openings designed for crossbows, in such a way that there is only a plain wall.'[110]

For the construction of major castles, the only ones of military worth, authorities did not hesitate to expend important amounts which a less miserly documentation sometimes allows us to know. The building of the keep alone at Dover between 1180 and 1190 cost almost £4,000. In 1196–98 Richard Coeur de Lion built a series of fortifications designed to obstruct the course of the Seine, protect Rouen and block Gisors and Vernon, the advance positions of the French. Of this ensemble the keystone was the future Château-Gaillard, then known as the *Bellum castrum de Roka* (fine castle on the rock). The accounts show expenses amounting to £21,203 which may be apportioned amongst the different works, as table 3 demonstrates.[111]

TABLE 3   Expenses on defence works at Château-Gaillard 1197–98, in sterling

	Materials and extraction	Transport	Labour	Total
Carts and labour		1,010	2,432	3,442
Stone	2,030	425	650	3,105
Timber	1,005	251	838	2,094
Sand, mortar and plaster	395		1,002	1,397
Metalwork and cordage		160	113	273
Miners, guards and porters	5,276		5,616	10,892
Total	10,552		10,651	21,203

Source: F. M. Powicke, *The Loss of Normandy*, Manchester 2nd edn 1961, pp.204–6.

During the reign of King John at least five royal English castles had £1,000 or more spent on them: Corfe £1,400, Dover £1,000 (from 1207–14), Kenilworth £1,000 (principally between 1210–15) Knaresborough £1,300 (from 1203–12), and Scarborough £2,000. According to the Pipe Rolls, which indicate the amounts spent on construction and upkeep of castles between 1155 and 1212, the fiscal year 1210–11 saw the highest total, with £2,893.[112]

In order to gauge the importance of these sums their equivalent may be calculated in daily wages. The whole fortified site of Château-Gaillard rep-

---

[110] Mortet and Deschamps (810), ii.233.
[111] D. F. Renn, *Norman Castles in Britain* (840), p.20, after F. M. Powicke, *The Loss of Normandy*, 1st edn, Oxford 1913.
[112] R. A. Brown et al., *The History of the King's Works* (826), ii.1023.

resents 2,544,436 working days by pioneers or foot sergeants, at an average of 7,000 working days a year. Less ambitious schemes attained, despite everything, appreciable levels. Orford in Suffolk, built between 1165 and 1173 and consisting of a polygonal keep, flanked by three rectangular towers and surrounded by a curtain and moat, cost £1,400, that is 336,000 days' pay for a foot soldier. If it is allowed that labourers absorbed three-fifths of this total, that they were paid at the same rate as infantry and for 250 days per year, this sum represents the permanent employment for nine years of a gang of 85 ditchers, building workers and woodcutters. Another example is Odiham (Hants), whose octagonal keep and enceinte built between 1207 and 1212 cost a little more than £1,000.

At much the same period the estimate for the tower which Philip Augustus had built at Villeneuve-sur-Yonne specified a height of 27.26 m, with walls 4.95 m thick, an interior diameter of 6.60 m, a ditch 13.20 m wide and 6.60 m deep, two drawbridges and a wooden screen (*hourd*) reinforced with iron, the whole to cost 1,600 *l.p.* or 8,000 days' pay for a foot sergeant.[113] At the end of the thirteenth century Edward I constructed ten major castles in Wales: Builth, Aberystwyth, Flint, Rhuddlan, Ruthin, Hope, Conway, Beaumaris, Harlech and Caernarvon. For five of these alone between 1277 and 1292 the cost was £25,000, and between 1277 and 1304 Rhuddlan absorbed £9,292, the equivalent of 1,115,040 days' pay for a foot soldier. It is true that the building was imposing. A huge ditch 15 m wide, a first enceinte of almost 400 m, reinforced by a series of turrets and pierced by two gates and a postern, then the fortress proper in the form of a lozenge, whose perimeter attained 220 m, defended by six cylindrical towers. The walls of the fortress reached 16 m high at the merlons and the towers 22 m (figures 1 and 2).

Some names of masters of the works are known from this period. Under Philip Augustus, Garnier worked on the fortifications of Laon, Saint-Marden-en-Soissonais, Montargis and Montreuil-sur-Mer, Gautier de Mullent worked at Compiègne, Guillaume de Flamenville at Montdidier, Melun, Evreux and Pont-de l'Arche and Master Abelin and Gilbert Le Fossier at Montreuil-Bellay. The Welsh castles built by Edward I saw the intervention of an architect of stature in the Savoyard Master James of St George.[114]

The importance of financial means and the participation of masters of the works who blended practical experience with an undeniable intellectual rigour resulted in military architecture around the year 1200 catching up, in a manner of speaking, the ground that had opened earlier between it and religious architecture. Around 1070–80 even the most sophisticated fortifications appeared very slight and primitive in comparison with great churches, especially abbatial ones like Saint-Etienne de Caen or Jumièges, whereas

[113] J. Vallery-Radot, Le donjon de Philippe Auguste à Villeneuve-sur-Yonne et son devis, *ChG*, ii (1964). 106–12.
[114] A. J. Taylor, Master James of St George (844).

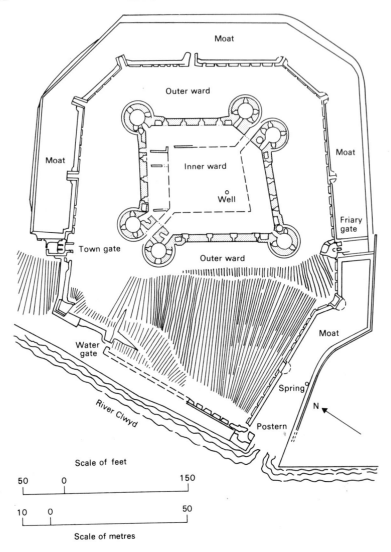

Figure 1   Rhuddlan Castle, Wales (from R. A. Brown, H. M. Colvin and A. J. Taylor, The History of the King's Works (826). Reproduced with the permission of the Controller of Her Majesty's Stationery Office.)

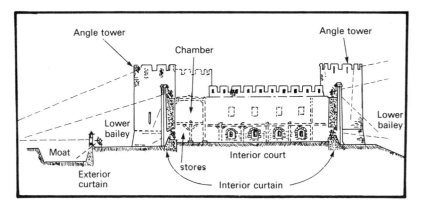

Figure 2 Rhuddlan castle, Wales: cross-section (after Brown, Colvin and Taylor, History of the King's Works (826))

Château-Gaillard, Coucy and Krak des Chevaliers arc not unworthy to be placed alongside Amiens, Westminster or Reims.

There was a difference, however: in contrast to the slowness with which the construction of cathedrals proceeded (Sens 1128–64, Paris 1163–1200, Chartres c.1195–1260), many castles were built rapidly. 'Ecce quam pulchra filia unius anni' (How fair a daughter but twelve months old), said Richard Coeur de Lion of Château-Gaillard, essentially built in a year. Coucy took five years. Nor was this only because the technology used for constructing castles was more rustic than that needed for religious buildings, but rather because the princes who built them considered the need urgent and accepted that they would have to spend very heavily for a few years. Cathedral yards, except for initial enthusiasm, were in general less thronged by masons, navvies and stone cutters than castle sites. The rhythm of work reflected that of the financing. When this was massive even the most complex and refined churches could be rapidly completed, like the Sainte-Chapelle between 1243–48 and the abbey of Royaumont between 1228–35, in both cases buildings directly patronized by the pious munificence of the Capetain monarchy.[115]

Among the developments that occurred after 1150 was the increasingly frequent and systematic use of stone instead of wood, even in regions where wood remained preponderant in ordinary rural and urban buildings. This triumph of stone, which was more resistant, less perishable, more difficult to burn, was nevertheless fairly slow. The keep at Hastings was only reconstructed in stone in 1171–72. 'At Montereau-sur-Yonne a wooden keep built in 1015 was only replaced in 1196 by a stone fortress which was not finished

[115] According to Guillaume de Saint-Pathus, Saint Louis spent 40,000 *l.p.* 'and more' on the Sainte-Chapelle in Paris and 100,000 *l.p.* on Royaumont: Mortet and Deschamps (810), ii.241–2.

until 1228.'[116] The castle of Rumigney near Rocroi still had wooden towers in 1172. In the Vaud district, in Savoy and around Geneva, the use of wood for castles continued until well into the fourteenth century. At Evreux in the fifteenth century 'in repairing the defensive system workers in wood incontestably outnumbered workers in stone . . . in 1417, alongside twelve building workers mending the walls, may be counted no fewer than 36 carpenters and 15 sawyers, without mentioning the labourers and carters specially charged to bring felled trunks and the parts made in the neighbouring forests on to the site.'[117] The use of wood was especially important for supplementary defences, barbicans, lists and brattices.

At the same time knowledge of merlons, hourds (soon replaced by machicolations), *coursières*, brattices, barbicans and drawbridges was increasingly disseminated. Archer-loops became more numerous and better placed; recourse to the crossbow allowed a more systematic flanking fire. To obstruct assault by scaling ladders, the curtains were raised. Towers surged upwards with an evident attempt to beat records analogous to that which had led to the elevation of the great Gothic cathedrals. At Coucy the *chemise* around the keep was 20 m high, whilst the keep itself was 55 m high. Sometimes also a second enceinte might be added. The roofing of towers became safer, thanks to the use of lead and stone resting no longer on joists and boards but on vaults. The towers distributed along the curtain walls were built closer together and were larger and higher. They could from this period constitute autonomous defensive units, whilst remaining linked to the whole by a series of galleries and wall-walks. To counter sapping, the bases of walls were reinforced and thickened and the scarps of ditches were paved with stone. Sometimes, even, the multiplication of towers and their reinforcement rendered maintenance of a keep unnecessary, as happened with the castles of Carcassonne and Angers.

Perhaps the most important modification, certainly the most visible, was the plan itself, where a movement to contract and concentrate elements took place. This resulted in simple, rational, geometrical structures, whether octagonal (Castel del Monte), triangular (Coucy) or, most frequently, quadrangular (Ghent, Carcassonne, the Louvre of Philip Augustus, Dourdan, Roquetaillade, Villandraut, the Welsh castles of Edward I or the fortresses built by Peter II and Philip of Savoy).

Some castles, finally, stand out for their extensive dimensions, like Dover, Château-Gaillard or, in the Holy Land, Saphet, the formidable Templar citadel reconstructed in two and a half years (1240–43), which according to a contemporary record cost 1,200,000 Saracen besants. This castle, built on an extinct volcano 850 m high, had a first enceinte 825 m in circumference,

[116] J. Hubert, L'ancien château de Montereau-fault-Yonne, *Bulletin de la Société nationale des Antiquaires de France 1954–1955*, 56–7.
[117] A. and S. Plaisse, *La vie municipale à Evreux pendant la guerre de Cent Ans*, Evreux 1978, p.103.

preceded by a ditch. This first wall was 22 m high and had a width at the summit of 3.30 m. Then there was an interior moat 15.40 m deep and 13.20 m wide, which was dominated by the walls of the interior enceinte 28.60 m high, which allowed them to overtop the outer enceinte by 6.60 m. The second enceinte had at least seven towers with walls 4.40 m thick. According to the witness who provides these precise details, the garrison was the size of a small town, 1,700 in peacetime and 2,200 in war, including 50 knights, 80 sergeants, 50 Turcopoles, 300 crossbowmen, 400 slaves and 820 domestic servants.[118]

CONCLUSION

Up to a certain point an autonomous activity obeying its own laws, exigencies and specific necessities, war can never be understood without reference to its historical context. Soldiers are men of their times and this synchrony counts for more than the diachrony. That is to say, between 1150 and 1300 war was inevitably changed at the same time as the rest of society, though not always with the same rhythm.

War benefited from improvements in the means of governing and administrating. For armies as well as for justice, finance and religion, organization became more complex, rigorous and compact. The mobilization of the Florentine army in 1260 was a model of precision and planning. On a yet greater scale, the bureaucracies of Edward I and Philip the Fair showed remarkable ability in military administration. Listing, summoning, revictualling and payment were all tasks henceforward entrusted to paid officials whose outstanding technical capacity rested on constant use of written records. Three examples may help to show the degree of complexity which had been reached. The first concerns organization. From 9 February 1260 Florence, in preparing its summer campaign against Siena, first of all named the leaders and administrators of its future army: 12 captains, 2 per district (*sesto*), 6 standard bearers for the horsemen, at 1 per *sesto*, each flanked by 2 commissioners (*distringitores*) and 2 councillors, 6 standard bearers for the crossbowmen, with the same system of commissioners and councillors, also extending to 6 standard bearers for the archers and 6 for the gates of the camp (*poste campi*) and the gonfalonier of the *carroccio* (the ox-cart carrying the town's colours). There were also 50 knights for the *carroccio*, the standard

---

[118] R. B. C. Huygens, Un nouveau texte du traité *De constructione castri Saphet* (871). The garrison may seem considerable, but according to W. Urban (Organization of defence of the Livonian frontier (290)), the castles of the Teutonic Order in that region each had 12 knights, a slightly larger number of men-at-arms, 100 soldiers, mercenaries or members of the local militia, crusaders and, lastly, domestic servants. According to Viollet-le-Duc, the defence of Carcassonne required at least 1,320 men: Finó, (783), p.215. In 1202-3 the garrison of Evreux contained up to 50 knights, 20 mounted sergeants, 25 crossbowmen on foot and 300 sergeants: Audouin, *Armée royale* (226), pp.47, 62, 79 and 90.

bearers and governors of the provision train, the standard bearers of the sappers, the gonfaloniers of the pavesiers, the chamberlains of the army, the standard and banner bearers of different auxiliary groups, and finally the officers appointed to recruit the standard bearers in the parishes of the *contado*, whilst others were to collect mules, livestock and foodstuffs.[119]

The second example concerns the kingdom of Naples during the Angevin period. By two documents of 19 and 20 November 1277 Charles of Anjou ordered his treasurers to pay to Gaucher Belot, his clerk, 5,070 ounces of gold for the hire of his troops, knights, esquires and mounted and foot cross-bowmen from 15 September to 15 December of that year. This payment was to be registered on 'three similar quires' listing 'particularly and distinctly the names and surnames of each hired man', the amount of the advance, his rate of pay, the day and place of payment and 'the defaults if there are any'. One of the quires was to be kept by Gaucher Belot, one by Pierre de Hugot, knight, or by Adam Fourre, the vice-marshal, and the third by Henri Barat, clerk, and Lucas de Saint-Aignan, knight.[120]

The third example also concerns the payment of hired men, this time in England. In 1300 John Botetourt took part in the Scottish campaign with a troop which fluctuated between six and eight men. One of his knights, Robert Bavent, accounted with the Wardrobe of Edward I on 12 September for the period which began on 4 July. The wages due amounted to £61 14s. He received a letter assigning him £30 on the farm of St Briavels, but he had already received wine and foodstuffs worth £13 4s. 8d. He was thus owed £18 9s. 4d. But his dealings did not stop there since he also claimed £134 13s. 4d. for horses lost at the time of the Falkirk campaign in 1298, plus £30 5s. 1d. corresponding to arrears in fees from the time he was a knight-banneret in the royal household. On the other hand he had already been advanced prests worth £98. In total, his credit amounted to £111 7s. 9d., in exchange for which he received from the Wardrobe a recognition of debt payable against a later account.[121]

Alongside administrative progress, there were technical improvements made possible by the presence of a more numerous and doubtless better quality workforce. Hence changes in armour, the appearance and diffusion of more refined and lethal siege engines, improvements in the art of castle building and fortification. More men, materials and money; all this allowed states to mobilize much greater forces, if not for longer periods, for enterprises and military policies of an increasing grandeur. The Aragonese expedition (*voye d'Aragon*) in 1285 cost Philip III 1,228,751 *l.t.* for the upkeep of almost 19,000 men, including 4,000 men-at-arms, 2,700 horsemen and 12,000 foot.[122] From 1294–98 the different military operations in which Edward I

[119] Paoli (223).
[120] A. de Boüard, *Documents français des archives de Naples* (*règne de Charles Ier*), i.37–8.
[121] M. Prestwich, *War, Politics and Finance under Edward I* (907), p.160.
[122] *RCH*, xxi.516–17.

was engaged cost English finances £750,000 (equivalent to 3,000,000 *l.t.*). Under Philip the Fair the *'chevance des deniers'* for the war in Gascony and on the sea in 1294–95 cost 2,125,000 *l.t.*[123] Likewise the purchases of arms were enormous. In 1295 for the war in Aquitaine Philip the Fair bought at Toulouse 2,000 crossbows with one or two feet, 1,000 padded doublets, 3,000 bascinets and 3,000 gorgets. In 1314 the Venetian Arsenal had 3,067 breastplates, 2,770 iron head-pieces and 2,950 gorgerins (*collaria*) in stock.

To complement such high costs there was evidently a wider recruitment 'by summons or by payment'[124] with an appeal both to the contribution of subjects, liegemen, vassals or citizens as well as to hired men, running the whole gamut to pure and unmitigated, explicit or implicit, mercenaries. Not only did towns succeed in emergencies in raising almost all their men capable of carrying arms (with the eventual contribution of women for supplementary defensive tasks), but within much more extensive regions, comprising the surrounding countryside, rates of mobilization which were by no means negligible could be achieved. If one believes the *De magnalibus urbis Mediolani* of Bonvesino della Ripa (1288), not only could Milan itself, with its supposed 200,000 inhabitants, provide in a general mobilization 10,000 cavalry and 40,000 foot, but with the 600 communities of its *contado*, in theory, another 30,000 men might be expected. In 1325, the year of the battle of Altopascio, the Florentine state, with a population of some 400,000 inhabitants, raised – without counting its Guelf allies – 1,500 mercenary horsemen, 500 Florentine knights and, perhaps, 15,000 infantry; one adult in every six or seven may have been mobilized.[125] In 1298 in England, with an army of 25,700 infantry and at least 3,000 knights, perhaps 5 per cent of the adult male population had been called to arms. The state of the evidence does not permit such a sure estimation for the kingdom of France during the reign of Philip the Fair, though this king may be found in 1304 seeking from the great lords of the counties of Toulouse, Carcassonne, Périgord, Rouergue, Auvergne and Beaucaire a contribution of 2,016 men-at-arms and 17,350 foot sergeants. In all likelihood this was just an estimate, for which no evidence survives to show it was attained, intended all along as a means of raising money not men (at the rate of a man-at-arms for each noble possessing revenues of 500*l.* and six foot soldiers for every 100 hearths (*feux*). But it remains the case that this money was to be spent on an equivalent number of combatants. Moreover, it is clear that all parts of the country were to be forced to pay, whilst that same year an appeal was made, this time genuinely, to lords who were obliged to assemble at the appointed place 'a fortnight after St John's Day' with a certain number of horsemen and foot soldiers. These lords were grouped geographically in

[123] E. Boutaric, Mémoire anonyme sur la guerre contre l'Angleterre, *Notices et extraits des manuscrits*, XX² (Paris 1872), 123–9; J. R. Strayer, The costs and profits of war (190a).
[124] *RCH*, xxiv.758.
[125] It has been calculated that Tuscany at this period contained two million inhabitants, of which only a sixth lived in the Florentine state.

the convocation lists: Toulouse, Carcassonne, Périgord, Rouergue, Beaucaire, Ile de France, Berry, Normandy, Poitou, Champagne, Brittany, Maine, Anjou, Touraine, Perche, Limousin, Burgundy, Vermandois, Beauvaisis, Artois, Corbie, Ponthieu, Vendômois, Auvergne and Lyonnais.[126]

Grandiose schemes were projected. Fidenzo of Padua in the *Liber recuperationis Terre sancte*, written between 1266 and 1291, thought that a new crusade should assemble, in addition to a whole host of *pedites*, 20,000–30,000 horsemen (including a large number of archers). He also suggested the creation in the Holy Land of a permanent army (*militia continua, stabilis et diuturna*) which would be maintained by the bishoprics, abbeys and cities of Christendom, all of them so very numerous that it would only be necessary to entrust to each of them a small number of knights which would not seriously burden them.[127] In 1323 an embassy led by Charles of Valois to Pope John XXII with a view to launching a new crusade proposed the following figures: 5,000 men-at-arms (including 1,000 maintained from the resources of the Hospitallers now enlarged by those of the Templars) and 15,000 foot soldiers, representing an annual total expenditure of 1,600,000 *l.t.* for five years. In other words the projected crusade would cost 8,000,000 *l.t.*[128]

Yet even before the end of the thirteenth century war was not only the concern of great states with large budgets. Almost everywhere, in Germany, Scotland, Ireland, in a part at least of the Iberian peninsula, warfare of a different character still continued; petty operations like the *razzias* led by the warrior-pastoralists in Spain, popular uprisings (in the Swiss cantons, Wales and Scotland), private ventures, close to banditry, led by the knights and burgraves of the Rhine Valley, Swabia, Franconia and Bavaria. Even the most powerful monarchies only succeeded in collecting large armies for a few weeks each year. These rapidly ran out of steam, and came up against the unpredictable laziness, discontent and anger of their subjects for whom war (and the tax burdens which resulted from it) in the heart of Christendom ought to have been an exceptional phenomenon or at least a temporary one.

---

[126] *RCH*, xxiii.792–5.

[127] Fidenzo of Padua, *Liber recuperationis Terre Sancte* (218).

[128] J. Petit, *Charles de Valois (1270–1325)*, Paris 1900, pp.395–400.

4

Free Companies, Gunpowder and Permanent Armies from the beginning of the Fourteenth to the end of the Fifteenth Century

From the last years of the thirteenth century and, in broad terms, increasingly until the end of the fifteenth century or even beyond, the historian of warfare and armies finds noticeably more varied and important documentation, albeit unevenly distributed in a geographical sense. This allows him to deal with more questions and, at least for certain regions and chosen themes, to provide some quantitative results.

This superiority of sources is not so much felt in the strictly literary field where the twelfth- and thirteenth-century *Chansons de geste* teach us as much about the practice of warfare and the ethical views of combatants as the chivalric romances, novella, farces and tales of the following period. The narrative sources, where the use of the vernacular was more and more frequent, provide information that is sufficiently precise and circumstantial for us to follow more exactly and completely the course of a battle, the fluctuating stages of a siege, the adventures of a company of men-at-arms or the exploits of some captain. Moreover, at this time didactic treatises consecrated to the art of war, military discipline and the organization of armies began to appear, for example the treatise which Theodore Paleologus (1291–1338), second son of Emperor Andronicus II and Violanta-Irena of Montferrat, composed in Greek and then translated into Latin around 1327. The Latin version was then translated into French at the end of the fourteenth century for Philip the Bold, duke of Burgundy, by Jean de Vignai under the title *Enseignemens et ordenances pour un seigneur qui a guerres et grans gouvernemens a faire.*[1] Other examples are: *L'arbre des batailles* (*The Tree of Battles*), a sort of manual of the laws of war largely inspired by the *De bello, de represaliis et de duello* (1360),[2] a work of the Italian jurist John of Legnano, which the Benedictine prior of Selonnet in the diocese of Embrun and doctor of decre-

---

[1] J. Bastin, Le traité de Théodore Paléologue (301).
[2] Giovanni da Legnano, *Tractatus de Bello* (916).

tals, Honoré Bovet, completed in 1386–87 and dedicated to the young Charles VI;[3] *Le Livre des fais d'armes et de chevalerie*, which Christine de Pisan composed in 1410;[4] for the mid-fifteenth century (perhaps written by Merlin du Cordeboeuf), there is the tract on 'The way soldiers dress in the kingdom of France both on foot and horseback';[5] *Le Jouvencel*, which Jean de Bueil, 'le lyon des frontieres', as Georges Chastellain styled him, composed or had written around 1460–70 in order to summarize his long military experience;[6] the *Bellisfortis*, in which at the beginning of the fifteenth century Conrad Kyeser described the military weapons of his day and suggested several engines which were the fruit of his imagination;[7] and in the same vein, although more influenced by a long tradition reaching back to the *Anonymus de rebus bellicis* of the fourth century AD, the *De machinis libri X* which Mariano di Jacopo Taccola wrote in 1449.[8]

For this period, too, regulations and military ordinances have survived, sometimes collected together to form proper codes like the *Codice degli stipendiarii* of the Florentine Republic (1369); the great ordinance promulgated by Charles V of France on 13 January 1374, which was considered so important that at the end of the fifteenth century the Admiral, Louis Malet de Graville, had a copy;[9] the military ordinances of Charles the Bold of Burgundy, especially that promulgated at Saint-Maximin at Trier in October 1473, of which a copy was sent to every captain at the same time as his bâton of command; the '*Estatuz, ordenances et custumes a tenir en l'ost*' issued by Richard II at Durham on 17 July 1385 after 'the good advice and deliberation' of John, duke of Lancaster, seneschal of England, Thomas, earl of Essex and Buckingham, constable of England, and Thomas Mowbray, earl of Nottingham, marshal of England; the *Statutes and Ordinaunces to be keped in time of Werre*, published by Henry V in 1419, of which there exists both a Latin and an English version; and the military regulations for the campaign against the Hussites drawn up at the Diet of Nuremberg on 9 and 10 March 1431, of which a contemporary French translation has been preserved; and finally various ordinances and campaign regulations concerning the military forces raised by the Swiss cantons.[10]

---

[3] Honoré Bonet, *L'arbre des batailles* (913).
[4] Christine de Pizan, *L'art de chevalerie* (12). For the fifteenth-century English tr. see *The Book of Fayttes of Armes* (13).
[5] R. de Belleval, *Du costume militaire des Français en 1446* (541).
[6] Jean de Bueil, *Le Jouvencel* (9).
[7] Conrad Kyeser, *Bellisfortis* (543).
[8] Mariano Taccola, *De Machinis* (545).
[9] BL, MS Sloane 2423.
[10] From the end of the fifteenth century at least the habit was established of announcing to each army at the moment it assembled a kind of general edict in which the disciplinary orders were set out. This is what Philippe de Clèves, lord of Ravenstein, recommended to the prince to whom he addressed his *Instruction des principaulx poincts de l'art militaire*. The 'camp proclamations' were debated first by the high command and then reduced to writing and delivered to the marshal of the host 'to publish them through your officers at arms and trumpeters wherever

Expert opinions like that sent by Ghillebert de Lannoy to Philip the Good in 1436,[11] or that which Sir John Fastolf drew up in the previous year for the government of Henry VI also survive.[12] In Italy Orso degli Orsini, duke of Ascoli and count of Nola, drew up in 1447 the *Governo et exercitio de la militia* for Alfonso I the Magnanimous of Aragon; there were also the *Memoriali* of Diomedes Caraffa who was similarly a faithful servant of the Aragonese house (1478–79),[13] and the small treatise on the militia which Chiereghino Chiericati dedicated in 1471 to Cardinal Orsini.[14] Very instructive, too, is military correspondence like that which is preserved for the Breton campaign of 1488 between Charles VIII, Louis de la Trémoille and various captains.[15]

Judicial archives (in France the various series of the Parlement of Paris and the letters of remission issued by the royal chancery) not only allow discovery of numerous petty military episodes and an appreciation from the legal point of view of various aspects of the activities of soldiers, but also allow a precise social approach to such a milieu. Even notarial registers containing inventories, wills and transactions to which soldiers were party can be taken into account.

But perhaps it is the financial archives of a public or, more rarely, private character which provide the most illuminating as well as the most abundant mass of documentation. Accounting records emanating from urban, princely or royal sources allow us to learn about methods of recruitment, numbers of effectives, their fluctuations and costs, and to reach not only the captains but the most lowly soldiers, to see how problems concerning individual or collective equipment and supply were solved.

Nor is there simply written evidence; material evidence has its value. Excavations of battlefields have produced notable results, like the discovery at Aljubarrota in Portugal of the holes in lines or in a chequered pattern which are supposed to have been dug in 1385 by the English archers of John of Gaunt, perhaps for stakes which were intended to stop and break up the charges of the Castilian cavalry,[16] or the exploration of the ditches into which

---

there is need and in as many languages as are spoken by the men in your army' (BL, MS Lansdowne 804 f.93r). For a French translation of the regulations for the war against the Hussites see G. Wolfram, Die Metzer Chronik des Jaique Dex (Jacques Desch) über die Kaiser und Könige aus dem Luxemburger Hause, *Quellen zur lothringischen Geschichte herausgegeben von der Gesellschaft für lothringische Geschichte und Altertumskunde*, Metz 1906, iv.377–94.
[11] Ghillebert de Lannoy, *Oeuvres* (329).
[12] J. Stevenson, *Letters and Papers* (344), II.ii.579–81. M. G. A. Vale, Sir John Fastolf's 'report' of 1435: a new interpretation reconsidered, *Nottingham Mediaeval Studies*, *17* (1973), 78–84.
[13] P. Pieri, *Governo et exercitio de la militia* (339).
[14] C. Zorci, Un Vicentino alla Corte di Paolo II (527).
[15] *Correspondance de Charles VIII et de ses conseillers avec Louis II de la Trémoille pendant la guerre de Bretagne*, ed. L. de la Trémoille, Paris 1875.
[16] A. do Paço, The Battle of Aljubarrota, *Antiquity*, *37* (1963), 264–9, for photographs and plans of the site.

the dead from the battle of Visby (Gotland) were thrown in 1361. This has enabled us to estimate the importance of the loss of human life, and also allowed a complete scientific study of defensive armour to be made.[17] In considerable numbers, urban enceintes, castles, citadels, fortified churches, forts and fortified residences, built or remodelled at the end of the Middle Ages, have come down to us; outstanding works like the enceintes of Avignon, York, Rothenburg and Nördlingen, the castles of Vincennes, Fougères, Salses, Karlstein and Tarascon . . . Elsewhere helmets, suits of armour, shields, various protective pieces of horse armour, swords, long-hafted weapons, arrowheads, crossbows and even banners have survived in fairly large numbers from excavations or from booty carefully preserved (like that which the Swiss cantons seized from Charles the Bold)[18] or from ex-votos (arms, banners or other objects) offered to certain sanctuaries,[19] and particularly in former imperial, royal, princely and seigneurial collections. Most of this is now preserved in different museums like the Tower Armouries and the Wallace Collection in London, the Musée de l'Armée at Paris, the Musée de la Porte de Hal at Brussels, the Castello San-Angelo in Rome, the Stibbert museum in Florence, the Armeria reale of Turin, the Real armeria at Madrid, the collection in Ambras castle in the Tyrol and so on. It must, however, be noted that the majority are pieces dating from after 1450 and that their often exceptional technical and artistic quality makes them less representative of the arms that were actually used in battle by ordinary combatants. In the same way, throughout Europe dozens of artillery pieces of all dimensions and calibres, as well as cannon balls and gun-carriages have been preserved.

The iconography is no less rich: there are innumerable war scenes and representations of soldiers in frescoes, easel paintings, miniatures, drawings, woodcuts and copper engravings, sculptures (especially funerary ones), reliquaries, statues of military saints, windows, ivories, sculpted panels, seals, and even on money and medals.

Doubtless one could say that this enrichment of the sources does not simply concern warfare but the whole range of human activities. But this does not diminish the significance of the great frequency of warlike themes in the art of the late Middle Ages. Military treatises in the fourteenth and fifteenth centuries are more numerous than didactic works on the art of navigation, agriculture, cloth-making or even commercial techniques. The sources better illuminate the evolution of military costume than civil dress. In miniatures, for every arcadian scene, there are countless depictions of sieges, jousts or full-scale battles. As for the importance of the financial records concerning hired troops, they witness to the importance of war in the life and preoccupation of states.

[17] B. Thordemann, *Armour from the Battle of Wisby* (675).
[18] F. Deuchler, *Die Burgunderbeute* (551).
[19] J. Mann, A further account of the armour preserved in the sanctuary of the Madonna delle Grazie (643).

In fact, at the end of the Middle Ages, it seems that war imposed its formidable weight on a Latin Christendom that was in other ways disorientated, anxious, even split and torn apart by profound political and social rivalries, economically weakened, unbalanced and demographically bled white. War, in large measure, contributed to this malaise, this long period of anaemia marked by crises and convulsions, though at the same time the general depression and tensions equally helped to engender conflicts. Hence there was a kind of vicious circle from which the West emerged only slowly and incompletely after 1450. The last two centuries of the Middle Ages saw the unleashing of the Great Companies on France and Spain, of the Free Companies in Italy and the *Ecorcheurs* (Skinners) in France and the western parts of Germany. In the same period there was the multitude of military events which allowed Scotland to preserve its independence, as well as the Hundred Years War, the Succession War in Brittany and the campaigns of Philip the Good and Charles the Bold which created and then destroyed the Burgundian state. There were civil wars and dynastic rivalries within or between the Iberian kingdoms, struggles for domination of Southern Italy and efforts by the church to recapture the papal states. There was the temporary seizure by Louis XI of Roussillon and the annexation of Brittany by Charles VIII. Maritime wars occurred between Genoa and Venice, the German Hanse, Denmark and England. There were the Hussite wars, the conflicts of the Teutonic Order and its neighbours, the rivalries of lords and communes in Tuscany and Lombardy, the advance of the Ottoman Turks (though this only incidentally affected the forces and territories of Latin Christendom), the end of the kingdom of Granada and the Wars of the Roses. Not only did especially long conflicts occur; they even conserved or acquired, in spite of their length, a very high degree of intensity. In addition, alongside major actions, entire regions suffered, sometimes for decades, from generalized insecurity and diffuse demonstrations of violence in all its forms.

That war was then at the back of everyone's mind is proved by the accounts of travellers, frequently attentive to the military virtues of the peoples they visited and to the strengths and weaknesses of the fortified buildings they saw on their journeys. Thus the Gascon pilgrim Nompar, seigneur de Caumont, writes:

> It is two leagues from Mazères to the city of Pamiers, a very fine and rich city in which there is a very strong, high castle. From Pamiers to Foix, two leagues. Foix is a very sovereign place for a fortress situated as it is on a high rock on all sides with no access and the castle thereupon has been very well built with good walls and towers and at its foot lies a large town of one thousand hearths, well enclosed with walls and a river flowing before it, and it is commonly said by everyone that they do not know a stronger place having such a town at its foot than this one.[20]

[20] *Le Voyatge d'Oultremer en Jherusalem de Nompar, seigneur de Caumont,* ed. P. S. Noble, Oxford 1975, 23–4.

Journeying through the West in 1466 a Bohemian noble, Leo of Rozmital, and his companions noted that Poole in England was an open town. Despite its dimensions, population and commercial activity they did not dare call Ghent a proper city because on one side it lacked walling and was simply bounded by a river. Conversely they remarked that the castle at Angers 'stands in a plain with artificial moats round it on the outside and an inner wall on which one could drive carts and on the wall are twenty-five towers. Each tower has a knight appointed to defend it and is so spacious and large that he has his dwelling and establishment inside.'[21]

In the same way fifteenth-century human geography insisted voluntarily on the warlike capacities of different societies. *Le livre de la description des pays* by Gilles le Bouvier, Berry Herald, a contemporary of Charles VII, witnesses to this and in it may be found a kind of military ethnography. This is the description of the duchy of Guyenne: 'The men of this province are courageous, light-headed and good men-at-arms . . . the common people are all crossbowmen.' Or of the Swiss: 'These men are cruel and rough people and fight all their neighbours if they ask for anything, and in the plains as well as the mountains 40,000 or 50,000 men can be found to fight.' In Upper Germany 'there are good crossbowmen on foot or horseback and they draw bows of horn or sinew which are good, accurate and strong because they never snap.' The kingdom of Naples included 'valiant horsemen, more numerous and better mounted and equipped than any others in Italy'. The Hungarians frequently 'make serious war on the Saracens, have small bows of horn or sinew with cranks with which they shoot, and good horses, are only scantily and lightly armed and do not voluntarily dismount to fight'. In the kingdom of Bohemia there were 'crowds of soldiers' where 'the Emperor and great German princes, thinking to reduce them by force, had great battles with them, lost there many of their own men and could never force them to submit. When they marched against the Germans to fight, they enclosed themselves with their carts, chained together, and carried great strong batons which had iron chains affixed to the tips. On the end of the chains there was a lead ball and every time they struck they felled a man and by this method they remained always in their fortified waggons.'[22] We can recognize here a description of Czech tactics during the Hussite wars with the celebrated *Wagenburg*, translated into French as *chastiaul sur char* or *chastel charral*. Naturally Berry Herald, who was also the author of a detailed chronicle on the reign of Charles VII, did not fail to mention English military usages. The English:

> are all good archers and soldiers. And when their king wants to raise an army to
> wage war in France or Spain or Brittany (so that the duke will make war on the

[21] Leo von Rozmital, *Ritter- Hof- und Pilgerreise*, Stuttgart 1844 (cf. *The Travels of Leo of Rozmital*, ed. M. Letts, Cambridge 1957 for the Hakluyt Society, pp.30, 62, 68).
[22] Berry Herald, *Le livre de la description des pays*, ed. E-T. Hamy, Paris 1908, pp.42, 60–1, 88, 98, 114.

king of France) and these countries are allied with the king of France, he sends them by sea to land in these countries to get there what they need, or to die there if they meet with great resistance. This nation is cruel and bloodthirsty and they even fight among themselves in the same way, waging great battles. Such is the condition of this kingdom. They also make war on all nations of the world by sea and land and all that they gain in the foreign parts to which they have gone they send back to their realm and through this it is rich.[23]

Finally, more than one author expressed, in various ways, his conviction that war had been implanted in the West until it spread its roots in all directions. This is suggested by Honoré Bovet when he described the meaning of a miniature placed as frontispiece to his *Arbre des batailles*:

> I have imagined the thing in such wise that I make a Tree of Mourning at the beginning of my book, on which you may see, first, at the head, the governors of the Holy Church in such sharp tribulation as was never before, dissensions and wars . . . and after you may see the great discord, battles and killings which exist today between kings and christian princes. Afterwards you may plainly see that among nobles and communities there is great anguish and slaughter.

War was present at all levels in the hierarchy of powers and society. The same author returned a little later to an analogous idea: 'I see all Holy Christendom so tormented by wars and divisions, robberies and dissensions that one can scarcely name a petty province, be it duchy or county, which enjoys peace.'[24] Two generations later in another geographical and political context, George Podiebrad, king of Bohemia, echoed these remarks in the prologue of his *Tractatus pacis toti christianitati fiendae*, written with the intention:

> that there might be brought to an end and completely extinguished all the wars, rapines, troubles, burnings and murders which as we shall relate, alas with sadness, have assailed Christendom in all its parts and through which the countryside has been devastated, towns pillaged, provinces torn apart and kingdoms and principalities borne down by innumerable miseries, and that we should return to a decent state of mutual love and fraternity through a praiseworthy union.[25]

Just as much as war, peace, its natural counterpoise (provided it was good, not 'feigned', 'corrupted', 'dissembled' or 'underhand'), ardently desired and invoked by subjects, ceaselessly urged with more or less good faith by authorities and politicians, exalted by the established church, clerics and intellectuals, was indeed one of the key words in public life at the end of the Middle Ages. It was through its achievement or durable re-establishment that the solution to the major crisis which had struck the whole of catholic humanity would infallibly be found.

[23] *Ibid.*, p.119.
[24] Musée Condé, Chantilly, MS 156¹, f.10v.
[25] George Podiebrad, *Tractatus pacis toti christianitati fiendae* (918), p.70.

THE AGE OF THE HORSE

'The horse as everyone knows is the most important part of a knight.'[26] Looking at the paintings of Paolo Ucello (The Battle of San Romano, the two St George and the Dragons), the equestrian statues of the great fifteenth-century condottieri, the miniatures (often of very ordinary quality) of the great battles of the Hundred Years War or the tapestry of Jean de Daillon, lord of Lude,[27] or at the drawings illustrating the life and deeds of Richard Beauchamp, earl of Warwick,[28] it seems that the military scene was still dominated by the heavily armed knight, using essentially a lance and sword, even if it often happened that he fought on foot. This horseman, whom French sources call *homme d'armes*, *lance*, *glaive* and also, at least in the fourteenth century, *bacinet* or *armure de fer*, is known in the German Empire as *Lanze*, *Spiess*, *Gleve* or *Helm*[29] and in England as men-at-arms, *homines ad arma* and *homines armati*.[30]

A more attentive examination reveals that the category of man-at-arms did not correspond to an entirely standardized type, first because the make-up of defensive armour evolved to a certain extent between 1320 and 1500. In the first half of the fourteenth century metal plates still only covered a small part of the combatant's body (chiefly the arms and legs), and chain mail still remained the fundamental protection for the torso, while in the fifteenth century it was *harnois blanc*, white or plate armour, which entirely encased a man like a carapace from head to toe so that mail was now only used for a few small accessories, for example, around the waist or throat. Yet at any given moment there were differences in quality or style of armour between different regions and also between individuals according to their fortune. Around 1360 in Italy it is sometimes possible to distinguish between an Italian man-at-arms and an English, Burgundian, German, Breton or Hungarian one simply by their appearance. In addition, a man-at-arms of the rank of a count, baron or banneret not only had armour which was normally of finer workmanship than that of a simple knight, esquire or gentleman and a more robust, speedier and more highly bred horse, but also a more numerous following. According to regulations for a *masnade* (retinue) which the city of Pisa was intending to pay in 1327–31, each banneret from beyond the Alps could bring three mounted assistants (*equitatores*), each knight two and each esquire one. A war indenture concluded in 1440 between Humphrey, earl of

[26] J. Giradoux, *Ondine*, Act I, scene 2.
[27] Montacute House, Somerset, cf. J. B. Vaivre, La tapisserie de Jean de Daillon, *Archivum Heraldicum* 1973, nos. 2–3, 18–25.
[28] Viscount Dillon and W. H. St-John Hope, *Pageant of the Birth, Life and Death of Richard Beauchamp, Earl of Warwick*, London 1914.
[29] W. Schultze, *Die Gleve* (387).
[30] A. E. Prince, The Army and the Navy (429).

Stafford, and Sir Edward Grey, knight bachelor, envisaged that the latter, in exchange for various carefully stipulated advantages, would serve across the sea with an esquire, three yeomen, a groom, a page and seven horses as long as he held that rank in the noble hierarchy, but that if he were to become a baron his retinue would be enlarged to include two esquires, four yeomen, a groom, two pages and ten horses.[31]

In general there was a tendency for weight and numbers to increase. In France in the middle of the fourteenth century, the number of men in a unit was two (only one of whom was a combatant) and two horses. In contrast, by the fifteenth century the rule was that each lance normally consisted of three mounted men, the man-at-arms properly so-called, a fighting auxiliary called a *coutilier*, and a page. This norm is also found in the armies of Charles the Bold. It seems that the change occurred in the last decades of the fourteenth century, no doubt because of changes in tactics on the battlefield. It is in the 1380s that the *gros valets*, flanking esquires and knights begin to be mentioned. Philippe de Mézières is a good witness to this development when he reveals, in the rule which he proposed for his future Order of the Passion (*Chevalerie de la Passion Jhesu Christ*) that 'the least knight of the Holy chivalry . . . if he would be ready for battle, expeditions and wars, shall have an esquire armed with all arms and a little valet who shall carry his lance, helm and bascinet, and another larger valet armed with a jack who shall carry his baggage (*malle*) and a foot servant who shall lead his pack-animal and thus for wars and expeditions the knight shall have five horses and four men.' As for a brother of the Order, he shall have 'on expeditions . . . three or four horses according to his virtuousness and three men, of whom one or two shall be combatants'.[32]

The conditions of the contract (*condotta*) drawn up in 1433 between Florence and Micheletto degli Attendoli stated that each lance provided by the latter should have 'unum caporalem, unum equitatorem sive piactum, et unum paggium cum duobus equis et uno rozeno'. Similarly, except for a few aberrant cases of default or excess, the *lancee* used in the papal states for wars in the mid-fifteenth century included one *caput lancee*, or esquire (*armiger*), a page (*pagius*, *rigazzus*) and lastly a *plattus*, *placto* or *platto*, these two latter mounted on rounceys or mules.[33] At the end of the century here as elsewhere growth in numbers is apparent: the *condotta* between Hercules Bentivoglio and Florence in 1483 stipulated 'four horses for each man-at-arms and

---

[31] A. C. Reeves, Some of Humphrey Stafford's military indentures (433).

[32] Bodleian Library, Oxford, MS Ashmole 813, f.24r. However, as early as 1336 for an expedition to Prussia led by the count of Hainault 620 horses and as many men were assembled for 155 *armures de fer*, that is four men and four horses for each lance. In addition, the tendency to increase the numbers is above all noticeable amongst the 'professional' men-at-arms; the noble serving as a man-at-arms because of his fief or fiefs in the second half of the fifteenth century often only had two horses and a valet.

[33] A. da Mosto, *Ordinamenti militari* (498).

cuirassier, amongst which the horse of the man-at-arms shall be large, strong and of good size'. In a scheme of 1472 concerning the Milanese army, 136 squadrons contained 3604 men-at-arms with 24,617 horses, that is on average seven for each man-at-arms.[34]

The authorities who recruited men-at-arms were obviously concerned about the quality of arms and mounts. The Pisan code of 1327 accepted for paid troops only horses worth at least 25 florins, coursers worth at least 15 florins and rounceys worth at least 20 florins. An advanced example of this concern may be found in a military regulation of Charles the Bold in 1473: the man-at-arms in a lance in the *ordonnance* companies should have a complete suit of armour with a *sallet* (large helmet) with beaver or a *barbute*, a neck piece (*gorgerin*), a long, firm and light sword, a cutting dagger carried on the left-hand side of the saddle and a mace on the right and a horse provided with a chamfron and barding, able to charge and break a lance. As for the armed servant or swordsman (*coutilier*), he had to have a brigandine or jack in German style, a sallet and gorgerin, his arms and legs protected, a javelin with *arrêt*, sufficiently firm and light that he might eventually use it horizontally as a sort of small couched lance, a good sword and a long two-edged dagger. His horse should be worth at least 30 *écus*. If nothing is said about the page's equipment, in contrast a minimal value is indicated for his mount of 20 *écus*. Lastly, the man-at-arms was authorized to procure a fourth horse to carry his baggage.[35]

Units of light cavalry are, however, also mentioned in various regions of the West, like the English hobelars who appear until the mid-fourteenth century. After the first defeats of the Hundred Years War *gens de cheval* make their appearance in the armies of the second Valois sovereign, John the Good. In fifteenth-century France and Burgundy there are references to brigandiners and mounted halberdiers, light horse, demi-lances and lances of the *petite ordonnance*. But it was above all on the southern periphery and in eastern Europe that light cavalry possessed a well-defined tactical role, like the Spanish *jinetes*, Hungarian cavalry and Venetian *estradiots*. Of these latter Commynes provides the following definition à *propos* their intervention in the battle of Fornovo (1495): 'Estradiots are men like *jinetes*, clothed on foot and horseback like Turks, except for their heads on which they wear only a turban (*toliban*) and they are very tough men sleeping outdoors all the year with their horses. They are all Greeks and all come from places the Venetians hold, some from Naples, others from Romania, the Morea, Albania and from Durazzo, and their horses are all good Turkish ones.'[36] Molinet adds that they are 'very strange, heavily bearded, but lacking armour and footwear,

---

[34] E. C. Visconti, Ordine dell'esercito ducale sforzesco (345).

[35] C. Brusten, Les compaignies d'ordonnance dans l'armée bourguignonne (448).

[36] Ph. de Commynes, *Mémoires*, ed. J. Calmette and G. Durville, Paris 3 vols. 1924–25, iii.163–4.

carrying a little targe (shield) in one hand and a demi-lance in the other'.[37] The 'great number of Lombards and Gascons who had terrifying horses used to turning on the gallop which the French, Picards, Flemings and Brabançons were not used to seeing', which Monstrelet mentions in 1410 in the military following of the duke of Orléans, were also light cavalry.[38]

Already mentioned in earlier centuries, mounted bowmen (crossbowmen and ordinary archers) also frequently figure in the armies of the late Middle Ages. In England mounted archers make their appearance at the beginning of the reign of Edward III. In October 1339, for example, independent of allied contingents, the king of England mustered on the northern frontiers of the kingdom of France some 1,600 men-at-arms, 1,500 mounted archers and 1,650 foot-archers and pikemen. Later, on one hand the proportion of men-at-arms tended to decrease and on the other, for the great majority, the archers were theoretically provided with horses even if on the battlefield they had to dismount to fight and, in certain circumstances, it was impossible for them to replace their mounts. Thus at the time of the expedition which was brought to a conclusion by the treaty of Picquigny in 1475, Edward IV included in his army a good 1,000 men-at-arms and ten times that number of mounted archers.[39]

Valois France rapidly became aware of the military efficacy of the longbow, and also sought to recruit mounted archers. These were the mounted crossbowmen, generally of Spanish or Italian origin, which may be found in appreciable numbers in the armies of Charles V and Charles VI. At the beginning of the fifteenth century the ratio was one mounted archer for every two men-at-arms. Then, after Agincourt and doubtless following the massive participation of the Scots, the ratio was established at two archers for every man-at-arms and the ordinary bow was systematically preferred to the crossbow in such a way that the *lance fournie* or *garnie*, officially established from 1445, included at least six men and six horses – a man-at-arms and his two assistants, plus two mounted archers having at their common disposition a valet or mounted servant. In imitation of France, the Burgundian and Breton states adopted the same formula in the course of the third quarter of the fifteenth century. In Italy, Spain and in the greater part of the Germanic world, mounted archers, mentioned here and there, were rarer.

Naturally, as with the men-at-arms, an effort was obviously made to impose a standard equipment, both offensive and defensive, on the mounted archers recruited. According to the code for men hired in the service of Florence in 1369, each English archer serving in mercenary companies like

[37] Jean Molinet, *Chroniques*, ed. G. Doutrepont and O. Jodogne, Brussels 3 vols. 1935–37, ii.415. See also M. Mallett, *Mercenaries and their Masters* (512), pp.152–3.
[38] Enguerrand de Monstrelet, *Chroniques*, ed. L. Douët d'Arcq, Paris 6 vols. 1857–62, ii.102.
[39] The English archers were considered to be a kind of mounted infantry rather like the seventeenth and eighteenth-century dragoons. For this reason Commynes included the English amongst 'les bonnes gens de pied' like the Swiss (*Mémoires*, i.109; cf. *Memoirs*, tr. Jones, p.124).

that of the *condotierre* John Hawkwood should have had a *panziere* or breast-plate (*cuirasse*), an iron headpiece or *cappellino*, mail gloves, a bow, arrows, sword and dagger. An indenture of 1440 dating from the time of the English occupation of Normandy specifies that a certain James Skidmore was to serve:

> as a man of armes with vj. archers in his company, all on horsbak and wele chosen men, and likly persones wele and suffisantly armed, horsed, and arayed ev'y man after his degree; that is to say, that the seid James Skidmore have herneis complete wt basnet or salade, with viser, spere, axe, swerd, and dagger; And all the seid archers specially to have good jakks of defence, salades, swerdes and sheves of xl. arwes atte lest.[40]

Describing the Norman campaign of 1449–50 Jean Chartier, the official chronicler of the Valois monarchy, described the 'mounted archers, mostly armed with brigandines, leg armour and sallets, of whom the majority were glittering in silver or at least had good jacks and haubergeons'.[41] The military ordinances of Charles, duke of Burgundy, envisaged two main types of mounted archer. First, the archer with a horse worth at least six francs, a sallet without a visor, a gorgerin and either a brigandine or, for preference, a small, sleeveless haubergeon covered by a jack formed by layers of ten ordinary cloths and three waxed clothes, a good bow and sheath with thirty arrows, a two-handed sword, firm and edged, which could be used for thrusting, a two-edged dagger, round-toed, pointless shoes and short spurs so that they might easily dismount. Next, the crossbowman or *cranequinier*, wearing a brigandine or jack and mounted on a horse worth at least ten *écus*.[42] It should be added that waggons, eventually used for fighting in the Hussite fashion, and also artillery, especially from the mid-fifteenth century, necessitated hundreds of horses for every army of importance. Sometimes, however – as in Italy, Spain and even in Scotland and Normandy – the relative scarcity of horses entailed recourse to mules, asses, oxen or buffaloes for the baggage.

In these circumstances the importance of replacement of mounts can be appreciated. The restoration of horses (*restauratio equorum*), already attested in the thirteenth century, was practised in France and England until the last years of the fourteenth century, accompanied by prior inspection of the horses by the marshals and their delegates so that frauds in eventual reimbursement might be avoided. The formula 'and his war horses shall be suitably priced and according to the price he shall receive reimbursement if any of them are lost in the service of our lord' is regularly found in the war indentures agreed between John, duke of Lancaster, and different captains

---

[40] *Archaeologia, 17* (1814), 214–15.
[41] Jean Chartier, *Chronique de Charles VII*, ed. Vallet de Viriville, Paris 1858, ii.236.
[42] Brusten (448).

from 1367 to 1399.[43] In Italy it fell to the *bullator equorum* to compile a roll (*scriptio, descriptio*) enumerating the name, surname, rank, name of father and place of origin of every hired man as well as a description of the horses. Here, for example, is the lance of Braccio Baglioni of Perugia recruited by Pope Pius II in 1458: 'Magnificus dominus Bracchius de Balionibus de Perusio domini Malateste: equus baius obscurus sfaciatus balzanus posterioribus; Catelanus de Arimino domini Petri, rigazzus: equus leardus rotatus morphea supra nares, balzanus a dextra; Pandulfus de Mundavio Acapiti, plattus: equus leardus muschatus de rubeo per totum, parva morphea in oculis.'[44] Sometimes the registers even reproduce the markings on the horse.

Because of their value, soldiers were forced to look after their horses. If we believe Guillaume Gruel in his *Chronique d'Arthur de Richemont* this was particularly the concern of the French: 'You know that the French complain a great deal about their horses.'[45] The capture of warhorses was considered as valuable a booty as that of armour or even jewels. Calling to mind a robbery suffered by Scots in the service of Louis XI in the region of Vesoul in 1477, Molinet writes: 'They lost jewellery, gold chains, tableware and 100 horses worth 100 *écus* each and the haul was worth 30,000 *écus*.'[46] Naturally the price of warhorses (destriers, coursers, hackneys and rounceys) varied in accordance with the laws of supply and demand. This is remarked upon by Olivier de la Marche in 1445 just before the creation of the *ordonnance* companies by Charles VII:

> And it was at this time that horses of pedigree were so dearly sold in France that one never spoke of selling a horse of note but for 500, 1,000 or even 1,200 *reals*, and the cause of this dearness was that it was rumoured an *ordonnance* on soldiers was about to be issued by which they would be divided up amongst different captains and companies to be elected by name and surname. And every gentleman thought if he were to appear on a good horse he would be more easily recognized, sought after and received into the companies.[47]

Perhaps with the intention of improving the breed, but especially in order to have stronger and more speedy mounts, at the end of the Middle Ages in France there was a notable trade in importing horses. From Germany came powerful, strongly-built animals capable of carrying the most heavily armed soldier. Hackneys were imported from England, but the most prized horses came from Spain and Italy. This importation of Spanish horses, which is attested from at least the thirteenth century, is all the more remarkable since they do not seem to have been very numerous there. Hence, according to

---

[43] *John of Gaunt's Register 1379–1383*, ed. E. C. Lodge and R. Somerville, London 1937, i.13–26; N. B. Lewis, Indentures of retinue with John of Gaunt (413).
[44] da Mosto (498).
[45] Guillaume Gruel, *Chronique d'Arthur de Richemont*, ed. A. Le Vavasseur, Paris 1890, p.156.
[46] Molinet, *Chroniques*, i.180.
[47] Olivier de la Marche, *Mémoires*, ed. H. Beaune and J. d'Arbaumont, Paris 4 vols. 1883–88, ii.60.

Antoine de Lalaing in his account of the journey which Archduke Philip the Handsome made to Spain in 1501–2, the efforts made at the end of the fifteenth century by Isabella the Catholic to remedy this defect:

> This queen, seeing that the majority of her gentlemen rode mules and when it was necessary to arm and ride on horseback they were the least dexterous in the world, considering that there was a daily expectation of war with the French or the Moors or against both of them at the same time, ordered that no-one, however great he was, unless he was a priest or ecclesiastic, should ride a mule but a horse and that the horses should stand fifteen hands or more, in order to be better suited to war, and she even forced her husband, the king, to do this and ordered that those living on the borders of France should ride in our fashion and those who were neighbours of the Moors should ride short-stirruped (*à la jennette*).[48]

See page 37

THE TRANSFORMATION OF THE INFANTRY

About 1330–40 foot soldiers still constituted a very important part of armies in the majority of countries in the West. Military schemes dating from the first years of Philip VI's reign envisaged the possibility or necessity of recruiting three or four times more infantry than men-at-arms. During the summer campaign of 1335 against Scotland more than 15,000 combatants received wages from Edward III's household, of whom 3,200 were men-at-arms, 4,000 mounted archers and 7,800 infantry, half of whom were archers. A document from 1357 specifies 'the number of companions who mustered at the hospital of St James near Fontarrabia and at St Jean de Luz to go by sea to Normandy in the service of the lord king', Charles of Navarre. There were in all ten companies of unequal size, numbering 224 men-at-arms and 1,120 infantry. The equipment of the latter included amongst other items haubergeons (*lorigones*), bascinets, plate armour, pavois, bucklers (called *tablachos*) and crossbows.[49] At Florence in the fourteenth century a third of the infantry were armed with a lance and boar spear, a third with crossbows or light bows and a third with swords and large, broad pavois or targes or elongated shields. The Florentine code for hired men (1369) also stipulated the armament of a crossbowman who had to have not only a crossbow with rachet and bolts (*viretons*) but also a knife, a breastplate and headpiece.

   Despite all this it seems that from the middle of the fourteenth to the mid-fifteenth century infantry lost both its quantitative and qualitative importance, at least on certain battlefields and in some theatres of operation. This decline, or partial eclipse, is visible in the composition of the English

---

[48] L. P. Gachard, *Collection des voyages des souverains des Pays-Bas*, Brussels 1876, i.223.

[49] Again in 1376, Gaston Fébus, count of Foix, could raise from the viscounty of Béarn and from Marsan, alongside 1,000 horsemen, 1,200 infantry, half archers, half infantry fighting with axes, iron-tipped staves, scythes and swords.

expeditionary forces on the continent, to the extent that spearmen and pikeman disappeared, leaving in their stead an almost absolute predominance of archers who, if they dismounted to fight, generally moved about on horseback. Similarly in France John the Good and then Charles V and his successors considered it militarily worthless and politically dangerous to have massive recourse to urban or communal contingents and preferred, on the one hand, to employ crossbowmen from Spain, Italy and Provence and, on the other, to request from a number of towns small bodies of archers and shield-bearers (*pavesiers*). In Italy, too, in the first half of the fifteenth century, although always present, the infantry was clearly inferior in numbers to the cavalry. The league concluded in December 1425 between Florence and Venice provided for the latter to maintain in wartime 8,000 cavalry and only 3,000 infantry. There were two important wars during the pontificate of Martin V. One in 1421–2 involved 3,700 cavalry and 400 infantry, the other in 1428–29 3,000 cavalry and 1,100 infantry.[50] Typical in this respect is the *condotta* of 13 November 1432 agreed between Florence and Micheletto degli Attendoli, who was to provide 600 lances (some 1,800 horses) and 400 infantry made up of 200 crossbowmen, 100 infantry with 'long lances' and 100 *pavesari*.

The situation began to change towards the middle of the fifteenth century. Army leaders recognized or rediscovered the advantages of having a large infantry at their disposal. This was partly economic (particularly because of the lack of mounts, lighter baggage and defensive equipment two or three times less expensive than a horseman's armour), and worthwhile provided that the infantry was experienced, uniform and well organized. The militia of Franc-archers of Charles VII in 1448 was a response to this need – it created a reserve of about 8,000 men who, in principle, were to exercise regularly, know in advance which company to join at the appointed moment and under which captains they should serve. Parishes were to ensure the quality of their equipment. Thus the Franc-archers appeared to be a direct extension in selective form of the former general *arrière-ban*, no longer considered usable, or even as the extension to the countryside of the companies or fraternities of archers which numerous towns had encouraged from the second half of the fourteenth century. For a time it was believed that the Franc-archers (in fact a mixture of archers, crossbowmen, pikemen and, soon, handgunners) were a success. The War of the Public Weal had scarcely been brought to a conclusion before Louis XI doubled their numbers and extended the institution to regions of the kingdom which until then had not known it. But the victories of the Swiss over Charles the Bold convinced the king that the Franc-archers were not the best solution. The setback of Guinegatte (1479) finally made up his mind. He dismissed the Franc-archers and replaced them by Swiss mercenaries recruited at great cost, and by French infantry troops armed with

<hr />

[50] P. Partner, *The Papal State under Martin V*, London 1958, pp.157–8.

bows and with pikes (in the Swiss style) and halberds (in the German style), who were kept together all year not only so that they would always be available but also so that they would get used to serving together.[51] These first infantry regiments did not survive the accession of Charles VIII and the budgetary economies on which the French monarchy then resolved. Around 1488–92 in the wars against Brittany and Maximilian von Habsburg, the French infantry comprised Franc-archers and some Swiss companies as well as troops raised in Picardy, Normandy or Gascony just for the length of the campaign. Of variable quality, these infantry were at least numerous and a large army could total 20,000 or more.

Naturally Charles the Bold, always in the forefront of developments in the art of war, was very conscious of the need to have first-class infantry. Alongside various communal forces analogous to the French militia,[52] he attempted to keep infantry permanently available by incorporating them into his regular companies (*compaignies d'ordonnance*). The Abbeville ordinance of 31 July 1471 provided for the recruitment of 1,250 men-at-arms (and the same number of *coutiliers*), 3,750 mounted archers and an infantry of 1,250 cross-bowmen, 1,250 handgunners (*couleuvriniers*) and 1,250 pikemen. His idea was probably to imitate the tactics he had seen the Swiss, then in the service of John, duke of Calabria, use with great effect in the War of the Public Weal in 1465. Olivier de la Marche was to write later in his *Mémoires* that these latter 'did not fear the cavalry for there were generally three Swiss together, a pikeman, a handgunner and a crossbowman, and they were so expert in this matter that they helped one another when need arose, and there was on foot amongst them Savarot, an archer of the count of Charolais's bodyguard, who played his full part with the said Swiss.'[53] Later, perhaps in order to oppose the Cantons in the best possible conditions, perhaps also because of difficulties in replacing mounts, revictualling and the terrain, the proportion of

---

[51] Thomas Basin, *Histoire de Louis XI*, ed. C. Samaran and M. C. Garand, 3 vols. Paris 1963–72, iii.334. In place of the Franc-archers, Louis XI 'raised foot soldier called halberdiers who were armed with arms similar to the Franc-archers, but instead of bows carried long iron-tipped batons which the Flemings call pikes, or great axes like the German foot soldiers'.

[52] cf. Arch. dép. Nord, B 3515, 31 August 1472, order of the Burgundian Chancellor Hugonet to officers in Flanders, Brabant, Hainault, Namur and the castellany of Lille to appoint 'a man of good authority' who with all speed was to recruit 'by constraint and authority' up to 2,000 pikemen to reinforce (*raffreschir*) the duke of Burgundy's forces, especially those of the *ordonnance* companies, filling the gaps. These pikemen were to be 'the most expert in war who may be found and who were of an age and physical strength to endure and undertake the hardships, duties and operations required and necessary in waging war' ('des plus esperts a la guerre que trouver se pourront et qui aient l'eaige et la corpulance pour endurer et supporter les peines, diligences et travaulx requis et necessaires en fait de guerre'). They were to receive five francs to equip themselves with 'haubergeon jackets with stiffened sleeves and on the right arm metal strips over the mail guard' ('jacquettes de hauberjons a manches de placquart et au bras destre de clincques de fer sur le maille a petites gardes'). On the left arm there was no protection so that they could more easily carry a targe, if required to do so.

[53] Olivier de la Marche, *Mémoires*, iii.22–3.

infantry in the Burgundian *lance fournie* increased yet further. For every man-at-arms there were nine infantry, three archers, three pikemen and three handgunners or crossbowmen.

In Castile at the time of the conquest of Granada the *peones* (foot soldiers) largely outnumbered the *jinetes*, as the figures show:[54]

Expedition	Jinetes	Peones
1485	11,000	25,000
1486	12,000	40,000
1487	11,000	45,000
1489	13,000	40,000

In the third quarter of the fifteenth century in Italy the following types of infantry (*fanti*) may be found:

1   *Lanceri*, with short or long lances, depending on circumstances.

2   *Balestrieri*, armed with simple crossbows or with more advanced ones (*ad molinellum*, with wheels and rachets).

3   *Arceri*, archers, though those of English origin almost completely disappeared after 1430.

4   *Picchieri*, armed with pikes.

5   *Rotularii*, using small round shields.

6   *Targhieri* or *targhe*, acting as shield-bearers in conjunction with archers.

7   *Schiopettari* or *schioppeteri*, handgunners armed with bronze or iron *scopetti*.

For a long time these latter were only garrison troops, charged with defending towns and strongholds. But from 1430–40 they began to take part in expeditions. In 1448, at the battle of Caravaggio, Francesco Sforza had in his army so many *schioppeteri* they had great difficulty in seeing each other because of the smoke.[55]

But it was obviously the infantry of the old leagues of Upper Germany which provided the most remarkable model. The military reputation of the Swiss was established early, as is evidenced by the testimony at the beginning of the fourteenth century of the Franciscan John of Winterthur, who speaks with admiration of their halberds in his chronicle. Then the mountainous cantons of central Switzerland (Uri, Schwyz and Unterwalden), the original core of the Helvetic confederation, began to form a reservoir of infantry mercenaries, for the service of different foreign powers, but also and perhaps chiefly for the towns of the plain like Zurich and Berne. In 1339 at the battle

---

[54] M. A. Ladero Quesada, *Castilla y la conquista del reino de Granada* (532).

[55] Mallett (512), p.157. In 1490 the Council of Ten at Venice decided to substitute handguns (*scopetti*) for crossbows. At the end of the fifteenth century in the wars between the Spanish and French for possession of the kingdom of Naples, mounted *schiopetteri* replaced mounted crossbowmen.

of Laupen against the Austrian army, this latter city placed a contingent of highlanders in the vanguard of its force.

After the victory at Sempach (1386) the movement grew still more quickly. The first prohibitions on foreign service issued by the Diets begin to appear. Henceforward, too, the export of soldiers did not simply concern the mountainous regions but also the towns and their surrounding countryside. From 1422 Zurich prevented its citizens and subjects from 'running to the war' in the pay of either a Confederate or a foreign power. The first evidence of an official demand coming from abroad appears in 1424: the ambassadors of Florence asked the Diet of the Confederates to agree to an aid of 10,000 paid troops. Although the future Louis XI, at the head of the *Ecorcheurs*, had faced and beaten Swiss troops at the battle of St Jakob-an-der-Birs, near Basle in 1444,[56] their reputation in France dated from the battle of Montlhéry (1465) when Commynes mentions alongside the Leaguers the presence of 'five hundred Swiss infantry troops, who were the first to be seen in this realm. They were the ones whose reputation prepared the way for those who came afterwards, because they conducted themselves very bravely in every situation where they found themselves.'[57]

With a certain time-lag, the whole of the Germanic world also experienced an incontestable rise in the importance of infantry. At the Diet of Nuremberg in 1422 Emperor Sigismund and the princes agreed to raise two armies against the Hussites. One was to fight until they were completely crushed and the other was to raise the siege of the fortress of Karlstein. Whilst the first did include some cavalrymen and archers (the latter being more numerous than the former), in the second the preponderance of infantry was overwhelming: 1,970 men-at-arms to 34,700 foot soldiers. In fact the estimated numbers were not achieved and the imperial forces totalled only 1,656 horsemen (some 552 lances) and 31,000 foot.

The most important development in the last years of the fifteenth century was the appearance of the lansquenets (*Landsknechte*). This has been explained by the fact that traditionally, at least in Upper Germany, there existed groups of young men, the warrior *Knabenschaften*, bands of companions (*Knechte*), who sometimes practised private warfare, preying on travellers, harvests and herds for their own benefit, and sometimes putting themselves at the service of towns, for example when the towns, confederated

---

[56] On this battle see the remarks of Mathieu d'Escouchy (*Chronique*, ed. G. du Fresne de Beaucourt, Paris 3 vols. 1863–64, i.20), 'I was told about this by several nobles who had fought in this battle and who had previously fought in wars in France at numerous battles and encounters with the English as well as against others, but in their time they had never seen nor met men who resisted so strongly or were so willing to sacrifice their lives' ('Me fut dit ceste matiere de aucuns nobles hommes qui avoient esté a ceste journee et qui avoient esté aultres fois es guerres de France, en pluseurs journees et rencontres tant contre les Anglois comme aultres, mais leur temps avoient veu ne trouvé gens de sy grant defense ne tant oultrageux de habandonner leurs vyes').

[57] Commynes, *Mémoires*, i.48 (cf. *Memoirs*, tr. Jones, pp.84–5).

in leagues, were forced to fight against the princes or knightly alliances. Sometimes these energetic fraternities of wild young men were called 'liberties'. In 1376, for example, the Swabian towns disposed of 'many foot soldiers of the liberty who possessed thick jacks, pikes and crossbows'.[58] At least to begin with the great majority of lansquenets originated in Upper Germany, bordering Switzerland from the Vorarlberg to the Sundgau. Given these underlying sociological facts, the state could work on them; that is to say, Maximilian von Habsburg could enroll these men, following the advice of the former faithful councillors of Charles the Bold like the counts of Romont and Nassau, who had witnessed the defeats suffered by their master at the hands of the Swiss. It was 'to wake up the French' on the Flemish frontier in 1486 that the king of the Romans employed Swiss for the first time and also lansquenets (*Landsknechte*), that is 'companions of the country' as opposed to hired troops, originating in Bohemia (called *Trabanten*), or Swiss. 'He was counselled to collect a great force of warriors in which there should be three or four thousand Swiss and the same number of German *Landsknechte*, together with many Picards, Hainaulters and others, both on horse and foot, up to a total of fourteen or fifteen thousand men, under the command of my lord Philip of Cleves, the prince of Chimay, the count of Nassau and other chiefs and war captains.'[59] In the previous year Molinet had mentioned the entry into Ghent 'in very fine order and all on foot' of 'my lord the count of Nassau, the lord of Montigni, the lord of Palma and other leaders of 5,000 Germans marching eight abreast'.[60]

Thus around 1500 several countries in the West were using an infantry which was very different from the foot soldiers who had been traditionally known at all periods of the Middle Ages, an infantry collected on a massive scale who specialized and were well qualified to fight on foot from corps tactically organized in depth. Because of this depth, these units were better able to resist cavalry attacks, forcing them in turn to adopt new forms of combat.

GUNPOWDER

Contemporaries rapidly became aware of the important changes which artillery using gunpowder introduced into the art of war. It was of these technological innovations that Jean de Bueil was thinking when he wrote in *Le Jouvencel*: 'From one day to the next and larger and larger grow the

---

[58] G. Franz, Von Ursprung und Brauchtum des Landsknechte (370).

[59] Molinet, *Chroniques*, i.543.

[60] *Ibid*, p.463. In 1486, 950 ash-wood pikes 22 or 24 ft long were purchased 'ferrez de bon fer . . . a la nouvelle faichon . . . pour distribuer aux Aulemans picquenaires' in Maximilian's army 'for the expedition to Artois and to serve in his wars against the king of France'.

machines devised by men which change the way in which things are done . . .
and at present there may be found many things and clever devices which
were neither known nor used in former times.'[61]

Technical aspects

Accounts of the invention and appearance of gunpowder, cannons and munitions quickly became wrapped in myths and legends. Petrarch, because of his
reverence for Greco-Roman civilization, thought that the Ancients could not
have been ignorant of the use of gunpowder. The same sentiment occurred to
Pope Pius II when he wrote the Duke Federigo of Urbino, 'In Homer and
Virgil we may find descriptions of all the weapons used in our age.' According to the *De re militari* of Valturio (1472), Archimedes was the inventor of
cannons, though it is true that at the same period Francesco di Giorgio
Martini remarked that if the Ancients had used cannons, gunloops ought to
have been discovered in the remains of their fortifications.[62]

Authors who deplored the invention of artillery and powder attributed this
to foreigners, or, better still, to Infidels like the Turks or Chinese. Flavio
Biondo in *Roma Triumphans* (1455–63) held a German of the mid-fourteenth
century responsible for the discovery of gunpowder and dated its first usage
to the war of Chioggia between Genoa and Venice (1378–81). In 1493
Antonio Cornazano completed the legend: this German was an alchemist
monk who taught the Venetians in 1380. Later it was thought he had lived at
the end of the thirteenth century, and he was given the name Berthold
Schwarz of Fribourg. Spanish sources present a different version: it was the
Moors who first used gunpowder in 1343 in the war against Alfonso XI.

It became traditional to insist on the diabolical character of the invention.
Around 1390, John Mirfield spoke of 'this warlike or diabolical instrument
commonly called a cannon (*gonne*)'. Francesco di Giorgio, although a military
engineer, approved of those who attributed the discovery 'not to human but
to devilish agency'. In the fifteenth century *Le livre du secret de l'artillerye et
canonnerye* attributed it to 'master Bertran, the great necromancer and alchemist', though here chance played the leading role. At the start his idea had
been to obtain 'a fine colour resembling gold for the manufacture of which he
took saltpetre, sulphur, lead and oil which he mixed together and put in a
covered earthenware pot to boil on the fire'. Once the ingredients had been
heated the pot naturally exploded. The alchemist began the experiment again
using a carefully sealed copper pot. He began to appreciate the use to which
the explosive force could be put, modified the proportions and 'made an
engine in the fashion of a cannon'. In this way the 'art of cannonry' was
discovered.[63] The link between magic and artillery still appears in the story

---

[61] de Bueil (9), i.17.
[62] J. R. Hale, Gunpowder and the Renaissance (689).
[63] Bib. Nat., MS français 2015.

of the 'bombadier' from Metz, Camoufle, of whom it was said around 1437 'that he shot three times a day where he wished using magical arts'.[64]

To return to reality as far as we are able: the first mention of the formula for gunpowder occurs in a Chinese work of 1044, the *Wujung Zongyao*. This powder was used to propel smoke, incendiary and explosive bombs. At the end of the thirteenth century the Mongols used it on a large scale, for example at the time of their attempted invasions of Japan in 1274 and 1281. Soon projectiles (chiefly fire-arrows) were thrown by use of powder after having been placed in guidance tubes made from thick bamboo, wood, iron or bronze. These inventions and techniques were transmitted to the West through the mediation of the Muslim world. An Andalusian botanist who died at Damascus in 1248 called saltpetre 'Chinese snow'. In Persia the same substance was called 'Chinese salt'. Perhaps the Mongols used rudimentary firearms at the battle of Sajo in Hungary (1241). From the middle of the thirteenth century the Moors put powder in various projectiles thrown by means of catapults and trébuchets. In the West the first known recipe for gunpowder is that of Roger Bacon (1267).

The presence of primitive guns (*sclopeti, sclopi:* blunderbuss) is mentioned at the time of the defence of Forli by Guido de Montefeltre in 1284, though this is an isolated and suspect reference. The first certain information dates from some 40 years later. A representation of a cannon in the form of a large pot, placed horizontally on a trestle, from the mouth of which a sort of large arrow emerges can be found in an illumination of the *De notabilitatibus, sapientiis et prudentiis* of Walter of Milemete.[65] It is one of those weapons used for throwing quarrels (*carreaux* or *garrots*) which are already mentioned fairly frequently by the mid-fourteenth century and more so later on. As for the word cannon, whose etymology goes back to the Greek *kanun* and Latin *canna*, with the meaning 'tube', it appears for the first time in a Florentine document under the date 11 February 1326 in which the Signori appointed two men 'ad faciendum et fieri faciendum . . . pilas seu palloctas ferreas et canones de metallo pro ipsis canonibus et palloctis habendis et operandis'.[66] The new artillery had, perhaps, been employed during the war against Metz in 1324, and was certainly used in 1331 by two German knights at the siege of Cividale (Friuli). In 1341 the town of Lille had its *maistre de tonnoire*. Aix-la-Chapelle in 1346 owned a *busa ferrea ad sagittandum tonitrum*. Two years later, Deventer possessed three *dunrebussen*. In 1341 Lucca gave its

---

[64] Philippe de Vigneulles, *Chronique*, ed. C. Bruneau, Metz 4 vols. 1927–33, ii.244.
[65] Christ Church, Oxford, MS 92, f.70v. (a well-known miniature reproduced, among others by J. F. Finó, *Forteresses de la France médiévale* (783), 291, figure 68). Another slightly later but equally well-known miniature showing a similar cannon is found in a manuscript of the *De secretis secretorum* of the Pseudo-Aristotle (BL, Add. MS. 47680, f.44v, reproduced for example n J. Gimpel, *Les batisseurs de cathédrales*, Paris 1958, p.178).
[66] Finó (783), p.290: 'to make and cause to be made . . . balls or iron bullets and metal cannons or the said cannons and tubes to have and use'.

captain, Ghiberto da Fogliano, 'an iron cannon to fire iron balls', while two blacksmiths of Brescia received the raw materials to forge a 'tube for firing balls' and an 'iron cannon tube and iron balls'.[67] In the Papal States cannons and bombards are mentioned in 1350 during a war in the Romagna. The accounts allude to '1,050 lbs of wrought and pig iron for manufacturing balls for the bombards' and to '226 iron balls for the bombards', weighing 88 lbs.[68] Not only did the English almost certainly set off powder and fire projectiles at the battle of Crécy (1346), but for the siege of Calais (1346–47) ten cannons, ribaudequins, lead-balls and gunpowder were despatched from London. A document dated 10 May 1346 speaks of 912 lbs of saltpetre and 886 lbs of sulphur bought from a London apothecary for the king's guns ('ad opus ipsius regis pro gunnis suis').[69] In France the first mentions of firearms date from 1338. At the siege of Cambrai in 1340 Hugues, lord of Cardaillac, a noble who had specialized in the new weapon, made ten cannons for the modest sum of 25 *l.* 2*s.* 6*d. t.*, whilst the saltpetre and live sulphur necessary for the use of these pieces cost 11 *l.* 4*s.* 3*d. t.* In 1346 the same lord provided 22 cannons for the defence of the castle of Bioule (Tarn-et-Garonne). On 29 April 1345 *Ramundus Arquerii*, the king of France's artiller at Toulouse, acknowledged receipt of a certain sum of money for 'two iron cannons, 200 lead balls and 8 lbs of powder'.[70]

Thus, although it is not possible to reconstruct the route, in 20 years the invention had spread throughout the West, perhaps starting from Italy. It is true that peripheral regions remained ignorant of it for a long time to come – the first mention of artillery in Scotland is not until 1384. But after the middle of the fourteenth century descriptions of cannons appear in both didactic treatises and narrative sources. One of the first was that which Jean Buridan introduced into his *Questiones de libris Meteorologicorum Aristotelis*: 'The force of the wind is revealed in those instruments called cannons (*canalibus*) which emit great arrows or lead balls through the blast set off by a little powder with so much force that no arms can with-hold them.'[71] In a more detailed fashion the *Chronicon Tarvisium* (1376) evokes:

these bombards which have never previously been seen and of which no-one in Italy has ever spoken like those which the Venetians have marvellously wrought. The bombard is in truth a very robust iron weapon, having at the front a large chamber into which a round stone the same shape as the duct is placed, and at the back a cannon twice as long as the chamber to which it is most tightly bound, into which a black powder is put made from saltpetre,

[67] F. Cognasso, *L'Italia nel Rinascimento*, Turin 1965.
[68] A. Pasquali-Lasagni and E. Stefanelli, Note di storia dell'artigliera (699).
[69] T. F. Tout, Firearms in England (706).
[70] Dom Cl. Devic and Dom J. Vaissete, *Histoire générale de Languedoc*, new edn. by A. Molinier et al., Toulouse, 16 vols. 1872–1904, x.967–8.
[71] E. Faral, Jean Buridan, maître ès arts de l'Université de Paris, *Histoire littéraire de la France*, 28 (1950), 2e partie, 83.

sulphur and charcoal through an opening in the cannon near its mouth. Once this opening at the mouth is sealed by means of a wooden bung driven into the interior and the round stone has been introduced at the other end, it is fired through a small opening in the cannon[72] and through the force of the ignited powder the stone is cast with great violence.[73]

For a long period the majority of cannons were of small dimensions, as this table of weights of 73 cannons manufactured for Richard II of England by William Woodward between 1382 and 1388 shows:[74]

1 cannon weighing between 665 and 737 lbs
47 'large cannons', average weight 380 lbs
5 cannons weighing 318 lbs each
4 'copper cannons' weighing 150 lbs each
7 'small cannons' at 49 lbs each
9 'small cannons' at 43 lbs each

The consumption of powder also remained very modest. In 1375 at the siege of Saint-Sauveur-le-Vicomte by the army of Charles V only 31 lbs of powder were needed to load three 'great iron cannons', firing stones, 24 copper cannons firing lead balls and five iron cannons also firing lead shot. In 1376–77 the charge for 'an iron cannon firing 60 lbs' was a pound and a half of powder. In 1383 for the 'army on the sea', the barges were provided with 'IIII gros canons enfustés fournis de chevilles de fer et de charnieres avec IIII quevalez de bois, VIII^{xx}VI livres de poudre et VIII^{xx} pieres pour yceulx canons', that is with one pound of powder for each shot.[75]

Exceptionally weapons with very large calibres were made. There was one at Mons in 1375 weighing 9,500 lbs.[76] Changes occurred on a wide scale, however, at the beginning of the fifteenth century. In 1410 Christine de Pisan advised the use of four large cannons, with their own names, of which the most important fired balls weighing 400 to 500 lbs,[77] for the assault on a very strong place. From this time onwards the largest pieces were, in effect, identified by a particular name intended to sow fear or referring to the circumstances of their manufacture, their first use or the rank of their owner. Inscriptions, sometimes in verse, were borne on the barrel:

Dergon suis, serpent venimeux,	I am Dragon the venomous serpent
Desirant par coups furieux	who desires with furious blows
Ennemis de nous esloigner.	to drive off our enemies.
Jehan le Noir, maistre canonnier	John the Black, master gunner,

[72] That is the touch-hole.
[73] J. R. Partington, *History of Greek Fire and Gunpowder* (698), 116–18.
[74] Tout (706).
[75] Bib. Nat., MS français 26019 no.407.
[76] C. Gaier, *L'industrie et le commerce des armes* (579), p.287.
[77] Christine de Pizan, *L'art de chevalerie* (12). This part of Christine's work was borrowed by de Bueil (9), ii.46.

et Conrard, Coin, Cradinteur,	Conrad, Coin and Cradinteur
Euls ensemble maistres fondeurs,	all together master founders
Me firent par terme prefix	made me on time
Mil IIII^c septante six.[78]	in 1476.

In short, just like ships and bells, great cannons acquired a personality and, in some sense, came alive.

That the counsel furnished by Christine de Pisan was not simply theoretical is proved by the fact that in the previous year five 'makers of bombards and cannons' drew up a contract with John the Fearless, duke of Burgundy, to found at Auxonne a great bronze bombard weighing 6,900 lbs for which stone balls each of 320 lbs were to be provided. In 1412 at Carcassonne there was talk of a bombard weighing 10,000 lbs. Mons Meg, an iron bombard, today conserved at Edinburgh castle, was ordered in 1449 by Philip the Good, duke of Burgundy, from Jean Cambier, 'artillery merchant', for the sum of 1,536 *l.* 2*s.* The cannon at the time was 15 ft long and weighed 15,366 lbs. According to an eighteenth-century estimate, a powder charge of 105 lbs was necessary to fire its stone ball of 549 lbs. The bombard De dulle Griet (Mad Margot), which is still to be seen in the market place at Ghent, is over 5 m long, has a diameter of 0.64 m and weighs 16,400 kg. Another monstrous piece was the 'great forged bombard' which Philip the Good had made in 1457–58 'in his household at Lebbre in Brabant by Jacquemin de l'Espine, maker of bombards and other engines'. This cannon contained between 33,000 lbs and 34,000 lbs of metal and fired stone balls 17 inches (*pouces*) in diameter (*en croisée*). 'In order to tip up the barrel of the said bombard so that it might be more accurately fired', a lead weight of 800 lbs was provided. One of the heaviest pieces of artillery was that which the duke of Brabant had forged at Brussels in 1409–11 and which attained 35 tons, only slightly less than the 40 tons of Raja Gopal, an enormous Moghul cannon preserved at Tandjore in Madras province.[79]

Whilst in the fourteenth century, at least in France, two terms only – cannon and bombard – were used to describe firearms, in the fifteenth century the vocabulary expanded, with mention *c.*1410 of culverin and veuglaire; *c.*1430 of serpentine, crapaudeaux and crapaudines; *c.*1460 of courtauds and mortars; *c.*1470 of hacquebutes and arquebus; and *c.*1480 of faucons and fauconneaux. From the work of Francesco di Giorgio Martini (1487–92) it is possible to construct a table, though idealized, to show the various forms of artillery (table 4).

There were other changes, too, which affected the artillery. In place of cannons made by beating together strips of forged iron, pieces were made by founding iron.[80] 'The liquid metal was poured into a mould in the form of a

---

[78] Bib. Nat., MS Nouv. acq. française 22715, f.10.

[79] Gaier (579), p.242.

[80] As late as 1456 at Rennes a great bombard which had burst was made from 38 bars and 33 iron circles (J-P. Leguay, *La ville de Rennes au XVe siècle à travers les comptes des Miseurs*, Paris 1969, p.284).

TABLE 4 Types of cannon and gun, after Francesco di Giorgio Martini

	Length (*feet*)	Nature of projectile	Weight of projectile (*lbs*)	Percentage of powder relative to weight of projectile
Bombard	15–20	stone	300	16
Mortar	5 or 6	stone	200–300	16
Medium or common bombard	10	stone	50	16
Courtaud	12	stone	60–100	16
Passe-volant	18	lead.or iron balls	16	10
Basilisk	22–25	bronze or iron balls	20	10
Cerbottana	8–10	lead	2–3	10
Espingarde	8	stone	10–15	10
Arquebus	3–4	lead	6 oz.	50
Blunderbuss	2–3	lead	4–6 *octavi*	80–100

Source: C. Promis, *Memorias historicas sobre el arte del ingeniero y del artillero en Italia y de los escritores militares de aquel pais desde 1285 a 1560*, Madrid 1882, pp.104–5.

hollow cylinder whose axis was filled by a core' or mandrel.[81] Boring by means of a steel-tipped drill ensured the regularity of the bore. By using the same moulds, or moulds of similar dimensions, calibres could be regulated. In addition, as for bells, bronze was employed in an alloy termed *mitaille* or *mitaille d'airain* in which a higher proportion of copper and smaller proportion of tin was used. Bell-founders could easily be transformed into cannon-founders and in emergencies bells could be melted down to make cannons. For example, a contract was drawn up in 1488 between the town of Rennes and a cannoneer and gunfounder and a cannoneer and blacksmith. The first pair was to found falcons, a bell and two boxes to serve as the firing chamber of a forged, iron serpentine. They received the 'metal and copper' necessary for this, weighing some 6,000 lbs. The second pair was to forge two iron serpentines, one of which was to use the copper chamber made by the first pair and was breech-loaded. The other would be all of a piece, the charge being muzzle-loaded, and provided with trunnions so that it could be carried on a wheeled gun-carriage. The two serpentines 'fired iron shot'.[82]

Improvements were made in transport and the setting up of batteries. For a long time artillery pieces (with the exception of handguns and culverins which appeared at the end of the fourteenth century) were carried in carts and waggons, generally having four wheels, and they had to be set up before they could be fired. Cannons were layed on a trestle or frame. However, from the mid-fifteenth century, pieces with trunnions are mentioned, resting on a

[81] Finó (783), p.300.
[82] *Documents inédits sur le complot breton de M.CCCC.XC.II*, ed. A. de la Borderie, Nantes 1884 (*Archives de Bretagne*, ii), 145 no. liv.

carriage which was mounted on a two-wheeled axle. On 19 August 1456 the town of Rouen bought a cannon weighing 100 lbs 'in the form of a small serpentine of bronze, firing little lead bullets, mounted and carried on two wooden wheels'.[83] In 1465–66 a carpenter at Nevers was ordered to make eight wheels, four medium-sized ones for a large iron bombard (which implies it was placed on a cart) and four others of large dimension for two serpentines.[84] In 1490 the castle of Angers received for storage three big serpentine cannons weighing about 7,000 lbs and fitted with six large wheels. Gradually an artillery appeared which was drawn, easily arranged in batteries and taken from place to place, as can be seen from numerous representations in manuscript miniatures from about 1470 and from some surviving examples from the booty captured by the Swiss from Charles the Bold at the battle of Grandson in 1476.[85]

For a long time it was essential to use plugs to seal the opening of the chamber in which the powder charge was placed. A fifteenth-century cannonry manual describes the process at length: 'If you wish to make good plugs for bombards, take good dry alder or willow wood and shape them so that they are thinner at the front than at the back so that when you knock a plug into the chamber of a *baston* it goes in and fits exactly, nor should any of the plug protrude from the chamber.' The plugs had to be made of wood which would expand with the vapour created by the combustion of the powder. At the proper moment the pressure would become too strong and the plug would jump out, rather like a champagne cork, liberating the explosive force of the powder which would then propel the cannon ball. One was advised to divide the internal length of the chamber into five equal parts: the first, close to the opening, was reserved for the plug, the second was left empty, the last three were filled with powder.[86]

It seems that in France at least by the end of the fifteenth century the use of the plug for certain pieces had been abandoned. Perhaps already such an instantaneous explosion of the powder had been achieved that it was no longer necessary to build up the pressure. Perhaps, too, the use of iron balls, perfectly shaped to the calibre of the pieces, sufficed to prevent the gas from escaping too quickly. In any event, cannons are mentioned which are all of one piece, without separate chambers. First of all powder was put into the bottom of the tube by means of 'pinewood rods called chargers', and then the ball was put in the muzzle.[87]

---

[83] *Ville de Rouen. Inventaire-sommaire des archives communales antérieures à 1790*, ed. C. de Robillard de Beaurepaire. Rouen 1887, *Délibérations*, i.60.

[84] Arch. mun., Nevers, CC 60, f.13r.

[85] Deuchler (551).

[86] Bib. Nat., MS français 2015, f.17r.

[87] cf. Biringuccio, *La pyrotechnie*, tr. J. Vincent, Paris 1572: 'Pour charger vostre piece on fait un instrument que les canonniers appellent une quaisse, de lames de fer, ou de cuivre, laquelle est aussi longue trois fois comme le diametre du boulet, dans lequel on met la pointe d'une broche, sur laquelle avec la quaisse on met poule plain de pouldre qu'on poulse jusques au fon

For the first projectiles in the mid-fourteenth century lead and iron were employed. But the majority of bullets, especially above a certain dimension, rapidly came to be made of stone – sandstone, marble, alabaster etc. Stone-cutters prepared munitions in advance, using a template or 'patron' made of wood, paper or parchment. Then iron bullets made their reappearance. In 1418 the town of Ghent acquired 7,200 cast-iron cannonballs.[88] Recourse to cast iron became very frequent in the French royal artillery from the second half of the reign of Charles VII. It is possible that the intervention of the Bureau brothers, Jean and Gaspard, was decisive.[89] The trend increased under Louis XI and in 1467 the king ordered Michau Baudouin to cast 1,000 iron cannon balls for each of his great serpentines and 100 for each of his bombards. Charles the Bold did not remain inactive; his great culverins used iron balls (*galets*). In 1473, 1,335 cast iron balls were purchased. Strangely, this innovation was not known beyond the Alps. If Biringuccio may be believed, Charles VIII 'was the first to show us in Italy iron cannon balls when he went to besiege Naples and to drive out King Ferrante in 1495'.[90]

Even the small *bastons* were perfected. In the middle of the fifteenth century in Germany a flint-lock mechanism was introduced for arquebuses (*hacquebutes*).[91] Two developments occurred. On the one hand the weight of the projectile diminished in proportion to the total weight of the cannon, and on the other, the weight of the powder rose in proportion to that of the projectile. This can be seen in tables 5 and 6, which compare Milanese bombards in 1472 with the English artillery of Henry VII and Henry VIII.

At the end of the fifteenth century and the beginning of the sixteenth giganticism had been renounced for pieces of standard size, which were robust, easy to transport, capable of firing at a relatively high frequency and using manageable projectiles propelled by appreciable quantities of powder. Finally, experiments to achieve medium range by level firing were made.[92]

---

du canon, et tournant la main vostre pouldre vient a tomber et a sortir hors de la quaisse que vous retirerez pour continuer en ceste facon deux ou trois fois selon la finesse et bonte de la pouldre, ou selon la grandeur de la quaisse, vous advertissant d'y en mettre les deux tiers de la pesanteur du boulet.'

[88] Gaier (579), p.96, n.110.

[89] H. Dubled, L'artillerie royale française (682).

[90] Quoted by V. Gay and H. Stein, *Glossaire archéologique* (554), i.190 B.

[91] C. Gaier, *Mise à feu et munitions des armes portatives*, Liège and Brussels 1969, pp.12–13.

[92] Naturally some greater ranges are mentioned here and there. At the siege of Ham in 1411 the Flemings fired by means of the 'Grosse griele' a stone 'bigger than a barrel' ('plus grosse qu'une tonnel') which missed the town and landed beyond the Somme: Gay and Stein, (554), i.172 A. In 1465, according to Commynes, Louis XI 'had good artillery on the walls of Paris which fired several shots as far as our army, which was a remarkable feat for it was two leagues away. But I am pretty sure that they had elevated the muzzles of the cannons very high' (*Mémoires*, i.72; cf. *Memoirs*, tr. Jones, p.100). In 1479 a huge bombard made the same year at Tours shot 500 lbs of iron from the Bastille Saint-Antoine as far as the gibbet on the bridge at Charenton (Jean de Roye, *Chronique scandaleuse*, ed. B. de Mandrot, Paris 2 vols. 1894–95, ii.81–2).

TABLE 5   Milanese bombards in 1472

Charge of powder (lbs)	Weight of ball (lbs)	Percentage weight of powder relative to weight of ball
50	400	12.5
40	300	13.3
33	225	14.6
100	626	15.9

The artillery of Francis I as shown in table 7 appears to be much closer to the artillery of Charles VIII than his had been to the artillery of Charles VII.[93]

Quantitative aspects

For a long period artillery pieces were not just small and ineffective; they were also fairly rare. However, from 1360–70 many towns throughout the West and practically all great powers possessed their arsenals. The receiver of Ponthieu for the king of England in 1368–9 bought for various places in the county 20 copper cannons, 5 iron ones, 215 lbs of saltpetre, sulphur and amber for making powder and 1,300 large garrots (quarrels or bolts) for the cannons.[94] For the expedition which was planned for France in 1372, the English government provided 29 iron cannons and 1,059 lbs of saltpetre. In the same year the castle of Lille had 59 lbs of powder, 652 lbs of saltpetre and

TABLE 6   English artillery at the end of the fifteenth and beginning of the sixteenth century

	Charge of powder (lbs)	Weight of ball (lbs)	Percentage weight of powder relative to weight of ball
Bombard	80	260	30.77
Courtaud	40	60	66.66
Culverin	22	20	110
'Nuremberg' and 'Apostle'	20	20	100
Lizard	14	12	117
Mignon	8	8	100
Serpentine	7	6	117
Falcon	1	1	100

[93] BL, Add. MS 23222.
[94] S. Storey-Challenger, L'administration anglaise du Ponthieu après le traité de Brétigny 1361–1369, Abbeville 1975, p.286.

TABLE 7   French artillery c.1530–40

	Total weight (lbs)	Weight of metal (lbs)	Weight of ball (lbs)	Weight of ball relative to metal (lbs) – %	Charge of powder (lbs)	Percentage weight of powder relative to ball	Number of rounds per day	Range in paces 'de pointe en blanc'
Cannon	8,200	5,000	23	4.6	20	87	100	500
Large culverin	6,380	4,000	15.25	3.8	10	66.6	100	700
Bastard culverin	4,773	2,500	7.25	2.9	5.0	68.9	140	500
Medium culverin	2,575	1,500	2.5	1.6	2.5	100	160	400
Falcon	1,240	800	1.5	1.8	1.5	100	200	300
Small falcon	880	500	0.75	1.5			250	200
Arquebus with stand (à croc)	50	45	0.1	2.0	0.1	100	300	120

Source: BL, Add. MS 23222.

114 lbs of sulphur in stock. Ghent acquired 70 firearms in 1380; Ypres bought 52 in 1383. Between 1372 and 1382 Malines increased its stock on average by 14 cannons a year.[95] By the end of the century the French garrisons in the north of the kingdom watching over Calais regularly included a cannoneer for each fortress.

/   A change occurred at the turn of the century. In 1406, in preparation for the siege of Calais, the Franco-Burgundian army employed by the lowest estimate the services of some 50 gunners. More than 20,000 lbs of powder was purchased. Four years later Christine de Pisan estimated that the defence of a place necessitated the use of 12 stone-firing cannons, from 1,000 to 1,500 lbs of powder and, for munitions, 3,000 lbs of lead for bullets and 200 stones. As for attack, in her opinion, 128 cannons, 1,170 stones, 5,000 lbs of leadshot and 30,000 lbs of powder were needed. In 1417 the town council of Dijon judged that the acquisition of 5,000 lbs of powder was necessary for the town's defence. In 1431, at the time of the crusade against the Hussites, the Imperial German army could count on 100 bombards.

/   A good criterion for measuring the importance of artillery is provided by the demand for powder. In 1413 François Pastoreau, a Parisian merchant, sold to John the Fearless some 10,000 lbs of powder, saltpetre and sulphur. A document from 1421–22 affirms that it was possible to procure immediately in Paris the raw materials to provide between 20,000 and 25,000 lbs of powder.[96]

It is even possible in some cases to know how much powder was used during military enterprises. In 1425 Lancelot de Lisle, governor of Chartres and marshal of the earl of Salisbury's army, in the name of Henry VI of England, received from John Harbotel, master of the Regent Bedford's artillery ordnance, 1,000 lbs of powder for the siege of Beaumont, 3,000 lbs for that of Le Mans, 2,800 lbs for that of Sainte-Suzanne and 5,800 lbs for that of Mayenne. At the siege of Compiègne in 1430 the army of Philip the Good expended 17,000 lbs of powder as opposed to the 10,000 lbs used in the Calais campaign of 1436.[97]

There was a new quantitative advance in the second half of the fifteenth
/   century. The budget for the daily running of the artillery (*Ordinaire de l'artillerie*) almost quintupled during the reign of Louis XI. Towns perceived even more clearly their interest in increasing their artillery. In 1452–53 the powder reserves of Rennes exceeded 5,000 lbs. From 1450–92 the town acquired 45 cannons, 32 serpentines, 65 culverins, 149 arquebuses, 7 veuglaires and 45 falcons. Ghent had 189 pieces of all calibres available in 1456 and 486 in 1479. For Cologne the figures are 348 in 1468, for Nuremberg 2,230 in 1462, and for Strasbourg 585 in 1476.

At the end of the fifteenth century, according to witnesses in the Italian

[95] Gaier (579), p.92.
[96] *Ibid.*, pp.327–33.
[97] cf. C. T. Allmand, L'artillerie de l'armée anglaise (677b).

wars, the French artillery was the best in the world both in importance and in quality. An account of 1489 shows that Charles VIII had five artillery bands, comprising dozens of gunners, about 150 pieces, thousands of horses and tens of thousands of pounds of powder. At this date the artillery expenses represented 8 per cent of the total military expenses of the French monarchy as against 6 per cent in 1482.[98] Even a small power like the duchy of Brittany could not allow itself to remain unarmed. An inventory in 1495, immediately after its annexation to France, lists 707 pieces deposited in 15 locations. Though there is a suspicion of exaggeration, Olivier de la Marche speaks of Charles the Bold having an artillery park of 300 pieces. It is known he had 110 pieces during the Guelders campaign (1472), 229 for the siege of Neuss (1474–75) and 130 for the first conquest of Lorraine (1475).

Despite a certain technical backwardness, the Italian states devoted considerable sums to the new weapon. At Milan in 1472 an artillery band was supposed to include eight bombards, eight espingardes and 100 arquebuses, each bombard having 100 cannon balls. Nearly 34,000 lbs of powder were required and, in order to transport everything, 334 waggons and 754 oxen or buffaloes were needed. An estimate of the powder available in the same principality in 1476 indicated that there were 138,847 lbs at Milan, 26,252 lbs at Padua and 24,399 lbs at Cremona.

Around the year 1500 strongholds and castles were used to store a not inconsiderable amount of artillery for their princes and sovereigns. At the Castel Nuovo at Naples there were 321 firearms, 1,039 barrels of powder, saltpetre and sulphur and 4,264 cannon balls. The Venetian Arsenal, according to the German pilgrim Arnold von Harff, included 12 powder mills worked by horses and 80,000 ducats' worth of saltpetre. The same eyewitness reveals that the two 'artillery houses' built at Innsbruck by Maximilian von Habsburg contained 280 artillery pieces, 18,000 hacquebuts and 22,000 hand culverins. In the citadel of Perpignan in 1503, Antoine de Lalaing was able to count 'from four to five hundred pieces of artillery such as courtauds, serpentines and falcons'.[99] Private individuals even possessed their own firearms in increasing numbers. As early as 1470 the musters held in the churchyard of the burgesses of Neuchâtel in Switzerland show that of the 523 listed names, 100 were armed with a hand culverin.

The growth of artillery showed no signs of running out of steam at the end of the fifteenth century, and indeed progress was to continue. In 1513, during the siege of Tournai, the army of Henry VIII of England had 180 pieces which, when being used at their maximum, could consume up to 32 tons of powder a day; 510 tons had been shipped for the campaign. At much the

---

[98] P. Contamine, L'artillerie royale française (680). For the following sentence see the remarkable document Arch. dép. Loire-Altantique, E 216 no.13, printed in Le Complot breton, ed. A. de La Borderie, Nantes 1884, no.LIII.
[99] L. P. Gachard, Collection des voyages des souverains des Pays-Bas, Brussels, 4 vols, 1876–82, i.

same moment in different French towns and castles from Boulogne-sur-Mer in the north to Bayonne and Béziers in the south, as well as in several places in Northern Italy then in French hands, the Valois monarchy had at its disposal 4 bombards, two small bombards, 88 serpentines, 38 great culverins, 86 medium culverins, 2 courtauds, 254 falcons and 947 hacquebuts; in all 1,430 pieces of artillery 'both large and small'.[100]

CONTRACTS, SALARIES AND VOLUNTEERS

The military system of a state is explained by its resources, principally financial, the structure of its government and administration, the level of its technology, the organization of its society and the nature of its economy, but one must also take into account its objectives and strictly military imperatives. Every state in effect seeks to raise armed forces adapted to its ambitions and to its own fears. This was the case in England at the end of the Middle Ages when military institutions were founded as a result of the interaction of several factors. First, it was a society where the feudal regime had changed almost completely into a system of land tenures, creating the need to establish new personal ties between those who governed and the men who were capable of serving them in war – 'bastard feudalism'. Secondly, the fact that the principal English strength lay in the massive use of the longbow, a weapon which was popular rather than aristocratic, led to the need to draw on the resources of every level of society, independent of juridical status, in order to recruit a sufficient number of highly qualified archers. Finally, the adoption of a deliberately aggressive and expansive foreign policy implied the sending of forces against Scotland, Wales and Ireland, but above all across the sea. These expeditionary corps had to be capable of waging war away from their base for six months, a year, two years or even more. Garrison troops, intended to hold permanently a certain number of places on the continent and also, if the need arose, capable of turning themselves into a proper army of occupation, were vital.

At the beginning of Edward III's reign there were still three types of soldiers who can be distinguished by their mode of recruitment.

1 Those obliged by feudal service. Thus in 1327, in order to repulse Scottish attacks, the king sent summonses to his tenants-in-chief who by the fealty they owed him and the homage they had performed were obliged to assemble on a given day at Newcastle upon Tyne, though from this time the aim was less to obtain the performance of voluntary feudal service than to remind the tenants-in-chief of their legal obligations and to incite them, indirectly, to raise more substantial but paid contingents.[101]

---

[100] Bib. Nat., MS français 2930, fos.136–41.
[101] N. B. Lewis, The summons of the English feudal levy (417).

2   The levies of the national militia raised by means of commissions of array. In 1327 there were plans to recruit 2,000 foot in Nottinghamshire and Derbyshire by this method, while the county of Cheshire was to provide 1,000 men, and so on. The commissioners were not only to equip and pay the men and lead them to the place of assembly, but above all they had to make a choice of the *meliores, fortiores, validiores, potentiores, aptiores*, and to retain 'the best and most able', 'the strongest and most vigorous', 'the most sufficient and valiant'.

3   Volunteers, pure and simple, from abroad as well as from the kingdom.

Later the first type of recruitment declined in importance and then disappeared. In 1385, on the occasion of his major campaign against Scotland, Richard II convoked the ecclesiastical tenants-in-chief who had to perform their free *servitium debitum* for 40 days – a free service which by the rates of pay applicable that year amounted to very little (some £1,500). As for the lay tenants-in-chief, they received a letter of summons which combined the old feudal writ *cum servitio debito* with the non-feudal writ *quanto potentius poteritis*. In other words, the king expected his lieges to bring the largest possible force, but it was understood that he would pay it from the start. Still in 1385, for the last time, the English crown thought, though it did not put it into practice, of raising a scutage on its rear-vassals.[102]

From the third quarter of the fourteenth century the core of the army was formed by gathering retinues, of variable size, recruited according to the terms of contracts called indentures for war. From many possible examples, one can select the indenture drawn up at the Savoy palace on 10 November 1369 between John of Gaunt, duke of Lancaster, and Sir John Neville, lord of Raby. The latter agreed to serve the duke 'before all others in the world' except the king wherever it pleased the duke, in peace and in wartime, except for express royal prohibition. In return he was to receive for life 50 marks a year on the revenues of two manors in the county of Richmond. He would have *bouche en court* whenever he visited his lord, as would one knight bachelor, two esquires and two chamberlains, whilst their pages and horses would receive wages or liveries. In wartime John de Neville was to serve with 20 men-at-arms (including five knights) and 20 mounted archers. In exchange he would receive annually for his fee 500 marks and the usual wages. His horses were to be valued or prised. He would receive reimbursement for their loss and transport costs on both outward and return journeys. Prisoners of war and war gains were to be shared in the manner customary for other bannerets. For war in Scotland he would furnish up to 50 men-at-arms and 50 archers.[103]

For Gaunt's expedition to France in 1373 there were gathered in this way,

---

[102] N. B. Lewis, The last medieval summons of the English feudal levy (414); J. J. N. Palmer, The last summons of the feudal army in England (424).
[103] Lewis (413), pp.88–90, no.3.

in addition to the duke himself, 28 leaders or captains of retinues: 13 Englishmen (three earls, seven bannerets, two knights and a clerk) and 15 foreigners, including the duke of Brittany (an exile in England so that his men were chiefly English), three Castilian knights (also in exile), four Netherlanders, three Gascons, a Poitevin and a man from Limoges. These 28 retinues totalled 6,000 combatants.

Alongside contracts drawn up between the leader of an expedition and his captains, sub-contracts allowed the captains to recruit their own contingents. In 1381 Sir Thomas Felton agreed to serve in Brittany for six months with 500 men-at-arms and the same number of archers. Fifteen sub-contracts in which he figures have also been preserved, assuring him of the service of 178 men-at-arms and 181 archers.[104]

Recourse to indentures of war continued into the fifteenth century, though not without some changes in detail, as is evidenced by the indenture drawn up on 7 April 1475 between Richard, duke of Gloucester, constable and admiral of England, and Edmund Paston, esquire. He engaged to serve under the duke in the army which the king was planning to take to France for a year as a man-at-arms with three mounted archers. He was to receive 18d. a day, and each archer 6d. He had already received payment for the first quarter of the year and had been ordered to muster at Portsdown in Hampshire on 24 May. He would then receive payment for the second quarter at the same time as his year's service began. After this he was to be paid month by month on the continent in English money or its equivalent within ten days of each due date. He agreed to obey the king's proclamations and ordinances, carry out the orders of the duke, and mount watch and do guard duty from time to time. If musters were held on the continent and his contingent was not up to strength, his wages would be decreased accordingly. The duke was to receive the thirds of his war gains and the thirds of the thirds (that is about 11 per cent) of his retinue's winnings. Within six days of a capture the duke was to be informed of the name, rank, state, condition, number and value of prisoners. Edmund could keep them unless they happened to be the king of France, the king's sons, dukes, counts, lieutenants or captains in chief, whom he was to deliver either to the king of England or to the duke, in return for suitable recompense.[105]

Rarely threatened at home, England scarcely had any need to mobilize generally for defensive purposes. Nevertheless the notion of military obligation falling on all Englishmen did not completely disappear. The monarchy considered it indispensable that the great majority of its subjects should be practised in archery. The Scots, French and Welsh could pose a specific threat, undertaking raids by land or sea, which necessitated the defence of the

[104] J. W. Sherborne, Indentured retinues and English expeditions to France (437); cf. also A. Goodman, The military subcontracts of Sir Hugh Hastings (402c).
[105] Paston Letters and Papers of the Fifteenth Century, ed. N. Davis, Oxford 2 vols. continuing 1971–, i.636–8 no.396.

directly threatened regions. In 1372, for example, John of Lancaster instructed his officers in Wales 'to order and array all manner of fencible men between the ages of 16 and 60, men-at-arms, hobelars, archers and others, and the same number of suits of armour, bows and arrows and other things necessary and defensible for war, that is to say, for each man according to his estate and faculty, and to assign them to units of thousands, hundreds and twenties.' In order to warn of the enemy's arrival beacons were to be lit or the hue and cry was to be raised and everyone was then to withdraw to defensible towns and castles.[106]

In the kingdom of France also, recourse to contracts of engagement became usual from the middle of the fourteenth century, principally under the form of *lettres de retenue* by which the king or his lieutenant retained a captain with a certain contingent in return for a named sum. Nevertheless the contractual aspect, at least officially, was noticeably less marked than across the Channel, especially to the extent that no time limit was stipulated so that in fact at the end of each month the two parties were theoretically free again. The *lettres de retenue* which were transcribed into formularies in the time of Charles V have virtually the same form as those in use under Charles VII and Louis XI. Apparently the monarchy intended to keep the upper hand. Once retained, captains were subjected to a measure of control, the terms of which were fully set out in the great ordinance of Charles V dated 13 January 1374. It was explained there that the king of France had promulgated this after the advice of the *chefs d'office* of his war, because certain captains who had charge (*gouvernement*) of men-at-arms had not maintained the number of effectives indicated at the time of their musters. They had kept for themselves and their private profit the sums received from the king, without distributing them to their men. They had not informed the treasurers of war about early withdrawals nor, when they were finally dismissed, had they distributed to their former companions the money which they had received from the war treasurers in drawing up their final accounts. In order to remedy these abuses and to avoid what had happened in the previous campaign when the captains had allowed the king's wages to be paid to men of little worth, pillagers, who were moreover insufficiently armed and mounted, different measures were announced. Except for men in the households of the constable and master of the crossbowmen, all other soldiers were to be mustered and inspected by the two marshals of France, who were to be assisted by eight lieutenants. Only those soldiers who were present in person, sufficiently armed and mounted, and provided with a horse and armour belonging to themselves or to their master would be enrolled. Every soldier at each muster or review was to swear to serve in that condition as long as he received the king's wages. He could not be replaced except if he was dismissed by his captain, summoned by the king to his service, or became bodily

---

[106] *John of Gaunt's Register 1372–1376*, ed. S. Armitage-Smith, London 2 vols. 1911, i.107–8 no.253.

infirm. The captains were to present trustworthy men known to themselves as if they were doing this for their own wars. They were to grant leave only for reasonable motives. They were to inform the treasurers of war of any illicit departures. They would then make the necessary financial adjustments. They were to get their men to swear to serve continuously, not to leave without permission, to pay for everything at the correct price and not to cause any injury to the king's subjects either on their way to serve, during their service or when going home afterwards. As soon as their wages ceased the men were to return home as quickly as possible on pain of losing their horses and armour. Moreover the captains were held responsible for damage caused by their troops. The payment of soldiers was to be made to *chambres*, small units or subdivisions, of the company or troop (*route*) which normally numbered at least 100 men-at-arms. The captain was to receive only the wages for the men of his own household. The controlling officials were also urged to take care that there were at least 100 men-at-arms in each company. In effect, the marshals' clerks received nothing for musters of companies fewer in number than this figure. Finally, captains were only to be appointed by letters and by authority of the king, his lieutenants or war leaders, or by other princes or lords of the kingdom, for the sole service of the king or the defence, well-being and surety of their own provinces.[107]

However, because of the often defensive character of the conflict, and because of traditional ideas about the nobility and the style of life which it was supposed to lead, the fiscal privileges of the nobility were definitely recognized from the reign of Charles V and feudal military obligations continued to influence powerfully the recruitment of armies, though these underwent some transformation.

Up to the mid-fourteenth century the monarchy fairly regularly conceded fief-rents to various lords and princes living just beyond the limits of the kingdom, in exchange for which these vassals agreed to provide a certain contingent when summoned by the king. These contingents were also promised the usual pay.[108] In certain cases – exceptional, it is true – voluntary feudal service, freed from the normal limitations of length and place of service, not only continued to be due but was also claimed, with the right of redemption. The 'account of the land of the county of Angoulême', which runs from 17 December 1349 to the feast of St John the Baptist (24 June) 1350, mentions the names of nobles in the region who owed one, two or three months' service at Merpins and who had bought exemption for a certain sum.[109] During the first campaigns of the Hundred Years War, the communal contingents provided by several towns only received their wages from the king's treasurers of war from the 41st day of their service. According to a

[107] *Ords. des rois de France*, v.658–61.

[108] B. D. Lyon, *From Fief to Indenture* (263), 308.

[109] L. Imbert, Compte de l'Angoumois sous la domination royale (1349–1350), *Bulletins et mémoires de la Société archéologique et historique de la Charente*, 8e sér., *8* (1917), 134–5.

fourteenth-century document concerning Poitou: 'Charles de Rochefort owes the service of one knight for 40 days in the diocese of Poitou. Item, he owes for the heritage of his children in the diocese of Saintonge, two knights for 40 days.'[110] But above all, the monarchy still had the right to expect service from all nobles holding fiefs (on pain of confiscation of their goods and capture of their bodies), as well as, often, all those who were accustomed 'to arm themselves'. The monarch could proclaim a general or regional summons, with varying conditions and varying efforts at enforcement, depending on circumstances. A summons to the nobles in 1355 was described by Froissart in these terms: John the Good, learning that Edward III had disembarked at Calais, issued 'a great and special order throughout his realm that every knight and esquire between the ages of 15 and 60 should be on a certain day in the city of Amiens or nearby for he wished to march against the English and to fight them'.[111]

Once raised, these nobles, fief-holders and vassals were treated in the same way as the simple volunteers. They were mustered before the marshals of France and their deputies and were in principal taken on as a charge by the military administration. This, according to a rule which only disappeared under Charles V, was not only supposed to pay them wages for each day of service but also to pay indemnities for their coming (venue) and return (retour). From the king's point of view, the essential thing was not to exercise his rights but to obtain in sufficient numbers soldiers of the best possible quality.

The military obligations of all the subjects of the realm were not forgotten either. On several occasions, up till 1356, the monarchy summoned the general arrière-ban which was marked not only by commutation for money but also, eventually, by the dispatch of contingents of varying size from towns and even very minor places. The great armies of the beginning of the Hundred Years War were thus, both by their recruitment as well as by their geographical and social origins, very much a mixture. Froissart testifies with regard to the army which fought the battle of Crécy:

> Orders were issued to the duke of Lorraine, the count of Sarrebruck, the count of Namur, the count of Savoy and Sir Louis de Savoy, his brother, the count of Geneva and all the great barons whom the king thought owed him service or would do it, as well as to the men of the cities and *bonnes villes*, the provostships, bailiwicks, castellanies and municipalities of the kingdom of France so that they might make ready. Then a day was appointed on which each one should appear to be mustered, for he wished to fight the English . . . Then there came, indeed poured in, soldiers from every region to serve the king of France and the kingdom, some who were obliged by homage to do so, others in order to earn their wages and money.[112]

[110] Bib. Nat., MS français 25948 no.971.
[111] P. Contamine, *Guerre, état et société* (457), p.38.
[112] Jean Froissart, *Chroniques. Dernière rédaction du premier livre. Edition du manuscrit de Rome Reg. lat. 869*, ed. G. T. Diller, Geneva and Paris 1972, pp.683–5.

After 1356, and above all from the reign of Charles V, the *arrière-ban* appears to have been entirely neglected for two reasons: first because fiscal interest no longer existed from the moment when other types of taxation (especially the hearth-taxes – *fouages* – and *tailles*) were imposed, bringing in a more regular and certain income; and secondly, because the government, for military and political reasons, no longer concerned itself with using the common people on a massive scale. All in all it agreed with the judgement of Philippe de Mézières in his *Epistre lamentable et consolatoire sur le fait de la desconfiture du noble et vaillant roy de Honguerie par les Turcs devant la ville de Nicopoli en l'Empire de Boulguerie.* The 'Old Solitary of the Celestines of Paris' started from the idea that 'in all military plans and direction since the beginning of wars in this world, four moral virtues have been necessary . . . that is Rule, Knightly Discipline, Obedience and Justice'. But he asked himself whether foot soldiers, commoners, 'the first level of soldiers in Christendom', were prepared to place their armies under 'true obedience to these highly praised virtues?' His answer was negative: 'For by nature the majority are uncouth, feebly nourished in virtue and of poor workmanship, and what is worse, either through nature or poor nurture, some of them feel rebellious against their natural lords because they think they are in servitude as has been all too often seen.' Nevertheless a minority of them 'are wise, subtle and adorned by virtue'. If there were 'well regulated' communal troops, it was because their 'governors are sometimes gentlemen or men of worth, well brought up and virtuous'. Thus at best the communes might provide a selection of soldiers, provided they are well organized and led by nobles.[113] For the same reason Christine de Pisan denounced the 'peril which comes of giving the common people more authority than they deserve' and recommended that they should not be armed. 'There is if I may dare to say so, no greater folly for a prince, who wishes to hold his lordship freely and in peace, than to give the common people permission to arm themselves.'[114]

In fact, after 1360–70 royal authority limited itself to demanding relatively modest contingents of well-trained and experienced archers and pavesiers from a certain number of towns. Only in cases of the most imminent and immediate danger was a form of levy en masse practised, or general mobilization on a local or urban scale. If from 1409–10 we meet once again summonses to the *arrière-ban*, they were above all intended to give convocations an especially solemn form. And this was surely because a civil war was raging and it was necessary to do everything to rally and convince hesitant nobles who might otherwise have sought to abstain from fighting or to join the opposite party.

Emerging from the serious crisis which marked the second part of the Hundred Years War, when he wished to reorganize the system of military

---

[113] Quoted by Kervyn de Lettenhove in his edition of the *Oeuvres* of Jean Froissart (xvi.467–8).
[114] Christine de Pizan, *Le livre de la paix*, ed. C. C. Willard, The Hague 1958, p.133.

obligations, Charles VII first of all re-established, under the name of *ban* and
arrière-ban, the service of all tenants-in-chief who, from the first years of the
reign of Louis XI, were even provided with their own permanent officers.[115]
Then he transformed the former levies of the communes by founding the
militia of the Franc-archers and crossbowmen, provided and equipped by
each community and parish of the kingdom, at the rate of one for every 120,
80 or 50 hearths (*feux*). For example, 30 Franc-archers were demanded from
Poitiers in 1448, a figure that was reduced to 12 after negotiation. Then in
1467 the number was raised to 18 (after 24 had been demanded) and in 1474
it rose to 24.[116] If one adds the fact that the requisition of pioneers, carters
and horses is frequently attested in the second half of the fifteenth century, it
appears that the idea of obligatory military service or at least of the active and
direct participation of a great number of subjects in the wars of their sovereigns had certainly not disappeared in France at the end of the Middle Ages.

A third geographical region, Italy, deserves examination. Under one form
or another free companies *avant la lettre* can be found in the Peninsula even
before the beginning of the fourteenth century. However, they only formed a
major feature of the military scene in Italy after 1320–30. Why did this fairly
sudden and above all, durable, change take place? One reason is connected
with the fact that, at least in the urban states of central and northern Italy, the
ruling classes who should normally have provided the majority of men-at-
arms allowed themselves to become more and more absorbed by their professional activities and preferred to use mercenaries, recruited either from the
other inhabitants of their own state, or from elsewhere in Italy, or from
foreigners. The business men of the Renaissance:

> knew that at certain moments war was necessary to advance the development of
> business and the prosperity of the city; they did not hesitate to declare it on
> occasion. But they did not fight themselves. Continual appeals to arms dis-
> turbed too much the good management of those companies, those societies with
> world-wide connections, where everyone's talents found employment.
> Fourteenth-century businessmen ceased to gird on their swords and form
> themselves into companies under the banners of citizen militias with their
> glorious past. They decided on wars, they financed them, but they no longer
> took part in them in person. Even those among them who had noble origins
> had lost the taste for fighting . . . Was it not reasonable and economical to
> avoid mobilizing the most efficient citizens and to pay mercenaries who could
> fight whilst merchants, active in their counting houses, earned the money to
> pay them? This was the *condotta* system. The businessman even through the
> development of his professional activities, by his eagerness for gain, through the
> feeling he had of his intellectual superiority, through his disdain for brute force,
> through his appreciation also of the power of money, created the *condottiere*.

[115] Charles the Bold, at least until the creation of his *ordonnance* companies, went further in this
direction since he had made arrangement for the fief-holders of his demesnes to receive wages
whilst remaining at home (*gages ménagers*) at a rate less than half that received in time of war.

[116] R. Favreau, *La ville de Poitiers à la fin du Moyen Age*, 2 vols. Poitiers 1978, ii.327.

These two opposite and complementary types of men characterized fourteenth-century Italian society . . . The businessman, especially in the inland cities, had become entirely civilian; the knight's spurs for which he longed or which he wore were simply a decoration.'[117]

If, at the time of the 1325 campaign which terminated in the disaster of Altopascio, Florence lined up with 1,500 mercenary cavalry, 500 Florentine horsemen of whom 400 were provided by the citizens' *cavallata*, it was a sort of swan song for the old institution of warhorses maintained by the *popoli grassi*, the rich.[118]

Recourse to *condotte* can also be explained by the emergence of *signori*, lordships and lords who, through fear of the *popolo*, preferred to use mercenaries – though this reason appears less convincing when it is recognized that the lords were able in general to call on the support of at least a faction inside the cities which they dominated. They could thus recruit their militia from this faction. Recourse to mercenaries is perhaps above all explained by economic and military factors. On the one hand, cities had fairly easy access to the necessary cash to pay mercenaries; on the other hand, mercenaries were readily available on the great war market where their worth and military efficiency was considered incomparable.

For almost two generations from 1340 to 1380, there was a period of companies in which non-Italian elements dominated. In 1334 the 'knights of the Dove', Germans, terrorized central Italy. In 1339 other Germans formed the first 'Company of St George' and served Lodrizio Visconti. After this in 1342 came the 'Great Company' of the German Werner von Urslingen, on whose breastplate was his device: 'Enemy of God, Enemy of Piety, Enemy of Pity'. Then the 'Great Company' of a former Provençal hospitaller, Montreal d'Albarno (Fra Moriale); a collection of ruffians of French, Hungarian, but above all, German origins who after their leader had been decapitated at Rome by Cola di Rienzo were led by Count Conrad von Landau, who was heavily defeated at Tuscan hands at Biforco in 1358. A change then occurred. The companies were no longer purely temporary associations whose primary aim was to exploit an indigenous population reduced to the state of victims, but permanent coherent military organisms entering into or seeking to enter systematically into the service and pay of one or other of the Italian states. Exemplary in this respect was the case of the Englishman, John Hawkwood. This son of a tanner and minor landowner from Sible Hedingham near

---

[117] Y. Renouard, *Les hommes d'affaires italiens du Moyen Age*, Paris 1968, p.237.

[118] In principle, every Florentine owed military service between the ages of 15 and 70 years, except in case of physical disability duly confirmed by a *cerusicus* or a *magister medicus*. Recalcitrants and defaulters, at least in wartime, risked capital punishment and confiscation of their goods. Traditionally mounted military service was owed by all Florentines enjoying a landed income of at least 500 florins, on a warhorse worth at least 35 to 70 florins. But substitutes were allowed. In 1339, 600 citizens still maintained mounts for this cavalry service although they did not fight personally.

Colchester, having campaigned in France, found himself in 1360 at the head of a composite troop, though one dominated by his countrymen. For a while he was part of the 'Great Company' of the marquis of Montferrat in the service of the counts of Savoy against the Visconti of Milan. Perhaps he was present at the battle of Brignais (6 April 1362) when the free companies in southern France inflicted a defeat on French royal forces. The following year he appeared in the service of Pisa in a war against Florence. After this he is found serving the Visconti. For nine years he was the most redoubtable captain in Italy at the head of the White Company.[119] He fought against Florence, against the pope and against Emperor Charles IV. But in 1372 he went over to the pope's side against Galeazzo Visconti whom he defeated at the battle of the river Chiese on 7 May 1373. Once Milan and the papacy were reconciled, Hawkwood, left without employment, turned against Florence, whose territories he menaced and pillaged. In vain Catherine of Siena besought him to leave Italy and to go on crusade against the Turk. In 1375, once more in papal service, he invaded Tuscany. Florence, however, managed to entice him by an offer of 130,000 florins, a sum to which payments by Pisa, Lucca, Arezzo and Siena were added. In a few months the English captain received 225,000 florins. What is more, Florence undertook to pay him an annual salary of 1,200 florins for life, though it is a strange fact that despite this flood of gold, Hawkwood remained in papal service for a further two years, throughout the War of the Eight Saints directed against Florence and its allies. He bears immediate responsibility for the massacre of Cesena (1377) in the Romagna, when perhaps 5,000 people lost their lives. A few weeks later he openly entered Florentine service and that of the League, who promised him 250,000 florins a year. It was then that he married Donnina, illegitimate daughter of Bernabo Visconti, and became the owner of a castle and lands. He remained faithful to Florence until his death in 1394. An effective and prudent tactician, always on the move, Hawkwood seems to have been truly appreciated by his men whom he paid regularly and who never mutinied. It is true that he knew defeat, but each time he succeeded in regrouping his forces, appealing especially to his compatriots (the second company of St George). He thus well deserved the appreciation of Paolo Giovio: 'Acerrimus bellator et cunctator egregius'. He never succeeded in building up a veritable fortune. Just before his death, he decided to free himself from debt by selling his goods – a villa near Florence, a castle near Arezzo – in order to return to his homeland, an indication that this adventurer was never integrated into the Italian world.[120]

The final great foreign company on Italian soil was that of the Bretons

---

[119] So called because John Hawkwood's men wore plate armour (*harnois blanc*), not covered by material which glinted in the sun.

[120] J. Temple-Leader and G. Marcotti, *Sir John Hawkwood*, London 1889; F. Gaupp, The condottiere John Hawkwood (505).

under Sylvestre Budes, whose epic deeds were practically brought to an end
with their defeat at the battle of Marino in 1380 by Alberigo da Barbiano at
the head of a third company of St George. This episode marked the end of
an epoch. Henceforth the Italian states endeavoured to recruit chiefly Italian
mercenaries and to tighten their links with the war-leaders whom they
employed. The period of companies of adventure was succeeded by that of
the *condottieri*.

In the fourteenth century the 'Great Company' was a *societas societatum*, in
other words the collection of a body of freebooters who accepted a supreme
chief whom they recognized by a sort of election. But he governed with the
aid of a council of *caporales et consiliarii* and the *condotta* mentioned not only
the name of the *condottiere* but also those of his councillors separately. The
pay was remitted jointly to the captain and to the councillors who were all
responsible for its distribution to their men. In the *condotta* in the fifteenth
century only the name of the captain appeared and he alone received the
money. The *condottiere* no longer wished to be the leader of a band but a
general, exalted by artists and writers.

Recourse to the *condotta* in the same way as use of the indenture in
England was not reserved to the military sphere. It could be used for mining
concessions, supply contracts or raising taxes confided to private individuals.
Inspired by the rules of the *Digest* on *locatio et conductio operum*, John of
Legnano, the fourteenth-century Italian jurist, defined the *condotta* as a
locatio operarum et rei where the employer (*locator*) hired the services of an
entrepreneur (*conductor*) for an agreed salary for a set period and specific
task. In fact the *condotta* was regularly drawn up between a public authority
and a captain or war-leader. The number and the type of troops and the
duration, either for a set period (*ferma*) or indefinitely (*ad bene placitum* or *di
rispetto*), were specified. There was a tendency to prolong this latter, since in
the fourteenth century it was often a question of three or four months, whilst
in the fifteenth six months' firm service with the possibility of a further six
months' service was the norm. Around 1440 at Venice two years' firm
service, followed by a further supplementary year, was envisaged. The rates
of pay were also specified, part of which was paid in advance in the form of a
loan. So too were conditions for division of ransoms and booty, methods of
inspection, the extent of the authority which the *condottiere* could exercise
over his men and his fiscal privileges, and for the provision of billets, wood,
straw and food supplies at a fair price. *Condottieri* might receive rewards after
noteworthy actions, such as silver helmets, even a pension, palace or fief, or,
to use an expression sometimes employed, a 'nest'. All this was intended to
integrate the *condottieri* into the state which they served. At Venice certain
frontier fortresses were entrusted to them for long periods. Out of 40 foreigners admitted to the Venetian Great Council between 1404 and 1454, 13
were *condottieri* employed by *la Serenissima*. On their death they were
accorded public funerals, a statue or a fresco depicting them in their full

glory. Conversely many unfaithful *condottieri* were executed, condemned to pay fines or banished.[121]

The desire of the *condottieri* to integrate themselves into the recognized framework of Italian political society is also evidenced by the fact that a number of them succeeded in striking territorial roots. Braccio da Montone became lord of his native city of Perugia in 1416. Of the two sons of Muccio Attendolo Sforza one, Alessandro, became master of Pesaro and the other, Francesco, after his second marriage to Bianca Visconti, was able to make good his claims to the duchy of Milan. Lords of small or medium-sized towns like Urbino, Mantua, Rimini and Ferrara became *condottieri*. Only very rarely were *condottieri* truly newcomers. The majority were rightful members of the aristocratic world, whose privileges, tastes and value systems, including that of patronage of the arts, they shared. In the end, some families constituted veritable nurseries of *condottieri;* a prosopographic study of 170 of them shows that 60 per cent belonged to only 13 military lineages, including the Colonna, Orsini and Sforza.[122]

If in the fifteenth century there was a predominance of Italians among the leaders, the same was true of their men. An examination of the account books of the company of Micheletto degli Attendoli allows us to follow its personnel from 1425 to 1449. Of some 450 soldiers whose geographical origins are known, 3.5 per cent were French, Provençal, German, Hungarian, Brabançon or Catalan, 2.2 per cent were Slav, Albanian or Greek, 26.8 per cent came from the kingdom of Naples, 36 per cent from the Papal States and 31.5 per cent from Tuscany and northern Italy.[123]

In comparison, the contribution of military obligations, except for a few northern principalities like Savoy, appears to have been slight. However, in the mid-fourteenth century Florence, threatened by a company of adventurers, thought about raising a company of crossbowmen from amongst its own citizens. In 1356 the same state formed a militia of 4,000 crossbowmen, of whom 800 came from the city itself and 3,200 from its *contado*. In 1378, to defend their regime, the *Ciompi* armed a popular force of 1,000 crossbowmen. At the end of the fourteenth century Milan decided to form a body of 300, then 1,200, citizens from 'the best and tallest men' destined to serve according to circumstances on foot or horseback. Even Venice with its *cernide* did not spurn the minor contribution of a native militia.

One can search in vain for an institution as rigorous and elaborate as the Italian *condotta* in the Holy Roman Empire of the German nation. This is not, however, because hired troops were not normally found there. They appear regularly in all conflicts, large and small, in the service of princes, lords or towns. Some were recruited individually or in small groups, others

---

[121] Mallett (512), pp.76–106.

[122] *Ibid.*, p.209.

[123] M. del Treppo, Gli aspetti organizzativi, economici e sociali di una compagnia di ventura (499).

were provided by captains (or, as it has been suggested they should be called, 'military enterprisers').[124] In 1474 the Swiss captain Wilhelm Herter (1424– 94), who has acquired a great reputation thanks to his participation two years later in the victory at Morat, offered to the town of Cologne 400 mercenaries, his compatriots, grouped under six or eight *Rottmeister*, on condition that he was recognized as their leader, for a year. He stipulated his financial demands thus: an indemnity of 200 florins for himself, 100 florins for each of 15 knights whom he would provide, 8 florins a month for each *Rottmeister* and four for each trooper. But the project collapsed, the archiepiscopal city having refused the 200 florins' indemnity despite its modesty in comparison with the enormous profits which were normal in Italy. During a war between Metz and René II, duke of Lorraine, in 1490, the chroniclers of Metz mentioned the presence of 1,500 horse and 800 foot in the service of their city, who were all foreigners: 'that is Burgundians, French, Lombards, Spaniards, Biscayans, Gascons, Hainaulters and Picards, as well as Germans, Sclavonians and Albanians', and each 'nation' had its own captain.[125]

In order not to be caught on the hop, authorities willingly resorted to the engagement of 'pensioners', who in peacetime received a small sum or were on half-wages. These were the *Diener von Haus aus* who in fifteenth-century Bavaria received 10, 15, 20 or 25 florins a year, called a *Dienstgeld* or *Rüstgeld*, for each horse.[126]

The idea of obligatory service had far from disappeared; it was termed *Landesaufgebot* when it concerned a territory, or *Lehnsaufgebot* for a fief. In 1401 the summons by Rupert, king of Germany, for the expedition to Italy was a feudal levy counted in 'lances', although the princes, counts and barons who had been summoned received monthly pay of 25 florins for every lance and only the towns had to maintain their contingents. At the same period the Teutonic Order depended before everything else on its *Wehrpflichtige*: 426 knights, 3,200 serving men, 5,872 sergeants, 1,963 troops provided by six great towns and some 1,500 subjects from the abbeys (*Stiftsmannen*).[127] The composition of the two armies which faced each other at Hemmingstedt on 17 February 1500 may also be noted: on the one hand there were the forces of King John I of Denmark where, alongside the Great Guard or Black Guard or German Guard (4,000 men on foot commanded by Thomas Sleutz, a much-decorated and well-respected mercenary captain, the very model of a military enterpriser), could be found a cavalry of 2,000 fief-holders, serving by virtue of their military obligations, but remunerated at the rate of 28 florins a month on campaign, and finally a *Landwehr* of 5,000 men combining contingents from Holstein, Schleswig and Jutland. On the other hand, there was the levy en masse of the *Dithmarscher*, a peasant foot militia, reinforced

---

[124] F. Redlich, *The German Military Enterpriser* (379).
[125] Ph. de Vigneulles, *Chronique*, iii.169.
[126] W. Beck, *Bayerns Heerwesen* (365).
[127] F. Benninghoven, *Die Gotlandfeldzüge des deutschen Ordens* (27).

by 500 mounted nobles and some hired men.[128] Machiavelli, wishing to acknowledge the wealth of German towns, noted in his *Report on German Matters* (17 June 1508): 'They spend nothing on unruly soldiers for it is their own men whom they keep and exercise in arms. On holidays, instead of amusing themselves, they exercise with arquebuses, pikes or other arms and, in return for some prize, they compete for some honour or *similia*, which they then share amongst themselves.'[129] Although this is not a false impression, it is too idyllic: in fact, in addition to citizen militias, the free and imperial towns resorted to their external pensioners (*Aüssoldner*), kept small permanent forces (at Metz, for example, it was the group of *soldeours*) and finally practised temporary enrolment.

From the increasing use of paid elements, it would be wrong to conclude that the old nobility was eclipsed. For they, as in England and France at the same period, continued to provide a very large proportion of the cavalry. Territorial princes and lords found themselves, as in the past, in posts of responsibility and command. Even the appearance of 'German serving men called lansquenets (*Landsknechte*)' at the end of the fifteenth century did not accentuate the separation of the military from the social hierarchy in its broadest terms. In effect, Maximilian von Habsburg knew how to convince or force knights to become captains of *Landsknechte*, and even to serve amongst them in the front rank in order to introduce at least a hint of the knightly ethic and *esprit de corps*.

Castile provides a last example. During the war against Granada of 1486–92, the Catholic monarchs employed foreigners who came, for example, from Germany, England and France. They also had the permanent forces of the royal guards and the Brotherhood (*Hermandad*). Nevertheless massive recourse was had to the crown's vassals, who benefited from a sort of fief-rent, the *acostamiento*, to ordinary nobles and to the militias of the *concejos*. For example the Master of Santiago had to provide 300 *jinetes*, the Master of Calatrava 1,000 foot and 450 *jinetes*, and the cities of Córdoba and Seville, 5,000 soldiers each. However, everyone was paid. A noble *jinete* received in Castilian money of account 25 maravedis a day, a footsoldier (*peon*) from the *concejos* 14 or 15 maravedis. In this way fairly considerable numbers of soldiers could be gathered: 13,000 lances and 40,000 foot in 1489.[130]

At the end of the Middle Ages the contrast was often far from clear between troops who served by reason of their military obligations and those who fought of their own free will. This was probably primarily because the majority of both sorts received or hoped to receive wages and those who consented to serve at their own expense were very rare. Amongst the exceptions may be cited, in France, the coronation campaign of 1429, as is revealed by a letter from Guy and André de Laval to their mother and grandmother,

[128] W. Lammers, *Die Schlacht bei Hemmingstedt* (64).
[129] Niccolo Machiavelli, *Oeuvres complètes*, tr. E. Barincou, Paris 1958, p.129.
[130] Ladero Quesado (532).

Jeanne and Anne de Laval. They had presented themselves to Charles VII when he was at Saint-Aignan. He had received them very warmly, saying he was very thankful to them for coming 'in his hour of need without order to do so', that is without being summoned, but that they could expect no financial advantage: 'Of money he had none at court which was in such very straitened circumstances that for the present I do not expect any relief or support from it.' As a result they asked their mother to put up for sale or mortgage such land as she thought necessary to supplement the meagre reserve of 300 écus which they had.[131]

The general shift to pay is also better understood if it is placed in the wider context of the spread of wage labour.[132] Traditional voluntary services were expected from the possessors of landed revenues, yet at the end of the Middle Ages, this type of revenue was affected by a long-term and sometimes dramatic fall. The pay of fief-holders was thus compensation for the fall in income they had suffered as lords. It was no longer possible to exact from them payments comparable to those which their predecessors had furnished in the great age of landed rents. Payment was also for the employers, that is for the states, the least ineffective means of controlling the actions of their troops and of obtaining from them that for which they had been recruited. It is true that the *Italian Relation* of 1500 considered the Scots could provide their king in an emergency with 50,000 or 60,000 men serving at their own expense for 30 days. But this was a characteristic feature of a medium-sized kingdom, very aware of foreign threats, with a somewhat archaic economy and still rudimentary public institutions. Even in the supposedly 'patriotic

---

[131] *Procès de condamnation et de réhabilitation de Jeanne d'Arc*, ed. J. Quicherat, Paris 5 vols. 1844–9, v.106–11.

[132] Although as the following table shows the parallelism between the evolution of soldiers' wages and those of civilians is not absolute:

	Daily rates for a skilled building worker at Rouen	Daily rates for an infantryman in the service of the king of France
1320	1s. 6d. t.	1s. t.
1350	3s. 6d. t.	2s. t.
1380	4s. t.	5s. 2d. t.
1410	3s. 9d. t.	3s. 4d. t.
1440	4s. 6d. t.	2s. 8d. t.
1470	4s. t.	2s. 8d. t.
1500	4s. 6d. t.	3s. 4d. t.

Sources: G. Bois, *Crise du féodalisme. Economie rurale et démographie en Normandie orientale du début du XIVe siècle au milieu du XVIe siècle*, Paris 1976, pp.187–9; P. Contamine, *Guerre, état et société* (457), pp.627–33.

and popular' wars which the old leagues of Upper Germany fought against the Burgundy of Charles the Bold, money continually made its presence felt.

THE FIRST PERMANENT ARMIES

Since an expression such as 'a permanent army' is fairly ambiguous, a typology must first be established. From at least the beginning of the fourteenth century one may take it for granted that in any given territory, provided it was big enough, there were some soldiers or permanently armed elements capable of at once contributing to the maintenance of internal order, apprehending robbers and murderers, executing the decisions of those in power or of the courts and ensuring at least a minimum of security for all the strongholds. Elsewhere in many circumstances and in many regions, bands (*routes*) of soldiers succeeded in prolonging their existence for years on end, sometimes by being employed and maintained by states, sometimes surviving by their own efforts. An example is provided by the company of Micheletto degli Attendoli, whose fortunes can be followed for 25 years, 1425–49, in the service successively of Florence, the kingdom of Naples, Venice and the papacy. Even between contracts, it maintained its cohesion and possessed a permanent administration, embodied in particular in its chancellor and treasurer. 'By means of contracts for a year or two years on average, noticeably longer than those which captains of adventuring companies had been used to in the previous century, and with insignificant breaks in continuity, Micheletto was able to maintain his company in the best possible conditions.'[133]

Strongholds, considered as 'keys to the country', were, sometimes for decades at a time, provided not only with a handful of guards but with genuine garrisons, like Calais, even when a peace or long truce had been concluded with France or Burgundy. During the second half of the fifteenth century garrisons had a tendency to multiply. In the France of Charles VII, Louis XI and Charles VIII, the lances of the small *ordonnance*, the *petites payes* and *mortes payes* were all primarily intended for this purpose. At the beginning of the sixteenth century the English monarchy constantly maintained 2,000 or 3,000 men split up amongst about 100 places, of which by far the best provided for were Calais, Dover and Berwick-upon-Tweed.[134]

In a typology of permanent forces a particular importance should be accorded to bodyguards, whose rise is noticeable, especially after 1350. From then onwards, numerous princes surrounded themselves for their personal safety with one or several elite units who, through the selection of their mounts and the splendour of their weapons and uniform (or livery), were also intended to enhance the magnificence of their masters. These troops had a

---

[133] del Treppo (499).
[134] C. G. Cruikshank, *Army Royal* (399), p.189.

more openly military aspect than the ushers, sergeants-at-arms and mace sergeants who, as in previous periods, continued to ensure the normal functioning and order of the court. However, sometimes the distinction is difficult to establish between this traditional category and the new one, as at the Curia, when the papacy was at Avignon; here 100 to 150 persons 'ensured the pope's safety and enhanced the brilliance of his court'.[135] From the first group there were the master ushers or main porters, the minor ushers and the keepers of the doors, then the sergeants-at-arms or mace-bearers, numbering 50 at least from the time of Benedict XII and instructed to escort the pontifical cortège, reinforce the internal security of the palace, arrest delinquent clerks, supervise prisons and perform various missions for the Apostolic Chamber. These sergeants-at-arms in the fifteenth century were regularly recruited from the nobility. Finally there was a third group, that of the esquires or papal *damoiseaux*.

The 'warlike' aspect is much more clearly visible in the case of Gaston Fébus, count of Foix, who surrounded himself with a 'military household' of some 200 knights,[136] and even more so in that of Richard II of England, whose bodyguard by the end of his reign took on the dimensions of a genuine small army. From 1397, doubtless above all to further his political plans, he recruited in the principality of Chester soldiers who were ordered to accompany him in all his travels in return for annual wages. In September 1398 the 'mastres del Wache de Chestreshire' numbered 750, including 10 knights, 97 esquires and 311 archers. The annual cost of keeping this very unpopular force amounted to nearly £5,000.[137]

The fifteenth century saw further progress in this direction. Hence in the duchy of Milan from 1420 there appeared around Filippo Maria Visconti the *familiares ad arma* (600 or 700 cavalry). In 1467 the 11 squadrons of the ducal *familia* totalled 2,000 men. The same figure recurs in 1497 if one adds the *famiglia fuori casa* to the *famiglia di casa*.

Already present in embryonic form under Charles V and Charles VI, the bodyguard of the Valois sovereigns expanded markedly between 1440 and the end of the fifteenth century. In 1511 it comprised the following units: the 200 Gentlemen of the Household, 100 Scots Archers, 100 French Archers, 200 other French archers and the 100 Swiss (*Les Cent-Suisses*), possibly 700 or even perhaps 900 combatants if one admits that each gentleman had a *coutilier* who could fight.[138] Even a prince with such exiguous revenues as

[135] B. Guillemain, *La cour pontificale d'Avignon* (*1309–1376*), Paris 1962, p.418.

[136] P. Tucoo-Chala, *Gaston Fébus. Un grand prince d'Occident au XIVe siècle*, Pau 1976, p.62.

[137] R. R. Davies, Richard II and the principality of Chester 1397–99, in *The Reign of Richard II. Essays in honour of May McKisack*, ed. F. R. H. du Boulay and C. M. Barron, London 1971, pp.268–9.

[138] G. Jacqueton, *Documents relatifs à l'administration financière en France de Charles VII à François Ier* (*1443–1523*), Paris 1891, p.162.

René II, duke of Bar and Lorraine, had his bodyguard, whose strength in 1496, for example, considerably exceeded 50.[139]

The state of the household of Charles the Bold is described both in the *Mémoires* of Olivier de la Marche and in the *Chroniques* of Jean Molinet, who may be followed as being less prolix:

> There were normally always present in the household and *familia* of the duke of Burgundy, 40 knights and 40 men-at-arms under the leadership of four noble knights, together with a great number of other knights, serving in relays according to the old ordinance, and 20 esquires of the chamber. There were also 50 pantlers, 50 cup-bearers, 50 esquires-carver and 50 esquires of the mews. Each of them had his *coutilier*. They were led by four company captains. Then there were 50 archers of the bodyguard under two knights, their leaders. And also on the other hand . . . his guard, which numbered 130 men-at-arms and as many armed *coutiliers* and 130 archers, who were all commanded by a very gallant and war-hardened knight and by four esquires, leaders of the squadrons.

At the time of the siege of Neuss in 1474–75 this was the position with a good 1,000 combatants including the *coutiliers*.[140] But ducal megalomania did not stop there. Following the ordinance issued at Lausanne in May 1476, Charles the Bold should have had in his bodyguard more than 2,000 combatants: 40 mounted chamberlains and Gentlemen of the Chamber, four squadrons of men-at-arms from the four divisions or offices of the court, four squadrons of men-at-arms of the guard, eight companies of English mounted archers and eight companies of household infantry.[141]

In the kingdom of Castile, too, there was a troop of *guardas reales* numbering 893 lances in 1481 and in 1496 some 1,100 men-at-arms and 130 *jinetes*. Even England could not escape this tendency. Henry Tudor took steps in 1486 to create a company of Yeomen of the Guard. A description of it at the marriage of Arthur, prince of Wales, referred to it in these terms: 'Chosen persones of the hole contreth; proved archers, strong, valiant, and bold men . . . in clothing of large jackets of damaske, whight and greene, goodly embrowdred bothe on ther brestys before and also on their bakkys behynde, with rownde garlands of vyne branches.'[142] Their number was put at 150 or 200 or even up to 600 at the beginning of Henry VIII's reign. At the same period the King's Spears, who were all gentlemen by birth, appeared; for one of the desired objectives of kings and princes in creating or developing their military household was to offer places to young nobles in their immediate entourage in order to reward, oversee and 'domesticate' them.

---

[139] P. Contamine, René II et les mercenaires de la langue germanique (367a), pp.387–8. Other examples: Contamine (457), p.297.
[140] Jean Molinet, *Chroniques*, i.36.
[141] R. Vaughan, *Charles the Bold*, London 1973, pp.197–229.
[142] *A Relation or rather a True Account of the Island of England . . . about the year 1500*, ed. C. A. Sneyd, London 1847, pp.104–5.

As for permanent armies properly so-called, they appeared most often insidiously or indirectly, rather the fruit of circumstances than of clearly formulated decisions on the part of the authorities. For there to be a permanent army in the full meaning of the term, several characteristics should occur together:

1   The existence of stable regular structures; in other words, of military units which survived independently apart from the replacement of their individual members.

2   The desire on the part of the authorities to maintain in active service elements of their armies, regardless of the state of peace or war, with the at least dimly discerned recognition that permanent troops, paid in peacetime as well as in wartime, were indisputably and indispensably superior and that in all events they constituted a support which temporary mobilizations could never achieve.

3   The presence among a sufficiently important section of the population of young men who planned proper military careers with the long and continuous periods of service, uprooting, loss of liberty and perpetual readiness to serve which this implied.

4   The establishment of regular and sufficient revenues to maintain this permanent army; that is, in practice, a stable taxation system whose contributors admitted the more or less well-founded justification for it because of the services regular forces were capable of rendering to the state.

In short, the permanent army is not simply the result of the evolution of institutions, nor of a certain level of activity attained by a monetary economy, nor even strictly military exigencies. It is also the result of a change in attitudes. It was only fully introduced when those who were called to serve in it, the governing groups and the majority of the population considered a need for it went without saying and that it was a supposedly normal and natural element of the politico-military complex.

In this area Valois France, in all respects, showed the way. There were indeed military imperatives, the establishment of a stable tax system, the attitude of a part of the French nobility and the reactions of a population extremely shocked by external dangers which allowed Charles V, at least from the resumption of the war against England in 1369, to establish more or less permanent companies of men-at-arms and crossbowmen both on foot and on horseback. This all resulted from circumstances; there is nothing to indicate that the king's intention or that of his entourage was to continue the experiment once the provinces, ceded a few years before at the treaty of Calais (1360), had been reconquered. The hard core of the 'army of reconquest' in any case practically disappeared as a mobile force during the acute financial crisis which disturbed the first years of Charles VI's reign, at the same time as the extension and prolongation of truces between France and

England perceptibly modified military requirements. At the end of the four-teenth century the only permanent elements consisted of a certain number of garrisons installed in the north, in Normandy and in the south-west. The 'divisions' and, soon, the English offensive once again forced the Valois to resort to arms. After 1418–19 the 'Armagnac' troops and captains offered, despite the collapse of military institutions, a continuous resistance to the schemes of Henry V and, then, to those of the Regent Bedford. Even the treaty of Arras (1435) did not result in their disappearance. Many turned themselves into *Ecorcheurs*, having become, despite themselves, military out-casts, yet hoping sooner or later to be recognized by the king or the great lords.

In order to put an end to disorders which had reached crisis proportions, Charles VII took decisive action. On the one hand he attempted to detach the soldiers from an uncontrolled errant way of life and to settle them in frontier garrisons in immediate proximity to those regions of the kingdom which were still subjected to foreign domination. On the other, as the majority of soldiers depended in fact and even in law on certain princes and great lords, he sought to break this privileged allegiance and to claim for himself alone the right to wage war and control all soldiers in the kingdom. 'The king's war' and 'the kingdom's war' must, in the end, be identical. In the third place, he proceeded in 1445–46 not, as is sometimes said, to recruit a permanent army, but to choose from the mass of available soldiers. By selecting the wheat from the chaff, only a certain number of men-at-arms and companies with a uniform composition were formed and officially recognized. These were the *ordonnance* companies: 1,800 *lances fournies*, that is 1,800 men-at-arms, 3,600 archers, and 1,800 *coutiliers* (7,200 combatants). Following the truce of Tours (1444), because it was still difficult for the king to raise the necessary taxes for their upkeep throughout the whole realm, these few thousand horsemen were divided up amongst the different provinces or *élections* with instructions to the inhabitants to maintain them by means of payments partly in kind, partly in cash. Dispersed in this fashion, the *ordonnance* companies were later brought together again for the recovery of Normandy (1449–50), then for the first and second reconquests of Guyenne (1451 and 1453). By the end of these campaigns the English kept on the continent only Calais, a town entirely surrounded by Burgundian demesnes.

At this point it might have been thought that a general disbanding of the *ordonnance* companies would occur, apart from those maintained in garrisons to ensure the security of the provinces recently recaptured. Various people were in favour of such a decision. Bishop Thomas Basin thought, for example, that the permanent army like permanent taxation was a form of tyranny – a tyranny all the more unnecessary, he added, because the king could freely dispose of the service of a formidable mass of nobles and fief-holders (50,000 combatants according to his own estimate). A patriot as ardent and vigilant as Robert Blondel finally suggested nothing less when he expressed the wish that in future 'during peaceful times the children of nobles and other strong youths from the towns and countryside should be trained and instructed so much in the use of arms that when the need arises we shall not have to learn again nor to start all over again but will be always ready and prepared to receive and repulse our enemies from our homesteads (*fumiers*) and that, according to reason, fear will take from them the desire to attack us and we shall have no need to go cap in hand to the Scots or other foreigners to come to defend the provinces of France as we have had to do in our great need and at infinite expense to our riches'.[143] In other words, to avoid both recourse to foreign mercenaries (blamed by all liberal thinkers, according to the humanist tradition going back to Vegetius)[144] and a permanent army, was it not best to organize a proper reserve army (*armée de reserve*): the *arrière-ban* and Franc-archers?

These suggestions were not accepted either during the last years of Charles VII's reign nor at the time of Louis XI's accession, on which occasion the problem was once again explicitly raised. Up to about 1470 the number of soldiers maintained against all opposition was comparable to that of Charles VII's time. Then an increase began, which became particularly rapid and obvious after 1475. Thomas Basin deplored the fact that at the end of his reign Louis XI:

> raised to 4,000 the effective number of his cavalry and raised in Normandy in the place of the Franc-archers . . . 4,000 foot soldiers called pikemen and in all the kingdom he raised proportionate numbers so that although they remained peacefully at home, he ordered that they should be paid five francs a month as ordinary wages. In addition, he brought from Germany 6,000 to 8,000 foot, Swiss whom he maintained in idleness in the kingdom for several years, even until his death, for although their pay was regularly paid to them, one cannot remember any campaign in which they were employed.[145]

Hence one of the novelties introduced by Louis XI consisted in the creation of a permanent infantry – a scandal even more manifest than the creation of a permanent cavalry, which was largely recruited from the noble class.

It is remarkable that the reaction which followed Louis XI's death in 1483 did not result in the suppression of the permanent army. There was no evidence amongst the deputies to the Estates General at Tours (1484) that they wanted to return to the pre-1445 situation. There was simply a demand which was sanctioned that the infantry troops (the *camp du roi*) should be

---

[143] Robert Blondel, *Oeuvres*, ed. A. Heron, Rouen 2 vols. 1891–93, i.448.

[144] cf. one of the criticisms which Molinet indirectly made of Charles the Bold: 'Vegetius counselled princes that it was better to teach their own knights the noble profession of arms than to take foreigners into their pay. Yet the duke, paying above the odds, was served by Lombards and English whom he employed in great numbers. But because he was feared and dreaded by all nations and because Heaven and Earth smiled on him more than any other, he had the right to break the philosophers' commandments' (*Chroniques*, i.61–2).

[145] Thomas Basin, *Histoire de Louis XI*, iii.320.

dismissed and the number of troops in the *ordonnance* companies and amongst the *mortes-payes* should be decreased. The ideal was to return to the levels, judged supportable, of the years 1450–60. In sum, during the last quarter of the fifteenth century the French monarchy maintained year in, year out, permanent forces of 20,000–25,000 men, which, if one accepts a figure of 10 million for the total subject population, gives an enrolment of 1 per cent of the adult male population between 18 and 45 years of age.

·· For a long period the house of Burgundy, which disposed of less abundant and, above all, less regular revenues, but whose existence was much more assured, resorted to traditional procedures to raise its armies: urban contingents, to which was added the feudal summons, which received wages for the duration of a campaign. The result was reasonably satisfactory. Philip the Good had little trouble in consolidating his rule at the expense of the kingdom. His armed forces were considered strong enough for him to practise an active diplomacy against the Empire. The urban uprisings in the Low Countries were mastered. At the battle of Montlhéry (1465) the Burgundian *arrière-ban* checked the regular companies of Louis XI. But the ambition of a new duke could not be satisfied with such archaic structures. Charles the Bold required a military instrument which encompassed and contained all that was best in the military innovations and traditions of the great states of the West. France, in particular, offered an institutional model; hence, after the brief experiment with *gages ménagers* (a sort of half-pay to reservists), recruitment of *ordonnance* companies began from the end of 1470. The ordinance of Abbeville on 31 July 1471 regularized a process which had developed empirically, by instituting an army of 1250 lances (nearly 10,000 combatants), divided into a dozen companies. The ordinance of Bohain-en-Vermandois on 13 November 1472 slightly modified these arrangements, providing for 1,200 lances with three horses each, 3,000 archers, 600 mounted *cranequiniers* (crossbowmen), 2,000 pikemen, 1,000 foot archers and 600 culverineers – again nearly 10,000 combatants. The next ordinances (Saint-Maximin-lès-Trèves, 1473; Lausanne, 1476) bought important changes in the organization of troops, the hierarchy of command, equipment and military drill, both individual and collective, but without providing for a figure higher than 10,000 combatants. It is true that the Burgundian *ordonnance* companies were practically annihilated after the death of Charles the Bold in 1477 and the subsequent political troubles. But after a few years, once the power of the archduke Philip the Handsome was consolidated, they were seen again on a modest scale at the same time as the administrative and state institutions that had been created by the Valois dukes of Burgundy also revived.

In Spain, also, at the very end of the fifteenth century, it was considered essential to have a regular army, which was described, for example, by Antoine de Lalaing during his visit to the Spain of Philip the Handsome in 1501–2. Isabel of Castile 'had 3,000 men-at-arms of the *ordonnance* in her pay and 4,000 men-at-arms who kept themselves in reserve on half-wages at home; but these latter were ready to serve in war as soon as she ordered them and then they received their full rate of pay.' The creation of the *guardas viejas* of Castile, composed of 20 captaincies of 100 men-at-arms and five captaincies with 100 *jinetes*, dates from 3 May 1493.

One might imagine that the Italian powers, confident in the very elaborate system of the *condotta*, did not feel the need to create true permanent armies in their direct service. But the reality was very different. Whatever precautions were taken, on the one hand the fidelity and the availability of *condottieri* could never be taken as fully guaranteed, and on the other, it was necessary to provide for the security and guard of fortresses. 'It is always our policy to have men of worth in our service both in peace and war,' declared the Venetian Senate in 1421. In fact, especially from the mid-fifteenth century, several Italian states (the Most Serene Republic of Venice, Milan and also the kingdom of Naples) regularly maintained forces placed directly under their command (*lanze spezzate*).

The appearance of permanent armies reinforced tendencies and characteristics which were certainly visible or discernible before, but in a less clearly defined fashion. They gave rise to the elaboration of more and more complex military codes, permitted the collective training both of cavalry and infantry (marching in step), made more frequent recourse to uniforms and distinctive signs, testifying to and supporting the military hierarchy (the pennons, standards and banners of the Burgundian army, for example), and developed a whole civilization around camp life with its rites, distractions, spectacles, hours of boredom and moments of pomp. However, around 1500, we are only at the beginning of a phenomenon which modern Europe, at least in its absolutist form, was to develop considerably. There were not yet at that date any true barracks, nor permanent infantry nor artillery regiments.[146] And, more importantly, a great number of peoples as in England – obstinately resisted the establishment of new military structures. There is a yet more important fact: in combat these peoples did not consider themselves nor were they thought by others to be markedly inferior to the professional armies which were eventually opposed to them.

[146] Caterina Sforza built barracks for her troops at Forli in 1491: Mallett (512), p.142.

Part II

Themes and Perspectives

5

Arms and Armour

War is waged with men. It is also fought with implements either for killing and vanquishing or for protection. Qualitatively and quantitatively these weapons are the product of the technical capacity of the society which makes them, the military habits of the people who use them and of the initiative and reaction of individuals, communities and governing authorities. In many respects the history of war grows out of a history of techniques. A few examples chosen from the thousand years of the Middle Ages will help to demonstrate this constant and organic relationship.

BARBARIAN ARMAMENT

If our knowledge of the tactics used by the Barbarian peoples who invaded the Western Roman Empire is fragmentary, in contrast information on their arms is better, thanks to narrative sources like Procopius, Agathias and Gregory of Tours, literary ones (the epic of Beowulf), juridical ones (for example, the *Lex Alamannorum*), iconographical and, above all, archaeological ones. In effect, among various Germanic peoples (especially the Franks and the Alamans and, to a lesser degree, the Burgundians, Anglo-Saxons and Lombards), there was a custom that the dead should be buried in their best clothes with their jewellery and weapons. This practice had the direct result of decreasing the capital of the survivors and often deprived them of costly and precious arms, but it resulted from the Germanic tradition according to which the dead man 'living in the hereafter kept both for this second life as well as for his funeral, imprescriptible rights to a part of his succession, in particular to the movable goods.'[1] The funeral offering of a man had to include the whole of his army equipment (German: *Heergerät;* Latin: *vestis bellica*): weapons, armour, warhorse. Two different beliefs thus produced the same effect: according to the first, the spirit of the dead man reached its final

---

[1] E. Salin, *La civilisation mérovingienne* (663), ii.232.

resting place in company with the equivalent of each of the funeral offerings, while in the second, the dead man in his individual grave led a new existence, surrounded by the familiar objects of his earthly life.[2]

This custom appears to have become general in the sixth century, even among populations of 'Roman' origin, perhaps because it then became 'easier to obtain replacement arms and equipment and because the number of users was greater.'[3] Then a double influence was felt – a Roman one according to which the dead man did not have the right to carry off with him an important part of his movables, and a Christian one, according to which the presence of movable goods in a burial was a sign of paganism. Moreover, amongst the Ostrogoths, Visigoths and Vandals weapons are not found in graves. From an archaeological point of view interest has centred on a minority of graves – those of people thought to be wealthy. Hence there is a triple limitation of time, geographical region and socio-economic status affecting the evidence.

Frankish armament, however, may be considered as being the most abundantly represented.

Offensive weapons

The battle axe (Latin: *securis, securis missilis, francisca, bipennis*)

Although it could be used for hand-to-hand combat, it was chiefly a throwing weapon which the Franks, according to Procopius, 'at a given signal and at the first encounter' all threw together at the enemy. Experiments have shown that a *francisca* weighing 1.2 kg (length of handle: 40 cm, length of blade: 18 cm) and rotating on its own axis can strike its adversary at 4 m with a single rotation, at 8 m with a double rotation and at 12 m with a triple one. The battle axe is found in Frankish graves from the mid-fifth century to the beginning of the seventh. It was used by foot as well as by cavalry. Its weight varied, the iron alone weighing between about 300 and 900 g.

The spear (Latin: *lancea, hasta*)[4]

The haft was made of wood with a short iron head, finely sharpened on two sides. The *ango* (barbed javelin) was a variety of spear, with a very thin iron stock sometimes circular in section, sometimes polygonal or square, the length of which was usually between 80 and 125 cm. At one end this stock was arrow-shaped, usually provided with barbs or hooks, while at the other

---

[2] *Ibid.*, p.260.
[3] *Ibid.*, p.255.
[4] The term *framea* (French: *framée*, javelin) sometimes used by modern historians to designate the spear is ambiguous. In fact it signifies a lance in the works of Tacitus but a sword in those of Gregory of Tours and Isidore of Seville. *Framen* is recorded with the meaning knife in English sources *c.*550 AD.

end it was extended by a wooden stave. A passage from Agathias describes its use in combat:

Angones are spears which are neither very short nor very long. They are appropriate for throwing, if need be, like javelins, or for hand-to-hand combat. The greater part of the weapon is covered with iron to such a degree that little wood can be seen save at the lower end. At the top of the spear round the head and from the socket itself to which the stave is fixed, there protrude curved barbs bent like hooks turned down towards the bottom. In the fray the Frank throws this *ango* when necessary and if it hits an enemy the dart naturally sinks in and neither he who is struck nor anyone else can easily pull the head out, being prevented by the bent hooks which deeply penetrate the skin where they cause grievous pain, so that even if the enemy is not seriously wounded he nevertheless dies from his wound. If the missile strikes a shield it fixes there suspended from it and is carried round with it, the end dragging on the ground. The man who has been hit can neither pull out the head [from his shield] because of the barbs which have sunk into it, nor cut it with his sword because he cannot reach the wood beneath its iron covering. As soon as the Frank sees this, he quickly puts his foot on the lower end of the *ango* and holds on to it. Under pressure the shield is dragged down, the hand which carries it lets it go and the man's head and chest are left exposed. The Frank then seizes his defenceless enemy and kills him easily either by cleaving his head with his axe or by thrusting another spear through his throat.[5]

The tenth-century poem *Walthari* describes another use of the *ango* which is very similar: a rope with three cords is attached to the end of the stock and each cord is held by one warrior. The *ango* is then thrown against an enemy shield, the hooks sink in and immediately the three soldiers pull together, forcing the enemy to let go of his shield and to fight without protection.

The sword

In comparing archaeological finds with written sources, the following types may be proposed:

1 The great symmetrical two-edged sword (Latin: *spatha, ensis, gladius*), with a fairly thin blade (length between 75 and 90 cm; breadth 6 cm). This relatively rare weapon, often decorated, praised by Cassiodorus at the beginning of the sixth century, is characterized by a hilt and a small guard; hence it has a centre of gravity comparatively close to the point. This makes it a horseman's weapon.

2 The short sword (average length 40 cm), which is probably the *semispatha* of Latin texts.

3 The one-handed sword which archaeologists have suggested corresponds to the terms *sax* and *scramasax*, and of which there are other possible

---

[5] *Historiae*, ii.5–6, cited by F. Lot, *L'art militaire* (6), i.84–5.

synonyms: *scramus, mucro, cultellus*. The *scramasax* could be up to 85 cm long, have a width between 4 and 6.5 cm and a thickness of 1 to 1.2 cm along the spine. There are also small *sax* from 20 cm upwards, used both for combat and for cutting in daily domestic circumstances.

The bow

This is attested by its presence in sixth and seventh century Merovingian graves, with many iron arrow heads.

Defensive arms

The shield (Latin: *clypeus, parma, scutum*)

This constituted the warrior's 'weapon' *par excellence*, the symbol of his status and function. It was handed to him when he was admitted to the ranks of warriors for the first time; to abandon it henceforth was a disgrace. If he died in combat, the warrior was carried away on his shield. During assemblies, decisions were approved by warriors striking the metal *umbo* of their shields. The king was recognized by elevation on shields (*pavois*). The round or elliptical buckler was made from strips of wood covered with leather, having a diameter of 80 to 90 cm and a thickness of 0.8 to 1.2 cm. In the centre there was an *umbo* (an average diameter was 15 to 17 cm; average height from 6 to 10 cm), which varied in shape. Around 500 AD it was concave. It became convex later and by about 700 AD was pronouncedly conical.

Armour (Latin: *lorica, thorax, bruina*)

This appears to have been mostly made up from metal rings (35,000 to 40,000 rings were needed for an Alamanic coat of mail, like a shirt, with a hood and two very short sleeves, the tunic coming down to the thighs or knees), though there were also leather mantles covered with little metal scales or plates. Leggings (Latin: *ocreae;* Germanic: *bagnbergae*) are only mentioned in the *Lex ribuaria*.[6]

The helmet (Latin: *galea, helmo*)

Sometimes this simply corresponded to an iron skull-cap, sometimes to a metal framework covered with leather or material.

---

[6] The *Lex ribuaria* values a mail shirt at 12s., a helmet 6s., a sword with scabbard 7s., leggings 6s., the spear and buckler 2s., and a mount from 3 and 7s.; in all between 36s. and 40s. for a complete set of equipment, the equivalent price of 20 cows.

The arms carried varied with the social rank of their owner to such an extent that archaeologists think it is possible to recognize rank from graves according to the jewellery and arms they contain. From excavations of Alamanic remains in the Württemberg region, it has been concluded that graves with a sword and *sax* are those of free men, graves with spears, arrows or axes are those of half-free and graves lacking arms those of the unfree. Another classification has also been proposed: the presence of a sword indicates a free, well-to-do peasant, that of a *sax*, a poor free peasant, that of a spear, a semi-freeman, while again the non-free possessed no weapons. The diffusion of arms should evidently be discussed along with political and economic conditions, but also in connection with the tactics used, a fact that is sometimes forgotten. At the time of the great invasions and the early Merovingian period, the predominance of the sword and the axe was linked to an individual way of fighting, with battles breaking up into a series of parallel and simultaneous duels. Later, with the intervention of groups of warriors fighting collectively, in unison, predominance passed to the *sax* (see table 8).[7] In any case, each people had their own military habits. Thus in the use of horses Frankish and Anglo-Saxon practice, where mounted warriors were exceptional, could be contrasted with that of the Vandals, Ostrogoths, Visigoths and Lombards, where their presence was notable and even preponderant on occasion.

THE PROBLEM OF THE STIRRUP

In contrast to the repeated set-backs suffered by the *regnum Francorum* at the end of the seventh and beginning of the eighth century may be set the great military successes of the Carolingian period from the time of the mayor of the palace Charles Martel (d. 741). Of course, this success should be explained fundamentally by political factors – restoration of Frankish authority for the benefit of a dynasty which, relying on a large and powerful network of fealties, was able to constitute and employ an armed force of great worth. But this worth itself had been considerably reinforced by a tactical revolution. At the end of the seventh century the Frankish army was still essentially composed of foot soldiers, but from the eighth century horsemen had a position in it which was qualitatively, if not quantitatively, preponderant. According to a theory, already old when summarized by H. Brunner,[8] the mayor of the palace had decided on this abrupt change after facing the Moslems at the so-called battle of Poitiers (25 October 732). In order to create this heavy cavalry Charles Martel, it was argued, massively and systematically secularized the church's property which he then conceded, directly or indirectly,

---

[7] H. Steuer, Historische Phasen der Bewaffnung (669).

[8] H. Brunner, Der Reiterdienst und die Anfänge des Lehnwesens, *ZSSRG, Germ. Abt.*, 8 (1887), 1–38.

TABLE 8 Forms of combat and use of individual weapons before c.1000 AD

	Primitive Germany	Roman Empire	Great invasions	Merovingians	Vikings
		Period AD			
	1	250	500	750	1000
Individual combat					
Collective combat					
Axe					
Spear					
Sword					
Sax/scramasax					
Bow	?	?	?		
Horsemen					

often by precarious tenures, to his faithful followers in exchange for mounted military service. Thus at a stroke, or at least in a very short period of time, the basic feature of feudalism was established.

Some years ago an American historian, Lynn White Jr., added a new dimension to Brunner's interpretation, while seriously modifying it.[9] According to him, pressing necessity effectively led Charles Martel and his sons Pepin and Carloman to favour the increasing role of the cavalry in their armies and, in forwarding this plan, to reorganize the Frankish realm according to a system of benefices or a feudal structure. But this necessity was not directly provoked by the struggle against the Muslims. In the first place this conflict occupied only a minor place in their strategic preoccupations, and for another, it seems that the first confiscations of ecclesiastical property had occurred even before the battle of Poitiers. In fact, White argued, if the need for mounted warriors was felt with particular intensity during the first half of the eighth century, it was because at the same time the use of the stirrup (unknown in the Graeco-Roman world, attested in China in the fifth century and in Iran and amongst the Avars by the end of the seventh) spread rapidly throughout Frankish society. It was easy to imagine the consequences: 'One should think of a horseman riding a horse without stirrups and provided with a cover instead of a saddle . . . fighting against another horseman or even a footsoldier. This knight may be armed with a spear or with a sword or an axe. Can one imagine him being able to couch his lance under his arm in the *rest* and charging his enemy? Evidently not, for lacking a saddle and stirrups, he would be the one unhorsed by the impact. Can one imagine this same horseman striking his enemy with a firm sword-stroke? Again obviously not, for obliged above all to keep his balance on the horse, he could scarcely strike with any force. Let us suppose now that this horseman has stirrups and a firm saddle and what had formerly been impossible becomes easy. The horseman ineffective in battle (except as an archer) now became effectively a warrior of redoubtable offensive worth and if one imagines him well protected by a coat of mail, he becomes the king of the battlefield.'[10] 'Antiquity imagined the Centaur; the early Middle Ages made him the master of Europe.'[11]

Many scholars have accepted Lynn White's thesis. Thus Jan Dhondt, who notes that 'if it is not really known when the stirrup and the saddle became general throughout Europe' it is, in contrast, well established that this generalization of usage had occurred by the second half of the ninth century at the latest:

It is very simple to say that Charles Martel suddenly had need of much land in order to attract many vassals to his service, but it becomes infinitely clearer if

[9] L. White, *Medieval Technology and Social Change* (667), pp.1–38.
[10] J. Dhondt, *Le Haut Moyen Age (VIIIe-XIe siècle)*, Paris 1976, p.55.
[11] White (677), p.38.

one intensifies this need because of a revolution in the organization of the army which in its turn is only truly justified if it is linked with the introduction of a new type of combatant – the heavily-armed horseman who because he can deal redoubtable blows with his lance and sword, assured royal forces of a simultaneous superiority over both internal and external enemies.[12]

However, objections have been raised, by B. S. Bachrach, for example, who examined and then rejected the three principal arguments advanced from written sources:[13]

1 That in 758, the tribute of 500 cows which the Saxons owed Pepin the Short was changed by him into a tribute of 300 horses. But, as Bachrach notes, already in 748 – that is, after the supposed massive increase of the cavalry in Frankish armies – the same Pepin had accepted a tribute of 500 cows.

2 That according to the *Annales Petaviani* in 755, 'Tassilo came to the Marchfield and this Marchfield was moved to the month of May.' Bachrach and others argue that this transfer had been accepted long before because of the need to wait for the first spring growth of grass before setting off on campaign. Moreover, the expression 'Marchfield' (*campus martius*) does not in the strict sense signify the assembly of warriors at a certain time of year, but only at a given spot, a place which at the same time became, by imitation of the Roman tradition, the field of Mars, the god of war.[14] In addition, even if the Carolingians showed themselves very anxious to ensure the feeding of their horses,[15] it remained the case that under Pepin, as under Charlemagne, campaigns sometimes started very late in the year and occasionally continued during the winter, as in 784–85 against the Saxons. It may be added that there was a Mayfield as early as 612.

3 That a passage from the *Annales Fuldenses* referring to the battle of the Dyle in 891 and indicating that it was 'unusual for the Franks to fight *pedetemptim*', should be translated (*contra* White) not 'on foot' but 'step by step'.

In any event, even if we accept the traditional interpretation of these three sources, nothing is revealed there of a 'military revolution' having taken place

[12] Dhondt, *Haut Moyen Age*, p.55.
[13] B. S. Bachrach, Charles Martel, the stirrup and feudalism (144), pp.50–3; see also the powerful critique of White by P. H. Sawyer and R. H. Hilton in *PP*, no.24 (1963), 90–100, whilst D. A. Bullough, Europae Pater: Charlemagne and his achievement in the light of recent scholarship, *EHR*, *85* (1970), 84–90, provides pertinent additional information on military matters and the archaeological evidence.
[14] L. Levillain, Campus Martius (168).
[15] cf. *Annales regni Francorum*, s.a. 797, 'Cum jam ver adpeteret, nondum tamen propter inopiam pabuli exercitus de hibernis produci potuisset'. A passage from the ninth-century *Officia XII mensium* establishes a very close link between the grass in May and the beginning of the campaigning season: *Revue archéologique*, *45* (1955), 185.

under the rule of Charles Martel. Both before and after 732 the operations mounted by the Franks appeared to spring from unchanging tactics; again, under Pepin the Short the cavalry did not play a preponderant role; the primary objective was rather to besiege, occupy and defend towns and strong points. The spread of the use of stirrups occurred, moreover, in an irregular and patchy way. The Byzantines knew of it in the sixth century and the richest Franks had adopted it well before the eighth century, but on the eve of the battle of Hastings the Anglo-Saxons still refused to use it, though they did know of it. Even if it is admitted that the long sword and a winged spear which terminated with a triangular iron head had become more widely used in the eighth century, nothing indicates that they were exclusively used by horsemen provided with stirrups. In other words, even without stirrups, cavalry can be perfectly effective and redoubtable.

Lynn White made equal use of philological studies of the texts. The spread of the stirrup, he argued, had entailed a change in vocabulary. In describing the act of mounting and dismounting from a horse, the verbs *insilire* and *desilire* were replaced by *scandere* and *descendere*. This is an ingenious hypothesis which it should be possible to verify by a systematic study of vocabulary; Bachrach has, however, already advanced serious evidence for rejecting it.

Finally, iconography scarcely sheds any light on the problem. For Western Europe the oldest representation of a stirrup may be found in the illustrations of a manuscript from the abbey of St-Gallen, the *Psalterium aureum* (Library of St-Gallen MS 22, cf. also the *Codex Perizonianus* of the University Library, Leiden).[16] But the St-Gallen manuscript, dating from the third quarter of the ninth century, is too late to be useful. Even there, although certain horsemen armed with lances are displayed with at least one stirrup, others, also armed with lances, lack stirrups.

Rather than accepting Brunner's thesis, rejuvenated and completed by Lynn White, one can reasonably prefer, in our present state of knowledge, a version of the facts which stresses the slowness of the evolution. It is likely that from the Merovingian period horses were no longer exceptional in the Frankish armies, at least for the transport of chieftains and the rich. It is not necessarily the case that these men dismounted even for combat. One of the most explicit passages from Gregory of Tours on Frankish tactics shows how the Thuringians, in order to repulse the troops of Thierry I, used a classic ruse: 'They dug a series of ditches in the field where the battle would be fought. Then they covered these holes over with turves and made them level again with the rest of the grass. When the battle began many of the Frankish cavalry rushed headlong into these ditches and there is no doubt that they were greatly impeded by them.'[17] In the seventh century the rise of the

---

[16] Reproduced in J. F. Finó, *Forteresses de la France médiévale* (783), 93–4.
[17] Gregory of Tours, *Historia*, ed. R. Latouche, Paris 1963, i.148–9, quoted here from *The History of the Franks*, tr. L. Thorpe, Harmondsworth 1974, p.168.

aristocracy was in all probability accompanied by a comparable increase in cavalry which, in any case, still remained in the minority. Of 704 listed warrior graves in eastern Francia from the end of the seventh century to the beginning of the ninth, a maximum of 135 can be considered those of horsemen, of which only 13 certainly possessed stirrups.[18] It was only under Charlemagne that mounted forces began to form the most solid and effective part of the army.

But this does not mean that from the ninth century the majority of horsemen fought with couched lances. In fact, for a knight there were four ways of using a lance. He could throw it like a javelin, or strike downwards with the arm raised, or strike directly, holding the lance flexibly with his arm by his side and his elbow lightly flexed, or – and this is the major technical innovation of the Middle Ages – he could hold the stock close under the armpit and direct the point of the lance with his hand, thus forming with his armour and horse a sort of unique projectile, the more effective the quicker the horse moved. It is a problem to know when this final technique became general usage. It is the Bayeux tapestry (c.1080) which is the oldest iconographical record of the 'new cavalry drill', yet it also shows other knights brandishing lances, arms stretched with no difficulty, as if it was a very light weapon (a little like the lances of the Lancers and Uhlans prior to 1914). Of course, the pictorial record could be lagging a long way behind reality, but literary texts such as the *Song of Roland* are not more advanced in describing the new tactics.[19]

MAIL SHIRT, HAUBERK AND HAUBERGEON

Faithful to a classification which goes back in France at least to Viollet-le-Duc, a large majority of archaeologists and historians have admitted and still admit that until the eleventh and twelfth centuries warriors were protected by an armour called in Latin *brunea* or in French *brogne*, (cf. English: *byrnie ;* Old Norse: *brynja*), that is a tunic of thick material or leather covered with little metal scales, strips or, eventually, iron rings. Then progressively from the eleventh century, this was abandoned for the hauberk which was made from interlinked iron mail rings more or less close together but without lining. From a disconcerting variety of pictorial representations and texts, eight different ways of arranging the mail have been suggested: criss-crossed mail, juxtaposed rings, riveted mail, meshed, overlapping, or single, double mail or even mail reinforced with metallic studs.[20]

[18] F. Stein, *Adelsgräber des achten Jahrhundert in Deutschland*, Berlin 1967; Bachrach (144), pp.63–5.
[19] D. J. A. Ross, L'originalité de 'Turoldus' (662).
[20] In England it was Samuel Meyrick who first proposed eight categories of mail. His terms for them were: trelliced, ringed, rustred, mascled, scaled, tegulated, single mail, banded armour and double chain mail (*Archaeologia*, *19* (1821), 120–45), terms suspiciously close to those later used by Viollet-le-Duc (translator's note).

However, other specialists, discarding this distinction, think that 'brogne' and 'hauberk' refer to the same garment, made from mail of riveted metal. It would also be the Anglo-Saxon byrnie, 'the tangled war-net' of which Beowulf speaks. As such it would thus be a very ancient technique, attested on a bas-relief on Trajan's column, amongst other early evidence, even though the Romans preferred armour formed from plates or strips of metal (bronze or iron). Discussing military equipment at the time of the Bayeux tapestry, a perfect representative of this point of view, Sir James Mann, writes

> We may therefore assume that all the dozens of mail shirts shown worn by horsemen and footmen in the Bayeux Tapestry are composed of unpolished, riveted rings forming a flexible armour, easy to wear in action, good for stopping a cut or thrust, but heavy and not effective against contusion without the supplement of a padded undergarment. When mail was pierced, links might be driven into a wound, which might easily become septic. It was those drawbacks which caused mail to be replaced by plate armour some two hundred and fifty years after the date of the Tapestry.[21]

Recently F. Buttin has proposed a series of interpretations which are very different, of which only the principal ones may be mentioned here.[22] For him the byrnie (*brogne*) is really an armour which covers all the body. As for the hauberk (*halsbergha*), it was a supple 'war head-gear' (*coiffure de guerre*) in the form of a hood covering the neck and shoulders.[23] In the thirteenth century the word *brogne* fell into disuse and was principally replaced by the terms 'coat of iron' (or, more rarely, 'coat of mail') and above all by *haubergon* [*sic*], whose etymology is, he suggests, *haubert-gone* (in the sense of gown). That being said, hauberk, *brogne* and *haubergon* have all basically the same structure based on mail. But there were two fundamental types of mail: either the metal stud which has been worked with a hammer (*malleus*) and which is then sewn onto a material or leather foundation garment (hence the expressions 'half-sewn mail, *mailles demi-clouées*, or *haute-clouure* or even *haubert à clavel*), or metal rings which when interlaced gave rise to the *brogne* or trelliced hauberk (*treslis*). It is true that from the thirteenth century hauberks (in the sense which F. Buttin attributes to the word) were most frequently made from annular mail which wire-drawers manufactured from strips of drawn iron. In contrast the *haubergon* was always made 'from full mail, sometimes iron but most often steel, sewn to a leather or cloth lining, or linked together without a lining by means of laces'.[24] When, for example, at

---

[21] J. Mann, Arms and armour, in *The Bayeux Tapestry*, ed. Sir Frank Stenton, London 1957, p.61.
[22] F. Buttin, *Du costume militaire* (574).
[23] *Ibid.*, p.406.
[24] *Ibid.*

the end of the fourteenth century Savoyard texts mention an 'auberjon d'acier de toute botte' and an 'auberjon de botte cassee d'acier', in the first case it was an armour which had been proved by withstanding arrows from a bow or ordinary crossbow, whilst in the second, the proof had been by the more powerful crossbow on a stand (*arbalète à tour*). A Burgundian account mentions the purchase of 1,600 steel *mailles* which were, in fact, 1,600 flat, round links to make the tail-piece (*queue*) of a *haubergon*. Finally, while the *cotte de fer* was made from rings (for example, those discovered in the excavations at Visby were generally between 0.8 and 1 cm across), the *cotte d'acier* only ever consisted of full, riveted or stamped mail. The craft of *haubergerie* consisted chiefly in manufacturing and assembling flat and full mail.

Despite the great profusion of quotations he used, and the great care he expended in demonstrating his views, the new definitions proposed by Buttin cannot be accepted unreservedly. The most dubious appear to be those concerning the hauberk and *haubergon*. Apparently unambiguous texts permit us, in effect, to affirm that the hauberk is indeed an armour covering the body and the *haubergeon* is nothing but a small hauberk not coming down as far. Thus Philippe de Mézières writes: 'The hauberk signifies the protection of the knight's body.'[25] The *Grandes Chroniques de France* recount an episode at the battle of Bouvines in the following way: 'He raised the hem of the hauberk, expecting to plunge his knife into his [opponent's] stomach, but the dagger was unable to penetrate because of the iron bands which were firmly sewn to the hauberk.'[26] The fourteenth-century French translation of the *Catholicon* of John of Genoa uses the word *haubers* for the Latin *lorica*. For the term *thorax* the translations *peiz ou auberjon* (breast/chest or hauberk) are suggested, whilst another dictionary translates the same word by *pis vel haubert*.[27]

It does not appear to be more correct to say that the *haubergeon* was always made of solid metal discs, as is proved by the following fifteenth-century French riddle: 'Question: What is heavier the more holes it has ? Answer: An haubergeon.'[28]

On the other hand, it seems the normal meaning of *maille* was indeed an iron ring. This passage in an old French translation of the *Art of Falconry* (*De arte venandi cum avibus*) of Frederick II is helpful: 'A further requisite is two rings or two *mailles de haubert*, and it does not matter whether these are

---

[25] Philippe de Mézières, *Le Songe du Vieil Pelerin*, ed. G. W. Coopland, Cambridge 2 vols 1969, i.213.

[26] Quoted by Buttin (574), p.172, who explains his reasons for rejecting this unique (according to him) reference.

[27] M. Roques, *Recueil général des lexiques français du Moyen Age (XIIe-XVe siècle)*, Paris 1938. There is no doubt, on the other hand, that *haubergon* is a diminutive of *haubert* (cf. the Latin forms: *halsbergotum, halsbergetum, halbsbergellum, halsbergeolum*).

[28] *Devinettes françaises du Moyen Age*, ed. B. Roy, Montréal and Paris 1977, p.106.

iron or bronze.'[29] Elsewhere comparisons between a net (Old French: *rois*) and a *haubert* or *brogne* is normal:

De vostre brogne aves fait nasse	Of your byrnie you have made a net
Mervelles estes envoissiés	You are deliriously happy
Bien sai que pas ne voliceś	For I know you would not want
Que l'anguille passast la maille[30]	An eel to get through the mail.

According to the dictionaries cited above 'a *macula* is a link in a haubergeon or a net' (*macula est maille de hauberjon ou de roiz*), and '*macula*, a spot, sin or link in a haubergeon or net made of iron'. As early as the ninth century Rabanus Maurus defined a *lorica* as being 'called thus because it did not have thongs but was woven from iron circles alone'.[31]

We cannot exclude the possibility that in the High Middle Ages use was sometimes made of armour made from little scales or strips (*lames*) of metal. There are some hints of this, primarily iconographic, if one accepts that pictures do truly represent reality and were not striving simply, for example, to represent warriors in the Ancient World as they were imagined to be (like the soldiers guarding Christ's tomb).[32] There are also archaeological remains: small *lames* and metal scales have been found in the Visby ossuary, whilst armour with scales of an uncertain date between the tenth and twelfth centuries is exhibited in the armoury of the Alava Museum at Vitoria in Spain.[33] A very explicit passage from John of Plano Carpini shows the Mongols, among others, using armour made from *lames* of metal:

> They fashioned a thin strip, a finger's width in size and as long as a palm, and made a great number of them in the same way. In each strip they bored eight small holes, and placing three straight and strong thongs inside they placed the strips one on top of the other thus making them rise by degrees and tied the strips to the thongs by thin pieces of string which they pushed through the holes so that all the strips held together.[34]

Gerald of Wales recalls that during an attack on Dublin in 1171 the Danes were protected by coats of mail or rather by 'strips of iron artfully stitched

---

[29] A. Tobler and E. Lommatzch, *Altfranzösiches Wörterbuch*, Berlin, 5 vols., 1915–62, v.796–7; cf. *The Art of Falconry*, tr. C. A. Wood and F. M. Fyfe, Stanford, 1943, p.139, citing Bologna University MS 419 f.39v: 'ad quantitatem annuli seu maylle loricarum'.

[30] *Ibid.*

[31] *Patr. Lat.*, cxi.543: 'Vocato eo quod loris careat: solis enim circulis ferreis contexta est.'

[32] Two examples: Bib. Nat., MS français 403, f.1v, and twelfth-century sculpture in the abbatial church of Saint-Gilles-du-Gard, reproduced in Buttin (574), figure 1. On the way in which armour from the Ancient World could be represented in the Middle Ages cf. Bertrandon de la Brocquière, Le voyage d'outremer (1432–1433), ed. C. Schefer (*Recueil de voyages et de documents*, Paris, xii (1892). 219–20), relating to the Turks: 'I have seen them wearing brigandines with very fine scales smaller than those we use and standard arm-guards in the same fashion as one sees in paintings of the time of Julius Caesar.'

[33] M. de Riquer, *L'arnès del cavaller* (596), figure 2.

[34] Quoted by Buttin (574), p.103.

together' (*laminis ferreis arte consutis*). Adam du Petit-Pont speaks of 'hauberks woven from circles and covered all over with strips' (*loricas textas ex
circulis et circumsquamatas ex laminis*) and Julien of Vézélay described the
armour of a soldier guarding Christ whose 'breastplate was made from a web
of overlapping *lames* which formed a tunic of continuous scales'.[35]

The problem of riveted, half-riveted and stamped mail needs investigation.
Is it necessary, against Buttin's hypothesis which implies that riveted or
stamped mail must be attached to some form of lining, to maintain the
traditional interpretation that implies that *clouure* is the 'riveting of the
eyelets of mail to close the circle' (Godefroy)? Obscurities certainly still
remain, but it is one of the merits of the vast enquiry undertaken by Buttin
that he has shown how even the best established notions can be fruitfully
subjected to new critical attention.[36]

COLLECTIVE EQUIPMENT AND UNIFORMS

There are two antithetical models here: on the one hand a system or military
society where each combatant has to provide his own weapons and other
equipment including his horse, on his own initiative. He does this in relation
to his economic means and his desire for security and efficiency, though at
the same time an indirect control is exercised over him by those who govern
him and the communities around him. On the other hand, there is the total
and exclusive takeover by the state of provision of equipment for its troops,
and the strict definition and regulation of this equipment to ensure uniformity and standardization. This would illustrate by its appearance alone
both the organization and hierarchy of the army.

In general, the first model was dominant throughout the Middle Ages.
Even in the fifteenth century a very large proportion of arms and armour
were still in private hands, not only those of professional soldiers but also
those of the 'civilian' population in towns and countryside. As for the second
model, the Middle Ages moved gradually towards it without ever adopting it
fully or systematically. Between these two extremes different arrangements
were adopted which gave varying responsibility to the individual, the community or the governing powers.

At the risk of outrageous simplification, a few observations may be made.
First, even when it was not just the responsibility of each individual or left to
their initiative, the equipment of soldiers could be determined by the intervention not merely of the supreme authority but by intermediate authorities
like a lord, a captain, an urban or village community. Second, it often happened that, without taking charge of equipment, authorities controlled it and

---

[35] Julien de Vézélay, *Sermons*, ed. D. Vorreux, Paris 1972, ii.608.
[36] It may be noted that a specialist as well informed as C. Gaier largely accepts Buttin's
opinions: C. Gaier, *L'industrie et le commerce des armes* (579), pp.265ff.

issued a series of orders about it, through, for example, the Assizes of Arms of Henry II Plantagenet, the inspections of the weapons of burgesses by municipal authorities during musters and periodic reviews, or the military ordinances of Charles, duke of Burgundy, which defined in minute detail the armament of his regular troops. Third, authorities, rather than directly equipping their troops, were sometimes satisfied with ensuring that they would have no difficulty in finding the armaments they needed, in the quantity required and at the most economic price. They made prohibitions on the export of arms and horses during periods of war, and granted fiscal and other advantages especially to helmet-makers, hauberk-makers, armourers and brigandine-makers. Finally, in the long term, it is true that state intervention increased and became more determined. It was particularly concerned with infantry troops rather than cavalry, war on the sea rather than war on land, and wide-ranging military expeditions rather than defensive operations at home.

In the kingdom of France, for example, from the beginning of the thirteenth century, the Capetian monarchy built up modest stocks in various castles and strongholds, not only of crossbows and quarrels, but also of shields, lances, axes and complete suits of armour.[37] A document of 1295 reveals a massive purchase of arms in the *sénéchaussée* of Toulouse on behalf of Philip the Fair.[38] For the arming of ships and galleys at the beginning of the Hundred Years War, Philip of Valois abundantly supplied the arsenals of the Norman coast.[39] The ordering of arms became more systematic still in the second half of the fifteenth century on the part of Charles VII, Louis XI and Charles VIII. For example, in 1465 Jacques d'Armagnac, duke of Nemours, received from Louis XI 6,000 *l.t.* in compensation for a similar sum paid to armourers for the kitting out of a complete *ordonnance* company of 100 men-at-arms and 200 archers.[40] This increasing state intervention is seen in other countries at the same period. In 1483 Maximilian von Habsburg ordered the acquisition of 600 sallets, 400 armguards and 1,000 suits of body-armour (*écrevisses*).[41] The same sovereign by his letters dated at Worms on 17 April 1495, agreed terms in a veritable treaty with the Milanese brothers Gabriele and Francesco da Merate, by which for the next three years in return for 1,000 *francs comtois* and 1,000 Rhenish florins, payable in three equal annuities, they agreed to install a forge and grinding-mill at

[37] P. Contamine, Consommation et demande militaire (886), p.412.
[38] P. Wolff, Achats d'armes pour Philippe le Bel dans la région toulousaine, *Annales du Midi, 61* (1948), 84–91 – arms for a maritime expedition. The same year, also for provisioning Philip IV's fleet, a Lombard bought at Bruges 1,885 crossbows, 666,258 quarrels, 6,309 shields, 2,853 helmets, 4,511 padded jackets, 751 pairs of gauntlets, 1,374 gorgerins and arm-braces, 5,067 iron plates, 13,495 lances or spearheads, 1,989 axes and 14,599 swords and daggers: Gaier, (579), p.118.
[39] A. Chazelas, *Documents relatifs au Clos des Galées de Rouen* (314).
[40] Bib. Nat., MS français 32511, f.245r.
[41] Gaier (579), p.89.

Arbois. Annual wages amounting to 100 *francs comtois* were stipulated; in return they promised to deliver to the king each year 'fifty complete suits of war armour well made in the Burgundian fashion and of good materials marked with the mark designated for the said armour'.[42] In 1475 Charles the Bold had appointed the Milanese Alessandro da Poli his privileged and paid manufacturer of arms at Dôle. The armourer in question had contracted to supply 100 armours with all accessories each year.[43] Naturally Italian princes had shown the way: in 1452 Cicco Simonetta had written to the duke of Milan that three armourers contacted by him had declared that they could make enough equipment for six men-at-arms every day.[44]

One might be surprised that recourse to uniforms, which passes now for a characteristic and even essential feature of any regular armed force, was so episodic in the Middle Ages. It is known that proper uniforms only appeared in England during the Civil War (1645), and it was 1670 before Louvois in France prescribed 'a uniform dress destined to clothe the Regiment of King's Fusiliers'. However, from an early stage the Middle Ages did not ignore distinctive signs or emblems. One thinks here not only of armorial banners, shields and coats of arms (appearing from the mid-twelfth century and then used as a matter of course after 1250), but also of the crosses always worn by the crusaders. At the time of the third crusade (1188–90), 'it was agreed that all those coming from the lands of the king of France should wear red crosses, those from the lands of the king of England white, and those from the county of Flanders green crosses.'[45] Again, in 1336, in the plans for a crusade by Philip of Valois, 'there were more than two hundred great lords (of France) who all undertook to wear scarlet crosses.'[46] Then the red cross (borrowed from the arms of St George) became the proper English standard, while from 1355 (or more especially from 1380) the Valois imposed the white cross on their armies. In their turn the Burgundians chose an emblem – the cross of St Andrew, either in saltire (*en sautoir*) or forked (*fourchue*), in white or red. A special clause in the treaty of Arras (1435) stipulated that the duke of Burgundy and his subjects who had 'worn as arms' the cross of St Andrew were not to be forced to take another emblem even if they served in a royal army, in the royal presence and for the king's wages.[47]

[42] R. Genevoy, Notes sur l'armurerie impériale d'Arbois (625); A. Motta, Armaiuoli Milanesi (649), p.222.
[43] A. de Schrijver, Notes pour servir à l'histoire du costume au XVe siècle dans les anciens Pays-Bas et en Bourgogne, *Annales de Bourgogne, 29* (1957), 29–42.
[44] B. Thomas and O. Gamber, L'arte milanese dell'armatura (672).
[45] Radulfus de Diceto, *Opera historica*, ed. W. Stubbs, London 1876, p.51.
[46] Froissart, *Chroniques*, i.354.
[47] E. Cosneau, *Les grands traités de la guerre de Cent Ans*, Paris 1889, p.145. More rarely scarves of the same colour were worn round the neck, thus in 1304 in the French army campaigning in Flanders:

Lors fait faire commandement
Par le bannier qui en l'ost crie,

It may be noted that this type of emblem was nevertheless largely beyond the military sphere. It was also evidence of a political affiliation, so that non-combatants could or had to wear it too. In 1419 Henry V, for example, required all Normans to wear the cross of St George as a sign of submission. At the time of the Flemish expedition of 1382 led by Charles VI, 'there was not a man or woman in the country upto Ghent who did not wear a white cross.'[48] At the time of Burgundian predominance in 1411, the Parisians wore little blue cloth hoods bearing a St Andrew's cross and shield with a fleur-de-lys. No one could leave the capital, according to the Bourgeois of Paris, without this badge. Other Burgundian and Armagnac tokens have been recovered from the Seine.[49]

Elsewhere kings, princes, captains and towns frequently equipped more or less important bodies of troops in identical fashion. Before the middle of the fourteenth century, soldiers originating in Cheshire, Flintshire and Wales were dressed in green and white uniforms (*cotecourtepiz*) and hats and were, doubtless, the first soldiers from across the Channel to appear in uniform on a continental battlefield.[50] In 1297 during the siege of Lille by Philip the Fair, 'there were from the city of Tournai 300 hired men in blue jackets and white hats.'[51] In 1340 Tournai similarly sent for the service of Philip of Valois 2,000 well-armed foot soldiers 'all clothed identically' (*tous vestus d'une parrure*). The same expression was used by Froissart to describe the mobilization of the Flemings in the Franc of Bruges: 'They had for each town and castellany similar uniforms in order to recognize each other.'[52] There are examples of urban contingents wearing the name of their town (Dijon, Caen) or its arms (Metz, Lyon). 'In this year (1477) Valenciennes maintained at its own expense 150 Germans and Swiss hacquebuters who wore the livery and uniform of the town.'[53]

The phenomenon could also be seen at a princely level, as the equipment of the Scots Archers under Charles VII and Louis XI, or that of the guard of Charles of Maine in 1480 show. In the latter case, all 'archers of the guard',

---

Que tout homme de sa partie
Face tant, comment qu'il la tranche,
Qu'il soit seignier d'escherpe blanche
Pour estre au ferir conneüz.

(Guillaume Guiart, *La branche des royaux lignages*, ll.11,052ff: 'Then the order was proclaimed in the army that all men of his party should, whatever he decided, mark themselves with a white scarf so that they would be recognized while fighting.')

[48] *Partie inédite des chroniques de Saint-Denis*, ed. J. Pichon, Paris 1864, p.15.
[49] cf. *A Parisian Journal 1405–1449*, ed. J. Shirley, Oxford 1968, p.56, and F. Salet and G. Souchal, *Le Musée de Cluny* (Collection des Guides du visiteur), Paris 1972, pp. 191–2.
[50] H. J. Hewitt, *The Black Prince's Expedition* (57), p.16.
[51] *Chronique artésienne*, ed. F. Funck-Brentano, Paris 1899, p.16 n.4.
[52] Froissart, *Chroniques*, xi.44.
[53] Jean Molinet, *Chroniques*, i.241.

'light-horse' (*genetaires*), 'my lord of Rieux's soldiers' and 'the men of Captain Jean Sallon', wore the colours of the new king of Sicily: red, white and grey. It is significant that these colours may be found again among the 'standards and guidons of the king's host'.[54]

It should not be forgotten, despite all this, that the wearing of a livery was certainly not limited to soldiers and could be accepted by or forced upon a great variety of serving men, even royal, princely or municipal officers. It was for this reason that in England at the end of the Middle Ages limitation on the wearing of livery was considered one of the means of controlling 'bastard feudalism'.

It is possible that, uniform as they were, military liveries included minor differences according to the rank of those wearing them. Thus the chain of command could appear at a glance. It seems, nevertheless, that rank was chiefly displayed in the different degrees of banners – varying in shape, size, and the use of painted or embroidered devices. A perfect example of this tendency may be found in the army of Charles the Bold, where distinct guidons, pennons, banners, baneroles and standards were stipulated for the men-at-arms and archers, the *ordonnance* companies and its subdivisions of squadrons and *chambres*.[55]

[54] F. Piponnier, *Costume et vie sociale. La cour d'Anjou, XIVe-XVe siècle*, Paris and The Hague 1970, pp.253ff.

[55] C. Brusten, Les emblèmes de l'armée bourguignonne de Charles le Téméraire (449); R. Vaughan, *Charles the Bold* (483), pp.209, 223. According to the testimony of Bluemantle, poursuivant of arms, who accompanied an English embassy to Duke Charles in 1472 at the time of the Picardy campaign, 'every C speres had a standart and II penons, I penon for the custerelles and yᵉ bowes on horsebake, wᶜʰ went before, anoder for the fotemen and the standart for yᵉ speres': C. L. Kingsford, *English Historical Literature in the Fifteenth Century*, Oxford 1913, pp.381–2. M. G. A. Vale, *War and Chivalry* (364a), pp.147–51, discusses these developments in some detail.

6

Artillery

The word 'artillery' comes from the Old French *atillier* (Chrétien de Troyes, *Erec et Enide*, 1164) with the meaning 'to deck, adorn with care or arrange'. *Atil* designates decoration, armour or equipment, and *attillement* means apparatus or tackle. Then the form *artillier* appeared under the influence of the word 'art' meaning 'craft'. An *artillier* according to Etienne Boileau (1268) was a manufacturer of war engines, especially bows and offensive weapons. Guillaume Guiart, at the beginning of the fourteenth century, provides the following definition:

Artillerie est le charroi	Artillery is the waggon-train
Qui par duc, comte ou roi	which by duke, count or king
Ou par aucun seigneur de terre	or by any earthly lord
Est chargié de quarriaus en guerre,	is loaded with quarrels for war,
D'arbalestes, de dards, de lances,	crossbows, darts, lances
Et de targes d'une semblance.[1]	and shields of similar kind.

For a long time the term artillery continued to cover all the equipment needed for war, and it cannot be said even by 1500 that this very general meaning had been entirely forgotten. For example Antoine de Lalaing described the arsenal of Maximilian von Habsburg at Innsbruck in these terms: 'The king had had a house built next to the river for his artillery (*artilleries*). I considered it the finest in the world. The house contained suits of armour, culverins, crossbows, pikes, bows, halberds, two-handed swords and all sorts of firearms (*bastons*).'[2] However, the expression 'artillery pieces' (*pièces d'artillerie*) used by the same author meant cannons alone, and before this one finds, for example in the *Chronique Scandaleuse* of Jean de Roye, a contemporary of Louis XI, the term 'artillery' employed in its modern sense.

The process by which artillery fired by gunpowder came to supplant trébuchet-type artillery was very slow, largely because of the mediocre performance of the new weapon over a long period. Progress in the manufacture

[1] Quoted by V. Gay and H. Stein, *Glossaire archéologique* (554), i.76.
[2] L. P. Gachard, *Collection des voyages des souverains des Pays-Bas*, i.310.

of gunpowder, and especially the change from stone balls to cast ones ultimately permitted the new artillery to prevail. Yet its role in warfare needs to be defined precisely, and the effects which its massive utilization had on fortifications and on the methods of attack and defence of fortresses need to be examined.

THE END OF TRÉBUCHET ARTILLERY

That trébuchet artillery (or that worked by balances) was considered around 1300 to be a technological marvel is shown by the very exact descriptions given by Giles of Rome in his *De regimine principum* and by Marino Sanuto Torsello in the *Liber secretorum*.[3] Specialists in this field were important persons, pampered even by the great. In 1297, at the siege of Lille, the count of Hainault beseeched 'through love' his 'very dear master of engines' to make the biggest possible machine. This, once built and loosed off (*descliqué*), threw a huge ball (*pomme*) weighing 200 lbs which demolished a chimney and struck the ground close to the enemy chief, Robert of Béthune.[4]

The first campaigns of the Hundred Years War frequently saw 'engines' (the most usual term) in action. They were also called 'martinets', 'flying engines' (*engins volants*), 'sows' (*truies*), catapults (*bricoles*), *couillarts*, *biffes*, tripences or *tripants*, stone-throwers (*perrières*) and mangonnels (*mangonneaux*).

According to Froissart, at the time of the siege of Mortagne in 1340 the men of Valenciennes constructed 'a very fine engine which threw well, so that great stones were carried into the town and castle'. To reply to this, the besieged approached a 'master engineer' who built them a smaller machine. With its first shot the stone fell a dozen feet short of the Valenciennes one, the second fell right alongside, and the third 'was so well aimed that it struck the main beam of the engine and broke it in two'.[5] The same year, during the siege of Tournai, the besiegers had eight engines and the besieged seven, although they only killed a total of ten people. The besiegers' main aim was to break down gates, while the engines of the besieged were principally attempting to destroy the enemy artillery.[6]

There was no sign of decline before the 1380s. Under Charles V administrative documents speak of stone balls for engines by the hundred.[7] In 1374

[3] Giles of Rome, *De Regimine principum* (11); Marino Sanuto Torsello *Liber secretorum fidelium Crucis super Terrae sanctae recuperatione et conservatione*, Hanover 1611.
[4] *Istore et Croniques de Flandres*, ed. Kervyn de Lettenhove, Brussels 2 vols. 1879–80, i.213.
[5] Froissart, *Chroniques*, ii.64–5.
[6] Froissart, *Oeuvres*, ed. Kervyn de Lettenhove, xxv.346–65.
[7] Bib. Nat., Pièces originales 3021, dossier Villiers de l'Isle Adam 66816, no. 18, and MS français 26040 no.5000. See also the account dating from 1390–1 for 'faczon de dous angins' amounting to 267 *l*. 9*s*. 2*d*. *t*. (*ibid.*, MS. Coll. Touraine et Anjou 28², f.161).

very impressive machines were built by the Genoese to besiege Jacques de Lusignan, constable of Cyprus, in his castle at Lérines. As late as 1405 the French used *machina jaculatoria* for the siege of Mortagne.[8] The following year 100 carpenters were busy at St-Omer making three large engines and four *couillarts*. At approximately the same time, Christine de Pisan stipulated for the defence of a place 'two catapults and two *couillarts*, each provided with enough accessories, ropes and a great number of stones', and for attack 'two great engines and two other medium-sized ones with all necessary things ready to fire. Item, four completely new *couillars* furnished and provided with all things, each having two cables and three *fondes* for changing when required.'[9] Since the same author also required a very large number of cannons, one may presume that the experts she had consulted considered that the new artillery had not eliminated the old but simply supplemented it, doubtless because its effects were thought to be different.

Even around 1420 there is still much evidence to suggest the continuing vitality of trébuchet artillery. In 1419–20 for an 'engine' which was in the cloister at St-Pol, the town of Orléans first bought 'a bale of hay to put in the *fonde* to test the said engine' and then some stones.[10] In 1421–22 the government of Henry V expected to obtain engines and *couillarts* in Paris.[11] In 1421 it was the Dauphin Charles who ordered payment of 160 *l.t.* to Jean Thibaut, master of his works in the Touraine, for two engines 'called and named coyllars', of which one could throw balls of 400 lbs and the other balls of 300 lbs.[12] For his part, Philip the Good, during the campaign intended to rid Picardy of the last remaining Armagnac centres of resistance in 1422, expected to use eight *couillarts*, furnished with projectiles ranging in weight from 100 to 300 lbs.[13]

Following this, at least in France, inventories list machines of this type until around 1460. When Normandy was recovered in 1450 the employment of mangonnels was mentioned here and there, as in the attack on the Tour grise at Verneuil.[14] But it was now only a question of very sporadic use. A decisive turning-point seems to have occurred during the second quarter of

---

[8] *Chronique du Religieux de Saint-Denys*, ed. L. Bellaguet, Paris 6 vols. 1839–52, iii.276.

[9] Bib. Nat., MS français 585, f.53v. The *fondes* were the containers into which the projectiles were placed.

[10] Orléans, Arch. mun., CC 547, f.22r. The use of the word *couillart* (meaning in Old French testicles) obviously has symbolic value since the stone was placed in a leather pouch or sling (cf. *Le Franc archer de Baignolet*, ed. F. Polak, Paris and Geneva 1966, p.35, l.107ff).

[11] C. Gaier, *L'industrie et le commerce des armes* (579), p.328 nn.4 and 6, where a different explanation is offered.

[12] Gay and Stein (554), i.455.

[13] Bib. Nat., MS français 1278, f.67r.

[14] A. Plaisse, *La libération de Verneuil, porte de la haute Normandie en juillet-août 1449*, Evreux 1973, p.30. For the use of 'engins volans' at the sieges of Saint-Denis (1435) and Montereau (1437), see *Les Chroniques du roi Charles VII par Gilles le Bouvier dit le Héraut Berry*, ed. H. Courteault, L. Celier and H. Jullien de Pommerol, Paris 1979, pp.166 and 184.

the fifteenth century; it would be valuable to know whether other regions of the West experienced exactly the same chronology.[15]

POWDER AND CANNON BALLS

As table 9 shows, there are numerous formulae for powder, preserved from the thirteenth century onwards, which can be converted to enable a list of proportions of the three fundamental ingredients of saltpetre, sulphur and carbon to be compiled.

If one remembers that modern experts consider the ideal proportions to be 74.64 per cent saltpetre, 11.85 per cent sulphur and 13.51 per cent charcoal,

TABLE 9   Percentages of saltpetre, sulphur and charcoal in formulae for gunpowder

	Saltpetre	Sulphur	Charcoal
Roger Bacon (c.1267)	41.2	29.4	29.4
Albertus Magnus (c.1275)	66.6	11.2	22.2
Marcus Graecus (c.1300)	66.6	11.2	22.2
John Arderne of Newark (c.1350)	66.6	11.2	22.2
Rothenburg (1377–80)	66.6	16.7	16.7
Nuremberg (1382)	66.6	16.7	16.7
Montauban (c.1400)	71.0	12.9	16.1
Germany (c.1400)	71.0	12.9	16.1
Burgundy (c.1413)	71.5	21.4	7.1
France (c.1430)			
'petite poudre'	57.1	28.6	14.3
slightly stronger powder	62.5	25.0	12.5
even stronger powder	66.7	22.2	11.1
Francesco di Giorgio Martini (second half of fifteenth century)			
powder for bombard throwing 200 lbs at least	50.0	28.6	21.4
powder for smaller bombard and espingarde	57.1	28.6	14.3
powder for passevolant, basilisk and cerbottana	61.5	23.1	15.4
powder for arquebus and escopetti	73.7	15.8	10.5
Rennes (1487)	75.0	11.5	13.5
France (mid-sixteenth century)	75.0	11.5	13.5

[15] At the siege of Burgos in 1475–76 trébuchets were still being used alongside bombards: Y. Bruand, Ouvrages fortifiés en Vieille-Castille (874). During the siege of Rhodes (1480) the Christians used a machine called Tribut, in all probability a trébuchet, to throw stones.

it appears that it was only at the end of the fifteenth century that cannoneers succeeded in coming very close to these figures. However, it may be noted that, first, we do not know what degree of purity of sulphur and saltpetre was attained and, secondly, that different examples (France c.1430; Francesco di Giorgio Martini) demonstrate that there was not always a systematic search for the most effective mixture possible. It was still necessary to ensure above all that the chamber resisted the explosion during firing; only with pieces firing grape-shot (*mitaille*) was it permissible to increase the powder charge and to use the optimal proportions.

The efficacy of powder depended not only on its composition but also on its homogeneity, fineness and the rapidity with which it ignited. It seems that in a pragmatic fashion, specialists at the end of the Middle Ages took these different factors into consideration. In the mid-fourteenth century an English formula prescribed milling the raw materials 'on a marble stone' and then sifting (*bulleter*) the powder through a fine linen cloth.[16] Later there was systematic recourse to powder mills, often worked by horses. On the other hand, because of the instability of the mixture of carbon, sulphur and salt-petre, powder had a tendency to decompose with the least shaking; saltpetre, the heaviest element, dropping to the bottom, while the carbon rose to the surface. Hence, perhaps from about 1420–30,[17] the engraining of powder was practised. From then on it was produced in little balls or granules with stable structure, between which the air (and thus oxygen) could circulate. This permitted a more instantaneous combustion. In order to make these granules, it was necessary to dampen the powder, watering it with brandy or spirits, vinegar or 'the urine of a wine-drinking man'.[18] Then the granules were dried in the sun or in a warm room. A contemporary treatise discussed this: 'The question is whether granulated powder made up into little balls (*boulles ou pelotes*) is better for charging cannon than sieved powder? The author answers that a pound of powder aggregated in granules or balls is worth more than 3 lbs of riddled powder'.[19] From the end of the fifteenth century, different powders were distinguished according to their function. A little later, though the chronology has still to be established in detail, a tripartite classification was reached (powder for large pieces, for hand guns or arque-buses on a stand, and for fuses).[20]

The cost price of powder fell very markedly between the mid-fourteenth century and 1500. If examples are limited simply to money of account in *livres tournois*, around 1370–80 a pound of powder cost 10s. t. Forty years

---

[16] J. R. Partington, *A History of Greek Fire and Gunpowder* (698), pp.323–9 after BL, Sloane MS 56, f.357r.

[17] A. von Essenwein, *Quellen zur Geschichte des Feuerwaffen*, Leipzig 1872, p.25.

[18] There is proof that spirits (*eau ardente*) were used for the making of powder (Lyon, Arch. mun., CC 454 no.41, 1475).

[19] Bib. Nat., MS français 2015, f.16v.

[20] BL, Add. MS 23222, fos.29v–30r.

later this had fallen to 5s. t., while further progress was made during the last quarter of the fifteenth century. By this time the price of a pound of powder was frequently between 1s. 6d. t. or 2s. t. The figure of 1s. 8d. t. was put forward by an official document at the beginning of the sixteenth century,[21] though it remains to be discovered how this lowering of cost became possible. It appears in any case (and contrary to what one might have expected) that the cost of saltpetre, an indigenous product, in both the fourteenth and fifteenth centuries was noticeably more than sulphur for an equal weight, even though the latter had to be imported into most parts of the West. In the Low Countries, for example, sulphur came from Italy. It mostly arrived at Bruges (or later at Antwerp) and was sold at less than half the cost of saltpetre, either in its natural state (live sulphur – soufre vif) or ground (en roc) or moulded into bricks or cakes (en canne).[22]

It is still more difficult to discover the cost of munitions and to learn whether the abandonment of stone balls for cast ones led to economies. A few scattered figures relating to this topic are available.

1   In 1415, 260 stones for cannons were worth 5d. t. each, while 130 smaller ones cost 2½d. t.[23]
2   In 1420–21 it was reported that stones for a great bombard could be taken 'from the quarry at Ivry a league upstream from Paris' and that for each stone the total cost would be 8s.p.[24]
3   In 1478 300 'large stones' cost 36 l.t., that is about 2s. 2d. t. each.[25]
4   In 1480 200 stones for three Burgundian cannon periers cost 3s. t. each, and 400 stones, doubtlessly smaller, cost 2s. 4d. t.[26]

As for balls of 'cast iron' (fer de fondue) we are a little better informed in so far as the weight concerned is generally given. In 1478 the munitions for a great culverin called La Gouvernante cost about 5s. t. a round and in terms of weight, 4d. or 5d. t. per lb. Two years later the figure was 6d. per lb. Under Francis I this figure seems to have fallen by about a half.[27]

THE ROLE OF GUNPOWDER ARTILLERY IN PITCHED BATTLES

Almost certainly at Crécy (1346), as Villani's Chronicle, the Grandes chroniques de France and Froissart's Chroniques attest in unison, the English 'fired off some cannons which they had brought to the battle to frighten the

[21] Bib. Nat., MS français 2068.
[22] Gaier (579), pp.186–8.
[23] BL, Add. Roll 10933.
[24] Gaier (579), pp.327–8.
[25] Arch. dép. Côte-d'Or, B 1783.
[26] Ibid., B 11870.
[27] Bib. Nat., MS français 2068.

Genoese'.[28] The desired end appears to have been chiefly psychological. It was an isolated incident and it was not until the 1380s that pieces of artillery were seen once again on the battlefield. Thus at the battle of Beverhoutsfeld on 3 May 1382 between the men of Bruges and those of Ghent, the latter had at their disposal 'in battle order' (*en ordonnance de bataille*) some ribaudequins (*ribaudeaux*) which Froissart described as being on 'high carts', mounted on two or four iron-banded wheels and provided in front with iron pikes and three or four small cannons. It was these weapons, numbering some 300, which the men of Ghent discharged simultaneously.[29] In Italy the first indubitable example of the use of artillery in the field is at the battle of Castagnaro in 1387 when John Hawkwood, captain of the Paduan army, positioned cannons in an ambush prepared for Veronese forces.[30] Two years, earlier, at Aljubarrota in the Iberian peninsula, cannons had been employed, especially on the Castilian side. However, as late as 1408, when the men of Liège fired their pieces at the battle of Othée, 'the rhythm of the field artillery's fire was too slow to succeed in creating a barrage'.[31]

Even during the second half of the fifteenth century cannons were only used occasionally in pitched battles. A few examples may be cited: at the battle of Castillon on 17 July 1453, the French were besieging the town defended by the English under Talbot. The besiegers, in conformity with current practice, had built a fortified camp (*parcq en champ*) in which to defend themselves and seek safety. Talbot imprudently attacked the camp which led to the intervention of the French battery commanded by Giraud de Samian, a highly respected cannoneer. 'He grievously injured them because with each shot five or six fell dead to the ground'.[32] Or, again, at Brustem on 28 October 1467: the vanguard of the Burgundian forces included mounted archers, pikemen and artillery, while the first battle (or division) of the men of Liège, with cannons and culverins, was dug in on the edge of the village of Brustem, safely protected by hedges, dykes, marshes and high palisades.

> The battle began with an artillery duel. The Burgundians . . . advanced their pieces up to the dykes at four or five spots and from there fired at the Liégeois. Moreover they managed to unleash a considerable bombardment (the Burgundians are said to have fired 70 rounds). But the trees and hedges impeded their line of fire, though if these obstacles prevented them from advancing, they also provided them with unexpected cover against shots by the enemy who were, for their part, often forced to rest content with taking pot-shots over the palisades. This resulted in the end in the Burgundian fire gaining more victims than that of the men of Liège.

[28] Froissart, *Chroniques*, iii.416.
[29] *Ibid.*, x.225–6 and 375.
[30] M. Mallett, *Mercenaries and their Masters* (512), p.160.
[31] C. Gaier, *Art et organisation militaires* (112), p.319.
[32] *BEC*, *8* (1846), 246–7.

Then the Burgundian vanguard advanced once again and the Liégeois fell back, abandoning their cannons. Thus the artillery (and then not all of it) had only been used in the initial struggle, for the Burgundian siege artillery remained with the rear-guard, protected by pikemen.[33]

It may be added that even a clear superiority in artillery was not sufficient to ensure victory, as the defeats of Charles the Bold at Grandson and Morat in 1476 show.[34] In addition, losses due to cannon were often very slight, notably at the battle of Fornovo (1495) which began with several artillery salvos. Philippe de Commynes, who was an eye-witness, estimated that the artillery on both sides had killed fewer than ten men, though he estimated the total losses at 100 on the French side and 3,500 on the Italian.[35]

The weakness of artillery and its vulnerability stemmed from its poor rate of fire, the difficulties of transporting it and its mediocre range. Once the first salvo had been fired, it was only necessary for the enemy to advance, seize the pieces and, according to a procedure attested from the beginning of the fifteenth century, to spike them.[36] The operation of unspiking was very slow and could scarcely be done before the battle was over. Hence the anxiety to protect the artillery by improvised fortifications (raised earth banks, ditches, palisades) and by a mass of pioneers and sappers. As for the light pieces (hand culverins, hacquebuts), they were used tactically.

SIEGE WARFARE: ATTACK AND DEFENCE

From a very early time small, medium and heavy artillery pieces were integrated into the total range of weapons used during sieges and attacks on strongholds. A first turning-point occurs in the years 1370–80, while a second follows at the beginning of the fifteenth century. From then on fairly reliable information is available with which to estimate the intensity of the pounding which those besieged had to withstand. During the siege of Maastricht from 24 November 1407 to 7 January 1408, the town received 1514 large bombard balls, that is some 30 a day. On Sunday 17 October 1428, according to the *Journal du siège*, the English fired 124 'pierres de bombardes et de canon' into the city of Orléans, some of them weighing up to 116 lbs. At the siege of Lagny in 1431, the besieged were subjected to a bombardment of 412 stone balls in the course of a single day. Dinant, from 19 to 25 August 1466, received 502 balls and nearly 1,200 serpentine shots. Rhodes in the siege of

---

[33] Gaier (112), pp. 345–6; cf. Commynes, *Memoirs*, tr. Michael Jones, Harmondsworth 1972, pp.121–3.

[34] H-R. Kurz, Grandson – 2 Mars 1476 – le déroulement de la bataille, in *Grandson 1476. Essai d'approche pluridisciplinaire d'une action militaire du XVe siècle*, ed. D. Reichel, Lausanne 1976, pp.201–13; G. Grosjean, Die Murtenschlacht (54).

[35] Commynes, *Mémoires*, iii.191–2. It is true that a storm had probably dampened the powder.

[36] Jean Jouvenel, *Histoire de Charles VI*, ed. Michaud and Poujoulat, Paris 1836, p.497.

1480 had to suffer the destructive effects of 3,500 balls. It is true that the effects were not always as successful as had been hoped. Chroniclers tell us, sometimes marvelling at it, about the almost total ineffectiveness of some batteries; though they also tell of buildings being demolished, quarters burnt and large breeches being opened up in walls.

One of the functions of the artillery was to protect the pioneers and sappers while they dug trenches, from the safety of which the attackers could reach the moat and walls. Jean de Bueil in the mid-fifteenth century recommended: 'When your bombards have begun to fire, make sure that the veuglaires and light artillery fire as much as possible after each bombard shot, so that those within have no chance to make boulevards nor to repair the damage which the bombard will have done to them.'[37] Nevertheless, to the extent that artillery was only effective over very short distances, it was exposed to the unexpected attacks of defenders as well as to their own cannons. Hence the need to protect it by 'great watches', faggots and bundles of branches, the raising of earth and thick wooden covers (*manteaux*), sometimes fitted with movable openings.

It is clear that at the very end of the Middle Ages, thanks to artillery, sudden, expeditious attacks could be attempted and succeed. Thus in France just before the Italian Wars a Florentine observer wrote:

When a town is reached, the horses (which have pulled the artillery) are led away, the cannons are turned round and then pushed forward bit by bit so that in a single day they can reach the walls under the protection alone of the waggons. When the time for bombardment comes thirty or forty pieces are fired so that the wall is soon reduced to rubble. The French say that their artillery can make a breech in a wall eight feet thick. Although every hole is small, their number is large for from the moment they begin to fire they do not stop day or night.[38]

Episodes like the taking of the town and castle of Coucy in 1487 confirm this analysis, which is echoed a little later in a treatise by Philippe de Clèves. He advised placing cannons in batteries only 30 or 40 paces from the moat, from where they might fire 40 shots a day. A quick calculation, according to the rhythm of fire and the number of pieces of artillery, suggests that in 24 hours (for night did not interrupt the cannoneer's work) up to 1,000 rounds could strike the enemy stronghold.

But naturally, from the beginning, defensive measures began to take account of the new weapon, and the art of fortification adapted to artillery, after a short time-lag. Every castle and town tried to maintain permanently a stock of firearms, bullets and powder to complement the traditional weapons and armour. In the fifteenth century there were numerous urban centres

[37] *Le Jouvencel* (9), ii.41, quoted here after M. G. A. Vale, *War and Chivalry* (364a), p.143 (translator's note).
[38] Quoted by P. Contamine, L'artillerie royale française (680), pp.22–3.

whose councils maintained one or several master cannoneers or artillers, just as they kept a master of works, clock-keeper and, sometimes, a doctor or a surgeon. The size of the stock of artillery reflected the wealth of the town, its strategic interest and the risks which it thought it ran.

From the middle of the fourteenth century the defence of castles was partially ensured by cannons, though doubtless of small calibre, taking their place along with crossbows, springalds and other engines. Thus at the castle of Bioule in 1347, according to an order of its lord, Hugues de Cardillac (or de Cardoullac), the 'gate in front of the place', among others, was to be defended in the following manner: 'On the first floor, two men to fire the cannons and throw the great stones; on the second floor, two men to fire the double-footed crossbow, then, on the wall, two crossbowmen, plus two men to throw fist-sized stones.' In total, 22 artillery pieces were to be used.[39]

More than a century later in 1468 the defence of Bourg-en-Bresse, threatened by the troops of Louis XI, was the object of extremely detailed instructions. It was envisaged that each of the town's six gates would be provided with a *veuglaire* and a serpentine on a fixed base, carefully sited and aimed (*logés, affûtés et adressés*) by the captain of the town and the syndic of the burgesses. Each piece had thus its own opening (*pertuys*) and line of fire, hence the need to clean and clear the boulevards and ravelins. In addition, for each gate there were to be two large iron culverins and two bronze culverins, this time movable. In the towers gunloops were anticipated, alongside arrow-loops, and it even appears that several of the towers were to be filled with earth up to a certain level of the interior 'so that seats could be placed there and it would be easier to fire through the said embrasures'.[40]

In general, a large part of the artillery was concentrated on and in the gates, the vulnerable points *par excellence*, and also on the terraces of towers, which, in consequence, it was necessary to reinforce.[41]

It was not thought necessary before the end of the fourteenth century to make openings in the base of towers and in the curtains in order to permit cannon fire. One of the first examples is probably the *meurtrière* placed in the portcullis chamber in the châtelet at Mont-Saint-Michel (a work completed in 1393).[42] Then the practice spread. In 1418 a contract for the reconstruc-

[39] *Bulletin archéologique*, 4 (1847–48), 490–5. This same lord formed the artillery of Cahors and Lauzerte when he received the captaincy of these places.
[40] O. Morel, L'état de siège à Bourg (335): 'pour povoir asseeter les syeges et trayre facillement esdictes canonyers'.
[41] There is a fairly early example at the Bastille in Paris according to an inventory of 1428: 'Item, es terresses dudit chastel, ung vuglaise, enchacillié en boys, gectant pierre de VI livres pesant ou environ, et a deux chambres': *Revue archéologique* (1855), 328ff.
[42] J. F. Finó, *Forteresses de la France médiévale* (783), p.308. For England where the earliest gunports may date from c.1365 and 'arketholes', mentioned in an indenture for Cooling castle (1381), tally with surviving apertures, see the recent survey of J. R. Kenyon, Early artillery fortification in England and Wales, *Archaeological Journal, 138* (1981), 205–40 (tr.).

tion of the gate of Lamballe castle makes allowance for a cannonière along with ordinary openings for crossbows.[43] At the castle of La Bruyère-l'Aubespin, as it is depicted in the mid-fifteenth century in the famous *Armorial* of Guillaume Revel, the enceinte is 'preceded by a low chemise pierced by numerous meurtrières, which can be used just as easily by archers as by defenders using firearms because the loophole has been enlarged in the middle by a round orifice'.[44] A document of 1473 concerning Montivilliers stipulated the 'piercing low down of the walls of towers which had not been so treated'.[45] At Caudebec in 1480 'to guard all the side and curtain along the river Seine' the construction of two large towers whose height and thickness were to be average was planned; one facing Tancarville was to guard and fire to the south, across the Seine, to the east, along the wall to the next tower, to the west, in the direction of Tancarville, and to the north as far as the Harfleur gate. The other tower, built close to the Rouen gate, was to fire to the west as far as the first tower and in other directions as far as the Rouen and Caux gates. *Moineaux*, or low blockhouses, were also to be installed at the level of the moat.[46]

As early as 1461 a similar layout had been mentioned in a project to fortify Dijon which had been presented by the well-known expert François de Surienne. He had recommended:

1   Gunports at the level of the *chemin de ronde* as well as at the base of walls. The lower gunports should be disposed in such a fashion that fire could be permitted at 3 ft above the boulevards which had been established beyond the moats. But if the edge of the moat was too high a trench was to be made to allow the cannons a clear line of fire (*pour donner chemin et droict mire aux canons*).

2   In the moats, low towers (with a maximum height of 4 ft, rectilinear on the sides and rounded at the front) were planned, making a salient of 5 m to the wall and pierced by three *lumières* on the sides and front for culverins and serpentines. These towers, which may be viewed as case-mates, blockhouses or, as they were called a little later, *caponières*, were to be so placed that 'the defence and artillery could fire in a straight line of

---

[43] P. Rocolle, *2000 ans de fortification française* (818), i.101 and 147. The contract is printed in *Anciens évêchés de Bretagne*, ed. J. Geslin de Bourgogne and A. de Barthélemy, St-Brieuc and Paris 6 vols. 1855–79, vi.241–3: 'et seront les fenestres des dictes tours garnies de bouches et de canonières'.

[44] Y. Bruand, Châteaux du Bourbonnais (770), p.525.

[45] Bib. Nat., MS français 20494 no.53. A generation earlier at Lisieux there had been plans for a 'boullevart de machonnerie . . . canonnieres embrases par leur dedens, garnies de retraiges, d'estouisses, de vousseurez bien et suffisamment comme il appartient' (*ibid.*, MS Clairambault 218 no.100).

[46] *Ibid.*, MS français 6987, f.224; J-P. Leguay, *Un réseau urbain au Moyen Age* (808a), p.186, for Breton examples.

sight from one tower to the next all along the curtains and the said moat.'[47]

In other words, Robert de Balsac around 1500 was only expressing a commonly accepted idea in recommending that 'blockhouses should be constructed in the moats to fire along them, which would be out of danger from without.'[48] For a long time, the defenders of a place thought first of reinforcing its solidity by thickening the walls (11 m – a record – for the keep of Ham, built by the Constable of St-Pol around 1470), and by enclosing their base in a *glacis* of sloped masonry, and secondly, of providing positions for light firearms intended to repulse an eventual assault. The ordinances made in 1443 for the fortification of Montuel (dép. Ain) may be cited as evidence of this: 'Item, in addition, it is advised that a *glacis* should be made all round the motte of the round tower and it should be put in a state of defence and furnished with cannonières in such a way that the *glacis* and the said tower should dominate all the motte.'[49] The boulevard (as the word appears in France at the beginning of the fifteenth century – a sort of advance work, most often before a gate, taking the place of the old barbican, Latin: *propugnacula*) seems to have been integrated into a system which was above all defensive. If this is accepted, the work of Leon Battista Alberti, *De re aedificatoria* (1440–50), remains very traditional in its insistence on flanking and the need for a very thick *glacis*. The same impression is gained from the *Trattato di architettura* of Filarete (about 1460) and also from Roberto Valturio when he extolled, in the fortress of Sigismondo Malatesta at Rimini, the scarping (*talus*) of the ramparts and the layout of the gunloops.[50]

But things had already begun to change with artillery towers (Italian: *torrioni*), where weapons of large calibre were permanently installed on a platform. In effect, these towers had to be more squat, and the idea of lowering them to the level of the curtains in order to facilitate circulation of the artillery and the resupplying of munitions became well known. Parapets were increasingly substituted in the place of merlons and crenellations. It is possible that it was the refashioning of these towers, placed at the angles of the fortifications, which gave birth to the bastion. The word, of Italian origin, appears from the end of the fourteenth century. But the bastion in its modern sense occurs only much later, and the decisive role in its development should not be attributed either to Leonardo da Vinci or to Francesco di Giorgio Martini, but to Guiliano da Sangallo (1445–1516), with his works at Borgo

---

[47] J. Richard, Quelques idées de François de Surienne sur la défense des villes à propos de la fortification de Dijon (1461), *Annales de Bourgogne, 16* (1944), 42–3: 'tellement que la deffense et artillerie puisse tirer en droict ligne a mire, d'une tour a aultre, au long des murs et dudict fossé'.

[48] P. Contamine, The war literature of the late Middle Ages (43).

[49] *Bibliotheca Dumbensis, ou recueil des chartes, titres et documents pour servir à l'histoire de Dombes*, ed. J. E. Valentin-Smith and M. C. Gigue, Trevoux, 2 vols, 1854–85, ii.90.

[50] J. R. Hale, The development of the bastion (863), p.477.

San Sepolcro, planned in 1500 and built between 1502 and 1505, Nettuno, constructed between 1501 and 1503, and Arezzo, planned in 1502 and built in 1503.[51] The fact that at the same period the kingdom of Naples, on the one hand, and Venice and Lombardy on the other, remained faithful to the traditional formulae, means that the development of bastions can be considered an autochthonous invention taking shape in central Italy. It was there that the 'proper' bastion was born, that is to say a mass of earth, surrounded or flanked by walls, of triangular, polygonal or rounded plan, forming a sharp angle in relation to the curtains.

However, we cannot exclude the possibility that bastions arose from a transformation of boulevards or ravelins, or even false brays (*fausses braies*), rather than from artillery towers. The boulevards of Bonaguil prefigure bastions and so do the boulevard-platforms added to the castle at Brest between 1489 and 1499.[52] Of the massive round construction built at Metz in 1466 opposite the Serpenoise gate it could be said that it was a 'bastion avant la lettre'.[53] One of the first mentions of the word bastion in French is found in the description of the siege of Neuss (1475) by Jean Molinet. He spoke in connection with the town's fortification of 'a great and powerful *bastillon* fortified with trenches' and of 'another *bastillon* . . . wonderfully fashioned from earth and bales of straw and stuffed with fine gunports and men and other terrible defences'. A third quotation clearly shows that it was a question of modified boulevards. Neuss, he said, had four principal gates, each with 'its boulevard in front in the form of a *bastillon*, large, strong and defensible, furnished with all the weapons of war, especially with gunpowder in quantity'.[54]

More extensive research (in particular with regard to the meaning, appearance and diffusion of technical terms) is needed for a clearer picture to emerge. This research should be on the whole of the West and allied to meticulous study of pictorial evidence, fortifications still in place, didactic treatises, historical narratives and accounting records. Perhaps it will show that at about the same time in several countries, sometimes widely separated, identical solutions were reached by both anonymous masters of works and well-known architects, working towards making the fortress no longer a passive mass but a place of dynamic defence, capable of passing, when required, on to the counter-offensive.

Three remarks may be made in conclusion to demonstrate the position acquired by artillery and the reputation of certain very capable gunners at the

---

[51] *Ibid.* An attentive study of the fortifications raised at the prompting of Louis XI (as in Burgundy or Roussillon) might perhaps show that France *c.*1480 was not lagging behind the most sophisticated transalpine constructions.

[52] P. Rocolle, *2000 ans* (818), i.172.

[53] J. Thiriot, *Portes, tours et murailles de la cité de Metz. Une évocation de l'enceinte urbaine aux XVIe et XVIIe siècles*, Metz 1970, p.33.

[54] Molinet, *Chroniques*, i.31, 64–5.

end of the Middle Ages.[55] First, the fact that even the lives of captains and war-leaders were directly threatened by the new weapon. One of the first examples of an identified victim is provided by Froissart from the siege of Ypres in 1383: 'There Louis Lin a very brave English esquire was killed by a cannon shot.'[56] Among others who can be mentioned later are Louis Paviot killed at the siege of Meulan (1423), the earl of Salisbury at the siege of Orléans (1428), the earl of Arundel (1434), Pedro of Castille (1438), the Admiral Prigent de Coëtivy and Tugdual le Bourgeois, both at the siege of Cherbourg (1450), the 'good knight Sir Jacques de Lalaing' (1453), Tanguy du Chastel (1477), Bayart (1524) and Louis de la Trémoille (1525). Not even princes and kings were safe from danger; James II of Scotland 'mair curieous nor becam him or the majestie of ane King . . . unhappely (was) slane with ane gun, the quhilk brak in the fyring' at the siege of Roxburgh on 3 August 1460; the arquebus which killed Tanguy du Chastel nearly carried off Louis XI, and in 1465, during the fighting around Paris, the French artillery 'fired two shots through the room where the count of Charolais was lodged while he was dining and killed a trumpeter carrying a plate of meat upstairs'.[57] Secondly, firearms appeared on board ships. According to a freight contract of 23 May 1394, the Catalan ship of Francescho Fogassot, going from Barcelona to Alexandria, was to be provided with three bombards and 60 stones.[58] At the beginning of the fifteenth century, each of 40 'large vessels à huis', which it was planned to equip in order to help the fleet at La Rochelle, were to have four culverins with powder and lead and two good veuglaires, each provided with 120 stones and 60 lbs of powder.[59] At the beginning of the sixteenth century Philippe de Clèves advised for the prince's principal ship 19 large pieces of artillery, a dozen falcons and an unspecified number of hacquebuts and culverins.[60] Thirdly, and lastly, even before 1500 artillery had taken its place in the panoply of honours paid to important figures. In 1496 Arnold von Harff, visiting Rome during the course of a pilgrimage,

---

[55] A place recognized by Machiavelli, despite some reticence, after a detailed analysis: *Oeuvres complètes*, ed. E. Barincou, pp.555–61; cf. also Vale (364a), pp.129–46. Among those cannoneers whose reputation was early noted was Watelet 'the finest gunner known anywhere', who at the siege of Bourges in 1412 'fired a cannon at the King's tent': Journal des années 1412 et 1413, ed. A. Tuetey, *Mémoires de la Société de l'histoire de Paris et de l'Ile de France*, 44 (1917), 179.

[56] Froissart, *Chroniques*, xi.120. Modern scholars do not appear to have further identified this medieval Huskisson.

[57] *The Auchinleck Chronicle*, ed. T. Thomson, Edinburgh, 1819–77, pp.20, 57; Commynes, *Mémoires*, i.61, cf. *Memoirs*, tr. Jones, p.94.

[58] C. Carrère, *Barcelone, centre économique et social à l'époque des difficultés 1380–1462*, Paris 2 vols. 1968, i.235 n.4. Cannons were normally loaded onto Castilian galleys operating against England in the 1370s and 1380s: P. E. Russell, *English Intervention in Spain and Portugal in the time of Edward III and Richard II*, Oxford 1955, p.231.

[59] Bib. Nat., MS français 1278, fos.73–4.

[60] Philippe de Clèves, *Instruction de toutes manieres de guerroyer*, Paris 1558. See also J. F. Guilmartin, *Gunpowder and Galleys. Changing Technology and Mediterranean Warfare at Sea in the Sixteenth Century*, Cambridge 1974, pp.295–303.

speaks of 200 cannons being fired off simultaneously to welcome Alexander VI to the Castel Sant'Angelo: 'This is done in honour of the Pope when he rides over the bridge, and similarly when a cardinal rides across they shoot off three cannon in his honour.'[61] In 1501 on the approach of Louis XII and the archduke Philip the Handsome, 'there were fired from the castle (of Amboise) as a sign of joy several great engines.'[62]

[61] *The Pilgrimage of Arnold von Harff*, tr. M. Letts, Hakluyt Society, London 1946, p.45.
[62] L. P. Gachard, *Collection des voyages des souverains des Pays-Bas*, Brussels, 4 vols, 1876–82, i.142.

7

The Art of War

Reflections on the art of war have long been the concern of historians who, conscious of long-term developments, have attempted to compare the medieval period with Antiquity and modern times. Almost without exception they have concluded that the art of war in the Middle Ages was very mediocre, rudimentary, simple, even non-existent as a deliberate, organized and established discipline, applicable at different levels by officers according to their rank and function. Many of these historians, sometimes serving or retired officers, work more or less consciously within the framework of pragmatic or utilitarian teaching designed for future officers or military schools. They have thus drawn the conclusion that there is practically nothing to be gathered or learnt from the study of medieval campaigns, battles or sieges. In short, as far as war is concerned, just as with the history of philosophic thought, between Antiquity and the Renaissance there is a thousand-year gap.

A few examples of this very generally held attitude may be cited. In the article 'Strategy' in the *Encyclopaedia Britannica*, B. H. Liddell Hart, a British military thinker of great reputation, after praising the outstanding strategic merits of Hannibal and Scipio, dismisses the Middle Ages in a few lines: 'In the West during the Middle Ages the military spirit of feudal "chivalry" was inimical to art, although the drab stupidity of its military course is lightened by a few bright gleams. King John of England had a real insight into grand strategy, and Prince Edward, later Edward I, produced a masterly example of mobility in exploiting a central position in the Evesham campaign' (1265). Finally, after centuries of an almost total void, there came Oliver Cromwell, 'the first great strategist of modern times'.[1] An analogous judgement was expressed by R. van Overstraeten when he described the medieval period in these terms:

> Once it became numerous, cavalry played the principal role. The lord wore full armour and was well mounted. All his life was passed on horseback in arms;

---

[1] *Encyclopaedia Britannica*, coronation edn. 1937, xxi.456, cf. 16th edn 1948, xxi.456.

war was his profession, occupation and hobby. The army never had such a uniform and exclusive recruitment, yet at the same time, never was the art of war so imperfect or so primitive, startling proof that a martial spirit and individual valour can achieve nothing without good organization and solid discipline . . . All the lords were equal, none consented to fight in the second rank. The army was formed into a single line; the knights charged without order, each choosing an adversary whom he judged worthy of his blows. The battle was a collection of individual combats in which the commander of the army participated as a simple combatant.[2]

A final diagnosis, this time more recent, is that of Eric Muraise, for whom in the Middle Ages:

the arrangements for battles were gross, the sequence of action very clumsy, the manoeuvres summary, the co-operation between units limited or non-existent . . . It cannot be emphasized too much how far the use of cavalry, especially the French, had regressed [by comparison with Antiquity] in its obstinate desire to charge in 'battles' without any sense of manoeuvre and on a very narrow front . . . Very often battles in the Middle Ages were not directed and broke down into a series of parallel, autonomous, combats . . . There no longer survived great mixed units and feudal fragmentation lent itself poorly to large-scale military schemes. There was no other military policy than that of enlarging one's domains and Europe only ever had two opportunities to extend its ambitions and the scale of its dreams – the Carolingian empire . . . and the Crusades. The general use of fortifications had . . . such a great importance that it took the place of a military culture . . . All the art of tactics was summed up in the desire not to be the first to attack for, as a general rule, the attacker was always defeated as he lost all ability to command in a total assault, without chance to manoeuvre on a terrain which he had not chosen and which was unfavourable to him.[3]

However, various recent works have shown that reality was more complicated and that it is not impossible (a) to gather some of the very general principles of medieval tactics; (b) to examine campaigns whose progress implies certain directing ideas, in other words, a strategy; (c) to list a fairly extensive series of responses and procedures used, according to circumstance, during pitched battles; and (d) to admit that with regard to mental attitudes, medieval soldiers had a clear idea of the advantages which recourse to a fund of practical experiences and theoretical reflections as complete and varied as possible could provide.

[2] R. Van Overstraeten, *Des principes de la guerre à travers les âges*, Brussels 1926, i.30 quoted by J. F. Verbruggen, *De Krijgskunst in West-Europa in de Middeleeuwen* (88). (I have not been able to find this quotation in the revised English version of Verbruggen – translator's note).
[3] E. Muraise, *Introduction à l'histoire militaire*, Paris 1964, pp.254, 257–8.

TEACHING ON THE ART OF WAR

Graeco-Roman Antiquity had seen the formation of a whole corpus of military literature from the time of Aeneas the Tactician, the leader of Greek mercenaries in the fourth century BC, to the time of Vegetius (late fourth century AD or perhaps mid-fifth century),[4] including the works of Philo of Byzantium, Hero of Alexandria and Frontinus.

From this corpus, for most of the Middle Ages at least in the West, a single author was well known: Vegetius, who appears as the outstanding authority (*auctor* or *auctoritas*) in the realm of warfare. Anthologies cited extracts from his works; ecclesiastical writers mentioned him both in their sermons and in their spiritual treatises. When in the thirteenth century Vincent of Beauvais wanted to include the art of war in his *Speculum majus*, he restricted himself to mechanically recopying almost entirely the *Epitoma de re militari* of Vegetius. Alfonso X the Wise of Castile (1252–84) in the *Siete Partidas*, Giles of Rome in the *De regimine principum* (about 1280) and Christine de Pisan in the *Art de chevalerie* acted in exactly the same fashion. The work of Vegetius has been preserved in dozens of manuscripts. From an early point it was translated into the vernacular. In French there are the translations of Jean de Meung (1284), 'Mastre Richard' (*c*.1271), Jean Priorat and Jean de Vignai (early fourteenth century); in Italian that of Bono Gimaboni (*c*.1250) and in English that for Thomas, lord Berkeley (1408), whilst other fifteenth-century translations into German, Spanish, Portuguese and even Hebrew survive.[5] A Vegetius can be discovered in the ninth-century library of Duke Evrard of Friuli, as can another in that of the future Edward I of England in the thirteenth century[6] or that of Sir John Fastolf in the fifteenth.[7] Naturally Denis the Carthusian could not avoid quoting it in his little work *De vita militarium*.[8] Christine de Pisan recommended reading at least Book IV of Vegetius to the 'noble baronnesse' who might have to defend her lands in the absence of her husband at the wars.[9] There are even some pocket-sized folding manuscripts of Vegetius.[10] In the books which Jean

[4] For the date of the *Epitoma de re militari* see the hypothesis advanced by W. Goffart, Vegetius' *De re militari* (53).
[5] C. R. Schrader, A handlist of extant MSS containing the *De re militari* of Flavius Vegetius Renatus, *Scriptorium*, *33* (1979), 280–303; J. Wisman, *L'Epitoma rei militari* de Végèce (93b).
[6] P. Riché and G. Tate, *Textes et documents d'histoire du Moyen Age, Ve-Xe siècles*, Paris 2 vols. 1975, ii.415; M. D. Legge, The Lord Edward's Vegetius (66).
[7] In his library, which contained 19 books, Sir John Fastolf had six history books (including a Livy and Caesar), a French poem, two romances plus Vegetius: S. L. Thrupp, *The Merchant Class of Medieval London 1300–1500*, Michigan 1962, p.249.
[8] Denis le Chartreux, *Opera Omnia*, Tournai 1909, pp.37, 581–3.
[9] P. Contamine, *La vie quotidienne en France et en Angleterre pendant la guerre de Cent ans* (*XIVe siècle*), Paris 2nd edn 1978, p.188.
[10] Like Wolfenbüttel, Cod. Lat. 84, cited by A. Murray, *Reason and Society in the Middle Ages*, Oxford 1978, p.446.

Gerson advocated for the Dauphin's library one finds the *De regimine principum* of Giles of Rome (hence, in part, Vegetius), the work of Valerius Maximus, the *De stratagematibus bellicis* of Frontinus and a *De re militari translatus* of Vegetius.[11] In 1346 Amadeus VI, count of Savoy, bought a copy of Vegetius in Paris. In the fifteenth century the catalogue of a bookseller at Tours mentions a 'Vegece de chevalerie' along with the *Rosier des guerres* and the works of Frontinus, Honoré Bovet and Jean de Bueil. Nor was it simply the Cistercians of the abbey of Maubuisson who, at the same period, possessed 'un livre bien escript nomme Vegece de re militari' in the midst of their liturgical and pious manuscripts.

The real, solid influence of this authority is difficult to determine; on the one hand because the army to which Vegetius referred was so profoundly different in its composition, recruitment, organization and spirit from medieval armies and, on the other, because in the majority of cases one can only guess at the theoretical understanding of the commanders and leaders. Rare examples show the direct application of Vegetius with more or less successful results. In the ninth century Rabanus Maurus advised Lothair I to re-read Vegetius the better to resist the Normans.[12] The same author made an abridgement with a number of interpolations, where the emphasis was placed, significantly, on the role of the cavalry.[13] In 1147 when Geoffrey Plantagenet, count of Anjou, was besieging a castle in the Loire valley, he inquired of the monks of Marmoutier how to make an incendiary bomb, which was finally constructed and then used thanks to a Vegetius manuscript.[14] A little later, we are told that the bishop of Auxerre, Hugues de Noyers (1183–1206), 'rejoiced in gathering a crowd of knights about him with whom he most gladly discussed military matters and also often re-read Vegetius, who talks about these problems, and he explained to the knights many of the lessons to be drawn from this author.'[15] During the siege of Neuss by Charles the Bold in 1474–75, a Castilian knight, 'who was considered very clever and inventive', inspired 'by Vegetius and other venerable writers who were very highly recommended and authoritative for the art of war', suggested to the duke of Burgundy the construction of a machine called a 'crane'

---

[11] Jean Gerson, *Oeuvres complètes*, ed. R. Glorieux, *Oeuvres épistolaires*, Paris 1962, ii.213.

[12] P. Riché, *Les écoles et l'enseignement dans l'Occident chrétien de la fin du Ve siècle au milieu du XIe siècle*, Paris 1979, p.302.

[13] L. White, *Medieval Technology* (677), p.149.

[14] Murray, *Reason and Society* pp.127–8; *Chroniques des comtes d'Anjou et des seigneurs d'Amboise*, ed. L. Halphen and R. Poupardin, Paris 1913, p.218. It should be noted that the authentic text of Vegetius does not mention any formula for the manufacture of incendiary bombs, so that in the event, it was an augmented Vegetius that was consulted.

[15] V. Mortet and P. Deschamps, *Recueil* (810), i.96–7. In the same way Philippe de Mézières advised 'princes et aux grans officiers de l'ost' to read or have read before them 'le gracieux livre du Gouvernement des princes, celluy que composa Egidius de Rome' and 'le livre profitable de Vegetius de la chose chevaleresque ainsi entitulé' (Froissart, *Oeuvres*, ed. Kervyn de Lettenhove, xv.464).

(*grue*), the plan of which he drew. After Duke Charles had given his agreement, the engine was built. It was a type of movable tower furnished with a ladder some 60 ft high which 'lowered like a draw-bridge' and could be fastened onto the wall at the moment of assault. But the site was unsuitable and the engine got stuck in the mud, provoking laughter amongst the besieged.[16]

The *Stratagems* of Frontinus, though having a more modest place, may be mentioned along with Vegetius. There were examples of this work in the libraries of Nicolas de Baye and Simon de Plumetot at the beginning of the fifteenth century.[17] It was translated into French early in Charles VII's reign and Antoine de la Sale took copious extracts from it for his compilation *La Salade*, written in 1444 for John of Calabria.[18]

The Middle Ages did not have recourse to the texts of Antiquity alone. Slowly their own military literature grew. An example of this is provided by the rules of the military religious orders, especially that of the Templars, which contained precise tactical teaching.[19] At the end of the twelfth century Gerald of Wales, who had accompanied Prince John on his expedition to Ireland (1185), indicated in the *Expugnatio hibernica* the methods most likely to defeat the Irish: 'In Irish warfare it is above all necessary to ensure that archers are added and mixed up with squadrons of knights, so that the stones thrown by the Irish, with which they are accustomed to oppose heavily and well-armed troops, as well as their manner of attacking on all sides, then withdrawing without injury because of their agility, may be countered by arrows shot in every direction.'[20]

From the second half of the thirteenth century, a whole politico-military literature, aimed at inciting temporal and spiritual leaders of Latin Christendom to take up the Crusade against the Infidels again, saw the light of day. One such volume was the *Liber recuperationis Terre sancte* which the Franciscan Fidenzo of Padua composed between 1274–91. This treatise, which he had undertaken at the instigation of Gregory X at the time of the Second Council of Lyon, was delivered to Nicholas IV at the beginning of 1291, that is only a few months before the loss of St John of Acre. It contained a total plan of reconquest. He estimated in particular the number of necessary troops, deplored the fact that Christendom did not have at its disposal a 'lasting, regular and permanent army', and suggested that such a

---

[16] Jean Molinet, *Chroniques*, i. 44–5.

[17] *Journal de Nicolas de Baye, greffier du Parlement de Paris 1400–1417*, ed. A. Tuetey, Paris 2 vols. 1885–88, ii.XCIV; G. Ouy, Simon de Plumetot (1371–1443) et sa bibliothèque, *Miscellanea codicologica F. Masai dictata*, ed. P. Cockshaw *et al.*, Ghent 1979, p.376. It is possible that it was a copy of Frontinus that Wibald sent about 1160 to Rainald von Dassel, chancellor of Frederick Barbarossa: *Bibliotheca rerum Germanicarum*, ed. P. Jaffé, Berlin 1864, i.326–8, nos.207–8.

[18] R. Bossuat, Jean de Rouvroy, (33).

[19] For example, about the role of esquires and sergeants in relation to the knights: H. de Curzon, *La règle du Temple* (217).

[20] Giraldus Cambrensis, *Opera*, vi.395–7.

force could be raised if its innumerable cities, bishoprics and abbeys simply maintained one, two or three knights each in the Holy Land. He observed that despite their numbers the Saracens had only a few good troops (*strenui milites*), that they lacked great, powerful horses and that their mounts were even more vulnerable since, in comparison with those of the Latins, they were not protected. All that was necessary was to attack them with determination, using an infantry armed with lances and able to form a wall or 'hedgehog,' with their lances projecting outwards, and to recruit mounted archers and crossbowmen.[21] The plan elaborated between 1306 and 1321 and proposed to Pope John XXII by the Venetian, Marino Sanuto Torsello, appears even more complete and precise. His remarkably informed *factum* indicated the itinerary and furnished estimates of troops, armament, provisions and financing. He waxed lyrical on war machines and offered a complete geographical description of the 'Promised land' (*Terre de promissione*). He specified the dispositions which were necessary to avoid past mistakes, the way to order a camp, fight a battle and undertake a siege. He listed a series of war ruses culled from ancient and more recent history, and it may be noted that the report which he submitted to the pope was accompanied by four maps – of the Mediterranean, 'de la mer et de la terre', of the Holy Land, and of Egypt.[22]

Pursuing this kind of literature, for the fifteenth century one finds the memoir addressed to the duke of Burgundy, Philip the Good, by Bertrandon de la Brocquière (1432). After describing Turkish tactics (which he judiciously compared with those of the Parthians and Persians) and suggesting that all their strength lay in their archers, for their lances were useless and they 'were not armed to withstand a great push on foot' ('ne sont point armez pour soustenir ung grant fait a poulser a pié'), he considered the expedition which the Christians should undertake against them. He dreamed of a composite army which gathered together the most effective military elements in Northern Europe – the largest possible number of French men-at-arms and archers, of German nobles with their foot and horse crossbowmen (*cranequiniers*), as well as 1,000 English men-at-arms and 10,000 English archers. For protection, dressing in a light, white (that is, plate) armour or even a brigandine would suffice, because the Turkish bows were not very powerful. The cavalry should have light lances with sharpened edges, hardened and piercing swords and small axes; the infantry should be armed with gisarmes or good, sharp boar-spears. In the event of a pitched battle, a single corps was envisaged for the centre, whilst the rear- and vanguards would protect the wings. The bowmen were to be 'interlarded' amongst the other soldiers in the same way, as were two or three hundred ribaudequins with

[21] Fidenzo of Padua, *Liber recuperationis Terre sancte* (218), although his influence must have been very limited since only one fourteenth-century copy of this manuscript is conserved (Bib. Nat., MS Latin 7242, fos.85r–126r).
[22] Marino Sanuto Torsello, *Liber secretorum fidelium Crucis*, Hanover 1611.

wheels which were to be taken along by the army. Finally, skirmishing at the start of an engagement was to be prohibited, as was the 'hunt' or pursuit at the end.[23]

It should not be forgotten that historical and narrative literature also had a didactic aspect in the military sphere, to the extent that a prince or lord would read Julius Caesar, Sallust, Valerius Maximus, histories of the crusades, Froissart or the *Grandes Chroniques de France* not simply to improve or to amuse himself, but also to educate himself in the technical sense of the term. In the mid-fourteenth century, Pierre Bersuire, on the order of King John the Good, undertook a French translation of the *Decades* of Livy 'so that in a similar manner [princes] may defend and govern their lands, possess and conquer in proper manner foreign ones, injure their enemies, defend their subjects and help their friends.' Sometimes application was immediate. It was by reading about an incident in the *Gothic Wars* of Procopius that Ferdinand of Aragon, then engaged in the siege of Naples, discovered the ruse which enabled him to penetrate the town by means of an acquaduct.[24] At the end of the Middle Ages, a small number of original treatises on the art of war were written, like those of Theodore Paleologus, Jean de Bueil and Robert de Balsac.[25]

In order to gauge with the greatest possible exactitude the impact of theory on practice, it will be necessary to undertake several types of investigation in parallel. The examination of narrative and historical sources reveals allusions to 'authorities', like this passage from *Jehan de Saintré* by Antoine de la Sale where he makes Vegetius say: 'Those who make errors in everything without reason can remedy all except confused mistakes in wars and battles which none can withstand for the penalty immediately follows their commission.'[26] Or there is the critical remark of Jean Molinet, concerning the siege of Neuss, deploring the fact that his master, the duke of Burgundy, had not followed the counsel of Vegetius 'who teaches that tents or the camp (*fors*) should be pitched in a place which cannot be affected by a sudden flood'.[27] It sometimes happens that there is evidence for the consultation of a manuscript on military science. On 30 November 1415 (doubtless at the moment when plans were being laid for the recapture of Harfleur) Master Jean Maulin, librarian

---

[23] Bertrandon de la Brocquière, *Le voyage d'outremer (1432–1433)*, ed. C. Schéfer, Paris 1892, pp.225ff.

[24] A. Lecoy de la Marche, *Le roi René*, Paris 2 vols. 1875, i.211. Jean de Bueil in *Le Jouvencel* (9), i.17, recognized that 'for a long time those who have written about the deeds of the Romans, the Chronicles of France and other battles in days gone by have sufficiently described in writing the way to organize oneself in war'.

[25] J. Bastin, *Le traité de Théodore Paléologue* (301); de Bueil (9); Robert de Balsac, *La nef des princes* (7). See also D. Bornstein, Military manuals in fifteenth-century England (30), and Military strategy in Malory and Vegetius' *De re militari* (31); P. Contamine, The war literature of the late Middle Ages (43).

[26] Antoine de la Sale, *Jehan de Saintré*, ed. J. Misrahi and C. A. Knudson, Geneva 1965.

[27] Jean Molinet, *Chroniques*, i. 83.

at the Louvre, carried to Rouen from Paris on the orders of Charles VI a book entitled the '*Trésor du Roy*, in which several war-engines were depicted'.[28] A systematic survey of manuscripts and incunabula editions of treatises on the art of war would obviously provide an index of their diffusion. Written 'advice', 'counsel', regulations and instructions compiled for specific projects – campaigns, sieges and battles – survive, particularly from the later Middle Ages. There is, for example, the battle-plan sent in September 1417 to John the Fearless, duke of Burgundy, as he circled round Paris with his army, or the instructions for the attack on Pontoise in 1441,[29] or the advice which in 1435 Sir John Fastolf addressed to Henry VI's government, in which may be found the best theoretical explanation for the great English *chevauchées* during the course of the Hundred Years War. The English captain there proposed to launch two expeditions from Calais or Le Crotoy, each of 3,000 combatants (including 750 lances), which, between 1 June and 1 November, were to ride towards Burgundy across Artois, Picardy, Laonnois and Champagne, burning and destroying all in their path.[30] Lastly, the libraries of soldiers (that is nobles of a certain rank who had exercised military responsibilites) are often instructive, and two examples can be quoted here. At the beginning of the fifteenth century the library of Guichard Dauphin, lord of Jaligny, master of the crossbowmen of France, included, in addition to various chronicles, a manuscript of Livy, another containing lives of Alexander and Caesar, books on tournaments and armorial bearings, the treatise of Theodore Paleologus, the book of Geoffroy de Charny on the joust, tournament and war, 'a little book on the care of horses' and, finally, Honoré Bovet's *L'Arbre des batailles*.[31] As for the inventory of the books of Bertrand de Béarn, bastard of Comminges, drawn up in 1497, it mentioned in the military sphere, *latu senso*, the Chronicles of Froissart, the Decades of Livy, the *Life* of Bertrand du Guesclin, *L'Arbre des batailles* and the *Jouvensel avancé pour guerra* by Jean de Bueil.[32]

Whatever the importance (in any case minimal) of theoretical or intellectual influences, it was without doubt practical training which was most significant in all respects. Because of its role in contemporary armies, all exercise on horseback, notably hunting, could be considered as preparation for war.

[28] H. Moranvillé, Extraits de journaux du Trésor (1345–1419), *BEC, 49* (1888), 426.

[29] P. Marchegay, L'assaut de Pontoise (19 septembre 1441), *Revue des Sociétés savantes*, 4e sér., iv.470–3.

[30] C. T. Allmand, *Society at War* (299), 34–5; M. G. A. Vale, *Nottingham Medieval Studies, 17* (1973), 78–84.

[31] A. Leroux de Lincy, Inventaire des livres composant la bibliothèque des seigneurs de Jaligny, 6 juin 1413, *Bulletin du Bibliophile* (1843), 518–27.

[32] Desbarreau-Bernard and A. Baudouin, Inventaire des livres et du mobilier de Bernard de Béarn, bâtard de Commenge (1497), *Académie des Sciences, Inscriptions et Belles-Lettres de Toulouse*, 7e sér., 4 (1872), 100–13. For an Italian example see M. E. Mallett, Some notes on a fifteenth-century *condottiere* and his library: Count Antonio da Marsciano, in *Cultural Aspects of the Italian Renaissance*, ed. C. H. Clough, Manchester 1976, pp.202–15.

The place of the quintaine, the joust and tournament (or *cembel* or *bohort*) should not be forgotten. Though it may be mentioned here that although the tournaments of William the Marshal's day were very close to real warfare in the number of participants, their conduct and the rewards and risks, things had changed by the end of the Middle Ages, when they had largely become a ritualized spectacle or formal parade respecting an increasingly strict etiquette. Moreover, not only the papacy (from 1130) but also, later, kings like Philip the Fair had tried to prohibit or to limit tournaments, which they considered dangerous and vain exercises, a waste of energy, which worked to the detriment of proper military activities over which they wished to preserve a monopoly.[33]

Individual exercises were also practised and in towns at the end of the Middle Ages master swordsmen gladly offered their services.[34] A form of martial gymnastics is sometimes mentioned which could be compared in certain respects with the military exercises of contemporary armies. One of the finest examples is Marshal Boucicaut, who shows, contrary to a long-lived legend, what degree of agility could be attained by even an armed man, wearing a supple coat of mail if not a rigid plate armour:

> He executed a somersault fully armed, except for his bascinet, and whilst dancing he was armed with a mail coat. Item, he leapt onto a courser without placing his foot in the stirrup, fully armed. Item, with a strong man mounted on a great horse, he leapt from the ground into his shoulders by taking his sleeve in one hand and without any other hold. Item, placing one hand on the saddle pommel of a great courser and the other near the horse's ears, seizing

[33] For the medieval hunt see bibliography in *Das Rittertum im Mittelalter*, ed. A. Borst (100), pp.457–8; for the tourney and joust, *ibid.*, pp.452–3. It is necessary, however, not to minimize the risks run even in tournaments and jousts at the end of the Middle Ages; cf. Mathieu d'Escouchy, *Chronique*, i.107, and M. G. A. Vale, *War and Chivalry* (364a), pp.68–71. Analogous to tourneys were the simulated fights which had existed for a long time in certain Italian towns until municipal authorities banned them (as at Perugia and Siena in the thirteenth century). Even after this rival groups of citizens continued to defy each other to prove their strength and valour. The defiance and gauntlet sent in 1387 by the *non paurosi combattenti* of the Porta S. Trinità at Prato to 'the noble and illustrious Messer Piero de' Rinaldeschi and the famous and virtuous merchant Francesco di Marco, master of the Battle of the Men of Porta Fuia', inviting them to choose 20 or 30 companions, has been preserved: Iris Origo, *The Merchant of Prato*, London 1957, p.60.

[34] A. de la Grange, *Extraits analytiques des registres des consaulx de la ville de Tournai 1431–1476*, Tournai 1893, p.133: 27 February 1448, request 'des compagnons esquiermisseux de l'espee a deux mains [de] faire une feste et esbatement et avoir grace de le faire publier par les bonnes villes'. In 1463 Poitiers authorized Simon Varlier, native of Soissons, 'maistre du jeu de toutes armes qui competent a fait d'armes, c'est assavoir d'espee a deux mains, de la hache d'armes, de l'espee a rouelle et de la dague . . . de jouer en ceste ville et de tenir *escolle* desdits jeux et aussi mectre et pandre aux fenestres l'espee, la dague et la hache': R. Favreau, *La ville de Poitiers*, Poitiers, 2 vols. 1978, ii. 436.

the mane, he leapt from the ground through his arms and over the horse. Item, if two walls were an arm's length apart and as high as a tower, he could climb to the top without slipping on the ascent or descent, simply using the strength of his arms and legs, without any other assistance. Item, wearing a coat of mail he ascended the under side of a great ladder placed against a wall to the top without using his feet, simply jumping with both hands from rung to rung and, then, taking off this coat, he did this with one hand until he was unable to ascend any higher.[35]

Especially at the end of the Middle Ages, there was a determined effort by public authorities to favour the practice of military exercises at the expense of sports or civil pastimes. Some peoples had an inveterate, even daily, habit of such exercises, like the Swiss[36] or the Scots. But this did not prevent a primacy being accorded to the martial arts, a general tendency which may be found both in the English countryside as well as in Italian or German towns. A statute of Richard II in 1389 imposed on 'servants and labourers' the need to obtain bows and arrows and to practise archery on Sundays and on holidays, renouncing ball games (either with the hand or foot) and 'other games called *coytes*, *dyces*, *gettre de pere*, *keyles* and other such importunate games'.[37] In France the Valois monarchy, faced by the English threat, took similar measures, especially from the reign of Charles V onwards. It is true that it seems to have hesitated over this, for reasons of public order. Jean Jouvenel des Ursins recounts how in 1384, on the conclusion of a truce between France and England, the government of Charles VI prohibited playing any other games except those with the bow and crossbow. Results were soon apparent: in a short time French archers were beating English ones. But then there were fears of social subversion, for 'if they were gathered together they would be more powerful than the princes and nobles.' As a result Charles VI gave up imposing a general apprenticeship and restricted himself to specifying a limited number of archers to be raised in certain towns and districts. 'Then afterwards people began to take up other games and pastimes as they had previously.'[38]

Thus there were many channels by which, at least individually, an apprenticeship in martial arts could be obtained. In contrast, collective exercises, manoeuvres on a small or large scale, never seem to have been regularly planned. We have to wait until the ordinances of Charles the Bold, that is until the very end of the Middle Ages, before finding regulations relating to

---

[35] *Le livre des faicts du bon messire Jean le Maingre, dit Boucicaut, marechal de France et gouverneur de Gennes*, ed. J. F. Michaud and J. J. F. Poujoulat, Paris 1836, pp.219–20.

[36] W. Schaufelberger, *Der Wettkampf in der alten Eidgenossenschaft* (383).

[37] 12 Ric. II, c.6.

[38] Quoted by J. Loiseleur, Compte des dépenses faites par Charles VII pour secourir Orléans pendant le siège de 1428, *Mémoires de la société historique et archéologique de l'Orléanais, 11* (1868), 92.

this topic.[39] It is astonishing to think that it proved possible to move on the battlefield, without previous peacetime training, a compact body of some 10,000 men like that used by the Swiss at Grandson, Morat, Nancy and elsewhere.[40] Moreover, the Middle Ages were ignorant of 'officers' training schools' or military academies. These were to appear in Italy only in the sixteenth century. In France 'the first establishment that one can compare with a military academy is probably the *Académie des Exercises* founded in 1606 by the duke of Bouillon.'[41]

All this means that apprenticeship in war was learnt in war itself, in the field; hence the necessity to start learning very early, even before adulthood was reached, and to accumulate experience with the passage of years. Authors spontaneously insisted on precedents, on slow maturation and on an indispensable progression in responsibility. *Le Jouvencel* of Jean de Bueil is built on this idea, with its three parts, 'monosticque yconomicque et polliticque'. 'The first speaks of the government of a single man. The second about oneself and others. The third of the government of princes and captains, who have the charge and governance of countries and peoples.'[42]

War as the domain of 'experience', of 'science', of 'reason', of 'discretion'; these were commonplaces in medieval writings. There, again, we could follow Jean de Bueil when he declared that 'the principal factor in all warfare is, after God, the discretion of the leader', as he described the celebrated Etienne de Vignolles, nicknamed La Hire, as 'a good doctor of the science of war' and when he emphasized that 'the conduct of war is artful and subtle, for which reason it is necessary to govern by art and science and to proceed little by little before one reaches a full understanding of it'.[43] As for the expression 'military art', Molinet came close to it with *art militant* and it was used at the same period by the astrologer Simon de Pharès.[44]

---

[39] P. Contamine, *Guerre, état et société* (457), pp.497–8. During the Anglo-French talks at Tours which resulted in the truces (1444), an archery competition was held between the archers of the earl of Suffolk and the Scottish Guard of Charles VII who carried off the prize (P. Champion, *Vie de Charles d'Orléans (1394–1465)*, 2nd edn Paris 1969, p.345). In May 1489, for the jousts which were taking place at Plessis-du-Parc near Tours, Charles VIII's captains 'faisoient mettre ensemble tous ceux qui estoient armez qu'ils faisoient marcher comme s'ils eussent esté rangez en bataille en face de leurs ennemis': Guillaume de Jaligny, *Histoire de Charles VIII, roy de France*, ed. D. Godefroy, Paris 1684, p.77.

[40] W. Schaufelberger, *Der Alte Schweizer und sein Krieg* (380).

[41] A. Corvisier, *Armées et sociétés en Europe de 1494 à 1789*, Paris 1976, pp.119–20.

[42] de Bueil (9), i.5. On the need to learn about war from an early age: 'Homo bellicosus, ab infancia in armis nutritus', says a twelfth-century text quoted by G. H. Hagspiel, *Die Führerpersönlichkeit im Kreuzzug* (253), and 'Les princes doyvent faire exercer leurs enfans es faiz des batailles dés l'aage de XIIII ans': Bib. Nat., MS français 193, f.270v.

[43] de Bueil (9), i.130, 246 and 15.

[44] '*Artus, rex Britanie*. Cestui fut moult expert en la science de astrologie et aussi de l'art militaire': Simon de Pharès, *Recueil des plus célèbres astrologues*, ed. E. Wickersheimer, Paris 1929, p.149.

STRATEGY: THE MASTERY OF SPACE AND TIME

Medieval strategy does indeed appear to have been dominated by two general principles: fear of the pitched battle, of the confrontation in open country, and what one could call the 'siege mentality', in other words 'an automatic reaction which consisted in replying to an attack by shutting oneself up in the most easily defensible strongholds of the country'.[45] From this emerged the shape which the majority of medieval conflicts assumed – the very slow progress of the attackers, the obstinate defence of those attacked, limited operations both in time and distance, a war of attrition (*guerre d'usure*), 'a strategy of accessories' where each combatant or group of combatants, often in an incoherent and discontinuous fashion, fought primarily for immediate material profit. Contemporaries had an expression to describe this kind of warlike activity on a reduced scale. It was the *guerre guerroyante*, made up of losses and recaptures, surprises, incursions, ambushes and sallies.[46] 'War is . . . above all made up of pillaging, often of sieges, sometimes of battles.' Moreover, because of a lack of money, men, supplies and provisions, many plans failed to mature: 'A campaign brought to a conclusion constitutes an exception, an enterprise which defies the rule.'[47]

Certain political societies have had recourse to continuous lines of fortification to contain a potential aggressor. This was the case of the Middle Empire with the famous Great Wall of China, built in the third century BC against the nomads of the Steppes, then lengthened, refashioned and reconstructed at different times, especially in the fifteenth century under the Ming dynasty. It was also the case with the Roman Empire, of which the *limes* was sometimes reduced to a simple ditch, coupled with a bank (Syria, North Africa). But it could also be constituted by a system of entrenchments with ditches, banks, walls, watch towers, small forts and camps (the *limes* of Germania for over 500 km, covering the Decumatian fields, Hadrian's Wall from the mouth of the Tyne to the Solway Firth and, further to the north, the Antonine Wall).

For many reasons the medieval West largely ignored such a solution. For a long time its state institutions were very primitive; hence the precarious system of financing, the impressing labour and the many and fragmented political units. In addition danger might come as much from within as without. There was a conception of fortification which favoured, doubtless for good reasons, isolated points of resistance.

That is not to say that there were no frontier zones (or marches) which had been organized and conceived as such: the Anglo-Scottish border, the Anglo-

---

[45] C. Gaier, *Art et organisation* (112), p.204.

[46] '*Guerre guerroyante*' was an expression used, for example, by Robert de Balsac. 'It was called *Guerra guerrejada*' in Catalonia (R. Sablonier, *Krieg und Kriegertum in der Crónica des Ramon Muntaner* (537), p.97).

[47] Gaier (112), p.216.

Welsh Marches, the Germanic marches facing the Slav world, the March of Brittany, the frontiers of Livonia, Granada or the Calais Pale all come into this category.[48] In the fourteenth and fifteenth centuries at the end of a campaign and once the main army had been dismissed, it was customary to organize the frontiers militarily using a network of garrisons or *establies*. This network could be dense and deep in order to prevent the infiltration or the irruption of enemy forces, who risked being isolated and seeing their line of retreat cut off if they passed through the links of the mesh, or had to capture each fortress one after another with all the delays that such a process implied. A good example of this defence is provided by the map of *establies* which the government of Philip VI of Valois kept in his pay on either side of the Garonne in September 1340, just before the truce of Esplechin (map 3).

Robert de Balsac, dealing with the line of conduct which he felt a prince should adopt when threatened with invasion, recommended him to 'guard the strong points of the frontier' ('garder les bonnes places de la frontière'). Then two possibilities were open to him: either to gather a great army which might confront the enemy at 'l'entrée de son pays' or:

> to repair and supply with foodstuffs, artillery and men the principal places of the frontier, to demolish those which were not defensible, to withdraw all livestock from the frontier and a broad swathe into the interior of his country and to place all the food supplies from the countryside in strong places so that the enemy might not find anything when they came to lay siege and ride about in strength.[49]

However we can list some examples of continuous linear fortifications. There is Offa's Dyke (eighth century), facing the Britons of what is present-day Wales. At the beginning of the ninth century the Danes built banks of earth, reinforced with timber, to create a barrier 15 km long across the Jutland isthmus (*Danevirke*). In the same region, facing the Obodrites, Charlemagne built the *limes saxonicus*, running roughly north–south.[50] More frequently, simple ditches were considered valuable obstacles to impede the movement of soldiers when their action was close to banditry. In 1454 (as

---

[48] On the notion of the frontier in the Middle Ages see, recently, the contributions of B. Demotz, P. Tucoo-Chala and C. Gauvard to *Les principautés au Moyen Age*, Bordeaux 1979. For their military organization, K. F. Drew, The Carolingian military frontier in Italy (157); A. R. Lewis, Cataluña como frontera militar (870–1050) (199); J. M. Lacarra, Les villes-frontières dans l'Espagne (257); W. Urban, The organization of defence of the Livonian frontier (290); E. M. Fernandez, La frontière de Grenade aux environs de 1400 (530); M. Jones, The defence of medieval Brittany (807a).

[49] de Balsac (7). A chapter in the treatise of Theodore Paleologus explains 'how a prince should organize his men on the frontiers, on *chevauchées*, on scouting missions (*en espies*) and other matters'.

[50] L. Musset, Problèmes militaires du monde scandinave (171); H. Jankuhn, *Die Wehranlagen der Wilingerzeit zwischen Schlei und Treene*, Neumünster 1937 and *Geschichte Schleswig-Holsteins*, Neumünster 1956, iii.137ff.

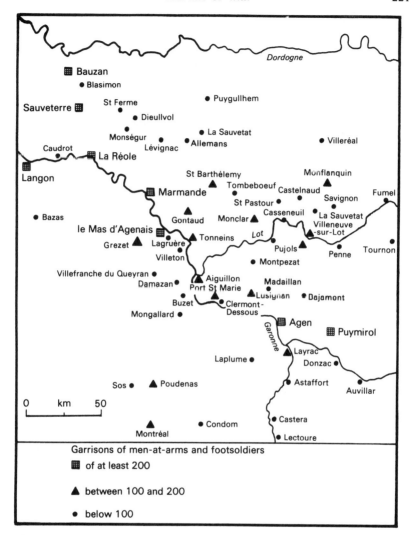

Map 3   Defence in depth: the principal French garrisons north and south of the Garonne
(September 1340)

well as in 1439 and 1465), on the orders of the bishop in the district of Liège,
a 'safety barrier' was constructed, 'constituted by wide ditches joining the
pre-existing natural or artificial obstacles from Huy to Saint-Trond', and
beyond, as far as the western marches of the county of Looz.[51] According to
Robert of Torigni in 1169, 'Henry II ordered the digging of wide and deep

---

[51] C. Gaier, La fonction stratégico-defensive du plat pays au Moyen Age dans la région de la
Meuse moyenne (795).

ditches between Normandy and France in order to repel brigands.' Such
were the Fossés-le-Roi in Perche which, depending on the Avre and Sarthe
rivers, extended from Nonancourt to Mêle-sur-Sarthe (map 4).[52]

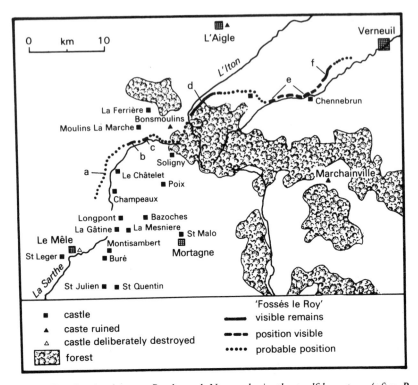

*Map 4 The frontier between Perche and Normandy in the twelfth century (after B.
Jouaux, Les Fossés-le-Roi, Cahiers percherons, 58 (1978)).
The visible sections of the ditch are to be found at: a. Fossés le Roy (Commune of
Ste-Scolasse); b. Bois de Bel Erable Bretonnière (Moulins-la-Marche); c. La Bachelière
(Commune of Moulins-la-Marche); d. Les Genettes/Les Aspres; e. isolated sections; f.
St-Christophe.*

Even operations on a small scale could betray a certain strategic care in the
sense that the aim was consciously adapted to means and certain tactics. The
short campaign of Edward III in the Cambrésis, Vermandois and Thiérache
during the autumn of 1339 can be taken as an example. It was a question
there of intimidating the enemy, Philip of Valois, almost of snapping one's
fingers at him, destroying his economic resources and, eventually, of confronting him in a pitched battle. The king of England could count on 1,600

<hr />

[52] B. Jouaux, Les Fossés-le-Roi, *Châteaux forts et guerres au Moyen Age, Cahiers percherons,*
no.58 (1978), 6–8.

men-at-arms, 1,500 mounted archers and 1,650 foot archers and spearmen from over the Channel, plus 800 men-at-arms recruited in the Low Countries and in Germany. To this considerable expeditionary force (at least by contemporary standards) were added the allied contingents of the dukes of Guelders and Brabant, the margrave of Juliers and the count of Hainault.[53] The *chevauchée* began on 20 September in the Cambrésis. There were various attempts (*assaus, escarmuces et paletis*) to capture Cambrai while the combatants were still assembling. Edward III left on 9 October. Having crossed the Scheldt, he trampled the kingdom of France under foot. On the evening of the ninth, he slept in the abbey of Mont-Saint-Martin very near to Péronne, while the duke of Brabant lodged at the abbey of Vaucelles. On the 10th, cardinals sent by Pope Benedict XII came to find him to negotiate, vainly, for peace. For some days he remained where he was, while his troops attempted to attack the castle of Honnecourt-sur-Escaut and undertook raids as far as the outskirts of Bapaume, Péronne and Saint-Quentin. On the 14th the king departed, the monastery of Origny-Sainte-Benoîte was destroyed and the earls of Northampton and Derby ravaged the district of Laon as far as Crécy. After stopping at the abbey of Fervaques (in the commune of Fonsommes), Edward III crossed the Oise (16 or 17 October), stayed the night at the abbey of Bohéries (commune of Macquigny), passed south of Guise and then turned back to the north-east, staying until 23 October between La Flamengrie and La Capelle-en-Thiérache. There he drew up his army in battle order, waiting for the forces of Philip VI which had been concentrated between Saint-Quentin, Péronne and Noyon, and had then followed the same route as Edward III, reaching the village of Buironfosse on 20 October. For some hours on 22 October the two armies were on the point of engaging, but the king of France's council convinced him, by advancing several reasons, that he ought not to expose his troops: they said it was a Friday (a return to a prohibition going back to the Truce of God); the horses, worn out by a five-league march, had neither eaten nor drunk; and, lastly, between him and the enemy there lay a difficult crossing-point. Suddenly during the night of 23/24 October Edward III set off in the direction of Brussels, and then to Antwerp. It was indeed a battle *manqué* but it left tangible traces. One source speaks of 2,117 'towns and castles burnt and destroyed'. Even if this figure is greatly exaggerated, it remains true that the destruction was immense, as is witnessed by the charitable mission undertaken a few months later by the papal envoy, Bertrand Carit, in the devastated zone (map 5).[54]

---

[53] A. E. Prince, The strength of English armies (432), 360–2.
[54] Froissart, *Oeuvres*, ed. Kervyn de Lettenhove, xviii.84–6, *p.j.* 26. L. Carolus-Barré, Benoît XII et la mission charitable de Bertrand Carit dans les pays dévastés du nord de la France, Cambrésis, Vermandois, Thiérache, 1340, *Mélanges d'archéologie et d'histoire publiés par l'école française de Rome 1950*, 165–232.

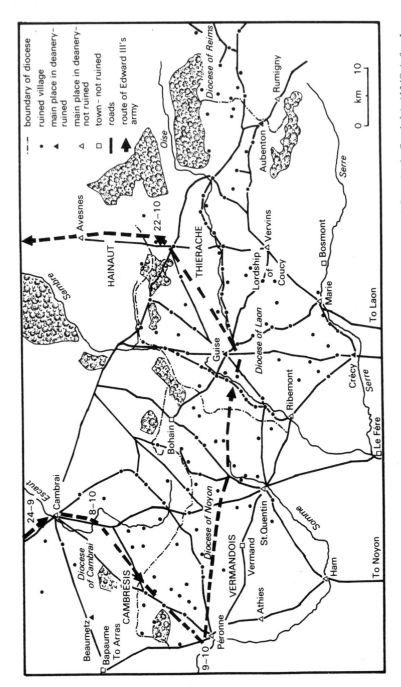

Map 5   The first campaign of the Hundred Years War (1339) and the charitable mission of Bernard Carit in the Cambrésis (1340) (after L. Carolus-Barré, Benoît XII et la mission charitable de Bertrand Carit, Mélanges d'Archéologie et d'Histoire publiés par L'Ecole française de Rome, 1950)

Other *chevauchées* ranged over a greater distance and moved more quickly. A classic example is that which the Black Prince carried out across Languedoc from the Atlantic to the Mediterranean in October and November 1355, covering 900 km in less than two months, that is an average of 15 km a day. This was a remarkable performance if it is remembered that towns and suburbs were taken by assault (Avignonet, Montgiscard, Castelnaudry, the lower town at Carcassonne) and that on the return journey an immense booty slowed down the march (map 6).[55]

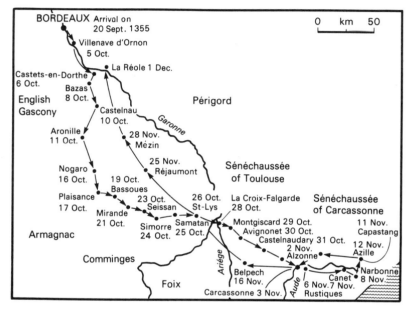

Map 6   The first raid of Edward, Prince of Wales (October–November 1355)

At a still more elevated level, some campaigns displayed an elaborate collective strategy, like the expeditions of Charlemagne against Saxony,[56] the conquest of England by William, duke of Normandy,[57] the campaign by Edward I to conquer Wales in 1294–95[58] or the simultaneous English *chevauchées* of 1346 and 1356.[59] Perhaps one of the greatest successes of this kind was the recovery (*recouvrement*) of Normandy by Charles VII in 1449–50. Once the truces of Tours had been broken following the capture of Fougères by François de Surienne (24 March 1449), the campaign proper

[55] H. J. Hewitt, *The Black Prince's Expedition of 1355–1357* (57).
[56] Above, p.25.
[57] J. H. Beeler, *Warfare in England* (25).
[58] J. E. Morris, *The Welsh Wars of Edward I*, Oxford 1901.
[59] A. H. Burne, *The Crécy War* (41).

began at the end of July with a concentric attack launched by three forces. From the east, leaving Beauvais, the counts of Eu and Saint-Pol crossed the Seine, took Pont-Audemer, Pont-l'Evêque and Lisieux and proceeded methodically to sweep the region of Bray. In the south, Dunois, who had the title of lieutenant-general, entered Verneuil, was joined by Charles VII at Louviers, captured Mantes and Vernon and then continued his march as far as Argentan. In the west, the army of the duke of Brittany, François I and the Constable of France, his uncle, Arthur of Richemont, took Coutances, Saint-Lô, Carentan and Fougères. While this last army took up its winter quarters, the others regrouped, obtained the capitulation of Rouen at the beginning of November and retook Harfleur, Bellême, Honfleur and Fresnay-le-Vicomte.

Tardily, the English government decided to react by sending a small relieving army under the command of Thomas Kyriel, which disembarked at Cherbourg on 15 March 1450. This expeditionary force recovered some places in the Cotentin, turned towards the Bessin but was overwhelmed at Formigny (15 April) by the united forces of the count of Clermont and the Constable, Richemont. The last phase of the campaign was marked by the fall of Caen, where the majority of English had sought refuge and which had been besieged by the four *osts* of Kings Charles VII and René of Sicily, the duke of Alençon and Guillaume Jouvenel des Ursins, Chancellor of France, the Constable and the count of Clermont, and Dunois and the lord of Orval. The last English strongholds fell like ripe fruit: Falaise, Domfront and, finally, Cherbourg. Jean Chartier, like other chroniclers, expressed his admiration: 'And after setting out, the whole of the duchy of Normandy was conquered and all the cities, towns and castles of the province were remitted into the king's obedience in the space of only one year and six days, which was a great miracle and remarkable marvel.'[60]

Despite the absence of land maps, it is clear that high commands capable of executing this or similar campaigns must have been sufficiently informed about the areas over which they fought. Consultation of 'itineraries', systematic recourse to 'guides', to spies or traitors, to merchants, religious and adventurers, would scarcely be a problem in a society in which mobility was indubitably an important characteristic.[61] It may be added that although from the mid-thirteenth century the utilization of nautical maps was a rule for the preparation and carrying-out of expeditions in the Mediterranean, it was only from the very end of the Middle Ages that there is any evidence for

---

[60] Jean Chartier, *Chronique de Charles VII*, ii.233–4.
[61] Espionage was considered an absolute necessity for princes at the end of the Middle Ages. Robert de Balsac spoke about this at several points in his treatise. de Bueil (9), ii.34–5, recommended: 'A prince should spend a third of his revenues on spies.' See also, on this important question, neglected for a long time by historians, J. R. Alban and C. T. Allmand, Spies and spying in the fourteenth century (347); H. Thomas, Französische Spionage im Reich Ludwigs des Bayern, *Zeitschrift für historische Forschung*, 5 (1978), 1–21.

the consultation of land maps for military ends. The Department of Maps and Prints of the Bibliothèque Nationale, Paris, preserves a military map of Lombardy, drawn in all probability on the occasion of the war between Venice and Milan (1437–41). On this map are marked, along with other things, bridge emplacements (whether stone or wood), routes (with indication in Arabic numerals of distances in miles) and fortified places. Robert de Balsac in 1502 was one of the first in France to recommend to a prince wishing to conquer a country that he map it (*mectre en paincture*), not simply, it seems, so that he could follow the stages of his progress from town to town but so that he could also get an idea of its natural obstacles, water-courses and mountain ranges.[62]

It thus appears that generals in the Middle Ages displayed a certain sense of geography, were capable of conceiving and executing a 'grand strategy' and could dominate a theatre of operations which was sometimes very extensive. Did they, in the same manner, know how to master time? Two considerations should be taken into account here: first, the feeble financial means of states, which meant that collection and payment of a large army for more than four or five months was, even for a powerful monarchy at the end of the Middle Ages, a fairly remarkable achievement; and second, that for all sorts of reasons it was very much easier and far more pleasant to wage war during the summer; 'When the soft season of summer had returned and it was good to wage war and stay in the fields' is a remark by Froissart which was a commonplace, almost an axiom.[63]

Nevertheless war was not necessarily conceived as a simple occupation, an almost sportive activity, linked to a particular way of life, an end in itself. It was also, fundamentally, a means for achieving an objective, and to reach this objective, authorities did not hesitate to turn natural rhythms upside down, to demand or impose on their financial officers, on merchants following the armies, on captains and troops, excessive efforts, sometimes far beyond commonly admitted or tolerated norms. Hence campaigns sometimes lasted a whole year, almost without any cessation of effort or wasted time, and sieges were pursued without intermission through the depth of the winter (Calais, Orléans, Neuss). It was evident, too – Philippe de Clèves remarked on it – that in Spain and Italy and, *a fortiori*, in the Holy Land, the break in fighting during winter months asserted itself even less than in Europe north of the

---

[62] Bib. Nat., Rés. Ge. C.4990, reproduced in R. Almagia, *Monumenta Italiae cartographica*, Florence 1929, p.9 and plate VIII, i; de Balsac (7).

[63] Froissart, *Chroniques*, viii.107. See also the remarks of the *Chronique des quatre premiers Valois*, ed. S. Luce, Paris 1862, pp.278–9, à propos the siege of Cherbourg by French troops in 1378–79: 'At that time when siege was being layed before Cherbourg it was remarkably cold, horses died and there was a great dearth of supplies, which Messire Jean le Mercier did his best to provide the army with . . . because it was an unsuitable time to undertake a siege and if neither men nor horses had enough to keep them alive, it would prove necessary for the army to depart.'

Pyrenees and Alps. But even in the far north, there was no hesitation in setting out on campaign late in the year when some strategic advantage was seen in doing so. Thus, for the Scottish war in 1337; 'In this time the king of England was advised by several sage councillors and, as it was commonly said that the land of Scotland could not be conquered except in winter, for this reason the king with his army assembled in the west around the feast of St Luke'; in other words, the expedition began on 18 October, the feast of St Luke.[64]

One cannot say that the percentage of winter expeditions was negligible. For the fifteenth century as a whole, the troops of Liège campaigned during January on at least nine occasions.[65] A chronology of 120 fights, battles or encounters during the fourteenth and fifteenth centuries gives the following list:[66]

January	3	May	11	September	15
February	5	June	15	October	7
March	8	July	19	November	7
April	12	August	16	December	2

Lastly, if generally the most ambitious projects and calculations of the leaders of states or armies were for campaigns lasting a maximum of one year, sometimes expeditions were planned from the start to be much longer, especially expeditions to the Holy Land. At the beginning of the fourteenth century Marino Sanuto Torsello proposed to the pope a military budget for three years, at 700,000 florins a year, i.e. 2,100,000 florins.[67]

TACTICS: THE PITCHED BATTLE

As already observed, medieval warfare included a relatively limited number of pitched battles. Sovereigns and war leaders sometimes formally instructed their armies to refuse all engagements, as Charles V did after Poitiers, Charles VII during the major part of his reign and Louis XI after Montlhéry. Siege warfare (la guerre *obsessive* – attack or defence of strongholds), *guerre gerroyante*, *chevauchées* (large or small), raids and adventures monopolized much more time and effort.

Yet, for all that, it remains the case that the pitched battle was conceived as the culminating point of a war, the major event which made sense of a campaign, the chief episode which, although limited in area and concentrated

---

[64] *Anonimalle Chronicle 1333–81*, ed. V. H. Galbraith, Manchester 1927, p.9.
[65] Gaier (112), p.117.
[66] Figures derived from W. Erben, *Kriegsgeschichte des Mittelalters* (4).
[67] Torsello, *Liber secretum*, p.36.

in time, was the object of all fears, expectations and hopes.[68] In addition, the most acute tactical problems were posed by it, so it must now form the focus of our discussion.

It should be agreed that medieval military history includes many battles which were nothing but hasty, instinctive and confused confrontations in which captains played the role of simple leaders of men, incorporated almost anonymously into the first line of battle, and where the warriors' chief concern was to find an adversary worthy of their rank or valour, without any preoccupation for their companions in arms. They grappled on the battlefield with a sort of holy fury, free to flee precipitately as soon as things seemed to be going against them, and the individual search for booty and ransom was all-important. Sudden irreversible panic could arise, followed by indiscriminate massacres or the large-scale capture of the defeated, who had been unexpectedly paralysed.[69]

All accounts of pitched battles should avoid two pitfalls: dramatization and also rationalization, that is to say reconstruction after the event of a tactic or a directing schema which was perhaps never applied or even thought of.[70] However, the critical study of sources in all normal cases allows the existence of some fundamental tactical principles to be discovered, whose application was considered indispensable or at least highly desirable. Simplifying to extremes, three types of troop arrangement can be discerned: mounted cavalry, dismounted cavalry and infantry.

In the first case, the troops drew themselves up in a continuous shallow line (probably some three or four ranks), with the result that a battlefield 1 km wide (a frequent occurrence) might see the deployment of 1,500 to 2,000 horsemen. This group formed a 'battle', and to constitute it a certain number of elementary tactical units called 'banners' (*bannières*) or *conrois* were drawn up. These were usually recruited through a family, lineage or feudal relationship, and were supposed to stay grouped around a flag or a leader or were united by a common war-cry. A compact order was, in fact, necessary. To take up comparisons which were current in texts of the time, horsemen and lances should ride so close to one another that if a glove, an apple or a plum

---

[68] Hence, sometimes, visits to 'their' battlefield by old soldiers like Arthur de Richemont at Agincourt 21 years later: 'And then he came by Agincourt and explained to those who were with him how the battle had been fought and showed them where he and his banner had stood and where all the other great lords had been or where their banners stood and where the king of England had camped': Guillaume Gruel, *Chronique*, ed. A. Le Vavasseur, Paris 1890, p.126. Similarly in 1501 the archduke Philip the Handsome visited the battlefield of Montlhéry: J. Chmel, *Die Handschriften der K. K. Hofbibliothek in Wien*, Vienna 1841, ii.563.

[69] Froissart explained the victory of the Scots over the English at Otterburn (Chevy Chase) in 1388 because they 'would rather have died than cede, for want of courage, an acre of ground' (*Oeuvres*, ed. Kervyn de Lettenhove, xiii.240). English military ordinances in particular prohibited the cry 'Monte' which was generally interpreted as 'To horse', in order to flee. Similarly the cry 'Havok' for ravaging and pillaging was forbidden.

[70] cf. R. C. Smail, *Crusading Warfare* (286), pp.12–17, 165ff.

had been thrown amongst them, it would not have fallen to the ground but on to the vertical lances. Apparently, 'the wind should not be able to blow through' the lances.[71] This line of battle was rarely engaged at a single clash, but section by section, often beginning from the right.[72] Each sector could correspond to a unit called an *échelle*, or, later, company or squadron.[73] The groups of horsemen began to move slowly at a given signal (*lente aleüre, gradatim, paulatim, gradu lento*), taking care to keep in line; then speed picked up until the moment of contact, at which it should have reached its maximum. To describe the charge, Latin texts used significant adverbs: *acriter, acerrime, vehementer, impetuose, velocissime.*[74] Jean de Bueil commented: 'The cavalry force (*la bataille de cheval*) should charge its enemies and do this with fury, but they should watch to see that they have room and that they can continue beyond, because to form a heap (*faire une pointe*) and to turn round is to lose the battle.'[75] When cavalry found foot soldiers facing it, the aim was to get them to lose their coherence, to isolate them in small groups, to expose (*desclore*) them, to cause disarray (*desroier*) or disarrange (*desrengier*) them, or to break up their units (*mettre hors d'ordonanse*). It was the same even when the enemy were on horseback: in this case, the aim was to reach the horses and thus unseat their riders. Then the esquires, foot soldiers and valets could intervene and finish things off as necessary.[76] When a charge had miscarried, the knights retraced their steps and reformed, while the neighbouring units took up the fight; then the first again returned to the attack.

However, if the number of troops was too large for them to be grouped into one line of battle, a reserve force might be formed or other 'battles' might be drawn up some distance to the rear to reinforce the line. In addition, wings to the left and right were often formed in order to guard the flanks or to turn the enemy's position, with the result that at the end of the Middle Ages, at least, an army might be divided into five corps: two wings to right and left, a vanguard, a principal 'battle' and a rearguard.[77]

The second major tactical formula concerned dismounted cavalry. Contrary to what has sometimes been thought, this tactic does not date from the

---

[71] 'Entre lor lances ne puet corre le vent'. Numerous examples drawn from *L'Estoire de la guerre sainte* by Ambroise, the *Chanson d'Aspremont, Raoul de Cambrai* and from the *Branche des royaux lignages* by Guillaume Guiart are cited by Verbruggen (88); cf. the English version pp.72–4, and also de Bueil (9), ii.246.

[72] Gaier (112), p.184.

[73] It must be underlined how ambiguous the term 'battle' was since it could simultaneously describe a 'line of battle' and a unit of cavalry or infantry. de Bueil (9), ii.245 establishes the synonymy of the terms *bataille, échelle* and *escadre.*

[74] This at least is the opinion of R. C. Smail (*contra* H. Delbrück).

[75] de Bueil (9), ii.39.

[76] See the description of the battle of Benevento in 1266 (Muratori, viii.823).

[77] Like the French army during the Roosebeke campaign (*Chronographia regum Francorum,* iii.43).

Hundred Years War nor from the intervention of English archers on continental battlefields. If the French, properly speaking, were ignorant of it for a
long time, in contrast it had been used fairly often in the Empire. The
chronicle of William of Tyre, recounting an episode in the Holy Land in
1148 where the king of the Romans, Conrad III, had fought on foot with his
knights, states: 'that was the custom of the Teutons when circumstances
obliged them to use it.'[78] In the same way, Anglo-Norman knights dismounted at the battles of Tinchebray (1106), Brémule (1119) and Bourgthéroulde (1124).[79] Once they had dismounted, men-at-arms obviously lost
a great part of their mobility, and the recommended tactic, at least at the end
of the Middle Ages, was to wait in position until the enemy committed the
imprudence of advancing and attacking. Jean de Bueil noted this: 'Everywhere and on all occasions that footsoldiers march against their enemy face to
face, those who march lose and those who remain standing still and holding
firm win.'[80] According to him, it was thus necessary to arrange for sufficient
supplies to be available so that they could wait patiently. 'The biggest crowd
of soldiers' was to be placed centrally with the standard of the commander in
chief, then the archers, on either side; and finally on the two ends of the line
of battle two 'trooplets' (troupelets) of men-at-arms. As for the pages and
horses, they were to be kept together safely to the rear.[81]

Finally, there was the proper infantry. Its battle formations varied according to traditions but also according to the available troops, the enemy and the
nature of the terrain. One might list:

1 An arrangement in the form of a wall, fairly extended, only a few ranks
   deep.[82]
2 Drawn up in a circle or crescent, a custom with the Swiss, Flemings or
   Scots (schiltrons). An example was seen at Bouvines when, after each
   charge, the count of Boulogne sought refuge and regrouped with his
   cavalry behind a double line of Brabantine pikemen arranged in a circle.[83]
3 A massive disposition in depth where there was no hollow in the centre of
   the formation, like the solid 'triangular battle' of the infantry of Liège,
   where the point of the triangle facing the enemy was composed of the
   most resolute men.[84] The Chronographia regum Francorum mentions a

---

[78] Quoted by Gaier (112), p.193.
[79] On the battle of Tinchebray see C. M. de la Roncière, P. Contamine, R. Delort and M.
Rouche, L'Europe au Moyen Age. Documents expliqués, Paris, 2 vols. 1969, ii.68–70.
[80] de Bueil (9), i.153.
[81] Ibid., i.151.
[82] Gaier (112), p.160.
[83] J. F. Verbruggen, Le problème des effectifs et de la tactique à la bataille de Bouvines (1214),
Revue du Nord, 31 (1949), 181–93, where the following passage from Guillaume le Breton
describing the formation of the Brabançons is cited: 'Vallum quoddam de satellitibus armatis et
confertissimis duplici serie, in modum rote instar castri obsessi.'
[84] Gaier (112), p.160.

troop of almost 7,000 Flemings in 1303 who were arranged in shield formation (*in modum scuti*), with the men placed at the point of the shield bound together (*illaqueati*) so that they would not be penetrated by their enemies. In the same way at Morat (1476) the army of the Confederates was made up of a small troop of cavalry, then a vanguard of 5,000 men, including the Swiss élite (crossbowmen, hand gunners and pikemen) and, above all, by a battle corps (*Gewalthaufen*) in the form of an elongated quadrilateral, headed by a pointed or wedge formation (*Keil*). On the periphery of this corps of about 10,000 men were four ranks of pikemen (armed with pikes some 5.5 m long), while all the centre was occupied by halberdiers whose weapons were only 1.8 m long. Then came a smaller rearguard with the same formation (figure 3). It was the pikemen's job to break up the opposing battle formation, after which the halberdiers rushed in. Faced on the other hand by a cavalry charge, the pikemen formed a hedgehog, pikes outward. Modern reconstructions of this tactic show that a body of 10,000 men occupies, in these conditions, an area of only 60 × 60 m.[85]

Other elements could be added to these three combinations of mounted and dismounted cavalry and infantry, particularly archers (and, in the fifteenth century, culverineers) and field artillery. Since the same army in the field might include troops on foot and on horseback, one could finish with relatively complex, subtle or elaborate orders of battle. A plan submitted in September 1417 for approval by John the Fearless, duke of Burgundy, and his council, stipulated that when attacked not only should the vanguard and

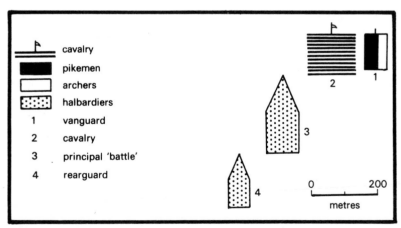

Figure 3   Order of battle of the Swiss at Morat, 1476 (after G. Grosjean, Die Murtenschlacht (54))

[85] G. Grosjean, Die Murtenschlacht (54). For the reconstitution of a Swiss square see *Rapport d'activité pour les années 1972–1974* (Institut Suisse d'Armes anciennes), p.14.

two wings of archers and crossbowmen dismount, but so, too, should the main battle corps. This should take its place either alongside the vanguard if the site was large enough, or some 50 or 60 m to the rear, while a bowshot further off (100–200 m) the rearguard, composed of 400 mounted men-at-arms and 300 archers, was to stay on the alert to ensure that the army was not outflanked. Finally, even further off behind the rearguard, the baggage train was to be drawn up to form a sort of fortified camp. Other formations were specified for attacking the enemy.[86]

The ideal battle order prescribed by Charles the Bold in the ordinance of Lausanne in May 1476 shows the degree of complexity which a professional soldier (a supreme perfectionist, it is true) could achieve at the end of the fifteenth century. Probably because of the size of his army in relation to the broken nature of the terrain, the duke of Burgundy had stipulated eight 'battles'. The first lined up from left to right, the 100 men-at-arms of the *Ordonnance* company of Captain Tagliant, then the 300 archers of this company, the 1,700 *enfans de pie* of Nolin de Bournonville, and lastly the 300 archers and 100 men-at-arms of another ordonnance company, that of Mariano; a total of 1,800 men, chosen from the best, under the command of Guillaume de la Baume, lord of Illens. For the second 'battle', formed by ducal household troops, an even more refined composition was conceived. From left to right three groups of men-at-arms alternated with three archer formations and three infantry troops. At the heart of this elite corps were placed the insignia of ducal power: Charles's standard, pennon and banner. As for the other six 'battles', less densely packed, their disposition was based on that of the first: infantry in the centre, hedged in and reinforced by archers and men-at-arms. To tell the truth, the eighth 'battle' only existed on paper, for it was to be constituted from Burgundian and Savoyard reinforcements whose arrival was expected.

To achieve better co-ordination and remedy the fragmentation which the terrain imposed, it was planned to regroup the eight 'battles' two by two, under the command of four senior captains. With all the forces united, the duke of Burgundy could thus have had 15,000 to 20,000 combatants at his command (figure 4).[87]

The actual formation which Charles the Bold had to adopt a few days later in the battle of Morat shows that he was by no means a prisoner of preconceived plans and was careful to adapt to both the realities of the terrain and the enemy. It also appears that liaison between the different arms (cavalry, artillery, infantry, archers) was considered one of the foundations of tactics (map 7).[88]

---

[86] Bib. Nat., MS français 1278; J. F. Verbruggen, Un plan de bataille (89); this plan is largely translated in R. Vaughan, *John the Fearless*, London 1966, pp.148–50.

[87] Grosjean (54), p.51. See also C. Brusten, Les compaignies d'ordonnance (448), p.159.

[88] Grosjean (54), p.55. Practically all the sources for the battle of Morat are collected in *Die Urkunden der Belagerung und Schlacht von Murten*, ed. G. F. Ochsenbein, Fribourg 1876.

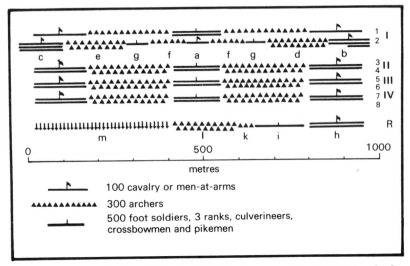

Figure 4   Ideal battle plan of Charles the Bold, Lausanne, May 1476 (after G. Gros-jean, Die Murtenschlacht *(54))*

Corps	Commanding officer	Line of battle	Captain
I	Duke of Atry	1	Guillaume de la Baume, lord of Illens
		2	Lord of Clessy
II	Prince of Tarento	3	Troylo de Rossano
		4	Antonio de Legnano
III	Count of Marle	5	Jacopo Galioto
		6	Lord of Fienne
IV	Count of Romont	7	Lord of Villarnoul
		8	Lieutenant of the count of Romont
R	Marshal of Billets		

Duke's household: a Squadron of chamberlains
                   b The Four Estates
                   c Noble guard
                   d Archers of Four Estates
                   e English archers
                   f Archers of the body
                   g Foot-soldiers (ducal household)
Reserve: h 200 demi-lances
                   i 500 foot-soldiers
                   k 100 English archers
                   l 400 English archers
                   m Artillery

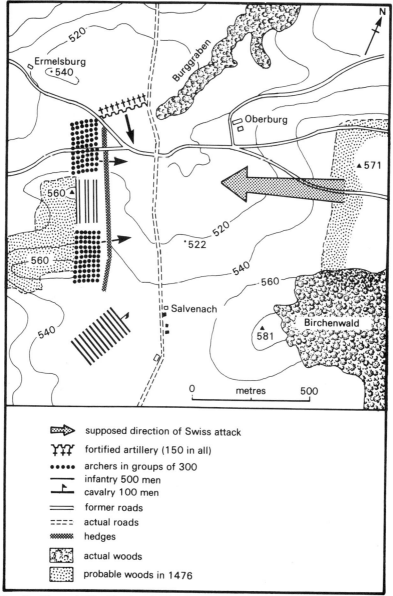

Map 7 Morat 1476: Charles the Bold's battle plan (after G. Grosjean, Die Murtenschlacht *(54))*

It is true that the unfolding of battles was always affected by the indiscipline of groups of combatants or by individuals in search of profit. However, it would be wrong to believe that leaders were unaware of these inconvenient facts. In any event, from the second half of the Middle Ages one finds commanders imposing the most severe punishments on all who broke rank and left the *conroi* for whatever reason, while it was recommended that all prizes be kept together for later division – although this was not always accepted or adopted.[89] 'Set the whole army to seek booty, prohibit pillaging and announce in all the "battles" that everyone obey the orders his war captain gives him on pain of being hanged by the neck,' advised Robert de Balsac.[90]

It cannot be said that the Middle Ages failed to recognize the advantages of a commander remaining apart from the mêlée, both in order to escape should circumstances require it and so that, surrounded by a sort of general staff, he could take all measures necessary for the occasion.[91]

Finally, just as recourse to spies was considered indispensable in strategy, for tactics, it was formally recommended that riders (*chevaucheurs*), watches and guards 'to guard the army and to watch for the body of their enemies should be provided'.[92] To deny the existence of a medieval art of war, with its variations and its evolution, springs in the end from a simple lacuna in

---

[89] On the question of ransoms and booty see especially P. Contamine, Rançons et butins dans la Normandie anglaise (460).

[90] de Balsac (7).

[91] *Ibid.*: 'Ledit prince ou chef de guerre doit avoir le jour de la bataille ung nombre de meilleurs gens qu'il ait et des gens plus sachans a la guerre a l'entour de sa personne pour le conseiller, garder et conduire.' Since the battle of Poitiers the French had learnt the need not to expose the king when he was present. One text recommends that he should remain on horseback even when all the rest of the army had dismounted, for he should 'veoir ses gens combatre, et si besoing est, qu'il voise de l'un a l'autre pour les reconfórter et donner courage, et aussi, se il avient que tout se perde, qu'il se puisse sauver, car il vault mieux perdre bataille que roy, car perdre roy se peult perdre le royaulme'. Advice sent to Isabeau de Bavière on the government of the kingdom went even further: 'Item, que le roy ne doit jamais aler en bataille mais se doit tenir en ung bel lieu bien acompaigné, car la prinse ou mort en bataille d'ung roy de France est faire perdre, ou mettre en merveilleuse desolacion le royaume, tesmoing la prise de roy Jehan' (Bib. Nat., MS français 1223, f.5v). Earlier Guillaume de Poitiers called attention to the fact that, unlike Julius Caesar, William the Conqueror had to play his part in warfare personally: 'It would have appeared of little honour or use to William in this war in which he defeated the English to fulfil the function of general unless he had equally acquitted himself as a knight as he had done in his other wars, for when he was present at any battle he fought sword in hand at the front or among the first': *Histoire de Guillaume le Conquérant*, ed. R. Foreville, Paris 1952, pp.251–3.

[92] de Bueil (9), i.149, 185, 203.

information. This attitude might be compared to that of Victor Hugo for whom music began with Palestrina.[93] 'It is pure blindness to leave a medieval gap in a list of military talents from Caesar to the sixteenth century.'[94]

---

[93] In his poem *Rayons et les ombres* entitled 'Que la musique date du XVI siècle'. In order to describe what would nowadays be called the 'art of war (tactics and strategy), the expressions *'art et science de chevallerie'* (Bib. Nat., MS français 19163, f.17v) or, better, *'discipline de chevalerie'* were used in the Middle Ages. Philippe de Mézières in his *Epistre lamentable et consolatoire* provides a definition of the latter:

C'est assavoir quant a fait d'armes et a toutes ses parties, estans en l'ost, par mer, ou par terre, chevauchant, arrestant et les batailles ordonnant, en plain ou en montaingne, en assaillant, minant ou defendant une forteresse, quant a la diligence des propres espies et le biens et soutillement mettre en euvre, quant aus engins et la garde d'iceulx, quant a soutilles chevauchees et embuches proufitables, quant a la diligence des gués de nuit et de jour et a la solicitude de congnoistre les espies des ennemis et les traistres privés, quant a la bonne garde que la chevalerie es batailles ne arester aus pillages et quant a retribution au butin de guerredonner les vaillans combatans et de punir les couars, quant aux consaulx publiques et secrés en gardant soi que traittié ne se face a ses ennemis ou ailleurs ouquel il se puisse trouver aucune traison, tenant verité en la bouche du prince de l'ost et de tous ses officiers a amis et aux ennemis et riens promettre, comment qu'il soit, que on n'ait entention de loyaument tenir tout ce qui sera accordé, quant aux dissimulations soubtilles et licites en l'ost de faire guerre a ses ennemis par autre voie tout estrange et non pensee que le conseil de l'ost ja publié n'aura determiné.

(Quoted in Froissart, *Oeuvres*, ed. Kervyn de Lettenhove, xv.462).

[94] J. Harmand, *La guerre antique de Sumer à Rome*, Paris 1973, p.196.

8

War, Government and Society

Medieval warfare was overwhelmingly fought in the name of established authorities (kings, princes or lords) by warriors who wished to be or who were recognized as belonging to the order (*ordo*) of *bellatores, pugnatores, agonistae* or *milites*, that is a functional category which had its recognized place in society, and whose relatively privileged position at the centre of the system of production can fundamentally only be explained by their vocation in arms. Even the structure of military society reflected more or less faithfully the structure of society as a whole, to the extent that, for secular society, the place of any given individual in the army was in direct relation to his place in the hierarchy of powers, even to his wealth. The most striking display of this tendency was found in the organization of the feudal system, where there was an organic link between obligations and military responsibilities and the number, importance and quality of fiefs. But even when military obligations went beyond the feudal regime, extending over a very large proportion of the lower ranks of society, links existed between the weight and nature of service and a place in society, as is evidenced by the Carolingian capitularies as well as by the arrangements of the Plantagenet sovereigns from Henry II to Edward I. Communal militias did not escape from this scheme – militias whose organization on campaign was often very closely tied to the organization of crafts. It cannot be said that the extension of payment had completely upset this parallelism. By many different means states still endeavoured to recruit their forces as they had before, from among the nobles (payment no longer being from that time only a kind of supplementary lure or compensatory indemnity), to dismiss foreigners (or only to admit them sparingly and under strict control), and to exclude social outcasts. The ideal was to fight with and against recognized troops, under a recognized authority in a limited, familiar and customary geographical region.

It goes without saying that reality was very different and that in practice there were frequent departures from this model. An idea of this gap between ideal and reality may be given by comparison to social and political structures.

SOCIAL STRUCTURES

The study of the social composition of armies, in its widest sense, should concern itself with several aspects. First, the place of those who had come down in the world or who lived on the fringes of society in relation to ranks in the hierarchy (from the very modest valet to the leaders in war) and to military speciality (horsemen, archers and footsoldiers, pioneers, etc.). To what extent were the poor, beggars and tramps excluded from military society? How important, especially at the end of the Middle Ages, were noble bastards?[1] It seems that in English expeditions to France in the fourteenth century the proportion of outlaws who obtained remission of their crimes from the king in recompense for their services was by no means negligible. In 1339–40 at least 850 letters of pardon were granted to such men who served in the wars. In 1346–47, again, with campaigns in Scotland, Northern France and Gascony, several hundred men received pardon, as did about 140 after Poitiers (1356) and 260 in 1360–61. 'It seems probable that from two to twelve per cent of most of the armies of the period consisted of outlaws.'[2] In connection with recruitment by Robert Knolles in 1370, before his *chevauchée* across the Channel, one source tells us that he 'took into his company, to its later utter confusion, various relapsed religious and apostates and also many thieves and robbers from different gaols'.[3] The *Registre Criminel du Châtelet de Paris* from 1389–92 retraces the careers of several adventurers who went from a civilian way of life to a military one, not without committing various misdemeanours. Regnaut de Saint-Marc, native of and married at Dijon, where he had three children, was such a case. Around 1383, earning nothing as a 'laboureur de vignes' he began to accompany bands of men-at-arms as a 'gros valet', serving several masters, including Jean la Personne, vicomte d'Acy. He went to Flanders, Spain, Germany, Milan, Chambéry and even to Hungary. Under torture he confessed to putting men to ransom, stealing horses and stealing even from his masters. For two months he had been a vagabond in Paris looking for a new master.[4]

Secondly, the geographical origins of combatants. We need to distinguish between those who had sometimes come from afar in response to a royal or princely order which they were obliged to obey and those who one might call true warrior nomads, the rootless, incorporated into composite, heter-

---

[1] For an attempt to estimate their position in the armies of the kings of France see P. Contamine, *Guerre, état et société* (457), index *sub* 'Combattants – bâtard de noble'; cf. M. Harsgor, L'essor des bâtards nobles au XVe siècle, *RH*, no.514 (1975), 319–54.

[2] H. J. Hewitt, *The Organization of War* (408), 30.

[3] *Anonimalle Chronicle 1333–81*, ed. V. H. Galbraith, Manchester 1927, p.63.

[4] *Registre criminel du Châtelet de Paris*, ed. H. Duplès-Agier, Paris 2 vols. 1864, ii.165ff. B. Geremek, *Les marginaux parisiens aux XIV et XVe siècles*, Paris 1976, provides many more picaresque examples.

TABLE 10   Expeditions mounted by Ghent and Bruges, 1338–40

			Number of troops	
Object of expedition	Starting date	Duration (days)	Ghent	Bruges
Sluys, Ypres, Poperinghe	17 July 1338	17	184	1,567
Courtrai	1 Oct. 1338	11	280	650
Beerst and Dixmude	12 Feb. 1339	11	1,193	3,552
Sint-Winoksbergen	23 Feb. 1339	7		
Menin	23 Oct. 1339	11	274	2,645
Aardenburg	5 Apr. 1340	2		
Tournai	7 Apr. 1340	9	2,783	1,373
Hainault	6 June 1340	24	4,567	2,095
Sluys	9 June 1340	22	281	1,921
Tournai, St-Omer, Sint-Winoksbergen, Cassel and Dixmude	5 July 1340	76	5,455	6,547

ogeneous formations in which all sorts of languages and nations were mixed – even though units were often very small, sometimes only 10 or 20 men. In this regard two models can be contrasted: (a) that of the military expeditions mounted by the men of Bruges and Ghent at the beginning of the Hundred Years War which had a very limited field of action and a purely local recruitment, some figures for which are offered in Table 10;[5] and (b) that offered by the list of 'brigands' ordered by Pope Gregory XI to defend the city of Avignon in March 1373 – no more than 77 names but originating from Savoy, Aragon, Sicily and Piedmont and also from the following twenty-five dioceses: Avignon, Limoges, Vercelli, Majorca, Viviers, Uzès, Riez, Saint-Flour, Piacenza, Tulle, Nîmes, Mende, Turin, Die, Clermont, Arles, Cremona, Arezzo, Cavaillon, Aix, Bologna, Cortona, Cambrai, Cahors and Besançon.[6]

Thirdly, participation in war of people who, because of their status, should have been more or less formally excluded from it. These would include slaves during the early Middle Ages; the unfree (who were not apparently affected by, for example, the Assize of Arms of Henry II Plantagenet, nor by later legislation of the same type until the mid-thirteenth century); clerics and religious. In the latter case it is also necessary to distinguish almoners and chaplains, whose presence was a regular feature, often indeed prescribed (as in the imperial ordinance of 1431 during the crusade against the Hussites,

[5] J. F. Verbruggen, Het Gemeenteleger van Brugge van 1338 tot 1340 en de Namen van de weerbare Mannen, Brussels 1962.
[6] R. Michel, La défense d'Avignon sous Urbain V et Grégoire XI (471).

when four or five priests were to accompany each troop 'in order to preach to the people and teach them how to behave themselves and how to fight for the Holy faith'), from clerics charged with temporal responsibilities (bishops and abbots), clerics participating in a defensive operation and, finally, those who, despite repeated prohibitions and condemnations by ecclesiastical authorities and in contempt of canon law, forgot their sacred order and tonsure and entered armies as ordinary soldiers. The actions of these priests were not, moreover, necessarily condemned, at least by a sector of public opinion. Froissart showed no disapproval – indeed he obviously admired him – for the chaplain of the earl of Douglas who, during the battle of Otterburn (1388), 'behaved not like a priest but like a courageous man-at-arms, for all night at the height of the battle, he had followed him everywhere with an axe in his hand, and just like a valiant man in the earl's retinue he had skirmished, struck out and helped to drive back the English by axe blows which he rained and beat down fiercely upon them.' This chaplain was immediately promoted to be an archdeacon and a canon of Aberdeen. 'And in truth, he had indeed physique, height, limbs, stature and bravery to do all this.'[7]

There were also the Jews. The *Landrecht* of the *Sachsenspiegel* freed from military service, except in cases of dire emergency, clerics, women, shepherds and servants of churches. In contrast, in the mind of its author, the Jews were not necessarily exempt, as a miniature in a manuscript of the *Sachsenspiegel* from the Dresden library shows. This depicts a peasant levy among which a Jew can be spotted (conspicuous by his hair-style), though he was present without arms.[8] Up to the mid-fourteenth century at least, in Spain Jews were ordered to guard urban fortresses as well as castles belonging to the Hospitallers. In 1416 a 'magister Joseph bombarderius, judeus' was in the service of the House of Aragon in Sicily.

Finally, there were women. Naturally they were present in armies as sutlers, serving women (*meschines*), and wantons. Sometimes *mauvaises femmes* were banished or there were limitations on their numbers. The participation of armed ladies (*dames, baronnesses*) was considered, when everything is taken into account, as fairly normal, given the fact that many feudal customs gave them a formal right to succession. Ordericus Vitalis mentions Helvise, countess of Evreux in the twelfth century, who rode to war with the horsemen, armed as they were and showing as much ardour as the knights, clothed in their hauberts, and the soldiers carrying spears. During the crusades women fought in the Frankish armies. The Greek historian Nicephorus described these Amazons, dressed as men, on horseback, wielding lances and war axes. At their head was 'the lady with the golden spurs', Eleanor of Aquitaine, whom he compared to Penthesilea.[9] Again, Froissart described Countess

---

[7] Froissart, *Chroniques*, xv.147.

[8] Reproduced in H. Conrad, *Geschichte der deutsche Wehrverfassung* (105).

[9] J. Verdon, Les sources de l'histoire de la femme en Occident aux Xe-XIIe siècles, *Cahiers de civilisation médiévale*, 20 (1977), 229; F. Heer, *L'univers du Moyen Age*, Paris 1970, p.169.

Jeanne de Montfort during the Breton Succession War, 'armed all over', 'mounted on a fine courser', who 'held a sharp cutting sword upright and fought right well with great courage'.[10] At the end of the fourteenth century, Thomas III, marquis of Saluzzo, described in *Le Chevalier errant* his grandmother, Richarda Visconti, who when her husband was in prison passed her time leading in person 'la greigneure guerre du monde'. 'You ought to know that she was always well and honourably armed and had her lance carried behind her like a captain, with her helmet, and always bore her bâton in her hand to command her men, and she had her ladies and damsels organized with her in this time of need.' Legend would even have it that during an assault attempted by Thomas Felton on the castle of Pontorson, the sister of the great constable, Julienne du Guesclin, so forgot her religious habit that she pushed away the scaling ladders placed against the wall.[11] But even ordinary women can be found here and there taking part in fighting. In 1382 Charles VI 'marched into Flanders and there a woman carried the Flemings' banner and when in the end they were defeated, she was killed'.[12] Another example is a Frisian woman who during the war between Friesia and Hainault (1396) 'was dressed in blue . . . like a madwoman' but who fought in the front rank and died pierced with arrows after, defying the enemy in her own way.[13] Finally the classic examples of Jeann d'Arc and Jeanne Hachette (defender of Beauvais in 1472) should not be fogotten.

POLITICAL STRUCTURES

War as a political phenomenon in society spread from top to bottom after an initial decision by official authorities, who endeavoured to direct, monopolize, organize, and terminate it, provisionally or definitively at the time they chose. But it was also a phenomenon which could rise from below, like a force independent of state control, springing from warlike propensities which all medieval societies knew in varying degrees.

In the long term governments evidently wanted to eliminate these spontaneous irruptions, in order to keep to themselves a monopoly of military action – hence the struggle against private wars, the promulgation of *Landfrieden*, the prohibitions against bearing arms and so on. However, this desire was limited by all the obstacles which could come between the decisions of authorities and their application, and particularly by the existence of a kind of

---

[10] Froissart, *Chroniques*, ii.144–6 and iii.9. But cf. Michael Jones, The Breton civil war, in *Froissart: Historian*, ed. J. J. N. Palmer, Woodbridge 1981, pp.68–9, for a sceptical view of her heroic role.
[11] *Cent cinquante textes sur la guerre de Cent ans dans le bailliage de Cotentin*, ed. M. Lantier, Caen 1978, p.39.
[12] Bib. Nat., MS. latin 5696, f.59r.
[13] Froissart, *Oeuvres*, ed. Kervyn de Lettenhove, xv.290.

contradiction. On the one hand states wanted to repress disorders and confine or suppress diffused violence, but on the other hand they needed to be able to call on armed subjects who were accustomed to martial exercises.

This relative impotence of states (which we must nevertheless not regard as general either in time or area) is seen with particular force at the end of wars, when troops had to be dismissed. Normally nothing was easier than to dismiss fief-holders at the end of a campaign of a few days or months, and to send back to their homes, villages or cities, the mass of *pedites*, pioneers or craftsmen, who had often obeyed with bad grace and some of whom had anticipated the dismissal by deserting. Nor were there serious problems with those small groups of regular forces who surrounded the sovereigns or accompanied those holding military office; dismissals were spread out, occurred individually, and resulted, moreover, as much from the wishes of those employed as from measures by their employers. It was only after a certain point, with a critical number, that it became delicate and perilous to rid oneself of warriors who over the course of years had acquired a sense of community, an idea of reciprocal solidarity, and who had no immediate chance of re-employment. For France during the last three or four centuries of the Middle Ages this kind of situation arose on three occasions: at the turn of the twelfth and thirteenth centuries, during the third quarter of the fourteenth (the time of the Companies) and after the treaty of Arras in 1435 (the time of the *Ecorcheurs*). It is striking to note that the most ephemeral of these crises was the last, while the first was the longest and, also, if not the most disastrous materially, at least the gravest psychologically. It is the one that will be recalled here.

Describing those mercenaries who had broken away from the king's control, Walter Map, in *Courtier's Trifles* (about 1180), provided a closely observed and horror-stricken portrait. The bands (*routes;* Latin: *ruttae*, a word which made its appearance then, comes from *rumpere* and described a small detachment, a handful of men) constituted an abominable heretical sect, thousands strong, armed from head to toe with leather and iron; they pillaged, violated and devastated everything, expressing to the full the word of the madman in the Scriptures, 'There is no God.' These men, bands of outlaws, fugitive clerics and false priests, originating in Brabant, were called Brabançons. 'They are now multiplied above numbering, and so strong have these armies of Leviathan grown that they settle in safety, or rove through whole provinces and Kingdoms, hated of God and man.'[14]

Other expressions were also used to describe the *routiers* and Brabançons: ravagers (by an easy play on words proposed, for example, by Jacques de Vitry: *ruptores, sive raptores*), Hainaulters, Catalans, Aragonese, Navarrese,

---

[14] cf. H. Grundmann, Rotten und Brabanzonen (252), a fundamental study summarized in the following paragraphs. Quotation from Walter Map, *De Nugis Curialium*, tr. M. R. James, London 1923, p.62.

Basques, Triaverdins, Mainades, Germans. Sometimes one finds *paillers* (Latin: *palearii*, strawmen), perhaps because as a token for recognition they wore a straw on their helmets or caps, perhaps because they used to set fire to straw.[15] For the term Cotereaux (*Cothrelli, qui vulgo dicuntur ruptarii*, says Rigord), which first appears in documents from 1127, various etymologies have been proposed. Does it derive from knife (*cultellus*), from cottar (in the sense of a poor peasant), from coterie (for it was indeed a question of an association, a sect or a church, as some documents plainly state), or from *coterel* (a word meaning at this time a small coat of mail)?

Everything leads to the conclusion that their geographical origins were varied, but that three regions furnished particularly numerous contingents: Provence, the Pyrenean mountains and the already over-populated provinces of Brabant, Flanders and Hainault, in short regions of poor soils, uplands or lands where men were already feeling too constricted, but also regions on the periphery of the kingdom of France. The sources agree in seeing the *routiers* both as poor men, even uprooted by their miserable condition, and as men excluded from the normal ranks of society.

The names of some leaders emerge. Was Guillaume of Ypres, a natural son of the count of Loos, who was leader of Stephen of Blois's mercenaries – some 300 cavalry – during the English civil war, one of them? A noteworthy Brabançon was Guillaume de Cambrai, a former cleric, whose career at the head of his men can be followed between 1166 and 1177. There was also a certain Lobar (or *Lupatus* or *Lupacius*), Spanish or Provençal by birth, who succeeded him. After him came Mercadier, a Provençal whom Richard Coeur de Lion took into his service. Another Provençal was Lupescar, whom John Lackland employed as a leader, and one can also cite Arnaud, a Gascon, Martin Algais, a Spaniard or Provençal, Courberan, of whom it is known only that he passed for a noble, Raymond le Brun, Falco or Falcaise, a bastard of Norman origin, and finally, in the service of Philip Augustus, the famous Cadoc (or Lambert of Cadoc). As for Renaud de Dammartin, count of Boulogne, although he led the *routiers* during the battle of Bouvines, he came from an entirely different world and his fortunes did not lie with those of the Brabançons, except during a very short period of his life.

It is difficult to estimate their numbers. Were they as large as the panic-stricken chronicles affirmed? In 1183, the majority of Cotereaux were massacred by a coalition of the forces of order. The sources give figures varying

---

[15] Fire and burning was an essential feature of medieval warfare. The *lex in pacis in exercitu* of Frederick Barbarossa (1158) entrusted to the marshal of the army the right to decide if a castle should be burnt or not. In the fifteenth century *Brandmeister* existed in German armies who could fix the ransom by which towns could escape burning. The *Loyal Serviteur* praised Bayart for having proscribed such acts: 'He had been in several wars in which there had been Germans who had gladly set fire to their billets on leaving them. The good knight never left his until he knew that all had gone or he left guards so that no fire was started there.' *Histoire du gentil seigneur de Bayart*, ed. J. Roman, Paris 1878, p.425.

from 7,000 to 17,000 killed. It is likely that at their peak they formed an army comparable in size to those which the regular governments of the day could line up: a few thousand men. Sometimes fighting on horseback, but mainly fighting on foot, they were regarded, perhaps wrongly, as excellent soldiers, quick to learn all the tricks of war. 'They are not inferior to nobles in knowledge or in courage to fight', remarked the *Généalogie des comtes de Flandre.*[16] At Bouvines the troops of Renaud de Boulogne fought with desperation, offering the last centre of resistance to the knights of Philip Augustus. And yet, in 1183, the Cotereaux allowed themselves to be killed almost like sheep.

At the time of the most important episodes in their history, it is likely that they already had behind them a fairly long tradition of warlike and predatory activities. In any case, Frederick Barbarossa apparently had no difficulty in enlisting 1,500 'Brabantini' and getting them to cross the Alps with the rest of his army in 1166–67. At the end of the campaign the Romans were defeated, but while the German knights obtained a glorious reputation, the Brabançons, if the sources may be believed, carried off all the booty: tents, weapons, clothes, horses, mules, donkeys and cash. Then, no doubt after they had been dismissed, they returned to France, where the abbot of Montier-en-Der mentions them on the edges of the kingdom and the Empire, that is to say in a region which was less organized politically. They must have remained in groups for several years, constituting an unceasing menace. It was to put an end to their presence and to deprive them of all public support that during an interview held between Toul and Vaucouleurs on 14 February 1171 Frederick Barbarossa and Louis VII agreed not to 'retain' them for their wars, at least in the area between the Alps and the Rhine to the east and Paris and its region to the west. Implicitly the sovereigns reserved for themselves the right to use them either to the west and south-west of Paris against the Plantagenets, or to the east of the Rhine and over the Alps, against rebellious German vassals and Italian communes in revolt.

Following this pact, the majority of Cotereaux found themselves driven into the western part of France. Henry II used them in Normandy against Louis VII (1173) and then sent them into Brittany and Anjou. He made them cross the Channel to fight his barons in revolt in August 1173 – the barons for their part did not scruple to recruit Flemings. After a short period he transported them back to Normandy, where they went to the aid of Rouen under siege. Peace was then concluded with Louis VII and Henry dismissed them.

It was doubtless the same men who were engaged by Frederick Barbarossa for a new expedition into Lombardy and the Romagna. Returning to France, they survived the peace of Nonancourt (1177) and profited by it, running riot in the south-west of the kingdom. The danger became so great that the same

---

[16] Quoted by G. Duby, *Le dimanche de Bouvines* (244), p.107.

canon of the third lateran ecumenical council (1179) which anathematized the
Cathars denounced the Cotereaux and the whole body of *routiers*. It condemned those who employed them, kept them in their pay or protected them,
to the same punishments stipulated for heretics. This did not prevent Philip
Augustus employing them against the Flemings at the beginning of his reign
and then against the count of Sancerre.

The devastation they caused was so great, and the indifference, incapacity,
even the complicity of authorities and a part of the feudal world had attained
such a degree that, as in the early days of the Peace of God, there was a
popular reaction. This was the 'white cowled' or 'hooded' sect (*Capuciati*),
inspired on the initiative of Durand Chaduiz, a woodcutter and carpenter of
Le Puy, to whom the Virgin had delivered a picture showing herself seated
on a throne with a representation of Jesus in her arms, surrounded by the
inscription: 'Lamb of God who takest away the sins of the World, give us
your *peace*.' Thus began the association of the '*Peace* of St Mary' whose
home was the church of Notre-Dame du Puy and whose members wore,
fixed to their white linen hoods, a tin image of the Virgin, reproducing that
which Durand had received. According to Robert of Torigny, abbot of Mont-
Saint-Michel, the confraternity found some support among bishops and
important men, nobles and men of lower classes. In addition to their efforts
in the strictly moral and religious sphere, the White Hoods succeeded in
ridding Auvergne of disturbers of the peace, whether local lords or *routiers*.
In the summer of 1183, perhaps assisted by the army of Philip Augustus,
they won a great victory over the Cotereaux in Berry, which brought them to
the peak of their fame. It is possible that this success caused a radicalization
of the movement, which then became decidedly hostile to both the feudal
laity and the ecclesiastical hierarchy. 'Everyone attempted to regain that
liberty which they said they possessed from their first parents on the day of
creation, ignorant of the fact that servitude was the reward of sin.'[17] It was
easy, in the circumstances of the times, to accuse them of heresy, and in 1184
or 1185 they were crushed by the nobles, who, on this occasion, supported
the remaining *routiers*.

After 1185–90 what one might call a second generation of *routiers* grew up,
but they were both less numerous and less dangerous than the first. It is true
that the church continued to fulminate against the Cotereaux and lords who
employed and protected them. In the context of the struggle against the
Albigensian heresy, it sought to eradicate from southern France these fomen-
tors of troubles whose presence could only accentuate material and moral
disorder. But the *routiers* appeared henceforward in fairly small troops which
kings like Richard I, John Lackland and Philip Augustus could use for

---

[17] The whole affair is examined by G. Duby, *Les trois ordres ou l'imaginaire du féodalisme* (106),
pp.393–402 (cf. *The Three Orders. Feudal Society Imagined*, tr. A. Goldhammer, Chicago and
London 1980, pp.327–36).

specifically defined tasks. The royal accounts for 1202–3 show, for example, that Philip Augustus paid 4,000 *l.p.* in this year to Cadoc, representing the pay of about 300 combatants. The role of these adventurers progressively lessened. A clause of Magna Carta (1215) formally invited King John to banish from England as soon as peace was re-established foreign knights, crossbowmen and mercenaries, and if the sources mention the presence of Brabançons among the soldiers on the Albigensian crusade, they only appeared sporadically afterwards. It may be added that the *routier* leaders attempted to integrate themselves into the normal ranks of feudal society, like Cadoc who became castellan of Gaillon, *bailli* of Pont-Audemer and a knight. The same tendency could be witnessed among those who chose the Plantagenet side: Mercadier, who had received the goods of Adhemar de Beynac in Périgord, called himself the king's *famulus* and boasted of his constant devotion: 'I fought for him with loyalty and strenuously, never opposed to his will, prompt in obedience to his commands; and in consequence of this service I gained his esteem and was placed in command of his army.'[18]

The history of the *routiers*, similar in more than one respect to that of the Companies in the fourteenth century, shows that they proliferated. They constituted hostile, foreign bodies which tore apart the social fabric because of bitter rivalries between sovereigns, kings and barons, heretics and orthodox, but once these rivalries had been suppressed or had died down through the victory of one side or the other, it was possible to put an end to them fairly quickly. In short, their presence is explained rather by the more or less prolonged weakness of normal political structures than by the disequilibrium of a society which, as in all periods, found itself incapable of re-absorbing those who lived on its margins. When its institutions were solid, when authority was sufficiently affirmed and respected, the problems of social outcasts remained at an individual level and they did not act collectively.

The Catalan company, at the beginning of the fourteenth century, represents another type of adventure, undertaken by professional mercenaries. This band of warriors was originally constituted by the conjunction of three elements. The first was the existence in the kingdom of Aragon of the Almogavars, whose pastoral and warlike style of life was lived out freely on the moving frontiers of the Christian and Muslim worlds. The second was the expansionism, or, it could almost be said, Aragonese nationalism, which turned the kingdom of Sicily into one of its fields of action during the last two decades of the thirteenth century, to the detriment of the rival expansionism of the French and Angevins. The third was the increasingly precarious position of the Byzantine empire, incapable of resisting Turkish pressure by its own strength and constrained by this to recruit mercenary forces.

[18] Sir Maurice Powicke, *The Loss of Normandy 1189–1204*, 2nd edn Manchester 1960, p.232, quoting a charter in favour of the abbey of Cadouin (cf. *BEC*, iii.444–5).

After years of fighting against the forces of Charles II of Anjou and Charles de Valois, troops in the service of Frederick of Aragon found themselves without employment once the peace of Caltabellota, which gave the kingdom of Naples to Charles II and Sicily to Frederick, had been concluded (1302). The Catalan company (*Universitas Catalanorum*) was then formed, to which were added in small numbers Sicilians, Calabrians and Italians from the north, and also individual adventurers from every nation. On the invitation of Andronicus II Paleologus, the Catalan company – at least 6,000 men, of whom two-thirds were Almogavars – disembarked in Byzantium in September 1303.

Two sources allow us to follow its history, which was full of tumult, movement, massacres and booty. One is Greek: the account of George Pachymeres. The other is Catalan: the *Chronicle* of Ramun Muntaner, which is even more precious because its author, who was the treasurer and chancellor of the Catalan company, was a direct eye-witness of and often participant in the deeds he recounts. In short, despite a 'cloak and dagger' side to the story, despite exaggerations and distortions, it is one of the rare medieval texts which shows life from the inside of a military company with its human and economic problems, the relationship of men to their leaders, the pressing search for supplies, the thirst for power and riches, tensions with the civilian population, the many faces of war, its risks, profits and fatigues and, finally, the complexity of political problems.

Under its successive leaders, the Catalan company, thanks to conspicuous Byzantine weakness, was able to conserve its cohesion and compensate for the inevitable erosion of its numbers by the addition of new elements. But above all, after its victory over the Frankish feudal forces of Gautier de Brienne, duke of Athens (1311), it was able to seize his heritage and, relying on distant Aragonese patronage, was able to found for its own profit a principality which was to survive until 1388. This was indeed an exceptional success of which no equivalent can be found either in the time of the Brabançons and Cotereaux or in that of the Companies during the Hundred Years War.[19]

Perhaps it is not enough to contrast states on the one hand with bellicose, anarchic and peripheral impulses which would have arisen and developed through political disturbances, on the other, and to imagine a long-term conflict between them until the victory of the states. The phenomenon of the free companies is more complex. It is largely explained by the support which was given them overtly or covertly by certain authorities, because of their supposed soldierly efficiency. In short, for a large part, integration of war into the state's activities occurred when and because states thought the advantages outweighed the inconvenience. However, even around 1500, this

[19] The history of the Catalan company has given rise to a considerable literature. R. Sablonier, *Krieg und Kriegertum in der Crónica des Ramon Muntaner* (537) has been particularly used here. For a survey of the problems concerning a history of the Great Companies see P. Contamine, *Les compaignies d'aventure en France pendant la guerre de Cent ans* (456).

development was by no means complete or assured. Large parts of the West still avoided it. It was only in a few regions and countries that effective demilitarization of society was occurring, alongside a relative isolation of military from civil society. This was caused by the appearance of permanent armies and by the greater role, in numerical terms, played by the infantry, who by tradition were recruited from the lower orders and therefore enjoyed no social prestige. These changes were to be reflected in the atmosphere of sixteenth-century war scenes and the world of Jacques Callot: 'the little troop of disbanded mercenaries, without bread, being led through a countryside of little woods towards a horizon dotted with gallows'.[20] And Machiavelli could argue in his *Art of War* that 'a man of worth should not follow arms to make a career', and that neither republics nor kings should allow their citizens or subjects to take up the profession of arms.[21] It is true that in France, for example, the permanent cavalry (the *ordonnance* companies) and the king's household, with its many different corps, formed 'a welcome home' for young nobles who saw in them a means of living honourably, a reason for hope and enterprise. Nevertheless the impression remained, at least among informed observers, that 'the king of France had disarmed his people in order to rule without resistance'.[22]

[20] P. Claudel, *Le soulier de satin*, version intégrale, Première journée, scene v.
[21] *Oeuvres complètes*, ed. E. Barincou, pp.731–40.
[22] *Ibid.*, p.742. On the demilitarization of society in France at the very end of the Middle Ages see Contamine (457), pp.550–1; R. Sablonier, Etat et structures militaires dans la Confédération autour des années 1480 (379a), accepts these views for Switzerland.

9

Towards a History of Courage

'The strength of mind of he who confronts danger without fear or withstands suffering without complaint'; 'the moral energy of he who masters fear and other tendencies which inhibit action and shows himself determined and constant in difficult situations':[1] with such timeless definitions in mind, apparently valid for all societies and all periods, it is right to ask whether the notion of courage on its own can constitute a subject of historical enquiry. How can it be avoided, however, when this characteristic, this psychological state, is evidently to be found at the heart of any warlike action? Moreover, recent examples have shown that a history of sentiments or emotions can be attempted, especially if approached from the exterior or periphery, that is to say by the study of the historical context in which they were formed and which, in a sense, conditioned them.[2] The remarks which follow seek only to highlight a few points which are meant to mark out a trail in this little-explored historical domain, which deserves a much longer and more profound inquiry.

COURAGE AMONG THE VIRTUES AND VICES

A first approach might consist of a scrutiny of the enormous and monotonous moral and psychological literature of clerical origin produced during the Middle Ages. It is not clear that courage as such appears in this. Nevertheless, among the four cardinal virtues inherited from Antiquity (following Plato, Aristotle, Cicero and the Stoics), through the mediation of St Ambrose and St Augustine, at least one, fortitude (*fortitudo*), substantially covers or includes the notion of courage. For St Thomas Aquinas courage is in its widest meaning both firmness of mind in the accomplishment of a duty and,

---

[1] P. Foulquié, *Dictionnaire de la langue philosophique*, Paris 1969, and *Dictionnaire de la langue pédagogique*, Paris 1971.
[2] J. Delumeau, *La peur en Occident* (351).

in consequence, the condition for all virtue; in a more restricted sense, the virtue which makes a man intrepid in the face of every danger. If it is danger of death this virtue leads him to defy it without flinching and to confront it with a courage free from rashness. Courage is thus relative to fear (chiefly of death) and to audacity; coming from the right quarter 'courage is a virtue which moderates fear and boldness for the common good'. It masters fear in such a way that one preserves one's nerve and sang-froid and it leads one to act with daring in order to escape, if possible, from danger. Courage promotes both fearlessness and bravery in war; certainly the second quality is more alluring, but the first is superior. The person who is on the defensive feels weaker and more threatened, and is not sustained by the spirit of aggression. Courage is midway between audacity and timidity; it is different from hope and intermediate between despair and presumption. It has seven potential characteristics: magnanimity, confidence, freedom from anxiety, magnificence, constancy, tolerance (or patience and steadfastness) and perseverance.[3]

Scholastics sometimes thought to examine specific cases. As an example we may take this quodlibetical question posed by Henry of Ghent about the conduct of the Franks at the time of the fall of St John of Acre in 1291. The episode occurred during a 'just' war, not one waged to recover unjustly seized goods, but to resist injury by an enemy who was seeking to seize the possessions, lives, country, liberty, laws and other temporal and spiritual goods of the Franks. The question concerned the behaviour of a knight who, while others were fleeing, threw himself upon the Saracens and met his death. Henry asks: Can it be thought, with the Song of Songs, that this was a sign of courage, exposing oneself for the sake of friends in peace and charity, or, in true magnanimity (according to the definitions of Aristotle, Cicero and Plato), should the knight have fled with the others? For perhaps the knight in question had acted through recklessness, a desire for glory, cupidity, or in a rash, unreflective manner, foolishly? Henry quotes Vegetius, who declared in effect that good captains did not risk public combat without full information. If our knight could not count on the help of his companions in arms he had displayed not magnanimity but stupidity.

However, Henry continues, the exact circumstances must be examined. It was reported that the Saracens had in fact entered Acre before dawn, so suddenly that the Christians did not have time to plan their resistance. It was thus possible that the knight, who was sleeping fully armed, ready to fight, hearing the tumult, wanted to resist the enemy, expecting that his companions would follow him. If this were the case, he had indeed shown magnanimity in choosing to die for his faith and city. If the other citizens and

---

[3] St Thomas Aquinas, *Summa theologiae*, IIa IIae, q.CXXIII-CXL (For English readers the most convenient edition of this is probably by the Dominicans, vol. 42, *Courage*, ed. and tr. A. Ross and P. G. Walsh, Blackfriars, 1966).

knights had acted in the same way, perhaps Acre would have been saved, for it only needs a handful of brave men to achieve victory. This is what is said in the Book of Maccabees and is repeated by Vegetius: 'Victory is always customarily won by a few men and above all by men of courage'; 'in all conflicts numbers are less useful than courage' and 'in war speed serves even more than courage.'

Let us, says Henry of Ghent, admit as a first proposition that the knight in question was a magnanimous and heroic man, and not rash. He then considered another approach: our knight could only be magnanimous to the extent that those who fled had acted as they should have done. Henry's aim here was to condemn the great, and above all the prelates, who deserted at the moment of attack. Three possibilities were envisaged: either the enemy was already victorious, or 'had surrounded the people' or threatened them. The first was dismissed, for all was not over at the moment when the leaders fled. As for the second and third possibilities, they were, it is argued, linked together: either, in effect, all could flee and all had despaired of victory, and thus no one was obliged to expose themselves to danger, or no one should have reasonably despaired. Then all, unanimously, should have confronted the enemy and fought for the fatherland and public weal. None should have departed except perhaps women, children and the infirm. Or perhaps opinion was divided, but even if the *major et sanior pars* was in despair, those who still continued to hope were not obliged to flee with the others, and the men charged with administering *spiritualia* to them should have remained with them.[4]

Profane writers had recourse to a learned, moral and clerical vocabulary, to apply it to soldiers. Jean de Bueil discerned among soldiers 'the virtue of courage, in so much as there are many who would rather die fighting than flee to their shame.'[5] Jean Molinet thought of cardinal virtues to attribute to each of the four Valois dukes of Burgundy: Philip the Bold had a claim to prudence, Philip the Good to temperance, Charles, although 'inspired by Mars the God of battles', was given justice, and courage was attributed to John the Fearless. 'Duke John . . . a prince without fear, magnanimous in all his doings, constant as the living rock, so inflamed by bold courage that nothing seemed to him either too difficult or too burdensome, can be likened by the qualities of his merits to courage, highly esteemed among the cardinal virtues.'[6] The *Loyal serviteur* characterized Bayard in these words: 'In boldness few men have approached him, in leadership he was a Fabius Maximus, in subtle enterprises a Coriolanus, and in courage and magnanimity a second Hector, raging against the enemy, gentle, peaceful and courteous to friends.'[7]

---

[4] Henry of Ghent, *Quodlibeta*, XV, q.XVI.
[5] Jean de Bueil, *Le Jouvencel* (9), i.51.
[6] Jean Molinet, *Chroniques*, i.27.
[7] *Histoire du gentil seigneur de Bayart*, composée par le *Loyal serviteur*, ed. J. Roman, Paris 1878, p.402.

Despite these borrowings, the notion of courage, as it can be appreciated from literary texts, brings one back to a distinct semantic field in which primacy is accorded to affectivity, impulsiveness or, almost, to instinct.[8]

MOTIVATION, BEHAVIOUR AND HOPE

Mainly from the twelfth century onwards, courage as an emotion or as an ideal form of behaviour is often mentioned in written sources.[9] Stereotypes were established and habits of description were created then, of which some were to persist throughout the Middle Ages. However, systematic study of the vocabulary used might perhaps reveal subtle changes, innovations and abandonments, which might also allow differences to be discerned between periods, regions, milieux and literary genres.

A first approach through a summary examination of *chansons de geste*, chronicles, didactic treatises, biographies of soldiers, panegyrics and epitaphs leads to the conclusion that courage was conceived above all as an aristocratic, noble form of behaviour, linked to race, blood and lineage, and as an individual trait arising from ambition and desire for temporal goods, honour, glory and posthumous renown. It was necessary to avoid 'shame' which was engendered despite oneself and one's family by 'despicable actions', 'cowardice' and laziness. It was also necessary to display 'great ardour' and vigour in combat, to perform many acts of 'great courage and hardy enterprises', 'feats in arms', 'prowesses', and experience 'the din of battle' (*estors*). In this way one would become courageous, valiant, bold, brave and proud and would act *vassalement*, in a chivalrous fashion. Less appreciated (but not really criticized) were those combatants who were 'arrogant', 'rash' (*outrageux*) or 'fell' (*fels* – that is, felons in the sense of cruel, unpitying and enraged).[10]

For Jean de Bueil, who was a good witness of his own times and also representative of a whole cultural heritage, war was seen first of all as a kind

---

[8] cf. the comparisons that were current with animal behaviour: 'Es guerres a eu tous jours trois excellentes choses et qui bien affierent a parfaict chevalier: assault de levrier, deffense de sanglier et fuyte de loup.' *ibid.*, p.428.

[9] 'Courage, this novelty of the twelfth century': G. Duby, *Le dimanche de Bouvines* (244), p.27. The classic link between poetry and war may be thought of in this regard with the role of *jongleurs* in the diffusion of heroic myths and of the fame (*los*) of warriors. During his campaign against Suenon, King Waldemar had enrolled in his army a bard whose songs denounced the perfidious parricide of his enemy and urged vengeance. In a war against the inhabitants of Châtillon, a band of Burgundian plunderers, confident in their numbers, strength and youthful vigour, were preceded by a buffoon, who on his musical instrument conjured up the bold deeds and wars of their ancestors in order to encourage imitation. According to Wace, Taillefer at Hastings sang *The Song of Roland* to the Normans: E. Faral, *Les jongleurs en France au Moyen Age*, Paris 1971, pp.55-7.

[10] A. Tobler and E. Lommatzsch, *Altfranzösiches Wörterbuch* Berlin, 5 vols. 1915-62, provides many examples.

of school of asceticism. It required effort, 'pain et travail'. Whoever took part had to bear 'souffraites, dangiers, povretez et disettes', to begin 'wearing armour day and night, fasting most of the time'. All this was done with the intention of acquiring 'honour and glory', obtaining 'a perfect glory in this world', for 'all worldly honour is gained by conquering and fighting', and also for material profit, considered a just recompense for bold exploits, with the result that war seemed a leading and obvious way of social promotion: 'Les grans triumphes et les grans seigneuries'. Essaying a comparison between the courtier and the soldier, Jean de Bueil came down without hesitation in favour of the latter, for in the final analysis his way of life scarcely entailed more risks and certainly developed many accepted social values. 'Arms always reward their users' in three ways: by death (but after all 'it often happens that another man dies as young as a man of war'); by a life of poverty, but one with honour, with the result that everyone talks about you and your renown lives on afterwards (as did that of Bertrand du Guesclin and Gadifer de la Salle, the conqueror of the Canary Isles). Moreover, no one can take his treasure with him and 'there are more poor nobles following the court and in the bonnes villes than there are following war'; finally by fortune and chance, for 'through arms you can become the greatest emperor in the world.'[11]

Emphasis placed on individual prowess, on outstanding actions which, if not carried out alone, were at least personally attributable to one man, doubtless encouraged the historical belief that medieval warfare was in effect a series of duels, and that the collective aspects of courage were more or less obliterated or misunderstood. Reality is, in fact, rather different; simple combatants as well as leaders and governing authorities had a clear idea of the potential dangers of the achievements of one isolated champion. Alongside its glorification of the 'good', the 'worthy' (preux), whether of former times, contemporary, or of profane or sacred history,[12] the Middle Ages knew the worth of individual lineages, races or peoples, all of whose members needed to act together on the battlefield. The custom was not simply to place in the front rank the best soldiers, chosen individually, or young, newly dubbed knights, but also a body of troops whose reputation for communal valour was well established – like the Templars or Hospitallers, for example, during the Crusades, or again, in the wars in the Empire, the Swabians who from the time of the battle of the Unstrut in 1075 claimed for themselves the first place in battle (primatus pugnae). In the discourses which it was conventional

---

[11] de Bueil (9), i.43.
[12] Jacques de Longuyon introduced the cult of the Nine Worthies around 1312 into Les voeux du Paon, a romance written for Thibaud de Bar, prince-bishop of Liège (three Jews: Joshua, David and Judas Maccabeus; three pagans: Hector, Julius Caesar and Alexander; three Christians: Arthur, Charlemagne and Godefroi de Bouillon). At the end of the fourteenth century Eustace Deschamps named, in parallel, nine female worthies and the same poet introduced a tenth worthy (Bertrand du Guesclin) and finally, with much more limited success, a tenth female (Joan of Arc).

to attribute to kings and leaders before every important engagement, it was not individual acts of bravery which were recalled as a guarantee of future victory, but collective successes achieved by the whole army or the whole population. In *Le débat des hérauts d'armes*, the two rivals each attempted to demonstrate the general valour of the English and the French.[13] Temporary bonds of solidarity could also intervene, based on oaths, vows or even, sometimes, on a physical link (rope or chains).[14] In recognition of this communal sentiment, the Swiss military code did not reserve punishment of bad soldiers to the authorities or to the high command, but authorized everyone to strike his nearest companion dead if he was fleeing or spreading panic.[15] At Florence in the fourteenth century two months' wages were granted collectively to victorious units.[16] In other words, *esprit de corps* was encouraged and used as much as individual emulation and competition in efforts to improve the behaviour of soldiers.[17]

THE EXTENT OF RISK

Obviously, the history of courage is bound up with that of risks. It is thus necessary to weigh the significance of these as far as the sources permit, that is to say only from the twelfth century onwards and, again, very generally. Professional soldiers, the *milites*, sought to swing the odds in their favour and to limit as far as possible, even at the cost of efficiency, the risk of death both for themselves and for their mounts. 'To place his body in danger of death and prison' and 'to hazard his body and his life', perhaps, but there was no taste for suicidal fanaticism; the notions of sacrifice and absolute devotion seem alien to medieval mentality. Hence the growing refinement of armour for men and, in certain periods, for horses; hence, also, the establishment of a code of chivalric warfare, which specified sparing the defeated, leaving them to be made prisoners from whom ransoms could be exacted. Although ransoms are attested in even the earliest periods of the Middle Ages, it seems that the incorporation of such practices into the rules of war should be related

---

[13] *Le débat des hérauts d'armes de France et d'Angleterre*, ed. L. Pannier and P. Meyer, Paris 1877, pp.7ff.

[14] cf. the behaviour of King John of Bohemia and his entourage at the battle of Crécy tying their bridles together (Froissart, *Chroniques*, iii.178; *Chronicles*, tr. G. Brereton, Harmondsworth 1979, p.90).

[15] W. Schaufelberger, *Der Alte Schweizer und sein Krieg* (380), p.237.

[16] C. C. Bayley, *War and Society in Renaissance Florence* (487), pp.12–13.

[17] It remains the case that the majority of rewards were most often individual, like decorations in modern armies. A reward of 25 florins was granted in fifteenth-century Italian armies to the first soldier scaling the walls of a besieged city and silver helmets were given to *condottieri* at the same time as their batons of command: M. Mallett, *Mercenaries and Their Masters* (512), p.90. For English practice in France cf. *English Suits before the Parlement of Paris 1420–1436* ed. C. T. Allmand and C. A. J. Armstrong, London (Royal Historical Society), 1982, p.264.

on the one hand to the diffusion of Christian values in a military society, and on the other to the practice of warfare in which identified combatants frequently had occasion to confront each other, make themselves known and recognized, to find each other and meet again. Hence, too, the notion of reciprocity, the alternation of reverses and successes, plainly visible in the writings of Froissart or even in the life of Bayart.

The values of chivalric warfare were not simply abstract ideals; incontestable examples show how they were applied in practice. After the murder of Count Charles the Good in 1127, war was waged for more than a year throughout the county of Flanders. In all about 1,000 knights were involved. Yet the day-by-day narration of these events by Galbert of Bruges mentions a total of seven dead, of whom five were nobles or knights. And of these only one was killed by an enemy during a chase – the other four were accident victims (a fall from a horse, a slip while climbing a wall, the collapse of a ceiling and too much enthusiasm in blowing a horn).[18] In 1119 the battle of Brémule took place, about which Orderic Vitalis wrote: 'I have been told that in the battle of the two kings, in which about nine hundred knights were engaged, only three were killed. They were all clad in mail and spared each other on both sides, out of fear of God and fellowship in arms (*notitia contubernii*); they were more concerned to capture than to kill the fugitives. As Christian soldiers they did not thirst for the blood of their brothers, but rejoiced in a just victory given by God for the good of holy Church and the peace of the faithful.'[19] It has been observed that the number of casualties was usually very small, including those incurred at sieges (unless an epidemic broke out, which was hardly the rule, and unless the victor, for political reasons rather than military ones, decided to put the defeated garrison to death).

Despite all this, chivalric warfare soon encountered its limits. Against the Infidel in Spain, as well as in the Holy Land, battles could end in the indiscriminate massacres of the vanquished, even those of high rank. On many occasions in a sizeable part of the West, when battles occurred between communal troops and nobles or even between the communes themselves, it was not normal recourse to resort to ransoms. Regarding the war in 1396, which lined up men of Holland, Hainault, France and England on one side and Frisians on the other, Froissart wrote about the latter, not without implicit reproof: 'As for taking any prisoners, one can hardly get any of them nor will they surrender but they fight to the death saying that it is better to die a free Frisian than to be subject to a lord or prince. And as for the prisoners that have been taken, hardly any ransoms can be exacted, nor will

---

[18] Duby (244), p.141.

[19] *Ibid.*, p.153, quoted here in the translation by Margaret Chibnall (*Orderic Vitalis*, vi.241). At Tinchebray in 1106 not a single knight was killed on the French side. At Lincoln in 1217 the victors only lost one knight and those defeated two, plus about 400 prisoners.

their friends and relatives redeem them, but they leave them to die one after another in prison, nor otherwise will they ransom their people unless, having taken some of their enemies, they exchange them man for man. Yet if they think that none of their men are prisoners, they will certainly put all their prisoners to death.'[20] In the same way, during a given battle, gentlemen were careful to avoid surrender to 'commoners' (English archers, for example) because they expected no mercy from them; it is hardly necessary to say that the opposite was also true. We should remember the fierceness of some battles and the instructions of the leaders during the course of fighting. All of which means that a number of battles were bloody, especially for the defeated side, for, as Froissart observed, 'it is a general rule that the greatest losses occur on the side of the vanquished.'[21]

At least for the last two centuries of the Middle Ages, apparently reliable figures are available for evaluating human losses during pitched battles. Listing the dead (and eventually the prisoners) was one of the victor's tasks. They had to be identified and given a Christian burial, all under the direction and charge of certain knights and officers of arms. Edward III acted in this way after Crécy (1346): 'Then the king was advised to send and search for the dead to know what lords had fallen there. So two very valiant knights were ordered to go out with three heralds in their company to identify the arms and two clerks to enregister and write down the names of those whom they found'.[22] Similarly the Black Prince after Najera (1367) 'remained there so long that all his men had returned from the pursuit and he ordered four knights and four heralds to go across the battlefield to advise on who had been captured and what number remained there dead.'[23]

Unfortunately this accounting, at least as far as the chroniclers have recorded it or where the occasional official record survives, cannot entirely be relied upon.[24] Was everyone listed or just the nobles? What of those killed during the pursuit (*chasse*) or those mortally wounded? There is the problem of the ever-present temptation to exaggerate the losses of the defeated in order to enhance the glory of the victors. As a result it is necessary to handle these sources with prudence and to compare them with other evidence, where this exists.

Examination of a series of battles from the eleventh century to the fifteenth leads to the conclusion that the defeated generally lost between 20 and 50 per

---

[20] Froissart, *Oeuvres*, ed. Kervyn de Lettenhove, xv.295.

[21] Froissart, *Chroniques*, xiv.165–6. One of the most striking contrasts (which must naturally be considered as a typical reflection of medieval mentality) concerns the victory achieved by the Christians at Rio Salado (1341): 20 horsemen killed on the victorious side against 400,000 massacred Moors: J. N. Hillgarth, *The Spanish Kingdoms 1250–1516*, 2 vols. Oxford 1976–8, i.342.

[22] Froissart, *Chroniques*, iii.190 (cf. *Chronicles*, tr. Brereton, p.95).

[23] *Ibid.*, vii.47.

[24] J. Stevenson, *Wars of the English in France* (344), iii.385–6, for a list of casualties at Cravant (1423), and 394–5 for those at Verneuil (1424).

cent of their numbers in relation to their total forces. At Courtrai (1302) 40 per cent of the French knights were killed; at Cassel (1328), at least half the Flemish communal forces were wiped out; at Halidon Hill (1333), 55 per cent of the Scottish cavalry; and at Agincourt (1415), as at Poitiers (1356), 40 per cent of the French cavalry were destroyed.[25] The figures advanced by the *Loyal serviteur* for the battle of Ravenna (1512) seem to give similar results: on the French side 3,000 infantry, 80 men-at-arms from the *ordonnance* companies, 7 gentlemen of the household and 9 archers of the bodyguard died.[26] After the battle of Visby (1361) the dead were heaped into five common graves; three of these have been excavated and they contained the remains of 1,185 soldiers.[27] During the battle of Hemmingstedt, fought in 1500 between the forces of John I of Denmark and the peasants of Dithmarschen, the latter, who were victorious, lost 300 men, 5 per cent of their troops, while the Danes lost 30 per cent (3,600 dead).[28] This series of figures explains the apprehension which men felt at the prospect of all pitched battles.[29] Not only could a defeat in this kind of engagement have catastrophic politico-military consequences, but during a few short hours the risks of death were extremely high. Hence the relative rarity of true battles, with the result that many soldiers, even professionals at the end of a long military career, had only experienced one or two.

It is a long time since the observations of Machiavelli on the risks of warfare have been successfully challenged. According to him the *condottieri* were so careful to husband their resources of human capital that they made sure that no losses were incurred on either side when they fought each other.[30] With regard to the battle of Anghiari (1440) he wrote:

> In the midst of such a complete rout, in a battle so bitter that it lasted for a full four hours, there was killed only a single man and he did not perish from his wounds or from some master stroke but because he fell off his horse and was trampled under the horses' feet. A battle in those days offered no danger; one always fought on horseback, covered in armour and assured of one's life when one surrendered; one was thus always safe from death, protected by armour during the action and surrendering when one could no longer fight.[31]

In fact it seems that losses at Anghiari amounted to 900 dead. Again, according to Machiavelli, at Molinella (1467): 'no one perished; there were only a few horses wounded and a few prisoners taken on both sides.' Once more this is a gross exaggeration; the figure of 600 killed seems a likely one. Yet despite

---

[25] C. Gaier, *Art et organisation militaires* (112), pp.67–79.
[26] *Histoire du gentil seigneur de Bayart*, p.330.
[27] Gaier (112), p.73; B. Thordemann, *Wisby* (675), i.149ff.
[28] W. Lammers, *Die Schlact bei Hemmingstedt* (64).
[29] cf. J. Keegan, *The Face of Battle*, London 1976, pp.79–116, for a realistic reconstruction of conditions during the battle of Agincourt.
[30] W. Block, *Die Condottieri* (491).
[31] Niccolo Machiavelli, *Oeuvres complètes*, ed. E. Barincou, p.1224.

all this, throughout the fifteenth century, above all in battles between Italians and when no foreign troops (French, Spanish or Turkish) intervened, losses in the peninsula were more limited. It has been calculated that out of 170 captains who led more than 200 lances only a dozen died in battle, nor does the proportion of losses appear to have been much higher among ordinary troops.[32]

Fear of death was not the only concern; the prospect of being made prisoner, of having to pay a ruinous ransom, brought with it another kind of apprehension, even more difficult to measure. Life in the Middle Ages was risky even for those in no danger from war, because of the high levels of natural mortality, and this fact needs to be taken into account in considering the risks involved in military action. Medieval societies as military societies made bravery in battle one of their essential values. They often associated the right to command with warlike prowess, as the surnames attributed to a number of princes and kings testify (Richard Coeur de Lion, John the Fearless, Boleslav the Valiant, Louis Hutin – Louis the Headstrong).[33] This did not prevent them from considering that courage was a 'virtue' unequally distributed, always threatened and continually called into question. The theme of the decline of chivalry, the enervation of warriors and of peoples, may be met in the writings of lay authors or, perhaps still more, among clerics, in almost every epoch.

---

[32] Mallett (512), p.197. In the company of Micheletto degli Attendoli between 1425 and 1449, of 512 sub-condottieri mentioned, 25 died, an average of one a year, but only 15 of these died in combat: M. del Treppo, Gli aspetti organizzativi economici e sociali di una compagnia di ventura (499), p.273.

[33] cf. 'Soun fitz Philippe Hardy, qe apres fuist nome Cowarde' (*Anonimalle Chronicle*, ed. V. H. Galbraith, Manchester 1927, p.40, referring to Philip, later duke of Burgundy, after Poitiers). The link between a prince and military virtue is still evident in the works of Montaigne (*Essais*, livre II, chap. 21):

> If any shall go about to maintaine, that it is better for a Prince to mannage his wars by others, then by himselfe; Fortune will store him with sufficient examples of those, whose Lieutenants have atchieved great enterprises; and also of some whose presence would have beene more hurtfull, then profitable. But no vertuous and coragious Prince will endure to be entertained with so shamefull instructions. Under colour of preserving his head (as the statue of a St.) for the good fortune of his estate, they degrade him in his office, which is altogether in military actions, and declare him uncapable of it. [John Florio's translation of 1603.]

10

Juridical, Ethical and Religious
Aspects of War

Perhaps more than any other human activity war, by its very nature, intro-
duces into every society in which it occurs a series of juridical and moral
considerations which are often complex and equivocal. It is not necessarily
proof of idealism or unreality to maintain that it is almost never desired,
experienced or conceived as pure and unlimited violence, in a crude or
elementary fashion. It exists enveloped in (and also masked by) a total con-
ceptual system springing from custom, law, morality and religion – an apparatus designed in principle to tame, orientate and channel it. Put simply, war
is a cultural phenomenon. The notion which one period or a given society has
of it is expressed in a more or less visible fashion in its upheavals, development and conduct. War offers the historian or the sociologist an opportunity
to study the relationships between reality and the ideal, between practice and
ethics, and between fact and law.

THE EARLY MIDDLE AGES: GERMANIC PRACTICES, THE CHURCH
FATHERS AND CAROLINGIAN CHRISTENDOM

At the same time as they gathered up the remnants of Roman political power,
the Barbarian kings fought their wars in conformity with Germanic custom.
War was considered a sort of judicial process (*judicium belli*) in which the two
parties agreed to confront one another on the battlefield to establish who
should win. The following remark put into the mouth of Gundovald the
Pretender by Gregory of Tours reflects this conception: 'When we meet on
the battlefield, God will make it clear whether or not I am King Lothar's
son.'[1] Sometimes, instead of the two armies, it was the leaders concerned or

---

[1] Gregory of Tours, *Histoire des Francs*, ed. R. Latouche, ii.109 (cf. *History of the Franks*, tr.
Thorpe, Paris 1963, p.415) and also *ibid.*, 89–90 (tr. Thorpe, p.392).

their champions who entered the lists alone. This practice, also attested by Gregory of Tours, is not, however, limited to the Germanic world.[2]

In 971 a duel was planned between the Byzantine Emperor, John Tzimisces, and the Russian prince, Sviatoslav, in an attempt to settle their quarrel while avoiding the massacre of their peoples.[3] Similar projects, in fact almost always abandoned before they were carried out, are attested throughout the history of the West down to the end of the Middle Ages.[4] Another tradition of Germanic origin was of decisive encounters sometimes fought on the banks of a river, as was the case for the battle of Fontenoy on 25 June 841.[5]

In order to make his victory official and undeniable, the victor had to remain on the battlefield a whole day, or even for three days if it was a question of an 'assigned battle'. This period can be compared with that which governed the appropriation of goods in Old Germanic law. The acquirer of real property had in effect to install himself there for three consecutive days (*sessio triduana*). Once again this practice was also handed down over the centuries; when, after the battle of Muhldorf (1322), Louis of Bavaria, conqueror of Frederick of Austria, did not respect the practice, it was said to be 'against the laws of war' (*contra morem bellantium*). In contrast, after Sempach (1315), as after Grandson (1476), the Swiss cantons faithfully adhered to it, and the three-day rule is still mentioned in the sixteenth century by Philippe de Clèves.[6]

Division of booty was the object of fairly strict regulations, as is testified, for example, by the celebrated episode of the Soissons vase.[7] Normally the army was assembled in a spot which had been roped off, in the centre of which a war standard was raised and around which the booty was heaped up. As for prisoners, they were frequently put to death. In 539 Theudebert I, king of the Franks, during his campaign in Italy, threw Ostrogothic women and children into the Po. Widukind of Corvey, alluding to the fate of the

---

[2] *Ibid.*, i.77 (tr. Thorpe, p.107), an example from a war between the Alamans and the Vandals. When the man representing the Vandals was beaten in single combat, Trasamund, their leader, gave his word that he would carry out his promise to withdraw.

[3] The duel of David and Goliath may also be considered as an example which served as a point of reference.

[4] P. Contamine, L'idée de guerre à la fin du Moyen Age (924a).

[5] Nithard, *Histoire des fils de Louis le Pieux*, ed. P. Lauer, Paris 1926, p.76. Other examples cited by K. G. Cram, *Iudicium Belli* (1012) include Otto of Carinthia fighting in the valley of the Brenta (1002), Boleslav II on the Bug (1018), Rudolph of Rheinfelden on the Neckar (1077), Boleslav III on the Cidlina (1110) and Albert of Austria on the Elz (1298).

[6] H. Conrad, *Geschichte der deutsche Wehrverfassung* (105); Philippe de Clèves, *Instruction de toutes manières de guerroyer*, Paris 1558, p.84.

[7] Gregory of Tours, *History*, tr. Thorpe, p.140, for this celebrated incident in which Clovis was thwarted by one of his men from obtaining the complete vessel among the booty gained, for return to the church of Soissons, because the soldier insisted on dividing it up along with all the other objects. He later gained his revenge, slicing the man in half with the remark 'That's how you dealt with the vase' (trans.).

Saxons who were still pagan, declared: 'All those who had reached a certain age were condemned to death; those who had not reached puberty were kept as booty' and, elsewhere, 'The booty from the town was delivered to the soldiers; all those who had reached puberty were massacred, but boys and girls were kept for captivity.'[8] If massacres of both pagan and Christian prisoners are frequently attested, sometimes on a vast scale, during the whole of the early Middle Ages, condemnation of the defeated to slavery was long considered normal. When the numbers captured were high, the slaves were shared out throughout the country: 'In this period when the very eminent Clovis, king of the Franks, had entered Gothia with his army and had killed Alaric, king of the Goths, he made an innumerable host of prisoners who were scattered and shared out among the provinces.'[9] War to a large extent explains the numerical importance of the servile population.[10]

However, ideas of limiting violence and destruction were not entirely absent from Barbarian societies. Fear of a supernatural punishment and the desire to obtain God's protection or that of his saints sometimes led chieftains to restrain or forbid devastation. During his campaign against the Visigoths, Clovis prohibited his men from ravaging the territory of Tours: 'In respect for Saint Martin, Clovis ordered that they should requisition nothing in this neighbourhood except fodder and water.'[11] He killed a man who disobeyed this order. The Carolingian capitularies attest that sovereigns were anxious to repress disorderly pillaging both in order to relieve their own subjects and to maintain discipline.[12] Cupidity led victors to spare lives in exchange for heavy ransoms: 'When all these fortified towns had been destroyed by the Franks, they led off into captivity all the inhabitants, but in the town of Ferruge, following the intervention of the bishops, Ingenuinus of Savona and Agnello of Trento, ransoms were allowed at a rate of between 1000 and 1600 shillings a man.'[13]

Here and there juridical forms appear among the warlike activities. The beginning of hostilities was sometimes marked by sending a herald bearing defiance, by throwing a weapon in the direction of the enemy ranks or at the gate of the town which it was planned to besiege. In Visigothic Spain as in Lombard Italy, Roman practices persisted, although the definitions by Isidore of Seville of military law (*jus militare*) and of the law of races (*jus gentium*) remained practically confined to the sphere of learned culture.[14]

---

[8] Widukind of Corvey, *Rerum gestarum Saxonicarum libri III*, ed. P. Hirsch, Hanover 1935.

[9] *Vita Eptadii, Acta Sanctorum*, August 4, 775–81.

[10] G. Duby, *Guerriers et paysans* (158), p.42.

[11] Gregory of Tours, *Histoire des Francs*, ed. Latouche, ii.37 (tr. Thorpe, p.151).

[12] H. Conrad, *Das Wehrstrafrecht* (153).

[13] Paul the Deacon, *Historia Langobardorum*, iii.31.

[14] 'Military law concerns usages for the declaration of war, obligations agreed by the conclusion of alliances, the march against the enemy or the beginning of an engagement at a given signal as well as its termination; likewise the administration of punishment for the disgrace of leaving a

For a long period deprived of influence over the behaviour of Barbarian sovereigns, Christian thought on war was fundamentally modified after the conversion of the Empire and of the Emperors to the new religion. It was then that the traces of pacificism contained in the works of Tertullian,[15] Origen[16] and Lactantius[17] were abandoned and forgotten, even if, for Sulpicius Severus as for Paulinus of Nola, to renounce the profession of arms remained a highly commendable procedure not only for clerics but for all those who wished to attain perfection in the Christian life.[18] From the Old Testament the image of a God of hosts was retained, ordering war against the enemies of his people, as were the feats of arms accomplished by Abraham, Moses, Joshua, Samson, Jephtha, Gideon, David and Judas Maccabeus. No condemnation of war is found – only of private and individual violence, following New Testament injunctions not to resist evil, to turn the other cheek, to love one's enemies and not to use the sword. On the contrary, passages where the military profession appeared normal and legitimate were collected. These included those where John the Baptist recommended soldiers not to manhandle anyone, not to denounce people falsely and to remain content with their pay, just as he had instructed tax collectors not to exact anything beyond what had been fixed; where Christ praised the faith of the Centurion; the passage relating to the Centurion Cornelius in the Acts of the Apostles and the Epistle to the Hebrews, which passed a favourable verdict on the wars fought by Israel.[19]

Saint Ambrose, bishop of Milan, whose experience as a great administrator helped him to understand the duties incumbent on temporal authority, was the first of the fathers fully to justify war waged in defence of the fatherland against barbarians and of society against outlaws.[20] There is even in his writings a certain christianization of war, this being fought essentially against

---

post, and similarly, the system of payment, the hierarchy of ranks and gratuitous rewards – like the granting of a crown or a collar – the division of booty, and the share of the prince.' (Isidore of Seville, Etymologies v.7.) The law of peoples concerned 'the occupation, construction and reinforcement of places, wars, captivities, reduction to slavery, the right to return to the fatherland, treaties of peace, truces, the obligation to respect ambassadors and prohibition of marriages between foreigners, hence the name of the law of peoples for almost all people make use of this law' (ibid., v.6).

[15] Tertullian, De Idolatria, Patr. Lat., i.61: 'In disarming Peter, Our Lord disarmed all soldiers. No position is allowed us if it lays us open to an illicit act.'

[16] Origen, Contra Celsum, v.33: 'We have changed into spades the lances with which we once fought; we shall no longer draw the sword against any nation . . . for we have become through Christ sons of peace.'

[17] Lactantius, De divinis institutionibus, vi.20: 'The act of putting to death is forbidden . . . It is always forbidden to kill a man, for God desires that his life should be sacred.'

[18] Sulpicius Severus, Vie de Saint Martin, ed. J. Fontaine, Paris 1967, i.260–1; Paulinus of Nola, Epist., XVIII.7.

[19] Luke 3.14; Matthew 8.5–13 and Luke 7.1–10; Hebrews 10.32–4; Acts 10.1.

[20] St Ambrose, De Officiis ministrorum, i.27.

barbarian Arians. Alluding to the substitution by Constantine after 317 of the *labarum*, the banner marked with the two interlaced initial letters of the Greek word *Christos*, for the Roman eagle, Ambrose wrote: 'Transform, O Lord, and raise up standards for your faith. Here there are no longer military eagles nor flying birds which lead the army but, Lord Jesus, your name and the worship which is paid you.'[21] The incorporation of nails of the Cross sent by Saint Irena to Constantine into a horse's bit and a helmet arose from the same attitude. In the writings of Prudentius, *pax romana* and *pax christiana* merged. Athanasius the Great proclaimed that murder of an enemy in a just war was an act worthy of praise. At the beginning of the fifth century the christianization of the army was officially accomplished. It was then that an edict of Theodosius II excluded from the military profession all those who were still sullied by pagan rites.

Here, as in other spheres of moral and theological reflection, the attitude of Saint Augustine was to lay a heavy burden on the medieval thought which followed. In his eyes, complete peace was impossible here below; the hope of seeing swords forever transformed into ploughshares no longer existed: 'Never will a people acquire such security that it will not have to fear invasions threatening its existence.'[22] It was thus necessary to make a place for war, even in the history of the Christian city, in the constant battle against the pagan, the heretic, the bad catholic or even the brother sharing the True Faith. This radical pessimism did not result in the condemnation of all wars. Some could be adjudged just provided that they sought peace or justice. Just war was first of all the fight for justice, itself conceived as the tranquillity of order (*tranquillitas ordinis*). Conversely if the motive for war is cupidity, the desire to dominate, it is then only brigandage on a vast scale.

To avenge wrongs and to recover goods unjustly removed: these were good reasons for a just war, even if one took the initiative by declaring it. *A fortiori*, an objectively defensive war would be just, in which one sought to protect oneself and one's possessions. It was not 'the desire to obtain human praise' but 'the need to protect safety and liberty' which had led the Romans to defend themselves against Barbarian assaults.[23] Another condition of a just war had a more formal character; it should be declared and waged on the authority of a prince. It was on the latter that the responsibility rested in deciding whether or not to take up arms. His role was so decisive that if he declared an unjust war, the sin was his alone, not his soldiers', since the duty of obedience rendered them innocent.

Saint Augustine did not see war as simply a consequence of sin, but a remedy against sin, a penal sanction of which the belligerents were, in a manner of speaking, the executants. His famous formula, 'justa bella ulciscuntur injurias' (just wars avenge injuries), does not only signify, as it does in Cicero, that just war seeks to obtain restitution for a hurt by returning to

[21] *Idem*, Contra Symmachum, *Patr. Lat.*, lx.227–30.
[22] St Augustine, *De civitate Dei*, XVII.13.
[23] *Ibid.*, III.10.

the *status quo ante bellum*. It also means that the prince who wages it plays the role of God's scourge and that his action, inspired by love, is beneficial even for him against whom it is directed. He who loves much, chastises much, might be a summary of the Augustinian attitude.[24]

The justice of a war thus rests on the disposition of the spirit and the motivation of the conscience. That is why one keeps one's word to an enemy, avoids needless violence, profanation of churches, atrocities and reprisals, for behaviour which is too cruel would be a sign of a war waged because of a taste for murder and not because of love of justice, and betrays a wicked intention. 'The desire to harm, cruelty in vengeance, an implacable spirit, unquenched ferocity in revolt, the desire to dominate and other similar attitudes, if there are any, that is what the law condemns in warfare.'[25] With this in mind, Saint Augustine admits that christianization can render war less cruel: the legitimate, avowed punishment implied by the *bellum justum* will be, as it were, tempered by the Sermon on the Mount. It is only to be expected after all that since war corresponds to a certain state in society, the men who by their function or vocation have been placed highest should renounce it. This means not only clerics, who because of their sacred character could not spill blood, but, *a fortiori*, monks whose monastery prefigures the Heavenly Jerusalem and who, for this reason, abstain from war as they abstain from private possessions and from marriage.

Despite obscurities deriving both from a lack of sources and from insufficient historical research in this area, it seems that with the Carolingians war between Christians may have lost a little of the harshness and bestial savagery which it possessed during the Merovingian period. The battle of Fontenoy (25 June 841) was won by Charles the Bald and Louis the German at the end of a fratricidal struggle. Nithard recounts that the victors decided not to pursue the defeated so that: 'punished by divine judgement and their defeat, these latter would repent of their insatiable cupidity and, with God's grace, would in the future unanimously search for true justice.' It was 'divine mercy' which had interrupted the carnage and pillage as well as inspiring pious conduct with regard to the dead and wounded and the pardon accorded to the fugitives. The same Nithard suggests that war and battles were the object of a moral valuation: the judgement of God having been manifested, 'it was recognized that the battle had been only for justice and equity.' In addition, every priest who had counselled battle or even taken part in the action was reputed innocent; however, anyone who through anger, hatred, vainglory or any other evil design, had counselled or accomplished a reprehensible act 'should make secret confession of his sin and should be judged according to the seriousness of his fault'. Finally, a fast of three days was decided upon for all those who had fought.[26]

[24] F. H. Russell, *The Just War in the Middle Ages* (947), pp.16–39.
[25] St Augustine, Contra Faustum, *Patr. Lat.*, xlii.447.
[26] Nithard, *Histoire*, ed. Lauer, p.82.

This event, described by a reliable source, does not show only that battle was thought of as a judgement of God and that justice was infallibly on the side of the victor; it reveals as a function of the imperatives of Christian morality a desire to restrict the horrors of war. It shows that even in a just war certain forms of behaviour were considered blameworthy, but that from the moment the war was declared just, clerics who found themselves involved in it had nothing for which to reproach themselves. Lastly, it indicates that war, whatever else it was, was a defilement from which it was necessary to purify oneself by a general penitence.

At the same period the custom of reducing prisoners of war to slavery progressively disappeared. The redemption of captives, a pious mission which had been accomplished by many saints, male and female, during the Merovingian age, lost its meaning. Murder of the defeated or their enslavement and trafficking in slaves were practices bannished to the periphery of Western Christendom. It was henceforward admitted that this kind of conduct was reserved for conflicts with pagans. The saintly Pope Nicholas I in his famous letter to the Bulgars (*Ad consulta Bulgarorum*, 866) wrote that they had greatly sinned in killing their enemies after victory and in depriving innocent women and children of their lives: 'We know that you have acted thus through ignorance rather than through malice; nevertheless you should do penance.'[27] In other words, the Bulgars, who had just been converted to Christianity, were not conscious of their fault; what had been normal when they were pagans had become reprehensible now that they were Christians.

In conjunction with a system of penitence and repentance involving a rigorous and objective scale of monetary payments for offences, and with the idea that spilling blood, whatever the circumstances, was a form of impurity from which it was necessary to gain absolution, the practice of inflicting an official punishment on all soldiers who had killed is found down to the eleventh century. The early Christian father and bishop of Caesarea, Basil the Great (330–79), recommended that those who had spilt blood in a war should be deprived of communion for three years. Archbishop Theodore of Canterbury (668–90) showed himself less rigorous in his letter to the priest Eoda: 'He who by order of his lord has killed a man, should not attend church for forty days and he who has killed a man in a public war should do penance for forty days.'[28] An Anglo-Saxon penitential of the same period expressed itself in similar terms:

> If the king within the kingdom leads an army against insurgents or rebels and being roused, wages war for royal authority or ecclesiastical justice, whoever

[27] *Patr. Lat.*, cxix.978–1016.

[28] St Basil stipulated 11 years of penitence for homicide. As for murders committed in war, they should not be punished regularly; their perpetrators were simply advised to abstain from communion for three years (*Dictionnaire de théologie catholique*, ed. A. Vacant, E. Mangerot and E. Amann, Paris 1933, xii.790–1).

commits homicide in carrying out the task for him shall be without grave fault, but, because of the shedding of blood, let him keep away from church for forty days and let him practise fasting for some weeks, let him be received by the bishop for the sake of humility and when reconciled after forty days let him take communion. Wherefore if an invasion of pagans overruns the country, lays churches waste, and arouses Christian people to war, whoever slays someone shall be without grave fault but let him merely keep away from entering the church for seven or fourteen or forty days and when purified in this way let him come to church.'[29]

According to the penitential of Bede, the soldier who killed during the course of a war was compelled to fast for 40 days.[30] The same penance and the same time limit is found in the *Paenitentiale Vallicellanum primum* from the second half of the eighth century, as in the *Paenitentiale Vallicellanum secundum* from the end of the tenth century; the latter specifying that the fast should be on bread and water (*in pane et aqua*). The Arundel penitential (at the end of the tenth century) returned to the three years of penance anticipated by St Basil for 'him who when his fatherland was invaded had killed an enemy'. Fulbert of Chartres at the beginning of the eleventh century insisted only on a year's penance.[31] At the same period Burchard of Worms in the *Corrector sive medicus* has the penitent interrogated by his confessor in terms which betray Augustinian influence: 'Have you killed in war on the order of a legitimate prince who was waging war to re-establish peace? Have you assassinated the tyrant who had striven to disturb peace? If this is so, you shall fast for three Lents on the days prescribed. But if it was otherwise, without the orders of a legitimate prince, you shall do penance as for a voluntary murder.'[32]

From these penitentials the idea emerges that a distinction can and should be drawn between unjust wars where killing is severely reprimanded, and defensive and legitimate wars after which those who have killed should do a light penance.[33] Such an appreciation implies a style of warfare in which each combatant is supposed to know whether or not he has committed homicide. If, on the other hand, this is moving away from the position of St Augustine, for whom every soldier serving in a war is innocent even if that war is unjust, since the soldier is only obeying the prince, it is no doubt less because of a deepening sense of individual responsibility than because of a change in the recruitment of armies in which the notion of obligatory service became largely blurred.

[29] J. E. Cross, The Ethic of War (958), p.281.
[30] C. Vogel, *Le pécheur et la pénitence au Moyen Age*, Paris 1969, p.77.
[31] *Dictionnaire de théologie catholique*, xiv.1972–81.
[32] Vogel, *Pécheur et pénitence*, p.82.
[33] For comparison, some penitentials stipulate three years' penance for a murder committed in anger, one year for one committed by accident, seven years for murder by poison or ruse, and ten years if it followed a quarrel.

That some thought any penance was unjustified, however light it might be, for homicide committed in a just war, is proved by the letter which Rabanus Maurus wrote shortly after the battle of Fontenoy. This was later inserted into his penitential, then into the *De Synodalibus causis et disciplinis ecclesiasticis* of Regino of Prüm and into the *Decretum* of Burchard of Worms:[34]

> Certain people excuse the homicide which has recently been perpetrated in the sedition and struggle of our princes and do not consider it necessary to do penance for this, seeing that this war was waged on the order of the princes and it should be left to the judgement of God . . . [But] it is necessary that those who wish to defend this abominable massacre should consider if they can excuse as innocent in the eyes of God those who have set eternal God at naught for the cause of cupidity, that root of all evil . . . and because of the protection of their temporal lords and despising His orders, have carried out this homicide not by chance but by deliberate design'.[35]

In at least two cases the church demanded a general penance for participation in a public war. The first was after the murderous battle of Soissons on Sunday, 15 June 923, when the troops of Charles the Simple defeated those of the 'tyrant' Robert, count of Paris, usurper of the royal crown, and the synod of Reims imposed a penance on the belligerents in both camps:

> That for three Lents for three years they should do penance in such a way that during the first they should remain outside the church and then should be reconciled at the Lord's supper. During these three Lents, on the second, fourth and sixth Sundays, they should abstain on bread, salt and water, or they should purchase exemption; and they should behave similarly for a fortnight before the Nativity of St John the Baptist and for a fortnight before the Nativity of Our Lord, and on every sixth Sunday throughout the whole year, unless they purchase exemption or a well-known feast falls on that day, or unless they are affected by illness or called to military service.[36]

Secondly, in 1070, four years after the battle of Hastings, a council of Norman bishops presided over by Ermenfrid of Sion imposed a penance on the soldiers of William the Conqueror even though the conquest had been carried out under a papal banner and against a perjuror.[37] The religious conscience of the early Middle Ages was yet more attentive to the problem of the participation of clerics in war. As early as 400 the

---

[34] *Patr. Lat.*, cx.471; cxxxii.295; clxi.736.
[35] *Monumenta Germaniae Historica Epistolarum* V, *Epistolae Karolini Aevi*, iii, ed. E. Dummler, 2nd edn. Berlin 1899, p.464.
[36] *Dictionnaire de théologie catholique*, vii.1605; Mansi, *Amplissima collectio*, xviii.345–6.
[37] H. E. J. Cowdrey, Bishop Ermenfried (957). See also the council of Winchester in 1076, stipulating that whoever kills a man should do a year's penance; if the perpetrator is ignorant of the fate of a man he has wounded he should do 40 days' penance; if he does not know how many men he has killed, he should do a day's penance a week for the rest of his life. As for archers who ran the risk of not knowing the losses they had inflicted, they had to do 40 days' penance three times.

Council of Toledo had declared that 'if anyone after baptism wages war dressed in a chlamys or a baldric, even if he has not committed the most serious offences, if he has been admitted as a cleric, he should not accept the dignity of deacon.' In 451 the Council of Chalcedon prohibited clerics and monks from joining the army. This prohibition, which was only a particular case of the order to those who served God not to be concerned with the things of this world,[38] remained in force. It was taken up again, in a circumstantial fashion, in the first general capitulary of Charlemagne (c.769): 'We absolutely prohibit clerics to bear arms and to go to war, except for those who have been chosen, because of their duties, to celebrate Mass and to carry the relics of the saints. Thus the prince may be accompanied by one or two bishops with their chaplains. Each captain shall have with him a priest to hear the confessions of soldiers and to impose on them penances to be performed.'[39] Even more severe was the synod of Tribur (895) which forbad the offering of prayers for clerics killed in a brawl, in war or in pagan games, though it did not go so far as to deprive them of Christian burial.

Naturally these regulations emanating from temporal and spiritual powers were frequently neglected. Some clerics bore arms, struck out, killed and mixed without shame with men of blood, just as other clerics (or even the same ones) were unchaste, drunkards or went hunting. In any event the prohibition could not apply to clerics whom circumstances and political events had endowed with temporal responsibilities. During the Merovingian period it was indeed necessary that a bishop as *defensor civitatis* should directly concern himself with military matters. St Arnoul, bishop of Metz (d.643), and St Eloi, bishop of Noyon (641–60) took part in the wars of their day. All this was institutionalized under the Carolingians. Charlemagne expected bishops and abbots to follow him in his campaigns, unless they possessed privileges or immunities, despite protestations like those of Patriarch Paulinus of Aquilea, who wrote to the king of the Franks in 789–90 that priests should fight only with spiritual arms and should not serve two masters.[40]

This militarization of the higher clergy, sometimes even to the extent that they defended themselves bodily, could only be accentuated by the invasions of the Normans, Saracens and Hungarians which spread across the West from the second half of the ninth century. The fratricidal struggles among the Franks ended with the same result. Sources tell us that between 886 and 908 ten German bishops fell in battle. Around the year 1000 Bishop Bernard, commanding the forces of Emperor Otto III, fought with a lance which

---

[38] 2 Timothy 2.

[39] Vogel *Pécheur et pénitence*, pp.192–3.

[40] See also the false capitularies of Benedict the Levite (after 847), according to which bishops rendered more service by remaining in their dioceses and praying than by following the army: 'When Moses prayed to Heaven, his hands outstretched, Israel was victorious.' Two or three bishops only were to accompany the army on campaign, but without arms, in order to pray and to protect the holy relics and sacred vessels: F. Prinz, *Klerus und Krieg* (205).

contained, as relics, a few nails of the true Cross. Even the papacy could not escape this tendency: John XII in the mid-tenth century had occasion to defend Rome with a weapon in his hand.

Intimately engaged in the wars of the period, the church hierarchy experienced at the same time an inevitable secularization of its habits, training and even appearance. In parallel, it was led to sacralize and sublimate warrior values. This was a movement which was especially visible at the level of the papacy. On different occasions, against the Lombard menace and then the Saracen one, popes promised eternal salvation to those who would take up arms in defence of the Roman church. Thus Stephen II declared in 753: 'Be sure that by the battle you fight for the church [of St Peter], your spiritual mother, the Prince of the Apostles will remit your sins.' In the same vein Leo IV promised a century later: 'Whoever meets death steadfastly in this fight (against the Saracens), the Heavenly Kingdoms will not be closed to him.'

Bellicose activities and pastoral care were not necessarily incompatible: witness the life of Adalbero I, bishop of Metz (929–62), a militant bishop as well as a reformer of the monastery of Gorze, or even more so that of the Archbishop of Cologne, Saint Bruno (953–65), who pursued with the same enthusiasm his triple ideal of *pax*, *timor* and *terror*.[41]

THE PEACE AND TRUCE OF GOD, THE CHIVALRIC ETHIC
AND THE CRUSADE

The early Middle Ages (above all between the eighth and tenth centuries) experienced changes in ideas about war – changes which it will be necessary to chart in more detail – but the period between the year 1000 and the beginning of the twelfth century was quite clearly more creative. Various different currents of recent historiography have been concerned to underline its complexity. One of them has uncovered the large scale of the peace programme proposed to the West; not simply the repression of pillage which disturbed daily life but a struggle, so to speak, which was also metaphysical and cosmological, against all elements of disorder and violence within the body and soul of the individual and society.[42] Another current has shown the organic links between the peace movements, the birth of chivalry and the formation of the idea of the crusade.[43] Yet another has emphasized the modification of social relationships, tensions and conflicts, not so much between the church and lay lords as between the powerful and the poor, taking into account the evolution of ideals, concepts and values.[44] In large

---

[41] cf. the *Vita Brunonis* of the deacon Ruotger (*Acta Sanctorum*, 5 October, 698–765).

[42] R. Bonnaud-Delamare, Fondements des institutions de paix au XIe siècle (965).

[43] G. Duby, *L'an mil*, Paris 1967.

[44] R. Fossier, Les mouvements populaires en Occident au XIe siècle, *AIBL* (1971), 257–69; E. Werner, *Pauperes Christi. Studien zu sozial-religiösen Bewegungen im Zeitalter des Reformpapsttums*, Leipzig 1956.

measure it was as a function of and around the notion of peace that a new balance of society was effected, though not without troubles and crises. From these analyses, sometimes complementary, sometimes contradictory, certain themes emerge which assist in a discussion of war.

First of all, the facts. The period 975–1025 was that of the Peace of God, or to use the expressions used at the time, of *pactum pacis, constitutio pacis, restauratio pacis et justitiae, pax reformanda*.[45] During the Council of Le Puy in 975 Bishop Guy of Anjou assembled in the open air on the field of Saint-Germain, the peasants and *milites* of his diocese, 'in order to hear from them what their advice was for the maintenance of peace'. From the outset the importance of what was at stake is made clear: 'Because we know that without peace nobody will see the Lord, we warn men in the name of the Lord that they should be sons of peace.' The word of command was transformed into an oath imposed, willy nilly, on the *milites* to respect the church's possessions and those of the peasants, at least if they were situated outside lands held by these *milites* as allods, benefices or *in commendam*. Bishop Guy ran up against some resistance, which he overcame thanks to the armed aid of his relatives, the counts of Brioude and Gevaudan. That is to say, the peace movement was not directed against all the powerful (who had an interest in seeing that the goods of their dependants were protected) but simply against plunderers and troublemakers. Subsequent peace assemblies saw the three levels of lay society at work: *principes, nobiles* and *vulgaris plebs* (Raoul Glaber).

The Council of Charroux (June 989), uniting the bishops of Aquitaine, *secunda*, under the presidency of Gombaud, archbishop of Bordeaux, pronounced a triple anathema against those who broke into churches, against those who seized as booty 'the goods of husbandmen or other poor people, sheep, bulls, asses, cows, goats, billy-goats and pigs, unless it is because of their crimes', and finally against those who committed violence against clerics not carrying arms. Thus protection of farmers (*rustici*) was very limited; it concerned only the seizure of unjust pledges. The Council of Verdun-sur-Doubs (1016) went further in imposing protection of peasants during a proper war. After this first phase, in which only an oath was exacted, a second saw the organization of peace leagues. In 1038, Aimon, archbishop of Bourges, was apparently the first to take this initiative by obliging all the faithful aged 15 or more to declare themselves enemies of disturbers of the peace and to promise to take up arms against them if required.

Thus the limits of the peace movement appear; it attempted to suppress daily violence, exactions and unlawful fines, *depraedationes* and *invasiones*. To this end places, goods and particular persons (clerics, merchants, pilgrims, peasants, noble women as well as their escorts in the absence of their hus-

---

[45] H. Hoffmann, *Gottesfrieden und Treuga Dei* (979); H. E. J. Cowdrey, The Peace and Truce of God in the Eleventh Century (975).

bands, widows, nuns . . .) benefited from a specific protection. It was a question of limiting the effects of *werra* or of the feud. Large-scale warfare (*bellum* properly so called), undertaken on the authority of public powers with the aid of vassals owing host and riding services, was not affected by these measures.

The Truce of God (*treuga Dei*) derived from the same spirit, despite differences in its methods. It first appears at the Council of Toulonges (1027). According to the *pactum sive treuga* which was promulgated there and applied in the diocese of Elne and the county of Roussillon, all violence was to cease between nine o'clock on Saturday evening and the hour of Prime on Monday, a decision similar to that prohibiting pleas, servile works and markets on Sunday.

In 1041 the bishops of Provence, no doubt at the instigation of Odilo, abbot of Cluny, addressed in their own names and in that of all the bishops of Gaul a letter to the bishops of Italy, beseeching them to 'receive' and keep 'the peace and this truce of God which has been handed down to us from Heaven by Divine Mercy and which we have received and hold firmly. It consists in the fact that from the hour of Vespers on Wednesday there is to be firm peace amongst all Christians, friend or foe, and a truce, which shall last till sunrise on Monday morning.' A few years later, the Truce of God was introduced into Aquitaine, Burgundy, Normandy and the ecclesiastical provinces of Vienne and Besançon. In its turn the papacy intervened, first during the reign of Nicholas II, then during that of Urban II, to extend the peace movement to the whole of Christendom. Other periods of abstention from war were added: Advent, Christmastide, Lent, Eastertide, between Rogationtide and the Octave of Pentecost, the three feasts of the Virgin and their vigils and for several Saints' days.

In these two forms, the peace movement had many consequences. Born of the absence of public authority in certain regions of the West, it encouraged kings and princes to take up the restoration of order in their own interests. In 1155 an Act of Louis VII, aimed at 'breakers of the peace', sought 'to repress the ardour of spite and restrain the violence of brigands'.[46] In 1158 Frederick Barbarossa proclaimed the peace through all Italy; the numerous *Landfrieden* which punctuate the history of the Holy Roman Empire sprang from the same desire. The result was less to suppress war than to reserve it to a small number of authorities, possessing the monopoly of violence, to use Max Weber's phrase. The measures of St Louis and his successors against private warfare were a logical continuation of the peace movement. The movement, in encouraging the creation of militias, provided a certain impetus for popular struggles against feudal lords and contributed to the emancipation of the communes. For the peace militias in effect 'unquestionably contained an element that conflicted with the social hierarchy; not only because they set

---

[46] A. Graboïs, De la trêve de Dieu à la paix du roi (978).

up villeins against robber lords; but also and perhaps most of all because they committed men to defending themselves, instead of looking for protection to the regular powers . . . Punitive expeditions, flying the banners of the churches and directed against the castles of the robber lords, heralded the French communal movement at Le Mans in 1070.'[47]

The competence of a Louis VI, advised by the monks of St Denis, was to enable the Capetian monarchy to profit from these initiatives. This was the direction of his policy from the start:

> Because King Philip, worn out by age and sickness, had allowed his princely power to decline and the royal justice had become too lax to punish tyrants, Louis was at first obliged to ask for help from the bishops all over his kingdom to put an end to the oppressions of bandits and rebels. As a result the bishops set up the communities of the people in France, so that the priests might accompany the king to battle or siege, carrying banners and leading all their parishioners.[48]

Among its many meanings, the Oriflamme of St Denis – as displayed at Bouvines – is presented as a banner of peace which protects the communes.[49]

Only a certain type of violence, different from *bellum* proper, was prohibited at various periods of the year by the regulations of the Truce of God. Treating the just war, the majority of canonists and theologians thought it useless to stipulate any limitation in time at all. St Thomas Aquinas even admitted that one could fight if the need arose on the most solemn days (since the very quality of a just war is its necessity). However, some thinkers were more demanding. Master Rufinus in his *Summa Decretorum* (*c*.1157) prescribed respect for feast days solemnized by the church to the extent that the punishment of wrongdoers, even if merited, should be interrupted. Several episodes show, on the other hand, that public opinion, perhaps assisted by superstitious fears, considered it abnormal to fight during the most sacred periods of the year.[50]

In contrast, the Peace of God particularly helped to release the notion of

---

[47] M. Bloch, *La société féodale* (99), i.206–8 (cf. *Feudal Society*, tr. L. Manyon, London 1961, pp.416–17). Joan of Arc remained faithful to this very ancient practice when in 1429 at Blois she ordered Brother Jean Pasquerel to make a church banner, decorated with the figure of Christ on the Cross. This banner, accompanied by priests who sang the *Veni Creator* and other anthems, went before the army proper during the march on Orléans; *Procès en nullité de la condamnation de Jeanne d'Arc*, ed. P. Duparc, Paris 1977, i.391.

[48] *Orderic Vitalis*, ed. Chibnall, vi.156.

[49] G. Duby, *Le dimanche de Bouvines* (244).

[50] P. Contamine, L'idée de guerre à la fin du Moyen Age (924a). For an incident at the siege of Bellême in 1113 by Henry I see *Ecc. Hist. Orderic Vitalis*, ed. Chibnall, vi.183: 'It was the feast of the Invention of the Holy Cross [2 May] and the king had ordered the whole army to desist from attacking the fortress or fighting in any way.' See also for the battle of Lincoln on 2 February 1141, the day of the Feast of the Purification (*ibid.*, 540). Conversely the *Histoire du gentil seigneur de Bayart*, ed. J. Roman, p.304, mentions without blame or surprise the assault on Ravenna attempted by the troops of Gaston de Foix on Good Friday, 1512.

the natural immunity of non-combatants and their possessions. A direct link exists between the Peace of God and the enumeration of those who in time of war had 'safe conducts without asking for it': churchmen, from bishops to pilgrims, including chaplains, lay brothers (*conversi*) and hermits, 'cowherds and all farmers' (*bouviers et tous gaigneurs*), labourers, merchants, women, old people and children. In *L'arbre des batailles* (*c*.1386) Honoré Bovet poses the question:

> Whether a child should be made prisoner and put to ransom? Although the matter has been in great debate, and is hard to determine on account of the conflicting customs that soldiers have used in these latter days, I hold firmly, according to ancient law, and according to the ancient customs of good warriors, that it is an unworthy thing to imprison either old men taking no part in the war, or women, or innocent children. Certainly it is a very bad custom to put them to ransom as it is common knowledge that they can have no part in war . . . and whoever does the contrary deserves the name of pillager.[51]

When he proposed a plan for total war to the English government in 1435, in which non-combatants would no longer be spared, Sir John Fastolf felt the need to justify his advice as the necessary and logical reply to the enemy's practices.

The anathema directed by the Lateran Council of 1139 against archers and crossbowmen using their detestable weapons in wars between Christians may also be linked with the peace movement. This prohibition, to which Gratian made no allusion in his *Decretum*, was, in contrast, repeated in the *Decretals* of Gregory IX. It is true, as has been seen, that the prohibition only had a temporary and limited application.[52] But while for Peter the Chanter around 1200 the use of the bow and crossbow was tolerated against the Infidel, pagans, and Cathars, as they were also in a just war, for others like Richard the Englishman, Raymond of Peñafort and Jean de Dieu, the ban imposed by the Second Lateran Council remained valid. It is significant, moreover, that neither the improvement of trébuchet artillery nor the appearance of gunpowder artillery aroused the same kind of condemnation from the church.[53] It is possible that in the final analysis the decision at Lateran II was aimed rather at a type of soldier than at a type of arms – against those professional

---

[51] Honoré Bonet, *L'arbre des batailles* (913), p.202 (cf. tr. G. W. Coopland, Liverpool 1949, p.185).

[52] Above, chapter 3.

[53] Reservations expressed in the fourteenth and fifteenth centuries with regard to artillery arose more from a certain chivalric ideology than from pacifist sentiments. See for example the remarks of Louis de la Trémoille, quoted by J. R. Hale, Gunpowder and the Renaissance (689): 'De quoy servira plus l'astuce des gensdarmes, leur prudence, leur force, leur hardiesse, leur prudhommie, leur discipline militaire et leur desir d'honneur puisqu'en general est permis user de telles invencions?'. Nevertheless Christine de Pisan, followed by Jean de Bueil (*Le Jouvencel* (9), ii.58), prohibits on pain of excommunication divulging the secret of Greek fire and its usage 'for it is not permissible for Christians to use such inhumane things which are quite contrary to all laws of war'.

soldiers whose trade Peter the Chanter declared was one where one's soul was automatically lost, for all their wages derived from slaughter of the innocent. The peace movement favoured definition and promotion of the chivalric ideal. The church, in effect, sought to integrate knights into the fight against violence and to use them for its own ends as much as to oppose their bellicose activities. On several occasions 'knights of peace' were instituted, and benefited, in exactly the same way as the crusaders, from the privilege of immunity.

One of the first indications of the attitude of the Church in respect of what was to become the chivalric vocation may be found in the *Vita* of St Gerald of Aurillac, written about 930 by Odo, abbot of Cluny. There, for the first time, as Georges Duby notes, it is demonstrated that a powerful noble could achieve sanctity and become a *miles Christi* without laying down his arms (though also without shedding blood).[54] Military activity, the specific function of one of the orders of society, acquired a spiritual and redemptive value. Henceforward there was a legitimate *militia*. Anselm of Lucca, about 1082, wrote that 'soldiers can be just men'. A little later Bonizo of Sutri devoted a chapter of his *Liber de vita christiana* to the duties of knights. They should remain faithful to their lord at the risk of their lives, protect him, abstain from pillage, pursue heretics and schismatics, defend the poor, widows and orphans and not break a pledged word. Both profane and learned literary works from *Chansons de geste* to the *Policraticus* of John of Salisbury popularized and, on certain points, defined the chivalric ideal. By the mid-twelfth century this ideal reached its classic formulation.[55] Later developments followed the same line of thought, as the enumeration of 31 sins or vices of knights which Alvarez Pelayo drew up at the beginning of the fourteenth century in his *De planctu Ecclesiae* indirectly testifies: 1. Knights commonly live by rapine, especially in Galicia; 2. They often fight against their own

---

[54] G. Duby, Origines de la chevalerie (190). On the attitude of Gerald of Aurillac (*Sanctus Giraldus miles fortissimus*, as Helgaud de Fleury styles him) to fighting, see *Patr. Lat.*, cxxxiii.646–7.

[55] John of Salisbury expressed himself thus:

But what is the office of the duly ordained soldiery? To defend the church, to assail infidelity, to venerate the priesthood, to protect the poor from injuries, to pacify the province, to pour out their blood for their brothers (as the formula of their oath instructs them), and, if need be, to lay down their lives. The high praises of God are in their throat, and two-edged swords are in their hands to execute punishment on the nations and rebuke upon the peoples, and to bind their kings in chains and their nobles in links of iron. But to what end? To the end that they may serve madness, vanity, avarice, or their own private self-will? By no means. Rather to the end that they may execute the judgement that is committed to them to execute; wherein each follows not his own will but the deliberate decision of God, the angels, and men, in accordance with equity and the public utility.

(Quoted by S. Painter, *French Chivalry*, Ithaca and New York 6th edn 1965, pp.69–70, from the trans. by J. Dickinson: *The Statesman's Book of John of Salisbury*, New York 1927, pp.199–200).

country and the lord they are obliged to serve; 3. They take part in unjust wars; 4. They take part in tournaments, especially in France; 5. They issue or take up challenges to duels on every occasion; 6. They accept wages and fail to serve, or do so with fewer horses than they should; 7. Some count themselves knights before they are dubbed; 8. After becoming knights and taking part in war, some of them enter religious orders; 9. They do not fight for God or the Common Weal but for booty and to increase their fortunes; 10. Many, especially in Lombardy, Tuscany and the Patrimony of St Peter receive knighthood at the hands of their relatives or friends and not from the Emperor, kings or princes; 11. They often flee from just wars and abandon their lords in the midst of their enemies, thus committing *lèse-majesté*; 12. They degrade themselves sometimes by accepting an administrative office; 13. They are perjurers because they commonly fail to keep the oath they have taken to face death for the security of the public good; 14. They absent themselves from service for the common good when their request to disband has been refused, and when they are at home, their request to retire from active service having been granted, they want to continue to enjoy chivalric privileges and their pay; 15. Certain return to a chivalric way of life after a solemn penance; 16. Many, after killing priests, enjoy knighthood; 17. They do not use knighthood for the purpose for which it was instituted – to redress injustice, and wreak vengeance on the impious; 18. They do not observe chivalric codes of behaviour; 19. They fight in a cruel, implacable manner in order to gain vengeance, to dominate and injure; 20. In fighting, they do not attend to the common good but to private interests; 21. They do not obey their superiors in useful, licit or simply doubtful matters; 22. They take more than their wages; 23. They kill men and wage war without legitimate authority of their superior; 24. They are often guilty of simony; 25. After public penance, certain men become knights; 26. In knighthood, they are promoted to honours not by degree but at a single step; 27. In a just war, they fight with bad grace and faint hearts, thus without merit; 28. They often leave before victory is won or before having served their full time; 29. They often kill their prisoners of war; 30. Today knights are often pillagers, above all in Spain; 31. They puff themselves up with pride, even in peacetime.[56]

Apart from the virtues of obedience and fealty expected in the chivalric ideal, it appears that the Church confided to the *milites* a mission which was not new but which had formerly been attributed chiefly to kings (although as early as the Carolingian period the aristocracy had seen itself responsible for protecting the poor and weak). Just as the peace movement of the eleventh century was born in a vacuum in monarchical power, which made necessary a series of local initiatives and responsibilities, so the impotence or indifference displayed by kings to their role in the maintenance of order led the church to assign this role to a social and professional group who in theory should only

---

[56] Alvarez Pelayo, *De Planctu Ecclesiae*, Lyon 1517, art.31.

have provided executants at various levels. 'The Church was in direct touch with the profession of arms without the king as an intermediary.'[57] In this perspective, it is not far-fetched to draw a parallel between the crowning or anointing of kings and the ceremony of dubbing, where the intervention of the Christian religion made itself more and more obvious.[58]

The influence of the church first appeared there at the level of the blessing of weapons. This practice is attested as early as the end of the Lombard period in Italy. Various pontificals from the middle of the tenth century contain formulae for the consecration of banners, swords and other weapons ('consecrationes vexilli, ensis, gladii, calcarum, clipei'). An *oratio super militantes* is expressed in these terms: 'Hearken, O Lord, to our prayers and bless with the hand of Your Majesty this sword with which your servant desires to be girded in order to defend and protect churches, widows and orphans and all the servants of God against the cruelty of the pagans and in order to be the scourge of all those who lay ambushes for him.'[59]

Alongside purely secular dubbings, which were always the most frequent, being accompanied only by vague benedictions granted by an ordinary priest or chaplain, there existed from the eleventh century solemn ceremonies, often occurring on the day of Pentecost and conducted by bishops. William the Conqueror had one of his sons dubbed by Lanfranc, archbishop of Canterbury. A pontifical from the province of Reims, compiled at the beginning of the eleventh century, describes the blessing of the sword, banner, lance and shield, of the knight himself and, finally, the delivery of the sword by the bishop. At the same period a ritual originating in the church of Cologne contains an 'ordo ad armandum Ecclesiae defensorem vel alium militem'.

At the end of an evolution many of the stages of which remain to be documented, the *Pontifical* of Guillaume Durand, drawn up about 1295 and which in the fourteenth century was to be integrated into the *Roman Pontifical*, enumerated the different phases of the *benedictio novi militis*. First came the blessing of the sword and other weapons for the 'defence of churches, widows, orphans and all servants of God against the cruelty of pagans'. Another benediction mentioned that God, in order 'to repress the wickedness of reprobates and to protect justice' had permitted the use of the sword on earth. He had willed the chivalric order (*militaris ordo*) to be instituted for the protection of people, since he had spoken through St John the Baptist to the knights who had come to seek him in the desert, warning them that they should not oppress anyone but remain content with their wages. God was asked to let his servant 'who was going to offer his neck to the yoke of chivalry' triumph, as he had once enabled David and Judas Maccabeus to triumph. The knight should never strike anyone unjustly, but should defend

---

[57] H. E. J. Cowdrey, The Genesis of the Crusades (995), p.16.

[58] J. Flori, Chevalerie et liturgie (109a).

[59] A. Franz, *Die kirchlichen Benediktionem im Mittelalter*, Fribourg-en-Brisgau 1909, ii.293.

with his sword 'all things just and righteous'. His passage from a minor estate (*minor status*) to 'the new honour of chivalry' is linked with the word of Scripture, 'Ye have put off the old man with his deeds; and have put on the new man which is renewed in knowledge after the image of him that created him.'[60] Then the pontiff would take the bare sword from the altar and with his hand in the right hand of the new knight say: 'Receive this sword in the name of the Father, and of the Son, and of the Holy Ghost, and use it to defend yourself, the Holy Church of God, the Christian faith and the Crown of the kingdom of France to the utter confusion of the enemies of the Cross of Christ.' The sword would be replaced in its scabbard and the future knight girt with it. He would draw it out and brandish it vigorously three times. The bishop could then mark the 'chivalric character' of the suppliant by giving him the kiss of peace and saying: 'Be a gentle, worthy, faithful and devoted knight of God'. The ritual blow was accompanied by these words: 'Awake from the sleep of malice and live in the faith of Christ a life worthy of praise.' The nobles present put spurs on the newly dubbed knight, who finally received his banner from the hands of the bishop.[61]

The connection between the ideology of the Peace of God and that of the crusade seems obvious. Did not the first canon of the Council of Clermont, at the end of which Urban II announced the expedition to Jerusalem, concern the Peace of God? It has been noted that in both cases the symbolism of the Cross played a decisive role and that the office of knight as a lover of justice and a penitent, of the *miles Christi*, extended both to the punishment of infidels as well as to the repression of malefactors and heretics. Nevertheless the crusade also included another, equally important, component; it was just as much a pilgrimage as a war. So the crusading vow should not be seen as analogous to the oath of peace taken at the end of synods or councils, but as a vow of pilgrimage which the faithful could take in varying circumstances. A body of theoretical reflection on the crusade, as it was elaborated from the second half of the twelfth century, omitted, consciously or not, the military implications of pilgrimage to the Holy Land.

> By the late eleventh century . . . Western Christendom had arrived at a concept of war, the holy war, which was both novel and important. Although it was built upon the Augustinian notions of the just war, the holy war went well beyond the position which Augustine had set forth. Not only was the holy war considered not offensive to God, but it was thought to be positively pleasing to Him. Participants were not merely held to act in a morally acceptable fashion, but their fighting in a blessed cause was believed to be a virtuous act which merited God's special favor, as embodied in the commutation of penance granted by papal proclamation.[62]

[60] Colossians 3.9–10.
[61] M. Andrieu, *Le pontifical romain au Moyen Age*, III: *Le pontifical de Guillaume Durand*, Vatican City 1940, pp.447–50.
[62] J. A. Brundage, *Medieval Canon Law and the Crusader* (994), p.29.

In fact the plenary indulgence, understood from the start as a redemption or commutation of penalties replacing fasts and other mortifications of the body, was for the first time accorded in 1095 by Pope Urban II, 'that this way may serve for all penitence'. The idea of a holy war was not, however, completely unknown in previous centuries. At the time of the Saracen incursions the papacy had promised spiritual favours to warriors who came to defend it. The new factor was that the holy war now applied to a military operation whose character appeared at first sight to be offensive. But behind this façade a different reality lurked, rendering the crusade not only licit but the very model of *bellum justissimum*. This was because, on the one hand, Christendom saw itself as a fortress encompassed on all sides, with the result that expeditions emanating from it were comparable to *sorties* undertaken by defenders, and that, on the other, the Holy Land was *par excellence* the kingdom of Christ whose capital, Jerusalem, should not only be taken but retaken and recovered by the faithful of the Cross.[63] This war, moreover, did not arise simply from the initiative of men who had rationally debated whether it was legitimate or not, but from the direct will of God – hence the cry 'God wills it' (*Dieu le veut*) – which had inspired the souls of Christians.

From the second half of the twelfth century another justification for the crusade was added to earlier ones; since the Saracens occupied lands which had formerly been part of the Roman Empire, it was right that the church, the legitimate heir of that Empire, should seek to recuperate what had been torn from it by force. Hence the name *bellum romanum* which, in the thirteenth century, Hostiensis was to give to the just war waged by the faithful against infidels.[64] Moreover Christians were justified in law in punishing the people of Islam who were termed 'the most blameworthy nation' (*summa culpabilis*).[65]

It remains the case that canonists and theologians did have some reservations about wars against the Infidel though these were more implicit than explicit. Huguccio admitted the Saracens possessed certain rights in the lands which they occupied. If he reserved to the papacy the monopoly of the crusade, it was not simply to exalt the successor to St Peter, but also to remove the possibility that any temporal authority could declare a 'holy war'. In addition the crusade, he argued, should be limited to the land around Jerusalem and should not concern other parts of the Roman Empire that had

---

[63] Among other representations, an illumination may be noted where the church is depicted as a crenellated tower on the summit of which there are three figures – in the centre a priest dressed in robes enriched with purple, symbolizing the sacerdotal order, bearer of the spiritual sword; to the left a soldier symbolizing the *ordo militaris*, carrying the temporal sword; to the right a monk in tears, symbolizing the *ordo monasticus* whose only weapon was prayer: M. D. Chenu, *La théologie au XIIe siècle*, Paris 2nd edn 1966, pp.240–1.

[64] M. Villey, L'idée de croisade chez les juristes du Moyen Age, *X Congresso Internazionale di Scienze Storiche Roma 4–11 Settembre 1955, Relazioni III: Storia del Medioevo*, Florence 1955, pp.565–94.

[65] N. Daniel, *Islam and the West*, Edinburgh 1960, p.112.

been conquered by Islam. Innocent IV, in the following century, adopting the same attitude, showed little enthusiasm for the crusade which Louis IX directed against Egypt. The same thinker, who might be considered the greatest canonist of the Middle Ages, denied Christians the right to make war on Saracens as infidels, even in order to convert them. In contrast, Innocent IV, as well as Hostiensis, were far more at ease in approving the struggle against heretics (*negotium fidei*, *negotium pacis*, *negotium Christi*), henceforward termed *crux cismarina* in opposition to the *crux transmarina*, since heretics had abandoned true faith in full knowledge and represented by their proselytism an immense danger to souls.

WAR AND SCHOLASTIC THOUGHT

Scholastic doctrine on war was born in the first half of the twelfth century with the rediscovery of Roman law by the jurists of Bologna and the publication of the *Decretum* of Gratian about 1140. In the second half of the century canonists undertook commentaries on the *Decretum*. Then in the course of the thirteenth century they became exegetes of the papal *Decretals*. In parallel, scholastic theology introduced its own methods of reflection. In the fourteenth and fifteenth centuries, popularization of canonistic teaching on war occurred while civil lawyers were forced to adapt their reasoning and conclusions to a political and military context which was continuously evolving. Despite the varying opinions and approaches, it seems possible to describe scholastic thought on war as a coherent, indissoluble whole.

Definition

Definitions of war aimed above all at distinguishing them from other forms of violence like brawls, sedition and the exercise of judicial power, in which the problem of legality was posed in a different form. St Thomas Aquinas is representative: 'War, properly speaking, is against an external enemy, one nation as it were against another, and brawls are between individuals, one against one or a few against a few. Sedition in its proper sense is between mutually dissident sections of the same people, when, for example, one part of the city rebels against another.'[66]

By virtue of this definition neither civil nor social wars have a right to the status of war; neither do domestic dissensions; nor the actions of an individual or a group seeking to injure, gain vengeance or defend itself. Equally, when any authority employs force to gain respect for its decisions it is not waging a true war, and recalcitrants should not be qualified as enemies (*hostes*). The fight against the tyrant, tyrannicide, belongs to another category in which other rights, obligations and criteria are involved.

---

[66] *Summa Theologica*, IIa IIae, qu.42, art. 1.

Causes of war

Explanations are advanced at different levels. One, the psychological and moral, is linked to the text of St James' Epistle: 'From whence come wars and fightings among you? Come they not hence, even of your lusts that war in your members? Ye lust, and have not: ye kill, and desire to have, and cannot obtain; ye fight and war, yet ye have not, because ye ask not.'[67] For *Le Jouvencel* the frequency of conflict is explained by the fact that 'no one willingly suffers the loss of his rights.'[68] According to the same source pride, envy and avarice are the main three reasons for 'the stirrings and commencement of war'.

Asking himself 'why are there so many wars in this world?', Honoré Bovet chose to explain it on this metaphysical level when he answered that 'they are all on account of the sins of this world' with the result that 'soldiers are the flail of God, who with His permission, punish sinners.'[69]

The six theological causes which according to John of Legnano prevent universal peace on earth mix political, religious and moral considerations: 1. Because evil deeds are not punished; 2. Because of the abundance of temporal possessions; 3. Because we are not engaged in fighting the Devil; 4. Because we do not consider the damage inflicted by warfare, in which we lose both our lives and riches; 5. Because we do not consider the outcome of war, which is very uncertain; 6. Because we do not obey God's commandments.

From another perspective, which one finds in John of Legnano as well as in Honoré Bovet, war appears all the more natural because it has a cosmological character. The heavenly spiritual warfare fought by angels and provoked by the pride of Lucifer is the yard-stick and model for the lower human spiritual war; in other words for the conflict which takes place within every man between reason and passion, intelligence and the senses. But there exists another celestial war, corporal this time, between the stars by reason of the perpetual movement which animates them. Now these stars have an influence on inferior bodies, engendering heat and cold, lust or chastity – so many contradictory effects which prevent concord between men and make conflicts natural, if not inevitable. Better still, not only do individual characters conflict with one another, as astral influences conflict, but certain periods are dominated by signs of war as others are by signs of epidemic or famine. Roger Bacon wrote that the comet of July 1264 had been engendered under the influence of the planet Mars and produced an increase in bile, thus

---

[67] James 4.1–2.

[68] de Beuil (9), i.20. One thinks of the comment of William Stubbs that: 'the kings of the Middle Ages went to war for rights, not for interests, still less for ideas', quoted by H. E. J. Cowdrey (995), p.9.

[69] Bonet (913), p.150 (tr. Coopland, p.157).

exacerbating an evil humour, and hence was responsible for the wars which broke out at that time in England, Spain and Italy.[70]

Just and unjust wars

Gratian in causa 23 of the second part of the *Decretum* asks himself initially whether waging war is a sin. His answer is no; there are many who can please God by exercising the profession of arms; only certain acts in war are reprehensible in law and the greatest merit of soldiers is that they are serving the public good. As such they should fight even under the command of a sacrilegious prince. For if the war is unjust and the orders given do not conform to divine law, the iniquity will be the prince's alone. As the Gloss put it: The lord may sin in giving orders but the subject does not sin in obeying ('Licet dominus peccet precipiendo, tamen subditus non peccat obediendo').

From Gratian four conditions for the just war can be derived: it should be ordered by a prince; without the participation of clerics; for the defence of the country attacked or for the recovery of despoiled goods; free from violent, unlimited passion. In the *Summa Decretorum* Rufinus repeated two of these criteria and proposed a third: 'A war is termed just in relation to him who declares it, him who fights it and him against whom it is waged. With regard to the function of him who declares it, that he who effectively declares it or authorizes it should have the power to do so; with regard to the function of him who fights, that he should wage it with a fervour penetrated by goodwill and he should be a person who might fight without causing scandal; with regard to him who is troubled by war, that he merits being tortured by war or, if not, that he should at least be reputed to merit it by just presumptions. Where one of these three conditions is lacking it is absolutely impossible for a war to be just.'[71] The *Summa Coloniensis* mentions the quality of the belligerent and of the declaring authority but adds also the justice of the cause and the suitability of time and place. As for Huguccio (*c*.1140–1210), he proposed an extremely concise formula. 'A just war is waged by the just edict of a prince.'[72]

It was not until the beginning of the thirteenth century that the five classic criteria for a just war were formulated under the rubrics *persona, res, causa, animus* and *auctoritas*. Defined by Laurentius Hispanus around 1210, they were repeated almost without variation by Johannes Teutonicus, while St Raymond of Peñafort (*c*.1180–1275) ensured their ultimate diffusion. They occur again in the fourteenth century in the works of the Italian civil lawyer Pietro Baldo degli Ubaldis (1327–1406), who proposed the following commentary: 'The person: he should be a layman and not an ecclesiastic; the

---

[70] A. C. Crombie, *Augustine to Galileo. The History of Science A.D. 400–1650*, London 2nd edn 2 vols. 1961, i.99.
[71] Russell (947), p.87 n.3.
[72] *Ibid.*, p.89.

object: war should be waged for the recovery of goods or to defend the country; the cause: one should fight by necessity as we find in Aristotle's remark, 'Act so that war is for you the ultimate necessity'; the spirit: war should not be waged out of hatred nor insatiable cupidity; the authority: without the prince's authority no war may be declared.'[73]

The notion of the prince, shorn of all ambiguity in Roman law, arising from the simplicity of the political structures of the Empire, could not fail to cause problems when applied to the complexities of the medieval world. Should it be reserved to the Emperor or to the pope? Should it also be attributed to kings, to the authorities responsible for urban states or to the immense variety of feudal powers? Among the most restrictive, Hostiensis was not far from reserving the *auctoritas* sufficient for declaring war to the Emperor and pope, but the majority of authors accorded this same *auctoritas* to independent kings like those of France and Castile, to kings who at one moment or another had recognized a temporal superior (the case of Sicily and England, vassals of the Holy See), and even to Italian cities.[74] Thus in the fifteenth century Martin of Lodi wrote: 'Although anyone who raises an army without the order of a superior commits the crime of *lèse-majesté*, nevertheless princes and Italian cities who do not recognize superiors may prepare for war against their subjects and enemies.'[75] Others escaped the problem by distinguishing not between just and unjust wars but between acts which were properly called wars (reserved to the Emperor or even more to the pope) and acts improperly called wars (which could be fought by inferiors).[76] For John of Legnano, and after him Honoré Bovet, the prince alone could wage a general war (*bellum universale*), which implies that 'particular' wars could be fought by those other than princes. Sometimes instead of the term *princeps*, that of *judex*, which had a wider attribution, was preferred.

It was partially in terms of criteria of authority that Hostiensis, repeated in the fourteenth century by John of Legnano, distinguished seven types of war, of which four were just or licit and three unjust or illicit:[77]

1   Roman war (*bellum romanum*). Prototype of the just war, this was a war of the faithful against infidels and was so called because 'Rome was head and mother of our faith.' Interpreted to the limit, Roman war, also termed

---

[73] Quoted in the edition of Alfonso the Wise's *Siete Partidas* by G. Lopez, Paris 1861, ii.243 n.2.

[74] According to the glossator Odofredus (first half of the thirteenth century) 'no one may start a war nor bear arms without permission of the Emperor'.

[75] G. Soldi-Rondinini, Il diritto di guerra (1018).

[76] Like J. Lopez of Segovia (1440–96) in his *De Bello et bellatoribus* cited by Soldi-Rondinini (1018).

[77] The same distinctions are drawn in the treatise of the Castilian Pedro Azamar, dedicated to John II, king of Aragon (1476) (Paris, Bibl. Arsenal MS 8319), and in the *Doctrinal de noblesse* dedicated to the town of Metz (late fifteenth century) (Bib. Nat., MS Nouv. acq. fr. 10017, f.52v). cf. also Russell (947), p.129.

mortal war, took up again the struggle of Ancient Rome against the Barbarians and was a total war in which enemies were to be neither spared nor liberated in return for ransoms but could be legitimately killed or reduced to slavery.

2 Judicial war (*bellum judiciale*). This was also just to the extent that it was fought on the authority of a judge (*judex*) who as possessor of *merum imperium* (complete, unshackled power in contrast to limited power, *mixtum imperium*) did not judge according to his own interest but in order to impose judicial order on those rebels or contumacious people who were opposing his legitimate power.

3 Presumptuous war (*bellum praesomptuosum*). This was unjust, for it was fought by rebels and the contumacious against the *judex* mentioned in the previous definition.

4 Licit war waged by a legal authority or with his permission to redress wrongs, or reject insults suffered by a subordinate power, like a baron punishing an enemy who had wronged him, after having obtained (either explicitly or implicitly) the right to wage this war from his sovereign.

5 Rash and illicit war fought against the *judex*.

6 Voluntary war, otherwise called offensive war, which was neither necessary nor just, waged by secular powers without authority of the prince.

7 The actions of those who defended themselves against a voluntary war; necessary and licit actions, for according to the *Digest* 'all laws and all rights permit opposing force with force.'[78]

Thus, as F. H. Russell has emphasized, this formulation was not simply evidence for the subtlety of analysis achieved by the great scholastics; it was a response to different real situations and covered practically all the types of conflict that could arise in a medieval political context.[79]

THE LAW OF ARMS AND JUSTICE: RELATIONS BETWEEN ETHICS AND PRACTICE IN THE WARS OF THE LATE MIDDLE AGES

It is convenient to start from concrete examples in examining to what extent temporal powers became conscious of the obligations of a just war or were at least forced to convince public opinion of the legitimacy of their actions. Various propaganda documents as well as diplomatic sources suggest constant attention was paid, if not to the *ideology*, then at least to the *phraseology* of *justum bellum*. Papal interventions seeking to put an end to the differences between Christian princes in the West, especially between the kings of France and England, merit study from this viewpoint.

A few signposts for such a study, which has hardly begun to attract any

[78] *Ibid.*, p.129, n.6.
[79] *Ibid.*, p.130.

attention in the historiography of war and diplomacy at the end of the Middle Ages, might be pointed out. In 1336 when the conflict with England was declared, Philip of Valois in a manifesto which he ordered to be read to his subjects in all the churches of the kingdom, affirmed: 'That we have good right and just cause according to the judgment of all our council.'[80] In 1369 Charles V only recommenced hostilities against Edward III after wide consultation with both French and foreign experts in canon and civil law, who assured him of his completely valid right. In the same way, the breaking of the truce of Tours in 1449, following the capture of Fougères by François de Surienne, was preceded by an examination of the situation by Charles VII and his councillors taking into account not only political and military factors but also juridical and moral ones – in what circumstances did one have the right to break truces which had been solemnly sworn? According to the Dominican John Bromyard, in his *Summa predicantium* (late fourteenth century), Edward III customarily undertook a pilgrimage before going to war and took counsel from experts in both the laws of God and those of this world.[81] Treatises on the art of war such as *L'Art de chevalerie* by Christine de Pisan, *Le Jouvencel* by Jean de Bueil and the *Nef des princes* of Robert de Balsac all mentioned, among the conditions preliminary to all military operations, the criterion of the just war. It is true that princes and kings fairly easily persuaded themselves that they had right on their side. It was easy to discover, in the imbroglio which every diplomatic affair constituted some wrong that had been suffered, an injustice of which one was the victim; to demand reparation from one's adversary and to commence hostilities against him on his refusal; hence the apparent futility of many of the conflicts. One of the most extreme examples of this was the so-called 'Basketful of Apples' war which brought the town of Metz and the duchy of Lorraine into conflict in 1428–29. The struggle was born 'a peu d'occasion' according to the Metz chronicler Philippe de Vigneulles: an abbot of the monastery of St-Martin-devant-Metz had picked or collected a basketful of apples from a garden situated in the village of St-Martin which belonged to the monks. Learning of this these monks went to complain to the duke of Lorraine who 'several times requested the city' to give him the right to judge the matter. Naturally the city turned a deaf ear, fearing that if it agreed it would create a dangerous precedent for its own franchises. The duke then took a pledge against the town of Metz in a village in its territory. In its turn Metz demanded compensation, which of course was followed by a ducal refusal. Metz then took revenge by sending its paid forces into the duke's lands, all these events having taken place in the most legally correct fashion. Before using force, legal measures had been taken and both parties could then with clear consciences have recourse to arms.[82] The same kind of idea, but with an

[80] G. du Fresne de Beaucourt, *Histoire de Charles VII*, Paris 1881, i.93.
[81] C. T. Allmand, *Society at War* (299), p.38.
[82] Philippe de Vigneulles, *Chronique*, ed. C. Bruneau, Metz, 4 vols. 1927–33, ii.187ff.

approach which was more philosophical than moral, occurred to Montaigne in his *Essais*, when following Commynes he wrote: 'Our greatest conflicts have ridiculous origins and causes. Just think how our last duke of Burgundy ruined himself by a quarrel over a cartload of sheepskins'.[83]

Philippe de Clèves, at the beginning of the sixteenth century, took up the same line of thought: 'You should', he told the prince to whom he addressed himself, 'beware of undertaking war for evil reasons'; it is necessary that you should act 'according to right and justice'. Once your right has been established, you can recover what belongs to you 'by main force if you cannot have it by any other means'. You should summon your adversary to give you justice and if he refuses, you should summon the *Etats* of your country and ask them for aid and assistance 'in order to gain your rights'. All sorts of *casus belli* appear legitimate to this author: help to an ally, a relative or a subject, the crusade etc. Philippe de Clèves is conscious of his laxity: 'Nevertheless, Monsieur, if theologians had debated this matter, I believe they would not have opened up such a broad avenue as I have done, but I am neither wise nor a good clerk, for which reason I have placed it before you there only in my fantasy and if for your peace of mind you would like to learn more, you may demand of those who have charge of your conscience.'[84]

It may be added that the concept of the common good, introduced by St Thomas Aquinas (following Aristotle) into the heart of his reflections on the just war, was fairly speedily and frequently used by princes to legitimate their bellicose enterprises. Becoming defence of the realm or the fatherland, defence of the common weal was scarcely anything other than a prefiguration of *raison d'état*.[85] Better still, extolling the person and powers of the prince, so characteristic of the thought and practical politics of the late Middle Ages, was translated in the military sphere into exaltation of 'guerres de magnificence' or 'de magnificence et d'honneur'. This, by opposition to common wars (*guerres communes*) in which one fought neighbours or kinsmen, designated enterprises in which 'princes went with their armies to conquer in far off and foreign lands or went to fight for the defence of the catholic faith or to enlarge its bounds.'[86] From this perspective, there is no distinction between the Italian Wars and the Crusade of Nicopolis.

Contemporaries were conscious that the criterion of *auctoritas* no longer corresponded to existing political conditions, resulting from the dismemberment of Christendom into a great number of states, sovereign in practice,

---

[83] Michel de Montaigne, *Essais*, ed. J. Plattard, Paris 1967, iii.2, 111; Philippe de Commynes, *Memoires*, ii.105 (tr. Jones, Harmondsworth 1972, p.281).

[84] Philippe de Clèves, *Instruction de toutes manieres de guerroyer*, p.3.

[85] Russell (947), pp.261–2; G. Post, *Ratio publicae utilitatis, ratio status und Staatsräson* (362). From the twelfth century *defensio patriae* was considered a legitimate reason for taking up arms: *Ecc. Hist. Orderic Vitalis*, ed. Chibnall, vi.64.

[86] *Le débat des hérauts d'armes de France et d'Angleterre*, ed. L. Pannier and P. Meyer, Paris 1877, p.12.

which had escaped from all material or moral control by either emperor or pope.[87] They equally saw that the notions of *res* and *causa* could give rise to all sorts of juridical subterfuges. As for the rank of belligerents, this scarcely caused any problems. Practically everyone subscribed to the moderate opinion, expressed among others by Guillaume Durand in the *Speculum juris:* 'A cleric may be appointed to oversee a just war, not to command directly men who shed blood, but to answer soldiers, provide money, arrange treaties, deliver sentences and dispose of all things, as we ourselves have done in the war which the Roman church undertook in the Romagna against cities in revolt.'[88] Astonishment or indignation was sometimes expressed when clerics or monks were seen disguised as soldiers, sword in hand in the bitterest fights;[89] though it was, in contrast, admitted that bishops having 'secular lordships in demesne' were directly concerned by military affairs. The presence of spiritual peers like the bishop of Beauvais or the archbishop of Reims in the army of the king of France was considered equally normal. Differences of opinion were in fact on another level: while temporal powers attempted to place the economic and fiscal burden of war on clerics as well as on the laity, the religious, alleging their privileges of exemption, tried to avoid having to contribute.

Although the problem of the moral responsibility of combatants engaged in an unjust war was discussed fairly infrequently, it gave rise to different solutions. One was the view of a good number of thirteenth-century moralists and theologians, such as Robert de Courçon: 'In illicit matters it is not necessary to obey temporal lords, thus knights when they feel a war is unjust should not follow the standards of the prince.' Similarly Stephen Langton argued that if the king of France declared an unjust war on the king of England, a French knight should indeed obey the royal summons but he should abstain or withdraw at the moment of combat. Yet again, Thomas de Chobham said bishops ought to exhort people to withdraw from an unjust war, at least if there was a chance that they would act unanimously following this advice with the result that all danger of sedition was excluded.[90] For

---

[87] cf. Christine de Pisan in *Le livre des faiz d'armes et de chevalerie.* To the question whether it was lawful for others than kings and sovereign princes to undertake war, she replied: 'it apperteyneth to none to empryse warre or bataylle for ony maner cause but yf it be to prynces soverayn lyke as emperours kynges dukes & other lordes terryens whiche ben merely princypall heedes of Iuredictions temporall ne to a baron what somever he be ne to ony other be he never so grete withoute lycence congie & volente of hys soverayn lord.': (*The Book of Fayttes of Armes and of Chyvalrye*, tr. William Caxton, ed. A. T. P. Byles, Early English Texts Society 1932, pp.10–11).

[88] *Speculum juris, De dispensatione*, 4 no.57, quoted in translation in *Rational ou manuel des divins offices*, ed. C. Barthélemy, Paris 1854, i.xv.

[89] In 1360 during a French raid on Winchelsea secular clergy and even regulars like the abbot of Battle took up arms to repel the attackers (John of Reading, *Chronicon*, ed. J. Tait, Manchester 1914, p.135; Ranulph Higden, *Polychronicon*, ed. C. Babington and J. R. Lumby, London 1883, viii.410).

[90] J. W. Baldwin, *Masters, Princes and Merchants* (921).

others, on the contrary, faithful to the Roman tradition of absolute obedience to the prince, it was for him to determine whether the war which he undertook was just or not, and his subjects had simply to follow, without their eternal salvation being endangered.[91] Naturally, governing authorities had every reason to want this thesis to triumph and, in fact, at the same time as discipline in armies was tightened and the system of military obligations became more coercive and rigorous, cases of conscience, concerning 'the condition of the soul', appear to have disappeared. At most, advocates of the golden mean like J. Lopez in the fifteenth century upheld the view that subjects could consider as just any war undertaken 'by order of their superiors', unless it appeared manifest to them that it was unjust and violent and that their lord desired to inflict oppression on others.[92]

In the final analysis it was the criterion of *animus* which was taken most seriously and, in a certain measure, contributed to shaping attitudes in the course of wars in the late Middle Ages. There were plenty of acute minds who were ready to compare the causes and ends of wars with the extent of devastation caused. St Thomas Aquinas had already underlined the need for proportionality between the motives for an action and its consequences, but only regarding tyrannicide. In his eyes, revolt against a tyrant could only be legitimate if the wrong which it entailed was presumed to be less than the evil provoked by the existence and action of the tyrant. Philippe de Mézières went further in his *Epistre à Richard II* King of England (1395). Having explained that the cause of a given conflict, while appearing just to the eyes of 'human wisdom' (*sapience humaine*) might very well not be accepted as such by God, he adds that it is necessary to take into account the extent of the miseries which war will bring once it is unleashed. He argues that it would be better for a prince to abandon to his potential enemy two-thirds of the object causing discord, for example two-thirds of a province which they both claimed, at the start of the problem.[93] His reasoning implies shared responsibility in the case of the Franco-English conflict. Hence the necessity for both parties to repent: 'the suffering of the kings and the true repentance of their knights, both French and English, for the great wrongs which they and their fathers have perpetrated and cruelly carried out against God and their neighbours.'[94]

Reflections of this type led to the contrasting of two kinds of war, according to the outward bearing of the combatants. In opposition to 'mortal' war, waged with fire and blood (*de feu et de sang*), where all sorts of 'cruelties, killings and inhumanities' were tolerated, or even systematically prescribed,

[91] Gutierre Diez de Games, *Le Victorial* (316), 313. Thomas Aquinas appears to agree with this opinion.
[92] Soldi-Rondinini (1018).
[93] Philippe de Mézières, *Letter to King Richard II*, ed. and tr. G. W. Coopland, Liverpool 1975, pp.53 and 126.
[94] *Ibid.*, pp.48 and 122.

there was that form of war described as *guerroyable*: regular war, loyal war, honourable, *bonne guerre*, fought by 'good fighters' in conformity with the law of arms (*droiturière justice d'armes*), or according to the 'discipline of chivalry'. Not to respect the lives of messengers and heralds, says Philippe de Vigneulles, was 'an unaccustomed thing in a righteous quarrel or in a just war'.[95]

To the extent that the precepts of good war were respected, soldiers did not compromise their eternal salvation in exercizing their profession. As Honoré Bovet said, in itself warfare was not evil, but the use to which it was put was all-important,[96] and *Le Jouvencel* adds, 'Whoever wages war loyally and prudently in a good cause does a just thing which, I hold, pleases God.'[97] *Le Victorial* likewise provides assurance that one can even save one's soul in fighting against Christians if certain conditions are met: one should not kill the enemy, having captured him; churches should be respected and no injury done to those who had sought refuge in them, nor should any objects which they contain be taken, unless it is impossible to find enough food to preserve life elsewhere. In this case it was permissible to take food to meet the immediate need, but no more – just sufficient for oneself and one's horse. No women should be taken or carried off, whether married or free, nor should the harvest or houses be burnt, for this action affected the innocent and poor who had done nothing to deserve such punishment.[98] At the end of the thirteenth century Guillaume Durand in the *Rational des divins offices* allowed burial in a cemetery and the office of the dead to the defender of justice and to the warrior killed in a war fought for a just cause. He simply prescribed that the bodies of the dead should not be carried into church for fear that their blood might pollute the floor.

A fifteenth-century manuscript defines by antiphrasis the ideal of good war by enumerating 'ten reproaches' which were enough to debar nobles who had incurred guilt from tournaments:

Violeurs d'esglises,
Residens excommuniez,

---

[95] Philippe de Vigneulles, *Chronique*, ed. Bruneau, iii.153; *ibid.*, 152, 'That nobody violates girls or women nor commits any offence against women lying-in and that nobody commits wrongs or uses force against any persons whatsoever as is proper in a righteous war.'

M. Schmidt-Chazan, Histoire et sentiment national chez Robert Gaguin, in *Le métier d'historien au Moyen Age*, ed. B. Guenée, Paris 1978, p.251, quotes the remarks of Richard of Wassebourg that before the arrival in Italy of René II, duke of Lorraine, 'the Venetians and Italians fought more wars which they called *'guerroyale'*, taking prisoners from one another in order to gain ransoms rather than killing their enemies. But the duke of Lorraine and his men did the opposite, for which reason the Venetians began to complain amongst themselves and called the Lorrainers murderers (*amassadors*) and did not find this acceptable any longer for fear that their enemies would do the opposite'.

[96] Bonet (913), pp.82–3.

[97] de Bueil (9), ii.265.

[98] Diez de Games (316), 313–14.

Meurtriers d'agués apensez,
Deshonnoureurs de femmes,
Faulsseurs voulentaires de leurs foys et scellez,
Fuytifs de bataille,
Desconfitz en gaiges par querelles,
Bouteurs de feux,
Conduiseurs de compaignies
Et pirates de mer.[99]

Jus in bello gradually eclipsed *jus ad bellum* in contemporary thought,[100] and was in very large measure the simple codification of the chivalric ideal which prohibited conduct contrary to 'all lordship and chivalry'. We may, however, note that this ideal was expressed simultaneously by moral imperatives governing the behaviour of soldiers, by rules of military discipline, and by a series of usages, customs and rites proper to the world of soldiers (the law of arms or *jus armorum*).[101]

According to various motives, governing powers and military authorities often sought to impose on their troops the 'discipline of chivalry', respect for which not only resulted in a certain humanization of war but also reinforced the effectiveness of armies. The fight against 'evil enterprises', against 'pillage, robbery, murder, sacrilege, violation and raping of women, arson and emprisonment',[102] benefited princes as much as the civilian population. It was for this reason that military ordinances included instructions and commands of a moral character. As an example, the 'estatutz, ordenances et custumes a tenir en l'ost' promulgated by Richard II in 1385 stipulated that on pain of death the Eucharist must not be profaned, nor the vessel which held the holy elements, that churches should not be pillaged, nor clerics, women or the civilian population robbed. Pillaging and foraging were both formally prohibited.[103] From the time of Frederick Barbarossa (*Lex pacis castrensis* of 1158) various legislative texts concerning the Empire witness to an analogous policy, for example, the *Sempacher Brief* of 1393 protected women, churches and other sacred places.

Many elements, however, conspired to thwart efforts to humanize war. They may be divided into three principal tendencies:

1. States were often anxious to wage as total a war as possible, not sparing the enemy. The notion of *lèse-majesté*, in particular, served to justify large-

---

[99] Bib. Nat., MS français 1997, f.18v–19r: 'Desecrators of churches, excommunicates, murderers by ambush, violaters of women, willing perjurers of their plighted word and sealed documents, fugitives from battle, those defeated in gage of battle, arsonists, leaders of free companies and pirates'.
[100] J. T. Johnson, *Ideology, Reason and the Limitation of War* (935).
[101] P. Contamine, *Guerre, état et société* (457), pp.187–92, 202–3. It may be noted that '*l'usance de guerre*' prohibited use of torture to make a prisoner of war talk: de Bueil (9), ii.91.
[102] Bib. Nat., MS français 5737, f.17ff.
[103] *Black Book of the Admiralty*, ed. T. Twiss, London, 4 vols. 1841–8, i.453–4.

scale massacres carried out in cold blood. On various occasions during the course of the Hundred Years War the English monarchy displayed implacable cruelty. Later Louis XI, like Charles the Bold, ordered his troops to carry out systematic devastations and had those who resisted them executed without pity. Similar atrocities on at least a comparable scale may be encountered during the crusade against the Hussite heresy.

2. The law of arms, the discipline of chivalry, with its more or less self-imposed constraints on combatants, could only apply to armies which were feudal and chiefly recruited from the nobility. But the late Middle Ages saw the appearance of a mass of adventurers who were scarcely amenable to this code – mercenaries including the great companies and Ecorcheurs in France, the Companies of Adventure in Italy, the Lansquenets in Germany, and the Albanian Estradiots during the Italian wars. They were content to let their bestial and sadistic instincts run riot without any restriction, but, more importantly, they contributed to a modification of the general atmosphere of war even when this was being waged by the traditional military cadres.

3. In contrast to aristocratic warfare, which easily changed into a sort of great tourney, half serious, half frivolous, a series of adventures and 'apertises d'armes' sought after and experienced for themselves, the warfare of communes, popular war, offered behaviour that was incontestably more violent. The Flemish communes systematically massacred the vanquished and refused the practice of ransoms, seen by them as cowardly and likely to lead to deception. Inevitably in battles where they faced the communes, nobles adopted a similar attitude. After the massacre of French knights during the battle of Courtrai, there was a massacre of Flemish craftsmen at Cassel and Roosebeke. One might link to this style of warfare, devoid of all courtesy, the warlike customs of the Irish and Swiss. The *Kriegsordnung* of Lucerne in 1499 stipulated that no prisoners were to be taken; all the enemy should be put to death. That of Zurich in 1444 thought it necessary to prohibit combatants from tearing out the hearts of their dead enemies and cutting up their bodies. Froissart attests, for his part, that the Irish 'never leave a man for dead until they have cut his throat like a sheep and slit open his belly to remove the heart, which they take away. Some who know their ways, say that they eat it with great relish. They take no man for ransom . . .'.[104]

At the end of the Middle Ages, relations between states had been formalized at the level of defiances and declarations of war,[105] truces,[106] safe-

[104] Froissart, *Oeuvres*, ed. Kervyn de Lettenhove, xv.168 (tr. Brereton, p.410).

[105] J. Glénisson, Notes d'histoire militaire (353). For examples of defiances: Froissart, *Chroniques*, xi. 96 and *Oeuvres*, ed. Kervyn de Lettenhove, xiii. 270; *Recueil des actes de Jean IV, duc de Bretagne, i. 1357–1382*, ed. Michael Jones, Paris 1980, no.225; Olivier de la Marche, *Mémoires*, i.256; J. J. Champollion-Figéac, *Lettres de rois, reines et autres personnages*, Paris, 2 vols. 1847, ii.495–6 no.257.

[106] K. Fowler, Truces, in *The Hundred Years War*, ed. K. Fowler, London 1971, pp.184–215. For examples of truces: Molinet, *Chroniques*, i.119–20; Arch. dép. Pyrénées-Atlantiques E 77; Philippe de Vigneulles, *Chronique*, iii.78; E. Cosneau, *Les grands traités de la guerre de Cent ans*, Paris 1889, pp.71–99 and 154–71.

conducts,[107] negotiations and peace treaties, and the increasing exigencies of discipline sometimes led leaders to control the action of their men better. In contrast the growth of mercenary service, the renewed importance of the infantry and an increase of political ambitions often resulted in an explosion of violence and cruelty in military operations, while the demands of *raison d'état* multiplied occasions for conflict.

MEDIEVAL PACIFICISM AND ITS LIMITS

So many elements prevented medieval pacificism from taking on an absolute form: the teaching of the Old Testament, a restrictive interpretation of pacifist verses in the New Testament, the idea, inherited from Roman law, that it was always permissible to meet force with force and that 'defence is a natural law to the extent that it exists and belongs not only to humans . . . but also to dumb animals',[108] with the result that even clerics could legitimately resist violence. Religious truth was seen as a supreme good which must be defended at all costs against the attacks and threats of infidels and heretics, and the temporal responsibilities assumed by the church at various levels and the accession to political power of Christianity from the time of Constantine and Clovis were significant influences. Church teaching never condemned every kind of war, nor did it ever doom to damnation every sort of warrior.

It remains the case that peace movements, proper campaigns of pacification and reconciliation, did affect the West on several occasions with the permission, encouragement and participation of the church and churchmen.[109] The papacy, the great canonists and theologians obviously had misgivings about wars between Christians. The criteria of the just war as they were precisely defined from the second half of the twelfth century led to implicit condemnation of a very large number of conflicts. Arbitration, recourse to judicial procedures and negotiation were favoured by the papacy and its legates. From Dante to Wycliffe, from Marsilius of Padua and Pierre Dubois to Erasmus via George Podiebrad, king of Bohemia, a constant hope, long-lived although illusory, was the establishment, under the control of a unique authority or sovereign assembly, of a new Christian community, within which war would be illegal and unknown.[110] At certain epochs, peace

---

[107] In which heralds had an increasing role: P. Adam-Even, Les fonctions militaires des hérauts d'armes (346).

[108] Le Songe du Verger: *Revue du Moyen Age latin, 13* (1957), 59.

[109] A. Vauchez, Une campagne de pacification en Lombardie autour de 1233, *Mélanges d'archéologie et d'histoire de l'école française de Rome, 78* (1966), 503–49.

[110] There survived throughout the Middle Ages a utopian belief that there existed somewhere a society or country ignorant of war and violence. cf. Philippe de Mézières, *Le Songe du Vieil Pelerin*, ed. Coopland, Cambridge 2 vols. 1969 i.224, speaking of the country of the Bragadins: 'There are no robbers there and they do not fight one another.' Or again his description of

became a true political concept, an omnipresent point of reference. Alongside literature on war, there was a literature on peace: *Le Livre de la paix* of Christine de Pisan, *Le Livre de paix* of Georges Chastellain and several discourses and sermons by Jean Gerson. It may be added that if politicians, the lay and religious elite, did not aim at peace at all costs and considered all in all that it was better to have a just war than an unjust peace,[111] popular reaction was different: 'Everyone knows well that when it is a question of deciding on war or ordering it, the poor do not intervene because as far as they are concerned they only wish to live in peace.'[112]

Traces of moral anxiety about war in general or particular conflicts appear here and there. Peter Damiani declared in the eleventh century that 'men were in no circumstances permitted to take up arms in defence of the faith of the universal church, let alone wage warfare for earthly and transitory goods.'[113] In the twelfth century a certain Niger protested against the crusade and questioned whether it emanated from the divine will.[114] According to different French chroniclers, the English knight John de Cornwall, having lost his son, killed by a cannon shot at the siege of Meaux in 1420, saw in this event a sign that the war waged by Henry V was in opposition to God and reason. Fearing the loss of his soul in this unjust conflict, he left the expeditionary force, returned to England and swore an oath never to fight against Christians again.[115]

It is among social outcasts, heretics and their sympathizers, that the most complete expression of medieval non-violence must be sought. A much deeper study of this problem is needed, but a few points may be listed here. At the beginning of the thirteenth century, a group of Vaudois were persuaded by Innocent III to rejoin the official church, but obtained exemption from military service. In Italy the tertiaries of St Francis, penitents and those living under vows of continence, ultimately benefited from the same measure. A Vaudois interrogated in 1321 by Jacques Fournier, bishop of Pamiers, declared: 'Whoever kills a Christian in any war whatsoever, commits a sin.'[116]

For Cathar *Perfecti*, it was forbidden for any man to kill his like whether in

---

'Upper Egypt otherwise called Ethiopia' (i.231): 'The Catholic faith flourishes there and brings forth fruit an hundredfold. Charity is seated on her throne in great majesty. No pauper is found there, neither any heretic. And all the goods of one are the goods of another. They do not know what war is, nor riots nor malevolence. There is an abundance of all temporal and spiritual possessions.'

[111] Jean Gerson, *Oeuvres complètes*, ed. P. Glorieux, Paris-Tournai 1966, vii.219.

[112] Bonet (913), p.71.

[113] *Patr. Lat.*, cxliv.316.

[114] G. Flahiff, Deus non vult, *MS*, 9 (1947), 162–88.

[115] On the vow taken by certain combatants not to fight against Christians see also the *Livre des miracles de Sainte-Catherine-de-Fierbois (1375–1470)*, ed. Y. Chauvin, Poitiers 1976, p.33.

[116] *Le registre d'inquisition de Jacques Fournier, évêque de Pamiers, 1318–1325*, tr. J. Duvernoy, Paris, The Hague and New York 1978, i.148.

time of war or in self defence. All wars, even those just in origin, were thought criminal. The soldier obeying his captains and the judge pronouncing sentence of death were both nothing but murderers. Here, as in other domains, Catharism took up again certain positions once adopted by the pre-Constantinian church.

Pacificism was one of the strands of the Lollard movement. It is by no means impossible that the English knight mentioned above had links with this religious tendency. According to Nicholas Hereford, 'Jesus Christ, duke of oure batel, taught us lawe of pacience, and not to fight bodily.'[117] One of the 12 Lollard opinions condemned in 1395 declared that 'manslaughter by battle . . . is express contrarious to the New Testament' on account of Christ's teaching to man 'to love and have mercy on his enemies and not for to slay them'.[118] Another opinion mentions armourers amongst the crafts 'not needful to man' which should be 'destroyed for the increase of virtue'.[119] Wycliffe criticized recourse to the Old Testament to justify war. The proceedings against Lollards in the diocese of Norwich in 1428–31 show that according to one of the accused, whatever the circumstances, it was wrong to fight; the majority of the rest maintained that it was wrong to fight for one's country or for an inheritance. The only justification offered was that it displayed a lack of charity. Similarly for these Lollards it was wrong to condemn a murderer, robber or traitor to death, even legally, because vengeance should be left to God.[120]

Against the pacifist views of the Lollards, in 1393 Walter Brut and William Swynderby, Cambridge theologians summarized the attitude of the official church in these terms:

> To fight in the defence of justice, against both unbelievers and Christians, is in itself holy and permissible: to hold the opposite is to be in error. Such opinion has it that it is not permitted to Christians to fight against unbelievers, pagans or others, so as to bring about their forcible conversion to the Christian faith: it also claims that no Christian may fight other Christians for the defence of justice.
>
> This opinion is false and erroneous, for the following reasons. First it would not permit any Christian king to defend his kingdom against invaders or false intruders, so that, for example, it would not be right for the king of England to defend his lands against the French or the Scots, nor against anybody else, etc. Secondly, the teachings of the holy Fathers have approved and vindicated just wars as being permissible and righteous when fought by Christians, if their end is the defence of justice or the protection of the Church and the catholic faith. Thus saints approved by the Church have granted indulgences to men going to

---

[117] Quoted by R. H. Bainton, *Christian Attitudes towards War and Peace* (920), p.120.

[118] K. B. McFarlane, *Lancastrian Kings and Lollard Knights*, Oxford 1972, p.177.

[119] Peter Damiani was already expressing this view in the eleventh century: *Patr. Lat.*, cxlv.681–2.

[120] *Heresy Trials in the Diocese of Norwich, 1428–1431*, ed. N. P. Tanner, London (Royal Historical Society, Camden 4th Ser., 20) 1977.

war for these purposes: God Himself has vindicated just wars of this kind, and, indeed, often ordered his chosen people to fight, as is made plain by a reading of almost the whole of the Old Testament. Thus it may be accepted that this is true and catholic doctrine, the contrary of which, propounded by the above-mentioned opinion, is an error.

As for the suggestion that a Christian is forbidden to defend himself and to resist attack by the use of force, that, too, is an error. This opinion holds that Christians cannot freely and forcefully defend themselves against injuries aimed at them, nor against bodily attacks, nor against violence of other kinds. Such an opinion is against the good of the general peace, against all order of government and against all reason. It is an error to uphold it, and the opposite must be maintained, namely that Christians may defend themselves with force, above all against injuries which they suffer unjustly, and may oppose force with force, especially when the hand of correction is not readily available.[121]

It may be pointed out that at the heart of the Hussite movement there was a tendency favourable to war and justifying resistance to the pretended crusaders in the name of truth, innocence and the fatherland, but this tendency was at odds with another, represented by the theorist of the Union of Bohemian Brothers, Peter Chelcicky, who preached non-violence. Chelcicky railed against those who scrupled to eat pork on Friday but lightly shed Christian blood. According to him the first pacific age of the church was also its golden age; Christian law as a law of love prohibited murder, with the result that adepts of this law were certainly obliged to obey the state and to render to Caesar that which was Caesar's, but to refuse public office and military service.[122]

In other words, these heterodox currents aspired on the one hand to extend to the whole of society and to public powers the prohibitions which, according to the traditional interpretation of the church, simply concerned private persons and individual conduct, and on the other, to impose on the mass of Christians a pacific form of behaviour which the official church reserved to clerics and those aspiring to perfection. It is in this sense that the replies of a Vaudois deacon, Raymond de Sainte-Foix, to the inquisitorial interrogation of Jacques Fournier in 1321 should be understood. On the one hand, the heretic admitted 'that it is permissible for secular authority to put to death or to mutilate malefactors, for without such actions there would be neither peace nor security amongst men'. He even admitted that it was 'just and licit to put to death' heretics like the Manichaeans 'if they will not return to the faith and unity of the Roman church', and again that 'those who kill or condemn malefactors or heretics to death may be saved.' He thought that it was permissible and just to make war on pagans and infidels who, having been warned by the church, refused to be converted, and he even felt that it was licit for a Christian prince to make war on other Christians 'to rebuff

---

[121] Allmand (299), pp.20–1.
[122] F. Seibt, *Hussitica* (949), pp.18–57.

insults, violent attacks, violated faith and for disobedience'. But as an individual, as a perfect, he refused to participate in these actions, with the result that even if a brigand wanted to kill him he would be content to defend himself physically with a stave or sword. If by misfortune or inadvertance he killed his attacker he would feel that he had committed a sin, though not as serious a sin as if he had killed a good man.[123]

INTEGRATED WAR

Whatever the reservations of the church in the face of war (reservations often masked by the use of an abstract scholarly vocabulary and formal analyses), it is clear that Christianity and war, the church and the military, far from being antithetical, on the whole got on well together. They existed in a state of constant symbiosis, each profiting from the other's support. Many medieval clerks would no doubt have been pleased to make their own the words pronounced by Lacordaire in his funeral elegy on General Drouot: 'No analogy is more striking than that of the religious and the soldier; the same discipline and the same devotion are necessary.'[124]

One has only to see, in the first instance, the frequency with which spiritual authors, preachers and theologians, following St Paul's example, had recourse to warlike comparisons to describe a particular form of religious conduct or sentiment;[125] thus Julian of Vézelay in his sermon *On the armour of Christ's Soldier*,[126] or Innocent IV comparing the intellectual centre which Paris had become to a fortress.[127] During the early Middle Ages paradise was also frequently compared to a stronghold.[128] We may cite in the same vein Geoffroy de Breteuil in his letter to Abbot John:

> If a keep is deprived of defensive works, it is as difficult to defend as it is easy to take by assault . . . A cloister without a library, is a castle without an arsenal, for the library is our arsenal. It is from there that we draw statements of Divine law, like good arrows, to repulse the attacks of the Enemy. It is there that we go to seek the breastplate of righteousness, the helmet of salvation, the shield of faith and the sword of the Spirit which is the Word of God.[129]

Or there is St Bernadino of Siena in the fifteenth century in his sermon *De pugna et saccomanno paradisi seu caelistis Jerusalem*.[130] Gerson, for his part,

---

[123] *Le registre d'inquisition de Jacques Fournier*, i.83.
[124] cf. Anselm of Havelberg's linking, in classic fashion, of *disciplina militaris* and *disciplina regularis: Dialogues*, ed. G. Salet, Paris 1966, i.98–100.
[125] Ephesians 6.11–12.
[126] *Sermons*, ed. D. Vorreux, Vézelay and Paris 1966, ii.594–616.
[127] L. Genicot, *Le XIIIe siècle européen*, Paris 1968, p.227.
[128] P. Riché, Les représentations du palais dans les textes littéraires du haut Moyen Age, *Francia*, 4 (1976), 171.
[129] *Patr. Lat.*, ccv.844–5, echoing Ephesians 6.14–17.
[130] St Bernadino of Siena, *Opera omnia*, Florence 1940, ii.452–70.

speaks of 'the great multitude of the Christian Chivalry of Angels'.[131] In the first half of the fourteenth century Bartolomeo of Urbino, an Augustinian hermit, and then bishop of Urbino, composed a *Tractatus de re bellica spirituali per comparationem ad temporalem* in which he extensively quoted the military authors of Antiquity — Valerius Maximus, Vegetius, Sallust, Frontinus, Livy, etc.[132]

If the analogy or comparison between *spiritualia* and *militaria* became habitual, it was not simply because the omnipresence of war in medieval life allowed churchmen to be easily understood by their listeners and readers, it was also more profoundly because spiritual life was, for a very long time, compared to a merciless struggle without respite, between the heavenly cohorts and the legions of the devil. This was the spirit of Cluny: 'If the Cluniac vocation was different from that of *milites*, it also was heroic in style, though it was a question of fighting the Devil.'[133] The liturgy of this order has been presented as ritual aggression against the forces of evil. In the twelfth century Julian of Vézelay writes in the sermon mentioned above:

> a terrible war assails us. Knights of Christ seize your arms . . . Courage, Soldiers of Christ! . . . The Enemy is at our gates, there's not a moment to lose, we must fight immediately, hand to hand. Our enemies are so numerous and they throw flaming darts at us from every direction. If they discover that we are ill-prepared and defenceless they will only be more emboldened to brandish their arms, unsheathing their swords against us and launching more impetuous attacks. They are enemies with whom we can neither arrange a truce, however short it may be, nor conclude a peace treaty.[134]

At the same time the notion of chivalry effaced the old idea, still current in the time of Jonas of Orléans and Hincmar of Reims, that a soldier could not live in conformity with moral law.[135] The cult of martial saints experienced a rapid growth (the precise chronology and geography of which remains to be determined) with patrons of chivalry like St Maurice,/ St George and St Michael, and protectors of confraternities and specialists in war like St Sebastian for archers and St Barbara for cannoneers. In the legend of St George, his armed fight against the dragon took precedence over his refusal to serve a pagan emperor. In the iconography of St Michael, representations of him as a

---

[131] *Oeuvres complètes*, ed. Glorieux, vii.763.

[132] Bib. Nat., MS Latin 7242, fos.127r–162r. See also F. Cardini, Psicomachia e guerra santa. A proposito di un trattato allegoricomorale duecentesco, *ASI* (1970), 53–101.

[133] B. H. Rosenwein, Feudal war and monastic peace (985).

[134] *Sermons*, ed. Vorreux, ii.595. See also an illumination of the *Hortus deliciarum* of Herradus of Landsberg showing devils, armed with bows and arrows, knocking down off the ladder which leads to the Lord and the Crown of Life different ranks in society (*heremus, inclusus, monachus, clericus, laica, miles*), as well as angels armed with swords and protected by shields trying to prevent their evil deeds: J. M. Van Winter, *Ridderschap Ideall en Werkelykhend*, Bussum 1965, figure 16.

[135] De Institutione laicale, *Patr. Lat.*, cvi.121ff.; De coercendis militum rapinis, *ibid.*, cxxv.953–6.

knight outnumbered pacific representations. Warrior princes were canonized or beatified – in the fourteenth century Charles de Blois, in the thirteenth, Louis IX, whose biography by Joinville is significantly organized as a diptych. 'The first part describes how he governed all his time according to God and Holy Church and for the profit of his reign. The second part of the book speaks about his great chivalry and his great deeds in arms.'[136] While in the Carolingian period, Agobard, archbishop of Lyon, ordered the exclusion from churches of all warlike representations (an indication that some already existed),[137] windows, frescoes, sculptures and capitals, of the Romanesque and Gothic periods, provide a notable proportion of warlike images: men at arms confronting each other, knights with banners, swords and mounts, etc. A celebrated sculpture from the cathedral at Reims depicts a knight in armour, with a mail coiffe on his head, receiving with joined hands communion from a priest. Similarly the armies of the period offer many religious images. Weapons could be engraved with pious inscriptions. The sword known as that of St Maurice kept in the Imperial Treasury at Vienna is decorated with the words: HOMO DEI. IN NOMINE DOMINI. CRISTUS VINCIT. CRISTUS REINAT. CRISTUS IMPERAT. The standard and pennon of Joan of Arc were not the only flags embroidered with pious images or texts; such flags can be found in almost every army of the day, Burgundian, English, Lotharingian, etc. Certain standards even had a sacred character, like the banner of St James at Compostella, that of St Lambert at Liège and the Oriflamme of St Denis.[138] It is remarkable that, prolonging a usage which doubtless arose during the first crusade, crosses made out of material of different colours and shapes served from the fourteenth century as the distinctive emblems for English, French, Breton, Burgundian and Lotharingian combatants.[139] Just as some sacred decoration was in part military, so military decoration was in part religious.

A pitched battle was preceded by religious rites: confession, communion, mass and the sign of the cross, which combatants made before risking death. The preliminaries to an expected clash in 1339 at Buironfosse between the

[136] Joinville, *Oeuvres*, ed. N. de Wailly, Paris 1868 p.4.

[137] R. van Marle, *Iconographie de l'art profane*, i.280.

[138] Leo of Rozmital, *Travels*, ed. Letts, Cambridge 1957, p.117; C. Gaier, Le rôle militaire de reliques et de l'étendard de saint Lambert dans la principauté de Liège, *MA*, *72* (1966), 235–49; P. Contamine, L'oriflamme de Saint-Denis (458).

[139] For a crusader's cross see the sculpture thought to represent Hugues I, count of Vaudemont, and his wife (second half of the twelfth century) in the Musée Lorrain at Nancy or, later, in a fifteenth-century miniature: J. M. Van Winter, *Ridderschap Ideall en Werkelykhend*, figure 17. For crosses on 'uniforms' at the end of the Middle Ages see P. Contamine, *Guerre, état et société* (457), pp.668–70. In 1214 during the campaign that was to end with the battle of Bouvines, the enemies of Philip Augustus had fixed 'both on the front and back of their coats of arms small signs of the cross' Duby (244), p.155. A number of Italian towns took into battle as a palladium a war-cart. At Parma the *Blancardo* was decorated with images of the Virgin and the patron saints of the town, as to this day is the Sienese *carroccio* paraded in Il Palio.

English and the French were typical: 'When Friday came, in the morning the two armies got ready and heard mass, each lord amongst his men and next to his tent. The majority took communion, confessed and prepared themselves even to face death if need be.'[140] Faithful to a rite frequently mentioned in the *Chansons de geste*, the good trouvère Cuvelier describes the attitude of Du Guesclin's companions before the battle of Pontvallain (1370) in these terms: 'And in eating their bread, they made the sign of the cross over it and blessed it at the start and then took it and used it for communion. They confessed to each other well and with devotion, often saying many prayers to God, beseeching him to protect them from evil and torment.'[141] During the battle of Agincourt Henry V and his men 'before going to battle, fell to their knees and kissed the earth three times'.[142] Fearing the arrival of a French relieving force while they were besieging Ivry, the English 'took up positions and awaiting a battle whose outcome was uncertain, they had the place blessed and in the middle erected a cross'. It was no doubt a question of delimiting a sort of cemetery so that after the battle the dead could be buried in earth that had been hallowed.[143]

During a battle, chaplains and almoners prayed for the success of their party. Thus the chaplain of Henry V at the battle of Agincourt relates:

> Then, indeed, and for as long as the conflict lasted, I, who am now writing this and was then sitting on a horse among the baggage at the rear of the battle, and the other priests present did humble our souls before God and, bringing to mind [that] which at that time the church was reciting aloud, said in our hearts: 'Remember us, O Lord, our enemies are gathered together and boast themselves in their excellence. Destroy their strength and scatter them, that they may understand, because there is none other that fighteth for us but only Thou, our God.'[144]

Even in the heat of battle, combatants were careful to invoke heavenly assistance, as the war cries testify: St George for the English, St Denis for the French, St Yves for the Bretons, and for others still Our Lady-St Denis, Our Lady-St James, Our Lady-Claiequin (that is Du Guesclin), Our Lady-

---

[140] Froissart, *Chroniques*, i.177. In 1382 before the battle of Beverhoutsfeld, Froissart mentions seven masses celebrated simultaneously for the troops of Ghent, each accompanied by a sermon lasting at least on hour and a half and preached by a Dominican. Three out of every four soldiers took communion (*ibid.*, x.221–2).

[141] Jean Cuvelier, *Chronique de Bertrand du Guesclin*, ed. E. Charrière, Paris 1839, ii.175, ll.18,397–402.

[142] C. L. Kingsford, *English Historical Literature in the Fifteenth Century*, Oxford 1913, p.317. Also before Agincourt every English soldier put a piece of soil to his mouth: *Gesta Henrici Quinti*, ed. F. Taylor and J. S. Roskell, Oxford 1975, p.xxxv.

[143] *Chronique de la Pucelle ou Chronique Cousinot*, ed. A. Vallet de Viriville, Paris 1864, p.197.

[144] *Gesta Henrici Quinti*, p.84. On 13 August 1429 Jacques du Chastelier, bishop of Paris, celebrated a solemn mass on the occasion of a battle which was expected to take place the same day between the forces of Henry VI and Charles of Valois: S. Luce, *Jeanne d'Arc à Domrémy*, Paris 1886, p. j.218.

Auxerre etc. Naturally the sequel to a battle entailed various religious ceremonies:[145] the obsequies and burial of the dead according to the means dictated by circumstances or by the social status of the victims; masses for favours shown and the *Te Deum* celebrated by the victor,[146] who might also offer trophies from the victory – flags, spurs, pieces of armour – to a sanctuary, found a rich abbey or a modest oratory. After the battle of Hastings William the Conqueror founded the abbey of Battle whose main altar was built on the spot where Harold had died. After Bouvines Philip Augustus founded the abbey of La Victoire near Senlis; after Cassel Philip VI offered to Notre-Dame de Paris an equestrian statute of himself. After Roosebeke Charles VI made a gift of his armour to Notre-Dame de Chartres. The golden spurs won by the Flemings on the field at Courtrai (1302) were deposited in the cathedral of that town, from where the French came to recover them 80 years later, after Roosebeke. After the raising of the siege of Tartas in 1442, the inhabitants built 'a fine cross and oratory', decorated with his arms and mentioning the date of the event, to show their loyalty to Charles VII; an annual mass, celebrated every 24 June, was founded to perpetuate a memory of it.[147] It is known that Joan of Arc, according to the custom of those wounded, offered her armour to St Denis, just as a long time before Guillaume d'Orange had done the same at St-Julien-de-Brioude. Other sanctuaries preserved the ex-votos of soldiers like that of Ste-Catherine de Fierbois near Tours and, in Italy, the Franciscan church of the Madonna delle Grazie near Mantua.[148] Having learnt of the defeat of Francis II, duke of Brittany, in 1468, Louis XI ordered the construction, near the Pierrefonds gate at Compiègne, of a chapel dedicated to the Virgin, with the name of the chapel of Notre-Dame de la Salvation or Bonnes Nouvelles or, again, Bon Confort.[149] Batalha, a Dominican church and convent, was founded in memory of the victory gained by John I of Portugal at Aljubarrota in 1385 and was dedicated to the Virgin under the name of St Mary of Victory.[150] During the campaign of 1476–77, at the end of which he achieved victory over Charles the Bold in the battle of Nancy (5 January 1477), René II, duke of Lorraine, had placed his troops under the protection of the Virgin of the Annunciation, whose image figured on 'his principal ensign and standard'.

[145] A general study of this subject is still lacking.

[146] For the *Te Deum* celebrated on the orders of Charles VII after the victory of Castillon see *BEC*, 8 (1846), 246–7. Other examples are cited by J. B. Pelt, *Ephémérides de la cathédrale de Metz (Ve-XVe siècle)*, Metz 1934, pp.43 and 46.

[147] M. G. A. Vale, *English Gascony 1399–1453*, Oxford 1970, p.207 n.6.

[148] Leo of Rozmital, *Travels*, ed. Letts, p.74; J. Mann, A further account of the armour (643).

[149] *Lettres de Louis XI, roi de France*, ed. J. Vaesen and E. Charavay, Paris 1890, iv.226.

[150] Similarly in 1274 Charles of Anjou founded two Cistercian abbeys as a thanksgiving for his victories at Benevento (1266) and Tagliacozzo (1268) – Realvalle (*Regalis vallis*, in memory of Royaumont) and Santa-Maria della Vittoria in the Abruzzi mountains: M. A. Dimier, *La place de Royaumont dans l'architecture du XIIIe siècle*, in *Septième centenaire de la mort de Saint Louis. Actes des Colloques de Royaumont et de Paris (21–27 mai 1970)*, Paris 1976, pp.117–18.

Once his duchy had been reconquered, he made 'great gifts' to the sanctuary of the Annunciation of Florence and 'wore white clothes for a whole year in honour of the Virgin Mary'. In 1482 the church of the Observant Franciscan convent at Nancy, a church dedicated to Notre-Dame de l'Annonciation, was founded through his help, in recognition of his victory. On the site of the battle he promoted the construction of a chapel 'as a record and perpetual memory of the victory'. This chapel, consecrated by Olry de Blamont, bishop of Toul, in 1498, contained a statue of a Virgin of Mercy called Notre-Dame de la Victoire or Notre-Dame de Bonsecours. In addition, at the precise spot where the body of the duke of Burgundy had been found, near to the lake of St-Jean, a cross with two crossbars was erected, that is the cross of Lorraine (known in English heraldry as a patriarchal cross) which he had made his troops adopt in conformity with the veneration his Angevin ancestors had displayed towards a fragment of the true cross preserved at Baugé in a reliquary shaped like a patriarchal cross. This symbol, which was borne on the original arms of Hungary also recalled for him Godefroi de Bouillon, from whom he claimed descent.[151] This example from Lorraine shows perfectly how the relationship between war (and victory), 'national' cults, and the ambitions and traditions of a dynasty could be forged.

Cathedrals, chapels and sanctuaries not only preserved armour which soldiers had offered them in the guise of ex-votos, but also the standards of the defeated. In 1388 the duke of Guelders, after a victory over the Brabançons, ordered that 17 banners of defeated nobles should be placed before the statue of Our Lady at Nijmegen.[152] Jean Bigot, a captain of Charles VI, did the same in 1419: 'He sent the banners which he had captured from enemies to Notre-Dame de Paris and to several other churches, asking that they should be hung up there as trophies from his victory.'[153] The same thing happened in the church of Notre-Dame la Ronde at Metz after a victory over René II.[154]

The obsequies of kings, princes and lords involved a series of rites which referred to the martial exploits they had performed. At the funeral of Louis de Male, count of Flanders, celebrated in St Peter's church at Lille in 1384, nobles were appointed to help in the ceremony, some dressed in war armour, others in tournament armour; yet other knights made offerings in money, destriers, swords and war banners, and one of money, horses, swords and tournament banners. It is significant that the first funeral oration for a layman who was neither a king nor a prince is thought to be that which Ferry Cassinel, bishop of Auxerre, delivered in 1389 during the Requiem in memory of the good constable, Bertrand du Guesclin, on the biblical theme

---

[151] P. Marot, Le duc de Lorraine René II et la bataille de Nancy dans l'historiographie et la tradition lorraines, in Bataille de Nancy, pp.84–7.
[152] Froissart, Chroniques, xv.94.
[153] Chronique du Religieux de Saint-Denis, ed. L. Bellaguet, vi.363.
[154] Philippe de Vigneulles, Chronique, ed. Bruneau, iii.5.

'Nominatus est ad extrema terrae'.[155] Not only did nobles have themselves represented in war apparel on funerary slabs, but their epitaphs recalled their acts of prowess and extolled their glory.[156]

Beginning with Constantine, the christianization of the warrior's function, in which it is possible to see an almost inevitable corollary to the christianization of governing powers and the alliance of the two swords, spiritual and temporal, resulted in a way in the sacralization of war, a reinforcement of the prestige of soldiers and of the profession of arms. A battle between men was felt to be a fully praiseworthy action and *vaillance* was a virtue that was something a little more than human. As exacting a theologian as Jean Gerson (though in extremely doleful and critical circumstances during the Hundred Years War, it is true) even went so far as to describe as 'martyrs of God' the 'men-at-arms who with good intent expose their lives in a righteous cause and in defence of justice and truth'.[157] One is less astonished at the veritable thanksgiving formulated by a simple layman like Gaston Fébus in his *Livre des Oraisons*:

And me, I make this prayer to you, God all powerful, that you will grant me honour in arms as you granted it me on many occasions, in full measure, to the extent that through your grace, amongst the Saracens, the Jews, the Christians in Spain, France, England, Germany and Lombardy, on this side and on the other side of the sea, my name is known. In every place where I have been, I have obtained victories and you have delivered all my enemies to me, for which reason I know you perfectly.[158]

[155] Dom Felibien, *Histoire de l'abbaye royale de Saint-Denys en France*, Paris 1706, p.304.
[156] *Ibid.*, pp.557–62.
[157] 'But if they do contrary, they are martyrs of Hell when they sustain unjust quarrels or evil deeds and perverse opinions': Gerson, *Oeuvres complètes*, ed. Glorieux, vii.1027–8.
[158] Gaston Fébus, *Le Livre des oraisons*, ed. G. Tilander and P. Tucoo-Chala, Pau 1974, p.36.

Conclusion

Reduced to essentials, the military originality of the Middle Ages in the West, if compared with Antiquity, Byzantium or Modern times, lies in the overwhelming preponderance of a very experienced heavy cavalry, possessing costly mounts, stirrups, complete armour and very firm, enveloping saddles. In the majority of cases each combatant, flanked by military servants, owned his own equipment and was linked by his style of life, system of values and resources to the lay aristocracy in its broadest sense. For these horsemen martial activity was considered a normal form of existence whatever the institutional framework within which it was exercised. They maintained complex and variable relations with the established powers, being frequently in their service while conserving a good measure of independence, either as individuals or as members of small groups (*contubernia, commilitones*) of a kinship, feudal, regional or professional character. Even when retained by a prince or a king at his 'wages and pay', these knights were far from being completely taken under charge by public authorities. If they were made prisoner, payment of their ransom was a burden in the first instance on their own personal fortune or on that of their close friends and dependents. As for profits, like the risks, these remained largely individual.

Among different forms of war, the Middle Ages in the West (except at the beginning) did not experience migratory invasions, that is massive displacement of population 'passing in principle violently from one geographical milieu to another'.[1] Nor did it experience slave wars (for obvious reasons), though internal struggles of a more or less marked social character were fairly frequent. It was also practically ignorant (despite appearances during the Carolingian period) of wars of hegemony, resulting in the domination of a people or dynasty over an immense territory. 'As much as the invasions, wars of imperial conquest tend to isolate Antiquity from the Middle Ages and from Modern Europe.'[2] Except at the periphery, the wars of the medieval

---

[1] J. Harmand, *La guerre antique de Sumer à Rome*, Paris 1973, p.11.
[2] *Ibid.*, p.38.

West did not take the form of rivalry between nomads and sedentary peoples. From at least the eleventh century they took place in a well-populated, even densely occupied, region dotted with a multitude of strongholds. The most frequent wars were petty episodes which appear to us to be very close to simple brigandage or vendetta. However, this did not prevent – alongside innumerable local quarrels which scarcely modified the political balance – a number of major enterprises of conquest or reconquest, either within Latin Christendom proper, or outside it at the expense of the pagan world, Islam and Byzantium.

Nearly all the objective or explicit causes of war which polemology has assigned may be encountered, in variable degrees, in medieval conflicts: wars caused by ambition, anger or desire for vengeance; ritual wars in the ethnographic sense of the word; wars of diversion or adventure; religious or ideological wars (the crusades both across the sea or within Europe); civil wars (Armagnacs and Burgundians, counts and communes in Flanders, Jacqueries); wars of sovereignty or magnificence, aiming at the development, extension or consolidation of political structures; economic wars for the acquisition of booty, possession of natural wealth, control of commercial routes and merchant banking houses. These were, of course, all fought on a scale and with the means of the period.

Despite their often limited character, both in terms of the numbers engaged and the duration, medieval wars did not fail to have perceptible, even disastrous, economic effects. The England of Domesday Book clearly bore traces of the devastation caused by the Norman conquest.[3] Recent studies have shown the truly catastrophic impact which the Hundred Years War had on several French provinces.[4] The consequences of fifteenth-century conflicts (especially the Hussite wars) on Silesia were just as painful.[5] From this fact sprang the considerable sacrifices which communities were prepared to make to ensure their safety as far as possible.[6] Regular war taxation, when it did not double the destruction brought about by armies, was doubtless more acceptable.[7] In any event the effects of warfare were never so numerous, continuous or intense, except very locally, as to entail irremedial ruin. Over the whole of the West war was only one element among many others in economic and demographic development; besides, some peoples or social groups knew how to make it a source of prosperity. The coin

---

[3] *A New Historical Geography of England before 1600*, ed. H. C. Darby, Cambridge 1976, map on p.60.
[4] P. Contamine, La guerre de Cent ans en France: une approche économique (887); G. Bois, *Crise de féodalisme. Economie rurale et démographie en Normandie orientale du début du XIVe siècle au milieu du XVIe siècle*, Paris 1976.
[5] R. C. Hoffmann, Warfare, weather and a rural economy (895). See, in particular, the map.
[6] Payment of war indemnities or, better, the erection and maintenance of walls: P. Contamine, Les fortifications urbaines en France (775).
[7] P. Contamine, Guerre, fiscalité royale et économie en France (888).

hoards of the Scandinavian world derive as much from forays as from commercial transactions. The military policy of Venice both on *terra firma* and at Candia was beneficial. For a long time the Carolingian aristocracy lived off its conquests, and there was a crisis as soon as these were interrupted. At the end of the Middle Ages the view that their victories had allowed the English to increase their wealth was very widespread on the continent.

As in other periods, war stimulated a certain technological progress, sometimes on the initiative and under the control of the state. This progress principally concerned weapons, but had a possible spin-off for other productive sectors such as metallurgy, mechanics, military engineering, transport, cartography and geography.

Medieval society has sometimes been described as chiefly military. This is an exact description to the extent that (a) there was rarely a clearly defined and limited military society within a greater society; (b) the physical presence of war was not limited to a few frontier regions but was widespread, affecting almost all the West; (c) the bonds between the organization of authority, and the social and military hierarchy were both tight and constant; and (d) possession of personal equipment for war (often, it is true, very rudimentary) was very widespread, particularly in the countryside.[8]

Nevertheless it should not be forgotten that the Middle Ages admitted and recognized the existence of non-combatants who by definition were held to be excluded from war: some marginal social groups, children and the young (under 14, 15, 16 or 18 years old), old people (over 60, 64 or 70), women, clerics and others in religious orders. Moreover, a system of conscription, such as the Roman Empire had known or which contemporary states have in general had to adopt was almost unknown in the Middle Ages. The process of social differentiation (itself linked to economic modes of production) resulted in the isolation of a minority of professional combatants, whose remuneration could take very variable forms. As for the mass of the population, sometimes termed 'unarmed' (*inermis*), their participation in war, while never entirely excluded, was on the whole episodic. The 'commons' and 'populace' at best constituted potential combatants, but they were only called upon in critical situations (and then with some apprehension and reservations).

Furthermore, it would be absurd to imagine a medieval ethic entirely impregnated and dominated by a martial spirit and values: Christian and courtly values (forerunner of bourgeois values) were foreign to martial values even when they in some sense integrated them. If one limits the debate to the fifteenth-century layman, then the Italian humanist, the counsellor in *Parlement*, even the courtier, were all recognized social models which owed very little to chivalric values. It is possible, finally, that medieval wars had less disruptive social effects than those of other periods – there was neither

---

[8] P. Contamine, Consommation et demande militaire (886).

reduction to slavery as in Antiquity nor, except very rarely, total dispossession or transfer of entire populations. Many conflicts only affected society superficially in its upper ranks; the majority waited for the storm to pass before returning to their holdings and to their villages. What did it matter if the lord had changed, and that justice was rendered and the *fouage* raised in the name of a new prince? If medieval society was a military society, it was above all because warlike activity and responsibility formed an essential part of the activity and responsibility of the governing lay framework.

It would also be very inexact to imagine the Middle Ages in a state of continuous belligerence, incessantly at the mercy of the violence of soldiers. In this respect contrasts are the rule and only a fine chronology within a limited region can allow a correct understanding. Nevertheless the impression remains, even if it is not possible to establish on a general level a 'table of massacres like our weather tables',[9] that whole centuries of the Middle Ages were not more violent than, for example, the sixteenth or seventeenth centuries. The illusion arises in part from the fact that in the Middle Ages the background of everyday life willingly assumed a military aspect. War was not hidden; it was a spectacle, paraded unashamedly in entertainments, buildings and modes of dress.

Some historians have taken pleasure in contrasting the smallness of armies of knights with the considerable numbers which could be assembled, well before the coming of the industrial world and the explosive growth of productive forces, by the states of Antiquity, by the Ancien Regime or even by the great Asiatic powers (the Caliphate of Baghdad, the Mongol Empire or the Middle Kingdom in China). In absolute numbers this is an incontestable fact: the 90,000 combatants which Antigone and Demetrius marched against Egypt in 306 BC, the 125,000 legionaries which the Roman Republic raised during the Second Punic War, the 360,000 soldiers on whom the Old Empire could depend, are so many almost certain and plausible figures for which one can find no equivalent in the Middle Ages.[10] At the beginning of the eighteenth century the Austrian armies totalled 100,000 men (1705), those of the kingdom of France up to 300,000 (1710), the United Kingdom up to 75,000 (1710), Russia 220,000 and Sweden 110,000 (1709).[11] Yet at no period of the Middle Ages could any state, however powerful assemble forces larger than 100,000 men, even for a very short period. Perhaps the largest numbers are encountered in the first decades of the fourteenth century within the framework of the great monarchies of the West. In August and September 1340 a peak was probably reached. It is not impossible that Philip of Valois then had at his disposal in all areas of military activity some 100,000 men (both combatants and auxiliaries), either in his pay or paid by towns and princes.

---

[9] The expression is that of Joseph de Maistre, quoted by L. E. Halkin, *Initiation à la critique historique*, Paris 4th edn 1973, p.35.

[10] Harmand, *Guerre antique*, p.123.

[11] A. Corvisier, *Armées et sociétés en Europe de 1494 à 1789*, Paris 1976, p.126.

At the same moment Edward III, with his allies in the Low Countries and the Empire, could face him with perhaps 50,000 men.

It should be remarked, nevertheless, that political fragmentation alone accounts for the modest numbers of troops. In relation to their size and population medieval states succeeded in mobilizations which were by no means derisory. When Gaston Fébus 'wished to wage war on an enemy, he could count on about 2500 men in Béarn and Marsan, while the army recruited in the county of Foix and its dependencies should have been of approximately similar size.'[12] And although details are lacking on which to estimate the population of the county of Foix, it is known that in 1385 Béarn had 50,000 inhabitants. If we multiply this figure by three to get the total number of Gaston Fébus's subjects, the ratio between troops and the population is 1 : 30, a figure comparable to Prussia in 1740 (1 : 27) and more than double that of France in 1710 (1 : 66). In 1298 for the Falkirk campaign Edward I of England collected 25,700 infantry and at least 3,000 cavalry. If the total population is admitted to be 4 million, the ratio of troops to population is 1 : 139, while in 1710 it was 1 : 150.[13] If in the second half of the fifteenth century it had been possible to mobilize all the Swiss who were of the right age and able to fight, an army of 50,000 or 60,000 combatants would have been obtained. It is remarkable that on several occasions the figure of 20,000 was actually achieved.[14]

The true problem for medieval powers (in any event after 1200) was not to assemble considerable armies but to maintain them in the field for more than a few weeks.[15] For a proper comparison with more modern periods, only permanent, regular, troops should be included. Here the inferiority of the Middle Ages appears startling. Even for a pioneer in this area like the kingdom of France in the second half of the fifteenth century, if an average population of 8 million subjects and a regular army of 15,000 men is accepted, the ratio of troops to population is 1 : 533. The reason is that for a very long time medieval states lacked financial means and had very fragile administrative structures. However, it must be admitted that although they developed and progressively expanded these structures, they did so largely under pressure of that supreme stimulant, war. In addition, their meagre resources in cash were very largely absorbed by the financing of war. During the last two centuries of the Middle Ages, when the evidence allows at least an approximate evaluation to be made, it was normal for a state to devote half of its resources, both ordinary and extraordinary, to war.[16] War was the

[12] P. Tucoo-Chala, *Gaston Fébus et la vicomté de Béarn (1343–1391)*, Bordeaux 1960, p.159.
[13] M. Prestwich, *War, Politics and Finance under Edward I* (907), who notes that it was not until the seventeenth century that England exceeded this figure: in 1642 there were between 60,000 and 70,000 under arms (p.113).
[14] W. Schaufelberger, *Der Alte Schweizer und sein Krieg* (380).
[15] cf. tables in Prestwich (907), pp.96–8.
[16] Contamine (886) gives some examples.

foundation and *raison d'être* of political power. 'All empires and all lordships find their origin in war.'[17]

Finally, it must be stressed that medieval war should not be studied in isolation. It was to some extent the heir to wars in Antiquity, especially to the paradigm offered by the Roman army, for various aspects of its techniques and usages. In the military sphere, too, the Middle Ages lived under the shadow of Rome.[18] It would be an error to date fascination with legions and imperial eagles from Machiavelli. Even more clearly, there was no break in continuity between medieval warfare and that of modern times; on the contrary there was progressive change, a slow evolution both in practices and in attitudes.

The myth of chivalry, the memory of Roland and the nine worthies, was to be perpetuated for a long time to come. Brantôme took this to heart when in his *Discours sur les colonels de l'infanterie de France* he went back to the century of Froissart, to the capture of King John and the great wars between France and England.[19]

[17] de Bueil (9), i.50–1.
[18] *Orderic Vitalis*, ed. Chibnall, vi.472.
[19] ed. E. Vaucheret, Paris and Montréal 1973.

Part III

Bibliography

There is no bibliographical journal which periodically publishes lists of works on war in the Middle Ages. Compilation of a bibliography thus necessitates recourse to general bibliographical aids which often contain one or more sections devoted to war, arms, fortifications and armies. Since 1968 the *International Medieval Bibliography*, ed. P. H. Sawyer and R. J. Walsh, has listed the contents of journals, collections of essays, *Festschriften* and the proceedings of conferences. For books, since 1926 the *International Bibliography of Historical Sciences* has provided a selective though abundant bibliography, as have a number of national publications: for France since 1953 see *Bibliographie annuelle de l'histoire de France*; for Germany the *Jahresberichte für deutsche Geschichte* has published a new series since 1949; for England the *Writings on British History* (since 1901) and the *Annual Bulletin of Historical Literature* (since 1911) have been joined by the *Annual Bibliography of British and Irish History* (since 1975); for Italy there is the *Bibliografia Storica Nazionale* (from 1939) and for Spain from 1955 the *Indice historico español. Bibliografía historica de España e Hispano-america*.

It may be recalled that the *Glossarium mediae et infimae latinitatis* of Ducange contains a copious list of words relating to war in its Index XXVII (VII, Paris 1850, 513–17): *Res militaris seu vocabula ad eam pertinentia*. It will be readily seen that the present bibliography does not systematically replace older works; those that are mentioned are not simply useful but indispensable, as recent republication of many of them shows.

1. Contamine, P. L'histoire militaire et l'histoire de la guerre dans la France médiévale depuis trente ans, *Actes du C^e Congrès national des Sociétés savantes, Paris 1975, Section de philologie et d'histoire jusqu'à 1610*, Paris 1977, i.71–93.
2. Daniels, E., *Geschichte des Kriegswesens*, II: *Das mittelalterliche Kriegswesen*, Berlin and Leipzig, 2nd edn, 1927.
3. Delbrück, H., *Geschichte der Kriegskunst in Rahmen der politischen Geschichte*, III: *Mittelalter*, 2nd edn Berlin 1923 (repr. Berlin 1964 with an introduction by K. G. Cram).
4. Erben, W., *Kriegsgeschichte des Mittelalters*, Berlin and Munich 1929.
5. *La guerre au Moyen Age, Château de Pons (Charente-Maritime), juillet-août 1976, catalogue de l'exposition*, Paris 1976.
6. Lot, F., *L'art militaire et les armées au Moyen Age, en Europe et dans le Proche-Orient*, Paris 2 vols., 1946.

2 THE ART OF WAR: CONFLICTS, CAMPAIGNS, SIEGES AND BATTLES

Sources

A list of narrative and literary works which discuss war and the art of warfare in a more or less developed and continuous fashion during this period would be interminable. Here a few treatises of a didactic character are cited.

7. Balsac, Robert de, *La nef des princes et des batailles de noblesse*, Lyon 1502.
8. Bossert, H. and Storck, W. F., *Das mittelalterliche Hausbuch*, Leipzig 1912.

9. Bueil, Jean de, *Le Jouvencel*, ed. C. Favre and L. Lecestre, Paris 2 vols. 1887–89.
10. Frontinus, Julius, *Stratagemata*, ed. G. Gundermann, Leipzig 1888.
11. Giles of Rome (Aegidius Colonna), *De Regimine principium libri III*, ed. F. H. Samaritanium, Rome 1607.
12. Pisan (or Pizan), Christine de, *L'art de chevalerie*, Paris 1488.
13. Pisan, Christine de, *The Book of Fayttes of Armes and of Chyvalrye*, tr. William Caxton, ed. A. T. P. Byles, London 2nd edn 1937.
14. Stuart, Berault, seigneur d'Aubigny, *Traité sur l'art de la guerre*, ed. E. de Comminges, The Hague 1976.
15. Vegetius, Flavius Renatus, *Epitoma rei militaris*, ed. C. Lang, Leipzig 1885.
16. Vegetius, *Le abrejance de l'Ordre de chevalerie, mise en vers de la traduction de Végèce par Jean de Meun par Jean Priorat de Besançon*, ed. U. Robert, Paris 1897.
17. Vegetius, *L'art de chevalerie. Traduction du 'De re militari' de Végèce par Jean de Meun*, ed. U. Robert, Paris 1897.
18. Vegetius, *Jean de Meun, Li Abregemenz noble homme Vegesce Flave René des establissemenz apartenanz a chevalerie*, ed. L. Löfstedt, Helsinki 1977.
19. Vegetius, *Knyghthode and Bataile. A XVth Century Verse Paraphrase of Flavius Vegetius Renatus' Treatise 'De Re Militari'*, ed. R. Dybosky and Z. M. Arend, London 1935.

Secondary works

20. Ashtor, E. and Kedar, B. Z., Una guerra fra Genova e i Mamlucchi negli anni 1380, *ASI*, *133*(1975),3–44.
21. Auer, L., *Die Schlacht bei Mailberg am 12. Mai 1082*, Vienna 1976.
22. Bachrach, B. S., The feigned retreat at Hastings, *MS*, *33*(1971),264–7.
23. Beeler, J. H., Castles and strategy in Norman and Early Angevin England, *Spec.*, *21*(1956),581–601.
24. Beeler, J. H., XIIth century guerilla campaign, *Military Review*, *42*(1962),39–46.
25. Beeler, J. H., *Warfare in England, 1066–1189*, Ithaca and New York 1966.
26. Beeler, J. H., *Warfare in Feudal Europe, 730–1200*, Ithaca and London 1971.
27. Benninghoven, F., Die Gotlandfeldzuge des deutschen Ordens, 1398–1408, *ZOF*, *13*(1964),421–77.
28. Benninghoven, F., Zur Technik spätmittelalterlicher Feldzuge im Ostbaltikum, *ZOF*, *19*(1970),631–51.
28a. Bérenger, J., L'influence des peuples de la steppe (Huns, Mongols, Tartares) sur la conception européenne de la guerre de mouvement et l'emploi de la cavalerie (Ve-XVIIe siècle), *RIHM* (1980),33–50.
29. Bömmels, N., Die Neusser unter dem Druck der Belagerung, in *Neuss, Burgund und das Reich*, Neuss: Stadtarchiv 1975, 255–87.
30. Bornstein, D., Military manuals in fifteenth-century England, *MS*, *37*(1975), 469–77.
31. Bornstein, D., Military strategy in Malory and Vegetius' *De re militari*, *Comparative Literature Studies*, *9*(1972),123–9.
32. Bornstein, D., The Scottish prose version of Vegetius' *De re militari*, *Studies in Scottish Literature*, *8*(1971),174–83.
33. Bossuat, R., Jean de Rouvroy, traducteur des *Stratagèmes* de Frontin, *Bibliothèque d'Humanisme et Renaissance*, *22*(1960),273–86, 469–89.

34. Brooks, F. W., *The Battle of Stamford Bridge*, York 1956.
35. Brusten, C. La bataille de Morat, *PCEEBM, 10*(1968), 79–84.
36. Brusten, C., Les campagnes liégeoises de Charles le Téméraire, in *Liège et Bourgogne, Actes du Colloque tenu à Liège les 28, 29 et 30 octobre 1968*, Liège 1972, 81–99.
37. Brusten, C., Charles le Téméraire et la campagne de Neuss, 1474–75, ou le destin en marche, *PCEEBM, 13*(1971), 67–73.
38. Brusten, C., Les itinéraires de l'armée bourguignonnes de 1465 à 1478, *PCEEBM, 2*(1960),55–67.
39. Brusten, C., A propos des campagnes bourguignonnes, 1475–78, *PCEEBM, 9*(1967), 79–87.
40. Burne, A. H., *The Agincourt War. A Military History of the Latter Part of the Hundred Years' War from 1369 to 1453*, London 1956.
41. Burne, A. H., *The Crécy War. A Military History of the Hundred Years' War from 1337 to the Peace of Brétigny, 1360*, London 1955.
42. Contamine, P., Crécy (1346) et Azincourt (1415): une comparaison, in *Divers aspects du Moyen Age en Occident, Actes du Congrès tenu à Calais en septembre 1974*, Calais 1977, 29–44.
43. Contamine, P., The war literature of the late Middle Ages: the treatises of Robert de Balsac and Béraud Stuart, lord of Aubigny, in *War, Literature and Politics*, 102–21.
43a. Contamine, P., L'art de la guerre selon Philippe de Clèves, seigneur de Ravenstein (1456–1528): innovation ou tradition?, *Bijdragen en mededelingen betreffende de Geschiedenis der Nederlanden, 95*(1980),363–76.
43b. Contamine, P., Froissart: art militaire, pratique et conception de la guerre, in *Froissart: Historian*, ed. J. J. N. Palmer, Woodbridge and Totowa 1981, 132–44, 180–1.
44. Coopland, G. W., *Le Jouvencel* (revisited), *Symposium, 5*(1951),137–86.
45. Duncan, A. A. M., The Battle of Carham, 1018, *Scottish Historical Review, 55*(1976),1–28.
46. Durdik, J. *Hussitisches Heerwesen*, Berlin 1961.
47. Eggenberger, D., *A Dictionary of Battles*, London 1967.
48. Ekdahl, S., Der Krieg zwischen dem Deutschen Orden und Polen-Litauen im Jahre 1422, *ZOF, 13*(1964),614–51.
49. Fiumi, E., *L'impresa di Lorenzo de' Medici contra Volterra (1472)*, Florence 1948.
50. Fowler, K. A., *The King's Lieutenant, Henry of Grosmont, First Duke of Lancaster, 1310–1361*, London 1969.
50a. Gaier, C. Relire Verbruggen . . . , *MA, 85*(1979),105–12.
51. Gillam, H., Der Neusser Krieg, Wendepunkt der europäischen Geschichte, in *Neuss, Burgund und das Reich*, Neuss 1975, 210–54.
52. Glover, R., English warfare in 1066, *EHR, 67*(1952),1–18.
53. Goffart, W., The date and purpose of Vegetius' *De re militari, Traditio, 33*(1977),65–100.
54. Grosjean, G., Die Murtenschlacht. Analyse eines Ereignisses, in *Actes du Ve Centenaire de la bataille de Morat*, Fribourg and Berne 1976, 35–90.
55. Hale, J. R., *The Art of War and Renaissance England*, Washington 1961.
56. Herde, P., Die Schlacht bei Tagliacozzo. Eine historischtopographische Studie, *Zeitschrift für bayerische Landesgeschichte, 25*(1962),679–744.

57.   Hewitt, H. J., *The Black Prince's Expedition of 1355–1357*, Manchester 1958.
58.   Hibbert, C., *Agincourt*, London 1964.
59.   Hobohm, M., *Machiavellis Renaissance der Kriegskunst*, Berlin 2 vols 1913.
60.   Huici Miranda, H. *Las grandes batallas de la Reconquista durante los invasiones africanas*, Madrid 1956.
61.   Hunger, V., Le siège et la prise de Vire par Charles VII en 1450, *Annales de Normandie, 12*(1971),109–22.
62.   Keegan, J., *The Face of Battle*, London 1976 (includes a chapter on Agincourt).
63.   Knowles, C., A fourteenth-century imitator of Jean de Meung: Jean de Vignai's translation of the *De re militari* of Vegetius, *Studies in Philology, 53*(1956),452–8.
63a. Koch, H. W., *Medieval Warfare*, London 1978.
64.   Lammers, W., *Die Schlacht bei Hemmingstedt. Freies Bauerntum und Fürstenmacht in Nordseeraum*, Neumunster 1953.
65.   Lange, J., *Pulchra Nussia*. Die Belagerung der Stadt Neuss 1474–75, in *Neuss, Burgund und das Reich*, Neuss 1975, 9–190.
66.   Legge, M. D., The Lord Edward's Vegetius, *Scriptorium, 7*(1953),262–5.
67.   Leyser, K., The battle at the Lech, 955. A study in tenth-century warfare, *Hist., 50*(1965),1–25.
68.   MacKensie, W. M., *The Battle of Bannockburn: a study in Medieval Warfare*, Glasgow 1913.
69.   Meyer, B., Die Schlacht bei Morgarten, *Revue suisse d'histoire, 16*(1966),129–79.
70.   Morris, J. E., *Bannockburn*, Cambridge 1914.
71.   Nesbitt, J. W., The rate of march of crusading armies in Europe, *Traditio, 19*(1963),167–81.
71a. Newark, P., *Medieval Warfare*, London 1979.
72.   Newhall, R. A., *The English Conquest of Normandy, 1416–1424*, New Haven and London 1924.
73.   Nicholson, R., The Siege of Berwick, 1333, *Scottish History Review, 40*(1961),19–42.
74.   Oerter, H. L., Campaldino, 1289, *Spec., 33*(1968),428–50.
75.   Oman, C. W. C., *The Art of War in the Middle Ages, AD 378–1485*, London 2 vols 1924 (repr. Ithaca 1960).
76.   Pieri, P., Alcune quistioni sopra la fanteria in Italia nel periodo comunale, *RSI, 45*(1933), 561–614.
77.   Putz, H. H., *Die Darstellung der Schlacht in mittelhochdeutscher Erzähldichtungen von 1150 bis um 1250*, Hamburg 1971.
78.   Razin, A. E., *Geschichte der Kriegskunst, II: Die Kriegskunst der Feudalperiode des Krieges*, Berlin 1960.
79.   Sander, E., Der Belagerungskrieg im Mittelalter, *HZ, 165*(1941),99–110.
80.   Schrader, C. R., The ownership and distribution of manuscripts of the *De re militari* of Flavius Vegetius Renatus before the year 1300, *Dissertation Abstracts International A, 37*(1976),3815–16.
81.   Smail, R. C., Art of war, in *Medieval England*, ed. A. L. Poole, Oxford and New York 1958, i.128–67.
82.   Soranzo, G., L'ultima campagna del Gattamelata al servizio della Repubblica veneta (1438–1441), *Archivio Veneto, 60–1*(1957),79–114.
82a. Springer, M., Vegetius im Mittelalter, *Philologus, 123*(1979),85–90.
83.   Sprömberg, H., Die Feudale Kriegskunst, in *Beiträge zur belgisch-niederländischen Geschichte*, Berlin 1959, 30–55.

84.   Thorpe, L., Mastre Richard, a thirteenth-century translator of the *De re militari* of Vegetius, *Scriptorium*, 6(1952),39–50.

85.   Verbruggen, J. F., L'art militaire en Europe occidentale du IXe au XIVe siècle, *RIHM*(1953–55),486–96.

85a. Verbruggen, J. F., L'art militaire dans l'Empire carolingien, *Revue belge d'histoire militaire* (1979),299–310, and (1980),343–412.

86.   Verbruggen, J. F., *1302 in Vlaanderen. De Guldensporenslag*, Brussels 1977.

87.   Verbruggen, J. F., De historiografie van de Guldensporenslag, *De Leiegouw*, 19(1977),245–72.

88.   Verbruggen, J. F., *De Krijgskunst in West-Europa in de Middeleeuwen (IXe tot begin XIVe ceuw)*, with French summary, Brussels 1954 (Eng. tr.: *The Art of Warfare in Western Europe during the Middle Ages (from the Eighth Century to 1340)*, Amsterdam and New York 1976).

89.   Verbruggen, J. F., Un plan de bataille du duc de Bourgogne (14 septembre 1417) et la tactique de l'époque, *RIHM*(1959),443–51.

90.   Verbruggen, J. F., Un projet d'ordonnance comtale sur la conduite de la guerre pendant le soulèvement de la Flandre maritime, *Bulletin de la Commission royale d'histoire*, 118(1953),115–36.

91.   Verbruggen, J. F., La tactique militaire des armées de chevaliers, *Revue du Nord*, 29(1947),161–80.

92.   Waley, D. P., Combined operations in Sicily, AD 1060–78, *Papers of the British School in Rome*, 22(1954),118–25.

93.   Willard, C. C., Christine de Pizan's Art of Medieval Warfare, in *Essays in honor of Louis Francis Solano*, ed. R. J. Cormier and U. T. Holmes, Chapel Hill, N. C., 1970.

93a. Wise, T., *Medieval Warfare*, New York 1976.

93b. Wisman, J. L'*Epitoma rei militaris* de Végèce et sa fortune au Moyen Age, *MA*, 85(1979),13–29.

3   INSTITUTIONS, SOCIETIES AND MILITARY ATTITUDES

General

94.   Adam-Even, P. Les enseignes militaires du Moyen Age et leur influence sur l'héraldique, in *Recueil du Ve Congrès international des Sciences généalogiques et héraldiques*, Stockholm 1960, 167–94.

95.   Barber, R., *The Knight and Chivalry*, London 1970.

96.   Batany, J., Du *bellator* au *chevalier*, dans le schéma des 'trois ordres' (étude sémantique), in *Guerre et Paix*, 23–34.

97.   Bezzel, O., *Geschichte des Kurpfälzischen Heeres, I: Das Heerwesen in Kurpfalz, Pfalzneuburg und Jülich-Berg von seinen Anfängen bis zur Vereinigung von Kurpfalz und Kur-Bayern 1778, nebst Geschichte des Heerwesen in Pfalz-Zweibrücken*, Munich 1925.

98.   Bisson, T. N., The military origins of medieval representation, *AHR*, 71(1966),1199–1218.

99.   Bloch, M., *La société féodale*, Paris 2 vols 1939–40 (Eng. tr.: *Feudal Society*, tr. L. A. Manyon, London 1962).

100. Borst, A., ed., *Das Rittertum im Mittelalter*, Darmstadt 1976 (includes a very full bibliography on knighthood, pp.437–82).

101. Bosl, K., Das *ius ministerialium*. Dienstrecht und Lehnrecht im deutschen Mittelalter, in *Studien zum mittelalterlichen Lehnswesen*, Lindau and Constance 1960.

102. Boutruche, R., *Seigneurie et féodalité*, Paris 2 vols 1968–70 (contains a very complete bibliography on feudal society: i.417–64 and ii.463–523).

103. Burns, N. T. and Reagan, C., *Concepts of the Hero in the Middle Ages and in the Renaissance*, New York 1975.

103a. Cardini, F., *Alle radici della cavalleria medievale*, Florence 1981.

104. Conrad, H., *Der Gedanke der Allgemeinen Wehrpflicht in der deutschen Wehrverfassung des Mittelalters*, Berlin 1937.

105. Conrad, H., *Geschichte der deutsche Wehrverfassung*, Munich 1939.

106. Duby, G., *Les trois ordres ou l'imaginaire du féodalisme*, Paris 1978 (Eng. tr.: *The Three Orders. Feudal Society Imagined*, tr. A. Goldhammer, Chicago 1981).

107. Erben, W., Schwertleite und Ritterschlag, Beiträge zu einer Rechtsgeschichte der Waffen, *Zeitschrift für historische Waffenkunde*, 8(1918–20),105–67.

108. Fehr, H., Das Waffenrecht der Bauern im Mittlealter, *ZSSRG, Germ. Abt.*, 35(1914),111–211, and 38(1917),1–114.

109. Finer, S. E., State and nation-building in Europe: the role of the military, in *The Formation of National States in Western Europe*, ed. C. Tilly, Princeton 1975, 84–163.

109a. Flori, J., Chevalerie et liturgie. Remise des armes et vocabulaire 'chevaleresque' dans les sources liturgiques du IXe au XIVe siècle, *MA*, 84(1978),147–78.

110. Frauenholz, E. von, *Entwicklungsgeschichte des deutsche Heerwesens, I: Das Heerwesen der germanischen Frühzeit des Frankenreiches und des ritterlichen Zeitalters; II: Das Heerwesen der schweizer Eidgenossenschaft in der Zeit des freie Söldnertums; III: Das Heerwesen des Reiches in der Landsknechtszeit*, Munich 1935–7.

111. Gaier, C., Analysis of military forces in the principality of Liège and the county of Looz from the twelfth to the fifteenth century, *Studies in Medieval and Renaissance History*, 2(1965),205–61.

112. Gaier, C., *Art et organisation militaires dans la principauté de Liège et dans le comté de Looz au Moyen Age*, Brussels 1968.

113. Gaier, C., La cavalerie lourde en Europe occidentale du XIIe au XIVe siècle: un problème de mentalité, *RIHM*(1971),385–96.

114. Grassotti, H., Para la historia del botín y de las parias en León y Castilla, *CHE*, 39–40(1964),43–132.

115. Guilhiermoz, P., *Essai sur l'origine de la noblesse en France au Moyen Age*, Paris 1902 (repr. New York 1960).

116. Gutton, F., *La chevalerie militaire en Espagne. L'ordre d'Alcantara*, Paris 1975.

117. Gutton, F., *La chevalerie militaire en Espagne. L'ordre de Calatrava*, Paris 1955.

118. Gutton, F., *La chevalerie militaire en Espagne. L'ordre de Santiago*, Paris 1972.

119. Hatto, A. T., Archery and chivalry: a noble prejudice, *Modern Language Review*, 35(1940),40–54.

120. Kantorowicz, E. H., Pro patria mori in medieval political thought, *AHR*, 56(1951),473–92.

120a. Lomax, D., *The Reconquest of Spain*, London and New York 1978.

121. Lourie, E., A society organized for war: medieval Spain, *PP*, *35*(1966),54–76.

122. Lübeck, K., Vom Reichskriegsdienste des Klosters Fulda, *Fuldaer Geschichte-Blätter* (1938),1–13, 20–32, 45–9.

123. March, U., Die holsteinische Heeresorganisation im Mittelalter, *Zeitschrift der Gesellschaft für Schleswig-holsteinische Geschichte*, *99*(1974),95–139.

124. Massmann, E. H., *Schwertleite und Ritterschlag*, Hamburg 1932.

125. Pastoreau, M., L'origine militaire des armoiries, *Actes du CIe Congrès national des Sociétés savantes, Lille 1976, Archéologie et histoire de l'art*, Paris 1978, 107–18.

126. Pietzner, F., *Schwertleite und Ritterschlag*, Heidelberg 1934.

127. Powicke, M. R., *Military Obligation in Medieval England*, Oxford 1962.

128. Prestage, E., ed., *Chivalry. Its Historical Significance and Civilizing Influence*, London 1928.

128a. Rautenberg, W., Ritter und Rotten. Zur begrifflichen und funktionalen Unterscheidung des geworbenen Kriegsvolkes, *Jahrbuch der Gesellschaft für niedersächsische Kirchengeschichte*, *76*(1978),87–121.

129. Romeiss, M., Die Wehrverfassung der Reichsstadt Frankfurt am Main im Mittelalter, *Archiv für Frankfurts-Geschichte und Kunst*, (1953),5–63.

130. Sandoz, E., Tourneys in the Arthurian tradition, *Spec.*, *19*(1944),389–432.

131. Schmitthenner, P., *Das freie Söldnertum im abendländischen Imperium des Mittelalters*, Munich 1934.

132. Schmitthenner, P., Lehnskriegswesen und Söldnertum im abendländischen Imperium des Mittelalters, *HZ*, *150*(1934),229–67.

133. Schneider, H., *Adel-Burgen-Waffen*, Berne 1968.

134. Schünemann, K., Deutsche Kriegsführung im Osten während des Mittelalters, *DA*(1938),54–84.

135. Sotto y Montes, J. de, La orden de caballeria en la alta Edad media, *Revista de historia militar*, *4*(1960),39–73.

136. Wackernagel, H. G., *Kriegsbräuche in der mittelalterlichen Eidgenossenschaft*, Basle 1934.

137. Weise, E., Der Heidenkampf des deutschen Ordens, *ZOF*, *12*(1963),420–73, 622–72, and *13*(1964),401–20.

137a. Winter, J. M. van, *Cingulum militiae*. Schwertleite en miles – terminologie als spiegel van veranderend menselijk gedrag, *Tijdschrift voor Rechtsgeschiedenis*, *44*(1976),1–92.

Sixth–ninth centuries

138. Angermann, H., *Ausweitung des Kampfgeschehens und psychologische Kriegführung im früheren Mittelalter*, Würzburg 1971.

139. Anton, H. H., *Fürstenspiegel und Herrscherethos in der Karolingerzeit*, Bonn 1968.

140. Bachrach, B. S., *Merovingian Military Organization, 481–751*, Minneapolis 1972.

141. Bachrach, B. S., Military organization in Aquitaine under the early Carolingians, *Spec.*, *49*(1974),1–33.

142. Bachrach, B. S., The origin of Armorican chivalry, *Technology and Culture*, *10*(1969),166–71.

143. Bachrach, B. S., Procopius, Agathias and the Frankish military, *Spec.*, *45*(1970),435–41.

144. Bachrach, B. S., Charles Martel, shock combat, the stirrup and feudalism, *Studies in Medieval and Renaissance History*, *7*(1970),47–75.

145. Bachrach, B. S., Was the Marchfield part of the Frankish constitution?, *MS*, *36*(1974),178–86.

146. Bertolini, O., Ordinamenti militari e strutture sociali dei Longobardi in Italia, in *OM*, i.429–607.

147. Bodmer, J. P., *Der Krieger der Merowingerzeit und seine Welt*, Zurich 1957.

148. Bognetti, G. P., L'influsso delle istituzioni militari romane sulle istituzioni longobarde del secolo VI e la natura della fara, in *Atti del Congresso Internazionale di Diritto Romano e di Storia del Diritto, Verona 27–29 settembre 1948*, Milan 1953, 167–210.

148a. Bowlus, C. R. and Schwatz, G. M., Warfare and society in the Carolingian Ostmark, *Austrian History Yearbook*, *14*(1978),3–30.

149. Brooks, N. P., The development of military obligation in eighth- and ninth-century England, in *England before the Conquest. Studies in Primary Sources presented to Dorothy Whitelock*, ed. P. Clemoes and K. Hughes, Cambridge 1971, 69–84.

149a. Brooks, N. P., England in the ninth century: the crucible of defeat, *TRHS*, 5th ser., *29*(1979),1–20.

150. Brühl, C. R., *Fodrum, Gistum, Servitium regis. Studien zu den wirtschaftlichen Grundlagen des Königstums* (*vom 6. bis zur Mitte des 14. Jahrhunderts*), Cologne and Graz 2 vols. 1968.

151. Cameron, A., Agathias on the early Merovingians, *Annali della Scuola Normale Superiore di Pisa*, *37*(1968),95–140.

152. Claude, D., *Adel, Kirche und Königtum im Westgotenreich*, Sigmaringen 1971.

153. Conrad, H., Das Wehrstrafrecht der germanischen und fränkischen Zeit, *Zeitschrift für die Geschichte der Strafrechtwissenschaft*, *56*(1937),709–34.

154. Dannenbauer, H., Die Freien im Karolinginschen Heer, in *Festschrift zum 70. Geburstag von Th. Mayer*, I: *Zur allgemeinen und Verfassungsgeschichte*, Constance 1954, 49–64.

155. D'Haenens, A., Les invasions normandes dans l'Empire franc au IXe siècle, in *I Normanni e la loro espansione in Europa nell'alto Medioevo*, Spoleto 1969, 233–98.

156. D'Haenens, A., *Les invasions normandes, une catastrophe?*, Paris 1970.

157. Drew, K. F., The Carolingian military frontier in Italy, *Traditio*, *20*(1964),437–47.

158. Duby, G., *Guerriers et paysans, VIIe–XIIe siècle, premier essor de l'économie européenne*, Paris 1973 (Eng. tr.: *The Early Growth of the European Economy. Warriors and Peasants from the Seventh to the Twelfth Century*, tr. Howard B. Clarke, London 1974).

159. Ganshof, F. L., L'armée sous les Carolingiens, in *OM*, i.109–30.

160. Ganshof, F. L., A propos de la cavalerie dans les armées de Charlemagne, *AIBL*(1952),531–6.

161. Garcia Moreno, L. A., Organización militar de Bisancio en la peninsula Ibérica (ss.VI–VII), *Hispania, Rivista Española de Historia*, *123*(1973),5–22.

162. Gillmor, C. M., Warfare and the military under Charles the Bald, 840–877, *Dissertation Abstracts International A*, *37*(1976),2349.

163. Hildersheimer, E., *L'activité militaire des clercs à l'époque franque*, Paris 1936.

164. Hoffmann, D., *Das spätrömische Bewegungsheer und die Notitia Dignitatum*, Düsseldorf 2 vols. 1969–70.

164a. Hooper, N., Anglo-Saxon warfare on the eve of the conquest: a brief survey, in *Proceedings of the Battle Conference on Anglo-Norman Studies*, ed. R. A. Brown, Woodbridge 1979, 84–93, 211–13.

165. Jarnut, J., Beobachtungen zur den langobardischen *Arimanni* und *Exercitales*, *ZSSRG, Germ. Abt.*, *88*(1971),1–28.

166. John, E., War and society in the tenth century: the Maldon Campaign, *TRHS*, 5th ser., *27*(1977),173–95.

167. Lebecq, S., Francs contre Frisons (VIe–VIIIs siècle), in *Guerre et Paix*, 53–71.

168. Levillain, L., Campus Martius, *BEC*, *107*(1947–48),62–8.

169. Macmullen, R., *Soldiers and Civilians in the Later Roman Empire*, Cambridge, Mass., 1963.

170. Mangold-Gaudlitz, H. von, *Die Reiterei in den germanischen und fränkischen Heeren bis zum Ausgang der deutschen Karolinger*, Berlin 1922.

171. Musset, L., Problèmes militaires du monde scandinave (VIIe–XIIe siècle), in *OM*, i.229–91.

172. Patlagean, E., Les armes et la cité à Rome du VIIe au XIe siècle, et le modèle européen des trois fonctions sociales, *Mélanges de l'Ecole française de Rome*, *86*(1974), 25–62.

173. Rasi, P., '*Exercitus italicus*' e *Milizie cittadine nell'alto medioevo*, Padua 1937.

173a. Rouche, M., *L'Aquitaine des Wisigoths aux Arabes, 418–781. Naissance d'une région*, Paris 1979.

173b. Ruiz Domenec, J. E., El asedio de Barcelona, según Ermoldo el Negro (Notas sobre el caractér de la guerra en el alta Edad Media), *Boletin de la Real Academia de Buenas Letras de Barcelona*, *37*(1977–78),149–68.

174. Sanchez Albornoz, C., La perdida de Espana, I: El ejército visigodo: su proto-feudalización, *CHE*, *43–4*(1967),5–73.

175. Stormer, W., *Früher Adel. Studien zur politischen Führungsschicht im fränkisch-deutschen Reich vom 8. bis 11. Jahrhundert*, Stuttgart 2 vols. 1973.

176. Teall, J. L., The Barbarians in Justinian's Armies, *Spec.*, *40*(1965),294–322.

176a. Vallvé, J., España en el siglo VIII: ejercito y sociedad, *Al Andalus*, *43*(1978),51–112.

177. Verbruggen, J. F., L'armée et la stratégie de Charlemagne, in *Karl der Grosse. Lebenswerk und Nachleben, I: Persönlichkeit und Geschichte*, Düsseldorf 1965, 420–36.

178. Vercauteren, F., Comment s'est-on défendu au IXe siècle dans l'Empire franc contre les invasions normandes?, *Annales du XXXe Congrès de la Fédération archéologique de Belgique*, Brussels 1936, 117–32.

Tenth and eleventh centuries

179. Auer, L., Der Kriegsdienst des Klerus unter den sächsischen Kaisern, *MIÖGF*, *79*(1971),316–407, and *80*(1972),48–70.

180. Auer, L., Zur Kriegswesen unter den früheren Babenberger, *Jahrbuch für Landeskunde von Niederösterreich*, *42*(1976),9–25.

181. Beyerle, F., Zur Wehrverfassung des Hochmittelalters, in *Festschrift Ernst Mayer*, Weimar 1932, 31–91.

182.   Bottner, R., Die Wehrorganisation der frühen Babenberger im Einzelgebiet der Bezirke Melk und Scheibbs, *Jahrbuch für Landeskunde von Niederösterreich*, 42(1976),26–37.

183.   Bonnassie, P., *La Catalogne du milieu du Xe à la fin du XIe siècle, Croissance et mutation d'une société*, Toulouse 2 vols. 1975–76.

184.   Boussard, J., Services féodaux, milices et mercenaires dans les armées en France aux Xe et XIe siècles, in *OM*, i.131–68.

185.   Brown, R. A., *The Normans and the Norman Conquest*, London 1969.

186.   Brown, R. A., *Origins of English Feudalism*, London and New York 1973.

187.   Buisson, L., Formen normannischer Staatsbildung (9. bis 11. Jahrhundert), in *Studien zum mittelalterlichen Lehnswesen*, Lindau and Constance 1960, 95–184.

187a. Cook, D. R., The Norman military revolution in England, in *Proceedings of the Battle Conference on Anglo-Norman Studies*, ed. R. A. Brown, Woodbridge 1979, 94–102 and 214–16.

188.   Douglas, D. C., *The Norman Achievement, 1050–1100*, Berkeley 1969.

189.   Douglas, D. C., *William the Conqueror*, London 1964.

190.   Duby, G., Les origines de la chevalerie, in *OM*, ii.739–61.

191.   Erdmann, C., Die Burgenordnung Heinrichs I, *DA*, 6(1943),59–101.

191a. France, J., La guerre dans la France féodale à la fin du IXe siècle et au Xe siècle, *Revue belge d'histoire militaire* (1979), 177–98.

192.   Hollister, C. W., *Anglo-Saxon Military Institutions on the Eve of the Norman Conquest*, Oxford 1962.

193.   Hollister, C. W., The five-hide unit and the Old English military obligation, *Spec.*, 36(1961),61–74.

194.   Hollister, C. W., The knights of Peterborough and the Anglo-Norman Fyrd, *EHR*, 77(1962),417–36.

195.   Hollister, C. W., *The Military Organization of Norman England*, Oxford 1965.

196.   Hollister, C. W., The significance of scutage rates in eleventh and twelfth century England, *EHR*, 75(1960),577–88.

197.   Johrendt, J., '*Milites*' und '*Militia*' im 11. Jahrhundert. Untersuchung zur Frühgeschichte der Rittertums in Frankreich und Deutschland, Nuremberg 1971.

198.   Knussert, R., *Die deutschen Italienfahrten 951–1220 und die Wehrverfassung*, Ottingen 1931.

199.   Lewis, A. R., Cataluña como frontera militar (870–1050), *AEM*, 5(1968), 15–29.

200.   Lewis, A. R., *The Development of Southern French and Catalan Society, 718–1050*, Austin, Texas, 1965.

201.   Leyser, K., Henry I and the beginnings of the Saxon Empire, *EHR*, 83(1968),1–32.

202.   Menendez Pidal, R., *La España del Cid*, Madrid 5th edn, 2 vols. 1956.

203.   Mor, C. G., La difesa militare della Capitanata ed i confini della regionale al principio del secolo XI, *Papers of the British School in Rome*, 24(1956),29–36.

204.   Powers, J. F., The origins and development of municipal military service in the Leonese and Castilian Reconquest, 800–1250, *Traditio*, 26(1970),91–111.

205.   Prinz, F. *Klerus und Krieg im früheren Mittelalter. Untersuchungen zur Rolle der Kirche beim Aufbau der Königsherrschaft*, Stuttgart 1971.

206.   Sanchez-Albornoz, C., El ejército y la guerra en el reino asturleonés, 718–1037, in *OM*, i.293–428.

207. Sanchez-Albornoz, C., *En torno a los origenes del feudalismo*, Mendoza 2 vols. 1943.
208. Sander, E., Die Heeresorganisation Heinrichs I, *Historisches Jahrbuch*, 59(1939),1–26.
209. Stenton, F. M., *The First Century of English Feudalism, 1066–1166*, Oxford 2nd edn 1961.
210. Tabacco, G., *I liberi del re nell'Italia carolingia e postcarolingia*, Spoleto 1966.
211. Tabacco, G., Dai possessori dell'età carolingia agli esercitali dell'età longobarda, *Studi medievali*, 10(1969),211–68.
212. Tabacco, G., Il regno italico nei secoli IX–XI, in *OM*, ii.763–90.
213. Van Luyn, P., Les *milites* dans la France du XIe siècle. Examen des sources narratives, *MA*, 77(1971),5–51, 193–238.
214. Werner, K. F., Heeresorganisation und Kriegsführung im deutschen Königreich des 10. und 11. Jahrhunderts, in *OM*, ii.791–843 (repr. in *idem*, *Structures politiques du monde franc (VIe–XIIe siècles)*, London 1979).

Twelfth and thirteenth centuries

Sources

215. Alfonso the wise, king of Castile, *Las siete partidas*, Paris 1861, II, Titles XXIII–XXX, 243–350.
216. *Catalogus baronum*, ed. E. M. Jamison, Rome 1972.
217. Curzon, H de, ed., *La règle du Temple*, Paris 1886.
218. Fidenzio of Padua, *Liber recuperationis Terre sancte*, ed. P. G. Golubovich, in *Biblioteca bio-bibliografica della Terra Santa e dell'Oriente Francescano*, Quaracchi 1913, ii.9–60.
219. Fryde, E. B., ed., *Book of Prests of the King's Wardrobe for 1294–5 presented to John Goronwy Edwards*, Oxford 1962.
220. Gallego Blanco, E., ed., *The Rule of the Spanish Military Order of St James (1170–1493)*, *Latin and Spanish Texts*, Leiden 1971.
221. Gough, H., ed., *Scotland in 1298. Documents relating to the Campaign of King Edward the First in that Year, and especially the Battle of Falkirk*, London 1888.
222. King, E. J., ed., *The Rule, Statutes and Customs of Hospitallers (1099–1310)*, London 1934.
223. Paoli, C., ed., *Il libro di Montaperti (An. MCCLX)*, Florence 1889.
224. Perlbach, M., ed., *Die Statuten des deutschen Ordens*, Halle 1890.

Secondary works

225. Alessandro, V d', *Politica e società nella Sicilia aragonese*, Palermo 1963.
226. Audouin, E., *Essai sur l'armée royale au temps de Philippe Auguste*, Paris 1913.
226a. Bautier, R. H. and Bautier, A. M., Contribution à l'histoire du cheval au Moyen Age. L'élevage au Moyen Age et les chevaux de guerre du XIIIe siècle à la guerre de Cent Ans, *Bulletin philologique et historique du Comité des travaux historiques et scientifiques* (1978), 9–75.
227. Beeler, J. H., The composition of Anglo-Norman armies, *Spec.*, 40(1965),398–414.

228.   Bell, A., Notes on Gaimar's military vocabulary, *Medium Aevum*, *40*(1971),93–103.

229.   Benninghoven, F., *Der Orden der Schwertbrüder*, Cologne and Graz 1965.

230.   Boussard, J., L'enquête de 1172 sur les services de chevalier en Normandie, in *Recueil de travaux offerts à Clovis Brunel*, Paris 1955, i.193–208.

231.   Boussard, J., Les mercenaires au XIIe siècle. Henri II Plantagenêt et les origines de l'armée de métier, *BEC, 106*(1945–46),189–224.

232.   Bumke, J., *Studien zum Ritterbegriff im 12. und 13. Jahrhundert*, Heidelberg 1964.

233.   Burns, R. I., How to end a crusade: techniques for making peace in the 13th-century kingdom of Valencia, *Military Affairs, 35*(1971),142–8.

234.   Cahen, C., *Le régime féodal de l'Italie normande*, Paris 1940.

235.   Carolus-Barré, L., Le service militaire en Beauvaisis au temps de Philippe de Beaumanoir, in *Guerre et Paix*, 73–93.

235a. Cathcart King, D. J., The defence of Wales, 1067–1283: the other side of the hill, *Archaeologia Cambrensis, 126*(1977),1–16.

235b. Cazelles, R. La réglementation de la guerre privée de Saint Louis à Charles V, *RHDFE*(1960),530–48.

236.   Chibnall, M., Mercenaries and the *Familia Regis* under Henry I, *Hist.*, *62*(1977),15–23.

236a. Combarieu, M. de, *L'idéal humain et l'expérience morale chez les héros des chansons de geste, des origines à 1250*, Paris 2 vols. 1979.

237.   Critchley, J. S., Summonses to military service early in the reign of Henry III, *EHR, 85*(1971),79–95.

238.   Denholm-Young, N., Feudal society in the thirteenth century: the knights, in *Collected Papers on Mediaeval Subjects*, Oxford 1946.

239.   Denholm-Young, N., The tournament in the 13th century, in *Studies in Medieval History presented to Frederick Maurice Powicke*, ed. R. W. Hunt et al., Oxford 1948, 240–68.

240.   Devos, J. C., L'organisation de la défense de l'Artois en 1297, *Bulletin philologique et historique (jusqu'au 1715) du Comité des travaux historiques et scientifiques, années 1955–1956*, Paris 1957, 47–55.

241.   Duby, G., Guerre et société dans l'Europe féodale: ordonnancement de la paix, in *Concetto, Storia, Miti e Immagini del Medio Evo, Atti del XIV Corso internazionale d'alta cultura*, ed. V. Branca, Florence 1973, 449–59.

242.   Duby, G., Guerre et société dans l'Europe féodale: la guerre et l'argent, *ibid.*, 461–71.

243.   Duby, G., Guerre et société dans l'Europe féodale: la morale des guerriers, *ibid.*, 473–82.

244.   Duby, G., *27 juillet 1214. Le dimanche de Bouvines*, Paris 1973.

245.   Flori, J., Qu'est-ce qu'un *bacheler*? Etude historique du vocabulaire dans les chansons de geste du XIIe siècle, *Romania* (1975), 289–314.

246.   Flori, J., La notion de chevalerie dans les chansons de geste du XIIe siècle. Etude historique du vocabulaire, *MA, 81*(1975),211–44.

247.   Flori, J., Sémantique et société médiévale. Le verbe adouber et son évolution au XIIe siècle, *AESC*(1976),915–40.

248.   Freeman, A. Z., The King's Penny: the headquarters paymasters in the Scottish wars, 1295–1307, *JBS, 6*(1966),1–22.

249. Freeman, A. Z., Wall-breakers and river-bridgers. Military engineers in the Scottish wars of Edward I, *JBS*, *10*(1971),1–16.

250. Galletti, A. I., La società comunale di fronte alla guerra nelle fonti perugine nel 1282, *Bollettino della depputazione di storia patria per l' Umbria*, *71*(1974),35–98.

251. Gattermann, G., *Die deutschen Fürsten auf der Reichsheerfahrt. Studien zur Reichskriegsverfassung der Stauferzeit*, Frankfurt-am-Main 1956.

252. Grundmann, H., Rotten und Brabanzonen. Söldner-Heere im 12. Jahrhundert, *DA*(1942),419–92.

253. Hagspiel, G. H., *Die Führerpersonlichkeit im Kreuzzug*, Zurich 1963.

254. Harvey, S., The knight and the knight's fee in England, *PP*, *49*(1970),3–43.

255. Hollister, C. W., The annual term of military service in medieval England, *Medievalia et Humanistica*, *13*(1960),40–7.

256. Keeney, B. C., Military service and the development of nationalism in England, 1272–1327, *Spec.*, *22*(1947),534–49.

257. Lacarra, J. M., Les villes-frontières dans l'Espagne des XIe–XIIIe siècles, *MA*, *69*(1963), 205–22.

258. Lewis, N.B., An early indenture of military service, 27 July 1287, *BIHR*, *13*(1935),85–9.

259. Lewis, N. B., The English forces in Flanders, August–November 1297, in *Studies in Medieval History presented to Frederick Maurice Powicke*, ed. R. W. Hunt et al., Oxford 1948, 310–18.

260. Lomax, D., *La orden de Santiago (1170–1275)*, Madrid 1965.

261. Lydon, J. F., An Irish army in Scotland, 1296, *Irish Sword*, *5*(1962),184–9.

262. Lydon, J. F., Irish levies in the Scottish wars, 1296–1302, *Irish Sword*, *5*(1962),207–17.

263. Lyon, B. D., *From Fief to Indenture. The transition from feudal to non-feudal contract in Western Europe*, Cambridge, Mass., 1957.

264. Lyon, B. D., The feudal antecedent of the indenture system, *Spec.*, *29*(1954),503–11.

265. McFarlane, K. B. An indenture of agreement between two English knights for mutual aid and counsel in peace and war, 5 December 1298, *BIHR*, *38*(1965),200–10.

266. Martin, J. L., Origenes de la Orden Militar de Santiago (1170–1195), *AEM*, *4*(1967),571–90.

267. Meier-Welcker, H., Das Militärwesen Kaiser Friedrichs II. Landesverteidigung, Heer und Flotte im sizilischen 'Modellstaat', *RIHM*(1975),9–48.

268. Mens, A., De 'Brabanciones' of bloeddorstige en plunderzieke avonturiers (XIIe–XIIIe eeuw), *Miscellanea historica in honorem Alberti de Meyer*, Louvain and Brussels, 2 vols. 1946, i.558–70.

269. Meyer, H., *Die Militärpolitik Friedrich Barbarossas im Zusammenhang mit seiner Italienpolitik*, Berlin 1930.

270. Navel, H., L'enquête de 1133 sur les fiefs de l'évêché de Bayeux, *Bulletin de la Société des Antiquaires de Normandie*, *42*(1934),5–80.

271. Painter, S., Castle-guard, *AHR*, *40*(1934–35),450–9.

272. Parisse, M., *La noblesse lorraine, XIe–XIIIe siècles*, Lille 2 vols. 1976.

273. Pescador, C., La caballeria popular en León y Castilla, *CHE*, *33–4*(1961),101–238, *35–6*(1962),56–201 and *37–8*(1963),88–198.

274. Pieri, P., Federico II di Svevia a la guerra del suo tempo, *Archivio Storico Pugliese*, *13*(1960),114–31.

275. Pieri, P., I Saraceni di Lucera nella storia militare medievale, *ibid.*, *6*(1953),94–101.

276. Powers, J. F., Frontier competition and legal creativity: a Castilian-Aragonese study based on twelfth-century municipal military law, *Spec.*, *52*(1977),465–87.

277. Powers, J. F., Townsmen and soldiers: the interaction of urban and military organisation in the militias of medieval Castile, *Spec.*, *46*(1971),641–55.

278. Powicke, M. R. Distraint of knighthood and military obligation under Henry III, *Spec.*, *25*(1950), 457–70.

279. Powicke, M. R., The general obligation of cavalry service under Edward I, *Spec.*, *28*(1953),814–33.

279a. Prestwich, J. O., The military household of the Norman kings, *EHR*, *96*(1981),1–35.

280. Riley-Smith, J. S. C., Peace never established: the case of the kingdom of Jerusalem, *TRHS*, 5th ser., *28*(1978), 87–102.

281. Rousset, P., La description du monde chevaleresque dans Orderic Vital, *MA*, *75*(1969), 427–44.

282. Rousset, P., Note sur la situation du chevalier à l'époque romane, in *Littérature, histoire, linguistique. Recueil d'études offertes à Bernard Gagnebin*, Lausanne 1973, 189–200.

283. Sanders, I. J., *Feudal Military Service in England: A study of the constitutional and military powers of the 'Barones' in mediaeval England*, London and New York 1956.

284. Schlight, J., *Monarchs and Mercenaries. A reappraisal of the importance of knight service of Norman and Angevin England*, Bridgeport, Conn., 1968.

285. Smail, R. C., *The Crusaders in Syria and the Holy Land*, London 1973.

286. Smail, R. C., *Crusading Warfare (1097–1193)*, Cambridge 1956.

287. Strayer, J. R., Knight service in Normandy in the XIIIth Century, in *Anniversary Essays in Mediaeval History by Students of Charles Homer Haskins*, ed. C. H. Taylor, Boston and New York 1929, 312–27.

288. Torres, A. P., Contribución al estudio del ejército en los estados de la Reconquista, *Anuario de Historia del Derecho Español*, *15*(1944),205–351.

289. Ubieto Areta, A., La guerra en la Edad media según los fueros de la linea del Tajo, *Saitabi*, *16*(1966),91–210.

290. Urban, W., The organization of defence of the Livonian frontier in the thirteenth century, *Spec.*, *48*(1973),525–32.

291. Uri, S. P., Het tournooi in de XIIe en XIIIeeuw, *Tijdschrift voor Geschiedenis*, *73*(1960),376–96.

292. Verbruggen, J. F., *Het leger en de vloot van de graven van Vlaanderen vanaf het onstaan tot in 1305*, Brussels 1960.

293. Verbruggen, J. F., De militaire dienst in het graafschap Vlaanderen, *Tijdschrift voor Rechtsgeschiedenis*, *26*(1958),437–65.

294. Waley, D. P., Papal armies in the thirteenth century, *EHR*, *72*(1957),1–30.

295. Waley, D. P., The army of the Florentine republic from the twelfth to the fourteenth century, in *Florentine Studies*, ed. N. Rubinstein, London and Evanston 1968, 70–108.

296. Waley D. P., Condotte and condottieri in the thirteenth century, *Proceedings of the British Academy* (1975), 337–71.

297. Waley, D. P., Le origini della condotta nel Duecento e le compagnie di ventura, *RSI*, *88*(1976),531–8.

298. Yver, J. L'interdiction de la guerre privée dans le très ancien droit normand, *Travaux de la semaine d'histoire du droit normand tenue à Guernsey 1927*, Caen 1928, 307–47.

Fourteenth and fifteenth centuries

Sources

299. Allmand, C. T., ed., *Society at War. The experience of England and France during the Hundred Years War*, Edinburgh 1973 (collection of documents in translation and full critical bibliography, 194–212).

300. Barnard, F. P., ed., *The Essential Portions of Nicholas of Upton's De Studio Militari before 1446, translated by John Blount, Fellow of All Souls*, Oxford 1931.

301. Bastin, J., Le traité de Théodore Paléologue dans la traduction de Jean de Vignai, in *Etudes romanes dédiées à Mario Roques par ses amis, collègues et élèves de France*, Paris 1946, 77–88.

302. Belleval, R. de, ed., *Rôle des nobles et fieffés du bailliage d'Amiens convoqués pour la guerre le 25 août 1337*, Amiens 1862.

303. Belleval, R. de, ed., *Trésor généalogique de la Picardie ou Recueil inédits sur la noblesse de cette province, II : Montres et quittances*, Amiens 1860.

304. Bohigas, P., ed., *Tractats de cavalleria*, Barcelona 1947.

305. Bollatti di Saint Pierre, F., ed., *Illustrazioni della Spedizione in Oriente di Amedeo VI(il Conte Verde)*, Turin 1900.

306. Boucher de Molandon, R. and Beaucorps, E. de, eds., *L'armée anglaise vaincue par Jeanne d'Arc sous les murs d'Orléans, Mémoires de la société historique et archéologique de l'Orléanais*, 23(1892).

307. Brassart, F., ed., La féodalité dans le nord de la France. Bans et arrière-bans de la Flandre wallonne sous Charles de Téméraire et Maximilien d'Autriche, *Souvenirs de la Flandre wallonne*, 1884, 5–78.

308. Bréard, C., ed., *Le compte du Clos des galées au XIVe siècle (1382–1384)*, Rouen 1893.

309. Bush, H. R., ed., La bataille de Trente Anglois et de Trente Bretons, *Modern Philology*, 9(1911–12),511–44, and 10(1912–13),82–136.

310. Canestrini, G., *Documenti per servire alla storia della milizia italiana dal XIII secolo al XVI, raccolti negli Archivi della Toscana*, Florence 1851.

311. Chabannes, H. de, ed., *Preuves pour servir à l'histoire de la maison de Chabannes*, Dijon 4 vols. 1892–7.

312. Champeval, J. B., ed., Le rôle du ban et arrière-ban du haut Auvergne, in *L'Auvergne historique, littéraire et artistique, Varia, 1909–1912*, Riom 1913.

313. Chandos, Le Héraut, *Le Prince noir, poème*, ed. Francisque-Michel, London and Paris 1883.

314. Chazelas, A., ed., *Documents relatifs au Clos des Galées de Rouen et aux armées de mer du roi de France de 1293 à 1418*, Paris 2 vols. 1977–78.

315. *Chronique du Mont-Saint-Michel (1343–1468)*, ed. S. Luce, Paris 2 vols. 1879–83.

316. Diez de Games, Gutierre, *El Victorial, Crónica de Don Pero Nino, conde de Buelna*, ed. J. de Mata Carriazo, Madrid 1940 (French tr.: *Le Victorial, chronique de Pedro Nino, comte de Buelna (1379–1449)*, ed. A. Circourt and comte de Puymaigre, Paris 1867; English tr.: *The Unconquered Knight. A Chronicle of the Deeds of Don Pero Nino, count of Buelna*, ed. J. Evans, London 1928).

317. Devillers, L., Documents relatifs à l'expédition de Guillaume IV contre les Liégeois, 1407–1409, *Bulletin de la Commission royale d'histoire*, 4e sér., *4*(1877),85–120.

318. Devillers, L., Sur les expéditions des comtes de Hainault et de Hollande en Prusse, *ibid.*, *5*(1878),127–44.

319. Dufour, E., *Documents inédits pour servir à l'histoire de l'ancienne province de Quercy*, Cahors 1865.

320. Dumay, G., Etat militaire et féodal des bailliages d'Autun, Montcenis, Bourbon-Lancy et Semur-en-Brionnais en 1474, *Mémoires de la Société éduenne*, 1882.

321. Ekdahl, S., *Die 'Banderia Prutenorum' des Jan Dugosz, eine Quelle zur Schlacht bei Tannenberg*, Göttingen and Zurich 1976.

322. Essenwein, A. von, ed., *Mittelalterliches Hausbuch, Bilderhandschrift des 15. Jahrhunderts mit vollständigem Text und facsimilierten Abbildungen*, Frankfurt-am-Main 1887.

323. Funck-Brentano, F., *De exercituum commeatibus tertio decimo et quarto decimo saeculis post Christum natum*, Paris 1897.

324. Hergsell, G., *Talhoffers Fechbuch aus dem Jahre 1467*, Prague 1887.

325. Hergsell, G., *Talhoffers Fechbuch (Gothaer Codex) aus dem Jahre 1443*, Prague 1883.

326. Huguet, A., Aspects de la guerre de Cent Ans en Picardie maritime, *Mémoires de la Société des Antiquaires de Picardie*, *48*(1941) and *50*(1944).

327. Jarry, L., Le compte de l'armée anglaise au siège d'Orléans, *Mémoires de la Société historique et archéologique de l'Orléanais*, 1892.

327a. Jones, M., An indenture between Robert, lord Mohaut, and Sir John de Bracebridge for life service in peace and war, 1310, *Journal of the Society of Archivists*, *4*(1972), 384–94.

328. Jusselin, M., Comment la France se préparait à la guerre de Cent ans, *BEC*, *73*(1912),209–36.

329. Lannoy, Ghillebert de, *Oeuvres*, ed. Ch. Potvin, Louvain 1878.

330. Le Cacheux, P., *Rouen au temps de Jeanne d'Arc et pendant l'occupation anglaise (1419–1449)*, Rouen and Paris 1931.

331. Llull, Ramon, *Livre de l'ordre de chevalerie*, ed. V. Minervini, Bari 1972 (fifteenth-century English tr. by William Caxton, *The Book of the Ordre of Chyualry*, ed. A. T. P. Byles, London 1926).

332. Longnon, A., *Paris pendant l'occupation anglaise (1420–1436)*, Paris 1878.

333. Luzzati, M. *Una guerra di popolo. Lettere private del tempo dell'assedio di Pisa (1494–1509)*, Pisa 1973.

334. Memorial über die Organisation des Kriegswesen der Stadt Worms Ende des XV. Jahrhunderts, in *Quellen zur Geschichte der Stadt Worms*, ed. M. Boos, III, *Annalen und Chroniken*, Berlin 1883, 349–70.

335. Morel, O., *L'état de siège à Bourg lors de l'invasion de la Bresse en 1468*, Bourg 1936.

336. Nicolas, Sir N. Harris, *History of the Battle of Agincourt and of the expedition of Henry the Fifth into France in 1415*, London 2nd edn 1832 (repr. 1970).

337. Nicolas, Sir N. Harris, *The Controversy between Sir Richard Scrope and Sir Robert Grosvenor, in the Court of Chivalry, AD MCCCLXXXV–MCCCXC*, London 2 vols. 1832.

338.   Oberman, H. and Weisheipl, J. A., The *Sermo epinicius* ascribed to Thomas Bradwardine (1346), *Archives d'histoire doctrinale et littéraire du Moyen Age*, *33*(1958),295–329 (treatise on the English victories over France and Scotland).

339.   Pieri, P., *Governo et exercitio de la militia* di Orso degli Orsini e i *Memoriali* di Diomede Carafa, *Archivio Storico per le provincie napoletane*, new ser., *19*(1933),99–212.

340.   Quicke, F., L'intérêt du point de vue de l'histoire politique, économique et financière, du troisième compte des expéditions militaires d'Antoine de Bourgogne, duc de Brabant et de Limbourg dans le duché de Luxembourg (1er septembre 1413–24 décembre 1414), *Publications de la section historique de l'Institut grand-ducal de Luxembourg*, *64*(1930),315–468.

341.   Riquer, M. de, *Lletres de batalla, cartelles de deseiximents i capitols de passos d'armes*, Barcelona 2 vols. 1968–69.

342.   Schürstab, E., *Beschreibung des ersten Markgräflichen Krieges gegen Nürnberg*, ed. J. Bader, Munich 1860 (repr. 1969).

343.   Schullian, D. M., *Diario de Bello Carolino*, New York 1967.

344.   Stevenson, J., *Letters and Papers illustrative of the Wars of the English in France during the Reign of Henry the Sixth, King of England*, London 3 vols. 1861–64.

345.   Visconti, E. C., Ordine dell'esercito ducale sforzesco, 1472–1473, *Archivio Storico Lombardo*, *3*(1876).

General

346.   Adam-Even, P., Les fonctions militaires des hérauts d'armes, leur influence sur le début de l'héraldique, *Archives héraldiques suisses*, *71*(1957),2–33.

347.   Alban, J. R. and Allmand, C. T., Spies and spying in the fourteenth century, in *War, Literature and Politics*, 73–101.

348.   Allmand, C. T., War and profit in the late Middle Ages, *History Today*, *15*(1965),762–9.

349.   Cipolla, C. M., *Guns and Sails in the Early Phase of European Expansion (1400–1700)*, London 1965.

350.   Contamine, P., Les armées française et anglaise à l'époque de Jeanne d'Arc, *Revue des Sociétés savantes de haute Normandie, Lettres et Sciences humaines* (1970),7–33.

351.   Delumeau, J., *La peur en Occident, XIVe–XVIIIe siècle. Une cité assiégée*, Paris 1978.

352.   Fowler, K. A., *The Age of Plantagenet and Valois*, London 1968.

353.   Glénisson, J., Notes d'histoire militaire. Quelques lettres de défi du XIVe siècle, *BEC*, *107*(1947–48),235–54.

354.   Goez, W., Über Fürstenzweikämpfe im Spätmittelalter, *Archiv für Kulturgeschichte*, *49*(1967),135–63.

355.   Hale, J. R., War and public opinion in the fifteenth and sixteenth centuries, *PP*, *22*(1962),18–33.

356.   Huizinga, J., La valeur politique et militaire des idées de chevalerie à la fin du Moyen Age, *Revue d'histoire diplomatique*, *35*(1921),126–38.

357.   Keen, M. H., Brotherhood in Arms, *Hist.*, *57*(1962),1–17.

358.   Keen, M. H., Chivalry, nobility and the man-at-arms, in *War, Literature and politics*, 32–45.

359. Keen, M. H., Huizinga, Kilgour and the decline of chivalry, *Medievalia et Humanistica*, new ser., *8*, ed. P. M. Clogan, Cambridge 1977, 1–20.

360. Keen, M. H., *The Laws of War in the Late Middle Ages*, London 1965.

361. Pippidi, A., *Contributti la Studiul legilor razboinlui în Evul Mediu*, Bucharest 1974 (a study of prisoners of war during the Hundred Years War and in Romance language countries in the Middle Ages).

362. Post, G., *Ratio publicae utilitatis, ratio status* und Staatsräson, *Welt als Geschichte*, *22*(1961),8–28, 71–99.

363. Puddu, R. *Eserciti e monarchie nazionali nei secoli XV–XVI*, Florence 1975.

364. Puddu, R., Istituzioni militari, Società e Stato tra Medioevo e Rinascimento, *RSI*, *87*(1975),749–69.

364a. Vale, M. G. A., *War and Chivalry. Warfare and Aristocratic Culture in England, France and Burgundy at the End of the Middle Ages*, London 1981.

Germany and the Germanic world (including Switzerland)

365. Beck, W., Bayerns Heerwesen und Mobilmachung im 15. Jahrhundert, *Archivalische Zeitschrift*, new ser., *18*(1911),1–232.

366. Benninghoven, F., Die Kriegsdienste der Komturei Danzig um das Jahr 1400, in *Acht Jahrhunderte Deutscher Orden in Einzeldarstellungen, Festschrift . . . Marian Tumler*, ed. P. K. Wieser, Bad Godesberg 1967, 161–222.

367. Benninghoven, F., Probleme der Zahl und Standortverteilung der Livländischen Streitkräfte im ausgehenden Mittelalter, *ZOF*, *12*(1963),601–22.

367a. Contamine, P., René II et les mercenaires de la langue germanique: la guerre contre Robert de La Marck, seigneur de Sedan (1496), in *Bataille de Nancy*, 377–94.

368. Deutsch, K. W. and Weillenmann, H., Die militärische Bewährung eines sozialen Systems: die Schweizer Eidgenossenschaft im 14. Jahrhundert, *Kölner Zeitschrift für Soziologie und Sozialpsychologie*, Sonderheft 12. *Beiträge zur Militärsoziologie*, Cologne, 1968, 38–58.

369. Ekdahl, S., Über die Kriegsdienste der Freien im Kulmerland zu Anfang des 15. Jahrhunderts, *Preussenland*, *2*(1964),1–14.

370. Franz, G., Von Ursprung und Brauchtum der Landsknechte, *MIÖGF*, *61*(1953),79–98.

371. Freynhagen, W., *Die Wehrmachtverhältnisse der Stadt Rostock im Mittelalter*, Rostock 1930.

372. Heinzen, T., Zunftkämpfe, Zunftherrschaft und Wehrverfassung in Köln, Beitrag zum Thema 'Zünfte und Wehrverfassung', *Veröffentlichungen des Kölnischen Geschichtsverein*, *16*(1939).

372a. Hummelberger, W., Die Bewaffnung der Bürgerschaft im Spätmittelalter am Beispiel Wien, in *Das Leben in der Stadt des Spätmittelalters, Internationaler Kongress Krems an der Donau 20. bis 23. September 1976*, Vienna 1977,191–206.

373. Martin, P., Quelques aspects de l'art de la guerre en Alsace au XIVe siècle, *Revue d'Alsace*, *88*(1948),108–23.

374. Martin, P., Wehr-, Waffen- und Harnischpflicht der Strassburger Zünfte im 14. Jahrhundert, *Waffen- und Kostümkunde 34*(1975),102–8.

375. Meissner, G., *Das Kriegswesen der Reichsstadt Nordhausen (1290–1803)*, Berlin 1939.

376. Nell, M., *Die Landsknechte. Entstehung der ersten deutschen Infanterie*, Berlin 1914.

376a. Orth, E., *Die Fehden der Reichsstadt Frankfurt am Main in Spätmittelalter. Fehderecht und Fehdepraxis im 14. und 15. Jht.*, Wiesbaden 1973.

377. Padrutt, C., *Staat und Krieg im alten Bünden. Studien zur Beziehung zwischen Obrigkeit und Kriegertum in den drei Bünden, vornehmlich im 15. und 16. Jahrhundert*, Zurich 1965.

377a. Rapp, F., Strasbourg et Charles le Hardi: l'ampleur et le prix de l'effort militaire, in *Bataille de Nancy*, 395–414.

378. Rautenburg, W., *Böhmische Söldner im Ordensland Preussen. Ein Beitrag zur Söldnergeschichte des 15. Jahrhunderts, vornehmlich des 13. jährigen Städte-Kriegs 1454–1466*, Hamburg 1954.

379. Redlich, F., *The German Military Enterpriser and his Work Forces*, Wiesbaden 2 vols. 1964–65.

379a. Sablonier, R., Etat et structures militaires dans la Confédération autour des années 1480, in *Bataille de Nancy*, 429–77.

380. Schaufelberger, W., *Der Alte Schweizer und sein Krieg. Studien zur Kriegsführung vornehmlich im 15. Jahrhundert*, Zurich 2nd edn 1966.

381. Schaufelberger, W., Zu einer Charakterologie des altschweizerischen Kriegertums, *Schweizerisches Archiv für Volkskunde*, 56(1960),48–87.

382. Schaufelberger, W., Zum Problem der militärischen Integration in der spätmittelalterlichen Eidgenossenschaft, *Allgemeine schweizerische Militärschrift*, 136(1970),313–28.

383. Schaufelberger, W., *Der Wettkampf in der alten Eidgenossenschaft. Zur Kulturgeschichte des Sports vom 13. bis ins 18. Jahrhundert*, Berne 2 vols. 1972.

384. Schmidt-Ewald, W., Das Landesaufgebot im westlichen Thüringen vom 15. bis zum 17. Jahrhundert, *Zeitschrift des Vereins für thüringische Geschichte und Altertumskunde*, 36(1929),6–58.

385. Schnitzer, M., *Die Morgartenschlacht in werdenden schweizerishcen National-Bewusstsein*, Zurich 1969.

386. Schultze, J., Die bürgerliche Dienst- und Wehrpflicht in der Mark Brandenburg, *Jahrbuch für die Geschichte Mittel- und Ostdeutschland*, 23(1974),270–80.

387. Schultze, W., *Die Gleve. Der Ritter und sein Gefolge im späteren Mittelalter*, Munich 1940.

388. Stöcklein, H., Das Landsknechts- und Söldnertum, in *Deutsche Soldatenkunde*, 1(1937),50–62.

389. Stolz, O., *Wehrverfassung und Schützenwesen in Tirol von den Anfängen bis 1918*, Innsbruck, Vienna and Munich 1960.

390. Wohlfeil, R., Adel und neues Heerwesen, in *Deutscher Adel, 1430–1555, Büdinger Vortrage 1963*, ed. H. Rossler, Darmstadt 1965, 203–33.

391. Wohfeil, R., Ritter – Söldnerführer – Offizier. Versuch eines vergleiches, in *Festschrift Johannes Barmann*, Wiesbaden, 2 vols. 1966, i.45–70.

392. Zimmermann, J., Wehrwesen und Zünfte, *Schaffhauser Beiträge zur vaterländischen Geschichte*, 38(1961),82–90.

England and its dependencies

393. Armstong, C. A. J., Sir John Fastolf and the Law of Arms, *War, Literature and Politics*, 46–56.

394.   Barnie, J., *War in Medieval English Society. Social Values and the Hundred Years War, 1337–1399,* Ithaca and London 1974.

395.   Boynton, L., The Tudor Provost-Marshal, *EHR, 77*(1962),437–55.

396.   Burley, S. J., The victualling of Calais 1347–65, *BIHR, 31*(1958),49–57.

397.   Carr, A. D., Welshmen and the Hundred Years' War, *Welsh History Review, 4*(1968),21–46.

398.   Chew, H. M., Scutage in the fourteenth century, *EHR, 38*(1923),19–41.

399.   Cruickshank, C. G., *Army Royal. Henry VIII's Invasion of France, 1513,* Oxford 1969.

399a.   Curry, A. E., L'effet de la libération de la ville d'Orléans sur l'armée anglaise: les problèmes de l'organisation militaire en Normandie de 1429 à 1435, in *Jeanne d'Arc, une époque, un rayonnement. Colloque d'histoire médiévale, Orléans, octobre 1979,* ed. J. Glénisson, Paris 1982, 95–106.

399b.   Curry, A. E., The first English standing army? Military organization in Lancastrian Normandy, 1420–1450, in *Patronage, Pedigree and Power in Later Medieval England,* ed. C. Ross, Gloucester and Totowa 1979, 193–214.

399c.   Ellis, S. G., Taxation and defence in late medieval Ireland: the survival of scutage, *Journal of the Royal Society of Ireland, 107*(1977),5–26.

400.   Ferguson, A. B., *The Indian Summer of English Chivalry. Studies in the Decline and Transformation of Chivalric Idealism,* Durham, N.C., 1960.

401.   Fowler, K. A., Les finances et la discipline dans les armées anglaises en France au XIVe siècle, *Actes du colloque international de Cocherel, Les Cahiers vernonnais, 4*(1964),55–84.

402.   Gillespie, J. L., Richard II's Cheshire archers, *Transactions of the Historical Society of Lancashire and Cheshire, 125*(1975),1–39.

402a.   Gillespie, J. L., Richard II's Archers of the Crown, *Journal of British Studies, 18*(1979),14–29.

402b.   Gillingham, J., *The Wars of the Roses. Peace and Conflict in Fifteenth Century England,* London 1981.

402c.   Goodman, A., The military subcontracts of Sir Hugh Hastings, 1380, *EHR, 95*(1980),114–20.

402d.   Goodman, A., *The Wars of the Roses. Military Activity and English Society 1452–97,* London 1981.

403.   Hanawalt, B. A., Violent death in fourteenth- and early fifteenth-century England, *Comparative Studies in Society and History, 18*(1976),297–320.

404.   Harriss, G. L., War and the emergence of the English Parliament 1297–1360, *Journal of Medieval History, 2*(1976),35–56.

405.   Hay, D., Booty in Border Warfare, *Transactions of the Dumfriesshire and Galloway Natural History and Antiquarian Society,* 3rd ser., *31*(1954),145–66.

406.   Hay, D., The division of spoils of war in fourteenth-century England, *TRHS,* 5th ser., *4*(1954),91–109.

407.   Hewitt, H. J., The organization of war, in *The Hundred Years' War,* ed. K. A. Fowler, London 1971, 75–95.

408.   Hewitt, H. J., *The Organization of War under Edward III, 1338–62,* Manchester 1966.

409.   Hooker, J. R., Notes on the organization and supply of the Tudor military under Henry VII, *Huntington Library Quarterly, 23*(1950),19–31.

409a.   Jones, T., *Chaucer's Knight. The Portrait of a Medieval Mercenary,* London 1980.

410. Kliman, B. W., The idea of chivalry in John Barbour's Bruce, *MS*, *35*(1973),477–508.

411. Lander, J. R., The Hundred Years' War and Edward IV's campaign in France, in *Tudor Men and Institutions. Studies in English Law and Government*, ed. A. J. Slavin, Baton Rouge 1972, 70–100.

412. Lander, J. R., *The Wars of the Roses*, London 1965.

413. Lewis, N. B., Indentures of retinue with John of Gaunt, Duke of Lancaster, enrolled in Chancery 1367–1399, *Camden Miscellany*, *22*(1964),77–112.

414. Lewis, N. B., The last medieval summons of the English feudal levy, 13 June 1385, *EHR*, *73*(1958),1–26.

415. Lewis, N. B., The organization of indentured retinues in fourteenth-century England, *TRHS*, 4th ser., *27*(1945),29–39.

416. Lewis, N. B., The recruitment and organization of a contract army, May to November 1337, *BIHR*, *37*(1964),1–19.

417. Lewis, N. B., The summons of the English feudal levy, 5 April 1327, in *Essays in Medieval History presented to Bertie Wilkinson*, ed. T. A. Sandquist and M. R. Powicke, Toronto 1969, 236–49.

418. McFarlane, K. B., A business-partnership in war and administration, 1421–1445, *EHR*, *78*(1963),290–310.

419. McNab, B., Obligations of the church in English society: military arrays of the clergy 1369–1418, in *Order and Innovation in the Middle Ages. Essays in honor of Joseph R. Strayer*, ed. W. C. Jordan, B. McNab and T. F. Ruiz, Princeton, N.J., 1976, 293–314, 516–22.

420. Mathew, G., Ideals of knighthood in late fourteenth-century England, in *Studies in Medieval History presented to Frederick Maurice Powicke*, ed. R. W. Hunt *et al.*, Oxford 1948, 354–62.

420a. Matons, A. T. E., Traditions of panegyric in Welsh poetry, *Spec.*, *53*(1978),667–87.

421. Miller, E., *War in the North. The Anglo-Scottish Wars of the Middle Ages*, Hull 1960.

422. Newhall, R. A., *Muster and Review. A problem of English military administration, 1420–40*, Cambridge, Mass., 1940.

423. Nicholson, R. G., *Edward III and the Scots. The formative years of a military career, 1327–1335*, Oxford 1965.

424. Palmer, J. J. N., The last summons of the feudal army in England (1385), *EHR*, *83*(1968),771–5.

425. Perroy, E., Gras profits et rançons pendant la guerre de Cent ans: l'affaire du comte de Denia, *Mélanges d'histoire du Moyen Age dédiés à la mémoire de Louis Halphen*, Paris 1951, 573–80.

425a. Powicke, M. R., Edward II and military obligation, *Spec.*, *21*(1956),83–119.

426. Powicke, M. R., The English aristocracy and the war, in *The Hundred Years' War*, ed. K. A. Fowler, London 1971, 122–34.

427. Powicke, M. R., Lancastrian captains, in *Essays in Medieval History presented to Bertie Wilkinson*, ed. T. A. Sandquist and M. R. Powicke, Toronto 1969, 371–82.

428. Prestwich, M., Victualling estimates for the English garrisons in Scotland during the early fourteenth century, *EHR*, *82*(1967),536–43.

428a. Prestwich, M., *The Three Edwards: War and the State in England 1272–1377*, London 1980.

429. Prince, A. E., The army and the navy, in *The English Government at Work*,

1327–1336, I: Central and Prerogative Administration, ed. J. F. Willard and W. A. Morris, Cambridge, Mass., 1940, 332–93.

430.   Prince, A. E., The indenture system under Edward III, in *Historical Essays in honour of James Tait*, ed. J. G. Edwards and E. F. Jacob, Manchester 1933, 283–97.

431.   Prince, A. E., The payment of army wages in Edward III's reign, *Spec.*, *19*(1944),137–60.

432.   Prince, A. E., The strength of English armies in the Middle Ages, *EHR*, *46*(1931),353–71.

433.   Reeves, A. C., Some of Humphrey Stafford's military indentures, *Nottingham Mediaeval Studies, 16*(1972),80–91.

434.   Rogers, A., Hoton versus Shakell: a ransom case in the Court of Chivalry, 1390–95, *Nottingham Mediaeval Studies, 6*(1962),74–108, and *7*(1963),53–78.

435.   Rowe, B. J. H., Discipline in the Norman garrisons under Bedford, *EHR*, *46*(1931),194–208.

436.   Sandberger, D., *Studien über das Rittertum in England, vornehmlich während des 14. Jahrhunderts*, Berlin 1937.

437.   Sherborne, J. W., Indentured retinues and English expeditions to France, 1369–1380, *EHR, 79*(1964),718–46.

438.   Templeman, G., Two French attempts to invade England during the Hundred Years War, in *Studies in French Language, Literature and History presented to R. L. G. Ritchie*, ed. F. MacKenzie, R. C. Knight and J. M. Milner, Cambridge 1949, 225–38.

France (including the Burgundian State)

439.   Balon, J., L'organisation militaire des Namurois au XIVe siècle, *Annales de la Société archéologique de Namur, 40*(1932),1–86.

440.   Bossuat, A., Un ordre de chevalerie auvergnat: l'Ordre de la Pomme d'Or, *Bulletin historique et scientifique de l'Auvergne, 64*(1944),83–98.

441.   Bossuat, A., *Perrinet Gressart et François de Surienne, agents de l'Angleterre*, Paris 1936.

442.   Bossuat, A., Les prisonniers de Beauvais et la rançon du poète Jean Regnier, bailli d'Auxerre, in *Mélanges Louis Halphen*, Paris 1951, 27–32.

443.   Bossuat, A., Les prisonniers de guerre au XVe siècle: la rançon de Guillaume, seigneur de Châteauvillain, *Annales de Bourgogne, 23*(1951),7–35.

444.   Bossuat, A., Les prisonniers de guerre au XVe siècle: la rançon de Jean, seigneur de Rodemack, *Annales de l'Est*, 5e sér., *3*(1951),145–62.

445.   Brusten, C., *L'armée bourguignonne de 1465 à 1468*, Brussels 1953.

446.   Brusten, C., L'armée bourguignonne de 1465 à 1477, *RIHM*(1959),452–66.

446a.   Brusten, C., La fin des compaignies d'ordonnance de Charles le Téméraire, in *Bataille de Nancy*, 363–75.

447.   Brusten, C., Charles le Téméraire au camp de Lausanne, mars-mai 1476, *PCEEBM, 14*(1972),71–81.

448.   Brusten, C., Les compaignies d'ordonnance dans l'armée bourguignonne, in *Grandson 1476, Essai d'approche pluridisciplinaire d'une action militaire du XVe siècle*, ed. D. Reichel, Lausanne 1976, 112–69.

449.   Brusten, C., Les emblèmes de l'armée bourguignonne de Charles le Téméraire.

Essai de classification, *Jahrbuch des bernischen historisches Museum in Bern*, *37–8*(1957–58),118–32.

450.   Brusten, C., Le ravitaillement en vivres dans l'armée bourguignonne 1450–1477, *PCEEBM*, *3*(1961),42–9.

450a.   Cauchies, J. P., Les 'Ecorcheurs' en Hainault (1437–1445), *Revue belge d'histoire militaire*, *20*(1974),317–37.

451.   Champion, P., *Guillaume de Flavy, capitaine de Compiègne. Contribution à l'histoire de Jeanne d'Arc et à l'étude de la vie militaire et privée au XVe siècle*, Paris 1906.

452.   Chevalier, B., L'organisation militaire à Tours au XVe siècle, *Bulletin philologique et historique jusqu'à 1610 du Comité des travaux historiques et scientifiques, année 1959*, Paris 1960, 445–59.

453.   Chevalier, B., Pouvoir royal et pouvoir urbain à Tours pendant la guerre de Cent ans, *Annales de Bretagne*, *81*(1974),365–92, 681–707.

454.   Chomel, V., Chevaux de bataille et roncins en Dauphiné au XIVe siècle, *Cahiers d'histoire*, *7*(1962),5–23.

455.   Collin, H., Les ressources alimentaires en Lorraine pendant la première partie du XIVe siècle, *Bulletin philologique et historique (jusqu'àu 1610) du Comité des travaux historiques et scientifiques, année 1968*, Paris 1971, 37–75.

456.   Contamine, P., Les compaignies d'aventure en France pendant la guerre de Cent ans, *Mélanges de l'Ecole française de Rome, Moyen Age, Temps modernes*, *87*(1975),365–96.

457.   Contamine, P., *Guerre, état et société à la fin du Moyen Age. Etudes sur les armées des rois de France, 1337–1494*, Paris and The Hague 1972.

458.   Contamine, P., *L'oriflamme de Saint-Denis aux XIVe et XVe siècles. Etude de symbolique religieuse et royale*, Nancy 1975.

459.   Contamine, P., Points de vue sur la chevalerie en France à la fin du Moyen Age, *Francia*, *4*(1976),255–85.

460.   Contamine, P., Rançons et butins dans la Normandie anglaise (1424–1444), in *Guerre et Paix*, 241–70.

460a.   Contamine, P., L'écrit et l'oral en France à la fin du Moyen Age. Note sur l'alphabétisme de l'encadrement militaire, in *Histoire comparée de l'administration (IVe–XVIIIe siècles). Actes du XIVe colloque historique franco-allemand, Tours 27 mars– 1er avril 1977*, ed. W. Paravicini and K. F. Werner, Munich 1980, 102–13.

461.   Cosneau, E., *Le connétable de Richemont (Artur de Bretagne), 1393–1458*, Paris 1886.

462.   Finó, J. F., Les armées françaises lors de la guerre de Cent ans, *Gl.*, *15*(1977),5–23.

463.   Gaier, C., L'approvisionnement et le régime alimentaire des troupes dans le duché de Limbourg et les terres d'Outre-Meuse vers 1400, *MA*, *74*(1968),551–75.

464.   Grava, Y., La guerre au XIVe siècle. Un exemple provençal: Martigues, in *Guerre et Paix*, 179–92.

465.   Harmand, J., Un document de 1435, concernant Houdan et la fin de l'occupation anglaise dans l'ouest de l'Ile-de-France, *Bulletin de la Société nationale des Antiquaires de France* (1975),205–47.

465a.   Hébert, M., L'armée provençale en 1374, *Annales du Midi*, *91*(1979),5–27.

465b.   Henneman, J. B., The military class and the French monarchy in the late Middle Ages, *AHR*, *83*(1978),946–65.

466. Jarousseau, G., Le guet, l'arrière-guet et la garde en Poitou pendant la guerre de Cent ans, *Bulletin de la Société des Antiquaires de l'Ouest* (1965),159–202.

467. Joris, A., Remarques sur les clauses militaires des privilèges urbains liégeois, *Revue belge de philologie et d'histoire*, *37*(1959),297–316.

468. Kilgour, R. L., *The Decline of Chivalry as shown in the French Literature of the Late Middle Ages*, Cambridge, Mass., 1937.

469. Leguai, A., Le problème des rançons au XVe siècle: la captivité de Jean Ier, duc de Bourbon, *Cahiers d'histoire*, *6*(1961),41–58.

470. Lewis, P. S., Une devise de chevalerie inconnue, créée par le comte de Foix? Le Dragon, *Annales du Midi*, *76*(1964),77–84.

471. Michel, R., La défense d'Avignon sous Urbain V et Grégoire XI, *Mélanges d'archéologie et d'histoire*, *30*(1910),129–45.

472. Michel, R., Les défenseurs des châteaux et des villes fortes dans le Comtat Venaissin, *BEC*, *75*(1915),315–330.

473. Reichel, D., Essai d'approche pluridisciplinaire d'une action militaire du XVe siècle, in *Grandson 1476*, ed. D. Reichel, Lausanne 1976, 214–39.

474. Reynaud, M., Le service féodal en Anjou et Maine à la fin du Moyen Age, *Cahiers d'histoire*, *16*(1971),115–59.

475. Roger, J. M., Guy Le Bouteiller, in *Guerre et Paix*, 271–329.

476. Schmidt-Sinns, D., Studien zum Heerwesen der Herzöge von Burgund, 1465–1477 (typescript thesis), Göttingen 1966.

477. Solon, P. D., Popular response to standing military forces in fifteenth century France, *Studies in the Renaissance*, *19*(1972),78–111.

478. Solon, P. D., Valois military administration on the Norman frontier, 1445–1461. A study in medieval reform, *Spec.*, *51*(1976),91–111.

479. Timbal, P. C., *La guerre de Cent ans vue à travers les registres du Parlement, 1337–1369*, Paris 1961.

480. Tucoo-Chala, P., Une bande de routiers dans la région de Casteljaloux en 1381–1383, *Revue de l'Agenais* (1973),5–35.

481. Tuetey, A., *Les Ecorcheurs sous Charles VII*, Montbéliard 2 vols. 1874.

482. Vale, M. G. A., A fourteenth-century Order of Chivalry: the Tiercelet, *EHR*, *82*(1967),332–41.

483. Vaughan, R., *Charles the Bold*, London 1973 (chapter on the armies, 197–229).

484. Vaughan, R., *John the Fearless*, London 1966 (chapter on the armies, 138–52).

485. Vaughan, R., *Valois Burgundy*, London 1975 (chapter on military power, 123–61).

Italy

486. Bautier, R. H., Soudoyers d'outremont à Plaisance. Leur origine géographique et le mecanisme de leurs emprunts (1293–1330), in *Guerre et Paix*, 95–129.

487. Bayley, C. C., *War and Society in Renaissance Florence. The 'De Militia' of Leonardo Bruni*, Toronto 1961.

488. Becker, M. B., Changing patterns of violence and justice in fourteenth- and fifteenth-century Florence, *Comparative Studies in Society and History*, *18*(1976),281–96.

489. Belotti, B., *Vita di Bartolomeo Colleoni*, Bergamo 2nd edn 1933.

490. Belotti, B., *Studi Colleoneschi*, Milan 1939.

491.   Block, W., *Die Condottieri. Studien über die sogennanten 'unblutige Schlachten'*, Berlin 1913.

492.   Bowsky, W. M., City and contado. Military relationships and communal bonds in fourteenth century Siena, in *Renaissance Studies in Honor of Hans Baron*, ed. A. Molho and J. A. Tedeschi, Dekalb, Ill. 1971, 75–98.

492a.   Bowsky, W. M., *A Medieval Italian Commune. Siena under the Nine, 1287–1355*, Berkeley, Los Angeles and London 1981 (chapter IV, The Commune uses force, 117–58).

493.   Bueno de Mesquita, D. M., Some condottieri of the Trecento, *Proceedings of the British Academy, 32*(1946),219–41.

494.   Cansacchi, C., Connestabili ed uomini d'armi della S. Sede nella seconda metà del secolo XV, *Rivista del Collegio Araldico* (1943),5–10, 57–62, 96–105.

495.   Cecchi, D., Compagnie di Ventura nella Marca, *Studi Maceratesi, 9*(1975),64–136.

496.   *Compagnie (Le) di Ventura. Catalogo della mostra di arti figurative e armi*, Narni 1970.

497.   Croce, B., *Un condottiere italiano del Quattrocento: Cola di Monforte, conte di Campobasso*, Bari 1936.

498.   Da Mosto, A., *Ordinamenti militari della soldatesche dello Stato Romano dal 1430 al 1470*, Rome 1903.

499.   Del Treppo, M., Gli aspetti organizzativi, economici e sociali di una compagnia di ventura, *RSI, 85*(1973),253–75.

500.   Fasoli, G., *Le compagnie delle armi a Bologna*, Bologna 1934.

501.   Föhl, W., Niederrheinische Ritterschaft im Italien des Trecento, *Annalen des historischen Vereins für den Niederrhein, 165*(1963),73–128.

502.   Franceschini, G., Boldrino da Panicale. Contributo alla storia delle milizie mercenarie italiane, *Bollettino della deputazione di Storia patria dell'Umbria, 46*(1949),118–39.

503.   Franceschini, G., *I Montefeltro*, Milan 1970.

504.   Gallinoni, G., Di un trattato militare inedito del secolo XV, *RSI, 40*(1938),87–90.

505.   Gaupp. F., The condottiere John Hawkwood, *Hist., 23*(1938–39), 305–21.

506.   Gentile, P., Lo Stato Napoletano sotto Alfonso I d'Aragona, *Archivio Storico per le Provincie napoletane, 62–3*(1937–38).

507.   Goldbrunner, H. M., Leonardo Brunis *De Militia*. Bemerkungen zur handschriftlichen Überlieferung, *Quellen und Forschungen aus italienischen Archiven und Bibliotheken, herausgegeben vom Deutschen Historischen Institut im Rom, 46*(1963),478–87.

508.   Gualdo, G., I Libri delle Spese di guerra del Cardinal Albornoz in Italia conservati nell'Archivio Vaticano, in *El Cardenal Albornoz y el Collegio de España*, ed. E. Verdera y Tuello, Bologna 1972, i.577–607.

509.   Hale, J. R., War and public opinion in Renaissance Italy, in *Italian Renaissance Studies*, ed. E. F. Jacob, London 1960, 94–122.

510.   Labande, E. R., *Rinaldo Orsini, comte de Tagliacozzo*, Monaco and Paris 1939.

511.   La Sizeranne, R. de, *Le vertueux condottière Federigo de Montefeltro, duc d'Urbino, 1422–1482*, Paris 1927.

512.   Mallett, M., *Mercenaries and their Masters. Warfare in Renaissance Italy*, London 1974 (full critical bibliography, 261–74).

513.   Mallett, M., Venice and its condottieri, 1404–54, in *Renaissance Venice*, ed. J. R. Hale, London 1973, 121–45.

514.   Mirot, L., *Sylvestre Budes (13??–1380) et les Bretons en Italie*, Paris 1898.

515.   Niese, H., Zur Geschichte des deutschen Soldrittertums in Italien, *Quellen und Forschungen aus italienischen Archiven und Bibliotheken*, 8(1905), 217–48.

515a.   Pacella, F., Un barone condottiero della Calabria del sec. XIV–XV: Nicolò Ruffo marchese di Cotrone, conte di Catanzero, *Archivio Storico per le Provincie napoletane*, 82(1964),45–93.

516.   Pieri, P., Milizie e capitani di ventura in Italia nel Medio Evo, *Atti della Reale Accademia Peloritana di Messina*, 40(1937–38).

517.   Pieri, P., Le milizie svizzere nel tardo Medioevo e nel Rinascimento in Italia, *Annali della Facoltà di Magistero della Reale Università di Messina*, 17(1939).

518.   Pieri, P., *Il Rinascimento e la crisi militare italiana*, Milan 1952.

519.   Ricotti, E., *Storia delle compagnie di ventura in Italia*, Turin 2nd edn 2 vols. 1893.

520.   Schäfer, K. H., Deutsche Ritter und Edelknechte in Italien während des XIV. Jahrhunderts, in *Quellen und Forschungen aus dem Gebiet der Geschichte*, Paderborn, 15(1911), 16(1914) and 25(1940).

521.   Secco D'Arragona, F., Un giornale della guerra di Ferrara (1482–84), nelle lettere di un condottiero milanese-mantovano, *Archivio Storico Lombardo*, 84(1957),317–45.

522.   Simeoni, L., Note sulle cause e i danni del mercenarismo militare italiano del 1300, *Atti e Memorie della Reale Accademia di Modena*, 1937.

523.   Taylor, F. L., *The Art of War in Italy, 1494–1529*, Cambridge 1921.

524.   Trease, G., *The Condottieri, Soldiers of Fortune*, London 1970.

525.   Ugurgieri Della Berardenga, C., *Avventuriei alla conquista di feudi e di corone, 1356–1429*, Florence 1962.

526.   Valeri, N., *La vita di Facino Cane*, Turin 1940.

527.   Zorzi, C., Un Vicentino alla Corte di Paolo II: Chierighino Chiericati e il suo trattatello della milizia, *Nuovo Archivio Veneto*, new ser., 30(1915),369–434.

The Iberian world

528.   Burns, R. I., The Catalan Company and the European Powers, *Spec.*, 29(1954),751–71.

529.   Carrère, C., Aux origines des grandes compaignies: la compaignie catalane de 1302, in *Recrutement, mentalités, sociétés. Colloque international d'histoire militaire. Université Paul-Valéry de Montpellier, septembre 1974*, 1–7.

530.   Fernandez, E. M., La frontière de Grenade aux environs de 1400, *MA*, 78(1972),489–522.

531.   Ferrer I Mallol, M. T., Mercenaris catalans a Ferrera (1307–17), *AEM*, 2(1965),155–227.

532.   Ladero Quesada, M. A., *Castilla y la conquista del reino de Granada*, Valladolid 1967.

532a.   Quatrefages, R., A la naissance de l'armée moderne, *Mélanges de la Casa de Velasquez*, 13(1977), 119–59.

533.   Riquer, M. de, *Caballeros andantes españoles*, Madrid 1967.

534.   Riquer, M. de, *Cavalleria fra realtà e letteratura nel Quattrocento*, Bari 1970.

535. Riquer, M. de, *Vida caballeresca en la España del siglo XV*, Madrid 1965.

535a. Ruano, E. B., La participacion extranjera en la guerra de Granada, *Revista de Archivos, bibliotecas y Museos*, 80(1977),679–701.

536. Rubio I Lluch, A., La companya catalana sota el comandament de Teobald de Cepoy (1307–1310), *Miscellania E. Prat de la Riba*, Barcelona, 2 vols. 1923, i.219–70.

537. Sablonier, R., *Krieg und Kriegertum in der Crónica des Ramon Muntaner. Eine Studie zum spätmittelalterlichen Kriegswesen aufgrund katalanischer Quellen*, Berne and Frankfurt-am-Main 1971.

538. Stewart, P., The Santa Hermandad and the first campaign of Gonzalo de Cordoba, 1495–1498, *Renaissance Quarterly*, 28(1975),29–37.

539. Stewart, P., The soldier, the bureaucrat and fiscal records in the army of Ferdinand and Isabella, *Hispanic American Historical Review*, 49(1969).

4 ARMS, ARMOUR AND WAR ENGINES

Sources

540. *Art (L') d'Archerie*, ed. H. Gallice, Paris 1901.

541. Belleval, R. de, *Du costume militaire des Français en 1446*, Paris 1866.

542. Giraud, J. B., *Documents pour servir à l'histoire de l'armament au Moyen Age et à la Renaissance*, Lyon 2 vols. 1895–1904.

542a. Hall, B. S., *The So-Called 'Manuscript of the Hussite War' and its Technological Milieu. A study and edition of Codex lat. Monacensis 197*, Ann Arbor 1971.

543. Kyeser, Conrad (aus Eichstätt), *Bellisfortis*, ed. G. Quarg, Düsseldorf 2 vols. 1967.

544. Nickel, H., *Ullstein Waffenbuch*, Berlin 1974.

545. Taccola, Mariano, *De Machinis*, I. *The Engineering Treatise of 1449, introduction, Latin texts, descriptions of engines and technical commentaries*, ed. G. Scaglia; II. *Facsimile of Codex latinus Monacensis 28800 of the Bayerische Staatsbibliothek of Munich*, Wiesbaden 1971.

Catalogues, inventories and lists

546. Angelucci, A., *Catalogo della armeria reale*, Turin 1890.

547. Blackmore, H. L., *The Armouries of the Tower of London, I, Ordnance*, London 1976.

548. Boccia, L. G., *Il Museo Stibbert a Firenze, III, L'armeria europea*, Milan 2 vols. 1975.

549. Clayton, M., *Victoria and Albert Museum, London. Catalogue of Rubbings of Brasses and Incised Slabs*, London 2nd edn 1968.

550. Cortes, J., *Real Armeria de Madrid. Guida turistica*, Madrid 1963.

551. Deuchler, F., *Die Burgunderbeute. Inventar der Beutestücke aus den Schlachten von Grandson, Murten und Nancy, 1476–1477*, Berne 1963.

551a. Dufty, A. R., *European Armour in the Tower of London*, London 1968.

551b. Dufty, A. R., *European Swords and Daggers in the Tower of London*, London 1974.

551c. Ffoulkes, C. J., *Inventory and Survey of the Armouries of the Tower of London*, London 2 vols. 1916.

552. Gaier-Lhoest, C. and J., *Catalogue des armes du musée Curtius (Ier–XIXe siècle)*, Liège 1963.

553. Gamber, O., *Glossarium armorum*, in course of publication from 1972.

554. Gay, V. and Stein, H., *Glossaire archéologique du Moyen Age et de la Renaissance*, Paris 2 vols. 1887–1928.

555. Grosz, A. and Thomas, B., *Katalog der Waffensammlung der Neuen Burg*, Vienna 1936.

556. Haenel, E. A., *Kostbare Waffen aus der Dresdner Rüstkammer*, Leipzig 1923.

557. Macoir, G., *Le Musée royal d'armes et d'armures de la Porte de Hal à Bruxelles*, Brussels 1928.

558. Macoir, G., *La salle des armures du Musée de la Porte de Hal à Bruxelles*, Brussels 1910.

559. Maglioli, V., *Armeria reale di Torino*, Turin 1959.

560. Mann, J. G., *Catalogue of European Arms and Armour in the Wallace Collection*, London 2 vols. 1962.

561. *Mostra di armi antiche (sec. XIV–XV)*, Poppi 1967.

562. Niox, G. L., *Le Musée de l'Armée. Armes et armures anciennes et souvenirs historiques les plus précieux*, Paris 2 vols. 1917.

563. Robert, L., *Catalogue des collections composant le Musée d'artillerie en 1889*, Paris 4 vols. 1889–93.

563a. Thomas, B. and Gamber, O., *Kunsthistorisches Museum Wien. Waffensammlung: Katalog der Leibrüstkammer, I. Der Zeitraum von 500 bis 1530*, Vienna 1976.

564. Trapp, O. R., *The Armoury of the Castle of Churburg*, London 1929.

565. Valencia de Don Juan, Juan Crooke y Navarrot, count of, *Catalogo historico descriptivo de la Real Armeria de Madrid*, Madrid 1898.

565a. Wegeli, R., *Inventar der Waffensammlung der bernischen historischen Museums in Bern*, Bern 4 vols. 1920–48.

General studies

566. Aroldi, A. M., *Armi e armature italiane fino al XVIII secolo*, Milan 1961.

567. Ashdown, C. H., *Armour and Weapons in the Middle Ages*, London 1925.

568. Blackmore, H. L., *Hunting Weapons*, London 1971.

569. Blair, C., *European and American Arms, c.1100–1850*, London 1962.

570. Blair, C., *European Armour, c.1066 to c.1700*, London 1958.

571. Boccia, L. G. and Coelho, E. T., *L'arte dell'armature italiana*, Milan 1967.

571a. Brewer, D., The arming of the warrior in European literature and Chaucer, *Comparative Literature*, 32 (1980),113–29.

571b. Brooks, N. P., Arms, status and warfare in late-Saxon England, *British Archaeological Reports*, 59(1978),81–103.

572. Bruhn Hoffmeyer, A., Arms and armour in Spain. A short survey. I. From the Bronze Age to the end of the High Middle Ages, *Gl.*, 7(1971),7–199.

573. Bruhn Hoffmeyer, A., *Middelalderens Tveagge de Svaerd*, Copenhagen 2 vols. 1954.

574. Buttin, F., *Du costume militaire au Moyen Age et pendant la Renaissance*, Barcelona 1971.

575. Canestrini, G., *Arte militare meccanica medievale*, Milan 1946.

576. Enlart, C., *Manuel d'archéologie française depuis les temps carolingiens jusqu'à la Renaissance, III. Le costume*, Paris 3rd edn 1932.

577. Ffoulkes, C. J., *Armour and Weapons*, Oxford 1909.
578. Ffoulkes, C. J., *The Armourer and his Craft from the XIth to XVIth Century*, London 1912.
579. Gaier, C., *L'industrie et le commerce des armes dans les principautés belges du XIIIe à la fin du XVe siècle*, Paris 1973.
579a. Gaier, C., *Les armes*, Turnhout 1979 (Typologie des sources du Moyen Age occidental, 10).
580. Gessler, E. A., *Die Entwicklung des Geschützwesen in der Schweiz*, Zurich 1918.
581. Hardy, R., *Longbow. A Social and Military History*, London 1976.
582. Laking, G. F., *A Record of European Armour and Arms through Seven Centuries*, London 5 vols. 1920–2.
583. Malatesta, E., *Armi e armaiolo*, Rome 1930.
584. Mann, J. G., Arms and armour, in *Medieval England*, ed. A. L. Poole, Oxford 1958, i.314–37.
585. Mann, J. G., *An Outline of Arms and Armour in England*, London 1960.
586. Martin, P., *Waffen und Rüstungen von Karl dem Grossen bis zu Ludwig XIV.*, Frankfurt-am-Main 1967 (French tr.: *Armes et armures de Charlemagne à Louis XIV*, Fribourg 1967).
587. Müller, H., *Historische Waffen. Kurze Entwicklungsgeschichte der Waffen von Frühfeudalismus bis zum 17. Jahrhundert*, Berlin 1957.
587a. Norman, V., *Arms and Armour*, London 1972.
588. Oakeshott, R. E., *The Archaeology of Weapons. Arms and Armour from Prehistory to the Age of Chivalry*, London 1960.
589. Oakeshott, R. E., *A Knight and his Armour*, London 1961.
590. Oakeshott, R. E., *A Knight and his Weapons*, London 1964.
591. Payne-Gallwey, R., *The Crossbow, Mediaeval and Modern, Military and Sporting. Its construction, history and management, with a Treatise on the Balista and Catapult of the Ancients*, London 1903 (repr. 1958: German tr.: *Die Armbrust*, tr. E. Harmuth, Graz 1963).
592. Pope, S. T., *Bows and Arrows*, Berkeley and Los Angeles 1962.
593. Poschenburg, V., *Die Schutz- und Trutzwaffen des Mittelalters*, Vienna 1938.
594. Post, P., *Kriegs-, Turnier- und Jagdwaffen vom frühen Mittelalter bis zum Dreissig-jährigen Krieg. Ein Handbuch dër Waffenkunde*, Berlin 3rd edn 1929.
595. Rathgen, B., *Das Geschutz im Mittelalter. Quellenkritische Untersuchungen*, Berlin 1929.
596. Riquer, M. de, *L'arnès del cavaller. Armes i armadures catalanes medievales*, Barcelona 1968.
597. Seitz, H., *Blankwaffen, i. Geschichte und Typenentwicklung im europäischen Kulturbereich von der prähistorischen Zeit bis zum Ende des 16. Jahrhunderts*, Brunswick 1965.

Particular studies

598. Beaulieu, M. and Baylé, J., *Le costume en Bourgogne de Philippe le Hardi à la mort de Charles le Téméraire (1364–1477)*, Paris 1956.
599. Berthelot, M., Histoire des machines de guerre et des arts mécaniques vers la fin du Moyen Age. Le livre d'un ingenieur de la fin du XIVe siècle, *Annales de Chimie et de Physique*, 7e sér., *19*(1900),289–420.

600. Berthelot, M., Pour l'histoire de l'artillerie et des arts mécaniques vers la fin du Moyen Age, *ibid.*, 6e sér., *24*(1891),433–521.

601. Brandt, A. von, 'Schwerter aus Lübeck'. Ein handelsgeschichtliches Rätsel aus der Frühzeit des hansisches Frankreichshandels, *Hansische Geschichtsblätter*, *83*(1965),1–11.

602. Bruhn Hoffmeyer, A., From mediaeval sword to Renaissance rapier, *Gl.*, *3*(1963),5–68.

603. Bruhn Hoffmeyer, A., Introduction to the History of the European Sword, *Gl.*, *1*(1961),30–75.

604. Buttin, C., *Les bardes articulées au temps de Maximilien Ier. Etude sur l'armament chevaleresque, XVe-XVIe siècles*, Strasbourg 1930.

605. Buttin, F., La lance et l'arrêt de cuirasse, *Archaeologia*, *99*(1965),77–178.

605a. Cirlot, M. V., La evolucion de la espada en la sociedad catalana de los siglos XI al XIII, *Gl.*, *14*(1978),9–58.

606. Clark, G., Beowulf's armor, *Journal of English Literature History*, *32*(1965),409–41.

607. Cripps-Day, F.H., *On Armour preserved in Churches, with a General Bibliography*, London 1922.

608. Davidson, H. R. Ellis, *The Sword in Anglo-Saxon England. Its Archaeology and Literature*, Oxford 1962.

609. De Poerck, G., L'artillerie à ressorts médiévale. Notes lexicologiques et étymologiques, *Bulletin Du Cange*, *18*(1943–44),35–49.

610. Ffoulkes, C. J., Some aspects of the craft of armourer, *Archaeologia*, *79*(1929),13–28.

611. Finó, J. F., Le feu et ses usages militaires, *Gl.*, *8*(1970),15–30.

612. Finó, J. F., Machines et jet médiévales, *ibid.*, *10*(1972),25–43.

613. Finó, J. F., Notes sur la production du fer et la fabrication des armes en France au Moyen Age, *ibid.*, *3*(1963–64),47–66.

614. Finó, J. F., Origine et puissance des machines à balancier médiévales, *Société des antiquités nationales*, nouvelle sér., *11*.

615. Flutre, L. F., Une arbaleste fait de cor, *Romania*, *95*(1974),309–16.

616. Fossati, F., Per il commercio delle armature e i missaglia, *Archivio Storico Lombardo*, *59*(1932),279–97.

617. France-Lanord, A., La fabrication des épées mérovingiennes et carolingiennes, *Revue de Métallurgie*, *49*(1952),411–22.

618. Friesinger, H., Waffenkunde des 9. und 10. Jahrhunderts aus Niederösterreich, *Archaeologia austriaca*, *52*(1972),43–64.

619. Gaibi, A., L'arte bresciana delle armature, *Armi antiche* (1963),15–50.

620. Gaier, C., L'évolution et l'usage de l'armament personnel défensif au pays de Liège du XIIe au XVe siècle, *Zeitschrift der Gesellschaft für historische Waffen- und Kostümkunde*, *4*(1962),65–86.

621. Gaier, C., Le problème de l'origine de l'industrie armurière liégeoise au Moyen Age, *Chronique archéologique du Pays de Liège* (1962),22–75.

621a. Gaier, C., L'invincibilité anglaise et le grand arc après la guerre de Cent ans: un mythe tenace, *Tijdschrift voor Geschiedenis*, *91*(1978),379–85.

622. Gamber, O., Orientalische Einflüsse auf die mittelalterliche Bewaffnung Europas, *Kwartalnik historii Kultury materialnej*, *21*(1973), 273–9.

623. Gamber, O., Wikingerbewaffnung und spätrömische Waffen Tradition,

in *I Normanni e la loro espansione in Europa nell'alto Medioevo*, Spoleto 1969, 767–82.

624. Ganshof, F. L., Armatura (Galbert de Bruges, ch.106, éd. Pirenne, p.152), *Archivum latinitatis Medii Aevi*, *16*(1940),179–94.

625. Genevoy, R., Notes sur l'armurerie impériale d'Arbois (1495–1509?) et sur les armures de Claude de Vaudrey et de Maximilien Ier au Kunst historisches Museum de Vienne, *Nouvelle revue franc-comtoise* (1955),208–22.

626. Gessler, A. E., *Bewaffnung, Wehr- und Befestigungswesen zur Zeit der Schlacht bei St. Jakob an der Birs*, Basel 1944.

627. Giese, W., Portugiesische Waffenterminologie des XIII. Jahrhunderts, in *Miscelânea de Estudos en Honra de D. Carolina Michaelis de Vasconcellos*, Coimbra 1930.

628. Geise, W., Waffengeschichtliche und terminologische Aufschlüsse aus katalanischen literarischen Denkmälern des 14. und 15. Jahrhunderts, in *Homenatge a Antoni Rubio i Lluch*, Barcelona, 2 vols. 1936, i.33–67.

629. Geise, W., Waffen nach den katalanischen Chroniken des XIII. Jahrhunderts, *Volksturm und Kultur der Romanen*, *1*(1928),140–82.

630. Geise, W., Waffen nach den provenzalischen Epen und Chroniken des XII. und XIII. Jahrhunderts. Beiträge zur Geschichte der Bewaffnung Südfrankreichs im Mittelalter, *Zeitschrift für romanische Philologie*, *52*(1932),351–405.

631. Geise, W., *Waffen nach der spanischen Literatur des 12. und 13. Jahrhunderts*, Hamburg 1925.

632. Gille, B., Etudes sur les manuscrits d'ingénieurs du XVe siècle, *Techniques et civilisations*, *5*(1956),77–86, 216–23.

633. Gille, B., *Les ingénieurs de la Renaissance*, Paris 1964 (Eng. tr.: *The Renaissance Engineers*, London 1966).

634. Hampe, T., Waffengeschichtliches aus einem Nürnberger Haus- und Rechnungsbuch des 15. Jahrhunderts, *Zeitschrift für historische Waffen- und Kostümkunde*, new ser., *2*(1927),117–82.

635. Heer, E., Armes et armures au temps des guerres de Bourgogne, in *Grandson 1476*, ed. D. Reichel, Lausanne 1976, 170–200.

636. Hejdova, D., Der sogenannte St. Wenzels-Helm, *Waffen- und Kostümkunde* (1966),95–110; (1967),28–54, and (1968),15–30.

637. Herben, S. J., jr, Arms and armor in Chaucer, *Spec.*, *12*(1937),475–87.

638. Hill, D. R., Trebuchets, *Viator*, *4*(1973),99–114.

639. Hummelberger, W., Die Ordnungen der Weiner Plattner und Sarwürcher, *Zeitschrift für historisches Waffenkunde* (1961),91–107.

640. Knudson, C. A., La brogne, in *Mélanges offerts à Rita Lejeune*, Gembloux, 2 vols. 1969, ii.1625–35.

641. Larson, H. M., The armor business in the Middle Ages, *Business History Review*, *14*(1940),49–64.

641a. Legge, D. M., 'Osbercs dublez'. The description of armour in 12th century Chansons de geste, in *Société Rencesvals. Proceedings of the fifth international conference*, Oxford 1970, 132–42.

642. McGuffie, T. H., The long bow as a decisive weapon, *History Today*, *5*(1955),737–41.

643. Mann, J. G., A further account of the armour preserved in the sanctuary of the Madonna delle Grazie, *Archaeologia*, *87*(1937),311–52.

644.   Mann, J. G., Notes on the armour worn in Spain from the Tenth to the Fifteenth Centuries, *Archaeologia*, *83*(1933),285–305.

645.   Mann, J. G., Notes on the evolution of plate armour in Germany in the fourteenth and fifteenth centuries, *Archaeologia*, *84*(1934),69–97.

646.   Mas-Latrie, L. de, Note des armes existant à l'arsenal de Venise en 1314, *BEC*, *25*(1865),562–6.

647.   Monreal Y Tejada, L., *Ingenieria militar en las cronicas catalanas*, Barcelona 1971.

648.   Mot, G. J., L'arsenal et le parc de matériel à la cité de Carcassonne en 1298, *Annales du Midi*, *68*(1956),409–18.

649.   Motta, A., Armaiuoli milanesi nel periodo Visconteo-Sforzesco, *Archivio Storico Lombardo*, *41*(1914),187–232.

650.   Neukam, W. G., Eine Nürnbergersulzbacher Plattenlieferung für Karl IV. in den Jahren 1362–1363. Ein Beitrag zur Nürnberger Waffenfabrikation des 14. Jahrhunderts, *Mitteilungen des Vereins für Geschichte der Stadt Nürnberg*, *47*(1956),124–59.

651.   Nickel, H., *Der mittelalterliche Reiterschild der Abendlandes*, Berlin 1958.

652.   Novak, R., Die französischen Waffennamen. Eine Auswahl, *Zeitschrift für historische Waffenkunde* (1970),68–74.

653.   Oakeshott, R. E., *The Sword in the Age of Chivalry*, London 1964.

654.   Pansieri, C., Ricerche metallografiche sopra una spada da guerra del XII° secolo, *Associazione italiana di metallurgia, Documenti e contributi*, Milan 1957, 7–40.

655.   Post, P., *Das Kostüm und die ritterliche Kriegstracht in deutschen Mittelalter von 1000–1450*, Berlin 1939.

656.   Reid, W. and Burgess, M. E., A habergeon of Westwale, *Antiquaries Journal*, *40*(1960),46–57.

657.   Reitzenstein, A. von, Über die Anfänge des Waffensammelns, *Zeitschrift für Waffenkunde* (1969,69–75.

658.   Reitzenstein, A. von, Die Landshuter Plattner, ihre Ordnung und ihre Meister, *ibid*. (1969),20–32.

659.   Reitzenstein, A. von, Die Ordnung der Ausberger Plattner, *ibid*. (1960),96–100.

660.   Reitzenstein, A. von, Die Ordnung der Nürnberger Plattner, *ibid*. (1959), 54–85.

661.   Reitzenstein, A. von, Der Ritter im Heergewäte. Bemerkungen über einige Bildgrabsteine der Hochgotik, in *Studien zur Geschichte der europäischer Plastik. Festschrift Theodor Müller*, Munich 1965, 73–91.

661a.   Reverseau, J. P., L'habit de guerre des Français. Le ms. anonyme fr.1997 de la Bibliothèque nationale, *Gazette des Beaux-Arts*, *93*(1979),179–98.

661b.   Riquer, M. de, El haubert francés y la loriga castellana, in *Mélanges de philologie et de litérature romanes offerts à Jeanne Wathelet-Willem*, ed. J. de Caluwe and H. Sépulchre, Liège 1978, 545–68.

662.   Ross, D. J. A., L'originalité de 'Turoldus': le maniement de la lance, *Cahiers de civilisation médiévale*, *6*(1963),127–38.

662a.   Rossi, F., *Armi e armaioli bresciana del 1400*, Brescia 1971.

663.   Salin, E., *La civilisation mérovingienne d'après les sépultures, les textes et le laboratoire*, Paris 4 vols. 1949–59.

664.   Salin, E. and France-Lanord, A., *Le fer à l'époque mérovingienne. Etude technique et archéologique*, Paris 1943.

664a. Scalini, M., Note sulla formazione dell'armatura di piastra italiana 1380–1420, *Waffen- und Kostümkunde*, *22*(1980),15–25.

665. Scheibe, E., *Studien zur Nürnberger Waffenindustrie von 1450–1550*, Bonn 1908.

666. Schwietering, J., Zur Geschichte von Speer und Schwert im 12. Jahrhundert, in *Philologische Schriften*, ed. F. Ohly and M. Wehrli, Munich 1969, 59–117.

667. Siebel, G., *Harnisch und Helm in der epischen Dichtungen des 12. Jahrhunderts bis zu Hartemanns 'Erek'*, Hamburg 1968.

668. Sprandel, R., *Das Eisengewerbe im Mittelalter*, Stuttgart 1968.

669. Steuer, H., Historische Phasen der Bewaffnung nach Aussagen der archäologischen Quellen Mittel- und Nordeuropas im ersten Jahrtausend n. Chr., *Frühmittelalterliche Studien*, Münster, *4*(1970),348–83.

670. Stotten, P., Wandlungen des Gebrauchs der Kriegswaffen im Mittelalter, in *Die Entwicklung der Kriegswaffe und ihre Zusammenhang mit der Sozialordnung*, ed. L. von Wiese, Cologne 1953, 118–33.

671. Tackenberg, K., Über die Schutzwaffen der Karolingerzeit und ihre Wiedergabe in Handschriften und auf Elfenbeinschnitzereien, *Frühmittelalterliche Studien*, Münster, *3*(1969),277–88.

672. Thomas, B. and Gamber, O., L'arte milanese dell'armatura, in *Storia di Milano*, Milan, 16 vols. 1958, xi.697–841.

673. Thomas, B. and Gamber, O., *Die Innsbrücker Plattnerkunst*, Innsbruck 1954.

674. Thompson, E. A., *A Roman Reformer and Inventor, being a New Text of the Treatise* De rebus bellicis, *with a Translation and Introduction*, Oxford 1952.

675. Thordemann, B., *Armour from the Battle of Wisby, 1361*, Stockholm 2 vols. 1939.

676a. Wathelet-Willem, J., L'épée dans les plus anciennes chansons de geste. Etude de vocabulaire, in *Mélanges offerts à René Crozet*, ed. P. Gallais and Y-J. Riou, Poitiers 2 vols. 1966, i.435–49.

676. White, L., The crusades and technological thrust of the West, in *War, Technology and Society in the Middle East*, ed. V. J. Parry and M. E. Yapp, London 1975, 97–112.

677. White, L., *Medieval Technology and Social Change*, Oxford 1962 (French tr.: *Technologie médiévale et transformations sociales*, Paris and The Hague 1969).

677a. Williams, M. R., Methods of manufacture of swords in medieval Europe illustrated by the metallography of some examples, *Gl.*, *13*(1977),75–101.

5 CANNONS AND GUNPOWDER ARTILLERY

677b. Allmand, C. T., L'artillerie de l'armée anglaise et son organisation à l'epoque de Jeanne d'Arc, in *Jeanne d'Arc, une époque, un rayonnment*, ed. J. Glénisson, Paris 1982, 73–83.

678. Angelucci, A., *Documenti inediti per la storia delle armi da fuoco italiane*, Turin 1869.

679. Bonaparte, L. N. and Favé, I., *Etudes sur le passé et l'avenir de l'artillerie*, Paris 6 vols. 1846–71.

680. Contamine, P., L'artillerie royale française à la veille des guerres d'Italie, *Annales de Bretagne*, *71*(1964),221–61.

681. Delmaire, B., L'artillerie d'Aire au XVe siècle, *Bulletin trimestriel de la Société académique des Antiquaires de la Morinie* (*Saint-Omer*), *22*(1973),97–113.

682. Dubled, H., L'artillerie royale française à l'époque de Charles VII et au début du règne de Louis XI (1437–69); les frères Bureau, *Mémorial de l'Artillerie française*, 50(1976),555–637.

683. Essenwein, A. von, *Quellen zur Geschichte der Feuerwaffen*, Leipzig 1872.

684. Ffoulkes, C. J., *Gun Founders of England*, Cambridge 1937.

685. Finó, J. F., L'artillerie en France à la fin du Moyen Age, *Gl.*, 12(1974),13–31.

686. Fischler, G., Über Pulverprober Früherer Zeiten, *Zeitschrift für Waffenkunde*, (1926),49–57.

687. Forestié, E., Hugues de Cardaillac et la poudre à canon, *Bulletin archéologique de la Société archéologique du Tarn-et-Garonne*, 29(1901),93–132, 185–222 and 297–312.

688. Garnier, J., *L'artillerie des ducs de Bourgogne d'après les documents des Archives de la Côte-d'Or*, Paris 1895.

689. Hale, J. R., Gunpowder and the Renaissance: an Essay in the History of Ideas, in *From the Renaissance to the Counter-Reformation. Essays in honor of Garrett Mattingly*, ed. C. H. Carter, New York 1965, 113–44.

690. Hassenstein, W., *Das Feuerbuch von 1420*, Munich 1941.

691. Hayward, J. F., *The Art of the Gunmaker*, London 2 vols. 1962.

692. Hime, H. W. L., *The Origin of Artillery*, London 1915.

693. Martin, P., L'artillerie et la fonderie à canon de Strasbourg du XIVe au XVIIIe siècle, *Armi antiche* (1967),71–90.

694. Mercier, M., *Le feu grégeois, les feux de guerre depuis l'Antiquité, la poudre à canon*, Paris 1952.

695. Montu, C., *Storia dell'artigliera italiana*, Rome 1934.

696. Müller, H., *Deutsche Bronzegeschützrohre 1400–1750*, Berlin 1968.

697. Natale, A. R., I diari di Cicco Simonetta, *Archivio Storico Lombardo*, 84(1957),285–6.

698. Partington, J. R., *A History of Greek Fire and Gunpowder*, Cambridge 1960.

699. Pasquali-Lasagni, A. and Stefanelli, E., Note di storia dell'artigliera nei secoli XIV e XV, *Archivio della Reale Deputazione Romana di Storia Patria*, 60(1937),149–89.

700. Perroy, E., L'artillerie de Louis XI dans la campagne d'Artois (1477), *Revue du Nord*, 26(1943),171–96, 263–96.

701. Roland, C., L'artillerie de la ville de Binche, 1362–1420, *Bulletin de la Société royale paléontologique et archéologique de l'arrondissement judiciaire de Charleroi* (1954),17–38.

702. Rothbert, H., Wann und wo ist die Pulverwaffe erfunden?, *Blätter für deutsche Landesgeschichte* (1952),84–6.

702a. Schmidtchen, V., *Bombarden, Befestigungen, Büchsenmeister, Von den Ersten Mauerbrechern des Spätmittelalters zur Belagerungsartillerie der Renaissance. Eine Studie zur Entwicklung der Militärtechnik*, Düsseldorf 1977.

703. Schmidtchen, V., *Die Feuerwaffen des deutschen Ritterordens bis zur Schlacht Tannenberg 1410. Beistände, Funktion und Kosten, dargestellt anhand der Wirtschaftsbücher des Ordens von 1374 bis 1410*, Luneburg 1977.

704. Schneider, R., *Die Artillerie des Mittelalters nach den Angaben der Zeitgenossen dargestellt*, Berlin 1910.

705. Schubert, H., The First Cast-Iron Cannon made in England, *Journal of the Iron and Steel Institute*, 146(1942),131–40.

706.   Tout, T. F., Firearms in England in the fourteenth century, in *Collected Papers of T. F. Tout*, Manchester, 3 vols. 1932–35, ii.233–75 (= *EHR, 26*(1911),666–702).

707.   T'Sas, F., *Dulle Griet. La grosse bombarde de Gand et ses soeurs, Armi antiche* (1969),13–57.

708.   Vale, M. G. A., New techniques and old ideals: the impact of artillery on war and chivalry at the end of the Hundred Years War, in *War, Literature and Politics*, 57–72.

709.   Volpicella, L., Le artiglierie di Castel Nuovo nell'anno 1500, *Archivio Storico per le Provincie Napoletane, 35*(1910),308–48.

710.   Wedler, R., Die Namen der Kanonen Maximilians I., *Beiträge zur Namenforschung*, new ser., *2*(1967),169–78.

711.   Willers, W., *Die Nürnberger Handfeuerwaffen bis zur Mitte des 16. Jahrhunderts*, Nuremberg 1973.

711a.   Williams, A. R., Some firing tests with simulated fifteenth-century handguns, *Journal of the Arms and Armour Society, 8*(1974),114–20.

6   CASTLES AND FORTIFICATIONS

In addition to numerous archeological journals, attention may be drawn to two important series: for France *Congrès archéologique de France* which since 1834 has published important monographs following the annual sessions (139ᵉ session, 1981, appeared in 1982); and more generally *Château-Gaillard. Etudes de castellologie européenne* (10 vols. since 1964).

General accounts (including studies dealing with several countries)

712.   Anderson, W., *Castles of the Middle Ages*, London 1970.

713.   Boüard, M. de, *Manuel d'archéologie médiévale, de la fouille à l'histoire*, Paris 1975.

714.   Bruhns, L., *Hohenstaufenschlösser in Deutschland und Italien*, Königstein in Taunus 1959.

715.   Chatelain, A., *Architecture militaire médiévale, principes élémentaires*, Paris 1970.

715a.   Coulson, C., Structural symbolism in medieval castle architecture, *Journal of the British Archaeological Association, 132*(1979),73–90.

716.   Ebhard, B., *Der Wehrbau Europas im Mittelalter. Versuch einer Gesamtdarstellung der europäischen Burgen*, Berlin 3 vols. 1939–58.

717.   Ebner, H., Die Burg in historiographischen Werken des Mittelalters, in *Festschrift Friedrich Hausmann*, ed. H. Ebner, Graz 1977, 119–51.

718.   Erb, H., Burgenliteratur und Burgenforschung, *Revue suisse d'histoire, 8*(1958),488–530.

719.   Fowler, K. A., Investment in urban defence: the frontier regions of France and England during the fourteenth century, in *Investimenti e civiltà, sec. XIII–XVIII* (9th Study Week of the Francesco Datini International Institute for Economic History), Prato 1977.

720.   Ganshof, F. L., *Etude sur le développement des villes entre Loire et Rhin au Moyen Age*, Paris and Brussels 1943.

721.   Héliot, P., L'évolution des donjons dans le nord-ouest de la France et de

l'Angleterre au XIIe siècle, *Bulletin archéologique du Comité des Travaux historiques et scientifiques*, nlle. sér., *5*(1969),141–94.

722. Héliot, P., La genèse des châteaux de plan quadrangulaire en France et en Angleterre, *Bulletin de la Société nationale des Antiquaires de France* (1965),238–57.

723. Héliot, P., Un organe peu connu de la fortification médiévale: la gaine, *Gl.*, *10*(1972),45–67.

724. Jäschke, K. U., *Burgenbau und Landesverteidigung um 900. Überlegungen zur Beispielen aus Deutschland, Frankreich und England*, Sigmaringen 1975.

725. Kiess, W., *Die Burgen in ihrer Funktion als Wohnbauten. Studien zum Wohnbauten in Deutschland, Frankreich, England, und Italien von 11. bis 15. Jahrhundert*, Munich 1961.

726. Ritter, R., *L'architec ture militaire médiévale*, Paris 1974.

726a. Taylor, A. J., Castle-building in thirteenth century Wales and Savoy, *Proceedings of the British Academy*, *63*(1977),265–92.

727. Toy, S., *A History of Fortification from 3000 B.C. to A.D. 1700*, New York 1955.

728. Verbruggen, J. F., Note sur le sens des mots *castrum, castellum* et quelques autres expressions qui désignent des fortifications, *Revue belge de philologie et d'histoire*, *28*(1950),147–55.

729. Warner, P., *The Medieval Castle. Life in a Fortress in Peace and War*, London 1971.

730. Warner, P., *Sieges of the Middle Ages*, London 1968.

The Empire and the Germanic world

731. Baravalle, R., *Burgen und Schlösser der Steiermark*, Graz 1961.

732. Binding, G., Spätkarolingisch-ottonische Pfalzen und Burgen am Niederrhein, *ChG*, v (1972),23–35.

733. Büttner, H., Zur Burgenbauordnung Heinrichs I., *Blätter für deutsche Landesgeschichte*, *92*(1956),1–17.

734. Collin, H., Etat des châteaux du comte de Bar en Lorraine en 1336, in *Guerre et Paix*, 155–77.

735. Dunan, M. F., Les châteaux forts du comté de Luxembourg et les progrès dans leur défense sous Jean l'Aveugle, 1309–1346, *Publications de la Section historique de l'Institut grand-ducal de Luxembourg*, *70*(1950),9–276.

736. Fischer, H., *Burgbezirk und Stadtgebiet in deutschen Süden*, Vienna and Munich 1956.

737. Genoux, A., *Les remparts de Fribourg au Moyen Age*, Fribourg (Confédération helvétique), 1960.

738. Grimm, P., *Der Vor- und Frühgeschichtlicher Burgwälle der Bezirke Halle und Magdeburg*, Berlin 1958.

739. Haase, C., Die mittelalterliche Stadt als Festung, in *Die Stadt des Mittelalters, I. Begriff, Entstehung und Ausbreitung*, ed. C. Haase, Darmstadt 1969, 377–407.

740. Hering, E., *Befestige Dörfer in südwestdeutschen Landschaften (mit besonderer Berücksichtigung des Rhein-Main Gebietes) und ihre Bedeutung für die Siedlungsgeographie*, Frankfurt-am-Main 1934.

741. Kiener, F., Le problème historique des châteaux forts en Alsace, *Revue d'Alsace*, *88*(1948),5–23.

742. Klebel, E., *Mittelalterliche Burgen und ihr Recht*, Vienna 1953.

743. Kunstmann, H., *Mensch und Burg. Burgenkundliche Betrachtungen an Ostfränkischen Wehrlangen*, Würzburg 1967.

744. Jankuhn, H., Ein Burgentyp der späten Wikingerzeit in Nord-friesland und sein historischer Hintergrund, *Zeitschrift der Gesellschaft für schleswig-holsteinische Geschichte*, *78*(1954),1–21.

745. Meyer, W., *Der mittelalterliche Adel und sein Burgen im ehemaliger Fürstbistum Basel*, Basel, 1962.

746. Mruzek, H. J., *Gesalt und Entwicklung der feudalen Eigenbefestigung im Mittelalter*, Berlin 1973.

747. Müller-Wille, M., *Mittelalterliches Burghügel ('Motten') in nördlichen Rheinland*, Cologne 1966.

748. Patze, II., cd., *Die Burgen im deutschen Sprachraum. Ihre Rechte- und Verfassungsgeschichtliche Bedeutung*, Sigmaringen 2 vols. 1976.

749. Rothe, H. W., *Burgen und Schlösser in Thüringen*, Frankfurt-am-Main 1960.

750. Salch, C. L., *Dictionnaire des châteaux de l'Alsace médiévale*, Strasbourg 1978.

751. Sayn-Wittgenstein, F., Prinz zu, *Reichsstädte*, Munich 1965.

752. Seberich, F., *Die Stadtbefestigung Würzburgs*, Würzburg 2 vols. 1962–3.

753. Sieber, H., *Schlösser und Herrensitze in Mecklemburg*, Frankfurt-am-Main 1960.

754. Tillmann, C., *Lexikon der deutschen Burgen und Schlösser*, Stuttgart 4 vols. 1958–61.

755. Waescher, H., *Feudalburgen in den Bezirken Halle und Magdeburg*, Berlin 2 vols. 1962.

756. Will, R., L'architecture des châteaux alsaciens du Moyen Age. Essai de classification, *Revue d'Alsace*, *100*(1961),110–19.

757. Willsdorf, C., L'apparition des châteaux alsaciens en Haute Alsace d'après les textes (1000–1200), *Actes du CIe Congrès national des Sociétés savantes, Lille 1976, Archéologie et histoire de l'art*, Paris 1978, 61–76.

758. Wirth, J., *Les châteaux forts alsaciens du XIIe au XIVe siècle. Etude architecturale, i. XIIe et première moitié du XIIIe siècle*, Strasbourg 1975.

759. Wuelfing, O. E., *Burgen der Hohenstaufen in der Pfalz und im Elsass*, Düsseldorf 1958.

760. Wuelfing, O. E., *Burgen der Hohenstaufen in Schwaben, Franken und Essen*, Düsseldorf 1960.

France and its sphere of influence

761. Aubenas, R., Les châteaux forts des Xe et XIe siècles, contribution à l'étude des origines de la féodalité, *RHDFE*(1938),548–86.

762. Bachrach, B. S., Early medieval fortification in the 'West' of France: a revised technical vocabulary, *Technology and Culture*, *16*(1975),531–69.

762a. Bachrach, B. S., Fortification and military tactics: Fulk Nerra's Strongholds *ca* 1000, *ibid.*, *20*(1979),531–49.

763. Barbier, P., *La France féodale. Introduction à l'étude de l'architecture militaire médiévale en France, I. Châteaux forts et églises fortifiées*, St Brieuc 1968.

764. Baylé, J., Mise en défense du château de Montaillou au début du XVe siècle, *BEC*, *129*(1971),113–19.

765. Bécet, M., Les fortifications de Chablis au XVe siècle (comment on fortifiait une petite village pendant la guerre de Cent ans), *Annales de Bourgogne*, *21*(1949),7–30.

766. Blondel, L., L'architecture militaire au temps de Pierre II de Savoie. Les donjons circulaires, *Genava*, *13*(1935),271–321.

767. Blondel, L., *Châteaux de l'ancien diocèse de Genève*, Geneva 1956.

768. Boüard, M. de, La motte, in *L'archéologie du village médiévale*, Louvain and Ghent 1967, 25–55.

769. Boüard, M. de, Quelques données archéologiques concernant le premier âge féodal, in *Les structures sociales de l'Aquitaine, du Languedoc et de l'Espagne au premier âge féodal*, Paris 1969, 40–51.

770. Bruand, Y., L'amélioration de la défense et les transformations des châteaux du Bourbonnais pendant la guerre de Cent ans, *AIBL*(1972),518–40.

771. Bruand, Y., La position stratégique des châteaux du Bourbonnais au Moyen Age, *BM*, *110*(1952),101–18.

772. Butler, R. M., Late Roman town Walls in Gaul, *Archaeological Journal*, *116*(1959),25–50.

773. Chapu, P. Les donjons rectangulaires du Berry, *ChG*, i (1964),39–51.

774. Chatelain, A., *Donjons romans des pays d'Ouest. Etude comparative sur les donjons romans quadrangulaires de la France de l'Ouest*, Paris 1973.

774a. Chatelain, A., *Châteaux et guerriers de la France au Moyen Age, II. Evolution architecturale et essai d'une typologie*, Strasbourg 1981.

775. Contamine, P., Les fortifications urbaines en France à la fin du Moyen Age : aspects financiers et économiques, *RH*, *260*(1978),23–47.

776. Coulson, C. L. H., Fortresses and social responsibility in late Carolingian France, *Zeitschrift für Archäologie des Mittelalters*, *4*(1976),9–36.

776a. Debord, A., *Castrum* et *castellum* chez Adémar de Chabannes, *Archéologie médiévale*, *9*(1979),97–113.

777. Deléage, A., Les forteresses de la Bourgogne franque, *Annales de Bourgogne*, *3*(1931),162–8.

778. Deprez, R., La politique castrale dans la principauté épiscopale de Liège du Xe au XIVe siècle, *MA*, *65*(1959),501–38.

779. Deshoulières, F., Les premiers donjons de pierre dans le département du Cher, *BM*, *106*(1948),49–61.

780. Deyres, M., Les châteaux de Foulques Nerra, *BM*, *132*(1974),7–28.

781. Enaud, F., *Les châteaux forts en France*, Paris 1958.

782. Enlart, C., *Manuel d'archéologie française, II. Architecture militaire*, Paris 1932.

783. Finó, J. F., *Forteresses de la France médiévale. Construction-Attaque-Défense*, Paris 3rd edn 1977 (with copious bibliography, including monographs on key works classified alphabetically, 489–529).

784. Fixot, M., *Les fortifications de terre et les origines féodales dans le Cinglais*, Caen 1968.

785. Fixot, M., La motte et l'habitat fortifié en Provence médiévale, *ChG*, vii (1975),67–93.

786. Fournier, G., Les campagnes de Pépin le Bref en Auvergne et la question des fortifications rurales au VIIIe siècle, *Francia*, *2*(1974),123–35, 910.

787. Fournier, G., Chartes de franchise et fortifications villageoises en basse Auvergne au XIIIe siècle, in *Les libertés urbaines et rurales du XIe au XIVe siècle*, *Actes du Colloque international de Spa, 1966*, Brussels : Pro Civitate, 1968, 223–44.

788. Fournier, G., *Le château dans la France médiévale. Essai de sociologie monumentale*, Paris 1978.

789. Fournier, G., Le château du Puiset au début du XIIe siècle et sa place dans l'évolution de l'architecture militaire, *BM*, *122*(1964),355–74.

790. Fournier, G., *Châteaux, villages et villes d'Auvergne au XVe d'après l'armorial de Guillaume Revel*, Geneva and Paris 1973.

791. Fournier, G., La défense des populations rurales pendant la guerre de Cent ans en basse Auvergne, *Actes du XCe Congrès national des Sociétés savantes, Nice 1965, Section d'archéologie*, Paris 1966, 157–99.

792. Fournier, G., Les enceintes de terre en Auvergne, *Bulletin historique et scientifique de l'Auvergne*, *81*(1961),89–110.

793. Fournier, G., Les forteresses rurales en France à l'époque carolingienne, *Actes du CIe Congrès national des Sociétés savantes, Lille 1976, Archéologie et histoire de l'art*, Paris 1978, 53–9.

794. Fournier, G., Vestiges de mottes castrales en basse Auvergne. Inventaire provisoire et essai de classement, *Revue d'Auvergne*, *75*(1962),137–76.

795. Gaier, C., La fonction stratégico-défensive du plat pays au Moyen Age dans la région de la Meuse moyenne, *MA*, *69*(1963),753–71.

796. Gardeau, L., Les châteaux des confins du Périgord et du Libournais au Moyen Age, *Bulletin philologique et historique (jusqu'à 1610) du Comité des Travaux historiques et scientifiques*, 1957, 407–22.

797. Gardelles, J., *Les châteaux du Moyen Age dans la France du Sud-Ouest. La Gascogne anglaise de 1216 à 1327*, Geneva and Paris 1972.

798. Gardelles, J., Du manoir au château fort en Gascogne anglaise au début de la guerre de Cent ans (1337–60), *Actes du CIe Congrès national des Sociétés savantes, Lille 1976*, Paris 1978, 119–29.

799. Genicot, L., ed., *Le grand livre des châteaux de Belgique, I. Châteaux forts et châteaux-fermes*, Brussels 1976.

800. Grand, R., L'architecture militaire en Bretagne jusqu'à Vauban, *BM*, *109*(1951),237–71 and 357–88, and *110*(1952),7–49.

800a. Gregg, E. M., Urban finance and defence spending at Nantes during the fifteenth century, Ph.D. thesis Yale 1977.

801. Héliot, P., Les châteaux forts en France du Xe au XIIe siècle à la lumière de travaux récents, *Journal des Savants* (1965),483–514.

802. Héliot, P., Le Château-Gaillard et les forteresses des XIIe et XIIIe siècles en Europe occidentale, *ChG*, i (1964),53–75.

803. Héliot, P., Sur les résidences princières bâties en France du Xe au XIIe siècle, *MA*, *61*(1955),27–61, 231–317.

804. Higounet, C., Bastiden und Grenzen, in *Altständisches Bürgertum*, ed. H. Stoob, Darmstadt, 2 vols. 1978, i.173–98.

805. Higounet, C., Esquisse d'une géographie des châteaux des Pyrénées françaises, in *I° Congreso internacional de Pirineistas del Instituto de Estudios Pirenaicos*, Saragossa 1950.

806. Hubert, J., Evolution de la topographie et de l'aspect des villes en Gaule du Ve au Xe siècle, in *La Città nell'alto Medioevo*, Spoleto (Settimane di Studio vi) 1959, 529–58 and 591–602.

807. Hubert, J., La frontière occidentale du comté de Champagne du XIe au XIIIe siècle, in *Recueil de travaux offerts à M. Clovis Brunel*, Paris, 2 vols. 1955, ii.14–29.

807a. Jones, M., The defence of medieval Brittany: a survey of the establishment of fortified towns, castles and frontiers from the Gallo-Roman period to the end of the Middle Ages, *Archaeological Journal*, *138*(1981),149–204.

808.   Lartigaut, J., Les lieux fortifiés dans la partie occidentale du Quercy au XVe siècle, *Annales du Midi*, *79*(1967),5–18.

808a.   Leguay, J. P., *Un réseau urbain au Moyen Age: les villes du duché de Bretagne aux XIVe et XVe siècles*, Paris 1981.

808b.   Le Maho, J., L'apparition des seigneuries châtelaines dans le Grand-Caux à l'époque ducale, *Archéologie médiévale*, *6*(1976),5–148.

809.   Mesqui, J., La fortification dans le Valois du XIe au XVe siècle et le rôle de Louis d'Orléans, *BM*, *135*(1977),109–49.

809a.   Mesqui, J., Les enceintes de Crécy-en-Brie et la fortification dans l'Ouest du comté de Champagne et de Brie au XIIIe siècle, *Mémoires publiés par la Fédération des sociétés historiques de Paris et de l'Ile-de-France*, *30*(1979),7–86.

809b.   Mesqui, J., *Provins, la fortification d'une ville au Moyen Age*, Paris and Geneva 1979.

809c.   Mesqui, J. and Ribéra-Pervillé, C., Les châteaux de Louis d'Orléans et leurs architectes (1391–1407), *BM*, *138*(1980), 293–345.

809d.   Michaud-Fréjaville, F., Une cité face aux crises: les remparts de la fidélité, de Louis d'Orléans à Charles VII, d'après les comptes de forteresse de la ville d'Orléans (1391–1427), in *Jeanne d'Arc, une époque, un rayonnement*, ed. J. Glénisson, Paris 1982, 43–59.

810.   Mortet, V. and Deschamps, P., *Recueil de textes relatifs à l'histoire de l'architecture et à la condition des architectes en France au Moyen Age*, Paris 2 vols. 1911–29.

811.   Mussat, A., Le château de Vitré et l'architecture des châteaux bretons du XIVe et XVe siècle, *BM*, *133*(1975),131–64.

811a.   Noyé, G., Les fortifications de terre dans la seigneurie de Toucy du Xe au XIIIe siècle. Essai de typologie, *Archéologie médiévale*, *6*(1976),149–217.

812.   Perroy, E., Les châteaux du Roannais du XIe au XIIIe siècle, *Cahiers de Civilisation médiévale*, *9*(1966),13–27.

813.   Pesez, J. M. and Piponnier, F., Les maisons fortes bourguignonnes, *ChG*, v (1970),143–64.

814.   Pous, A. de, L'architecture militaire occitane (IXe–XIVe siècles), *Bulletin archéologique du Comité des travaux historiques et scientifiques*, nlle. sér., *5*(1969), Paris 1970, 41–139.

815.   Pous, A. de, Notice sur l'évolution de l'archère dans les châteaux féodaux des Pyrénées méditerranéennes entre le Xe et le XIVe siècle, *Gl.*, *4*(1965),67–85.

816.   Richard, J., Le château dans la structure féodale de la France au XIIe siècle, in *Probleme des 12. Jahrhunderts*, Constance and Stuttgart 1968, 169–76.

817.   Richard, J., Châteaux, châtelains et vassaux en Bourgogne aux XIe et XIIe siècles, *Cahiers de Civilisation médiévale*, *3*(1960),433–47.

818.   Rocolle, P., *2000 ans de fortification française*, Paris 2 vols. 1973.

819.   Salch, C. L., *L'atlas des villes et villages fortifiés en France (Moyen Age)*, Strasbourg 1978.

820.   Salch, C. L., *Dictionnaire des châteaux et des fortifications du Moyen Age en France*, Strasbourg 1979.

820a.   Seydoux, P., *Forteresses médiévales du Nord de la France*, n.p. 1979.

821.   Yver, J., Les châteaux forts en Normandie jusqu'au milieu du XIIe siècle: contribution à l'étude du pouvoir ducal, *Bulletin de la Société des Antiquaires de Normandie*, *53*(1955–56),28–115.

The British Isles

822. Armitage, E. S., *The Early Norman Castles of the British Isles*, London 1912.

823. Barley, M. W., Town defences in England and Wales after 1066, in *The Plans and Topography of Medieval Towns in England and Wales*, ed. M. W. Barley, London 1976, 57–71.

824. Brown, R. A., *English Medieval Castles*, London 3rd edn 1976.

825. Brown, R. A., Royal castle-building in England, 1154–1216, *EHR*, 70(1955),353–98.

826. Brown, R. A., Colvin, H. M. and Taylor, A. J., *The History of the King's Works: The Middle Ages*, London 2 vols. 1963.

827. Brown, R. A., An historian's approach to the origins of the castle in England, *Archaeological Journal*, 126(1969),131–48.

828. Brown, R. A., A list of castles, 1154–1216, *EHR*, 74(1959),249–80.

829. Cruden, S., *The Scottish Castle*, London and Edinburgh 1960.

830. Davison, B. K., The origins of the castle in England, *Archaeological Journal*, 124(1967),202–11.

831. Edwards, J. G., Edward I's castle-building in Wales, *Proceedings of the British Academy*, 32(1946),15–81.

831a. Forde-Johnston, J., *Castles and Fortifications of Britain and Ireland*, London 1977.

832. Freeman, A. Z., A moat defensive: the coast defence scheme of 1295, *Spec.*, 42(1967),442–62.

833. Fry, P. S., *British Medieval Castles*, London 1974.

834. Hogg, A. H. A. and King, D. J. C., Early castles in Wales and the Marches, *Archaeologia Cambrensis*, 117(1963),77–124.

835. Le Patourel, H. E. Jean, Les sites fossoyés [moated sites] et leurs problèmes: l'organisation de la recherche en Grand-Bretagne, *Revue du Nord*, 58(1976), 571–92.

836. Oakeshott, R. E., *A Knight and his Castle*, London 1965.

837. O'Neil, B. H. St John, *Castle and Cannon: a Study of Early Artillery Fortification in England*, Oxford 1960.

838. Painter, S., English castles in the early Middle Ages: their number, location and legal position, *Spec.*, 10(1935),321–32.

839. Renn, D. F., The Anglo-Norman keep, 1066–1138, *Journal of the British Archaeological Association*, 3rd ser., 23(1960),1–23.

840. Renn, D. F., *Norman Castles in Britain*, London 1968.

841. Simpson, W. D., 'Bastard Feudalism' and later castles, *Antiquaries Journal* (1946),145–71.

842. Simpson, W. D., *Castles from the Air*, London 1949.

843. Stenton, F. M., The development of the castle in England and Wales, in *Social Life in Early England*, ed. G. Barraclough, London 1960, 96–123.

844. Taylor, A. J., Master James of St. George, *EHR*, 65(1950),433–57.

845. Taylor, A. J., Military architecture, in *Medieval England*, ed. A. L. Poole, Oxford, 2 vols. 1958, ii.98–127.

846. Thompson, A. Hamilton, *Military Architecture in England during the Middle Ages*, Oxford 1912.

847. Tranter, N. G., *The Fortified House in Scotland, I. South-East Scotland*, Edinburgh and London 1962.

848. Turner, H. L., *Town Defences in England and Wales: an Architectural and Documentary Study, AD 900–1500*, London 1971.

Italy

849. Agnello, G., L'archittetura militare e religiosa dell'età sveva, *Archivio Storico Pugliese, 13*(1960),146–76.

850. Agnello, G., L'archittetura religiosa, militare e civile dell'età normanna, *ibid.*, *12*(1959),159–96.

851. Agnello, G., *L'architettura sveva in Sicilia*, Rome 1935.

852. Conti, P. M., Limiti urbani ed organizzazione defensiva nell' Italia tardo antica e alto medioevale, in *Studi in onore Eugenio Dupré Theseider*, Rome, 2 vols. 1974, ii.561–72.

853. Cusin, F., Per la storia del castello medioevale, *RSI*(1939),491–542.

854. De Rossi, G. M., *Torri e castelli medievali della campagna romana*, Rome 1969.

855. Fiecconi, A., Luoghi fortificati e strutture edilizie nel Fabrianese nei secoli XI–XIII, *Nuova Rivista Storica, 59*(1975),1–54.

856. Hahn, H., *Hohenstaufen Burgen in Süditalien*, Ingelheim 1961.

857. Haseloff, A., *Die Bauten der Hohenstaufen in Unter-italien*, Leipzig 5 vols. 1912–26.

858. Martini, Francesco di Giorgio, *Trattati di architettura ingegneria et arte militare*, ed. C. and L. Maltese, Milan 1967.

859. Rocchi, E., *Le fonti storiche dell'architettura militare*, Rome 1908.

860. Schmiedt, G., Città e fortificazioni nei rilievi aerofotografici, in *Storia d'Italia*, 5, I. *Documenti*, Turin 1973, i.121–257.

861. Severini, G., *Architetture militari di Giuliano da Sangallo*, Pisa 1970.

862. Settia, A. A., Fortificazioni colletive nei villagi medievali dell'Alta Italia: ricetti, ville forti, recinti, *Bollettino Storico-bibliografico Subalpino* (1976),527–617.

863. Hale, J. R., The development of the bastion, 1440–1534, in *Europe in the Late Middle Ages*, ed. J. R. Hale, J. R. L. Highfield and B. Smalley, London 1965, 466–94.

863a. Volpi, G., *Rocche e fortificazioni del ducato di Urbino (1444–1502). L'esperienza martiniana e l'architettura militare di 'transizione'*, Fossombrone 1982.

864. Weller, A. S., *Francesco di Giorgio, 1439–1501*, Chicago 1943.

865. Willemsen, C. A., *Die Bauten der Hohenstaufen in Süditalien. Neue Grabungs und Forschungsergebnisse*, Cologne 1968.

The Latin East

866. Bon, A., *La Morée franque. Recherches historiques, topographiques et archéologiques sur la principauté d'Achaïe, 1205–1430*, Paris 2 vols. 1969.

867. Deschamps, P., *Les châteaux des Croisés en Terre Sainte*, Paris 2 vols. and 2 albums, 1934–39.

868. Fedden, R., *Crusader Castles. A Brief Study in the Military Architecture*, London 1950.

869. Fedden, R., and Thompson, J., *Crusader Castles*, London 1957.

870.   Hazard, H. W., *The Art and Architecture of the Crusader States*, Madison 1977.
871.   Huygens, R. B. C., Un nouveau texte du traité *De constructione castri Saphet*, *Studi Medievali*, 3rd ser., *6*(1965),355–85.

The Iberian peninsula

871a.   Araguas, P., Les châteaux des marches de Catalogne et Ribagorce (950–1100), *BM*, *137*(1979),205–24.
872.   Avila Y Diaz-Ubierna, G., *Castillos de la provincia de Burgos*, Burgos 1961.
873.   Bordeje, F., *Castles Itinerary in Castila. Guide to the most interesting Castilian Castles*, Madrid 1965.
874.   Bruand, Y., De l'importance historique et de la valeur des ouvrages fortifiés en Vieille-Castille au XVe siècle, *MA*, *63*(1957),59–86.
875.   Durliat, M., *L'art dans le royaume de Majorque. Les débuts de l'art gothique en Roussillon, en Cerdagne et aux Baléares*, Toulouse 1962.
876.   Grassotti, H., Sobre la retenencia de castillos en la Castilla medieval, *Bulletin de l'Institut historique belge de Rome*, *44*(1974),283–99.
877.   Monreal Marti de Riquer, L., *Els castells medievales de Catalunya*, Barcelona 1958.
878.   Sarthou-Carreres, C., *Castillos de Espana*, Madrid 4th edn 1963.
879.   Serra-Rafols, C., Camp I Arboix, J. de, Tasis, R. and Catala I Roca, P., *Els Castells catalans*, Barcelona 3 vols. 1967.
880.   Villena, L., El castillo espanol, *Gl.*, *4*(1965),87–106.
881.   Weissmuller, A. A., *Castles from the Heart of Spain*, London 1967.

7   WAR, ECONOMY AND TAXATION

From the host of works which, either in detail or in general, allude to the economic consequences of war, deal with war as one of the elements of life and economic development or evoke problems related to the financing of conflicts, the following may be particularly mentioned:

882.   Braunstein, P., Guerre, vivres et transports dans le Haut-Frioul en 1381, in *Erzeugung, Verkehr und Handel in der Geschichte der Alpenländer, Hervert-Hassinger-Festschrift*, ed. F. Huter, G. Zwanowetz and F. Mathis, Innsbruck 1977, 85–106.
883.   Bridbury, A. R., Before the Black Death, *Economic History Review*, 2nd ser., *30*(1977),393–410.
884.   Brouwers, D. D., Indemnités pour dommages de guerre au pays de Namurois en 1432, *Annales de la Société archéologique de Namur*, *40*(1932–33),87–103.
885.   Brun, R., Notes sur le commerce des armes à Avignon au XIVe siècle, *BEC*, *109*(1951),209–31.
885a.   Cardini, F., I costi della crociata. L'aspetto economico del progetto di Marino Sanudo il Vecchio (1312–1321), in *Studi in memoria di Federigo Melis*, Naples, 5 vols, 1978, ii.179–210.
886.   Contamine, P., Consommation et demande militaire en France et en Angleterre, XIIIe–XVe siècles, in *Domande e consumi. Livelli e strutture (nei secoli XIII–XVIII). Atti della 'Sesta settimana di studio' (27 aprile- 3 maggio 1974)*, Istituto internazionale di Storia economica Francesco Datini, Prato, Florence 1978, 409–28.

887. Contamine, P., La guerre de Cent ans en France: une approche économique, *BIHR*, *48*(1974),125–49.

888. Contamine, P., Guerre, fiscalité royale et économie en France (deuxième moitié du XVe siècle), in *Proceedings of the Seventh International Economic History Congress*, ed. M. W. Flinn, Edinburgh, 2 vols. 1978, ii.266–73.

889. Delmaire, B., La guerre en Artois après la bataille de Courtrai (1302–1303), in *Guerre et Paix*, 131–41.

890. Favier, J., *Finance et fiscalité au bas Moyen Age*, Paris 1971 (with abundant bibliography, 311–46).

891. Harriss, G. L., *King, Parliament and Public Finance in Medieval England to 1369*, Oxford 1975.

892. Hébert, M., Guerre, finances et administration: les Etats de Provence de novembre 1359, *MA 83*(1977),103–30.

893. Henneman, J. B., Financing the Hundred Years War: royal taxation in France in 1340, *Spec.*, *42*(1967),275–98.

894. Henneman, J. B., *Royal Taxation in Fourteenth Century France*, Princeton 2 vols. 1971–6.

895. Hoffmann, R. C., Warfare, weather and a rural economy. The Duchy of Wroclaw in the mid-fifteenth century, *Viator*, *4*(1973),273–301.

896. Lane, F. C., Economic consequences of organized violence, *Journal of Economic History*, *18*(1958),401–17.

897. Ladero Quesada, M. A., *Milicia y economia en la guerra de Grenada: el cerco de Baza*, Valladolid 1964.

898. McFarlane, K. B., War and society, 1300–1600. England and the Hundred Years' War, *PP*, *22*(1962),3–13.

899. Maddicott, J. R. L., The English peasantry and the demands of the Crown, 1294–1341, *PP*, Suppl. no.I, (1975).

900. Menkés, F., Aspects de la guerre de Provence à la fin du XIVe siècle, in *Économies et sociétés au Moyen Age. Mélanges offerts à Edouard Perroy*, Preface by J. Schneider, Paris 1973, 465–76.

901. Menjot, D., Le poids de la guerre dans l'économie murcienne, l'exemple de la campagne de 1407–1408 contre Grenade, *Miscelanea Medieval Murciana*, Murcia 1976, 37–68.

902. Newhall, R. A., The war finances of Henry V and the duke of Bedford, *EHR*, *36*(1921),172–98.

903. Miller, E., War, taxation and the English economy in the late thirteenth and early fourteenth century, in *War and Economic Development. Essays in Memory of David Joslin*, ed. J. M. Winter, Cambridge 1975, 11–31.

904. Pavodan, G., L'economia di guerra di un grande commune del Trecento, *Rivista di Storia economica*, *5*(1940),35–42.

905. Postan, M. M., The costs of the Hundred Years War, *PP*, *27*(1964),34–53.

906. Prestwich, J. O., War and finance in the Anglo-Norman state, *TRHS*, 5th ser., *4*(1954),19–43.

907. Prestwich, M., *War, Politics and Finance under Edward I*, London 1972.

908. Rey, M., *Le domaine du roi et les finances extraordinaires sous Charles VI, 1388–1413*, Paris 1965.

909. Rey, M., *Les finances royales sous Charles VI. Les causes du déficit, 1388–1413*, Paris 1965.

910.   Sivéry, G., L'enquête de 1247 et les dommages de guerre en Tournaisis, en Flandre gallicante et en Artois, *Revue du Nord*, *59*(1977),7–18.

910a.   Strayer, J. R., The costs and profits of War: the Anglo-French conflict of 1294–1303, in *The Medieval City*, ed. H. A. Miskimin, D. Herlihy and A. L. Udovitch, New Haven and London 1977, 262–91.

8   WAR AND PEACE: LAWS, ETHICS AND CHRISTIANITY

Selected sources

911.   Abbon de Saint-Germain-des-Prés, Sermo ad milites, *Patr. Lat.*, cxxxii.761–78.

912.   *Acta Pontificia iuris gentium usque ad annum MCCCIV*, ed. G. B. Pallieri and G. Vismara, Milan 1946.

913.   Bonet, Honoré, *L'arbre des batailles*, ed. E. Nys, Brussels 1883 (English tr. G. W. Coopland, *The Tree of Battles*, Liverpool 1949).

914.   Denis le Chartreux, De vita militarium, in *Opera Omnia*, XXXVII, Tournai 1909, 569–83.

915.   Hincmar de Reims, De coercendis militum rapinis, *Patr. Lat.*, CXXV, 953–6.

916.   Legnano, Giovanni da, *Tractatus de Bello, de Represaliis et de Duello*, ed. T. E. Holland, tr. J. L. Brierly, Oxford 1917.

917.   Mézières, Philippe de, *Letter to King Richard II. A Plea made in 1395 for Peace between England and France*, ed. and tr. G. W. Coopland, Liverpool 1975.

918.   Podiebrad, George, *Tractatus pacis toti christianitati fiendae*, ed. J. Kejr *et al.*, Prague 1964.

919.   Stehkämper, H., Ein Ütrechter kanonischer Traktat über Kriegsrecht (1419–20), *ZSSRG, Kan. Abt.*, *78*(1961),196–265.

War and Christianity: the Notion of the Just War

920.   Bainton, R. H., *Christian Attitudes towards War and Peace. A Historical Survey and Critical Re-evaluation*, London 1961.

921.   Baldwin, J. W., *Masters, Princes and Merchants. The Social Views of Peter the Chanter and his Circle*, Princeton 2 vols. 1970.

922.   Bond, B., The 'Just War' in historical perspective, *History Today*, *16*(1966),111–19.

923.   Brock, P., *Pacifism in Europe to 1914*, Princeton 1972.

924.   Chénon, E., Saint Thomas d'Aquin et la guerre, in *L'Eglise et le droit de la guerre*, Paris 1929.

924a.   Contamine, P., L'idée de guerre à la fin du Moyen Age: aspects juridiques et éthiques, *AIBL*(1979),70–86.

924b.   Contamine, P., La théologie de la guerre à la fin du Moyen Age: la guerre de Cent ans fut-elle une guerre juste?, in *Jeanne d'Arc, une époque, un rayonnement*, ed. J. Glénisson, Paris 1982, 9–21.

925.   Ermini, G., *I trattati della guerra e della pace di Giovanni da Legnano*, Imola 1923.

926.   Finke, H., Das Problem des gerechten Krieges in der mittelalterlichen theologischen Literatur, in *Aus der Geisteswelt des Mittelalters. Martin Grabmann zur*

Vollendung des 60. Lebensjahr von Freunden und Schülern gewidmet, ed. A. Lang, J. Lechner and M. Schmauss, Münster 1935, 1426–34.

927. Fournier, P., La prohibition par le deuxième concile de Latran d'armes jugées trop meurtrières, *Revue générale de Droit international public*, 33(1916).

928. Fritz, G., Service militaire, in *Dictionnaire de théologie catholique*, XIV, 2e partie (1972–81).

929. Gmür, H., *Thomas von Aquino und der Krieg*, Leipzig 1933.

929a. Hehl, E. D., *Kirche und Krieg im 12. Jahrhundert. Studien zu kanonischen Recht und politischer Wirklichkeit*, Stuttgart 1980.

930. Hödl, G., Ein Weltfriedsprogramm um 1300, in *Festschrift Friedrich Hausmann*, ed. H. Ebner, Graz 1977, 217–33.

931. Hornus, J. M., *Evangile et labarum. Etude sur l'attitude du christianisme primitif devant les problèmes de l'Etat, de la guerre et de la violence*, Geneva 1960.

932. Hrabar, V. E., Le droit international au Moyen Age, *Revue de Droit international*, 18(1936).

933. Hubrecht, G., La juste guerre dans la doctrine chrétienne des origines au milieu du XVIe siècle, *Recueils de la Société Jean Bodin*, 15(1961),107–23.

934. Hubrecht, G., La 'juste guerre' dans le décret de Gratien, *Studia Gratiana*, 3(1955),161–77.

935. Johnson, J. T., *Ideology, Reason and the Limitation of War. Religious and Secular Concepts, 1200–1740*, New Jersey 1975.

936. Leclercq, J., L'attitude spirituelle de saint Bernard devant la guerre, *Collectanea cisterciensia*, 36(1974),195–225.

937. Mahaut, M. C., Le rôle pacificateur du pape Benoît XII dans le conflit de la Castille avec le Portugal (1337–1340), in *Guerre et Paix*, 225–39.

938. Margolin, J. C., *Guerre et paix dans la pensée d'Erasme de Rotterdam*, Paris 1973.

939. Morisi, A., *La guerra nel pensiero cristiano dalle origini alle crociate*, Florence 1963.

940. Muldoon, J., A fifteenth-century application of the canonistic theory of just war, in *Proceedings of the Fourth International Congress of Medieval Canon Law, Toronto, 21–25 August 1972*, ed. S. Kuttner, Vatican City 1976, 467–80.

941. Ortega, J. F., La paz y la guerra en el pensamiento agustiniano, *Revista española de derecho canónico*, 20(1965),5–35.

942. Ortolan, T., Guerre, in *Dictionnaire de theologie catholique*, VI (1899–1952).

942a. *Pace (la) nel pensiero, nella politica, negli ideali del Trecento*, Todi 1975 ('Convegni del Centro di studi sulla spiritualità medievale', XV).

943. Poggiaspella, F., La chiesa la partecipazione dei chierici alla guerra nella legislazione conciliare fino alle Decretali di Gregorio IX, *Ephemerides iuris canonici*, 15(1959),140–53.

944. Poggiaspella, F., La condotta della guerra secondo una disposizione dello III° concilio lateranense, *ibid.*, 12(1956),371–86.

944a. Prinz, F. E., King, clergy and war at the time of the Carolingians, in *Saints, Scholars and Heroes. Studies in Medieval Culture in Honor of Charles W. Jones*, ed. M. H. King and W. M. Stevens, Collegeville 1979, 301–29.

945. Regout, R., *La doctrine de la guerre juste de saint Augustin à nos jours d'après les théologiens et les canonistes catholiques*, Paris 1935.

946. Russell, F. H., Innocent IV's proposal to limit warfare, in *Proceedings of the*

Fourth International Congress of Medieval Canon Law, Toronto 21–25 August 1972, ed. S. Kuttner, Vatican City 1976, 383–99.

947.   Russell, F. H., *The Just War in the Middle Ages,* Cambridge 1975.

948.   Sicard, G., Paix et guerre dans le droit canon du XIIe siècle, in *Paix de Dieu et guerre sainte en Languedoc au XIIIe siècle, Cahiers de Fanjeaux,* 4(1969),72–90.

949.   Seibt, F., *Hussitica. Zur Struktur einer Revolution,* Cologne 1965.

950.   Solages, B. de, *La théologie de la guerre juste, genèse et orientation,* Paris 1946.

951.   Tooke, J. D., *The Just War in Aquinas and Grotius,* London 1965.

952.   Vanderpol, A. M., *Le droit de guerre d'après les théologiens et les canonistes du Moyen Age,* Paris and Brussels 1911.

953.   Vanderpol, A. M., *La doctrine scolastique du droit de guerre,* Paris 1925.

954.   Windass, S., *Le christianisme et la violence,* Paris 1966.

955.   Wright, N. A. R., The *Tree of Battles* of Honoré Bouvet and the Laws of War, in *War, Literature and Politics,* 12–31.

The early Middle Ages

956.   Bonnaud-Delamare, R., *L'idée de paix à l'époque carolingienne,* Paris 1939.

957.   Cowdrey, H. E. J., Bishop Ermenfried of Sion and the Penitential Ordinance following the battle of Hastings, *Journal of Ecclesiastical History,* 20(1969),225–42.

958.   Cross, J. E., The ethic of war in Old English, in *England before the Conquest. Studies in Primary Sources presented to Dorothy Whitelock,* ed. P. Clemoes and K. Hughes, Cambridge 1971, 269–82.

959.   Draper, G. I. A., Penitential discipline and public wars in the Middle Ages, *International Review of the Red Cross* (1961).

960.   Ganshof, F. L., La paix au très haut Moyen Age, *Recueils de la Société Jean Bodin, 14*(1961),397–413.

960a.   Renna, T., The idea of peace in the West, 500–1150, *Journal of Medieval History, 6*(1980),143–67.

961.   Vismara, G., Problemi storici e istituti giuridici della guerra alto-medievale, *OM,* ii.1126–1200.

962.   Wallace-Hadrill, J. M., War and peace in the early Middle Ages, *TRHS,* 5th ser., *25*(1975), 57–74.

The Peace and Truce of God

963.   Bisson, T. N., The organized peace in Southern France and Catalonia (*ca.*1140–*ca.*1233), *AHR, 82*(1977),290–311.

964.   Bonnaud-Delamare, R., La convention régionale de paix d'Albi de 1191, in *Paix de Dieu et guerre sainte en Languedoc au XIIIe siècle, Cahiers de Fanjeaux,* 4(1969),91–101.

965.   Bonnaud-Delamare, R., Fondements des institutions de paix au XIe siècle, in *Mélanges Louis Halphen,* Paris 1951, 21–6.

966.   Bonnaud-Delamare, R., Les institutions de paix dans la province ecclésiastique de Reims au XIe siècle, *Bulletin historique et philologique du Comité des travaux historiques et scientifiques, années 1955 et 1956,* Paris 1957, 143–200.

967. Bonnaud-Delamare, R., Paix d'Amiens et de Corbie, *Revue du Nord*, *38*(1956),169–74.

968. Bonnaud-Delamare, R., La paix de Dieu en Touraine pendant la première croisade, *Revue d'histoire ecclésiastique*, *70*(1975),749–57.

969. Bonnaud-Delamare, R., La paix en Aquitaine au XIe siècle, *Recueils de la Société Jean Bodin*, *14*(1961),415–87.

970. Bonnaud-Delamare, R., La paix en Flandre pendant la première croisade, *Revue du Nord*, *39*(1957),147–52.

971. Boüard, M. de, Sur les origines de la trêve de Dieu en Normandie, *Annales de Normandie*, *9*(1959),179–89.

972. Callahan, D. F., Adémar de Chabannes et la paix de Dieu, *Annales du Midi*, *89*(1977),21–43.

973. Carozzi, C., La tripartition sociale et l'idée de paix de Dieu, in *Guerre et Paix*, 9–22.

974. Conrad, H., Gottesfrieden und Heerverfassung in der Zeit der Kreuzzüge, *ZSSRG, Germ. Abt.*, *61*(1941),711–26.

975. Cowdrey, H. E. J., The Peace and Truce of God in the eleventh century, *PP*, *46*(1970),42–67.

976. Duby, G., Les laics et la paix de Dieu, in *I Laici nella 'societas christiana' dei secoli XI e XII. Atti della Terza Settimana internazionale di studio*, Mendola 21–27 agosto 1965, Milan 1968, 448–61.

977. Gleiman, L., Some remarks on the origin of the 'Treuga Dei', *Etudes d'histoire littéraire et doctrinale* (1962),117–37.

978. Graboïs, A., De la trêve de Dieu à la paix du roi. Etude sur la transformation du mouvement de paix au XIIe siècle, in *Mélanges offerts à René Crozet*, Poitiers, 2 vols. 1966, i.585–96.

979. Hoffmann, H., *Gottesfrieden und Treuga Dei*, Stuttgart 1964.

980. Joris, A., Observations sur la proclamation de la trêve de Dieu à Liège à la fin du XIe siècle, *Recueils de la Société Jean Bodin*, *14*(1961),503–45.

981. Justus, W., *Die frühe Entwicklung des säkularen Friedensbegriffs in der mittelalterlichen Chronistik*, Cologne and Vienna 1975.

982. Kennelly, D., Medieval towns and the Peace of God, *Medievalia et Humanistica*, *15*(1963),35–53.

982a. Magnou-Nortier, E., La place du concile du Puy (vers 994) dans l'évolution de l'idée de paix, in *Mélanges offerts à Jean Dauvillier*, Toulouse 1979, 489–506.

983. Molinié, G., *L'organisation judiciaire, militaire et financière des associations de la paix. Etude sur la paix et la trêve de Dieu dans le Midi et le centre de la France*, Toulouse 1912.

984. Platelle, H., La violence et ses remèdes en Flandre au XIe siècle, *Sacris erudiri*, *20*(1971),103–73.

985. Rosenwein, B. H., Feudal war and monastic peace: Cluniac liturgy as ritual aggression, *Viator*, *2*(1971),129–57.

986. Strubbe, E. I., La paix de Dieu dans le nord de la France, *Recueils de la Société Jean Bodin*, *14*(1961),489–501.

987. Töpfer, B., Die Anfänge der 'Treuga Dei' in Nordfrankreich, *Zeitschrift für Geschichtswissenschaft*, *9*(1962),876–93.

988. Töpfer, B., *Das Kommende Reich des Friedens. Zur Entwicklung chiliasticher Zukunftshoffnungen in Hochmittelalter*, Berlin 1964.

The crusade and Holy War

989. Alphandéry, P., *La chrétienté et l'idée de croisade*, ed. A. Dupront, Paris 2 vols. 1954–59.

990. Belch, S. F., Theologi anonymi Utrum bella contra infideles fidelibus licitum sit movere?, *Mediaevalia philosophica Polonorum*, *19*(1974),3–63.

991. Beumann, H., Kreuzzugsgedanke und Ostpolitik im hohen Mittelalter, in *Heidenmission und Kreuzzugsgedanke in der deutschen Ostpolitik des Mittelalters*, ed. H. Beumann, Darmstadt 1963, 121–45.

992. Blake, E. O., The formation of the 'Crusade Idea', *Journal of Ecclesiastical History*, *21*(1970),11–31.

993. Brundage, J. A., Holy War and the medieval lawyers, in *The Holy War*, ed. T. P. Murphy, Columbus 1976, 99–140.

994. Brundage, J. A., *Medieval Canon Law and the Crusader*, Madison 1969.

995. Cowdrey, H. E. J., The genesis of the crusades: the springs of Western ideas of Holy War, in *The Holy War*, ed. T. P. Murphy, Columbus 1976, 9–32.

996. Cowdrey, H. E. J., Pope Urban II's preaching of the First Crusade, *Hist.*, *55*(1970),177–88.

997. Delaruelle, E., Essai sur la formation de l'idée de croisade, *Bulletin de littérature ecclésiastique*, *42*(1941),24–45, 86–103; 45(1944),13–46, 73–90; *54*(1953),226–39; *55*(1954),50–63.

998. Delaruelle, E., Paix de Dieu et croisade dans la chrétienté du XIIe siècle, in *Paix de Dieu et guerre sainte en Languedoc au XIIIe siècle, Cahiers de Fanjeaux*, *4*(1969),51–71.

999. Erdmann, C., *Die Entstehung des Kreuzzugsgedankens*, Darmstadt 1955 (English tr. M. W. Baldwin and W. Goffart, *The Origin of the Idea of Crusade*, Princeton 1977).

1000. Noth, A., *Heiliger Krieg und heiliger Kampf. Beiträge zur Geschichte der Kreuzzüge*, Bonn 1966.

1001. Richard, J., *L'esprit de la croisade*, Paris 1969.

1002. Robinson, I. S., Gregory VII and the Soldiers of Christ, *Hist.*, *58*(1973),169–92.

1002a. Schmandt, R. H., The fourth crusade and the Just War theory, *Catholic Historical Review*, *61*(1975),191–221.

1002b. Walters, L., The Just War and the crusade: antithesis or analogies?, *The Monist*, *57*(1973),584–94.

Landfriede: the public peace

1003. Angermeier, H., *Königtum und Landfriede im deutschen Spätmittelalter*, Munich 1966.

1003a. Angermeier, H., Landfriedenspolitik und Landfriedensgesetzgebung unter den Staufern, in *Probleme um Friedrich II.*, Sigmaringen 1974 (*Vorträge und Forschungen*, xvi, 167–86).

1004. Gernhuber, J., *Die Landfriedensbewegung in Deutschland bis zum Mainzer Landfrieden von 1235*, Bonn 1952.

1005. Gernhuber, J., Staat und Landfrieden im deutschen Reich des Mittelalters, *Recueils de la Société Jean Bodin*, *15*(1962),23–77.

1006.   Mohrmann, W. D., *Der Landfriede im Ostseeraum während des späten Mittelalters*, Kallmünz 1972.
1007.   Picht, G. and Huber, W., *Was heisst Friedensforschung?*, Stuttgart 1971.

Chivalry and religion

1008.   Meissburger, G., *De vita christiana*. Zum Bild des christlichen Ritters im Hochmittelalter, *Der Deutschunterricht*, *14*(1962),21–34.
1009.   Richter, J., Zur ritterlichen Frömmigkeit der Stauferzeit, *Wolfram-Jahrbuch* (1956),23–52.
1010.   Richter, J., Der Ritter zwischen Gott und Welt. Ein Bild mittelalterlicher Religion bei Hartmann von Aue, *Zeitschrift für Religions- und Geistesgeschichte*, *16*(1964),57–69.
1011.   Wang. A., *Der 'miles christianus' im 16. und 17. Jahrhundert und seine mittelalterliche Tradition. Ein Beitrag zum Verhältnis von sprachlicher und graphischer Bildlichkeit*, Berne and Frankfurt-am-Main 1975.

The laws of war

1012.   Cram, K. G., *Iudicium belli. Zum Rechtscharakter des Krieges im deutschen Mittelalter*, Münster and Cologne 1955.
1013.   Conrad, H., Germanisches Denken im deutschen Kriegsrecht des Mittelalters, in *Das Bild des Krieges im deutschen Denken*, ed. A. Fauste, Stuttgart and Berlin 1941, i.83–103.
1013a. Glénisson, J. and Deodato da Silva, V., La pratique et le rituel de la reddition aux XIVe et XVe siècles, in *Jeanne d'Arc, une époque, un rayonnement*, Paris 1982, 113–22.
1014.   Grassotti, H., El deber y el derecho de hacer guerra y pas en León y Castilla, *CHE*, *59–60*(1976),221–96.
1015.   Masi, G., Un capitulo di storia del diritto internazionale. Alcuni usi di guerra in Italia all'epoca dei Communi, *Rivista di Storia del Diritto italiano*, *28*(1955),19–37.
1016.   Richard, J., Le droit de guerre du noble comtois, *Mémoires de la Société pour l'histoire du droit et des institutions des anciens pays bourguignons, comtois et romands* (1948–49),107–15.
1017.   Rosenau, P. U., *Wehrverfassung und Kriegsrecht in der mittelhochdeutschen Epik, Wolfram von Eschenbach, Hartmann von Aue, Gottfried von Strassburg, Der Niebelunge Not, Kridrunepos, Wolfdietrichbruchstück A, König Rother, Salman und Moroff*, Bonn 1959.
1018.   Soldi-Rondinini, G., Il diritto di guerra in Italia nel secolo XV, *Nuova Rivista Storica*, *48*(1964),275–306.

Index

References to the plates are given in italic

Aachen, 54, 139
Aardenburg, 240
Abbeville, 134, 171
Abbo of St Germain-des-Prés, 28, 105
Abelin, master of works, 111
Aberdeen, 241
Aberystwyth, 111
Abingdon, 53, 79
Abraham, patriarch, 263
Abruzzi, 98, 300n
Achaea, 3
Acqui, 40
Acre, 64, 66, 76, 101, 212, 251–2
Adalbero, bishop of Metz, 270
Adam du Petit Pont, 188
Adrianople, battle of (378), 11
Aeneas the Tactician, 210
Africa, 4, 6, 11, 14, 16, 18, 219
Agathias, 7, 9, 175, 177
Agen, Agenais, 83
Agincourt, battle of (1415), 129, 229n, 258, 299
Agnello, bishop of Trento, 262
Agobard, archbishop of Lyon, 298
Aighyna, 20
Aigle (L'), 42
Aignan, St., 13n
Aimo of Salerno, 54
Aimon, archbishop of Bourges, 271
Aisne, 41
Aistulf, king of the Lombards, 19
Aix-en-Provence, 240
Aix-la-Chapelle, *see* Aachen
Alamans, 4, 11, 14, 22, 175, 178–9, 261n
Alan Barbetorte, duke of the Bretons, 43

Alans, 3, 4, 11, 12
Alaric, king of the Visigoths, 17, 18, 262
Albania, 128, 161–2, 291
Albarno, *see* Moriale, Fra
Albert, bishop of Riga, 76
Albert I of Austria, German emperor, 261n
Alberti, Leon Battista, 204
Albertus Magnus, 196
Albi, Albigensians, 22, 84, 87, 91, 246–7
Alboin, king of the Lombards, 20
Alcantara, Order of, 76
Alemannia, 37; *see also* Alamans
Alençon, John, duke of, 226
Aleppo, 63–4
Alexander VI, pope, 207
Alexander the Great, 215, 254n
Alexandria, Egypt, 206
Alexiad, 71
Alexis I Comnenus, Byzantine emperor, 59
Alfonso I, king of Aragon, 121
Alfonso I, king of the Asturias, 56
Alfonso II, king of the Asturias, 56
Alfonso X, king of Castile, 210, 283n
Alfonso XI, king of Castile, 138
Alfonso I, king of Portugal, 76
Alforrats, 70–1
Alfred the Great, king of Wessex, 50
Aljubarrota, battle of (1385), 121, 199, 300
Allstedt, battle of (933), 35
Almeria, 63
Almogavars, 73, 247–8
Alp Arslan, 59
Alps, 3, 35, 37–8, 77–8, 126, 145, 227, 245

Alsace, 4
Altopascio, battle of (1325), 117, 158
Alvarez Pelayo, 275–6
Amalfi, 55
Amalgar, 20
Amazons, 241
Amblève, battle of (716), 22
Amboise, 207
Ambras, 122
Ambrose, St., 40, 250, 263–4
Amiens, 42, 48, 113, 155
Ammianus Marcellinus, 9, 13
Anacletus II, anti-pope, 55
Ancona, 78, 85
Andalusia, 57, 139
Andelys (Les), 42
Andronicus II Paleologus, Byzantine
    emperor, 119, 248
Angers, Angevins, 20, 114, 124, 144, 247
Anghiari, battle of (1440), 258
Angles, 4n, 14
Anglo-Saxons, 21, 50, 175, 179, 183, 185,
    266–7
ango, 176–7
Angoulême, county of, 154; Hugues le
    Brun, count of, 93
Anjou, 43, 49, 81, 118, 245; Charles of,
    see Charles I and Charles II; Foulques
    V, count of, 42, 48; Geoffrey
    Plantagenet, count of, 211; Guy of,
    271
Anna Comnena, 71
Annales Fuldenses, 182
Annales Marbacenses, 104
Annales Petaviani, 182
annonae, 5, 16, 17, 57
Annoy, 87
Anselm of Havelberg, 296n
Anselm of Lucca, 235
Anselm of Ribemont, 59
Ansfred, 37
Antigone I, king of Macedonia, 306
Antioch, 59, 61–4
Antonine wall, 219
antrustions, 21
Antwerp, 198, 223
Apulia, 4, 55, 70, 96
Aquileia, 40, 269
Aquitaine, 22–3, 42–3, 48, 117, 241,
    271–2; see also Guyenne

Arabs, 4, 14; see also Islam; Muslims
Aragon, 56–7, 66, 73, 82, 97, 116, 240–1,
    243, 247–8, 283n
arbalest, see crossbow
Arbois, 190
Arborychi, 5
Arbre (L') des batailles, see Tree of Battles
Arc, Joan of, 242, 254n, 273n, 298, 300
archers, 12, 54–5, 60, 70–3, 91, 100, 102,
    115–18, 121, 129–30, 132, 134,
    151–3, 156–7, 166–7, 180–1, 199,
    212–3, 217, 223, 231–3, 257, 268n,
    274, 297; see also crossbowmen
Archimedes, 138
Arderne, John, 196
Arezzo, 159, 205, 240
Argentan, 226
Argentoratum (Strasbourg), battle of
    (357), 4, 11
Arians, 5, 264
Aribert, archbishop of Milan, 40
arimanni, 21
Arimino, Catelanus de, 131
Aristotle, 90, 140, 250–1, 283, 286
Arles, 240
Arlon, 37
Armagnacs, 169, 191, 195, 304
Armament, 12, 19, 20, 28, 31, 33, 51, 58,
    67–73, 86, 88–9, 95, 97, 106,
    115–18, 122, 126–37, 153, 175–92,
    216–17, 277, 300–1, 303; see also 1,
    2, 6, 7, 8, 9, 10, 12, 14–19
Armies, barbarian, 11–21; Carolingian,
    22–9; permanent, 165–72; Roman,
    5–12; Roman, contrasts with
    barbarian, 15; Roman, contrasts with
    medieval, 303–8; social structure of,
    239–42
Armourers, 5n, 189–90, 294; see also
    fabricenses; 18–19, 21
Arms, law of, 290–2
arms, weapons, see Armament
Arnaud, a routier, 244
Arnoul, St., 269
Arpad family, 33
Arquerii, see Ramundus Arquerii
Arras, 42, 190, 243; treaty of (1435), 169
Array, commissions of, 151
arrière-ban, 87–8, 92, 133, 155–7, 170–1
Arrouaise, 84

Art de chevalerie, 210, 285
Arthur, King (legendary), 218n, 254n
Arthur, prince of Wales, 167
artillery, gunpowder, 137–50, 172, 193, 196–207, 274; traditional, 193–6; *see also* trébuchet
Art of war, 208–37
Artois, 118, 137n, 215; Robert II, count of, 96
Arundel, 267; Thomas, earl of, 206
Ascalon, 63–4; battle of (1099), 59, 62
Asia minor, 59, 63
Assize of Arms (1181), 67, 88, 189, 240
Asti, 40
Asturias, 56–7
Athanasius, St., 264
Athelhelm, 53
Athelstan, king of Wessex, 50
Athens, 248
Atlantic ocean, 225
Attendoli, Micheletto degli, 127, 133, 161, 165, 259n
Attila the Hun, 13n
Augsburg, 35–6
Augustine, St., 76, 250, 264–5, 278
Aulnay, *see* Annoy
Aurillac, Gerald of, 275
aurum tironicum, 7
Austrasia, 22–3
Austria, 36, 41, 78, 86, 136, 306; Albert of, 260n; Frederick of Habsburg, king of the Romans, duke of, 261; Philip, archduke of, 132, 171, 207, 229n
Auvergne, 18, 41–2, 44, 46, 117–18, 246
Auxerre, Auxerrois, 43, 211, 300–1
Auxonne, 142
Avars, 23, 25, 32, 181
Aversa, 55
Avignon, 122, 166, 240
Avignonet, 225
Avila, 56
Avis, Order of, 76
Avitus, St., 17
Avre, river, 222
Axe, battle, 176–7, 180–1, 189, 241
Azamar, Pedro, 283n

Bachrach, B. S., 182–3
Bacon, Roger, 139, 196, 281
Bagaudes, 16

Baghdad, 306
Baglioni, Braccio, 131
Baldwin I, king of Jerusalem, 64
Baldwin II, king of Jerusalem, 64, 74
Balearic islands, 27
Balfart, 49
Balkans, 4, 59
Balsac, Robert de, 204, 214, 219n, 220, 226n, 227, 236, 285
Baltic sea, 66, 77
Bamberg, 33
ban, *bannum*, 24, 36, 43, 45, 87, 157
bannières, 229
Bapaume, 223
Bar, duke of, 166; Thibaud I, count of, 85; Thibaud de, prince-bishop of Liège, 254n
Barat, Henri, 116
Barbara, St., 297
Barbaricarii, 5n
Barbiano, Alberigo da, 160
barbicans, 107, 114, 204
Barcelona, 23, 56, 206
Bari, 29, 55, 98
Barontus, 20
barracks, 6, 172
Bar-sur-Aube, 96
Bartolomeo, bishop of Urbino, 297
Basil, St., 266–7
Basilicata, 98
Basin, Thomas, 134n, 169–70
Basle, 136
Basques, 19, 244
Bastille St.-Antoine, 145n
bastions, 204–5
Batalha, abbey of, 300
battering rams, 103
Battle, abbey of, 300; abbot of, 287n
battle, plans, 215; risks in, 255–9
Baudouin, Michau, 145
Baugé, 301
Bavaria, 23, 27, 37, 118, 162
Bavarians, 14, 22, 35
Bavent, Robert, 116
Bavière, Isabeau de, 236n
Bayart, Pierre Terrail, lord of, 206, 244n, 252, 256, 273n
Baye, Nicolas de, 212
Bayeux, 20, 48, 54, 184–5; *see also* 1
Baynard's Castle, London, 83

Bayonne, 150
Bazacape, Pietro of, 97
Béarn, 132, 307; Bernard de, bastard of
  Comminges, 215
Beaucaire, 102, 117–18
Beaugency, Raoul de, 42
Beaumanoir, Philippe de, 85–6
Beaumaris, 111
Beaumont-sur-Sarthe, 148
Beauvais, Beauvaisis, 42, 48, 85, 118,
  226, 242, 287
Bede, Venerable, 51n, 267
Bedford, John, duke of, 148, 169
Beerst, 240
Belisarius, 11
Bellême, 106, 226, 273n
Bellisfortis, 120
Belot, Gaucher, 116
Benedict XII, pope, 166, 223; *see also*
  Fournier, Jacques
Benedict the Levite, 269n
Benevento, 23, 29, 38, 55; battle of
  (1266), 66, 230n, 300n
Bentivoglio, Hercules, 127
Benzo of Alba, 39
Beowulf, 175, 185
Berkeley, Thomas, lord, 210
Berkshire, 51, 80
Bernard, a bishop, 269
Bernard of Clairvaux, St., 32n, 74
Bernardino of Siena, St., 296
Berne, 135; *see also 17, 23*
berrierii, 97–8
Berry, 20, 41–2, 47, 118, 246
Berry herald, *see* Le Bouvier, Gilles
Bersuire, Pierre, 214
Bertoald, 14
Berwick-upon-Tweed, 165
Besançon, 240, 272
Bessarabia, 33
Bessin, 226
Béthune, Robert of, 194
Beverhoutsfeld, battle of (1382), 199,
  299n
Beynac, Adhémar de, 247
Béziers, 150
Biforco, battle of (1358), 158
Bigot, Jean, 301
Billungs, march of, 41
Biondo, Flavio, 138

Bioule, 140, 202
Biringuccio, 145
Biscay, 162
Black sea, 6
Blâmont, Olry de, bishop of Toul, 301
Blanche of France, 93
Bloch, M., 28n, 273n
Blois, 273n; Charles de, duke of
  Brittany, 298; Stephen, count of, 62;
  Stephen, count of, king of England,
  78, 244; Thibaud IV, count of, 41–2,
  48
Blondel, Robert, 169–70
Bluemantle poursuivant, 192n
bodyguards, 5, 16, 21, 52, 57, 100, 165–7
Bohain-en-Vermandois, 171
Bohemia, 32, 35–8, 78, 124–5, 137, 292
Bohemian brothers, 295
Bohemond I, prince of Antioch, 61n, 62
Bohéries, abbey of, 223
Boileau, Etienne, 193
Boleslav I, king of Poland, 259
Boleslav II, king of Poland, 261n
Boleslav III, king of Poland, 261n
Bologna, 100, 240, 280
Bombards, 140–5, 149–50, 196, 200–1,
  206; *see also 20*
Bonaguil, 205
Bonizo of Sutri, 275
Bonneval, 42
booty, 57, 73, 151–2, 236, 245, 248,
  261–2, 276, 304; *see also* ransoms
Bordeaux, Bordelais, 4, 83, 88, 271
Borgo San Sepolcro, 204–5
Botetourt, John, 116
Boucicaut, Jean le Meingre, marshal,
  216–17
Bouillon, Godefroy de, 61–2, 64, 106,
  254n, 301; *see also 13*; Henri, duke of,
  218
boulevard, 201–5
Boulguerie, 156; *see also* Bulgaria
Boulogne, Guynemer de, 62; Renaud de
  Dammartin, count of, 231, 244–5
Boulogne-sur-Mer, 149
Bourg-en-Bresse, 202
Bourgeois of Paris, 191
Bourges, 22, 42, 206n, 271
Bourgthéroulde, battle of (1124), 231
Bournonville, Nolin de, 233

Boutruche, R., 128
Bouvines, battle of (1214), 65–6, 186, 231, 244–5, 273, 298n, 300
Bovet, Honoré, 120, 125, 211, 274, 281, 283, 289
Brabançons, 100, 129, 161, 231, 243, 245, 247–8, 301
Brabant, 134n, 142, 243–4; Anthony, duke of, 142; John III, duke of, 223
Braga, 56
Bragadins, 292n
Brandenburg, 78
Brantôme, Pierre de, 308
Bray, 226
Brémule, battle of (1119), 42, 231, 256
Brenner pass, 36
Brenta, river, 261n
Brescia, 40, 140
Brest, 205
Breteuil-sur-Iton, 42
Bréthencourt, 41
Bretons, 20, 23, see also Brittany
Brie, 42, 48, 96
Brienne, Gautier de, duke of Athens, 248
Brignais, battle of (1362), 159
Brionne, Gui de, 52
Brioude, 271, 300; count of, 271
Britain, 4, 6, 14
Brittany, 27, 42–3, 48, 52, 65, 82n, 118, 121, 123–4, 126, 129, 134, 149, 152, 159–60, 220, 242, 245, 298–9; Charles, duke of, see Blois; Conan III, duke of, 42; Francis I, duke of, 226; Francis II, duke of, 300; John I, duke of, 65; John II, duke of, 82n; John IV, duke of, 152
Brive, 84
Bromyard, John, 285
Bruges, 84, 189, 191, 198–9, 240; Louis de, lord of Gruythuse, see 22
Brunner, H., 179, 181, 183
Bruno, St., archbishop of Cologne, 270
Brussels, 122, 142, 223
Brustem, battle of (1467), 199
Brut, Walter, 294
Bruyère-l'Aubespin (La), 203
Buccellarii, 21
Buckingham, see Essex, Thomas, earl of
Budes, Sylvestre, 160
Bueil, Jean de, 120, 137–8, 201, 211, 214–15, 218, 230–1, 252–4, 274n, 285; see also Jouvencel (le)
Bug, battle of the river (1018), 261n
Builth, 111
Buironfosse, 223, 298
Bulgaria, 156
Bulgars, 27, 33, 266
Burchard of Worms, 267–8
Bureau, Gaspard, 145
Bureau, Jean, 145
Burgos, 56, 196
Burgundians (Burgondes), 4, 11n, 14, 17, 175, 253n
Burgundy, Burgundians, 20, 27, 41–3, 90, 93, 109, 118, 128–9, 134–5, 162, 165, 170n, 171, 186, 190–2, 196, 199, 200, 205n, 215, 252, 272, 298, 304
Burgundy, Charles, count of Charolais, duke of, 120, 122–3, 127–8, 130, 133–4, 137, 144–5, 149, 157n, 165, 167, 170n, 171, 189–90, 192, 200, 206, 211–12, 214, 217, 233–5, 252, 286, 291, 300–1; Hugues II, duke of, 41, 48; Hugues de, 93; John the Fearless, duke of, 142, 148, 215, 232, 252, 259; Philip the Bold, duke of, 119, 252, 259n; Philip the Good, duke of, 121, 123, 142, 148, 171, 190, 195, 213, 252
Buridan, Jean, 140
Bury St Edmunds, 79
Bussières, Mauger de, 68
Buttin, F., 185–8
byrnie, see haubergeon
Byzantines, Byzantium, 4, 14, 17, 18, 29, 35, 54–5, 59–60, 62, 71, 183, 247–8, 261, 303–4

Caballeros hidalgos, 58
Caballeros villanos, 58
Cadiz, 4
Cadoc, Lambert of, 72, 244, 247
Caedwalla, king of Wessex, 51n
Caen, 52, 81, 111, 191, 226
Caernarvon, 111
Caesar, Julius, 187n, 210n, 214–15, 236, 254n
Caesarea, 266
Cahors, 84, 202n, 240

Calabria, 4, 55, 98, 248; John, duke of, 134, 212
Calais, 140, 148, 155, 165, 169, 215, 220, 227; treaty of (1360), 168
Calatrava, Order of, 76, 163
Callot, Jacques, 249
Caltabellota, peace of (1302), 248
Cambier, Jean, artillery merchant, 142
Cambrai, 22, 140, 222–4, 240
Cambridge, 294
Camerino, 85
Camoufle, bombardier, 139
Canary islands, 254
Candia, 305
Canivez, J-M., 74
cannons, 138–50, 193–207, 293, 297 (see also artillery; bombards); types of, 142–3, 146–7, 196–7 (see also 20–4)
Canossa, 36
Cantabrian mountains, 56
Canterbury, 266, 277
Cantilupe, William de, 80
Canute the Great, king of England and Denmark, 50, 52
Cap Colonna, battle of (982), 38
Capelle-en-Thiérache (La), 223
Capitanata, 98
Capitatio, 6
Capua, 55
Capuciati, 246
Caraffa, Diomedes, 121
Caravaggio, battle of (1448), 135
Carcassonne, 107, 114–15, 117–18, 142, 225; see also 4
Cardaillac (Cardillac, Cardouillac), Hugues de, lord of, 140, 202
Carentan, 226
Carinthia, 23, 41; Otto of, 261n
Carit, Bertrand, 223–4
Carloman, 22, 181
Carmona, 59
carnaticus, 26
Carniola, 41
Carpathian mountains, 33
carroccio, 115
Cartae baronum, 79
Cartagena, 4
Cassel, battle of (1328), 240, 258, 291, 300
Cassinel, Ferry, bishop of Auxerre, 301

Cassiodorus, 18, 177
Castagnaro, battle of (1387), 199
Castel del Monte, 114
castella, 6, 16, 17, 21, 28, 39, 44
castellanie, 5
Castelnaudary, 104, 225
Castile, 21, 30, 56–8, 77, 92–3, 121, 135, 151, 163, 167, 199, 206n, 210–11, 283; Fernando of, 93; Pedro of, 206
Castillon, battle of (1453), 199, 300n
castles, rendability of, 109; density of, 46, 109; see also fortifications; 3–5
Catalan company, 100, 247–8
Catalogus baronum, 55
Catalonia, 56, 71, 73, 100, 161, 206, 219n, 243
catapult, 103–4, 139, 195; see also trébuchet
Cathars, 246, 274, 293–4
Catherine of Siena, St., 159
Catholicon, 186
Caudebec-en-Caux, 203
Caumont, Nompar, lord of, 123
Caux, region of, 28, 81, 203
Cavaillon, 240
cavalry, 5, 6, 10, 25, 31, 33, 35–8, 47–50, 58–60, 99, 115–18, 121, 126–33, 150–70, 179–84, 208–9, 211–12, 229–37, 255–9, 303, 307; see also horse
cedant arma togae, 16
Celts, 50–1
Ceneda, 40
Cesena, 159
Chadoind, 20
Chaduiz, Durand, 246
chain mail, 126, 178, 181, 184–8, 216, 244, 256; see also 8, 10, 18
Chaira, 20
Chalcedon, council of (451), 269
Châlons-sur-Marne, 48
Châlus, 72
Chambéry, 239
chambres, 154, 192
Champagne, 43, 52, 82, 87, 96, 118, 215; Hugues, count of, 48; Thibaud, count of, 72, 109
Channel, the English, 53, 79, 153, 191, 223, 239, 245
Chansons de geste, 56, 119, 253, 275, 299

Charenton, 145n
Charibert, 20
Charlemagne, king and emperor, 23–7, 44, 56, 182–4, 220, 225, 254n, 269; vassals of, 25–7
Charles V, king of France, 120, 129, 133, 141, 153–6, 166, 168, 194, 217, 228, 285
Charles VI, king of France, 120, 129, 166, 168, 191, 214, 217, 242, 300–1
Charles VII, king of France, 124, 131, 133, 145–6, 153, 157, 164–5, 169–70, 189, 191, 195, 212, 218n, 226, 228, 285, 299n, 300
Charles VIII, king of France, 121, 123, 134, 137n, 145–6, 149, 165, 189, 218n, 225–6
Charles I of Anjou, king of Sicily, 67–8, 98–9, 116, 300n
Charles II of Anjou, king of Sicily, 248
Charles the Bad, king of Navarre, 132
Charles III the Simple, emperor, 29, 268
Charles IV, emperor, 159
Charles the Bald, emperor, 27–9, 43, 265
Charles the Fat, emperor, 30
Charles Martel, 22, 24, 179, 181–3
Charny, Geoffroy de, 215
Charolais, count of, see Burgundy, Charles, count of
Charroux, council of (989), 271
Chartier, Jean, 130, 226
Chartres, Chartrain, 42, 46, 48, 113, 148, 267, 300
Chastel, Tanguy du, 206
Chastelier, Jacques du, bishop of Paris, 299n
Chastellain, Georges, 120, 293
Chastel-Marlhac, 44
Château-Gaillard, 101, 105, 110–11, 113–14
Châteauneuf-sur-Epte, 42
Château-Thierry, 87
Châtillon, 253n
Chelcicky, Peter, 295
chemin de ronde, 107, 203
chemise, 114, 203
Cherbourg, 206, 226–7
Cheshire, 151, 166, 191
Chester, 166
chevauchées, 215, 220n, 223–5, 228, 239

Chevreuse, 41
Chevry, Pierre de, 86
Chiericati, Chiereghino, 120
Chiese, battle of river (1373), 159
Chilperic, king of the Franks, 14, 19–20
Chimay, prince of, 137
China, Chinese, 138–9, 181, 219, 306
Chinon, 106
Chioggia, 138
Chivalry, growth of, 270–7
Chramnelen, 20
Chrétien de Troyes, 193
Christ, Order of, 76
Christian of Oliva, bishop of Prussia, 76
Chronicon Ebes Pengense, 34
Chronicon Sampetrinum, 104
Chronicon Tarvisium, 140–1
Chronique Scandaleuse, 193
Chronographia regum francorum, 231
Cicero, 250–1, 264
Cidlina, battle of river (1110), 261n
Cinglais, region of, 46
Cingulum, 16
Cinque ports, 51
Ciompi, 161
Circumcellions, 16
Cîteaux, 76
Città Papale, 85
Cividale, 139
Clavering, 52
Clergy, clerics, role in warfare, services of, 19, 34, 37–8, 40, 42, 87, 240–1, 266, 268–9, 276–7, 282, 287, 292, 299, 305
Clermont, John, count of, 226
Clermont-en-Auvergne, 59, 240, 278
Clermont-sur-Oise, 42
Clèves, Philippe de, lord of Ravenstein, 137, 201, 206, 227, 261, 286
Clisson, Olivier de, 65
Clovis I, king of the Franks, 18, 261n, 262, 292
Cluny, abbey of, 90, 272, 275, 297
Clusae, 17
Coblenz, 44
Codex Perizonianus, 183
Codex Spirensis, 7
Codice degli stipendiarii (1369), 120
Coëtivy, Prigent de, admiral of France, 206

Colchester, 159
Cologne, 38, 148, 162, 270, 277, 282
coloni, 7
Colonna family, 161
Comes stabuli, 6
comitatenses, 5, 7, 12, 16
comites civitatum, 16
Comminges, 17, 102; Bernard IV, count of, 72
Commynes, Philippe de, 128, 129n, 136, 145n, 200, 286
Companies, Free, 123, 157, 159, 243, 247–8, 291; Great, 123, 158–60, 248n, 291; *ordonnance*, 128, 131, 134–5, 157n, 165, 168–9, 170–1, 189, 192, 233, 249, 258
Company, White, 159
Compiègne, 107, 111, 148, 300
Compostella, 56, 298
compulsores, 229, 236
Conan III, *see* Brittany
Condotta, condottieri, 99–100, 127–8, 130, 157–61, 172, 255n, 258
Conrad I, king of Germany, 34
Conrad II, king of Germany, 32, 38
Conrad III, emperor, 231
conrois, 229, 236
Constantine, emperor, 5–7, 16, 264, 292, 294, 302
Constantine, patrician, 4
Constantinople, 3, 16, 54, 59, 61, 63, 101, 105; *see also* Byzantines, Byzantium
Consuetudines et justicie, 46
Contracts, military, 150–65
Conway, 111
Cooling castle, 202n
Corbeil, 81
Corbie, 118
Cordebeuf, Merlin de, 120
Córdoba, 4, 23, 57, 59, 65, 163
Corfe, 110
Coriolanus, 252
Cornaut, Jocelin de, engineer, 106
Cornazano, Antonio, 138
Cornelius, centurion, 263
Cornwall, John de, 293; Richard of, 80
Corsica, 4, 27, 100
Cortenuova, battle of (1237), 66
Cortona, 210
Corvey, abbot of, 25

Cosne, 42
Costs: of arms, 58, 94–7; of cannonballs, 198; of fortifications, 107–11, 114–15; of gunpowder, 198; of wars, 116–18
Cotentin, 81, 226
Cotereaux, 100, 244–6, 248
Coucy, 108, 113–14, 201; Enguerran III of, 108
courage, 250–9
Courberan, 244
Courland, 76
Courtenay, Hugues de, 80
Courtrai, battle of (1302), 87, 240, 258, 291, 300; *see also* 7
Coutances, 226
coutilier, 127–8, 134, 166–7, 169
Coventry, 53
cranequiniers, 171, 213; *see also* crossbowmen
Cravant, battle of (1423), 257n
Crécy-en-Ponthieu, battle of (1346), 140, 155, 198, 255n, 257
Crécy-sur-Serre, 42, 223
Cremona, 149, 240
Crete, 96
Croats, 23
Cromwell, Oliver, 208
cross, 61, 190–1, 298–9, 301
crossbow, use of, 71–2, 89, 110, 114, 117, 122, 132, 186, 189, 193, 202–3, 217, 274
crossbowmen, 67, 91, 96n, 100, 102, 115–16, 124, 129–30, 132–5, 137, 157, 161, 168, 202, 213, 232–3, 247, 274; mounted, 71, 98, 116, 124, 129, 171, 213
Crossbowmen, Master of, 153, 215
Crotoy (Le), 215
Crusade, Albigensian, 101–2; *see also* Albi
Crusades, 41, 49, 56, 59–66, 74–6, 93, 99, 101, 103, 118, 159, 190, 209, 212, 214, 241, 254, 270, 278–80, 293, 298, 304; *see also* 13
Cuvelier, Jean, 299
Cyprus, 195

Dacia, 3, 6
Dagobert I, king of the Franks, 20, 22
Daillon, Jean de, lord of Lude, 126

Dalmatia, 3, 16
Damascus, 63–4, 139
Damietta, 103
Danelaw, 28, 50–1
Danes, *see* Denmark
Danevirke, 220
Dangu, 42
Dante Alighieri, 292
Danube, river, 4, 6, 33
Dardania, 3
Dassel, Rainald von, 212n
Datini, Francesco di Marco, 216n
Dauphin, Guichard, 215
David, king of the Jews, 254n, 261n, 263, 277
Decretals, 274, 280
Decretum, 274, 280
Decumatian fields, 3, 219
De Dulle Griet (Mad Margot), bombard, 142; *see also 20*
Dee, river, 30
defiances, 291
Delbrück, H., 25
Demetrius, 306
Denis, St., 298–9; *see also* Saint-Denis, abbey of
Denis the Carthusian, 210
Denmark, 23, 32, 39, 50, 105, 123, 162, 187, 220, 258
Derby, Henry, earl of, 223
Derbyshire, 151
Deschamps, Eustache, 254n
Desclot, Bernat, 73
Deventer, 139
Dhondt, J., 181–2
Dialogus de scaccario, 90
Die, 240
Dienstleute, 38, 78
Digest, The, 284
Dijon, 148, 191, 203, 239
Dinant, 200
Diocletian, emperor, 4–7
Dithmarschen, 162–3, 258
Dixmude, 240
Djihad, 57; *see also* Holy war
Dobrzyn, 76
Doctrinal de noblesse, 283n
Dol-de-Bretagne, 98
Dole, 190
Domesday book, 51, 304

Domfront, 226
donativum, 16, 17
Dorylaeum, battle of (1097), 62–3
Douglas, James, earl of, 241
Dourdan, 114
Dover, 49, 51, 89, 110, 114, 165; *see also 3*
drawbridges, 107, 111, 114, 212
Dresden, 241
Drouot, Antoine, 296
Dublin, 187
Dubois, Pierre, 92, 292
Duby, G., 275
Duero, river, 58
Dunois, Jean d'Orléans, count of, 226
Durand, Guillaume, bishop of Mende, 277, 287, 289; *see also 9*
Durazzo, 128
Durham, Ordinance of (1385), 120
dux, 6, 16, 20–1, 33, 37, 57
Dyle, battle of the (891), 182

East Anglia, 50
Ebro, 23, 56
Ecorcheurs, 123, 136, 169, 243, 291
Edessa, 62–4
Edinburgh, 105, 142
Edward, the Black Prince, prince of Wales and Guyenne, 225, 257
Edward I, king of England, 66, 70, 72–3, 80, 89, 91–3, 97–8, 104–5, 109, 111, 114–17, 208, 210, 225, 238, 307
Edward III, king of England, 129, 132, 140, 146, 150–1, 222–4, 228, 257, 285, 307
Edward IV, king of England, 129
Edward the Elder, king of the Anglo-Saxons, 50
Edward the Confessor, 50–2
Egbert, king of the Anglo-Saxons, 50
Egica, king of the Visigoths, 20
Egypt, 60, 106, 213, 280, 293n, 306
Elbe, river, 23, 30, 32, 36
Eleanor of Aquitaine, 241
Elne, 272
Eloi, St., 269
Elz, battle of river (1298), 261n
Embrun, 119
emerita missio, 6
engineers, 105–6, 194

England, English, 28, 30, 41, 48–55, 60,
    62, 65, 68–73, 78–80, 88–9, 91–4,
    97, 99, 105, 108–9, 116–17, 120,
    123–4, 129, 131, 136n, 140, 150–3,
    155, 160, 163, 165, 167–70, 172,
    190, 192, 198, 200, 202n, 208, 213,
    215, 217, 225–6, 229n, 231, 239,
    241, 244, 256–7, 274, 282–5, 287–8,
    291, 293–5, 298–9, 302, 304–6, 308
Eoda, 266
Epirus, 3
Epistre à Richard II, 288
Erasmus, 292
Erkenbald, bishop of Strasbourg, 37
Ermenfrid, 268
Ervig, king of the Visigoths, 19–20
Escouchy, Mathieu d', 136n
Espine, Jacquemin de l', 142
Esplechin, truce of, 220
Essex, 52; Thomas, earl of Buckingham
    and, 120
Este, Azzo of, 78
Estradiots, 128, 291
Etablissements de Saint Louis, 81, 85
Etampes, 42, 48
Ethiopia, 293n
Eu, Charles d'Artois, count of, 226
Euric, king of the Visigoths, 21
Evesham, battle of (1265), 208
Evrecy, 48
Evreux, 28, 111, 114, 115n; Helvise,
    countess of, 241
Expeditio italica, 35
Expugnatio hibernica, 70, 212
ex voto, 300–1

Fabius Maximus Cunctator, 252
fabricenses, 5n
fabriciae, 5, 16
Falaise, 106, 226
Falcaise, Falco, 244
Falkirk, battle of (1298), 70, 116, 307
Fano, 85
fara, faramanni, 21
Fastolf, Sir John, 120, 210, 215, 274
Fatimids, 64
Felton, Sir Thomas, 152, 242
Ferdinand, Ferrante II, king of Aragon,
    145, 214
Fère (La), 42

Fernand de Jean, 92–3
Ferrara, 161
Ferruge, 262
Ferté-Alais (La), 41
Fervaques, abbey of, 223
Fibonacci, Leonardo, 90
fideles, 21, 43, 58
Fidenzo of Padua, 118, 212
fief-rent, 92–3, 154, 163
Figéac, 84
Filarete, Antonio Averlino, called, 204
fines for default of military service, 17,
    26, 52, 82; see also scutagium
fire, use of, in warfare, 41–2, 244n
flags, see signs, distinctive; standards
Flamengrie (La), 223
Flanders, 42–3, 45, 47, 49, 52, 83, 96,
    100, 134n, 137, 190–1, 239, 242,
    244–5, 255–6, 258; see also Flemings;
    Baldwin VII, count of, 42; Charles the
    Good, count of, 48, 256; Louis de
    Male, count of, 301; Robert II, count
    of, 41, 48–50, 61n; Robert de
    Béthune, count of, 194
Flemings, 61, 66, 96, 129, 134n, 145n,
    191, 231–2, 242, 245–6, 258, 291,
    300, 304; see also 7
Flint, 111
Flintshire, 191
Florence, 67, 70, 73, 84, 86, 91, 94, 96–7,
    99–100, 115–17, 120, 122, 127, 129,
    132–3, 136, 139, 158–9, 161, 165,
    201, 301
foederati, 7, 9
Fogassot, Franchesco, 206
Fogliano, Ghiberto da, 140; see also
    endpapers
Foix, county of, 81, 85, 102, 123, 307;
    Gaston Fébus, count of, 132n, 166,
    302, 307; Gaston de, count of
    Nemours, 273n
fonsado, fossato, 57–8
Fonsomme, 223
Fontarrabia, 132
Fontenoy-en-Puisaye, battle of (841),
    261, 265, 268
Forez, 109
Forli, 139, 172n
Formigny, battle of (1450), 226
Fornovo, battle of (1495), 128, 200

fortifications, 6, 12, 31, 35, 44–7, 50–1, 101–15, 122–3, 201–4, 209, 219; see also 3–5
Fossés-le-Roi (Les), 222
Fougères, 122, 225–6, 285
Fournier, Jacques, bishop of Pamiers, 293, 295; see also Benedict XII
Fourre, Adam, 116
framea, 176n
Franc-archers, 133–4, 157, 170
France, French, 30, 33, 37–9, 41–50, 58n, 60–1, 65–6, 68, 72, 79–87, 91, 93–4, 98–100, 115–18, 120–1, 123–5, 128–9, 132–3, 136, 140–2, 144–9, 151–7, 159, 161–3, 165–71, 184, 189–90, 194–201, 204, 209, 213–15, 218, 222–3, 227, 231, 239, 243–7, 249, 256–9, 272–3, 276–8, 283–5, 287–8, 291, 294, 298–302, 304, 306–8
Francis I, king of France, 146, 198
Francis of Assisi, St., 293
francisca, 176
Franco, Generalissimo, 9
Franconia, 37, 118
Franconians, 35
Franks, 4, 12–14, 17–24, 36, 39, 44, 61–2, 64, 175–9, 181–4, 261–2, 269; see also 2
Fredegar, 20, 22
Frederick Barbarossa, emperor, 66, 108, 212n, 244n, 245, 272, 292; see also 6
Frederick II, emperor, 67–8, 70–1, 76, 91, 99, 109, 186
Frederick II of Aragon, king of Sicily, 248
free, non-free, 19–20, 27, 38–9, 88–9, 240, 256–7, 261–2, 265
Fresnay-le-Vicomte, 226
Fribourg-en-Brisgau, 138
Frisia, 23, 36, 242
Frisians, 22, 242, 256
Friuli, 139
Friuli, Evrard, duke of, 210
Froissart, Jean, 155, 191, 194, 198–9, 206, 214–15, 227, 229n, 241, 256–7, 291, 299n, 308
frontiers, 4–6, 27, 39, 41, 56–7, 219–22; see also limes
Frontinus, 210–12, 297

Frothard, 26n
Fulbert, bishop of Chartres, 267
Fulda, abbey of, 34, 182
Fulford, battle of (1066), 52
Fulrad, 26
Fyrd, 51–2, 54

Gaeta, 55
Gaillon, 72, 247
Galbert of Bruges, 256
Galicia, 56, 275
Gallienus, emperor, 7
Gallo-Romans, 18
gambeson, 73, 86, 88
Ganshof, F. L., 25
gardingi, 21, 57
Garland, Y., 99
Garnier, master engineer, 106; master of works, 111
Garonne, river, 22, 83, 220–1
Gascons, 20, 82–3, 100, 106, 129, 152, 162, 244
Gascony, 20, 93–4, 106, 117, 134, 239; see also Aquitaine; Guyenne
Gasny, 42
Gaul, 4–6, 12, 14, 16, 18, 29
Gautier de Mullent, 107, 111
geld, danegeld, heregeld, 52
Geneva, 114; count of, 155
Geneviève, Ste., 13n
Genoa, 62, 95, 123, 138, 195, 199
Genseric, king of the Vandals, 11
Geoffroy de Breteuil, 296
George, St., 126, 190–1, 297, 299; company of, 158–60
George Pachymeres, 248
George Podiebrad, king of Bohemia, 125, 292
Gepids, 20
Gerald of Wales (Giraldus Cambrensis), 70, 187, 212
Germans, 5, 13, 17–19
Germany (including Holy Roman Empire), 30–41, 61, 68, 77–9, 83, 86, 100, 118, 123–4, 129, 131, 135–7, 145, 148, 158, 161–3, 165, 170, 180, 191, 196, 213, 217, 219, 223, 231, 239, 244–5, 254, 269, 272, 290–1, 302, 307
Germigny-l'Exempt, 42

Gerson, Jean, 210–11, 293, 296–7, 301
Gesiths, 21, 51
Gévaudan, count of, 271
Ghent, 114, 124, 142, 145, 148, 191, 199, 240, 299n; *see also 20*
Ghibellines, 66
Gideon, 263
Gilbert Le Fossier, master of works, 111
Giles of Rome, 194, 210–11
Gimaboni, Bono, 210
Giovio, Paolo, 159
Gisors, 42, 81, 110
Givry, 109
Gloucester, Richard, duke of, 152; Robert, earl of, 48; trébuchet, 105
Godefroy, F., 188
goedendags, 73
Goliath of Gath, 261n
Gombaud, archbishop of Bordeaux, 271
Gorze, abbey of, 270
Gothia, 262
Goths, *see* Ostrogoths; Visigoths
Gotland, 122
Gournay, 41–2
Granada, 65, 123, 135, 163, 220
Grandson, battle of (1476), 144, 200, 218, 261
Gratian, 274, 280–2
Gravelines, 49
Greek fire, 274n
Greeks, 71, 96, 128, 161, 210, 241, 248
Gregory IX, pope, 67, 78, 274
Gregory X, pope, 212
Gregory XI, pope, 240
Gregory of Tours, 17, 19, 44, 175, 176n, 183, 260–1
Grey, Sir Edward, 127
Gruel, Guillaume, 131
Guelders, 39n, 149; Renaud, count of, 223; William, duke of, 301
Guelfs, 66, 117
Guesclin, Bertrand du, constable of France, 215, 242, 254, 299, 301; Julienne du, abbess, 242
ʼart, Guillaume, 191n, 193, 230n
ume de Cambrai, 244
ʼe de Flamenville, 111
de Poitiers, 236n
Saint-Pathus, 113n
ange, 300

Guillaume le Breton, 72, 231n
Guillaume of Ypres, 244
Guillaume Piere de la Mar, 72
Guinegatte, battle of (1479), 133
Guise, 223
Gundobad, king of the Burgundians, 18, 19
Gundovald the pretender, 260
gunports, 202–5
gunpowder, 137–50, 196–8
guns, 137–50, 196–207; *see also* bombards; cannons
Guntram, king of the Franks, 17, 20
Guyenne, 82, 109, 124, 169

Habsburg, Philip the Handsome, *see* Austria, Philip, archduke of
Hachette, Jeanne, 242
Hadrian's wall, 219
Hainault, 134n, 137, 162, 240, 242–4, 256; John I, count of, 194; William I, count of, 127, 194; William II, count of, 223
Halidon Hill, battle of (1333), 258
Ham, 145n, 204
Hampshire, 152
handgunners, 134–5, 232
Hannibal, 208
Hanse, German, 123
Harbotel, John, 148
Harff, Arnold von, 149, 206
Harfleur, 203, 214, 226
Harlech, 111
harnois blanc, 126, 159n, 213
Harold, king of the English, 54, 99n, 300
Harran, 63
Hasding Vandals, *see* Vandals
Hastings, battle of (1066), 51–3, 99n, 113, 183, 253n, 268, 300; *see also 1*
haubergeon, hauberk, 31, 58n, 67, 69, 73, 86, 88, 95, 130, 132, 134n, 184–8, 241
Hawkwood, Sir John, 130, 158–9, 199; *see also 14*
Hector, 252, 254n
Heerschild, 37, 68
Helgaud of Fleury, 295n
helmet, 178, 255n, 264; *see also 19*
Hemmingstedt, battle of (1500), 162, 258

Henry I, king of England, 39, 41–2, 48–50, 54, 64, 79–80, 256, 273n
Henry II, king of England, 66, 78–80, 88, 108–9, 189, 221–2, 238, 240, 245
Henry III, king of England, 65, 68, 80, 91, 94, 109
Henry V, king of England, 120, 169, 191, 195, 229n, 293, 299
Henry VI, king of England, 121, 148, 215, 299n
Henry VII, king of England, 145–6, 167
Henry VIII, king of England, 145–6, 149, 167
Henry I, king of Germany, 34–5
Henry II, emperor, 32
Henry IV, emperor, 32, 36, 39, 62
Henry V, emperor, 37, 39, 48
Henry VI, emperor, 78
Henry VII, emperor, 78
Henry of Ghent, 251–2
Heraclea, 63
heralds, 257, 262, 289, 292n; see also Le Bouvier
heribannum, 26, 87
hermandad, 163
Hermenric, 20
Hero of Alexandria, 210
Herradus of Landsberg, 297n
Herstal, see Pepin II
Herter, Wilhelm, 162
Hetti, 26n
Hincmar of Reims, 297
hlafaeten, 21
hobelars, 71, 128, 153
Holland, 256; see also Netherlands
Holy Land, 33, 70, 72, 74–7, 92, 96, 101, 118, 213, 227–8, 231, 256, 278–9; see also Palestine
Holy Roman Empire, see Germany
Holyrood, Abbey of, 105
Holy War, 278–9; see also Crusades; Djihad
homage, 31
Homer, 138
Homs, 64
honesta missio, 6
Honfleur, 226
Honnecourt-sur-Escaut, 223
Hope castle, 111
horse, 28, 58, 62, 67–73, 85, 88, 96–7, 100, 126–32, 149, 151, 179, 181–3, 197, 201, 213, 216–17, 223, 238, 241–2, 258, 301, 303; see also cavalry
horses, costs of, 96–7, 127–8, 130–1
hospitalitas, 16
Hospitallers, Order of, 75–7, 118, 241, 254
Hostiensis, 279–80, 283
hostilense, 26
Hugo, Victor, 236
Hugonet, Guillaume, 134n
Hugot, Pierre de, 116
Huguccio, 279, 282
Humbert, lord of Ste-Sevère, 41
Hungarians, 39, 124, 126, 128, 158, 161, 269; see also Magyars
Hungary, 30, 32–3, 38, 71, 139, 156, 239, 301
Huns, 3, 11, 13, 32
Hussites, 120, 121n, 123–4, 130, 136, 148, 240–1, 291, 295, 304
Huy, 221
Hythe, 51

Ibelin, 77
Iberia, see Portugal; Spain
Ifriqiya, 54; see also Africa
Ile-de-France, 43, 168.
incastellamento, 40
indentures, 151–2, 160
Indiculus loricatorum, 37
Ine, king of Wessex, 17
infantry, 5, 10, 25, 49, 55, 58, 64, 67–73, 77, 86, 91, 94, 100, 115–18, 132–7, 151–65, 170, 229–37, 243, 258, 307
infanzones, 58
infeudation, sub-infeudation, 53–5, 64, 78–9
Ingeborg of Denmark, queen of France, 81
Ingenuinus, bishop of Savona, 262
Innocent II, pope, 55
Innocent III, pope, 76, 78, 293
Innocent IV, pope, 71, 289, 296
Innsbruck, 149, 193
Iran, 181; see also Persia
Irene, St., 264
Ireland, Irish, 70, 73, 118, 150, 212, 291

Isabella the Catholic, queen of Spain, 132, 171–2
Isidore of Seville, 13, 20, 176n, 262
Islam, 279–80, 304; *see also* Muslims
Israel, 263, 269n
Issoudun, 84
Istria, 40
Italian Relation, 164
Italy, 4, 11, 12, 14, 16, 17, 20, 23, 25, 27, 29–30, 33, 35–41, 52, 54–5, 58–9, 61, 65–7, 70–3, 78, 83–6, 96–7, 99–100, 123–4, 126, 129–31, 133–5, 140, 145, 149–50, 157–62, 172, 198–201, 204–7, 217–18, 227, 245, 248, 255, 258–9, 261–2, 272, 277, 282, 286, 289n, 291, 293, 298n, 300
Ivrea, 39
Ivry-la-Bataille, 299
Ivry-sur-Seine, 198.

Jacqueries, 304
Jacques de Longuyon, 254n
Jaffa, 62
Jaligny, lord of, *see* Dauphin, Guichard
James, St., the Major, 56, 298–9
James, St., the Minor, 281
James II, king of Scotland, 206
James of St George, master of works, 111
James of Vitry, 243
Japan, 139
Jean de Dieu, 274
Jean de Garlande, 102n, 103
Jean de Meung, 210
Jean de Roye, 193
Jean le Roux, *see* Brittany, John I, duke of
Jeptha, 263
Jerome, St., 3, 13
Jerusalem, 54, 59–60, 62–4, 74–5, 77, 105, 265, 278–9; Assizes of, 77
Jesus Christ, 74–7, 187–8, 246, 263–4, 273n, 275, 278–9, 294, 296–7
Jews, 241, 302
jinetes, 58, 71, 128, 135, 163, 167, 172
Jocelin of Brakelond, 79
Johannes Teutonicus, 282
Johannes Vitoduranus, *see* Winterthur, John of
John, abbot, 296

John the Baptist, St., 263, 268, 277
John XII, pope, 270
John XXII, pope, 118, 213
John II, king of Aragon, 283n
John the Blind, king of Bohemia, 255n
John I, king of Denmark, 162, 258
John I Lackland, king of England, 71, 80, 87, 89, 100, 106, 108, 110, 208, 212, 214, 244, 246–7
John the Good, king of France, 128, 133, 155, 236n, 308
John I, king of Portugal, 300
John of Genoa, 186
John of Legnano, 119, 160, 281, 283
John of Salisbury, 275
John the Black, master gunner, 141
John the Lydian, 7
John Tzimisces, emperor, 261
Joinville, Jean de, 87, 99, 105n
Jonas of Orléans, 297
jongleurs, 253n
Joseph the Bombardier, 241
Joshua, 254n, 263
Jouvencel (le), 120, 137–8, 215, 218, 281, 285, 289; *see also* Bueil, Jean de
Jouvenel des Ursins, Jean, 217
Jouvenel des Ursins, Guillaume, 226
Jovinus, emperor, 4
Judas Maccabeus, 254n, 263, 277
Julian, emperor, 4, 15
Julien of Vézelay, 188, 296–7
Juliers, Guillaume, margrave of, 223
Jumièges, abbey of, 53, 111
Justinian, emperor, 4, 7, 9–11
Just War, theory and practice of, 251, 264–5, 273–4, 276, 279, 282–8, 292–5
Jutes, 4n, 14
Jutland, 162, 220

Karlstein, 122, 136
Kenilworth, 110
Kerboga, 63
Knaresborough, 110
knighthood, distraint of, 64; orders of, 74–7
knights, *see miles*
knights banneret, 68, 70, 80, 82, 116, 126, 151–2
Knights of the Dove, 158

Knolles, Sir Robert, 239
Krak (le) des Chevaliers, 101, 113; see also 5
Kulm, 76
Kyeser, Conrad, 120
Kyriel, Thomas, 226

laager warfare, 124, 130; see also 24
labarum, 264
La Baume, Guillaume de, 233
La Brocquière, Bertrandon de, 213
Lacordaire, H., 296
Lactantius, 263
Lagny, 96, 200
Laize, river, 46
Lalaing, Antoine de, 132, 149, 171, 193; Jacques de, 206
La Marche, Olivier de, 131, 134n, 149, 167
Lamballe, 203
Lambert, St., 298
Lambert of Hersfeld, 36
Lancaster, John of Gaunt, duke of, 120–1, 130, 151, 153
lance, composition of, 67–70, 127–8, 169
Landau, Conrad von, 158
Landfriede, 66, 242, 272
Lanfranc, archbishop of Canterbury, 277
Langeais, 47
Langobardia, 55
Languedoc, 225
Lannoy, Ghillebert de, 121
lansquenets (Landsknechte), 136–7, 163, 291
Lantweri, 24
Laon, Laonnois, 42, 48, 107, 111, 215, 223
La Personne Jean, 239
La Salade, 212
La Sale, Antoine de, 212, 214
La Salle, Gadifer de, 254
Lateran, second council of (1139), 71, 274, third council of (1179), 246
La Trémoille, Louis de, 121, 206, 274n
Laupen, battle of (1339), 136
Laurentius Hispanus, 282
Lausanne, 167, 171, 233–4
Lauzerte, 202n
Laval, André de, 163–4; Anne, lady of, 163–4; Guy, lord of, 163–4; Jeanne,

dowager lady of, 163–4
La Victoire, abbey of, 300
Lebbre, 142
Le Bourgeois, Tugdual, 206
Le Bouvier, Gilles, Berry herald, 124
Lechfeld, battle of (955), 30, 35
Le Debat des hérauts, 255
Legio mesaburiorum, 35
legions, 5
Legnano, battle of (1176), 66; see also 6
Léhon, 98
Leiden, 183
Le Mans, 20, 88, 148, 273
Le Mercier, Jean, 227n
Leo IV, pope, 270
Leo VI, emperor, 33–4
Leon, 56–8
Leovigild, king of the Visigoths, 18
Lérines, 195
lèse-majesté, 276, 283, 290
lettres de retenue, 153; see also indentures
Leudebert, 20
leudes, 22
Lex Alamannorum, 175
Lex Ribuaria, 178
Libanius, 16
Liber judiciorum, 18
Liber recuperationis Terre Sancte, 118, 212
Liber secretorum, 194
Liddell Hart, B. H., 208
lidi, 19
Liège, 199–200, 221, 228, 231, 254n, 298
Liguria, 39, 100
Lille, 42, 134n, 139, 146, 191, 194, 301
limes, 4–6, 15, 17, 51, 219
limes danicus, 27
limes saxonicus, 220
limitanie, 5, 6, 16
limits on military service: distance, 38, 77–8, 81–8, 91–2, 150–2, 163–4; time, 50–2, 77–8, 81–8, 91–2, 150–2, 163–4
Limoges, Limousin, 72, 84, 118, 152, 240
Lin, Louis, 206
Lincoln, battle of (1141), 273n; battle of (1217), 256n
Lisbon, 56
Lisieux, 28, 87, 203n, 226
Lisle, Lancelot de, 148
lists, 108

Liutprand of Cremona, 33–4
livery, *see* uniforms
Livonia, 76, 115n, 220
Livre de la paix, 293
Livre des fais d'armes et de chevalerie, 120, 287
Livre du secret de l'artillerye et canonnerye, 138
Livry, 42
Livy, Titus, 210n, 214–15, 297
Lobar, 244
Lodi, 40
Loire, river, 28, 43, 83, 211
Lollardy, 294–5
Lombard league, 71–2
Lombards, 4, 13, 14, 17–23, 27, 35, 39, 55, 175, 179, 262, 270, 277
Lombardy, 35, 97, 123, 129, 162, 170n, 189n, 205, 227, 245, 276, 302
London, 53, 83, 108, 122, 140
longbow, 72, 129, 150–3, 217
Loos, count of, 244
Looz, county of, 221
Lopez, Juan, 283, 285
Lorraine, 37, 61, 149, 285, 298, 301; Raoul, duke of, 155; René II, duke of, 162, 167, 289n, 300–1
Lot, F., 9, 25
Lothair II, king of the Franks, 260
Lothair II, king of Italy, 25
Lothair I, emperor, 29, 211
Lothair of Supplinburg, emperor, 36
Louis VI the Fat, king of France, 41–3, 48, 256, 273
Louis VII, king of France, 32n, 42, 72, 87, 245, 272
Louis VIII, king of France, 101
Louis IX, Saint Louis, king of France, 65, 67–8, 81, 83, 85–6, 92, 96–9, 103, 106–7, 113n, 272, 280, 298
Louis X Hutin, king of France, 259
Louis XI, king of France, 123, 131, 133, 134n, 136, 145, 148, 153, 156, 165, 170–1, 189, 191, 193, 202, 205n, 206, 228, 291, 300
Louis XII, king of France, 207
Louis the German, king of Germany, 265
Louis II, emperor, 29
Louis of Bavaria, emperor, 261

Louis the Pious, emperor, 25–7, 29, 30
Loup, St., 13n
Louviers, 226
Louvois, François, 190
Louvre, The, 114
Loyal serviteur, 244n, 252, 258; *see also* Bayart
Lucca, 19, 139, 159, 275
Lucera, 70, 100
Lucerne, 291
Lucifer, 281
Lupescar, 244
Lusatia, 41
Lusignan, Jacques de, 195
Luttrell, Sir Geoffrey, *see 12*
Lyon, Lyonnais, 118, 191, 197n, 212, 298

Maastricht, 200
Maccabees, Book of, 252; *see also* Judas Maccabeus
Macedonia, 3
Machiavelli, Niccolo, 162, 206n, 249, 258, 308
machicolations, 114
Mâcon, 43, 46
Macquigny, 223
Madras, 142
Madrid, 122
magister utriusque militiae, 16
magistri equitum, 16
magistri peditum, 16
Magna Carta, 247
Magyars, 30, 32–5, 39; *see also* Hungarians
Mainades, 244
Maine, 46, 50, 118; Charles, count of, 191
Majorca, 240
Malaga, 4, 65
Malassis, 42
Malatesta, Sigismondo, 204
Malet de Graville, Louis, admiral of France, 120
Malik Shah, 59
Malines, 148
Malmédy, 22
Manasses, archbishop of Reims, 59
man-at-arms, definitions and terms for, 126
mancipia, 19

Manichaeans, 295
Mann, Sir John, 185
Mantes, 42, 226
Mantua, 40, 161, 300
Manzikert, battle of (1071), 59
Marchfield, 182
Marco, Francesco, see Datini
Marcomans, 3
Marcus Graecus, 196
Mariano, captain, 233
Marino, battle of (1380), 160
Marmande, 101
Marmoutier, 211
Mars, God of War, 182, 252; planet, 281
Marsan, 132, 307
Marsilius of Padua, 292
Martel, 84
Martin, St., 262
Martin V, pope, 133
Martin Algais, 244
Martin of Lodi, 283
Martini, Francesco di Giorgio, 138,
    142-3, 196-7, 204
Mary, St., 246, 272, 299-301
Masovia, Conrad, duke of, 76
Masters of works, 111, 195, 202, 205; see
    also engineers
Mastre Richard, 210
Matilda, empress, 78
Matthew Paris, 68, 94
Maulin, Jean, 214
Maurice, St., 297-8
Maximilian von Habsburg, emperor,
    king of the Romans, duke of
    Burgundy, 134, 137, 149, 163, 189,
    193; see also 21
Mayenne, 148
Mazères, 123
Meaux, 293
Medinaceli, 57
Mediterranean sea, 27, 30, 213, 225-6
Mêle-sur-Sarthe (Le), 222
Melgueil, Pons de, abbot of Cluny, 90
Melun, 81, 107, 111
Mende, 245
mendum, 97
Menin, 240
Merate, Francesco da, 189-90; Gabriele
    da, 189-90
Mercadier, 244, 247

mercenary service, 95-101, 117, 150-65;
    see also wages; definition of, 99
Mercia, 50
merlons, 114
Merpins, 154
Merseburg, 35
Metz, 139, 162-3, 191, 205, 269-70, 283,
    285, 301
Meulan, 42, 206; Robert III, count of,
    41
Meung-sur-Loire, 41
Meuse, river, 23, 41
Meyrick, Samuel, 184n
Mézières, Philippe de, 127, 156, 186,
    211n, 236-7, 288, 292n
Mezos, Jean de, engineer, 106
Michael, St., 297
Middle East, 30
Midi, 82
Milan, 40, 97, 117, 128, 145-6, 149, 159,
    161, 166, 172, 189-90, 227, 239,
    263; see also 6, 19a-c
Milemete, Walter of, 139
miles (including knights), 31, 36-7, 40,
    47-50, 53-5, 58, 60-2, 64, 67-73,
    77-89, 91-102, 115-17, 126-32,
    150-2, 165-72, 181-2, 211-13,
    230-1, 238, 247, 251-2, 255-9, 271,
    275-6, 287-8, 297, 303, 306-7; see
    also 8, 12, 13, 15
military enterprisers, 162
military exercises, training, 95, 150, 155,
    216-17
millenarius, 20
Milo, son of Rambert, 39n
Ming dynasty, 219
ministeriales, 38
Mirfield, John, 138
Mirvaux, Henri de, 109-10
Misnia, 41
Missaglia, Antonio, armourer, see 19c
missi dominici, 27
mobilization, general, 152-3, 156-7; see
    also arrière-ban; rates of, 117, 171,
    306-7
Modena, 97
Moghuls, 142
moineaux, 203
Moldavia, 33
Molinella, battle of (1467), 258

Molinet, Jean, 128, 131, 167, 170n, 205, 214, 218, 252
Mongols, 139, 187, 306
Mons, 141
Mons Meg, 142
Monstrelet, Enguerrand de, 129
Montaigne, Michel de, 259n, 286
Montaigu, 41
Montaperti, battle of (1260), 66, 73, 86
Montargis, 111
Montauban, 196
Mont Cenis, pass of, 36
Montdidier, 80, 111
Monte Cassino, abbey of, 54
Montefeltre, 139
Monte-Frago, Order of, 76
Monteil, Aimar de, bishop of Le Puy, 60
Montereau-sur-Yonne, 113, 195n
Montesa, Order of, 76
Montferrat, 78; John I Paleologus, marquis of, 159; Violanta-Irena of, 119
Montfort, Amaury de, 101; Guy de, 72; Jeanne de, duchess of Brittany, 241–2; Simon de, 87, 101–2, 104, 108
Montgiscard, 225
Montier-en-Der, 245
Montigni, lord of, 137
Montivilliers, 203
Montlhéry, 41; battle of (1465), 136, 171, 228, 229n
Montmorency, 41
Montone, Braccio da, 161
Montreuil-Bellay, 111
Montreuil-sur-Mer, 111
Mont-Saint-Martin, abbey of, 223
Mont-Saint-Michel, abbey of, 202, 246
Mont-Saint-Vanne, church of, 39
Montségur, 101
Montuel, 204
Moors, 56–8, 60, 131, 138–9, 257n; see also Muslims
Morat, battle of (1476), 162, 200 218, 232–3, 235; see also 23
Moravians, 23
Morea, 128
Moriale, Montreal d'Albarno, Fra, 158
Mortagne, 194–5
Moses, 263, 269n
motte, 31, 44–5, 47, 52–3, 204

Mouchy, Dreu de, 41
Mousket, Philippe, 87
Mühldorf, battle of (1322), 261
Mundavio Capiti, Pandulfus de, 131
Muntaner, Ramun, 248
Muraise, E., 209
Murbach, 37
Muslims, 22–3, 27, 54–9, 64–5, 76, 90, 101, 139, 179, 181, 247; see also Moors; Turks, Ottoman; Turks, Seljuk

Najera, battle of (1367), 257
Namur, 134n; Guillaume I, count of, 155
Nancy, battle of (1477), 218, 298n, 300–1
Naples, 55, 116, 124, 128, 135, 145, 149, 161, 165, 172, 205, 214, 248
Narbonne, 4; Amaury de, 70
Nassau, Englebert, count of, 137
Navarre, 56–7, 93, 132, 243
Navas (Las), de Tolosa, battle of (1212), 65
navy, 7, 51–2, 55, 189, 206
Neaufles-Saint-Martin, 41
Neckar, battle of river (1078), 261n
Nef des princes, 285; see also Balsac, Robert de
Nemours, Jacques d'Armagnac, duke of, 189
Nesle, 42
Netherlands, 152, 171, 198, 223, 256, 307
Nettuno, 205
Neufchâtel, 149
Neuss, siege of (1474–5), 149, 167, 205, 211, 214, 227
Neustria, 22–3, 27
Nevers, 144
Nevers, Guillaume II, count of, 41–2, 47
Neville, John, lord of Raby, 151
Newark, 196
Newcastle-upon-Tyne, 150
Nicea, battle of (1097), 62–3
Nicephorus, 241
Nicetius, St., 44
Nicholas I, pope, 266
Nicholas II, pope, 55, 272
Nicholas IV, pope, 212
Nicholas Hereford, 294
Nicopolis, battle of (1396), 156, 286

Niger, 293
Nijmegen, 301
Nîmes, 240
Nithard, 265
Nivernais, 43
Nola, see Orsini, Orso degli; Paulinus of
Nonancourt, 222, 245
Nördlingen, 122
Nordmark, 41
Normandy, 41, 43, 46, 48, 50, 52–4,
    60–1, 80–2, 87, 106, 109, 118, 130,
    132, 134, 169–70, 189, 191, 195, 222,
    225–6, 244–5, 253n, 268, 272; Robert
    Curthose, duke of, 61; William the
    Bastard, duke of, see William the
    Conqueror, duke of Normandy, king
    of England
Normans, 4, 27–30, 35–6, 52, 54–5, 98,
    211, 269; see also Vikings
Northampton, William Bohun, earl of,
    223
Northumbria, 50
Norway, 52
Norwich, 294
Notitia dignitatum, 7–10
Nottingham, Thomas Mowbray, earl of,
    120
Nottinghamshire, 151
Nouvion-l'Abbesse, 42
Noyers, Hugues de, bishop of Auxerre,
    211
Noyon, 42, 223, 269
Nuremberg, 120, 136, 148, 196

obligations, military, 16–22, 38, 47–64,
    72, 77–90, 98–9, 117–18, 150–65, 238;
    military, exemption from, 20, 38
Obodrites, 220
Occitania, 66, 100, 104; see also
    Languedoc
Odiham, 111
Odilo, St., abbot of Cluny, 272
Odo, St., abbot of Cluny, 275
Odo, bishop of Bayeux, 54
Odoacer, king of the Heruls, 4, 16
Odofredus, 283
Offa, king of Mercia, 50–1
Offa's dyke, 51, 220
offerings, religious, see ex voto
Oise, river, 223

Orderic Vitalis, 42, 53, 241, 256
ordinances, military, 120, 168–71, 290
Orford, 111
Oriflamme, 42, 273, 298
Origen, 263
Origny-Sainte-Benoîte, abbey of, 223
Orléans, 13n, 42, 48, 81, 195, 200, 206,
    227, 273n, 297; Louis, duke of, 129
Orne, river, 46
Orsini, family, 161; Latino, Cardinal,
    121; Orso degli, duke of Ascoli, count
    of Nola, 121
Orval, Arnaud Amanieu d'Albret, lord
    of, 226
Osma, 56
Ostmark, 41
Ostrogoths, 4, 11–12, 14, 16, 18, 21, 176,
    179, 261
Othée, battle of (1408), 199
Otranto, 98
Otterburne, battle of (1388), 229n, 241
Otto I the Great, emperor, 32, 35–6, 40
Otto II, emperor, 37–8, 40
Otto III, emperor, 39–40, 269
Otto IV, emperor, 104
Otto of Freising, 33, 36
Oxford, 53

pacificism, 292–6; see also Peace of God
Padua, 118, 149, 199, 212, 292
pagi, 37, 43
Palatinate, 4
palatini, 5
Paleologus, Theodore, 119, 214–15, 220n
Palestine, 60, 68, 74–7; see also Holy
    Land
Palestrina, Giovanni Pierluigi da, 236
Palma, lord of, 137
Pamèle, lord of, see Palma
Pamiers, 123, 293
Pamplona, 23, 56
Pannonia, Pannonians, 3, 16, 20, 33
Papal states, 78, 85, 91, 123, 127, 140,
    161, 165, 276, 283, 287
Parayre, Bernard, engineer, 106
paréage, 109
Parenzo, 40
Paris (including region of), 13, 42, 48, 93,
    113, 121–2, 145n, 148, 156, 191, 195,
    198, 202n, 206, 211, 215, 227, 239,

Paris (continued)
    245, 268, 296, 299n, 300–1; see also
    Ile-de-France; Robert, count of, 268
Parma, 40, 298n; battle of (1247), 66
Parthians, 213
Pasquerel, Jean, 273n
Passion, Order of, 127
Paston, Edmund, 152
Pastoreau, François, 148
Paul, St., 296
Paulinus of Aquilea, 269
Paulinus of Nola, 263
pavesari, pavesiers, 73, 91, 116, 132–3,
    156
Pavia, 40
Paviot, Louis, 206
pax romana, 264
Payens, Hugues de, 74
Peace of God, 52, 223, 246, 270–5
pedones, peones, 58, 135, 163
Pelagius, king of the Asturias, 56
penitence, 265–8
Penthesilea, 241
Pepin II of Herstal, mayor of the
    Austrasian palace, 22
Pepin III the Short, king of the Franks,
    22, 24, 44, 181–3
Perche, 118, 222
Périgord, Périgueux, 17, 84, 117–18, 247
Péronne, 42, 223
Perpignan, 149
Persia, 139, 213; see also Iran
Perugia, 84, 86, 91, 97, 131, 161, 216n
Pesaro, 161
Petchenegs, 33
Peter, St., 263n, 270, 279
Peter Damiani, St., 293, 294n
Peter the Chanter, 274–5
Peter the Hermit, 61
Peter the Venerable, abbot of Cluny, 90
Petit Jehan de Saintré, 214
Petit Pont, Adam du, 188
Petrarch, Francesco, 138
petrariae, perriers, 102–4, 106, 194–5,
    198
Pharès, Simon de, 218
Philip I, king of France, 41, 48–50, 61–2,
    272
Philip II Augustus, king of France, 41,
    65–6, 68, 71, 80–1, 83, 90–1, 100–1,

106–7, 109, 111, 114–15, 244–7,
    298n, 300
Philip III the Bold, king of France,
    81–2, 93, 96–7, 107, 116
Philip IV the Fair, king of France, 66,
    72, 82, 86–7, 89, 92–3, 117–18, 189,
    191, 216
Philip VI of Valois, king of France, 132,
    189–91, 220, 222–3, 285, 300, 306
Philo of Byzantium, 210
Piacenza, 40, 240
Picardy, 42, 100, 129, 134, 137, 162,
    192n, 195, 215
Picquigny, treaty of (1475), 129
Picts, 4
Piedmont, 240
pikemen, 134, 170, 199–200, 231–2
Pisa, 62, 90, 100, 108, 126, 128, 159
Pithiviers, 42
Pitres, 28
Pius II, pope, 131, 138
Pizan, Pisan, Christine de, 120, 141–2,
    148, 156, 195, 210, 274n, 285, 287n,
    293
Planches, 41
Plano Carpini, John of, 187
Plato, 250–1
Ploërmel, 82n
Plumetot, Simon de, 212
Po, river, 261
Poitiers, Poitou, Poitevins, 20, 46, 49,
    82–3, 118, 152, 155, 157, 179, 181,
    216n, 228, 236n, 239, 258, 259n
Poitiers, Alphonse de, 93, 96
Pola, 40
Poland, 30, 32, 37, 78
Poli, Alessandro da, 190
Policraticus, 275
Pont-Audemer, 226, 247
Pont-de l'Arche, 111
Ponthieu, 41, 48, 80, 118, 146
Pont-l'Evêque, 226
Pontoise, 215
Pontorson, 242
Pontvallain, battle of (1370), 299
Poole, 124
Poperinghe, 240
Porto, 56
Portsdown, 152
Portugal, 56, 65, 77, 93, 121, 300

praebitio tironum, 7
Prato, 216n
prepositi exercitus, 20
Principate, 98
Priorat, Jean, 210
Prisia servientum, 83–5
prisoners, 33, 35, 42, 57, 73, 151–2,
    256–7, 265, 274, 276
Privilegium minus, 78
Procopius, 5, 175–6, 214
Provençals, 61, 96, 158, 161
Provence, 27, 71–2, 100, 109, 133, 244,
    272; Raimond VII, count of, 67, 71
Provins, 96
Prudentius, 264
Prussia, 66, 76, 127n, 307
Psalterium Aureum, 183
Pseudo-Fredegar, 22
Puiset (Le), 42, 45
Pujol, 102
Puy (Le), 60, 246, 271
Pyrenees, 23, 56–7, 76, 83, 227, 244

Quadi, 3
quintaine, 216

Rabanus Maurus, 187, 211, 268
Raby, *see* Neville, John, lord of
Raetia, 16
Raja Gopal, 142
Raimond d'Aguilers, 105
Rambert, *see* Milo, son of
Ramundus Arquerii, 140
ransoms, 15, 151–2, 160, 236, 239, 244n,
    255–6, 259, 261–2, 274, 284, 289,
    291, 303
Raoul Glaber, 271
Rational des divins offices, 289
Ratisbon, 36
ravelin, 202, 205
Ravenna, 4, 40, 258, 273n; battle of
    (1512), 258, 273n
Ravenstein, *see* Clèves, Philippe de, lord
    of
Raymond le Brun, 244
Raymond of Peñafort, St., 274, 282
razzias, 118
Realvalle, abbey of, 300n
Reccared, king of the Visigoths, 14, 18
Receswinth, king of the Visigoths, 17

Reconquista, 30, 41, 55–9
Red Sea, 6
Reichstag, 77
Reggio Emilia, 40
Regino of Prüm, 268
Reims, 41, 48, 113, 268, 277, 287, 297–8;
    see also 8
René of Anjou, king of Sicily, 226
Rennes, 142n, 143, 148, 196
Renouard, Y., 157–8
restauratio equorum, 93, 97, 130–1, 151
Revel, Guillaume, 203
Rheinfelden, Rudolph of, 261n
Rhine, river, 4, 22–3, 28, 83, 118, 245
Rhodes, 196n, 200
Rhone, river, 5, 41
Rhuddlan castle, 111–13
Ribemont, Anslem of, 59
Richard, *see* Mastre Richard
Richard I the Lionheart, king of
    England, 65, 72, 80, 100, 110, 113,
    244, 246–7, 259
Richard II, king of England, 120, 141,
    151, 166, 217, 288, 290
Richard FitzNigel, 90
Richard the Englishman, 274
Richard's Castle, Herefords., 52
Richemont, Arthur de, constable of
    France, 131, 226, 229n
Richer of Reims, 31
Richmond, 151
Rienzo, Cola di, 158
Rieux, lord of, 192
Riez, 240
Riga, 76
Rigonthis, 14
Rigord, 244
Rimini, 161, 204
Rinaldeschi, Piero de', 216n
Rio Salado, battle of the (1341), 257n
Ripa, Bonvesino della, 117
Ripenses, 5
risks, in warfare, 255–9
Robert, constable, 61n
Robert de Courçon, 287
Robert Guiscard, 54–5
Robert of Torigni, abbot of
    Mont-Saint-Michel, 221, 246
Rocamadour, 84
Roccavione, battle of (1275), 66

Roche-aux-Moines (La), battle of (1214), 66
Rochefort, Charles de, 155
Rochelle (La), 206
Rocroi, 114
Rodez, 22
Roger II, king of Sicily, 55
Roger of Hauteville, 55
Roger of Hoveden, 95
Roland, paladin, 308, see also Song of Roland
Rollo, 28, 43
Romagna, 140, 159, 245, 287
Roman de Renart, 87
Romania, 128; Assizes of, 77
Romans, Roman Empire, 3–13, 15–19, 176, 185, 219, 260, 264, 305–6
Romanus Diogenes, emperor, 59
Roma triumphans, 138
Rome, 4, 5, 11, 12, 35, 37, 78, 122, 158, 206–7, 245, 270, 283–4, 308
Romfahrt, 78
Romney, 51
Romont, Jacques de Savoie, count of, 137
Roncaglia, 36
Roncevaux, 56
Roosbeke, battle of (1382), 230n, 291, 300
Roquetaillade, 114
Rosier des guerres, 211
Rothari, king of the Lombards, 17
Rothenburg, 122, 196
Rottmeister, 162
Roucy, Eble II, count of, 41
Rouen, 28, 81, 85, 110, 144, 164n, 203, 215, 226, 245
Rouergue, 117–18
Roussillon, 123, 205n, 272
Roussillon, Chanson de Girart de, 87
Rouvroy, 87
Roxburgh, 206
Royaumont, abbey of, 113, 300n
Roye, 80
Rozmital, Leo of, 124
Rufinus, Master, 273, 282
Rumigney, 114
Rupert of Luxembourg, king of Germany, 162
Russell, F. H., 284

Russia, 306
Ruthin, 111

Saale, river, 23, 78
Sachsenspiegel, 77–8, 86, 241
saddles, 181, 303
Saint-Aignan, 164; Lucas de, 116
St Andrew's cross, 190–1
Saint-Benoît-du-Sault, 47
St Briavels, 116
Saint-Brisson-sur-Loire, 42
Saint-Denis, abbey of, 42, 48, 195n, 273, 300
Sainte-Catherine-de-Fierbois, 293n, 300
Sainte-Foix, Raymond de, 295
Sainte-Suzanne, 148
Saint-Florentin, 72
Saint-Flour, 240
Saint Gall, St Gallen, abbey of, 34, 183
Saint-Germain-des-Prés, 85
Saint-Germain-en-Laye, 80
Saint-Gilles, Raymond de, 61n, 106
Saint-Gilles du Gard, 187
St Gothard pass, 36
St Jakob an der Birs, battle of (1444), 136
St James of the Sword, Order of, 76
Saint-Jean-de-Luz, 132
St John of Acre, see Acre
Saint-Julien-de-Brioude, 300
Saint-Junien, 84
Saint-Lô, 226
Saint-Marc, Regnaut de, 239
Saint-Mard-en-Soissonais, 107, 111
Saint-Martin-devant-Metz, 285
St Mary, Order of, 76
Saint-Maur-des-Fossés, 86
Saint-Maximin-lès-Trèves, 171
Saint-Omer, 195, 240; Geoffroi de, 74
Saintonge, 155
Saint-Pol, Louis de Luxembourg, count of, 204, 226
Saint-Quentin, 80, 223
Saint-Remy, Inghilese de, 70, 100
Saint-Sauveur-le-Vicomte, 141
Saint-Thiébault-sous-Bourmont, 85
Saint-Trond, 221
saiones, 21
Sajo, battle of (1241), 139
Salamanca, 56

Salerno, 54–5
Salian Franks, see Franks
Salian dynasty, 32
Salin, E., 175
Salisbury, Thomas Montague, earl of, 148, 206
sallets, 189
Sallon, Jean, captain, 192
Sallust, 214, 297
Salses, 122
saltpetre, 138–40, 146–9, 196–8
Saluzzo, Thomas, marquis of, 242
Salvian of Marseilles, 13
Salza, 104; Hermann von, master of the Teutonic Order, 68, 76
Samian, Giraud de, 199
Samson, 263
Samson, abbot, 79
Sancerre, Etienne, count of, 246
Sandwich, 51
Sangallo, Guiliano da, 204
San Julian de Periero, Order of, 76
San Romano, Battle of, 126
Santa Maria della Vittoria, 300n
Santiago, Master of Order of, 163
Saône, river, 41
Saphet, 72, 114–15
Saracens, 27, 29, 30, 34, 37, 70, 73, 99–100, 103, 124, 213, 251–2, 269–70, 279–80, 302; see also Moors, Muslims, Turks
Saragossa, 27, 56–7
Sardinia, 4, 27
Sarlat, 84
Sarmates, 3
Sarrebruck, count of, 155
Sarthe, river, 222
Savarot, archer, 134
Savia, 16
Savona, 262
Savoy, 78, 106, 114, 159, 161, 186, 233, 240; Amadeus VI, count of, 155, 159, 211; Louis de, 155; Peter II, count of, 114; Philip, count of, 114; palace of the, 151
sax, 177–80
Saxons, 4, 13, 14, 22, 37, 39, 182, 262
Saxony, 23, 35–7, 78, 225
Scandinavia, 30, 52
scara, 21, 27

Scarborough, 110
Scarpone, battle of (366), 4
Scheldt, river, 223
schiltrons, 231
schioppeteri, 135
Schleswig, 162
Schmitthenner, P., 93
scholae, 5, 16
Schwabenspiegel, 77
Schwanau, 104
Schwarz, Berthold, 138
Schwyz, 135
Scipio, 208
Scotland, Scots, 4, 65–6, 73, 86, 116, 118, 123, 129–32, 140, 150–2, 164, 166, 170, 191, 206, 217, 218n, 219, 228, 229n, 231, 239, 258, 294
scramasax, 177–8, 180
Scripta de feodis, 80
sculca, 17
scutagium, scutage, 79, 80, 91, 151
Scythia, 3
Sebastian, St., 297
Secretum secretorum, 90
Segovia, 56, 183, 285
Seine, river, 14, 24, 28, 110, 191, 203, 226
Selden, John, 51n
Seljuks, see Turks
Selonnet, 119
Sempach, battle of (1386), 136, 261, 290
Senlis, 300
Sens, 42, 81, 113
Septimania, 19, 27, 56
servi, 19–20
servitium debitum, 53–4, 79–80, 82, 89, 151
Seville, 59, 65, 163
Sforza, family, 161; Alessandro, 161; Caterina, 172n; Francesco, 135, 161, 190; Muccio Attendolo, 161
shield, form of, 178; see also pavesari; 17
Sible Hedingham, 158
Sicily, 4, 30, 54–5, 61, 66–7, 78, 91, 98, 109, 192, 240–1, 247–8, 283
Sidonius Apollinaris, 13
siege weapons, 102–6, 116, 193–207, 211–12, 215; see also trébuchet.
Siena, 86, 96, 100, 115, 159, 216n, 298n
Siete Partidas, 210, 283n

Sigebert, king of the Franks, 22
Sigismund of Luxembourg, emperor, 136
signs, distinctive, 61, 69, 172, 190–2, 233, 242, 264, 273, 298–301; *see also* standards; uniforms
Silesia, 304
Siling Vandals, *see* Vandals
Simancas, 56
Simonetta, Cicco, 190
Sint-Winoksbergen, 240
Sion, 268
Skidmore, James, 130
slaves, 19–20, 262–3, 266
Slavs, 32, 35, 37, 39, 161, 230
Sleutz, Thomas, 162
Sluys, 240
Soissons, 48, 216n, 261; battle of (923), 268
Solway, 219
Somme, river, 145n
Song of Roland, 184, 253n
Song of the Albigensian Crusade, 102, 107
Sorabs, 32
Sorbs, 23
Sorrento, 55
Spain, 4, 5, 12, 14, 21, 27, 30, 41, 55–60, 96, 100, 118, 123–4, 129–33, 162–3, 171–2, 187, 227, 239, 241, 244, 256, 259, 262, 276, 282, 302
Speculum juris, 287
spies, 226
Spoleto, 23
Stafford, Humphrey, earl of, 126–7
Stamfordbridge, battle of (1066), 52
standards, 5, 115–16, 122, 298, 300–1
Stephen II, pope, 270
Stephen, king of England, 78, 244
Stephen Langton, archbishop of Canterbury, 287
Steppes, 12, 33, 219
Stirling, 104
stirrup, 58, 179–84, 303
Stoics, 250
Strasbourg, 4, 37, 104, 148
strategy, 208–9, 219–28
Stubbs, William, 281n
Styria, 41
Suenon, 253n
Suevi, 4, 12, 14, 20

Suffolk, 111; William de la Pole, earl of, 218n
Suger, abbot of St-Denis, 48
Sulpicius Severus, 263
Summa Coloniensis, 282
Summa Decretorum, 273, 282
Summa Predicantium, 285
Sundgau, 137
supplies, 26, 62, 94–5
Surienne, François de, 203, 225, 285
Sviatoslav, prince of Kiev, 261
Swabia, Swabians, 35, 118, 137, 254
Sweden, 306
Swiss, 118, 120, 122, 124, 129n, 133–7, 144, 162, 166, 170, 191, 217–18, 231–2, 291, 307; *see also* 23
Switzerland, 73, 118, 137, 149, 249n, 255, 261
sword, blessing of, 277–8; *see also* 9; types of, 177–8
Sword Brothers, Order of, 76
Swynderby, William, 294
Syria, 59–61, 219.

Taccola, Mariano di Jacopo, 120
Tacitus, 176n
Tactics: general, 127, 208–9; in pitched battles, 228–37; of Almogavars, 73; of Barbarians, 11–12, 175–9, 181–3; of Burgundians, 232–5; of Czechs, 124 (*see also* laager warfare); of English, 124–5; of Irish, 70, 212; of Magyars, 33–34; of Spanish, 58; of Swiss, 231–2; of Turks, 59–60, 213
Tafurs, 61
Tagliacozzo, battle of (1268), 66, 300n
Tagliant, captain, 233
Tagus, river, 56
Taillefer, 253n
Talbot, John, earl of Shrewsbury, 199
Tancarville, 203
Tandjore, 142
Tarascon, 122
Tarn-et-Garonne, 140
Tarragona, 56
Tartas, 300
Tassilo, duke of the Bavarians, 182
Taticius, Tatikos, 62
Temple, Order of the, 67–9, 74–7, 96, 114, 118, 212, 254

Teobald, duke of the Alamans, 22
Termes, 100
Terra del Lavoro, 98
Terre Jourdaine, 98
Tertry, battle of (687), 22
Tertullian, 263
Teutonic Knights, Order of, 66, 76–7, 115n, 123, 162
Thames, river, 50, 53, 83
Theodore, archbishop of Canterbury, 266
Theodoric, king of the Ostrogoths, 4, 16
Theodosius II, emperor, 264
Thessaly, 3
Theudebert I, king of the Franks, 261
Thibaut, Jean, 195
Thiérache, 222
Thierry I, king of the Franks, 183
thiufadus, 20, 57
Thomas Aquinas, St., 250–1, 273, 280, 286, 288
Thomas de Chobham, 287
Thrace, 3
Thuringia, Thuringians, 14, 20, 78, 104, 183
Tinchebray, battle of (1106), 231, 256n
Tingitania, 6
Titus Livius, *see* Livy
Toledo, 19, 56, 269
Torsello, Marino Sanuto, 194, 213, 228
Tortona, 40
Tortosa, 56, 100
torture, 290
Totila, king of the Ostrogoths, 11, 18
Toul, 26n, 245, 301
Toulonges, 272
Toulouse, 4, 22, 60, 72, 82, 84, 93, 101–2, 104, 106–8, 117–18, 140, 198; Raymond V, count of, 60
Touraine, 20, 46, 81, 118, 195
Tournai, 42, 84, 149, 191, 194, 216n, 240
tournaments, 95, 215–16, 276, 301; *see also 15*
Tournus, 43
Tours, 81, 145n, 169–70, 211, 218n, 225, 262, 285, 300
Toury, 42
Toxandria, 4
Trabanten, 137
Trajan's column, 185

Transylvania, 76
Trasamund, 261n
Treatises on art of war, 119–21, 210–18; *De arte venandi cum avibus*, 186; *De notabilitatibus sapientiis et prudentiis*, 139; *De planctu ecclesiae*, 275; *De re aedificatoria*, 204; *De rebus bellicis*, 3, 9; *De regimine principum*, 194, 210–11; *De re militari*, 138; *De secretis secretorum*, 139n; *De stratagematibus bellicis*, 211–12; *De vita militarium*, 210; *Epitoma de re militari*, 210–12; *Trattato de architettura*, 204
trébuchet, 102–6, 139, 193–6, 274
Tree of Battles, 119, 125, 215, 274
Trento, 262
Treviso, 40
Triaverdins, 244
Tribur, 269
Trier, 26n, 37, 44, 120
Trieste, 40
Trinoda necessitas, 50–1
Tripoli, 63–4
Tripolitania, 6
troops, numbers of, 7–12, 25–6, 33–4, 37–8, 53, 61–2, 77, 116–18, 129, 132–5, 163, 222–3, 244–5, 306–7
Troyes, 13n, 48, 74; Chrétien de, 193
Truce of God, *see* Peace of God
Tulle, 240
Tunis, 99
Turcopoles, 64, 70, 115
Turks, Ottoman, 123, 128, 138, 156, 159, 187n, 213, 247, 259; Seljuk, 59–64
Turgel, 76
Turin, 40, 122, 240
Tuscany, 99, 117n, 123, 158–9, 161, 276
Tyne, river, 219
Tyrol, 122

Ubaldus, Pietro Baldo degli, 282–3
Uccello, Paolo, 126; *see also 14*
uniforms, 16, 172, 188–92, 298n
Unstrut, battle of the river (1075), 254
Unterwalden, 135
Urban II, pope, 59, 60, 71, 272, 278–9
Urban IV, pope, 67
Urbino, 161, 297; Federigo, duke of, 138
Uri, 135
Urric, master engineer, 106

Urslingen, Werner von, 158
Uzès, 240

Val de Crati, 98
Val-ès-Dunes, battle of (1047), 52
Valenciennes, 191, 194
Valens, emperor, 9, 11
Valentinian I, emperor, 6
Valerius Maximus, 211, 214, 297
Vallicellanum, 267
Valois, Charles, count of, 118, 248;
    Philip of, see Philip VI, king of France
Valturio, Roberto, 138, 204
Vandals, 3–4, 11, 12, 14, 18, 176, 179,
    261n
Van Overstraeten, R., 208
Varenne-Saint-Hilaire (La), 86
Varlier, Simon, 216n
vassi dominici, 25
Vaucelles, abbey of, 223
Vaucouleurs, 245
Vaud, region of, 114
Vaudémont, Hugues I, count of, 298n
Vaudois, 293, 295
vavassores, 40, 70
Vegetius, 170, 210–12, 214, 251–2, 297
Velleius Paterculus, 13
Vendôme, 47, 118; Bouchard, count of,
    47
Venice, 67, 72, 84, 96, 117, 123, 128, 133,
    135n, 138, 140, 149, 160–1, 165, 172,
    205, 213, 227, 289n, 305
Verbruggen, J., 25
Vercelli, 240
Verdun, 39n
Verdun-sur-le-Doubs, 271
Vermandois, 42, 81, 118, 222; Hugues,
    count of, 61; Raoul, count of, 48
Verneuil, battle of (1424), 195, 226, 257n
Vernon, 110, 226
Verona, 40, 199
Vesoul, 131
Vexin, 42, 80
Vienna, 298
Vienne, 272
Vignai, Jean de, 119, 210
Vigneulles, Philippe de, 285, 289
Vignolles, Etienne de, called La Hire,
    218
Vikings, 27–9, 34, 46, 50, 105, 180; see
    also Normans

Villandraut, 114
Villani, Giovanni, 84, 198
Villard de Honnecourt, 103
Villehardouin, Geoffroi de, 105
Villeneuve-sur-Yonne, 111
Vincennes, 122
Vincent of Beauvais, 210
Vinchy, battle of (717), 22
Vinci, Leonardo da, 204
Viollet-le-Duc, E., 184
Virgil, 138
Visby, battle of (1361), 122, 186–7, 258;
    see also 10, 11
Visconti, family, 159; Barnabo, 159;
    Bianca, 161; Donnina, 159; Filippo
    Maria, 166; Galeazzo, 159; Lodrizio,
    158; Richarda, 242
Visigoths, 4–5, 9, 11, 12, 14, 17–21, 57,
    176, 179, 262
Vitoria, 187
Viviers, 240
Voralberg, 137
Vouillé, battle of (507), 17
Vualprand, 19

Wace, 253n
Wagenburg, 124
wages, 5, 90–101, 164
Walachia, 33
Waldemar I, king of Denmark, 253n
Walderic, 20
Wales, 65–6, 71–2, 98, 109, 111–14, 118,
    150, 152–3, 167, 191, 220, 225;
    Arthur, prince of, see Arthur; Edward,
    prince of, see Edward
Wallingford, 53, 80
Walloons, 61
Walter Map, 32n, 243
Walter Sans Avoir, 61
Wamba, king of the Visigoths, 18–19
Wandalmar, 20
war, laws of, 284–92; in scholastic
    thought, 280–4; types of, 283–4,
    303–4
war cries, 33, 229, 299–300
warrior mentality, 13–15, 33, 74–5,
    250–9, 280, 288–9
wars, frequency of, 22–3, 35–6, 41–2,
    56–7, 65; length of, 26, 34–6, 57, 228,
    240

Warwick, Richard Beauchamp, earl of, 126
Wassebourg, Richard of, 289n
Watelet, cannoneer, 206n
Wat's Dyke, 51
weapons, blessing of, 277; see also Armament; 9
Weber, M., 272
Weissensee, 104
Wends, 32, 78
wergild, 15
Werner, K. F., 25–6
Wessex, 50–1
Westminster, 113
White, Lynn, 181–3
Wibald, 212n
Widukind of Corvey, 35, 261
William I the Conqueror, king of England, duke of Normandy, 46, 52–4, 60, 225, 236n, 268, 277, 300
William II Rufus, king of England, 41, 54, 62
William of Malmesbury, 99n
William of Tyre, 60n, 231
William the Catalan, 100

William the Marshal, 216
Willibad, 20
Winchelsea, 287n
Winchester, 80; earl of, see Bruges, Louis de; Saer de Quincy, earl of, 80
Windsor, 53, 91
Winterthur, John of, 135
Wissant, 49
Witiges, king of the Ostrogoths, 11
women, role of, in armies, 12, 14–15, 81, 86, 241–2, 272, 274, 289–90, 305
Woodward, William, 141
Worms, 189, 267
Worthies, Cult of Nine, 254, 308
Wujung Zongyao, 139
Württemberg, 179
Wycliffe, John, 292, 294

Yeomen of the Guard, 167
York, 122
Ypres, 148, 206, 240
Yves, St., 299

Zosimus, 6
Zurich, 135–6, 291